THE
BOOK OF
RESOLUTIONS
OF THE UNITED METHODIST CHURCH
1996

THE
BOOK OF
RESOLUTIONS
OF THE UNITED METHODIST CHURCH
1996

The United Methodist Publishing House
Nashville, Tennessee

This book is printed on recycled, acid-free paper.

Scripture quotations, unless otherwise noted, are from the New Revised Standard Version of the Bible, copyright © 1989 by the Division of Christian Education of the National Council of the Churches of Christ in the USA. Used by permission.

The Social Principles on pages 31–53 are from *The Book of Discipline of The United Methodist Church—1996.* Copyright © 1996 by The United Methodist Publishing House. Used by permission.

ISBN 0-687-01917-6

Software Edition (Book of Resolutions with *Book of Discipline)*
Windows/Macintosh Versions on CD-ROM, ISBN 0-687-01934-6

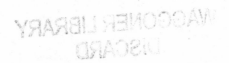

96 97 98 99 00 01 02 03 04 05—10 9 8 7 6 5 4 3 2 1

PRINTED IN THE UNITED STATES OF AMERICA

PREFACE

The Book of Resolutions has been published after each General Conference since 1968. This edition includes all resolutions that are currently valid. Resolutions that have been rescinded or superseded have been removed from this 1996 edition.

When approved by the General Conference, resolutions state the policy of The United Methodist Church on many of the current social issues and concerns. Only the General Conference speaks for The United Methodist Church in its entirety (*Book of Discipline*, ¶ 509).

The 1996 General Conference approved a new rule stating: "Resolutions shall be considered official expressions of The United Methodist Church for twelve years following their adoption, after which time they shall be deemed to have expired unless readopted. Those that have expired shall not be printed in subsequent editions of the *Book of Resolutions*" (*Book of Discipline*, ¶ 510.2*a*). This rule will be first applied to publication of *The Book of Resolutions, 2000*.

This 1996 edition presents the resolutions in seven sections: (1) The Natural World, (2) The Nurturing Community, (3) The Social Community, (4) The Economic Community, (5) The Political Community, (6) The World Community, and (7) Other Resolutions. The first six section titles match the sections of the Social Principles, United Methodism's foundational statement on social issues (printed after the User's Guide). The date of General Conference adoption appears at the end of each resolution.

To assist readers in study and use of the resolutions, this edition includes:

—User's Guide
—Cross-referencing of related resolutions
—Index and list of topics and categories

The 1996 *Book of Resolutions* is published by The United Methodist Publishing House—Neil M. Alexander, president and publisher, and

Harriett Jane Olson, book editor of The United Methodist Church. Lee Ranck of the General Board of Church and Society and members of the editorial and production staff of The United Methodist Publishing House served as the team assigned to the volume. The late Carolyn D. Minus, former General Board of Church and Society staff member, wrote the User's Guide.

Book design by Leonardo M. Ferguson.

CONTENTS

THE SOCIAL COMMUNITY

CONTENTS

CONTENTS

THE ECONOMIC COMMUNITY

THE POLITICAL COMMUNITY

13

THE WORLD COMMUNITY

CONTENTS

OTHER RESOLUTIONS

USER'S GUIDE

What's the purpose of the *Book of Resolutions*?

The Book of Resolutions, 1996, published by The United Methodist Publishing House, collects in one volume all current and official social policies and other resolutions adopted by the General Conference of The United Methodist Church. These resolutions are:

- Official policy statements for guiding all the work and ministry of The United Methodist Church on approximately 200 subjects;
- Educational resources for The United Methodist Church on many of the important issues affecting the lives of people and all God's creation;
- Guides and models for helping United Methodist members and groups relate a lively biblical faith to action in daily life;
- Resource materials for persons preparing public statements about United Methodist concerns on current social issues.

The Book of Resolutions, 1996 is primarily a reference tool for church members and leaders. It is not a book that you will sit down to read from cover to cover.

You might not get acquainted with these resolutions until you are in the midst of some controversy in your congregation, or something happens regarding a particular subject in your community (or state, or nation). You may find that your denomination's policies give you more "food for thought." Maybe you will agree with the denomination's position. On the other hand, you may disagree. Either is all right. At the least, you know your Church cares and wants you to be a knowledgeable and caring Christian about the issues of the day.

Furthermore, you may look to some of the statements in this book for spiritual guidance as you make an important decision in your life about work, home, family life, or use of money and other resources.

Can you answer some of my questions?

Why do we have all these social policies and resolutions?

The resolutions say, "We care!" Delegates in the General Conference of The United Methodist Church believe that we each need and deserve the guidance of the whole denomination as we face daily hopes, struggles, joy, or pain. The resolutions and Social Principles express our Church community's beliefs and give us evidence that the Church means for God's love to reach into situations faced each day, not just on Sunday mornings. Not all of us are intimately involved with each issue, but someone, somewhere, is.

Isn't the *Book of Discipline* enough?

Most of the *Book of Discipline* is legislation and legally sets up the framework for each part of United Methodism. The General Conference decided in 1968 that for reasons of length, these resolutions should be published in a volume separate from the *Discipline*. While the *Book of Resolutions* is not legally binding, it is an official guide from our denomination to be used responsibly for reference, encouragement, study, and support.

Why do the Social Principles appear in both the *Discipline* and in the *Book of Resolutions*?

The United Methodist Church puts the Social Principles in the *Discipline* (¶¶ 64–70) as one of our denominational foundation statements suggesting how faith is translated into action. Its broad principles (guides, not rules) are declarations to help us be in dialogue with one another about how faith motivates us to "get off the fence" and act.

The United Methodist Church puts the Social Principles in the front of the *Book of Resolutions* to help us relate the broad strokes of the Social Principles to more specific exploration and applications in resolutions.

Where do these policies and resolutions come from?
How do they get adopted by General Conference?

They are sent in as petitions to General Conference every four years by general agencies, annual conferences, local churches, individual members, and groups. Once submitted as petitions, most of them are worked on by delegates in the Church and Society or the Global

Ministries legislative committees. The legislative committees accept, reject, or amend the petitions, then report their recommendations to the General Conference plenary; all delegates then vote on their recommendations.

Can I trust the statistics and data in these resolutions?

General source references are usually given when statistics are used in a resolution. Because such data may change during the years the resolution is valid, sometimes the resolution will provide more general descriptions of social conditions that make it urgent for the Church to speak on a particular topic. Resolutions will take on more meaning when you secure local statistics and data on relevant topics.

Why do Church social policies and U.S. government policies or positions seem so far apart on some of these issues?

The United Methodist Church membership extends beyond the U.S. boundaries; it is global. So, in many cases we are speaking to, from, or with more than one national government. Further, the Christian church must never be a mirror image of any government, whether Democrat or Republican, totalitarian or democratic. We know that Christians are obligated to be responsible and participating citizens under any governmental system, but that response and participation is to be interpreted in light of our faith.

As the Social Principles state, "Our allegiance to God takes precedence over our allegiance to any state" (¶ 68). And our Church's public witness is first and foremost to be judged by God by whether it supports justice, love, and mercy, particularly for the poor and powerless.

Why can't the Church just let us make up our own minds on these matters after it presents us neutral information on both sides of an issue?

Most importantly, The United Methodist Church believes God's love for the world is an active and engaged love, a love seeking justice and liberty. We cannot just be observers. So we care enough about people's lives to risk interpreting God's love, to take a stand, to call each of us into a response, no matter how controversial or complex. The Church helps us think and act out a faith perspective, not just responding to all the other "mind-makers-up" that exist in our society.

No information is truly neutral. This is true even of the most "hard scientific" data secured from the most advanced technology. These resolutions do strive for objectivity, not neutrality. There are usually more than "two sides" in important social controversies. Dialogue between different sides is critical in taking a stand. Faithfulness requires favoring what best demonstrates God's love and being willing to change when new perspectives or data emerge.

Is this something new in United Methodism?

Taking an active stance in society is nothing new for followers of John Wesley. He set the example for us to combine personal and social piety. Ever since predecessor churches to United Methodism flourished in the United States, we have been known as a denomination involved with people's lives, with political and social struggles, having local to international mission implications. It is an expression of the personal change we experience in our baptism and conversion.

Is there a difference between a *social policy* and a *resolution*?

The terms are used almost interchangeably in The United Methodist Church. Most social issue resolutions refer to public policy matters, such as local, state, and federal government programs and legislation. Other statements focus on conditions affecting the Church and the Church's programs or funding.

How do people use this *Book of Resolutions*?

• An ordained minister went to console neighbor parents after their son committed suicide. At home later that evening, the pastor and his own family struggled in their grief to apply their faith to this troubling situation. What did the Church say about suicide? How should a Christian act? The pastor found the 1980 *Book of Resolutions* absolutely silent on this topic. During the six years after that first personal encounter with ministry after a suicide, the pastor wrote letters and articles and talked with seminary faculty and national Church staff. As a result, the 1988 General Conference adopted its first resolution on suicide. Instead of wishing for guidance from our Church on this most difficult subject, this pastor gave constructive leadership in the Church, and we now can find helpful perspectives in the 1996 *Book of Resolutions*.

• A bishop and an annual conference board of church and society wanted to share a United Methodist position against the death penalty with their governor, who had to consider clemency for a death row inmate. They visited the governor and delivered a letter stating their own views of this particular situation and describing why The United Methodist Church opposes the death penalty. They used the resolution on capital punishment in the *Book of Resolutions* as the official policy of The United Methodist Church to support their plea for clemency.

• An adult church school group studied the foreign policy discussion topics called "Great Decisions," issued annually by the Foreign Policy Association. They compared its resources with positions in the relevant United Methodist policies from the *Book of Resolutions* for several evenings of lively study.

• Another adult class meeting on Sunday morning always studied faith and contemporary issues. For nearly six months, the members used the *Book of Resolutions* to guide their study and discussion. Different members made presentations on some aspect of the resolutions; then they used the study questions provided to stimulate some challenging discussion. Occasionally, they had guest speakers or used an audiovisual resource from their conference media center to amplify the subject.

• A nurse who is an active church member found the resolutions on "Universal Access to Health Care in the United States and Related Territories" and "Ministries in Mental Illness" to be helpful as she reflected on the strains in her job. She found it more possible to connect her faith to her discussions with coworkers about some of the major issues facing her profession in a big city hospital.

• A local church's outreach work area asked its administrative council to approve a congregational statement to the county zoning board favoring the construction of several low-income housing units. As part of their homework, the work area members reviewed the "Housing" resolution in the *Book of Resolutions*. That resolution then served as a basis for their initiative; they even quoted from it when they testified at the zoning board.

How do I use the *Book of Resolutions?*

Read the preface. ⟶ It provides an orientation to the whole book.

Skim through the table of contents. ⟶ Note: Resolutions are listed alphabetically under the section of the Social Principles to which they most closely relate.

Look at the index in the back of the book. ⟶ The index helps you find find subject references that may be more specific than titles.

Example: If you want to know whether our denomination has spoken about AIDS or HIV, you look for those entries in the index. These subjects are referred to in a number of resolutions.

Example: What is there on "schools"? The index includes a number of references. You may also choose to look under "education."

Find the text of the Social Principles.
• Note that the Social Principles include broad, fundamental statements grouped in six sections between a preamble and a creedal summary, "Our Social Creed."
• Review the "How can I understand the Social Principles?" section in this User's Guide. Use the diagrams in this section to help interpret and look for meaning in the Social Principles.

How can I understand the Social Principles?

The Book of Resolutions organizes almost all resolutions into the six areas of concern that form the major sections of the Social Principles. You may find it helpful to consider these six areas of concern as you explore specific resolutions.

One way of understanding the Social Principles is to consider the six sections as areas of concern: (1) the natural world, (2) the nurturing community, (3) the social community, (4) the economic community, (5) the political community, and (6) the world community.

The Natural World, the starting point for the areas of concern, provides the essential resources of life for all humankind.

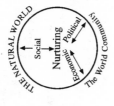

Then add to the natural world the people of the world—of **The World Community**. All of us live in community, oftentimes becoming part of several communities. Together we make up the world community.

All of us also become a part of **The Nurturing Community**. Through the people with whom we interact most often—family, friends, local church, etc.—we shape our lives and the way we relate to other communities.

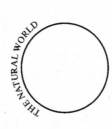

Three other communities impact both the nurturing community and the world community.

The Social Community (or cultural community) provides the arena where we live out our responsibilities and rights in our treatment of others.

The Economic Community, in which each of us functions, establishes production, distribution and employment systems; it creates both wealth and poverty.

The Political Community determines whether our rights are guaranteed and our basic freedoms are upheld. Directions and goals of our social and economic communities are debated and decided in this arena.

Decisions in all of these communities have an impact on the natural world, and vice versa.

Our Social Creed

"Our Social Creed" (Section VII of the Social Principles) is a summarization of the foregoing sections of the Social Principles in the form of a creed. While it is recommended by the general Church for separate use in worship services, "Our Social Creed" is an integral part of the Social Principles.

Another way of considering the six sections of the Social Principles (the six areas of concern) is to look at: (1) the role of each section, (2) the predominant faith statement in each section, (3) our responsibility defined in each section, and (4) the issues discussed in each section. The chart on the next two pages summarizes the Social Principles in this way.

The Social Principles

CATEGORY	I The Natural World	II The Nurturing Community	III The Social Community	IV The Economic Community	V The Political Community	VI The World Community
ROLE	Provides for sustenance of all creation to be used with integrity.	Provides the potential to nurture human beings into the fullness of their humanity.	Provides for means for determining the rights and responsibilities of the members toward one another.	Provides directions for influencing economic policies.	Provides for the ordering of society.	Provides the setting for the interaction of nations.
FAITH STATEMENT	All creation is God's.	All persons are important and loved by God.	All persons are equally valuable in the sight of God.	All economic systems are under God's judgment.	All political systems are under God's judgment.	All of God's world is one world.

OUR RESPONSI-BILITY	To value and conserve all natural resources.	To innovate, sponsor, and evaluate new forms of community.	To work toward societies in which social groups and individual values are recognized, maintained, and strengthened.	To ensure that sound policies are developed that provide for full employment, adequate income, and so forth.	To take active responsibility for our government.	To work to develop the moral and spiritual capacity to achieve a stable world of love.
ISSUES	Water, air, soil, plants, energy utilization, animal life, space.	Family, Christian community, marriage, human sexuality, abortion, death.	Rights of minorities, children, youth and young adults, the aging, women, people with disabilities; alcohol/drugs; rural life.	Property, collective bargaining, work/leisure, consumption, poverty, migrant workers, gambling.	Basic liberties, political responsibility, freedom of information, civil obedience and civil disobedience, crime and rehabilitation, military service.	Nations and cultures, national power and responsibility, war and peace, justice and law.

How can I better understand the resolutions?

The following model or method for studying any of the resolutions shows:

- the Social Principles paragraph to which that resolution relates (found in the cross-reference at the conclusion of any resolution);
- the biblical references and/or theological concerns identified in this resolution;
- the major actions called for in that resolution for churches; individuals; church agencies; local, state, or national governments; and
- hymns found in *The United Methodist Hymnal* that may be especially appropriate to sing in relation to this resolution. (For page number, *see* index of first lines and common titles in the *Hymnal*.)

For some subjects, you may need to consult the list of Topics and Categories.

The Natural World

Resolution	Social Principles Paragraph	Biblical References/ Theological Concerns	Actions called for	Hymns to use
Indoor Air Pollution	¶ 64A	Jesus' abundant life embraced physical well-being as well as emotional and spiritual health. Wesley and his followers have a long record of health/welfare ministries.	• Urge local churches, all Church agencies, and institutions to learn of suffering due to indoor air pollution; prohibit smoking indoors; provide adequate fresh-air ventilation audit for sources of pollution. • Urge general United Methodist agencies, with consultation with those most seriously affected, to prepare guidelines addressing indoor air pollution; advocate legislation to adopt standards and regulatory laws. • Ask all United Methodists to inventory indoor pollution levels and to take steps to reduce environmental pollution.	"Open my eyes, that I may see" (*Hymnal*, 454). "O God who shaped creation" (*Hymnal*, 443).

The Natural World

Resolution	Social Principles Paragraph	Biblical References/ Theological Concerns	Actions called for	Hymns to use
Nuclear Safety in the United States	¶ 64B	The God-given charge to humans to "guard and keep the earth" (Genesis 2:15). To ensure that God's creation is protected for present and future generations.	• Urge general United Methodist agencies to assist annual conferences in all aspects of information and action strategies on this issue. • Advocate for public policy, particularly regarding nuclear power, reviewing safety of operating plants, researching designs for plant safety, phasing out nuclear weapons production, establishing uniform safety standards for civilian and military nuclear operations, reevaluating U.S. nuclear waste policy, and conserving energy and enhancing alternative energy sources.	"A charge to keep I have" (*Hymnal*, 413). "Creating God, your fingers trace" (*Hymnal*, 109.)

¶ 64

U.S. Agriculture and Rural Communities in Crisis

God's gift of the land is a common gift to all humanity, requiring just patterns of land use (Lev. 25).

Jesus commands us to love neighbor as self.

The gospel challenges an ethic based on "bigness is better."

Issues over 72 comprehensive calls for change by the Church at all levels, by local communities, and by state and federal governments. For example:

• Churches to develop intentionally ministry to meet major needs in today's rural U.S.A.; to become public policy advocates; to model and support team and cooperative ministries; to emphasize ecology as part of Christian stewardship.

• Federal legislation and programs to enable farm families to receive just return for their labor and investments; to develop just water and energy policies to recognize and protect rights of farm workers.

• State and governments, private lending agencies, local governments, and community groups to be involved, together and separately; overall, to develop a vision for agricultural life where programs and relations are just, participatory, and sustainable.

"Great is thy faithfulness" (*Hymnal*, 140).

"Faith, while trees are still in blossom" *Hymnal*, 508).

What do I do next?

Consider these questions for study and response to any of the resolutions:

- How familiar am I with the situation(s) described in this resolution?

- What are my reactions to this call for action by our Church?

- How might reactions be different if we lived in another part of this country? came to the United States from another country? lived in another country? were of a different economic class? attended a different church? if members of my family were present (or not present)?

- How could our local congregation creatively respond to the calls for action in the resolution?

- Are there groups in my area or state at work on this issue where I could join in action or learn more?

- What have I communicated to our congressional members or state legislators about our Church's position on an issue of great importance?

- Who could we contact for more information or resources? Write to or call: Communications, General Board of Church and Society, 100 Maryland Avenue, N.E., Washington, D.C. 20002; (202) 488-5621.

SOCIAL PRINCIPLES

PREFACE

The United Methodist Church has a long history of concern for social justice. Its members have often taken forthright positions on controversial issues involving Christian principles. Early Methodists expressed their opposition to the slave trade, to smuggling, and to the cruel treatment of prisoners.

A social creed was adopted by The Methodist Episcopal Church (North) in 1908. Within the next decade similar statements were adopted by The Methodist Episcopal Church, South, and by The Methodist Protestant Church. The Evangelical United Brethren Church adopted a statement of social principles in 1946 at the time of the uniting of the United Brethren and The Evangelical Church. In 1972, four years after the uniting in 1968 of The Methodist Church and The Evangelical United Brethren Church, the General Conference of The United Methodist Church adopted a new statement of Social Principles, which was revised in 1976 (and by each successive General Conference).

The Social Principles are a prayerful and thoughtful effort on the part of the General Conference to speak to the human issues in the contemporary world from a sound biblical and theological foundation as historically demonstrated in United Methodist traditions. They are intended to be instructive and persuasive in the best of the prophetic spirit. The Social Principles are a call to all members of The United Methodist Church to a prayerful, studied dialogue of faith and practice. (*See* ¶ 509.)

PREAMBLE

We, the people called United Methodists, affirm our faith in God our Creator and Father, in Jesus Christ our Savior, and in the Holy Spirit, our Guide and Guard.

We acknowledge our complete dependence upon God in birth, in life, in death, and in life eternal. Secure in God's love, we affirm the goodness of life and confess our many sins against God's will for us as we find it in Jesus Christ. We have not always been faithful stewards of all that has been committed to us by God the Creator. We have been reluctant followers of Jesus Christ in his mission to bring all persons into a community of love. Though called by the Holy Spirit to become new creatures in Christ, we have resisted the further call to become the people of God in our dealings with each other and the earth on which we live.

Grateful for God's forgiving love, in which we live and by which we are judged, and affirming our belief in the inestimable worth of each individual, we renew our commitment to become faithful witnesses to the gospel, not alone to the ends of earth, but also to the depths of our common life and work.

¶ 64.   I. THE NATURAL WORLD

All creation is the Lord's, and we are responsible for the ways in which we use and abuse it. Water, air, soil, minerals, energy resources, plants, animal life, and space are to be valued and conserved because they are God's creation and not solely because they are useful to human beings. Therefore, we repent of our devastation of the physical and nonhuman world. Further, we recognize the responsibility of the church toward lifestyle and systemic changes in society that will promote a more ecologically just world and a better quality of life for all creation.

A) Water, Air, Soil, Minerals, Plants—We support and encourage social policies that serve to reduce and control the creation of industrial byproducts and waste; facilitate the safe processing and disposal of toxic and nuclear waste and move toward the elimination of both; encourage reduction of municipal waste; provide for appropriate recycling and disposal of municipal waste; and assist the cleanup of polluted air, water, and soil. We support measures designed to maintain and restore natural ecosystems. We support policies that develop alternatives to chemicals used for growing, processing, and preserving food, and we strongly urge adequate research into their effects upon God's creation prior to utilization. We urge development of international agreements concerning equitable utilization of the world's resources for human benefit so long as the integrity of the earth is maintained.

B) Energy Resources Utilization—We support and encourage social policies that are directed toward rational and restrained transformation of parts of the nonhuman world into energy for human usage and that de-emphasize or eliminate energy-producing technologies that endanger the health, the safety, and even the existence of the present and future human and nonhuman creation. Further, we urge wholehearted support of the conservation of energy and responsible development of all energy resources, with special concern for the development of renewable energy sources, that the goodness of the earth may be affirmed.

C) Animal Life—We support regulations that protect the life and health of animals, including those ensuring the humane treatment of pets and other domestic animals, animals used in research, and the painless slaughtering of meat animals, fish, and fowl. We encourage the preservation of all animal species including those threatened with extinction.

D) Space—The universe, known and unknown, is the creation of God and is due the respect we are called to give the earth.

E) Science and Technology—We recognize science as a legitimate interpretation of God's natural world. We affirm the validity of the claims of science in describing the natural world, although we preclude science from making authoritative claims about theological issues. We recognize technology as a legitimate use of God's natural world when such use enhances human life and enables all of God's children to develop their God-given creative potential without violating our ethical convictions about the relationship of humanity to the natural world.

In acknowledging the important roles of science and technology, however, we also believe that theological understandings of human experience are crucial to a full understanding of the place of humanity in the universe. Science and theology are complementary rather than mutually incompatible. We therefore encourage dialogue between the scientific and theological communities and seek the kind of participation that will enable humanity to sustain life on earth and, by God's grace, increase the quality of our common lives together.

¶ 65.   II. THE NURTURING COMMUNITY

The community provides the potential for nurturing human beings into the fullness of their humanity. We believe we have a responsibility to innovate, sponsor, and evaluate new forms of community that will encourage development of the fullest potential in individuals. Primary for us is the gospel understanding that all persons are important—because they are human beings created by God and loved through and by Jesus Christ and not because they have merited significance. We therefore support social climates in which human communities are maintained and strengthened for the sake of all persons and their growth.

A) The Family—We believe the family to be the basic human community through which persons are nurtured and sustained in mutual love, responsibility, respect, and fidelity. We understand the family as encompassing a wider range of options than that of the two-generational unit of parents and children (the nuclear family), including the extended family, families with adopted children, single parents, step-families, and couples without children. We affirm shared responsibility for parenting by men and women and encourage social, economic, and religious efforts to maintain and strengthen relationships within families in order that every member may be assisted toward complete personhood.

B) Other Christian Communities—We further recognize the movement to find new patterns of Christian nurturing communities such as Koinonia Farms, certain monastic and other religious orders, and some types of corporate church life. We urge the Church to seek ways of understanding the needs and concerns of such Christian groups and to find ways of ministering to them and through them.

C) Marriage—We affirm the sanctity of the marriage covenant that is expressed in love, mutual support, personal commitment, and shared fidelity between a man and a woman. We believe that God's blessing rests upon such marriage, whether or not there are children of the union. We reject social norms that assume different standards for women than for men in marriage. Ceremonies that celebrate homosexual unions shall not be conducted by our ministers and shall not be conducted in our churches.[1]

D) Divorce—When a married couple is estranged beyond reconciliation, even after thoughtful consideration and counsel, divorce is a regrettable alternative in the midst of brokenness. It is recommended that methods of mediation be used to minimize the adversarial nature and fault-finding that are often part of our current judicial processes.

Although divorce publicly declares that a marriage no longer exists, other covenantal relationships resulting from the marriage remain,

[1] *See* Judicial Council Decision 694.

such as the nurture and support of children and extended family ties. We urge respectful negotiations in deciding the custody of minor children and support the consideration of either or both parents for this responsibility in that custody not be reduced to financial support, control, or manipulation and retaliation. The welfare of each child is the most important consideration.

Divorce does not preclude a new marriage. We encourage an intentional commitment of the Church and society to minister compassionately to those in the process of divorce, as well as members of divorced and remarried families, in a community of faith where God's grace is shared by all.

E) *Single Persons*—We affirm the integrity of single persons, and we reject all social practices that discriminate or social attitudes that are prejudicial against persons because they are single.

F) *Women and Men*—We affirm with Scripture the common humanity of male and female, both having equal worth in the eyes of God. We reject the erroneous notion that one gender is superior to another, that one gender must strive against another, and that members of one gender may receive love, power and esteem only at the expense of another. We especially reject the idea that God made individuals as incomplete fragments, made whole only in union with another. We call upon women and men alike to share power and control, to learn to give freely and to receive freely, to be complete and to respect the wholeness of others. We seek for every individual opportunities and freedom to love and be loved, to seek and receive justice, and to practice ethical self-determination. We understand our gender diversity to be a gift from God, intended to add to the rich variety of human experience and perspective; and we guard against attitudes and traditions that would use this good gift to leave members of one sex more vulnerable in relationships than members of another.

G) *Human Sexuality*—We recognize that sexuality is God's good gift to all persons. We believe persons may be fully human only when that gift is acknowledged and affirmed by themselves, the church, and society. We call all persons to the disciplined, responsible fulfillment of themselves, others, and society in the stewardship of this gift. We also recognize our limited understanding of this complex gift and encourage the medical, theological, and social science disciplines to combine in a determined effort to understand human sexuality more completely. We call the Church to take the leadership role in bringing together these disciplines to address this most complex issue. Further, within the

35

context of our understanding of this gift of God, we recognize that God challenges us to find responsible, committed, and loving forms of expression.

Although all persons are sexual beings whether or not they are married, sexual relations are only clearly affirmed in the marriage bond. Sex may become exploitative within as well as outside marriage. We reject all sexual expressions that damage or destroy the humanity God has given us as birthright, and we affirm only that sexual expression which enhances that same humanity. We believe that sexual relations where one or both partners are exploitative, abusive, or promiscuous are beyond the parameters of acceptable Christian behavior and are ultimately destructive to individuals, families, and the social order.

We deplore all forms of the commercialization and exploitation of sex, with their consequent cheapening and degradation of human personality. We call for strict enforcement of laws prohibiting the sexual exploitation or use of children by adults. We call for the establishment of adequate protective services, guidance, and counseling opportunities for children thus abused. We insist that all persons, regardless of age, gender, marital status, or sexual orientation, are entitled to have their human and civil rights ensured.

We recognize the continuing need for full, positive, and factual sex education opportunities for children, youth, and adults. The Church offers a unique opportunity to give quality guidance and education in this area.

Homosexual persons no less than heterosexual persons are individuals of sacred worth. All persons need the ministry and guidance of the church in their struggles for human fulfillment, as well as the spiritual and emotional care of a fellowship that enables reconciling relationships with God, with others, and with self. Although we do not condone the practice of homosexuality and consider this practice incompatible with Christian teaching, we affirm that God's grace is available to all. We commit ourselves to be in ministry for and with all persons. [2]

H) Family Violence and Abuse—We recognize that family violence and abuse in all its forms—verbal, psychological, physical, sexual—is detrimental to the covenant of the human community. We encourage the Church to provide a safe environment, counsel, and support for the victim. While we deplore the actions of the abuser, we affirm that person to be in need of God's redeeming love.

---

[2] *See* Judicial Council Decision 702.

I) Sexual Harassment—We believe human sexuality is God's good gift. One abuse of this good gift is sexual harassment. We define sexual harassment as any unwanted sexual advance or demand, either verbal or physical, that is reasonably perceived by the recipient as demeaning, intimidating, or coercive. Sexual harassment must be understood as an exploitation of a power relationship rather than as an exclusively sexual issue. Sexual harassment includes, but is not limited to, the creation of a hostile or abusive working environment resulting from discrimination on the basis of gender.

Contrary to the nurturing community, sexual harassment creates improper, coercive, and abusive conditions wherever it occurs in society. Sexual harassment undermines the social goal of equal opportunity and the climate of mutual respect between men and women. Unwanted sexual attention is wrong and discriminatory. Sexual harassment interferes with the moral mission of the Church.

J) Abortion—The beginning of life and the ending of life are the God-given boundaries of human existence. While individuals have always had some degree of control over when they would die, they now have the awesome power to determine when and even whether new individuals will be born. Our belief in the sanctity of unborn human life makes us reluctant to approve abortion. But we are equally bound to respect the sacredness of the life and well-being of the mother, for whom devastating damage may result from an unacceptable pregnancy. In continuity with past Christian teaching, we recognize tragic conflicts of life with life that may justify abortion, and in such cases we support the legal option of abortion under proper medical procedures. We cannot affirm abortion as an acceptable means of birth control, and we unconditionally reject it as a means of gender selection. We call all Christians to a searching and prayerful inquiry into the sorts of conditions that may warrant abortion. We commit our Church to continue to provide nurturing ministries to those who terminate a pregnancy, to those in the midst of a crisis pregnancy, and to those who give birth. Governmental laws and regulations do not provide all the guidance required by the informed Christian conscience. Therefore, a decision concerning abortion should be made only after thoughtful and prayerful consideration by the parties involved, with medical, pastoral, and other appropriate counsel.

K) Adoption—Children are a gift from God to be welcomed and received. We recognize that some circumstances of birth make the rearing of a child difficult. We affirm and support the birth parent(s) whose choice it is to allow the child to be adopted. We recognize the agony, strength, and courage of the birth parent(s) who choose(s) in hope, love, and prayer to offer the child for adoption. In addition, we affirm the receiving parent(s) desiring an adopted child. When circumstances warrant adoption, we support the use of proper legal procedures. We commend the birth parent(s), the receiving parent(s), and the child to the care of the Church, that grief might be shared, joy might be celebrated, and the child might be nurtured in a community of Christian love.

L) Death with Dignity—We applaud medical science for efforts to prevent disease and illness and for advances in treatment that extend the meaningful life of human beings. At the same time, in the varying stages of death and life that advances in medical science have occasioned, we recognize the agonizing personal and moral decisions faced by the dying, their physicians, their families, and their friends. Therefore, we assert the right of every person to die in dignity, with loving personal care and without efforts to prolong terminal illnesses merely because the technology is available to do so.

¶ 66.   III. THE SOCIAL COMMUNITY

The rights and privileges a society bestows upon or withholds from those who comprise it indicate the relative esteem in which that society holds particular persons and groups of persons. We affirm all persons as equally valuable in the sight of God. We therefore work toward societies in which each person's value is recognized, maintained, and strengthened. We support the basic rights of all persons to equal access to housing, education, employment, medical care, legal redress for grievances, and physical protection.

A) Rights of Racial and Ethnic Persons—Racism is the combination of the power to dominate by one race over other races and a value system that assumes that the dominant race is innately superior to the others. Racism includes both personal and institutional racism. Personal racism is manifested through the individual expressions, attitudes, and/or behaviors that accept the assumptions of a racist value system and that maintain the benefits of this system. Institutional racism is the established social pattern that supports implicitly or explicitly the racist value system. Racism plagues and cripples our growth in Christ, inasmuch as it is antithetical to the gospel itself. Therefore, we recognize racism as sin and affirm the ultimate and temporal worth of all persons.

We rejoice in the gifts that particular ethnic histories and cultures bring to our total life. We commend and encourage the self-awareness of all racial and ethnic groups and oppressed people that leads them to demand their just and equal rights as members of society. We assert the obligation of society and groups within the society to implement compensatory programs that redress long-standing, systemic social deprivation of racial and ethnic people. We further assert the right of members of racial and ethnic groups to equal opportunities in employment and promotion; to education and training of the highest quality; to nondiscrimination in voting, in access to public accommodations, and in housing purchase or rental; and to positions of leadership and power in all elements of our life together. We support affirmative action as one method of addressing the inequalities and discriminatory practices within our Church and society.

B) Rights of Religious Minorities—Religious persecution has been common in the history of civilization. We urge policies and practices that ensure the right of every religious group to exercise its faith free from legal, political, or economic restrictions. We condemn all overt and covert forms of religious intolerance, being especially sensitive to their expression in media stereotyping. We assert the right of all religions and their adherents to freedom from legal, economic, and social discrimination.

C) Rights of Children—Once considered the property of their parents, children are now acknowledged to be full human beings in their own right, but beings to whom adults and society in general have special obligations. Thus, we support the development of school systems and innovative methods of education designed to assist every child toward complete fulfillment as an individual person of worth. All children have the right to quality education, including full sex education appropriate to their stage of development that utilizes the best educational techniques and insights. Christian parents and guardians and the Church have the responsibility to ensure that children receive sex education consistent with Christian morality, including faithfulness in marriage and abstinence in singleness. Moreover, children have the rights to food, shelter, clothing, health care, and emotional well-being as do adults, and these rights we affirm as theirs regardless of actions or inactions of their parents or guardians. In particular, children must be protected from economic, physical, and sexual exploitation and abuse.

D) Rights of Youth and Young Adults—Our society is characterized by a large population of youth and young adults who frequently find full participation in society difficult. Therefore, we urge development of policies that encourage inclusion of youth and young adults in decision-making processes and that eliminate discrimination and ex-ploitation. Creative and appropriate employment opportunities should be legally and socially available for youth and young adults.

E) Rights of the Aging—In a society that places primary emphasis upon youth, those growing old in years are frequently isolated from the mainstream of social existence. We support social policies that integrate the aging into the life of the total community, including sufficient incomes, increased and nondiscriminatory employment opportunities, educational and service opportunities, and adequate medical care and housing within existing communities. We urge social policies and programs, with emphasis on the unique concerns of older women and ethnic persons, that ensure to the aging the respect and dignity that is their right as senior members of the human community. Further, we urge increased consideration for adequate pension systems by employ-ers, with provisions for the surviving spouse.

F) Rights of Women—We affirm women and men to be equal in every aspect of their common life. We therefore urge that every effort be made to eliminate sex-role stereotypes in activity and portrayal of family life and in all aspects of voluntary and compensatory participation in the Church and society. We affirm the right of women to equal treatment in employment, responsibility, promotion, and compensation. We af-firm the importance of women in decision-making positions at all levels of Church life and urge such bodies to guarantee their presence through policies of employment and recruitment. We support affirmative action as one method of addressing the inequalities and discriminatory prac-tices within our Church and society. We urge employers of persons in dual career families, both in the Church and society, to apply proper consideration of both parties when relocation is considered.

G) Rights of Persons with Disabilities—We recognize and affirm the full humanity and personhood of all individuals with disabilities as full members of the family of God. We affirm the responsibility of the Church and society to be in ministry with children, youth, and adults with mental, physical, developmental, and/or psychological disabili-ties whose different needs in the areas of mobility, communication, intellectual comprehension, or personal relationships might interfere with their participation or that of their families in the life of the Church and the community. We urge the Church and society to receive the gifts of persons with disabilities to enable them to be full participants in the community of faith. We call the Church and society to be sensitive to, and advocate for, programs of rehabilitation, services, employment, education, appropriate housing, and transportation. We call on the Church and society to protect the civil rights of persons with disabilities.

H) Equal Rights Regardless of Sexual Orientation—Certain basic human rights and civil liberties are due all persons. We are committed to supporting those rights and liberties for homosexual persons. We see a clear issue of simple justice in protecting their rightful claims where they have shared material resources, pensions, guardian relationships, mutual powers of attorney, and other such lawful claims typically attendant to contractual relationships that involve shared contributions, responsibilities, and liabilities, and equal protection before the law. Moreover, we support efforts to stop violence and other forms of coercion against gays and lesbians. We also commit ourselves to social witness against the coercion and marginalization of former homosexuals.

I) Population—Since the growing worldwide population is increasingly straining the world's supply of food, minerals, and water and sharpening international tensions, the reduction of the rate of consumption of resources by the affluent and the reduction of current world population growth rates have become imperative. People have the duty to consider the impact on the total world community of their decisions regarding childbearing and should have access to information and appropriate means to limit their fertility, including voluntary sterilization. We affirm that programs to achieve a stabilized population should be placed in a context of total economic and social development, including an equitable use and control of resources; improvement in the status of women in all cultures; a human level of economic security, health care, and literacy for all.

J) Alcohol and Other Drugs—We affirm our long-standing support of abstinence from alcohol as a faithful witness to God's liberating and redeeming love for persons. We support abstinence from the use of any illegal drugs. Since the use of alcohol and illegal drugs is a major factor in crime, disease, death, and family dysfunction, we support educational programs encouraging abstinence from such use.

Millions of living human beings are testimony to the beneficial consequences of therapeutic drug use, and millions of others are testimony to the detrimental consequences of drug misuse. We encourage wise policies relating to the availability of potentially beneficial or potentially damaging prescription and over-the-counter drugs; we urge that complete information about their use and misuse be readily available to both doctor and patient. We support the strict administration of laws regulating the sale and distribution of all opiates. We support regulations that protect society from users of drugs of any kind where it can be shown that a clear and present social danger exists. Drug-dependent persons and their family members are individuals of infinite human worth deserving of treatment, rehabilitation, and ongoing life-changing recovery. Misuse should be viewed as a symptom of underlying disorders for which remedies should be sought.

K) Tobacco—We affirm our historic tradition of high standards of personal discipline and social responsibility. In light of the overwhelming evidence that tobacco smoking and the use of smokeless tobacco are hazardous to the health of persons of all ages, we recommend total abstinence from the use of tobacco. We urge that our educational and communication resources be utilized to support and encourage such abstinence. Further, we recognize the harmful effects of passive smoke and support the restriction of smoking in public areas and workplaces.

L) Medical Experimentation—Physical and mental health has been greatly enhanced through discoveries by medical science. It is imperative, however, that governments and the medical profession carefully enforce the requirements of the prevailing medical research standard, maintaining rigid controls in testing new technologies and drugs utilizing human beings. The standard requires that those engaged in research shall use human beings as research subjects only after obtaining full, rational, and uncoerced consent.

M) Genetic Technology—The responsibility of humankind to God's creation challenges us to deal carefully with the possibilities of genetic research and technology. We welcome the use of genetic technology for meeting fundamental human needs for health, a safe environment, and an adequate food supply.

Because of the effects of genetic technologies on all life, we call for effective guidelines and public accountability to safeguard against any action that might lead to abuse of these technologies, including political or military ends. We recognize that cautious, well-intended use of genetic technologies may sometimes lead to unanticipated harmful consequences.

Human gene therapies that produce changes that cannot be passed to offspring (somatic therapy) should be limited to the alleviation of suffering caused by disease. Genetic therapies for eugenic choices or that produce waste embryos are deplored. Genetic data of individuals and their families should be kept secret and held in strict confidence unless confidentiality is waived by the individual or by his or her family, or unless the collection and use of genetic identification data is supported by an appropriate court order. Because its long-term effects are uncertain, we oppose genetic therapy that results in changes that can be passed to offspring (germ-line therapy).

N) Rural Life—We support the right of persons and families to live and prosper as farmers, farm workers, merchants, professionals, and others outside of the cities and metropolitan centers. We believe our culture is impoverished and our people deprived of a meaningful way of life when rural and small-town living becomes difficult or impossible. We recognize that the improvement of this way of life may sometimes necessitate the use of some lands for nonagricultural purposes. We oppose the indiscriminate diversion of agricultural land for nonagricultural uses when nonagricultural land is available. Further, we encourage the preservation of appropriate lands for agriculture and open space uses through thoughtful land use programs. We support governmental and private programs designed to benefit the resident farmer rather than the factory farm and programs that encourage industry to locate in nonurban areas.

We further recognize that increased mobility and technology have brought a mixture of people, religions, and philosophies to rural communities that were once homogeneous. While often this is seen as a threat to or loss of community life, we understand it as an opportunity to uphold the biblical call to community for all persons. Therefore, we encourage rural communities and individuals to maintain a strong connection to the earth and to be open to: offering mutual belonging, caring, healing, and growth; sharing and celebrating cooperative leadership and diverse gifts; supporting mutual trust; and affirming individuals as unique persons of worth, and thus to practice shalom.

O) Urban-Suburban Life—Urban-suburban living has become a dominant style of life for more and more persons. For many it furnishes economic, educational, social, and cultural opportunities. For others, it has brought alienation, poverty, and depersonalization. We in the Church have an opportunity and responsibility to help shape the future of urban-suburban life. Massive programs of renewal and social planning are needed to bring a greater degree of humanization into urban-suburban lifestyles. Christians must judge all programs, including economic and community development, new towns, and urban renewal, by the extent to which they protect and enhance human values, permit personal and political involvement, and make possible neighborhoods open to persons of all races, ages, and income levels. We affirm the efforts of all developers who place human values at the heart of their planning. We must help shape urban-suburban development so that it provides for the human need to identify with and find meaning in smaller social communities. At the same time, such smaller communities must be encouraged to assume responsibilities for the total urban-suburban community instead of isolating themselves from it.

P) Media Violence and Christian Values—The unprecedented impact the media (principally television and movies) are having on Christian and human values within our society becomes more apparent each day. We express disdain at current media preoccupation with dehumanizing portrayals, sensationalized through mass media "entertainment" and "news." These practices degrade humankind and violate the teachings of Christ and the Bible.

United Methodists, along with those of other faith groups, must be made aware that the mass media often undermine the truths of Christianity by promoting permissive lifestyles and detailing acts of graphic violence. Instead of encouraging, motivating, and inspiring its audiences to adopt lifestyles based on the sanctity of life, the entertainment industry often advocates the opposite, painting a cynical picture of violence, abuse, greed, profanity, and a constant denigration of the family. The media must be held accountable for the part they play in the decline of values we observe in society today. Many in the media remain aloof to the issue, claiming to reflect rather than to influence society. For the sake of our human family, Christians must work together to halt this erosion of moral and ethical values in the world community.

Q) Right to Health Care—Health is a condition of physical, mental, social, and spiritual well-being, and we view it as a responsibility—public and private. Health care is a basic human right. Psalm 146 speaks of the God "who executes justice for the oppressed;/who gives food to the hungry./The LORD sets the prisoners free;/the LORD opens the eyes of the blind." It is unjust to construct or perpetuate barriers to physical wholeness or full participation in community.

We encourage individuals to pursue a healthy lifestyle and affirm the importance of preventive health care, health education, environmental and occupational safety, good nutrition, and secure housing in achieving health. We also recognize the role of governments in ensuring that each individual has access to those elements necessary to good health.

R) *Organ Transplantation and Donation*—We believe that organ transplantation and organ donation are acts of charity, *agape* love, and self-sacrifice. We recognize the life-giving benefits of organ and other tissue donation and encourage all people of faith to become organ and tissue donors as a part of their love and ministry to others in need. We urge that it be done in an environment of respect for deceased and living donors and for the benefit of the recipients, and following protocols that carefully prevent abuse to donors and their families.

¶ 67.   IV. THE ECONOMIC COMMUNITY

We claim all economic systems to be under the judgment of God no less than other facets of the created order. Therefore, we recognize the responsibility of governments to develop and implement sound fiscal and monetary policies that provide for the economic life of individuals and corporate entities and that ensure full employment and adequate incomes with a minimum of inflation. We believe private and public economic enterprises are responsible for the social costs of doing business, such as employment and environmental pollution, and that they should be held accountable for these costs. We support measures that would reduce the concentration of wealth in the hands of a few. We further support efforts to revise tax structures and to eliminate governmental support programs that now benefit the wealthy at the expense of other persons.

A) *Property*—We believe private ownership of property is a trusteeship under God, both in those societies where it is encouraged and where it is discouraged, but is limited by the overriding needs of society. We believe that Christian faith denies to any person or group of persons exclusive and arbitrary control of any other part of the created universe. Socially and culturally conditioned ownership of property is, therefore, to be considered a responsibility to God. We believe, therefore, governments have the responsibility, in the pursuit of justice and order under law, to provide procedures that protect the rights of the whole society as well as those of private ownership.

B) *Collective Bargaining*—We support the right of public and private (including farm, government, institutional, and domestic) employees and employers to organize for collective bargaining into unions and other groups of their own choosing. Further, we support the right of both parties to protection in so doing and their responsibility to bargain in good faith within the framework of the public interest. In order that the rights of all members of the society may be maintained and promoted, we support innovative bargaining procedures that include representatives of the public interest in negotiation and settlement of labor-management contracts, including some that may lead to forms of judicial resolution of issues. We reject the use of violence by either party during collective bargaining or any labor/management disagreement. We likewise reject the permanent replacement of a worker who engages in a lawful strike.

C) *Work and Leisure*—Every person has the right to a job at a living wage. Where the private sector cannot or does not provide jobs for all who seek and need them, it is the responsibility of government to provide for the creation of such jobs. We support social measures that ensure the physical and mental safety of workers, that provide for the equitable division of products and services, and that encourage an increasing freedom in the way individuals may use their leisure time. We recognize the opportunity leisure provides for creative contributions to society and encourage methods that allow workers additional blocks of discretionary time. We support educational, cultural, and recreational outlets that enhance the use of such time. We believe that persons come before profits. We deplore the selfish spirit that often pervades our economic life. We support policies that encourage the sharing of ideas in the workplace, cooperative and collective work arrangements. We support rights of workers to refuse to work in situations that endanger health and/or life without jeopardy to their jobs. We support policies that would reverse the increasing concentration of business and industry into monopolies.

D) *Consumption*—Consumers should exercise their economic power to encourage the manufacture of goods that are necessary and beneficial to humanity while avoiding the desecration of the environment in either production or consumption. Consumers should evaluate their consumption of goods and services in the light of the need for enhanced quality of life rather than unlimited production of material goods. We call upon consumers, including local congregations and Church-related institutions, to organize to achieve these goals and to express dissatisfaction with harmful economic, social, or ecological practices through such appropriate methods as boycott, letter writing, corporate resolution, and advertisement. For example, these methods can be used to influence better television and radio programming.

E) Poverty—In spite of general affluence in the industrialized nations, the majority of persons in the world live in poverty. In order to provide basic needs such as food, clothing, shelter, education, health care, and other necessities, ways must be found to share more equitably the resources of the world. Increasing technology, when accompanied by exploitative economic practices, impoverishes many persons and makes poverty self-perpetuating. Therefore, we do not hold poor people morally responsible for their economic state. To begin to alleviate poverty, we support such policies as: adequate income maintenance, quality education, decent housing, job training, meaningful employment opportunities, adequate medical and hospital care, and humanization and radical revisions of welfare programs. Since low wages are often a cause of poverty, employers should pay their employees a wage that does not require them to depend upon government subsidies such as food stamps or welfare for their livelihood.

F) Migrant Workers—Migratory and other farm workers, who have long been a special concern of the Church's ministry, are by the nature of their way of life excluded from many of the economic and social benefits enjoyed by other workers. Many of the migrant laborers' situations are aggravated because they are racial and ethnic minority persons who have been oppressed with numerous other inequities within the society. We advocate for the rights of all migrants and applaud their efforts toward responsible self-organization and self-determination. We call upon governments and all employers to ensure for migratory workers the same economic, educational, and social benefits enjoyed by other citizens. We call upon our churches to seek to develop programs of service to such migrant people who come within their parish and support their efforts to organize for collective bargaining.

G) Gambling—Gambling is a menace to society, deadly to the best interests of moral, social, economic, and spiritual life, and destructive of good government. As an act of faith and concern, Christians should abstain from gambling and should strive to minister to those victimized by the practice. Where gambling has become addictive, the Church will encourage such individuals to receive therapeutic assistance so that the individual's energies may be redirected into positive and constructive ends. The Church should promote standards and personal lifestyles that would make unnecessary and undesirable the resort to commercial gambling—including public lotteries—as a recreation, as an escape, or as a means of producing public revenue or funds for support of charities or government.

¶ 68.   V. THE POLITICAL COMMUNITY

While our allegiance to God takes precedence over our allegiance to any state, we acknowledge the vital function of government as a principal vehicle for the ordering of society. Because we know ourselves to be responsible to God for social and political life, we declare the following relative to governments:

A) Basic Freedoms—We hold governments responsible for the protection of the rights of the people to free and fair elections and to the freedoms of speech, religion, assembly, communications media, and petition for redress of grievances without fear of reprisal; to the right to privacy; and to the guarantee of the rights to adequate food, clothing, shelter, education, and health care. The form and the leaders of all governments should be determined by exercise of the right to vote guaranteed to all adult citizens. We also strongly reject domestic surveillance and intimidation of political opponents by governments in power and all other misuses of elective or appointive offices. The use of detention and imprisonment for the harassment and elimination of political opponents or other dissidents violates fundamental human rights. Furthermore, the mistreatment or torture of persons by governments for any purpose violates Christian teaching and must be condemned and/or opposed by Christians and churches wherever and whenever it occurs.

The Church regards the institution of slavery as an infamous evil. All forms of enslavement are totally prohibited and shall in no way be tolerated by the Church.

B) Political Responsibility—The strength of a political system depends upon the full and willing participation of its citizens. We believe that the state should not attempt to control the church, nor should the church seek to dominate the state. Separation of church and state means no organic union of the two, but it does permit interaction. The church should continually exert a strong ethical influence upon the state, supporting policies and programs deemed to be just and opposing policies and programs that are unjust.

C) Freedom of Information—Citizens of all countries should have access to all essential information regarding their government and its policies. Illegal and unconscionable activities directed against persons or groups by their own governments must not be justified or kept secret, even under the guise of national security.

D) Education—We believe responsibility for education of the young rests with the family, the church, and the government. In our society, this function can best be fulfilled through public policies that ensure access for all persons to free public elementary and secondary schools and to post-secondary schools of their choice. Persons in our society should not be precluded by financial barriers from access to church-related and other independent institutions of higher education. We affirm the right of public and independent colleges and universities to exist, and we endorse public policies that ensure access and choice and that do not create unconstitutional entanglements between church and state. The state should not use its authority to promote particular religious beliefs (including atheism), nor should it require prayer or worship in the public schools, but it should leave students free to practice their own religious convictions.

E) Civil Obedience and Civil Disobedience—Governments and laws should be servants of God and of human beings. Citizens have a duty to abide by laws duly adopted by orderly and just process of government. But governments, no less than individuals, are subject to the judgment of God. Therefore, we recognize the right of individuals to dissent when acting under the constraint of conscience and, after having exhausted all legal recourse, to resist or disobey laws that they deem to be unjust or that are discriminately enforced. Even then, respect for law should be shown by refraining from violence and by being willing to accept the costs of disobedience. We do not encourage or condone, under any circumstances, any form of violent protest or action against anyone involved in the abortion dilemma. We offer our prayers for those in rightful authority who serve the public, and we support their efforts to afford justice and equal opportunity for all people. We assert the duty of churches to support those who suffer because of their stands of conscience represented by nonviolent beliefs or acts. We urge governments to ensure civil rights, as defined by the International Covenant on Civil and Political Rights, to persons in legal jeopardy because of those nonviolent acts.

F) Criminal Justice—To protect all citizens from those who would encroach upon personal and property rights, it is the duty of governments to establish police forces, courts, and facilities for the confinement, punishment, and rehabilitation of offenders. We support governmental measures designed to reduce and eliminate crime that are consistent with respect for the basic freedom of persons. We reject all misuse of these necessary mechanisms, including their use for the

49

purpose of persecuting or intimidating those whose race, appearance, lifestyle, economic condition, or beliefs differ from those in authority; and we reject all careless, callous, or discriminatory enforcement of law. We further support measures designed to remove the social conditions that lead to crime, and we encourage continued positive interaction between law enforcement officials and members of the community at large. In the love of Christ, who came to save those who are lost and vulnerable, we urge the creation of genuinely new systems for the care and support of the victims of crime and for rehabilitation that will restore, preserve, and nurture the humanity of the imprisoned. For the same reason, we oppose capital punishment and urge its elimination from all criminal codes.

G) Military Service—Though coercion, violence, and war are presently the ultimate sanctions in international relations, we reject them as incompatible with the gospel and spirit of Christ. We therefore urge the establishment of the rule of law in international affairs as a means of elimination of war, violence, and coercion in these affairs.

We reject national policies of enforced military service as incompatible with the gospel. We acknowledge the agonizing tension created by the demand for military service by national governments. We urge all young adults to seek the counsel of the Church as they reach a conscientious decision concerning the nature of their responsibility as citizens. Pastors are called upon to be available for counseling with all young adults who face conscription, including those who conscientiously refuse to cooperate with a system of conscription.

We support and extend the ministry of the Church to those persons who conscientiously oppose all war, or any particular war, and who therefore refuse to serve in the armed forces or to cooperate with systems of military conscription. We also support and extend the Church's ministry to those persons who conscientiously choose to serve in the armed forces or to accept alternative service.

¶ 69.   VI. THE WORLD COMMUNITY

God's world is one world. The unity now being thrust upon us by technological revolution has far outrun our moral and spiritual capacity to achieve a stable world. The enforced unity of humanity, increasingly evident on all levels of life, presents the Church as well as all people with problems that will not wait for answer: injustice, war, exploitation, privilege, population, international ecological crisis, proliferation of arsenals of nuclear weapons, development of transnational business organizations that operate beyond the effective control of any governmental structure, and the increase of tyranny in all its forms. This generation must find viable answers to these and related questions if humanity is to continue on this earth. We commit ourselves as a Church to the achievement of a world community that is a fellowship of persons who honestly love one another. We pledge ourselves to seek the meaning of the gospel in all issues that divide people and threaten the growth of world community.

A) Nations and Cultures—As individuals are affirmed by God in their diversity, so are nations and cultures. We recognize that no nation or culture is absolutely just and right in its treatment of its own people, nor is any nation totally without regard for the welfare of its citizens. The Church must regard nations as accountable for unjust treatment of their citizens and others living within their borders. While recognizing valid differences in culture and political philosophy, we stand for justice and peace in every nation.

B) National Power and Responsibility—Some nations possess more military and economic power than do others. Upon the powerful rests responsibility to exercise their wealth and influence with restraint. We affirm the right and duty of people of all nations to determine their own destiny. We urge the major political powers to use their nonviolent power to maximize the political, social, and economic self-determination of other nations rather than to further their own special interests. We applaud international efforts to develop a more just international economic order in which the limited resources of the earth will be used to the maximum benefit of all nations and peoples. We urge Christians in every society to encourage the governments under which they live and the economic entities within their societies to aid and work for the development of more just economic orders.

C) War and Peace—We believe war is incompatible with the teachings and example of Christ. We therefore reject war as an instrument of national foreign policy and insist that the first moral duty of all nations is to resolve by peaceful means every dispute that arises between or among them; that human values must outweigh military claims as governments determine their priorities; that the militarization of society must be challenged and stopped; that the manufacture, sale, and deployment of armaments must be reduced and controlled; and that the production, possession, or use of nuclear weapons be condemned.

51

Consequently, we endorse general and complete disarmament under strict and effective international control.

D) Justice and Law—Persons and groups must feel secure in their life and right to live within a society if order is to be achieved and maintained by law. We denounce as immoral an ordering of life that perpetuates injustice. Nations, too, must feel secure in the world if world community is to become a fact.

Believing that international justice requires the participation of all peoples, we endorse the United Nations and its related bodies and the International Court of Justice as the best instruments now in existence to achieve a world of justice and law. We commend the efforts of all people in all countries who pursue world peace through law. We endorse international aid and cooperation on all matters of need and conflict. We urge acceptance for membership in the United Nations of all nations who wish such membership and who accept United Nations responsibility. We urge the United Nations to take a more aggressive role in the development of international arbitration of disputes and actual conflicts among nations by developing binding third-party arbitration. Bilateral or multilateral efforts outside of the United Nations should work in concert with, and not contrary to, its purposes. We reaffirm our historic concern for the world as our parish and seek for all persons and peoples full and equal membership in a truly world community.

¶ 70.   VII. OUR SOCIAL CREED

We believe in God, Creator of the world; and in Jesus Christ, the Redeemer of creation. We believe in the Holy Spirit, through whom we acknowledge God's gifts, and we repent of our sin in misusing these gifts to idolatrous ends.

We affirm the natural world as God's handiwork and dedicate ourselves to its preservation, enhancement, and faithful use by humankind.

We joyfully receive for ourselves and others the blessings of community, sexuality, marriage, and the family.

We commit ourselves to the rights of men, women, children, youth, young adults, the aging, and people with disabilities; to improvement of the quality of life; and to the rights and dignity of racial, ethnic, and religious minorities.

We believe in the right and duty of persons to work for the glory of God and the good of themselves and others and in the protection of their welfare in so doing; in the rights to property as a trust from God, collective bargaining, and responsible consumption; and in the elimination of economic and social distress.

We dedicate ourselves to peace throughout the world, to the rule of justice and law among nations, and to individual freedom for all people of the world.

We believe in the present and final triumph of God's Word in human affairs and gladly accept our commission to manifest the life of the gospel in the world. Amen.

(It is recommended that this statement of Social Principles be continually available to United Methodist Christians and that it be emphasized regularly in every congregation. It is further recommended that "Our Social Creed" be frequently used in Sunday worship.)

THE NATURAL WORLD

Affirming the Household EcoTeam Program

The United Methodist Church is committed to protecting and preserving the environment for the benefit of present and future generations. The Social Principles of The United Methodist Church remind us that "all creation is the Lord's, and we are responsible for the ways in which we use and abuse it" (¶ 64). Many of our churches already sponsor recycling and other "environment friendly" projects.

We commend to our churches and United Methodist families a new, "human scale" program to help save the earth. The Global Action Plan, based in Woodstock, New York, along with local organizations nationwide, sponsors the Household EcoTeam Program. This program can be organized by small groups of friends, family members, neighbors, or coworkers, who form an EcoTeam to support one another in working on monthly action areas such as reducing garbage, improving home water and energy efficiency, Eco-wise consuming, and so forth. There is a parallel program for children, "Journey for the Planet." Workbooks and other materials are available to EcoTeams at nominal cost.

The Household EcoTeam Program is similar in many ways to the Methodist Class System, which did so much to energize and build The Methodist Church. This same organizational method can now be used in local churches to preserve and protect the environment and to meet the needs of the present without compromising the ability of future generations to meet their own needs.

We commend the EcoTeam program to our churches and direct the General Board of Church and Society to make information about it available to the Church.

ADOPTED 1996

See Social Principles, ¶ 64; "Environmental Justice for a Sustainable Future"; "Environmental Stewardship."

Black-Owned Farmland

WHEREAS, according to the agricultural census of 1978, Black farmland loss was two-and-one-half times greater than the loss rate for white farmers; Black farmers as a group, compared to other farmers, depend more heavily on farming for an income and have less off-farm income; the continuing loss of ownership and control of agricultural land by Black American farmers has reduced their ability to achieve economic viability and financial independence; this loss has been accelerated by the Black land owners' lack of access to capital, technical information, and legal resources needed to retain and develop agricultural land holdings into stable, income-producing, self-sustaining operations;

WHEREAS, the 1982 Civil Rights Commission study entitled "The Decline of Black Farming in America" reported many actions and inactions on the part of the U.S. Department of Agriculture and, in particular, the Farmers Home Administration that have contributed to Black land loss; a follow-up study in 1983 showed the Farmers Home Administration's record to be worse than the year before; there were many specific recommendations in the two reports that are yet to be followed through on;

WHEREAS, the U.S. Civil Rights Commission's study predicted that, if present trends continue, there will be no Black-owned farms by the year 2000;

WHEREAS, the dislocation of Blacks in agriculture and the disruption of rural Black family life contributes to unemployment, drug and alcohol abuse, child and spouse abuse, loss of identity, loss of community leadership, increasing absentee land ownership, and a decline in attendance and participation in rural Black churches across the countryside;

WHEREAS, we as United Methodists take seriously Paul's advice: "If one member suffers, all suffer together";

Therefore, be it resolved, that The United Methodist Church go on record supporting the crucial need for the Church and the government to provide financial, technical, and management assistance to help stop the decline of Black-owned farmland in America.

Be it further resolved, that the General Conference of The United Methodist Church call upon the secretary of agriculture to provide grants to agricultural colleges to help develop new marketing strategies for limited-resource farmers and to help disseminate information on existing viable marketing strategies—preference to be given to historically Black agriculture (1890 land grant) colleges where available.

Be it further resolved, that the General Conference of The United Methodist Church ask the secretary of agriculture to seek initiatives linking government, private, church, and other community resources to offer support and to aid Black farm owners.

Finally, be it further resolved, that the General Conference of The United Methodist Church ask the President of the United States and the secretary of agriculture to press for a just and enlightened public farm policy that will preserve the diverse ownership of land as well as the continuation of Black-owned family-operated farms.

ADOPTED 1988

See Social Principles, ¶ 64; "U.S. Agriculture and Rural Communities in Crisis"; "Environmental Racism."

Common Heritage

Common Heritage Concept

The common heritage is a pioneering concept in actual international cooperation and sharing of the benefits of the world's resources. This concept stems from the underlying premise that resources outside the control of different nations should be under a just and equitable system of management. Several principles are a general guide to what a common heritage area may be. These include the need for full participation in decision-making for all nations; the use of the resource area only for peaceful purposes; no nation allowed an exclusive claim; the transfer of technology; and development of the resources for the benefit of all humanity while ensuring future generations the use of the area and resources as well.

Past, Present, and Future Implementation

The international community has been developing the concept of common heritage through the United Nations Law of the Sea Treaty and the Agreement Governing the Activities of States on the Moon and Other Celestial Bodies. The system that has evolved in the Law of the Sea is one to which most countries have agreed, although no one nation has been totally satisfied. Nations are continuing in the process to complete the implementation of the concept through the ongoing Law of the Sea process. The concept of the common heritage is being expanded to include, but is not limited to, the air we breathe; water, which sustains all life; the genetic variability of plants and animals upon which future agriculture and medicine may depend; Antarctica; the moon and other planets; and outer space.

Biblical and Theological Base

The common heritage concept has its roots for people of faith in the biblical understanding that all creation is under the authority of God and that all creation is interdependent. Our covenant with God requires us to be stewards, protectors, and defenders of all creation. The use of natural resources is a universal concern and responsibility of all as reflected in Psalm 24:1: "The earth is the LORD'S and the fullness thereof" (Revised Standard Version).

The New Testament confronts us with the implication of the Old Testament understanding when it asks us how we use our resources in relation to our brothers and sisters. John the Baptist prepared us for Jesus' ministry by stating, "Those who have two coats let them share with those who have none; and those who have food let them do likewise" (Luke 3:11, RSV). This philosophy was carried forth into the early church by incorporating the belief that the way in which one shares one's goods is a reflection of how one loves God. This is stated in 1 John 3:17 (RSV): "But if anyone has the world's goods and sees his brother in need, yet closes his heart against him, how does God's love abide in him?"

Our Denominational Witness

The Social Principles of The United Methodist Church apply these basic biblical perceptions to how we use the resources of creation, in the statement: "We believe that Christian faith denies to any person or group of persons exclusive and arbitrary control of any other part of the created universe. Socially and culturally conditioned ownership of property is, therefore, to be considered a responsibility to God" (¶ 67A).

The Social Principles also remind us that "upon the powerful rests responsibility to exercise their wealth and influence with restraint" (¶ 69B). Furthermore, the statement says that as United Methodists "we applaud international efforts to develop a more just international economic order in which the limited resources of the earth will be used to the maximum benefit of all nations and peoples" (¶ 69B).

United Methodists have affirmed the common heritage since 1976 and have worked to see the common heritage become codified into international agreements for Law of the Sea, the moon, and Antarctica.

Statements of Understanding

In light of the uneven patterns of utilization of the world's resources and in light of our own understanding of the gospel and United Methodist tradition, we affirm these principles:

1. Specific natural resources belong to all humanity, and therefore must be developed and preserved for the benefit of all, not just for the few, both today and for generations to come.

2. All people have the right to enough of the resources of the universe to provide for their health and well-being.

3. God's creation is intended to be used for the good of all as a precious gift, not for warfare or economic oppression of others.

Recommended Actions

Therefore, as United Methodists we are called to:

1. Work for and support the process of legal implementation of the common heritage concept as understood in the Law of the Sea Treaty and the Agreement Governing the Activities of States on the Moon and Other Celestial Bodies, as vehicles to address a more just and responsible use of God's creation;

2. Request that the appropriate general agencies of The United Methodist Church study and develop a broad biblical and theological understanding of the common heritage concept, which should include but not be limited to Antarctica, outer space, plant and animal genetics, air, and water;

3. Request that the appropriate general agencies of The United Methodist Church develop and distribute resources for education about, and become advocates for, the common heritage concept; and

4. Study these materials on the common heritage as individuals, local congregations, general program agencies, and other groups.

ADOPTED 1984

See Social Principles, ¶ 64; "Environmental Justice for a Sustainable Future"; "Environmental Stewardship"; "The Law of the Sea."

A Dioxin-Free Future

The U.S. Environmental Protection Agency's (EPA) 1994 report entitled *The Scientific Reassessment of Dioxin* affirmed health warnings made twenty years ago—that the "background" levels of *dioxin*, a deadly chlorine-based chemical, pose a serious threat to the health of the general U.S. population.

The EPA concluded that dioxin compounds cause several types of cancer. Exposure to toxic chemicals such as dioxin is widely suspected to be related to the increasing rates of cancer in the United States. The rate of testicular cancer has tripled in the past thirty years, the rate of prostate cancer has doubled in the past ten years, and the rate of breast cancer in the United States has risen from one in every twenty women in the 1960s to one in every eight women today. More women have died of breast cancer in the last two decades than the number of U.S. soldiers killed in World War I, World War II, and the Korean and Vietnam wars.

The EPA report stated that there is reason to believe that dioxins at extremely low levels cause a wide range of other serious health effects, including reproductive impairment, learning disabilities, developmental injuries, and the increased risk of diabetes and endometriosis. Furthermore, even low levels of dioxin impair the ability of the immune system to fight infectious disease. The EPA report says that there is no level of dioxin below which the immune system is not affected.

The EPA concluded that the levels of dioxins already lodged in human bodies are already close to levels known to cause serious health problems. According to the EPA, the average person is exposed to dioxin levels 50 to 100 times greater than the maximum allowable amounts designated by the federal government in 1985.

Some persons have what the EPA calls "special" exposures, including certain occupational groups, people living near dioxin emitters, and people who consume higher than average levels of meat, fish, and dairy products. Human exposure to dioxins begins early in life, since dioxin crosses the placenta. Nursing infants take in four to twelve percent of their lifetime dose of dioxin within the first year of their lives, a period during which they are most susceptible to the effects of such toxins.

Toxic pollution costs society hundreds of billions of dollars each year in expenses for health care, diminished productivity, waste disposal, and remediation of contaminated sites and ground water.

A healthy population, a clean environment, and efficient, nonpolluting technologies are essential to a sound economy. With a single program—dioxin phaseout—much of the world's most severe toxic pollution could be stopped.

The United Methodist Church calls on cancer research organizations to move to a prevention-based approach to cancer research and funding, including more studies on the relationship between cancer and chlorine-based toxins in the environment.

We support a phaseout of the production of dioxin, beginning with the immediate action on the three largest sources of dioxin: incineration of chlorine containing wastes, bleaching of pulp and paper with chlorine, and the entire life cycle of polyvinyl chloride (PVC) plastic.

We support worker protection programs for people working in industries that make toxic chemicals or result in toxic by-product and related chemicals, who may lose their jobs with a phaseout of these chemicals. Such programs could include a "Workers' Superfund" program.

We direct the General Board of Church and Society to cooperate with the Health and Welfare Ministries unit of the General Board of Global Ministries to work with companies, governments, and medical institutions to implement the above recommendations.

ADOPTED 1996

See Social Principles, ¶ 64; "Environmental Stewardship"; "Environmental Justice for a Sustainable Future."

Energy Policy Statement

Preamble

In 1979, our nation experienced two shocks that are compelling us to reassess our energy future: the revolution in Iran, and the accident at Three Mile Island. It is already clear that by the turn of this century, our sources of power will be radically altered. Just as the first half of this century was marked by a rapid shift from wood, water, and coal to the fossil fuels that currently supply 90 percent of the U.S. energy needs, so we, today, are at the beginning of a rapid transition from these fuels, which are running out, to the renewable sources that must supply our energy future. Because society runs on its energy and is shaped by the fuels it uses and the way it uses them, we will, in effect, be shaping a new world by the energy policies we adopt in the next few decades. The stakes are high: The decisions that human societies are now making will either enhance or degrade the quality of life on our planet; they will either more closely approximate the vision of the reign of God that fires the Christian imagination or they will make that vision more remote from actual human existence. Furthermore, as our world comes up against limits and undergoes the stress of rapid change, fears will be raised and conflicts will become inevitable. Our responses to these stresses can produce either more repressive societies or societies in which liberty is enhanced.

Stewards of the Spaceship Earth

The recognition that a new world is emerging and that the church of Jesus Christ may have a role to play in shaping that world calls us to reexamine the biblical sources out of which we as Christians live our lives.

Humankind enjoys a unique place in God's universe. On the one hand, we are simply one of God's many finite creatures, made from the "dust of the earth," bounded in time and space, fallible in judgment, limited in control, dependent upon our Creator, and interdependent with all other creatures. On the other hand, we are created in the very image of God, with the divine Spirit breathed into us, and entrusted with "dominion" over God's creation (Genesis 1:26, 28; 2:7; Psalm 8:6). We are simultaneously co-creatures with all creation and, because of the divine summons, co-creators with God of the world in which we live. This hybrid human condition produces both the opportunity and the twin dangers for humans on this planet.

The first danger is *arrogance:* that we may overestimate the extent of human control over our environment and the soundness of human judgments concerning it (after all, we still know very little about the ecosystem in which we live); that we may underestimate the limits of the planet where we live; and that we may misunderstand "dominion" to mean exploitation instead of stewardship.

The second danger is *irresponsibility:* that we may fail to be the responsible stewards of the earth that God has called us to be, choosing instead to bury our "talents" while awaiting the Master's return (Matthew 25:24-28). As stewards entrusted with dominion, then, we will demonstrate our faith in God by becoming God's avant-garde in shaping the new human society that will emerge in the twenty-first century. We cannot, therefore, eschew the task of seeking to embody in the new-world-aborning the values that we hold in covenant with God. At the same time, however, we dare not overlook the limits of our control; nor can we forget the forgiving grace in Jesus Christ, which alone makes us bold enough, or the hope in Christ, which alone keeps us from despair.

The Values Involved in Energy Policy

The Scripture that provides the motive for our action in the present energy crisis also lays the foundation for the values that we seek to realize. These values underlying the policies we advocate are *justice* and *sustainability*.

1. *Justice*. Ever since the first covenant between God and Israel, and especially since the eighth-century prophets, the people of God have understood that they bear a special concern for justice. "Let justice roll down like waters,/ and righteousness like an everflowing stream" (Amos 5:24) is a cry echoed in hundreds of contexts throughout the Old and New Testaments. Biblical righteousness includes a special concern for the least and the last: the poor, the captive, the oppressed (Luke 4:18; cf. Isaiah 61:1-2). Energy policies that Christians can support, then, will seek to actualize the multifaceted biblical vision of justice. They will be policies that close rather than widen the gap dividing wealth and poverty, rich nations and poor. They will be measures that liberate rather than oppress. They will be programs that distribute fairly the benefits, burdens, and hazards of energy production and consumption, taking into consideration those not yet born as well as the living. They will thus be strategies that give priority to meeting basic human needs such as air, water, food, clothing, and shelter.

2. *Sustainability*. Only recently have we humans come to recognize that creation (finitude) entails limits to the resources entrusted to us as stewards of the earth. In particular, we have come up against limits to the nonrenewable fuels available for our consumption and limits to our environment's capacity to absorb poisonous wastes. These double limits mean that humans can betray their stewardship either by using up resources faster than they can be replaced or by releasing wastes in excess of the planet's capacity to absorb them. We now know that humans have the capacity to destroy human life and perhaps even life itself on this planet, and to do so in a very short period of time. Energy policy decisions, therefore, must be measured by sustainability as a criterion in addition to justice. In terms of energy policy, sustainability means energy use that will not: (a) deplete the earth's resources in such

a way that our descendants will not be able to continue human society at the level that is adequate for a good quality of life, and (b) pollute the environment to such an extent that human life cannot be sustained in the future. These guidelines for sustainability must include considerations of quality of life as well as mere biological continuance.

Until such time as a truly inexhaustible source of power is developed, we must create and expand all of the energy resources available to us, with special emphasis on renewable energy resources. We enjoy a highly sophisticated, industrialized world. It is not a realistic option for us to retrogress to a world where people read by candlelight and heat with wood. Also, we should be aware of the tragic effects that steadily increasing energy costs will have, especially upon the aged and poor members of our society. All options available in the United States are not open to peoples in other parts of the world; hence, we should endeavor to develop all available energy sources. We must creatively explore all of the energy options available to us.

There are environmental problems connected with these energy options that cause people to raise objections to their development and use. We believe that the objections in each energy source should be calmly assessed and then the risks and benefits of its use compared with the use of the other energy options. For example, the large-scale use of our coal resources poses many problems. Underground mining, in addition to operational accidents, causes disabling illness or death from black lung. Strip-mining can despoil an area and ruin it for further use if restoration measures are not practiced. The actual burning of coal causes large-scale pollution and could seriously alter the environment by increasing the carbon dioxide content of the atmospheric envelope.

Hydroelectric power also has its problems. In addition to deaths from industrial accidents, many dam sites are (or were) attractive scenic areas. Destroying (or diminishing) such natural beauty areas as the Grand Canyon would be objectionable to most of us. Possible dam failure with the resultant flood damage must also be considered in evaluation of this source of power.

The use of petroleum products creates environmental problems that are on the increase. Tankers and offshore wells have created spills that have devastated seacoast areas; the damage is long-lasting or permanent. Atmospheric pollution, far from being under control, is a most serious health problem in centers of dense population.

Our nuclear energy option also has many problems to be faced. The hazards in storing radioactive wastes for thousands of years and the destructive potential of a catastrophic accident involve a great risk of irreversible damage to the environment or to the human genetic pool.

1. We support a strenuous national effort to conserve energy. Economists have concluded that in the next decade, a greater increase in end-use energy can be gained through conservation than through any single new source of fuel. Furthermore, conservation is nonpolluting and job producing. We include under conservation: insulation, cogeneration, recycling, public transportation, more efficient motors in appliances and automobiles, as well as the elimination of waste, and a more simplified lifestyle. The technology for such steps is already known and commercially available; it requires only dissemination of information and stronger public support, including larger tax incentives than are presently available.

2. All United Methodist churches are encouraged to be models for energy conservation by doing such things as: installing dampers in furnaces, insulating adequately all church properties, heating and lighting only rooms that are in use, using air circulation, and exploring alternative energy sources such as solar energy.

3. We also urge all our members and agencies to assess their own energy consumption, finding ways to conserve, to eliminate waste, to revise transportation patterns, and to simplify lifestyles as a model for sound stewardship of the limited resources entrusted to us.

4. We support increased government funding for research and development of renewable energy sources, especially solar energy, and government incentives to speed the application of the resulting technologies to our energy needs, wherever appropriate. The greatest national effort should be made in the areas of conservation and renewable energy sources.

5. We oppose any national energy policy that will result in continuing exploitation of Native American lands without the consent of the persons who control those lands. The despoiling of Native American lands and the increased health problems that have resulted among Native Americans because of the mining of coal and the milling of uranium must cease.

6. We support a national energy program that will not increase the financial burden on the poor, the elderly, and those with fixed incomes. If a rapid rise in the price of fuel is necessary to smooth out distortions in the energy economy, as many economists believe, then legislative means should be found to cushion the impact of such price increases on the poor.

7. We support full U.S. cooperation in international efforts to ensure equitable distribution of necessary energy supplies and rapid development and deployment of appropriate technologies based on renewable energy resources such as solar, wind, and water energy generation.

8. We strongly encourage The United Methodist Church at all levels to engage in a serious study of these energy issues in the context of Christian faith and the values of justice and sustainability.

ADOPTED 1980

See Social Principles, ¶ 64B; "Nuclear Safety in the United States"; "Environmental Stewardship."

Environmental Justice for a Sustainable Future

Humankind is destroying the global ecological balance that provides the life-support systems for the planet. Signs of the crisis are evident all around us. The global ecological imbalance produces environmental destruction.

Polluted air pervades the atmosphere. Garbage abounds, with little space for disposal. Polluting gases destroy the ozone layer and cause global warming. Deforestation leads to soil erosion, a lack of carbon storage, inadequate water quantity and poor quality, and the loss of species, and thus a reduction in biological diversity. The misuse of pesticides and fertilizers contributes to the poisoning of our soils and creates products harmful to all life.

Present social, political, and economic development structures fail to provide the basic necessities of food, clothing, and shelter for an estimated 5.4 billion people. Additionally, at least one billion people live in absolute poverty. The environmental crisis results in social unrest and mounting violence.

Historical and Theological Concerns

Through the ages, a theological base for the domination of creation was found in Genesis 1:28: "Be fruitful and multiply, and fill the earth and subdue it; and have dominion over . . . every living thing that moves upon the earth." Misinterpretation of "subdue" and "dominion" has been used to justify much of the nature-destroying aspects of modern civilization.

The scale of human activity has grown so large that it now threatens the planet itself. Global environmental problems have become so vast

65

that they are hard to comprehend. Between 1955 and 1990, the human population has doubled to 5.4 billion. During the same time, the consumption of fossil fuels has quadrupled. Increasing evidence suggests that the carbon dioxide from fossil fuels has already caused a noticeable warming of the globe. Destruction of habitat, especially tropical rain forests, is causing the loss of species at an ever-increasing rate. Valuable topsoil is being depleted. There is a recurring hole in the ozone layer. More ultraviolet radiation now reaches the earth, which may cause more cancers, poorer crop growth, and damage to the immune systems of humans and other animals.

Confronted with the massive crisis of the deterioration of God's creation and faced with the question of the ultimate survival of life, we ask God's forgiveness for our participation in this destruction of God's creation. We have misused God's good creation. We have confused God's call for us to be faithful stewards of creation with a license to use all of creation as we see it. The first humans had to leave the garden of Eden when they decided they had permission to use all of creation despite warnings to the contrary. We have denied that God's covenant is with all living creatures (Genesis 9:9). We have even denied that all of the human family should enjoy the covenant. We forget that the good news that we are called to proclaim includes the promise that Jesus Christ came to redeem all creation (Colossians 1:15-20).

We believe that at the center of the vision of *shalom* is the integration of environmental, economic, and social justice.

We are called to eliminate over-consumption as a lifestyle, thus using lower levels of finite natural resources.

We are called to seek a new lifestyle rooted in justice and peace.

We are called to establish new priorities in a world where 40,000 children die of hunger each day.

Therefore, we are called to a global sense of community and solidarity leading to a new world system of international relationships and economic/environmental order. In this way, the misery of one billion poor now living in absolute poverty can be alleviated and the living ecosystem be saved.

Principles for a Sustainable Future

The Social Principles of The United Methodist Church remind us that "all creation is the Lord's, and we are responsible for the ways in which we use and abuse it" (¶ 64). Development must be centered in the concept of *sustainability* as defined by the World Commission of Environment and Development: "to meet the needs of the present without compromising the ability of future generations to meet their own needs." The Christian understanding of sustainability encompasses this concept. Fundamental to our call as faithful witnesses is the meeting of human needs within the capacity of ecosystems. This ensures the security of creation and a just relationship between all people. Sustainable development, therefore, looks toward a healthy future in three vital areas: the social community, the economy, and the environment.

Conclusion

The United Methodist Church will strive for a global sense of community to help achieve social, economic, and ecological justice for all of creation.

We will focus on the conversion to sustainable practices in the following areas:

Atmosphere

- Support measures calling for the reduction of carbon dioxide, chlorofluorocarbons (CFCs), methane, nitrogen oxides, and sulfur dioxide, believed to cause the greenhouse effect and acid rain.
- Support measures calling for the elimination of CFCs to stop the depletion of the ozone layer.
- Support the cleanup of environmental problems through economic incentive, appropriate enforcement measures, and sanctions against those causing pollution.

Earth

- Support integrated and sustainable natural resource management.
- Commit to the "Greening of the World" through the limiting of all emissions of pollutants that damage forests and reforestation.
- Work for ecologically sound agricultural practices that produce healthy food and a clean environment.
- Protect biodiversity among both animals and plants.

Water

- Support integrated, sustainable management to reduce or eliminate factors contributing to limited water quantity and poorer quality.

Energy

- Support improved energy conservation and greater reliance on new and renewable sources of energy.
- Support the development of efficient mass transportation.
- Support a call for a sustainable national energy policy.

Actions/Recommendations

We call upon the agencies and local congregations of The United Methodist Church to take the following actions:

Council of Bishops

- Communicate to the Church the urgency of responding to the ecological crisis.
- Model for the Church a "ministry of presence" by going to places where humans and ecosystems are endangered by environmental destruction.

General Council on Ministries (GCOM)

- Initiate basic research on the changing attitudes on environmental issues among United Methodist members.
- Request each United Methodist agency to include an evaluation of their corporate action taken toward sustainable environmental practices as a part of their 1995–96 Quadrennial Report.

General Board of Church and Society (GBCS)

- Develop programs that help annual conferences and local churches become more involved in sustainable practices in public policy and personal aspects of the ecological crisis. These programs would emphasize conversion to a sustainable society.

General Board of Discipleship (GBOD)

- Develop curriculum and programs (for all ages), in consultation with GBCS, that emphasize ecological responsibility as a key element of discipleship.

General Board of Global Ministries (GBGM)

• Join with the GBCS in working with mission partners through the National, World, and Women's Divisions to prepare for and participate in the environmental recommendations that will flow from the United Nations Conference on the Environment and Development (UNCED).
• Conduct a survey, with the assistance of all mission partners, to identify environmental concerns and develop projects geared to the solution of common concerns.
• Initiate an audit of all National, World, and Women's Division and UMCOR-sponsored projects as to their environmental effect on the global ecological balance.
• Establish an eco-mission intern group to work on ecology issues under the sponsorship of the National and World Divisions.
• Include global environmental issues in the training of all GBGM missionaries.
• Facilitate dialogue between religious groups, other nongovernment organizations, and government agencies on the formation and methods of popular participation.

General Board of Higher Education and Ministry (GBHEM)

• Include a greater awareness in clergy education and training of the global ecological crises.

United Methodist Communications (UMCom)

• Produce programs that stress Christian responsibility for the future of creation and include models of The United Methodist Church's involvement in environmental justice.

General Council on Finance and Administration (GCFA)

• Assist the Church in its effort to be ecologically responsible in its own use of resources by collecting statistics on local churches' and general agencies' use of energy, water, paper, and recycling to monitor the progress of the Church in these aspects of stewardship.

General Board of Pension and Health Benefits (GBPHB)

• Develop investment guidelines, in consultation with agencies, to evaluate its securities in light of whether those corporations have a positive history of care for creation.

Local Congregations

• Develop programs to incorporate the concerns of ecological justice into their work in evangelism, social concerns, mission activities, stewardship, trustees, and worship.

ADOPTED 1992

See Social Principles, ¶ 64; "Environmental Stewardship"; "Energy Policy Statement."

Environmental Racism

The United Methodist Church is committed to understanding and eliminating racism. One generally ignored aspect is environmental racism. People of color are disproportionately affected by toxic contamination due to the production, storage, treatment, and disposal process of hazardous materials and wastes. African American, Hispanic North American, Asian American, Native American, and third world communities are usually the least able, politically and economically, to oppose the sitings of these facilities.

Research has documented the following:

1. Race is consistently the most statistically significant variable in the location of commercial hazardous waste facilities. Three of the five largest commercial hazardous waste landfills in the United States are located in communities of color; communities with commercial hazardous waste facilities have two to three times the average minority population of communities without such facilities; and three out of every five African Americans and Hispanic North Americans live in communities with toxic waste sites.[1] The predominantly African American and Hispanic south side of Chicago has the greatest concentration of hazardous waste sites in the United States.

2. Communities where hazardous waste incinerators are sited tend to have large minority populations, low incomes, and low property values. The minority portion of the population in communities with existing incinerations is 98 percent higher than the national average. In Houston, Texas, six of eight municipal incinerators are located in predominantly African American neighborhoods.[2]

3. Communities of color have greater cancer rates than white communities.[3] Many environmental groups are calling for a study of the

---

[1] "Toxic Wastes and Race," Commission for Racial Justice, United Church of Christ, 1987.
[2] *Playing with Fire: Hazardous Waste Incineration,* Greenpeace, 1991.
[3] *Health and Status of Minorities and Low-Income Groups,* Third Edition. U.S. Department of Health and Human Services, 1991.

linkage between environmental contamination and increased cancer rates.

4. Fifty percent of the children in the United States suffering from lead poisoning are African American.

5. Farm workers' children (mainly Hispanics) in the United States suffer a higher rate of birth defects due to their mothers' exposure to pesticides during the early stages of pregnancy. In farm worker communities, children with cancer are common. Pesticide exposure among farm workers causes more than 300,000 pesticide-related illnesses each year.[4]

6. Navajo teenagers have cancer rates seventeen times the national average, due to countless uranium spills on Navajo lands that contaminated their water, air, and soil.[5]

7. The growing trend during the 1980s and 1990s has been to dump toxic wastes in developing countries.[6] Countries such as Liberia have been offered much-needed foreign capital if they accepted several shipments of toxic wastes in the past few years. Unfortunately, these countries often lack the appropriate infrastructure to adequately handle the environmental and health problems that accompany these wastes.

Other evidence suggests that the problem is worsening. The findings of the Interdenominational Hearings on Toxics and Minorities, held in September 1990, in Albuquerque, New Mexico, and the General Board of Church and Society-sponsored consultation on Responding to Communities Facing Toxic Hazards held in Baton Rouge, Louisiana, in October 1990, poignantly demonstrated that communities are still having problems related to toxic contamination more than ten years after the media exposed the problems.

Our society's attitude toward the production and disposal of hazardous products is one of "out of sight, out of mind." But "out of sight, out of mind" is most often where the poor and powerless live and work. These communities have thus become toxic "sacrifice zones." This pattern of racism represents a serious challenge to the conscience of all Christians. We ask our local churches, conferences, and general agencies to join with other religious bodies and groups in actions to end this form of racism:

---

[4] Marion Moses, M.D., Pesticide Education Network.
[5] Center for Third World Organizing.
[6] Greenpeace Waste Trade Campaign.

1. We request the Council of Bishops to address environmental racism in any formal communication to the denomination concerning racism or the environment;

2. We urge annual conferences, districts, local churches, and general agencies to become more involved with community groups working to alleviate environmental racism;

3. We urge all general program agencies and the General Commission on Religion and Race to:

(a) disseminate the "stories" of people and communities affected by environmental racism;

(b) find expertise, build leadership, and develop networks that can help empower people within communities in crisis; and

(c) develop programs that help annual conferences, districts, and local churches respond to these concerns;

4. We call upon the General Board of Church and Society to:

(a) advocate a moratorium on the siting of hazardous waste treatment, storage, and disposal facilities in low-income/people-of-color communities;

(b) advocate comprehensive legislation that remedies these injustices and adequately protects all citizens and the environment; and

(c) develop programs that help annual conferences, districts, and local churches respond to these concerns;

5. We request the General Council on Ministries to assist the General Board of Church and Society in conducting research in this area;

6. We call upon the General Board of Pension and Health Benefits and other Church investors to sponsor shareholder resolutions on environmental racism issues and to urge corporations to sign guidelines for corporate conduct on the environment (such as the Valdez Principles developed in cooperation with the Interfaith Center on Corporate Responsibility);

7. We urge individual United Methodists to:

(a) become aware of how and where their community's wastes are disposed and who in their community is adversely affected by the production and disposal of industrial chemicals; and

(b) make a personal commitment to reduce their use of hazardous chemicals by one each day;

8. We call upon the U.S. federal government to:

(a) institute comprehensive risk-assessment studies of communities at risk and their affected populations;

(b) enable these communities to participate in cleanup decisions that affect them directly;

(c) institute a budget and staff in the Environmental Protection Agency to monitor toxic waste siting in low-income/people-of-color communities;

(d) give these communities priority in receiving Superfund funding to clean up existing sites; and

(e) prohibit hazardous waste exports and imports;

9. We urge industry to:

(a) assess the adverse impacts of their production and disposal processes on workers and surrounding communities;

(b) implement comprehensive Toxics Use Reduction (TUR) programs;

(c) develop nontoxic alternatives to commonly used hazardous materials;

(d) comply with local, state, and federal environmental and safety laws;

(e) respond to community concerns and grievances;

(f) sign comprehensive environmental guidelines developed with public input, such as the Valdez Principles; and

(g) develop industrywide standards for environmental accounting and auditing procedures similar to those required for financial accounting.

ADOPTED 1992

See Social Principles, ¶ 64, "Environmental Justice for a Sustainable Future"; "A Charter for Racial Justice Policies in an Interdependent Global Community."

Environmental Stewardship

I. A Theology of Stewardship and the Environment

Many of today's "environmental problems" have their roots in humanity's shortsighted use of God's creation. While focusing on the stewardship of monetary resources, we forget that the source of all wealth is God's gracious creation.

In the Bible, a steward is one given responsibility for what belongs to another. The Greek word we translate as steward is *oikonomos,* one who cares for the household or acts as its trustee. The word *oikos,* meaning household, is used to describe the world as God's household.

Christians, then, are to be stewards of the whole household (creation) of God. *Oikonomia*, "stewardship," is also the root of our word *economics*. *Oikos*, moreover, is the root of our modern word *ecology*. Thus, in a broad sense, stewardship, economics, and ecology are, and should be, related. Indeed, a "faithful and wise steward" (Luke 12:42, KJV) must relate them.

The Old Testament relates these concepts in the vision as *shalom*. Often translated "peace," the broader meaning of *shalom* is wholeness. In the Old Testament, *shalom* is used to characterize the wholeness of a faithful life lived in relationship to God. *Shalom* is best understood when we experience wholeness and harmony as human beings with God, with others, and with creation itself. The task of the steward is to seek *shalom*.

Stewards of God's Creation. The concept of stewardship is first introduced in the Creation story. In Genesis 1:26, the Bible affirms that every person is created in God's image. But this gift brings with it a unique responsibility. Being created in God's image brings with it the responsibility to care for God's creation. God chose to give human beings a divine image not so we would exploit creation to our own ends, but so we would be recognized as stewards of God. To have dominion over the earth is a trusteeship, a sign that God cares for creation and has entrusted it to our stewardship. Our stewardship of all the world's resources is always accountable to God, who loves the whole of creation and who desires that it exist in *shalom*. The intention of creation was that all should experience *shalom* to know the goodness of creation. In the Old Testament, "fullness of life" means having enough, sufficient to experience the goodness of creation. By contrast, our age has come to define "fullness of life" as more than enough. The desire of many for excess begins to deny enough for others, and *shalom* is broken. That all should participate in creation's goodness is a fundamental of stewardship.

Another theme of *shalom* is that in creation we are all related. Humans are not self-sufficient. We need God, others, and nature. The story of the garden (Genesis 2) attempts to picture the complete and harmonious interrelatedness of all creation. There is *shalom* only when we recognize that interrelatedness and care for the whole. When we violate the rules of the garden, we are dismissed. In ecological terms, when we violate the principles of ecology, we suffer environmental damage.

As the story of the garden shows, God's intention of *shalom* was not carried out. Sin intervened, and the *shalom* was broken. But God offered a way to restore *shalom*—redemption. And as God's stewards, we have a role in that redemption. Stewardship, then, is to become involved wherever wholeness is lacking and to work in harmony with God's saving activity to reconcile, to reunite, to heal, to make whole. Stewardship has to do with how we bring all of the resources at our disposal into efficient use in our participation in the saving activity of God. Environmental stewardship is one part of our work as God's stewards. As stewards of the natural environment, we are called to preserve and restore the very air, water, and land on which life depends. Moreover, we are called to see that all persons have a sufficient share of the resources of nature. The environmental crises that face us need not exist. With new hope rooted in Christ and with more obedient living as stewards of the earth, the creation can be healed.

II. United Methodist Historical Concerns

Since the beginnings of the Methodist movement, there has been a concern with what we today call "environmental concerns." Wesley's emphasis on "cleanliness" came as he observed a land of open sewers, impure water, unplanned cities, and smoke-filled air. In the mines and mills, squalor and filth were everywhere, as was disease. The substantial decline in the death rate in England from 1700 to 1801 can be traced to improvements in environment, sanitation, and a wider knowledge of concepts of basic health such as those advocated by Wesley.

The first Social Creed, adopted by the 1908 General Conference of The Methodist Episcopal Church (North), focused on the environmental and health hazards facing workers.

As the problems of soil erosion and dwindling reserves of natural resources became more obvious, General Conferences in the 1940s, the 1950s, and the 1960s called for the development of programs stressing careful stewardship of the soil and conservation of natural resources. In 1968, a United Methodist Church concerned with continuing pollution of the environment insisted that community rights take precedence over property rights and that "no individual should be permitted to degrade the environment . . . for the sake . . . of profit."

In the mid-1980s, the environmental problems of the world are no less acute than they were in the 1960s and 1970s. While some parts of the industrialized world have less pollution of some sorts, polluting factories have been relocated to the industrializing nations. Hazardous chemicals have been banned in one nation, while their use increases in another. In the United States, children have been poisoned by toxic wastes under their schools; in Central America, children have been poisoned when the fields they have worked in have been sprayed with pesticides banned in other countries.

Sometimes our solutions create new problems. Some thought higher smokestacks would help disperse air pollutants; instead, we have more acid rain. Herbicides, used in "no till" agriculture, while helping to control soil erosion, have begun to pollute aquifers. The environmental problems of the next few decades will require more effort and more initiative to solve than the problems of the past.

The Christian church should actively support programs to implement principles that will safeguard the environment. Some of the areas we now recognize as key are: responsible use of resources, toxic and hazardous substances, air quality, pesticide use, use of wild and agricultural lands, water quality, the military and the environment, and the impact of new technologies on the environment.

III. Principles for Christian Stewardship of the Environment

A. *Responsible Use of Natural Resources.* We support measures that will lead to a more careful and efficient use of the resources of the natural world. We encourage programs that will recycle solid materials of all sorts—paper, glass, metals, plastics, and so forth. We urge United Methodists to participate actively in community recycling programs and urge the establishment of such programs in communities without these programs.

B. *Toxic and Hazardous Substances.* We advocate that governments devote sufficient monetary and human resources to assessing the extent of possible toxic and hazardous waste disposal problems within their jurisdictions. We believe that the entity or entities responsible for the problem should pay the costs related to the site's cleanup and for any health damages caused by the improper or inadequate disposal of such substances. We call upon those agencies responsible for enforcing existing laws to adopt a more aggressive strategy in responding to violators. We support strong penalties for those convicted of illegal disposal of hazardous and toxic materials. We oppose the practice of exporting materials banned in one nation for use in another nation. We advocate that all parties with information on the health effects of a potentially toxic or hazardous substance make these data available to users of the substance. We support the right of those groups that would be affected by a nuclear, toxic, or hazardous material waste repository to be involved actively in all decisions to locate such repositories in their neighborhoods or jurisdiction.

Finally, in order to preclude serious environmental threats to the world population, we urge a discontinuation of the dumping of nuclear waste at sea and support the monitoring of waste disposal of a toxic nature in the soil.

C. *Clean Air.* We believe all persons have the right to breathe clean air. Where the air quality is now poor, steps should be taken to improve its quality, including the elimination of toxic pollutants; the limiting of pollutants from cars, trucks, and buses; and the cleanup of smokestack emissions. Where the air is now good, every effort should be made to maintain such good air quality. We advocate the adoption and strict enforcement of adequate standards to control indoor air pollutants, including toxic substances and tobacco smoke. Special attention should be given to such long-range air quality problems as the depletion of the ozone layer, the heating of the atmosphere, and acid rain. We support international and bilateral efforts to eliminate the cause of such long-term problems.

D. *Chemical Use.* Many chemicals are used for agricultural purposes. These include pesticides, herbicides, and fertilizers. These are required to maximize yields in feeding a hungry world, but their use may be detrimental to the crops or to the environment if improperly selected and/or applied.

We recommend the concept of integrated pest management (IPM), natural control systems, and crop rotation. We urge that greater restrictions be placed on the export of restricted agricultural chemicals from the United States and that the U.S. development agencies encourage the use of agricultural techniques that rely less heavily on agricultural chemical use.

A wide variety of chemicals is used for the processing and preservation of food products. There is growing suspicion, and some scientifically confirmed knowledge, that some of these chemicals are harmful to animals and humans. We recommend that continual aggressive investigation and study be made on the long-range effect of these chemicals by industry, consumer groups, and governmental agencies. We urge policies that retard the indiscriminate use of chemicals, including those used for growing, processing, and preserving food.

E. *Land Use.* All agricultural productivity relies on our careful stewardship of a few inches of topsoil. We encourage economic and farming practices that conserve and promote the improvement of topsoil. We urge that governments provide farmers with incentives for more careful management of this precious resource.

Just as the best farmland is lost through erosion, so too is it lost when it is used for purposes other than farming (e.g., highways, reservoirs, housing, industrial uses, and surface mining). Likewise, land that has become poisoned with salt through poor irrigation practices or with pesticides may become less productive as an agricultural resource. We urge that the careful maintenance of the productivity of the land be the central goal of all management of agricultural lands. We urge governments to preserve the most productive soils for agricultural purposes. Careful management of agricultural lands can help discourage the so-called "reclamation" of forests, wetlands, and wild areas. These areas are valuable in their own right and should be preserved for the contribution they make to ecological balance, wildlife production, water and air quality, and the human spirit.

F. *The Diversity of Life.* We believe that the wondrous diversity of nature is a key part of God's plan for creation. Therefore, we oppose measures that would eliminate diversity in plant and animal varieties, eliminate species, or destroy habitats critical to the survival of endangered species or varieties.

G. *Water.* We live on what has aptly been called the "Water Planet." More than 70 percent of the surface of the earth is covered with water; yet only a small part of that water can be used for drinking or for industrial and agricultural purposes. Our careless use of water in the past means that it will cost more in the future. Decisions over how to allocate increasingly costly supplies of pure water for drinking, industry, and agriculture will be among the most contentious resource-policy questions of the next decades. We urge that steps be taken by all concerned parties to ensure more careful management and preservation of existing groundwater sources. We support the right of native peoples to the first use of waters on their lands. We urge that industrial, municipal, agricultural, and individual consumers of water find ways to use more efficiently the water we now have. We believe that conservation of an area's existing water supplies, not costly transfers of water from basin to basin or other large-scale projects, usually offers the most efficient and environmentally sound source of new water. Finally, we believe that all persons have a right to a sufficient supply of high-quality water free from toxic chemical or pathogenic impurities.

H. *Impact of Technology.* We urge that the ethical and environmental effects of new technologies be fully examined before these technologies are used on a widespread basis. We acknowledge the constantly imperfect state of our knowledge of the effects of our creations and urge the development of those technologies most in accord with God's plan of wholeness for all creation.

I. *The Military and the Environment.* We oppose the military's imperious claim to our planet's resources and its willingness to risk massive environmental contamination through accidental or intentional release of nerve gas, preparation for biological warfare, or continued testing and possible use of nuclear weapons for the sake of claimed offensive and defensive needs.

We also oppose the production of nuclear weapons and the resultant production of tremendous amounts of nuclear waste that endangers the environment.

IV. Involvement

We urge all United Methodists to examine their roles as stewards of God's earth and to study, discuss, and work to implement this resolution.

ADOPTED 1984

See Social Principles, ¶ 64; "Environmental Justice for a Sustainable Future."

The Church and God's Creation

As disciples of Christ, we are called to be good stewards of God's creation. Accordingly, we call upon The United Methodist Church to adopt fresh ways to respond to the perils that now threaten the integrity of God's creation and the future of God's children.

Specifically, The United Methodist Church:

• designates one Sunday each year as a Festival of God's Creation, celebrating God's gracious work in creating the earth and all living things, incorporating into it the Church's liturgical calendar, and developing appropriate ways for congregations to celebrate it;

• endorses the work of the National Inter-Religious Coalition for the Environment and the World Council of Churches Consultation on "Accelerated Climate Change: Sign of Peril, Test of Faith" and urges conferences and congregations to support their activities and programs;

• supports the annual observance of the United Nations' Environmental Sabbath and encourages conferences and churches to participate
in their program;

• recommends that annual conferences establish annual awards to
honor prophetic defenders of God's creation from within their own
constituencies; and

• encourages a simplified and environmentally sound lifestyle throughout the Church and requests that Church agencies, conferences, and
congregations be stewards of God's creation by reducing levels of
consumption and participating in programs that reuse and recycle
goods.

ADOPTED 1996

See Social Principles, ¶ 64; "Environmental Stewardship"; "Environmental Justice for a Sustainable Future"; "God's Vision of Abundant Living."

Indian Lands Used by The United Methodist Church

The General Conference directed:

1. That the General Board of Global Ministries develop a comprehensive study and report on the use by The United Methodist Church of
American Indian Lands for mission purposes since 1784, in consultation
with the Native American International Caucus and the Oklahoma
Indian Missionary Conference; and

2. That the board report include the intended disposition of any
unused land.

ADOPTED 1988

See Social Principles, ¶¶ 64, 66A; "The United Methodist Church and America's Native
People"; "Toward a New Beginning Beyond 1992"; "Confession to Native Americans."

Indoor Air Pollution

The United Methodist Church stands in a long tradition of profound
concern for the health and physical well-being of the human family.

For Jesus, the abundant life embraced the physical well-being as well
as emotional and spiritual health; he performed acts of healing as signs
of the reign of God.

John Wesley was, in his day, at the forefront of the advocates of
physical health, and the churches that formed The United Methodist
Church have a long record of health and welfare ministries.

Our Church has addressed in various ways the issues of environmental contamination, especially outdoor pollution and workplace hazards. Indoor air pollution has also emerged as an important dimension of overall air contamination, and extensive research has demonstrated the acuteness of this problem. Indoor air pollution affects in a very serious way persons with respiratory problems, allergies, chemical sensitivities, and ecological illnesses. This is an emerging problem for churches, because air pollutants in church buildings can be serious deterrents against attendance at worship and other church activities for some persons.

Churches are generally unaware of the extent to which persons are either prevented from being in church facilities by pollutants or endure them only at considerable personal discomfort or illness.

Sources of indoor pollution in church buildings include chemical fumes from gas stoves and furnaces, pesticides, cleaning materials, formaldehyde, candles, paint, photocopy machines, restroom deodorizers, and radon, as well as particulates such as dust, mold, and asbestos fibers.

Additional pollutants are brought into church buildings in the form of perfume, cologne, and other scents; dry-cleaning odors; and cigarette smoke (which itself releases over 1000 chemicals into the air).

The problem in church buildings is compounded by: (a) the general absence of effective air circulation systems that can mechanically circulate fresh air, and (b) the improved insulating of buildings in recent decades, which, while conserving heat, also reduces the rate of air exchange and allows the buildup of concentration of the indoor pollution. U.S. government studies have shown indoor air pollution levels to be as much as eight times higher than outdoor air pollution.

Indoor air pollution is not only a problem for those most seriously affected; the long-term effects of such pollution could potentially be detrimental to everyone. In our century, the human body is forced to cope with an incredible level of chemical exposure, for which the long-term effects are only partially known. Lung cancer and other sickness resulting from exposure to smoke, whether to smokers themselves or to involuntary smokers exposed to sidestream smoke, are the most widely publicized of the potential long-term effects on everyone.

There is much that churches and church institutions can do to minimize the effect of indoor air pollution. Some churches have already taken steps to reduce indoor air pollution and to address the needs of those seriously affected.

We urge local churches and Church agencies and institutions at all levels to: (a) invite those with special sensitivities to share the handicaps and suffering that they bear due to indoor air pollution; (b) prohibit smoking in all indoor facilities; (c) provide adequate fresh air ventilation or high-quality air cleaning equipment, if necessary; and (d) take an audit of sources of indoor air pollution and take remedial steps.

We ask the Health and Welfare Division of the General Board of Global Ministries, in consultation with those most seriously affected, to: (a) draw up and promote guidelines for addressing indoor air pollution, and (b) to investigate and develop a vigorous program to eliminate the use of tobacco in churches and Church institutions.

Further, we ask the General Board of Church and Society and conference church and society agencies to advocate strong legislation in all nations at all levels of government for the adoption and attainment of indoor air pollution standards and for laws that regulate chemical contamination of public areas, workplaces, and the overall environment.

Finally, we ask all United Methodists to make an inventory of the pollution levels in their homes, schools, workplaces, and public areas and to take steps to reduce environmental pollution for the sake of ourselves, our loved ones, our communities, and future generations.

ADOPTED 1988

See Social Principles, ¶ 64A; "Environmental Stewardship."

The Law of the Sea

We recognize that "All creation is the Lord's, and we are responsible for the ways in which we use and abuse it" (¶ 64).

We are called to repent of our devastation of the physical and nonhuman world, because this world is God's creation and is therefore to be valued and conserved.

Nowhere is this need greater than in relation to the sea. In 1970 the United Nations agreed that those areas of the seabed beyond national boundaries were the "common heritage" of humankind. This means that the resources belong to everyone.

The best hope for global cooperation is through the United Nations, where representatives of the nations of the world developed the Law of the Sea.

The Law of the Sea conference worked to produce a fair and just law for the ocean, in which all nations will benefit. No one nation will have all of its interests satisfied, but mechanisms will be set up to maintain order and peace, and both developed and developing countries will have worked on the regulations.

The Law of the Sea Treaty is concerned with protecting this "common heritage" of humanity. It would:

• guarantee unimpeded access to over 100 straits, facilitating commercial transportation;
• prevent conflicts over fishing waters;
• enforce environmental regulations forbidding countries to dump harmful wastes that spoil the ocean waters;
• share equitably the ocean resources, oil, fish, minerals, and prohibit unjust exploitation of these resources by the powerful;
• regulate access to the waters of coastal countries to permit research of the marine environment;
• limit the continuing extension of national sovereignty over international waters and settle legal disputes arising therefrom;
• prevent the division of the world into competing camps depending on powerful navies; and
• create an international agency to manage cooperatively the international seabed resources.

We also affirm our support for the evolution of effective "commons" law, such as the treaties for the Antarctic, climate, biodiversity, and outer space, which supports our obligations of stewardship, justice, and peace.

Further, we urge all United Methodists to become informed about the Law of the Sea and to call upon their governments to commit themselves to just and equitable implementation of the Law of the Sea and to the ratification of the treaty.

ADOPTED 1980
AMENDED & READOPTED 1996

See Social Principles, ¶ 64A; "Common Heritage"; "Environmental Justice for a Sustainable Future."

Nuclear Safety in the United States

Theology

God has given humans a special charge to "guard and keep" the earth (Genesis 2:15). Nuclear technology presents a special challenge to our call to be stewards of God's creation because of the risks involved in the production, handling, and disposal of long-lived nuclear byproducts (such as plutonium) in the energy and weapons-production cycles. As long as society continues to use nuclear power to produce energy and weapons, we have a special responsibility to ensure that God's creation be protected for present and future generations by insisting that the entire production cycle be as safe as possible.

The problem of nuclear safety is of worldwide concern. It is the responsibility of the Church to use its influence internationally to prevent the devastation that could result from nuclear disasters.

United Methodist Policy

The United Methodist General Conference affirmed the use of nuclear power for energy production but noted that the "nuclear energy option also has many problems to be faced" (*The Book of Resolutions, 1984;* page 160). Among these many problems, it particularly identified the health hazards from "ionizing radiation [that] threaten the exposed individual to additional hazards such as cancer and sterility, and also threaten future generations with birth defects and gene mutations" (*The Book of Resolutions, 1984;* page 238).

The General Conference urged society to examine the ethical and environmental effects of technological developments and ensure that these technologies be in accord with God's plan of wholeness for all creation. It also "oppose[d] the production of nuclear weapons and the resultant production of tremendous amounts of nuclear waste that endangers the environment" (*The Book of Resolutions, 1984;* page 339).

Background

Nuclear Power

The accident at Chernobyl on April 28, 1986, demonstrated the dangers involved in the production of nuclear energy. This accident was much larger than the one at Three Mile Island. However, the Nuclear Regulatory Commission's Reactor Safety Study points out that accidents even larger than Chernobyl are possible for U.S. reactors. Despite the difference between the design of the Chernobyl plants and the designs of most U.S. plants, there are, according to the Reactor Safety Study, many accident scenarios possible in U.S. plants that could lead to substantial releases of radiation. Those safety analyses indicate

84

that even after the improvements instituted after the Three Mile Island accident, there is a substantial chance of a core meltdown among the 107 currently licensed U.S. commercial nuclear power plants over the next twenty years.

In the past few years, while other nations with a sizable commitment to nuclear power have increased their efforts to improve nuclear power-plant safety, the U.S. efforts have been inadequate. Countries such as Japan, West Germany, and Sweden have demonstrated that there are practical and reasonable options available to improve reactor safety. These nations' records show outstanding quality in plant construction, plant materials and equipment, extensive preventive maintenance programs, outstanding levels of human performance, plant reliability, and few unplanned shutdowns, equipment failures, or personnel errors. In the U.S., the nuclear power industry is plagued by human error (operators falling asleep on the job), poor maintenance practices, poor management, poor design, and a serious gap in contractor accountability. In 1985 alone, there were almost 3000 plant mishaps and 764 emergency shutdowns, up 28 percent from 1984.[1]

Department of Energy Reactors

The Department of Energy (DOE) operates over 200 nuclear facilities. Among its main responsibilities are the production and testing of this country's nuclear weapons program. The DOE facilities are generally more antiquated than civilian plants and are not subject to review by outside agencies. Five of these facilities are the main nuclear weapons production reactors. Four are located on the Savannah River in South Carolina; the fifth is the "N-Reactor" at Hanford, Washington (a complex where poor disposal of wastes in the past has created a radioactive landfill known as "one of our largest contaminated areas"). The containment systems in these plants have been criticized as being inadequate and not capable of meeting minimum civilian standards. In 1986, the DOE agreed to submit its five weapons reactors to state and federal waste disposal rules and shut down the Hanford "N-Reactor" for safety improvements. The cleanup of the Hanford site alone could cost over $100 billion. Yet most DOE plants continue to be exempt from the far more rigorous examination of commercial reactors by the Nuclear Regulatory Commission.

---

[1] Joshua Gordon, as cited by Christopher Flavin, Worldwatch Paper 75: "Reassessing Nuclear Power: The Fallout from Chernobyl"; March 1987.

Emergency Planning and State Rights

After the Three Mile Island accident, rules were instituted to improve public safety in case of a nuclear accident. The new rules required the participation, in emergency planning exercise, of local and state officials. In 1986, the Nuclear Regulatory Commission, in response to two state governors' challenge to the viability of utility-produced emergency plans, requested that it be allowed to approve utility emergency evacuation plans in the event that state and local officials refuse to participate in the emergency-planning process. This rule change would ease the licensing of future nuclear reactors and seriously diminish public participation and review of safety measures, as well as increase the dangers of a serious accident.

Nuclear Wastes

One of the most controversial and costly components of the nuclear fission process is the creation of radioactive byproducts. The Nuclear Regulatory Commission divides wastes into two different categories according to the level and duration of radioactivity: high-level and low-level wastes. Since the 1950s, the Department of Energy has been searching for a viable way to dispose of the wastes created by commercial nuclear reactors (irradiated fuels) and high-level wastes from weapons production. These wastes are highly radioactive and will remain radioactive for long periods of time. Presently, these wastes are stored within nuclear facility sites, creating what one member of Congress called hundreds of "de facto nuclear waste dumps."

The Nuclear Waste Policy Act of 1982 set a schedule for the location, construction, and operation of two high-level waste geologic repositories, one in the east, and one in the west. Unfortunately, the U.S. nuclear-waste policy remains in disarray. Political considerations have taken precedence over safety and scientific considerations, and there has been improper and inadequate consultation and cooperation with state governments and Native American tribes. Clear examples of the fragmented and problem-ridden condition of the U.S. nuclear-waste policy include an April 1985 proposal to build a Monitored Retrievable Storage (MRS) facility within the state of Tennessee (an interim facility to make up for expected delays in the permanent repository schedule); and a May 1986 DOE recommendation for a permanent waste-storage site in Texas, Nevada, or Washington, and postponement of further siting activities for an eastern site (in order to avoid placing a nuclear waste site in states where the Department of Energy expects strong political opposition). The MRS facility is intended to receive 15,000 metric tons of nuclear waste (20 percent of the capacity of the permanent repository) and package it for delivery to a permanent repository for final disposal. Critics feel that the MRS proposal is being offered by DOE solely as an expedient way of relieving utilities of the burden of on-site, spent fuel storage. Little research has been done as to the increased hazards of such a plan. Building the MRS would increase the likelihood of a transportation accident due to the need to ship waste twice. Moreover, there will likely be political pressure to convert the MRS into a "semipermanent" repository without careful environmental review.

Recommendations

The United Methodist Church expresses its deep concern over the use of a technology with severe environmental and health impacts without appropriate and extensive safety measures in the production, handling, and disposal processes. We also reiterate our opposition to the use of nuclear technology for the production of weapons.

We recommend:

1. *Reviewing the safety of operating plants.* Each of the 107 operating commercial plants in the U.S. should be reviewed by the Nuclear Regulatory Commission and the Office of Technology Assessment of the U.S. Congress to identify design deficiencies and weaknesses that could contribute to or cause an accident.

2. *Instituting improvement programs.* Improvement programs should be instituted in areas of demonstrated weak performance such as management, personnel performance, equipment reliability, and contractor accountability.

3. *Researching new designs for plant safety.* New designs for existing and future nuclear plants should be researched and developed so as to eliminate the potential of a core meltdown accident.

4. *Phasing out nuclear weapons production.* We urge the closing down of the five weapons-producing reactors and the Rocky Flats Plutonium Processing Plant, a thorough cleanup of any remaining nuclear wastes at these sites, and no more nuclear arms testing.

5. *Establishing uniform safety standards for civilian and military nuclear operations.* We support having all nuclear operations in the U.S. subject to uniform basic safety provision. All Department of Energy nuclear

operations should be licensed and reviewed by an independent agency such as the Nuclear Regulatory Commission or the Environmental Protection Agency. Department of Energy contractors should be held accountable to the same standards as civilian facility contractors and operators.

6. *Protecting neighboring populations.* We urge that due attention be given to the protection of populations living near nuclear power plants or along routes used to transport nuclear materials by ensuring the communities' participation in emergency evacuation plans. We support maintaining evacuation planning zones for all areas within ten miles from a nuclear facility, and engaging the full participation of state and local officials in the planning process. We believe that the safety of all potentially exposed populations should be the guide in safety improvements to nuclear power plants, not narrow cost-benefit analysis.

7. *Instituting full liability and compensation.* We hold that those corporations and governments responsible for nuclear accidents should be liable for cleanup and restitution to all victims of an accident.

8. *Reevaluating the U.S. nuclear waste policy:* (a) We urge a moratorium on DOE's proposed nuclear waste repository program;

(b) We urge Congress to establish an independent commission to review DOE's nuclear waste repository and Monitored Retrievable Storage Programs and to provide increased funding for the development of waste management technologies that will allow prolonged storage at the reactor site;

(c) We urge that full public participation and consultation in any future nuclear waste repository siting and transportation routing be guaranteed through provision of grants to affected localities, states, and Native American tribes; and

(d) We urge a moratorium of the building of nuclear power facilities until an adequate national plan is developed and implemented for the permanent disposal of nuclear waste products.

9. *Decommissioning.* We urge that the full cost of decommissioning (the dismantling and disposing of obsolete or closed power plants) be paid by the entities responsible for the construction and operation of nuclear facilities, not ratepayers or taxpayers.

10. *Conserving energy and finding alternative energy sources.* The greatest national effort should be made in the areas of conservation and renewable energy sources. We support increased government funding for research and development of technologies that would decrease dependence upon nuclear energy as an electricity source and urge the

development of incentives, including tax and appliance standards, to speed the adoption of these technologies.

11. *Cooperating with annual conferences.* We urge the general Church agencies of The United Methodist Church to assist central and annual conferences in their efforts to learn more about nuclear safety. Specifically, we urge general agencies of The United Methodist Church to assist annual conferences who have identified nuclear safety problems related to nuclear facilities, waste sites, and transportation routes within the bounds of those annual conferences.

We particularly urge the General Board of Church and Society to identify qualified nuclear safety experts who could assist annual conferences to understand and respond to nuclear waste and nuclear safety concerns in their areas.

ADOPTED 1988
AMENDED & READOPTED 1992

See Social Principles, ¶ 64; "Environmental Stewardship"; "Energy Policy Statement."

Protecting the Native American Land Base

WHEREAS, protection of the Native American land base is an issue of prime importance today as it has been historically; and

WHEREAS, Native American tribal organizations are seeking to consolidate and increase their land base for economic and cultural purposes; and

WHEREAS, intrusion on tribal lands and subsequent attempts to seize Indian lands by non-Indian parties continues to be a source of tension and insecurity among Native American people; and

WHEREAS, The United Methodist Church has historically held tribal lands for mission purposes and contemporarily holds Indian lands originally secured for purposes of missionary work of the Church among Native Americans; and

WHEREAS, some of their land is no longer used for purpose of mission among Native Americans;

Be it resolved, that all such lands held by the Church, where there is no intention of continuing or developing ministries among the respective Native Americans, be transferred without compensation to the ownership of the Indian nation within whose bounds it exists, or to the Indian nation that was the original owner.

ADOPTED 1988

See Social Principles, ¶¶ 64A, 66A; "Indian Lands Used by The United Methodist Church"; "The United Methodist Church and America's Native People."

Reduce Environmental Tobacco Smoke

WHEREAS, the Environmental Protection Agency of the United States (EPA) has established the health risks attributed to Environmental Tobacco Smoke (ETS), also known as second-hand, passive, or involuntary smoke; and

WHEREAS, EPA studies conclude ETS is responsible for lung deaths of approximately 3,000 nonsmokers in the United States each year;

Be it resolved, that this action encourage the inclusion of ETS prevention in the Clean Air Act and enable more stringent laws by the states to supersede those of federal law, in this case, specifically the Clean Air Act.

ADOPTED 1996

See Social Principles, ¶ 64; "Environmental Stewardship"; "Environmental Justice for a Sustainable Future."

Reduction of Water Usage by United Methodists

Be it resolved, that members of all churches of The United Methodist Church be called upon to analyze their usage of water as a matter of conscientious Christian stewardship; and

Be it further resolved, that The United Methodist Church calls on industry, makers of government policies and regulations, manufacturers, developers, and consumers to reflect on the importance of water conservation and difficulties being faced by society because of water problems, and to develop and utilize water-conserving technology and practices.

ADOPTED 1992

See Social Principles, ¶ 64; "Environmental Stewardship"; "Environmental Justice for a Sustainable Future."

U.S. Agriculture and Rural Communities in Crisis

I. Preface

The United Methodist Church has long witnessed to rural peoples and their concerns. Each General Conference since 1940 has suggested responses for improving rural church and community life, and the economic and environmental well-being of rural peoples. The 1988 General Conference accepted a study on U.S. Agriculture and Rural

Communities in Crisis. This resolution reaffirms that study and calls The United Methodist Church to continue its commitment to rural church ministry and its advocacy for agricultural and rural community concerns.

II. Theological Statement: Land, People, and Justice

God is the owner of the land (Leviticus 25); thus it is a gift in covenant that involves the stewardship of keeping and tending the land for present and future generations; as God's creation, land has the need to be regenerated that it may sustain life and be a place of joy. It is a common gift to all of life, requiring just patterns of land use.

Social, economic, and ecological justice with regard to the use of land was central to the Law. The land itself was to receive a rest every seven years (Leviticus 25:4). Voluntary charity or occasional care of the land was not enough. Israel's failure to follow the laws related to the land was considered a cause of the exile to Babylon (2 Chronicles 36:21). The care of the land, the rights of the poor and those in need were at the center of the Law. Adequate food was regarded as an inherent right of all, such that the poor could eat grapes in a neighbor's vineyard or pluck grain when passing by a field (Deuteronomy 23:24-25). Owners were urged not to be too efficient in their harvest (Leviticus 19:9-10), so that gleaning by those in need was possible.

Indeed, the concept of equal access to community resources according to need formed the basis of the covenant the community was expected to embody. The caring for one's neighbor, especially one in need, became a religious obligation. Jesus both inherits and fulfills this tradition when he lists the commandment to love your neighbor as yourself as second only to the commandment to love God (Matthew 22:38-40).

The prophets saw the patterns of economic exploitation, social class consciousness, judicial corruption, political oppression, failing to care for the land, and exclusiveness as opposed to God's desire for full life and wholeness for all (Amos 2-8; Isaiah 5:1-13; 58:3-7; Jeremiah 2:7-8; Hosea 4:1-3). Some would suggest that both the contemporary world and Israel under the monarchy came to worship "bigness" more than God.

Today, rural parts of the globe suffer from many of the same maladies as did ancient Israel. Land holdings have become more concentrated. The accumulation of material wealth often is worshiped as the solution to other spiritual and economic problems. Creation itself groans under a burden of eroding topsoil, toxic wastes, and polluted waters. Neither the land nor most of the people who work it can celebrate the wholeness God intended.

III. Major Findings

A. The Farm Crisis

As the adverse economic conditions affecting rural America continue to be chronic, the patterns of diverse land ownership and control are disappearing. The structure of agriculture is changing. In 1986, the Office of Technology Assessment of the U.S. Congress estimated that about 72,000 farms may be lost each year until the year 2000. Most of the farms expected to be lost are family-sized units. Ethnic minority-owned and small-scale farms will decline further if present trends continue. A family farm is defined not by the number of acres in operation, but as an agricultural production unit and business in which the management, economic risk, and most of the labor (except in peak seasons) are provided by the family, and from which the family receives a significant part, though not necessarily the majority, of its income.

Declining land values, the relationship between farm product prices and incomes, farm debt and bankruptcies, forced land transfers and foreclosures, changes in the structure of agriculture, and tax policy continue to contribute to the loss of family farms.

African American and other minority farmers are even less likely than white farmers to benefit from any changes in the rural/farm economy. According to the Federation of Southern Cooperatives/Emergency Land Fund, if present land loss continues, there will be virtually no black farmers by the year 2000. Surveys of Native American farmers suggest that their situation may be nearly as bleak as that of black farmers. Farming is the leading occupation among Native Americans living on reservation lands. Asian Americans and Hispanics have historically been excluded from significant farm ownership.

Farm workers have difficult and dangerous work. Inadequate wages, benefits, and living facilities keep many farm workers in poverty.

Many farmers have internalized the external cause of their losses, which has led to deep depression, spouse and family abuse, alcoholism, mental breakdown, divorce, suicide, participation in extremist groups, and, on rare occasions, murder.

The farm crisis accelerates the loss of rural community.

B. Rural Community in Crisis

The rural United States today is a contrast between beauty and desecration, isolation and industrialization, wealth and poverty, power and oppression, freedom and exploitation, abundance and hunger, and individualism and dependence. The nation's poorest housing and health facilities occur disproportionately in rural communities, as do the worst education, the worst roads and transportation systems, the least progressive justice systems, and the greatest poverty and malnutrition. Towns that not long ago were vibrant communities of economic, social, and spiritual life now have become ghost towns with empty businesses, abandoned homes, closed churches, and broken spirits. Broken homes, broken lives, suicides, bankruptcies, spouse and child abuse, unemployment, substance abuse and related violence, and other social catastrophes often make up the local news for many rural communities.

C. The Ecological Crisis in Rural Areas

Much of the rural population of the United States depends on ground water from shallow wells, many of which are already polluted. The U.S. Environmental Protection Agency (EPA)'s 1984 survey of rural water quality found that almost two-thirds of the supplies tested exceeded EPA's drinking water standards for at least one contaminant.

Soil conservation practices such as contour plowing, crop rotation, windbreaks, and covering-cropping are sometimes negatively affected as farmers are pushed to farm more and more acres with bigger and bigger equipment.

The decline of conservation practices is paralleled by an increase in pesticide and herbicide use. While their use brings many benefits, there are still unanswered questions that need to be carefully examined.

Absentee land ownership and all its shortcomings are endemic to mining. Restoration of mined land continues to be a concern. Studies by the Commission on Religion in Appalachia reveal that mining interests often pay little heed to restoration laws and have the political clout to get away with ignoring them.

The loss of genetic diversity, including the consequences of the loss of native seed and animal varieties, is a concern.

The genetic engineering of plants and animals and the patenting of genes, plants, and animals raise major theological and ethical concerns.

IV. The Church Responding to Crisis

In some areas the churches have been helpful in assisting farmers to cope with the loss of their farms and in aiding others to help keep their farms. Unfortunately, in many cases, churches have been ineffective in fulfilling this ministry. A number of reasons have been cited for the Church's shortcoming:

Many church members are still accepting a theology that "goodness" means "success," and that failure means that God has punished the person for his or her "sins."

Many clergy are not adequately trained to minister to the needs of the hurting families in their communities.

In general, clergy are more involved in responding to congregational needs than to the needs of the larger community.

In many rural areas, churches are still operating under an independent rather than a cooperative model.

V. A Call for Change: What Needs to Be Done?

A. The local churches, charges, and cooperative parish ministries are called to:

1. Intentionally develop ministries to meet major needs that exist today in rural United States, including:
(a) take responsibility for assisting with mending the brokenness of community life in rural society;
(b) strengthen their ministry and mission with rural churches and communities;
(c) lift up the responsible stewardship of natural resources; and
(d) build bridges of understanding and partnership between rural and urban congregations and communities.
2. Implement the recommendations of the General Board of Discipleship's 1992 study on "Strengthening the Small Membership Church."

B. The districts are called to:

1. Develop and/or strengthen their missional stance in rural areas;
2. Create cluster groups and other supportive networks within the district to facilitate spiritual formation; and

3. Encourage cooperative leadership through more creative use of available personnel and appropriate technology.

C. *Annual conferences are called to:*

1. Analyze their rural crisis response and provide funding for an effective and ongoing response;

2. Place personnel strategically in order to respond to rural needs; insist that pastoral appointments be made with the needs of entire communities in mind, and not just the needs of the congregation;

3. Become public policy advocates, speaking out as a Church, creating awareness and understanding, and bringing about positive change;

4. Cooperate with other Church and secular agencies in a rural response;

5. Be in partnership with seminaries to develop programs, including "teaching" parishes and internships, to equip ministers to serve in rural areas;

6. Develop programs to invest conference foundation funds in rural economic development needs;

7. Discover ways to enable the ethnic ownership of farmland;

8. Model and support the team ministry concept at every level, including cluster groups and other supportive networks to facilitate spiritual formation;

9. Develop programs for volunteers-in-mission in rural areas;

10. Encourage sustainable agricultural practices by United Methodist family-owned farms.

D. *The general Church is called to:*

1. Use its seminaries to prepare clergy to be more effective pastors in rural areas, using the "missionary training" model, knowing that many ministers not accustomed to rural life enter into an area where there is a new "language," a new lifestyle, a new culture;

2. Cooperate ecumenically and with other groups to develop responses to the problems of rural areas;

3. Better learn the skills of personnel placement, so that appointed ministers in rural areas will have a long enough tenure to build trust/understanding relationships necessary for becoming pastors to the community. Place more mission (and similar) personnel in rural ministries;

4. Recognize Rural Life Sunday as a special day in the Church year, combining in the one day the emphases of Rural Life Sunday, Soil Stewardship Day, Earth Day, World Environment Day, and Rogation Sunday;

5. Provide opportunities for U.S. and third world farmers to share innovations and knowledge;

6. Carefully analyze and monitor all Church agencies' programs to ensure sensitivity to the present rural crisis;

7. Emphasize, in all appropriate literature and training programs, the importance of soil stewardship and ecology as a part of total Christian stewardship. General agencies should report annually on their stewardship of farm and rural lands they own;

8. Consider using a significant portion of the investment funds of all Church agencies for investment in local church-based community economic development in rural areas;

9. Urge all Church agencies to continue to promote the cooperative style of ministry, especially cooperative parish ministries, as a model of God's desire for life in community;

10. Aggressively research corporate ownership of agriculture and its effects upon life in rural areas and advocate necessary responses based upon the findings of this research;

11. Request that the General Board of Discipleship Curriculum Resources Committee periodically develop curriculum resources on the issues raised in this resolution, in coordination with the General Board of Church and Society and the General Board of Global Ministries, and make such materials available to all churches; and

12. Call upon the General Board of Church and Society and the General Board of Global Ministries to develop other materials to interpret this resolution.

E. Bishops are called to:

1. Work toward longer-term rural appointments (with a goal of a minimum of four years) of clergy leadership to provide more stability in rural areas; and

2. Foster cooperative styles of leadership in rural churches by more creative use of available ministerial personnel and appropriate technology.

F. Federal legislators and administrators, as they develop farm and rural policies, are called to:

1. Develop policies that will enable farm families to receive a just return for their labor and investments. These new policies would:

(a) reverse the loss of family farms;

(b) provide for credit to family farmers at affordable interest rates;

(c) develop a marketing and government support system that will guarantee the cost of production to farm families;

(d) initiate participatory democratic processes with farmers to determine if mandatory production goals, which would discourage overproduction of some commodities, are needed to move toward a balance between supply and demand;

(e) greatly reduce government payments to large corporate farming interests;

(f) create programs that would enable new families to enter farming as a vocation;

(g) create incentives for family farmers to shift from current production-oriented modes to a sustainable and regenerative agriculture; and

(h) ensure the participation of family farmers regardless of race and sex.

2. Discourage concentration in ownership and control of land and money and move toward land reforms that broaden ownership of land;

3. Require soil and water conservation practices for farm operations that participate in federal programs; include farmers in the planning of such requirements;

4. Reduce the federal deficit without burdening family farms;

5. Reform federal tax laws to remove unfair competition and discourage tax shelter-motivated capital in agriculture;

6. Maintain an emphasis on direct loan activity, resist attempts to reduce the level of direct loans in favor of guarantees, and increase the Limited Resources Loan program for qualified farmers;

7. Provide for commodity reserves, isolated from the market, to be established at a level adequate to protect consumers from supply disruption and meet domestic agricultural disaster and global humanitarian food aid requirements;

8. Ensure that most federally supported programs of research and education in agriculture focus on small and medium-sized family farm operations, with special attention paid to minority farmers, and that

county committees, which administer these programs, be inclusive of women and minority farmers;

9. Fund major new research initiatives and programs through the federal land grant institutions, including black land grant colleges, to ensure the development of long-term, sustainable, and regenerative agriculture;

10. Develop farm policies that will encourage farm-owned and controlled businesses and cooperatives for processing, distributing, and marketing farm products;

11. Develop policies that will respect the guaranteed land and water rights of all minority peoples;

12. Develop and support programs in cooperation with community-based organizations to improve the quality of life in depressed rural areas, with attention given to health care, transportation, education, employment, law enforcement, housing, job training, and environmental protection;

13. Develop national and regional water and energy policies that assure that those who benefit from energy and water projects pay a substantial portion of those costs;

14. Recognize and protect the right of farm workers to organize into unions of their own choosing, to be covered by minimum wage laws, and to receive adequate benefits, including social security, health care, and unemployment;

15. Discourage export policies that would hurt small farm agriculture in developing countries and hinder efforts toward food self-sufficiency in those countries;

16. Prohibit the importation of produce containing residues of pesticides or other chemicals that are banned for U.S. producers, and revise permitted residue levels when the pesticide is banned;

17. Urge the federal government to declare moratoriums on foreclosures in states where lenders are participating in debt restructure or mediation programs; and

18. Seek out international cooperation in developing an international food policy.

G. *State governments are called to:*

1. Develop systems of mediation to resolve conflicts between borrower and lender;

2. Develop and enforce fair and just tax systems that ensure that those with great wealth and political power pay their fair share of taxes;

3. Ensure that state subsidies for water benefit small and medium-sized operations;

4. Protect security of farm products stored in elevators by farmers;

5. Develop and support farmers' markets and marketing cooperatives;

6. Pay special attention to the education and relocation of jobless persons, commit state resources to the establishment of industries or agencies that will increase the job/tax base, and maintenance of an acceptable quality of social services for all;

7. Allocate funds to monitor all state programs and economic development projects for their impact upon the socioeconomic and natural environments;

8. Urge the development and maintenance of conservation programs that supplement federal programs and environmental standards that exceed federal minimums;

9. Sell bonds to help farmers secure low-interest loans, with special attention given to minority farmers and others with similar needs. Assist such families in identifying and securing loans from such sources;

10. Ensure that state marketing regulations benefit small and medium-sized operators;

11. Ensure that most state-supported programs of research and education in agriculture focus on small and medium-sized family farm operations, with special attention paid to minority farmers; and

12. Fund major research initiatives and programs through state and/or corporate grants to ensure the development of long-term, sustainable, and regenerative agriculture.

H. Government and private lending agencies are called to:

1. Continue to restructure existing loans to allow for lower payments over a longer period of time, and with lower interest rates, as agreed to by lender and borrower through a mediation process;

2. Require the U.S. Department of Agriculture and other lending agencies to have more balanced and consistent lending policies and practices and to assess fairly the spending of authorized funds on farm operations;

3. Urge the U.S. government to change accounting procedures to allow banks that participate in debt restructure agreements to write off any potential losses over a ten-year period; and

4. Give priority for purchases to minority, foreclosed, beginning, and re-entering farmers when foreclosed land is offered for sale.

I. Local government and community groups are called to:

1. Develop land use and land reclamation policies, supported by adequate funding, to preserve productive farmlands;

2. Organize and support local groups to provide legal aid, financial advice, counseling, and other support service for rural persons;

3. Monitor programs to assure that all community planning is ecologically sound, socially responsible, and includes persons of color and women;

4. Foster a positive community spirit with a variety of local programs that enhance the community members' well-being and self-worth;

5. Develop and support measures that ensure a fair tax treatment of all in the community;

6. Support the development of local programs to meet such special needs as better housing, health care, transportation, and recreation;

7. Develop local representative, long-range planning committees to monitor and advise elected or appointed officials and community groups; and

8. Cooperate with state agencies to develop policies so that farmers markets in their communities may be able to accept food stamps and WIC certificates for purchases.

J. Multinational, national, and local business groups are called to:

1. Examine their corporate policy in relationship to an understanding of and responsiveness to the values of rural lifestyles represented by smaller farm-sized units; and

2. Implement just policies concerning the ethics of research; short-term and long-term ecological effects; conservation of resources; water and energy use; local, national, and export marketing; labor use; and the availability and access to financing and credit.

The More Difficult Task

The more difficult task for the Church is to take clearly and intentionally the prophetic role. The Church has a clear record of helping the world address such issues as clean water and air, civil rights, nuclear warfare, arms expenditures, and world hunger. The Church must likewise take responsibility for addressing the problem of agriculture. The outcome of human history will be determined by our resolve to achieve a favorable future for agriculture.

Unless we change some basic directions, we are not just in a period of transition; we are headed for disaster for all nations. Some basic directions that must be changed include:

• the movement toward investor-owned land in increasingly larger corporate units; the separation of ownership, management, and labor;

• the increased reliance upon high inputs of nonrenewable resources such as fossil fuels and chemicals;

• the continued decline in rural populations from rural areas, especially those who have been directly involved in food production;

• the increasing chemical toxicity of our water systems, air, rain, waste dumps, and vegetable and animal products;

• the continuing loss of cropland through erosion, salinization, urbanization, conversion, and other processes;

• the disappearance of world forest resources and the resulting changes in weather patterns;

• the loss of atmospheric ozone;

• the continuing and growing use of the world's basic resources for armaments; and

• the loss of our centuries-old genetic seed bank.

Three Ethical Guidelines

We can change the direction of agriculture and rural development, but we need guidelines. A preferred agriculture must have three attributes:

1. It must be *just*. A just society and a just agriculture provide the means whereby people can share in the inheritance of the earth so that all life can fully be maintained in freedom and community. The purpose of a just agriculture should be for the maintenance and renewal of the necessary resources for food, clothing, and shelter, for now and for the future.

2. It must be *participatory*. For an agriculture to be just, everyone has the right to be consulted. Participation in society and in the ongoing process of creation is the necessary condition for justice. Participation requires a recognition of everyone's right to be consulted and under-

stood, regardless of that person's economic, political, or social status. Participation is not possible without power. In such decision-making, everyone has the right to be consulted about such issues as expenditures for armaments, nuclear power, forms of employment, social services, and so forth.

3. It must be *sustainable*. A sustainable agriculture is one where the idea of permanent carrying capacity is maintained, where yields (agriculture, energy production, forestry, water use, industrial activity) are measured by whether or not they are sustainable rather than by the criteria of yields per acre or profits. In a sustainable agriculture, waste products can be absorbed back into the ecosystem without damage.

A just, participatory, and sustainable agriculture would meet basic human needs for food and fiber, regenerate and protect ecosystems, be economically viable, enhance the quality of life for farm families, be supportive of rural communities, be socially just, and be compatible with spiritual teachings that recognize the earth as a common heritage and responsibility. For Christians, the idea of sustainability flows directly from the biblical call to human beings to be stewards of God's creation.

ADOPTED 1996

See Social Principles, ¶¶ 64A, 66M; "An Affirmation of Basic Rural Worth"; "Special Needs of Farm Workers"; "The Church's Response to Changing Rural Issues."

Use of Reclaimed Paper

Be it resolved, that the General Conference request the publisher, boards, agencies, and all local churches to diligently seek suppliers of recycled or reclaimed paper for all possible uses whenever practicable and possible.

Be it further resolved, that the General Conference request that all said agencies use only recycled or reclaimed paper whenever possible for all printing, mimeographing, correspondence, and other uses of paper.

ADOPTED 1972

See Social Principles, ¶ 64; "Environmental Stewardship."

THE NURTURING COMMUNITY

Adoption

WHEREAS, all privately arranged placement of a child for adoption without a license to place children for adoption is frequently in violation of state laws; and

WHEREAS, all those concerned with the placement of a child for an (non-relative) adoption shall abide by the laws of their state in using only licensed child-placing agencies; and

WHEREAS, by so doing, the needs of the birth parents can be met by appropriate counseling as they make decisions regarding their life and the life of their child; and

WHEREAS, licensed child-placing agencies have a more diverse group of approved prospective parents, which enables them to serve the best interest of the child;

Therefore, be it resolved, that United Methodists planning to enter the adoption process be encouraged to work only with licensed adoption agencies.

ADOPTED 1988

See Social Principles, ¶ 65K.

Against Sterilization Abuse

We recognize, especially in this country, that the choice of sterilization as a method of limiting family size is winning more acceptance. When voluntary, this practice is a matter of personal choice; however, when someone else makes the decision, the chances of abuse are great.

Sterilization abuse is recognized as a problem of low-income women, particularly third world women. According to *Family Digest*, May 1972, 35 percent of married Puerto Rican women of child-bearing age were sterilized. In November 1977, the U.S. General Accounting Office issued a report indicating that Health Service had sterilized approximately 5.5 percent of all Indian women of child-bearing age in the Aberdeen, Phoenix, Albuquerque, and Oklahoma City areas. In 1979, a study conducted by the Women's Division in New York City found, in face-to-face interviews with 500 women ages 18–45, that of the first 50 interviews, 26 women had had tubal ligations, and 8 had had hysterectomies. Of those who had tubal ligations, 13 were Black, 9 were Puerto Rican, and 4 were white. Ten of the 26 were receiving public assistance. In 13 cases, a doctor suggested the operation, and 12 of these women indicated that the doctor was the single most influential person in the decision. Only 8 of the 26 brought up the subject themselves; 3 women did not remember how the subject came up; and in one case, the woman's mother influenced her. Fifty percent of the women showed regret over having been sterilized.

WHEREAS, the decision to be sterilized is unique in the area of reproductive freedom because it is irreversible, the dangers of coercion, deception, and misinformation and the desire of some for population control—particularly among the poor, third world people (in the U.S. and overseas)—require safeguards against an uninformed and involuntary decision with such inexorable consequences; and

WHEREAS, the importance of the sterilization decision for most people cannot be overestimated, since reproductive ability is key to the identity of many people, both male and female, and the decision to become sterilized can have tremendous psychological as well as physical repercussions; and

WHEREAS, sterilization abuse—the sterilizing of people against their will or without their knowledge—is still occurring;

It is therefore recommended that:
1. The United Methodist Church support the following principles:
   (a) The patient, not her physician or any other party, should make the ultimate decision, in accordance with law, as to whether she will be sterilized. Involuntary sterilizations (for minors or persons adjudged to be mentally incompetent) are justifiable only if ordered by a competent court after a hearing according to due process of law;
   (b) Adequate and accurate information should be given to women concerning sterilization and its alternatives; and

(c) The decision to be sterilized should not be made during a time of stress, particularly during hospitalization for abortion or childbirth;

2. In order that the sterilization decision be both informed and voluntary, there is a need that:

(a) Women considering sterilization be given specific information in their own language, using understandable terms about the nature and consequences of the sterilization procedure to be performed as well as the risks and benefits of that procedure; and

(b) They have adequate time in which to make this irreversible decision in a noncoercive atmosphere—thus, a thirty-day waiting period, which would enable them to leave the hospital and consult with family, friends, or other physicians;

3. Local churches monitor the implementation of the guidelines in local hospitals;

4. Local churches be encouraged to ascertain women's attitudes toward and experience with sterilization in their communities;

5. Education and information about sterilization and other forms of contraception be included in family-life programs, with special note taken of the guidelines for voluntary consent;

6. The United Methodist Church oppose racist population-control policies and practices aimed at third world peoples (in the U.S. and overseas); and

7. The United Methodist Church oppose all forms of sterilization abuse, including lack of informed consent, arbitrary measures for disabled and institutionalized women, and industrial exposure in radiation.

ADOPTED 1980

See Social Principles, ¶¶ 65, 66A; "Equal Rights of Women"; "Racism"; "Racism: The Church's Unfinished Agenda."

AIDS and the Healing Ministry of the Church

I. AIDS and the Gospel of Wholeness

As United Methodists, we confess that the God known in Jesus Christ is the One who "makes all things new," who promises to redeem past failures and sends an empowering Spirit to support us when we seek to enact the divine will.

According to the Gospel of Luke (4:16-21), Jesus identified himself and his ministry with that of the servant Lord: the one who Isaiah tells us was sent to bring good tidings to the afflicted; to bring hope to the brokenhearted; to proclaim liberty to the captives; to comfort all who mourn; to give them the oil of gladness; and the mantle of praise instead of a faint spirit (Isaiah 61:1-3, RSV, paraphrased).

There is no doubt that the gospel entrusted to the church as the body of Christ is a gospel of wholeness that calls us to a ministry of healing; a ministry that understands healing not only in physiological terms, but as wholeness of mental, physical, spiritual, relational, and social being.

Diseases spring from complex conditions, factors, and choices. It is not helpful to speak of diseases in inflammatory terms like "punishment for sin." The gospel challenges us to respond with compassion that seeks to enable the physical and spiritual wholeness God intends in the lives of all persons affected by Acquired Immune Deficiency Syndrome (AIDS).

With the apostle Paul, we assert that "neither death, nor life, nor angels, nor rulers, nor things present, nor things to come, nor powers, nor height, nor depth, nor anything else in all creation, will be able to separate us from the love of God in Christ Jesus our Lord" (Romans 8:38-39).

In the spirit of the One who makes all things new, who empowers the people of God for ministries of healing and hope even in the midst of a frightening epidemic, The United Methodist Church and its members are called to respond to the epidemic of Acquired Immune Deficiency Syndrome by engaging in ministry, healing, and social responsibility consistent with the Church's understanding of the gospel imperatives.

II. AIDS and the Church as a Healing Community

The Church as a healing community, empowered by the Holy Spirit, is called to confession, celebration, and action.

A. As a Church, we confess that until now our response to AIDS has been tardy and inadequate; that we have failed to call political leaders to account for their slowness and lack of compassion; and that when challenged by the assertion that AIDS is God's punishment, we have failed to offer a grace-filled alternative consistent with an understanding of the whole gospel of Jesus Christ.

B. As a Church, we celebrate and offer thanksgiving for the pioneering and self-sacrificial work of persons who have developed volunteer ministries of service to persons with AIDS (PWAs), and for the disease-prevention education work that has reduced both the sexual transmission and blood transfusion-associated transmission of AIDS.

We celebrate the leadership of local churches and annual conferences that have begun ministries in response to AIDS; the guidance provided during the 1984–88 quadrennium by the General Boards of Global Ministries, Church and Society, and Discipleship.

C. As a Church, we resolve that:

1. Churches should be places of openness and caring for persons with AIDS and their loved ones. The Church should work to overcome attitudinal and behavioral barriers in church and community that prohibit the acceptance of persons who have AIDS and their loved ones;

2. Ministries in response to AIDS will be developed, whenever possible, in consultation and collaboration with local departments of public health and community-based groups that have already identified priorities for action, and they will be supportive of ecumenical and interfaith efforts;

3. Educational efforts must include reliable medical and scientific information and theological and biblical components that enable participants to address issues related to death and dying, human sexuality, and recognition of people's lack of knowledge and fear. Such educational efforts can prepare congregations to respond appropriately when they learn that a member has been infected by HIV (Human Immunodeficiency Virus) or diagnosed with AIDS, and they can lead to the development of compassionate rational policies, educational materials, and procedures related to the church school, nurseries, and often issues of institutional participation;

4. Pastors, paid workers, and other volunteer church workers should prepare themselves to provide appropriate pastoral care and counseling to persons living with AIDS or AIDS-related Complex (ARC) and the loved ones of these persons;

5. Liturgical and worship life should provide opportunities for education as well as an expression of pastoral care. Worship provides a time for celebration and the lifting up of special concerns;

6. Congregations should organize to provide emotional, physical, and/or financial support to those in their community who are caring at home or elsewhere for a person who has AIDS;

7. Local churches should use their resources to respond to the AIDS crisis. These may include support groups, counseling, grants, providing a location for recreational activities for persons with AIDS, and recruit-

ing volunteers or offering office or meeting space for community-based organizations.

D. As a Church, we call upon our general agencies, annual conferences, local churches, and members to:

1. Work for public policies and the allocation of resources to ensure the availability of appropriate medical, psychological, and support services for all persons infected by HIV. These programs should afford the greatest amount of independence and self-determination possible for persons with AIDS within the framework of their individual circumstances;

2. Advocate that children infected by HIV be permitted to attend regular school so long as they are able and wish to do so and while their presence does not constitute a threat to their own health or the health of others;

3. Advocate for the development of accurate testing procedures that are voluntary and that guarantee confidentiality, including counseling services. The ability to test for antibodies to the AIDS virus is a useful AIDS-prevention strategy in some instances. However, even voluntary use of antibody testing as a preventive effort will require the assurance of levels of confidentiality and anonymity;

4. Support AIDS-prevention education in church and society that provides both the information and motivation required for persons to change their behavior so as to reduce or eliminate the risk of infection. Because sexual and intravenous drug-using activities can begin at a very young age, we encourage school boards to initiate AIDS education activities at the elementary school level. We affirm the necessity for comprehensive health education, including human sexuality and drug-abuse prevention designed for children and youth. We call for the development of adequate numbers of drug treatment programs to care for persons who are dependent on the use of illicit drugs. We support the provision of detailed information and other resources that will prevent intravenous drug users from sharing needles as a part of the larger effort to prevent the further spread of AIDS;

5. Urge implementation and enforcement of policies and, if necessary, legislation to protect the human and civil rights of persons infected by HIV, persons perceived to be at risk for such infection, and persons with AIDS or AIDS-related conditions. We urge efforts to investigate thoroughly, document, and prevent prejudice and violence against all persons who have AIDS or are perceived as being at risk for AIDS;

6. Support the development of workplace policies that permit all persons with AIDS/ARC to work as long as they are able and wish to do so, with medical assurance that their presence in the workplace does not constitute a threat to coworkers or others;

7. Encourage health-care providers to regard persons with AIDS as the appropriate decision-makers about their care, to respect their wishes to seek or refuse specific treatments, and to honor their determination about persons who will make decisions on their behalf should they become unable to decide themselves;

8. Request the health-related and health-care institutions of The United Methodist Church to provide leadership in the creation of services, including hospices and home health-care facilities for patients with AIDS and HIV patients, and to publicize their services to these patients in beneficial ways; and to further request that wherever possible these institutions join with other agencies in research activities;

9. Work for public policies and the allocation of public resources for research and prevention, treatment, and elimination of AIDS-related diseases. Monitor private insurance company policies related to coverage and benefits for persons with AIDS and HIV-related diseases;

10. Encourage worldwide cooperation by all countries in sharing research facilities and findings in battling this disease, mindful that governments, churches, families, and persons in every region of the world are affected by the AIDS epidemic.

E. We commend the interagency efforts by the General Boards of Discipleship, Church and Society, and Global Ministries to address the AIDS crisis and urge the continuation and growth of this work to envision, create, and help facilitate a plan for AIDS ministry and education within The United Methodist Church. We urge these boards to immediately inform and enlist the annual conferences in the work of this ministry and to continue to report their action to the General Conference.

The global AIDS pandemic provides a nearly unparalleled opportunity for witness to the gospel and service to human need among persons, many of whom would otherwise be alone and alienated from themselves, from other people, and from God. The Christian gospel of wholeness calls us to a complete and full dedication of our bodies as temples of the Holy Spirit. We are called, also, to a ministry with and among all persons, including those whose lives are touched by AIDS. As members of The United Methodist Church, we covenant together to ensure ministries and other services to persons with AIDS, based on the reality of meaning and hope in and for their lives, whatever duration they may have. We acknowledge the spiritual and personal growth that can be experienced by persons facing AIDS in their own life or the life of a loved one, and we give thanks for the witness to God's empowering love contained in that growth. We ask for God's guidance that we might respond in ways that bear witness always to Jesus' own compassionate ministry of healing and reconciliation; and that to this end we might love one another and care for one another with the same unmeasured and unconditional love that Jesus embodied.

ADOPTED 1988

See Social Principles, ¶ 65; "Care-Giving Teams for Persons with AIDS"; "Pastoral Care and the AIDS Epidemic in Native American Communities"; "Resources for AIDS Education"; "Recognizing and Responding to the Many Faces of HIV/AIDS in the U.S.A."

Care-Giving Teams for Persons with AIDS

WHEREAS, AIDS has emerged in epidemic proportions in the United States and in the world; and

WHEREAS, AIDS is being transmitted more and more through contaminated needles used to inject drugs; and

WHEREAS, recent statistics indicate that Black Americans are being disproportionately infected and that cultural needs are not being adequately addressed; and

WHEREAS, current information often does not reach black communities;

Therefore, be it resolved, that each local church be encouraged to establish care-giving teams that will be trained to minister specifically to persons with AIDS and their families, giving particular attention to those communities where needs are not being addressed; and

Be it further resolved, that using materials from general Church agencies, these teams would be trained to provide AIDS education in churches and communities.

ADOPTED 1992

See Social Principles, ¶ 65; "AIDS and the Healing Ministry of the Church"; "Pastoral Care and the AIDS Epidemic in Native American Communities"; "Resources for AIDS Education."

Clinic Violence

WHEREAS, faithful and conscientious persons hold widely different convictions concerning abortion; and

WHEREAS, some opponents of abortion have publicly postulated a "justifiable homicide" rationale for killing abortion providers; and

WHEREAS, murder is a sin; and

WHEREAS, violence is a sin; and

WHEREAS, escalation of attacks on abortion clinics resulting in the murder of doctors, clinic officers, workers, and visitors constitutes domestic terrorism; and

WHEREAS, escalation of rhetoric on all sides continues to push people apart and make useful dialogue around common-ground issues difficult; and

WHEREAS, this increase in violence, both in attitude and acts of physical violence, calls all of us to repentance;

Therefore, be it resolved, that The United Methodist Church:

Repent of violence, turn toward attitudes of respect, and seek areas of common ground between those who call themselves pro-life and those who call themselves pro-choice;

Reject and condemn the use of violence against those peacefully assembled to protest abortion;

Reject and condemn the use of violence against providers of legal services related to reproductive health; and

Encourage local churches, annual conferences, and General Conference agencies to speak out whenever such violence occurs.

ADOPTED 1996

See Social Principles, ¶ 65J.

Condemning Legal Prostitution

WHEREAS, the Social Principles of The United Methodist Church state that "sexuality is God's good gift to all persons" and that "we reject all sexual expressions that damage or destroy the humanity God has given us as birthright, and we affirm only that sexual expression which enhances that same humanity" (¶ 65G); and

WHEREAS, one such damaging and destroying practice is prostitution, which treats sex as a market commodity rather than as a shared gift from God, and which treats persons as things to be used rather than as human beings with the potential to grow in grace; and

WHEREAS, many public officials and law-enforcement officers are reported to disregard statutes against prostitution; and

WHEREAS, the state of Nevada, by statute, permits cities and counties to license and regulate brothels;

Therefore, be it resolved, that The United Methodist Church strongly condemns the practice of prostitution, legal or illegal, while supporting programs of care, counseling, and rehabilitation for those who have been victimized by that practice; and

Be it resolved, that United Methodist congregations are urged to develop strategies for influencing state and local officials in their communities to enforce laws on prostitution, and to minister to the victims of the practice of prostitution who are in their midst; and

Be it further resolved, that the General Conference strongly urges United Methodists in the state of Nevada, and anywhere legalized prostitution exists, to implement strategies leading to the repeal of such laws; and

Be it finally resolved, that the General Conference calls upon all United Methodists, including the leadership of general agencies, district superintendents, and bishops in areas where prostitution is legal, to be persistent in:

1. Communicating The United Methodist Church's understanding of the degrading, sinful nature of prostitution; and

2. Contacting government executives and legislators to influence them to give leadership to the enactment of legislation repealing laws that authorize the practice of prostitution.

ADOPTED 1988

See Social Principles, ¶ 66F; "Sexual Violence and Pornography."

Homosexuals in the Military

Basis: The United States of America, a nation built on equal rights, has denied the right of homosexuals to actively serve their country while being honest about who they are. Meanwhile, The United Methodist Church is moving toward accepting all people for who they are. The United Methodist Church needs to be an advocate for equal civil rights for all marginalized groups, including homosexuals.

Conclusion: The U.S. military should not exclude persons from service solely on the basis of sexual orientation.

ADOPTED 1996

See Social Principles, ¶ 66H.

May as Christian Home Month

WHEREAS, we believe that families in our nation, at this hour, stand at a critical juncture, in the midst of destructive pressures that are daily taking their toll; and that The United Methodist Church has the opportunity, potential, and responsibility to respond to the urgent needs of families;

Therefore, be it resolved, that General Conference declare the month of May as Christian Home Month, with emphasis upon family worship in the home, A Day of Prayer for the Family set aside in May, and emphasis on the family by local churches in worship and program planning. We call upon the Family Life Committee and Curriculum Resources Committee to gather existing family curriculum materials and, where necessary, create a core of curriculum materials across age levels.

ADOPTED 1992

See Social Principles, ¶ 65A; "Responsible Parenthood"; "Putting Children and Their Families First."

Organ and Tissue Donation

WHEREAS, selfless consideration for the health and welfare of others is at the heart of the Christian ethic; and

WHEREAS, organ and tissue donation is a life-giving act, since transplantation of organs and tissues is scientifically proven to save the lives of persons with terminal diseases and improve the quality of life for the blind, the deaf, and others with life-threatening diseases; and

WHEREAS, organ donation may be perceived as a positive outcome of a seemingly senseless death and is thereby comforting to the family of the deceased and is conducted with respect, and with the highest consideration for maintaining the dignity of the deceased and his or her family; and

WHEREAS, moral leaders the world over recognize organ and tissue donation as an expression of humanitarian ideals in giving life to another; and

WHEREAS, thousands of persons who could benefit from organ and tissue donation continue to suffer and die due to lack of consent for donation, due primarily to poor awareness and lack of an official direction from the Church;

Therefore, be it resolved, that The United Methodist Church recognizes the life-giving benefits of organ and tissue donation and thereby encourages all Christians to become organ and tissue donors by signing and carrying cards or driver's licenses, attesting to their commitment of such organs upon their death to those in need, as a part of their ministry to others in the name of Christ, who gave his life that we might have life in its fullness.

ADOPTED 1984

See Social Principles, ¶ 65L; "Understanding Living and Dying as Faithful Christians."

Pastoral Care and the AIDS Epidemic in Native American Communities

WHEREAS, the AIDS disease is of epidemic proportions; and

WHEREAS, pastoral care training does not take into consideration the unique cultural and spiritual healing methods of the Native American community; and

WHEREAS, a national consultation on pastoral care and AIDS for Native Americans would provide sound cultural insights for The United Methodist Church in the area of pastoral care for Native American pastors; and

WHEREAS, a program of this nature would provide nurture for Native American pastors and their continuing education;

Therefore, be it resolved, that the General Board of Higher Education and Ministry and the National United Methodist Native American Center continue to develop culturally relevant curriculum materials regarding pastoral care and AIDS in the Native American community; and

Be it further resolved, that General Conference encourage the National United Methodist Native American Center and the General Board of Higher Education and Ministry to hold, as soon as possible, a National Consultation on Pastoral Care and AIDS in the Native American community using this curriculum, consistent with the availability of independent funding.

ADOPTED 1992

See Social Principles, ¶ 65; "AIDS and the Healing Ministry of the Church"; "Resources for AIDS Education"; "Care-Giving Teams for Persons with AIDS."

Putting Children and Their Families First

Once considered the property of their parents, children are now acknowledged to be full human beings in their own right, but beings to whom adults

and society in general have special obligations. . . . All children have the right to quality education. . . . Moreover, children have the rights to food, shelter, clothing, health care, and emotional well-being as do adults, and these rights we affirm as theirs regardless of actions or inaction of their parents or guardians. In particular, children must be protected from economic, physical, and sexual exploitation and abuse. (Social Principles, ¶ 66C)

The Problem

Growing up whole and healthy is increasingly difficult for children. They face weakened support systems throughout society, from home to school to church, at the very time they are struggling with unprecedented stresses. They are forced to grow up too quickly, to make significant life choices at a younger and younger age.

Every day in America:

- 3 children die from child abuse;
- 15 children die from guns;
- 27 children—a classroomful—die from poverty;
- 95 babies die before their first birthday;
- 564 babies are born to women who had late or no prenatal care;
- 788 babies are born at low birth weight (under 5 pounds, 8 ounces);
- 1,340 teenagers give birth;
- 2,217 teenagers drop out of school (each school day);
- 2,350 children are in adult jails;
- 2,699 babies are born into poverty;
- 3,356 babies are born to unmarried women;
- 8,189 children are reported abused or neglected;
- 100,000 children are homeless;
- 135,000 children bring guns to school;
- 1,200,000 latchkey children come home to a house in which there is a gun.[1]

The percentage of children in poverty is perhaps the most dependable indicator of childhood well-being. In 1992, one in every five of America's children lived below the poverty line. Very young children, those under age six, are among the very poorest groups in the country, with over a quarter of them living in poverty.[2]

---

[1] *The State of America's Children 1995, Children's Defense Fund.*
[2] *Kids Count Data Book 1995,* Annie E. Casey Foundation.

The share of children living in single-parent families increased from 21 percent in 1985 to 25 percent in 1992. The poverty rate for single-parent families is 42 percent, compared to 8 percent for two-parent families.[3]

Public Policy Implications

In light of the critical nature of the problems described above, The United Methodist Church should press for public policies that:

1. Guarantee basic income for all families regardless of structure (some states exclude from welfare programs two-parent families and persons who work yet earn well below the poverty line);

2. Provide basic support services for families in economic crisis, including food and nutrition programs (such as food stamps; Women, Infants, and Children's programs; childcare; school food programs; and so forth), crisis respite care, and home-care services;

3. Mandate full and complete access to health and medical care, including health maintenance; prenatal and well-baby services; and mental-health services for all family members, including the highly under-served group of young children and teens;

4. Ensure safe and affordable housing for families without regard to the number and ages of children; and

5. Safeguard protective services for children at risk of abuse.

Too often we engage in public policy debate, make new laws, and cut budgets and programs without putting the highest priority on how any change or policy will affect children and their families. We have seen this tendency in a number of federal, state, and local legislative battles in recent years.

We call upon United Methodists to ask the following questions of any pending legislation, any budget cut, or any new policy:

1. Are children's needs and well-being considered first and foremost in evaluating health and welfare reforms or any other national, state, or local policy?

2. Will this program or policy make fewer children poor and increase the likelihood of children's growing up healthy, educated, and prepared to work and contribute to the future productivity of the economy?

---

[3] Ibid.

3. Will this program or policy make families more self-sufficient, enabling parents to work by providing them with jobs and the tools of work (education and training, childcare, health care, child-support enforcement)?

4. Will this program or policy support families in providing care, nurture, safety, and stability to children?

5. Will this program or policy help the many who have little rather than the few who have much?

6. Will this program or policy help families stay together and care for their children?

7. Does this program or policy refrain from punishing children for the actions or inaction of their parents or guardians?

8. Will this program or policy actually save money in the long run rather than gain a shortsighted savings that leaves the next generation to pay the price?

9. Is this program or policy as fair to children as to adults, and to women as to men?

10. Will this program or policy provide young people with opportunities for a meaningful future?

11. Will this program develop in children a sense of responsibility for themselves and their communities?[4]

Legislators and other public leaders should be held accountable to citizens and voters for their answers to these questions and for the results of their actions.

Church Program and Policy Implications

Churches must strengthen and expand their ministry and advocacy efforts on behalf of children and their families. A coordinated ministry that serves families with children in the congregation and in the larger community, that joins hands with human service providers and ecumenical colleagues, and that addresses the public policy concerns listed above is needed in every church and community.

The Church has traditionally emphasized the integrity of the institutions of marriage and family and the responsibilities of parenthood. While these emphases should be maintained, a holistic ministry with families must, of necessity, be based on the broadest possible definition

---

[4] Adapted from the Children's Defense Fund brochure "Protecting Children in Shifting Political Winds" (1995), and the Children Now flyer "Contract with America's Children: Why Children Need Policies for Change" (1995).

of family so that the great variety of structures and configurations will be included. Grandparents often function as parents, and many families are headed by single parents or are "blended" through divorce and remarriage. Adoption, fostering, and extended family structures are among those that need the Church's ministry.

Churches need to understand that all the problems described here happen to individuals and families inside the congregations as well as in the wider community. A 1992 survey of active United Methodists across the country concerning women and families in crisis revealed that among the nearly 2,500 respondents:

- One in every fifty had abused illegal drugs; one in every nineteen had abused alcohol;
- One in every twenty-three had experienced a teenage and/or unmarried pregnancy; one in four reported that a family member or close friend had had such an experience;
- One in every five had experienced divorce; one in eight had been a single parent;
- One in every five had experienced job loss or some other financial crisis;
- One in every six had been a victim of incest or other sexual abuse as a child;
- One in every fifteen had been physically abused as a child;
- One in every fourteen had been battered by a spouse;
- One in every eleven had been raped, most by an acquaintance or a spouse.[5]

In light of these statistics, which initially sound shockingly high but are in fact somewhat lower than national statistics, it is critically important that each congregation deal openly with the needs of its members and its community and begin developing appropriate ministry responses for children and their families. Support groups, hotlines, shelters, parenting classes, treatment programs, home-care services, nutrition and feeding programs, and after-school tutoring and men

---

[5] From a 1992 churchwide survey conducted by the Office of Ministries with Women and Families, National Division, General Board of Global Ministries. The total sample of 2,310 included responses from readers of *Response* magazine and *The United Methodist Reporter*, a random sampling of local churches supplied by the research department of GCOM, and surveys distributed to all attendees at a number of local units of United Methodist Women and Schools of Christian Mission.

toring programs are especially needed in many communities, and these are programs that churches are often well-suited to sponsor or support.

A network of child-serving institutions and agencies, from community centers to residences for at-risk children and youth, exists across the Church. Many are local expressions of national mission, and others are related to annual conferences. These agencies meet critical needs and urgently require the financial, volunteer, and prayer support of congregations. Recent cuts in public funding to these programs make support from the Church even more critical.

The twenty-first century is nearly upon us. If the Church is to be a faithful advocate for children, protecting and nurturing them into healthy adulthood, increased awareness and vigilance will be required. In preparation for this daunting task, we call upon The United Methodist Church to:

1. Generate a plan in every local church for assessing ministry with children (in the congregation and in the community) and implementing a vision for ministry with children and their families that takes seriously the facts and perspectives presented above. This plan is to be overseen by the official decision-making body of each local church.

2. Celebrate the Children's Sabbath in every local church each October. For information and resources, contact Children's Defense Fund, Children's Sabbath Office, P.O. Box 90500, Washington, DC 20090-0500.

3. Increase awareness of the needs of children and their families by challenging the Church's leaders (including bishops, general agency staff, CCOM directors, and district superintendents, as well as local church clergy and lay leadership) to spend the equivalent of one full day during the 1997–2000 quadrennium as a volunteer at a local outreach ministry that serves children, such as a community center, childcare center, tutoring or parenting program, shelter for homeless families, and so forth.

4. Continue and strengthen a task force formed of persons from general Church agencies who work on issues of child and family advocacy in order to coordinate work, implement this resolution, and advocate cooperatively for the needs of children (to be convened annually by the Children's Ministries Office of the General Board of Discipleship).

ADOPTED 1996

See Social Principles, ¶¶ 65A, H, 66C; "Responsible Parenthood"; "Ministry to Runaway Children."

Recognizing and Responding to the Many Faces of HIV/AIDS in the U.S.A.

The United Methodist Church has resolved to minister compassion-ately with all persons living with HIV/AIDS and their loved ones, following in the way of healing, ministry, hospitality, and service shown by Jesus.[1] Churches and other concerned United Methodist communities have been in ministry since the beginning of the pandemic.

The Context of Caring Ministry

HIV/AIDS affects and infects a broad cross-section of people in the United States and Puerto Rico—all ages, all races, both sexes, and all sexual orientations. In 1995, the Centers for Disease Control (CDC) noted that the proportion of AIDS cases among women, racial and ethnic people, and children continues to increase, while the rate of AIDS among gay/bisexual men has leveled. From a geographic perspective, more persons in the South and Northeast contracted AIDS in 1994 than in 1993.[2]

The United Methodist Church can help to stop the spread of HIV/AIDS by providing sound comprehensive, age-appropriate pre-vention education, including information that abstaining from sex and injection drug-use[3] is the safest way to prevent infection. In addition, the Church can provide a grounding in Christian values for children, teens, and young adults, something that cannot be done in public schools or in official government prevention materials.

Teens and Young Adults

AIDS will increasingly affect and infect our next generation of lead-ers. Since 1991, AIDS has been the sixth-leading cause of death among 15- to 24-year-olds in the United States. In 1994, 50 percent of new infections of HIV were among persons under twenty-five. Older teens, males, and racial and ethnic people were disproportionately affected.

---

[1] "AIDS and the Healing Ministry of the Church," 1988 General Conference.

[2] CDC, "Current Trends: Update, Acquired Immunodeficiency Syndrome—United States, 1994," 02/03/95.

[3] By "injection drug-use," we are referring to the sharing of needles and works done by injection drug users. Usually this refers to use of heroin on the streets or steroids in sports contexts. We are not referring to persons who are diabetic, for instance, who use only sterile needles and inject insulin to maintain health.

The CDC reported:

"Many American teenagers are engaging in behaviors that may put them at risk of acquiring HIV infection, other sexually transmitted infections, or infections associated with drug injection. Recent CDC studies conducted every two years in high schools (grades 9–12) consistently indicate that by the twelfth grade, approximately three fourths of high school students have had sexual intercourse; less than half report consistent use of latex condoms, and about one fifth have had more than four lifetime sex partners. Many students report using alcohol or drugs when they have sex, and in the most recent survey, one in sixty-two high school students reported having injected an illegal drug."[4]

By 1993, HIV became the leading cause of death in the United States among all persons ages twenty-five to forty-four.[5] Racial and ethnic groups have been hit especially hard. By 1991, HIV infection had become the leading cause of death for African Americans and Hispanics among males ages twenty-five to forty-four years. By 1993, it was the number one cause of death for African American women in the same age group. Among Asians/Pacific Islanders and American Indians/Alaska Natives young adults, AIDS ranks in the top ten leading causes of death.[6]

Racial and Ethnic Groups

African Americans, Hispanics, and Native Americans have been disproportionately infected with HIV/AIDS. In 1993, racial and ethnic people accounted for 51 percent of the cases of AIDS among adolescent and adult males, 75 percent among adolescent and adult females, and 84 percent among children.

Race and ethnicity are not in themselves risk factors for HIV. The CDC observes that "unemployment, poverty, and illiteracy are correlated with decreased access to health education, preventive services, and medical care, resulting in an increased risk for disease. In 1992, 33 percent of blacks and 29 percent of Hispanics lived below the federal poverty level, compared with 13 percent of Asians/Pacific Islanders and 10 percent of whites."[7] HIV/AIDS prevention education must therefore take into account the racial, cultural, and economic realities

---

[4] *CDC Hotline Training Bulletin #114*, 01/06/95.

[5] *Morbidity and Mortality Weekly Report* [MMWR], 02/03/95.

[6] *MMWR*, 09/09/94.

[7] *MMWR*, 09/09/94.

of each group. Additionally, as the Church, we are called to work for the conversion of those principalities and powers that promote racism, poverty, drug addiction, and other oppression.

Women

AIDS among women has been mostly an "invisible epidemic," even though women have been affected and infected since the beginning.[8] Since 1992, HIV/AIDS has been the fourth-leading cause of death among U.S. women ages twenty-five to forty-four. African American and Hispanic women make up 21 percent of all U.S. women, yet these two groups accounted for 77 percent of the AIDS cases reported among women in 1994.[9] That same year, the AIDS case rate per 100,000 population was 3.8 for white women, 62.7 for African American women, 26.0 for Hispanic women, 1.3 for Asian/Pacific Islander women, and 5.8 for American Indian/Alaska Native women.

Dr. Michael Merson of the World Health Organization has identified the following reasons for the growing number of HIV infections in women. His observations, though made in the context of global AIDS, are also applicable to women in the U.S.A. and Puerto Rico. He says that: (1) women are biologically more vulnerable to heterosexual transmission of HIV and other sexually transmitted diseases (STDs); (2) women tend to marry or have sex with older men, who have often had more sexual partners and therefore are liable to be infected; and (3) women often live in cultures of situations of women's subordination to men, which often means they cannot insist that their partner use a condom. Merson has said, "Women face extra challenges in protecting themselves and their children from HIV infection. But this vulnerability is hard for women to challenge as individuals, or even through female solidarity alone. It will take an alliance of women and men working in a spirit of mutual respect."[10]

Older Adults

By the end of 1993, persons age fifty and older accounted for 10 percent of all cases of AIDS nationwide.[11] That same year, the increase

---

[8] See Gena Corea, *The Invisible Epidemic: The Story of Women and AIDS* (New York: Harper Collins, 1992).

[9] CDC Fact Sheet, "Facts About ...Women and HIV/AIDS," 02/09/95.

[10] Press release published in Edinburgh, England, on September 7, 1993, during the Second International Conference on HIV in Children and Mothers.

[11] National Institute of Health [NIH], "Older Americans at Risk of HIV Infection Take Few Precautions," 01/04/94.

in persons with AIDS age sixty and older increased 17 percent over the previous year.[12] The most prevalent behavioral risks for older adults are multiple sexual partners and having a partner with a behavioral risk.[13] "The myth that people become sexually inactive as they age has produced dreadful consequences in the age of AIDS."[14]

Most older people believe they are not at risk if they are heterosexual and do not inject drugs. Since they are not worried about pregnancy, older people are less likely to use condoms.[15] One HIV/AIDS social worker says: "Reaching significant numbers of older adults with the HIV prevention message will entail exploring creative venues—the widows' support group at the senior center, the seniors' bowling league, the Golden Age clubs at community centers and churches. Wherever seniors gather, the HIV message must be visible, accessible, relevant, and respectful."[16]

The Challenge for Church Action into the Next Century

Churches and other United Methodist organizations need to continue compassionate ministry with persons living with HIV/AIDS and their loved ones. In terms of prevention education, United Methodists have an opportunity to teach not only the facts about HIV transmission and how to prevent infection but also to relate these facts to Christian values. We can do HIV/AIDS prevention education in broader contexts, such as human sexuality and holistic health, and by addressing societal problems such as racism, sexism, and poverty. We call on United Methodists to respond:

1. We request that General Board of Discipleship: (a) prepare curriculum resources for all age levels that is sensitive to cultural diversity, in consultation with the General Board of Global Ministries and the General Board of Church and Society. The curriculum will include biblical, theological, and ethical grounding information on what individuals and communities of faith can do in the areas of compassionate ministry and HIV/AIDS advocacy, and age-appropriate, comprehensive prevention education, including teaching that abstaining from sex and injection drug-use is the safest approach to HIV/AIDS prevention. This

---

[12] *New York Times*, 08/09/94.

[13] NIH, "Older People," 01/04/94.

[14] Gregory Anderson, "HIV Preventions and Older People," *Siecus Report*, December 1994/January 1995, page 19.

[15] Rebecca A. Clay, "AIDS Among the Elderly," *Washington Post*, 01/16/93.

[16] Anderson, page 20.

material is to be made available in the first half of the quadrennium; (b) revise the United Methodist sexuality curriculum across age levels to include HIV/AIDS prevention education; and (c) prepare worship resources to assist in HIV/AIDS ministry that can be used by both laity and clergy.

2. We call upon the Interagency Task Force on AIDS to coordinate a second national United Methodist HIV/AIDS consultation for the 1997–2000 quadrennium (the first one was held in San Francisco in 1987), in response to frequent requests from individuals, local churches, and conferences for HIV/AIDS training to equip them for ministry in the twenty-first century. We ask that the event be planned in consultation with appropriate United Methodist racial and ethnic national organizations. The event will equip United Methodist adults and youth to address HIV/AIDS issues and concerns into the twenty-first century, including the trends noted in this resolution, such as HIV/AIDS and women, youth, children, and cultural and racial diversity. The emphasis will be on HIV/AIDS in the United States but will have a global component.

3. We urge all national leadership training sponsored by general Church agencies to include an HIV/AIDS education awareness component, basic facts about HIV/AIDS, workplace issues when appropriate, and ministry concerns.

4. We ask local churches and all United Methodist organizations and communities to respond to the concerns of this resolution through use of the planned resources and materials, such as the United Methodist HIV/AIDS Ministries Network Focus Papers, and working with religious and/or community-based HIV/AIDS organizations to do prevention education with church and community. The United Methodist Church has a congregational HIV/AIDS ministry called the Covenant to Care program, whose basic principle is, "If you have HIV/AIDS or are the loved one of a person who has HIV/AIDS, you are welcome here. . . ." We commend those who have been in ministry through this program and recommend the Covenant to Care to all United Methodist organizations. [17]

ADOPTED 1996

See Social Principles, ¶ 65; "AIDS and the Healing Ministry of the Church"; "Resources for AIDS Education."

---

[17] For more information about the Covenant to Care program and HIV/AIDS ministries resources, contact: HIV/AIDS Ministries Network, Health and Welfare Ministries, General Board of Global Ministries, The United Methodist Church, Room 350, 475 Riverside Drive, New York, New York 10115.

Resources for AIDS Education

WHEREAS, the virus that causes Acquired Immune Deficiency Syndrome (AIDS) has proven itself to be a deadly killer of children, women, and men; and

WHEREAS, the AIDS virus is being carried and may be transmitted by millions of persons worldwide; and

WHEREAS, the AIDS virus is known to be transmissible through exchange of blood, semen, or vaginal fluids or other suspected bodily fluids of the carrier; through sexual intercourse (anal, oral, or vaginal); by injection of a contaminated hypodermic needle; by transfusion/contamination with infected blood; or by organ transplant; and

WHEREAS, massive efforts will be required to change the behaviors that result in continued transmission of the virus and to care for the victims who develop AIDS or AIDS-related Complex (ARC);

Therefore, be it resolved, that the 1988 General Conference directs the General Boards of Church and Society, Discipleship, and Global Ministries to provide or continue providing the annual conferences and local churches with equipping resources to carry out a multifaceted effort of education and awareness for all, including school-age children; legislative lobbying at federal, state, and local levels; and direct ministry to persons who have been or may be exposed to or infected with the AIDS virus; and

Be it further resolved, that the delegates to the 1988 General Conference encourage their respective annual conferences:

1. To utilize the resources developed by the general boards or other organizations such as the National Council of Churches or the United States Public Health Service; or

2. To develop their own resources; and

3. To make these resources available to their own churches as quickly as possible.

Be it further resolved, that these efforts and resources:

1. Be explicit and clear in describing the AIDS virus and the process of its transmission;

2. Promote the prevention and treatment of AIDS and ARC;

3. Educate the public about the needs of the victims of AIDS and ARC; and

4. Encourage United Methodist clergy and laity to participate in direct ministries with HIV-positive persons and their families.

ADOPTED 1988

See Social Principles, ¶ 65; "AIDS and the Healing Ministry of the Church"; "Recognizing and Responding to the Many Faces of HIV/AIDS in the U.S.A."

Responsible Parenthood

We affirm the principle of responsible parenthood. The family, in its varying forms, constitutes the primary focus of love, acceptance, and nurture, bringing fulfillment to parents and child. Healthful and whole personhood develops as one is loved, responds to love, and in that relationship comes to wholeness as a child of God.

Each couple has the right and the duty prayerfully and responsibly to control conception according to their circumstances. They are, in our view, free to use those means of birth control considered medically safe. As developing technologies have moved conception and reproduction more and more out of the category of a chance happening and more closely to the realm of responsible choice, the decision whether or not to give birth to children must include acceptance of the responsibility to provide for their mental, physical, and spiritual growth, as well as consideration of the possible effect on quality of life for family and society.

To support the sacred dimensions of personhood, all possible efforts should be made by parents and the community to ensure that each child enters the world with a healthy body and is born into an environment conducive to the realization of his or her full potential.

When through contraceptive or human failure an unacceptable pregnancy occurs, we believe that a profound regard for unborn human life must be weighed alongside an equally profound regard for fully developed personhood, particularly when the physical, mental, and emotional health of the pregnant woman and her family show reason to be seriously threatened by the new life just forming. We reject the simplistic answers to the problem of abortion that, on the one hand, regard all abortions as murders, or, on the other hand, regard abortions as medical procedures without moral significance.

When an unacceptable pregnancy occurs, a family—and most of all, the pregnant woman—is confronted with the need to make a difficult decision. We believe that continuance of a pregnancy that endangers the life or health of the mother, or poses other serious problems concerning the life, health, or mental capability of the child to be, is not a moral necessity. In such cases, we believe the path of mature Christian judgment may indicate the advisability of abortion. We support the legal right to abortion as established by the 1973 Supreme Court decision. We encourage women in counsel with husbands, doctors, and pastors to make their own responsible decisions concerning the personal and moral questions surrounding the issue of abortion (*see* ¶ 65*I*).

We therefore encourage our churches and common society to:

1. Provide to all education on human sexuality and family life in its varying forms, including means of marriage enrichment, rights of children, responsible and joyful expression of sexuality, and changing attitudes toward male and female roles in the home and the marketplace;

2. Provide counseling opportunities for married couples and those approaching marriage on the principles of responsible parenthood;

3. Build understanding of the problems posed to society by the rapidly growing population of the world, and of the need to place personal decisions concerning childbearing in a context of the well-being of the community;

4. Provide to each pregnant woman accessibility to comprehensive health care and nutrition adequate to ensure healthy children;

5. Make information and materials available so all can exercise responsible choice in the area of conception controls. We support the free flow of information about reputable, efficient, and safe nonprescription contraceptive techniques through educational programs and through periodicals, radio, television, and other advertising media. We support adequate public funding and increased participation in family planning services by public and private agencies, including church-related institutions, with the goal of making such services accessible to all, regardless of economic status or geographic location;

6. Make provision in law and in practice for voluntary sterilization as an appropriate means, for some, for conception control and family planning;

7. Safeguard the legal option of abortion under standards of sound medical practice, make abortions available to women without regard to economic standards of sound medical practice, and make abortions available to women without regard to economic status;

8. Monitor carefully the growing genetic and biomedical research, and be prepared to offer sound ethical counsel to those facing birth-planning decisions affected by such research;

9. Assist the states to make provisions in law and in practice for treating as adults minors who have, or think they have, venereal diseases, or female minors who are, or think they are, pregnant, thereby eliminating the legal necessity for notifying parents or guardians prior to care and treatment. Parental support is crucially important and most

desirable on such occasions, but needed treatment ought not be contingent on such support;

10. Understand the family as encompassing a wider range of options than that of the two-generational unit of parents and children (the nuclear family); and promote the development of all socially responsible and life-enhancing expressions of the extended family, including families with adopted children, single parents, those with no children, and those who choose to be single;

11. View parenthood in the widest possible framework, recognizing that many children of the world today desperately need functioning parental figures, and also understanding that adults can realize the choice and fulfillment of parenthood through adoption or foster care;

12. Encourage men and women to actively demonstrate their responsibility by creating a family context of nurture and growth in which the children will have the opportunity to share in the mutual love and concern of their parents; and

13. Be aware of the fears of many in poor and minority groups and in developing nations about imposed birth-planning, oppose any coercive use of such policies and services, and strive to see that family-planning programs respect the dignity of each individual person as well as the cultural diversities of groups.

ADOPTED 1976
AMENDED & READOPTED 1996

See Social Principles, ¶ 65*A, G, H, J*; "Putting Children and Their Families First"; "Protecting and Sustaining Children."

Sexual Abuse Within the Ministerial Relationship and Sexual Harassment Within The United Methodist Church

The 1992 General Conference resolution on "Sexual Harassment and The United Methodist Church" states, "Sexual harassment is any unwanted sexual advance or demand, either verbal or physical, which is perceived by the recipient as demeaning, intimidating, or coercive. . . . [and] includes the creation of a hostile or abusive working environment resulting from discrimination on the basis of gender." The resolution further states that "sexual harassment is a significant problem in The United Methodist Church, and [it] detracts from the ministry and mission of Jesus Christ." The 1990 survey "Sexual Harassment in The United Methodist Church" conducted by the General Council on Ministries concluded that "unwanted behavior damages the moral environment where people worship, work, and learn," and that "the presence of sexual harassment in environments associated with The United Methodist Church interferes with the moral mission of the Church and disrupts the religious activity, career development, and academic progress of its participants."

Significant Progress

In 1992, the General Conference called for each annual conference, general agency, and United Methodist-related educational institution to have a sexual harassment policy in place, including grievance procedures and penalties for offenders. The results of a 1995 survey of sexual harassment and sexual misconduct policies conducted by the General Commission on the Status and Role of Women indicate that 56 of the 69 annual conferences in the U.S.A. and Puerto Rico have approved policies on sexual harassment and sexual abuse within the ministerial relationship. Of the 13 remaining conferences, 10 have drafted policies awaiting annual conference approval. The survey also revealed that 50 annual conferences have offered training for cabinets, 52 for clergy, and 25 for laity. Sexual harassment policies and grievance procedures are in effect in each of the 13 general agencies of The United Methodist Church. According to the General Board of Higher Education and Ministry, all of the 13 United Methodist schools of theology have sexual harassment policies and grievance procedures in place. In addition, all 124 United Methodist-related colleges and universities have or are refining sexual harassment policies and grievance procedures.

Update

As the Church has confronted sexual harassment, it has also encountered sexual abuse within ministerial relationships. Through processes of policy development and training, annual conferences in the U.S.A. have recognized a need to address the particular issue of clergy sexual misconduct and sexual abuse within the ministerial relationship. In a 1993 survey of United Methodists on "Women and Families in Crisis" conducted by the National Division of the General Board of Global Ministries, 1 in every 56 respondents reported sexual abuse by a clergyperson. One in 26 indicated they had been sexually harassed by a professor, 1 in 45 by a doctor, and 1 in 110 by a therapist. Sexual misconduct or sexual abuse within the ministerial relationship involves a betrayal of sacred trust, a violation of the ministerial role, and the exploitation of those who are vulnerable. Sexual abuse within the ministerial relationship occurs when a person within a ministerial role of leadership (pastor, educator, counselor, youth leader, or other position of leadership) engages in sexual contact or sexualized behavior with a congregant, client, employee, student, staff member, coworker, or volunteer.

Sexual harassment and sexual abuse within the ministerial relationship represent an exploitation of power and not just "inappropriate sexual or gender-directed conduct." Sexual harassment is a continuum of behaviors that intimidate, demean, humiliate, or coerce. These behaviors range from the subtle forms that can accumulate into a hostile working, learning, or worshiping environment to the most severe forms of stalking, assault, or rape. It is important to see both sexual harassment and sexual abuse within relationships at work, school, or church as part of this continuum of brokenness.

The impact of sexual harassment and sexual abuse within the ministerial relationship is far reaching. A survey by the Alban Institute found that unethical behavior, including sexual misconduct, was among the leading factors related to involuntary termination of pastors in U.S. Protestant denominations. Incidences of abuse have legal, financial, physical, emotional, and spiritual ramifications affecting a wide web of relationships. There is an impact not only on victims and their families, but also on perpetrators and their families, congregations, communities, and annual conferences. In situations involving clergy or ministerial leaders, consequences include the potential loss of faith by victims and congregations, as well as the loss of integrity in ministerial leadership. When the Church has not been faithful to its ministry of grace and justice, victims often seek recourse from the courts. It is imperative that the Church institute measures to ensure justice, wholeness, and healing.

Action

Therefore, be it resolved, that The United Methodist Church name sexual harassment and sexual abuse within the ministerial relationship as incompatible with biblical teachings of hospitality, justice, and healing, and continue its efforts to eliminate sexual harassment and abuse in the denomination and its institutions. *Furthermore,* The United Methodist Church, at all levels, commits to these actions:

Education

1. The Council of Bishops will reaffirm its leadership in eradicating and preventing sexual harassment and abuse in the Church. The Council will engage in education, training, and sharing of resources with colleague bishops. Each bishop will ensure that education and training for the prevention of sexual harassment and abuse are made available in the episcopal area that he or she serves. Each area will develop a plan to facilitate communication and coordination among persons involved in ministries of prevention and intervention, including, but not limited to: district superintendents, conference boards of ordained and diaconal ministry, advocates, intervention and healing teams, trained mediators, and staff-parish relations committees.

2. The General Commission on the Status and Role of Women will continue to work with the General Board of Higher Education and Ministry, the General Board of Global Ministries, the General Board of Church and Society, and other appropriate Church bodies to ensure that United Methodist Church-developed education and training resources on prevention of sexual harassment and abuse are made available to local churches; annual conference boards of ordained and diaconal ministry; cabinets; United Methodist-related educational institutions; United Methodist-related benevolent care institutions; and other agencies, groups, and individuals throughout The United Methodist Church.

3. United Methodist-related schools of theology will provide education on the prevention of sexual harassment and sexual abuse within the ministerial relationship. United Methodist-related educational institutions will maintain safe and hospitable learning environments.

Policies and Procedures

1. Each local church, annual conference, general agency, United Methodist-related educational institution, and United Methodist-related benevolent care institution will have a policy on sexual harassment and abuse in effect that may include, but not be limited to, the following:

• a description of the context and scope of the policy, naming the ministry context and persons covered by the policy (e.g., clergy, diaconal ministers, employees, volunteers);

• a clear policy statement consistent with the United Methodist *Book of Resolutions* prohibiting sexual harassment and abuse;

• definitions and examples of sexual harassment and sexual abuse;

• guidelines for initiating complaint procedures when such procedures are contained in the *Book of Discipline*;

• complaint procedures not specified in the *Book of Discipline* may vary according to the context and scope of policy (e.g., employees, volunteers) and may include a provision for bringing a grievance to someone other than the person asserted to be the harasser or abuser;

• guidelines for reporting incidents of sexual harassment and abuse, including mandatory requirements specific to all applicable laws;

• a clear statement of assurance of prompt and equitable fair process, concern for safeguarding the confidential nature of the process, protection of potential victims, and intolerance of retaliation;

• a statement that identifies the consequences for the offending person(s) if the complaint is substantiated;

• provisions for training persons involved in ministries of intervention, prevention, and healing (e.g., advocates, employee or volunteer supervisors, staff-parish relations committees, neutral mediators, congregational healing teams); and

• a stated commitment to education, to ongoing assessment of church ministry environment, and to continuous evaluation of policy and procedures.

2. The General Board of Church and Society will continue to be an advocate for just laws that will help to eradicate sexual harassment and abuse.

Ongoing Assessment

The General Commission on the Status and Role of Women will work with the General Council on Ministries and other appropriate Church bodies to develop and implement research and survey tools for assessing the effectiveness of the Church's efforts to eradicate sexual harassment and abuse. A summary of these findings and recommendations will be reported to the 2000 General Conference.

ADOPTED 1996

See Social Principles, ¶¶ 65H, I, 66F; "Sexual Harassment in Church and Society in the U.S.A"; "Sexual Harassment and The United Methodist Church."

Sexual Violence and Pornography

"So God created humankind in God's own image, in the image of God was the human created; male and female God created them. . . .

And God saw everything that was made, and behold, it was very good" (Genesis 1:27, 31, RSV-AILL). Human sexuality is a sacred gift of God. It "is crucial to God's design that creatures not dwell in isolation and loneliness, but in communion and community . . . sexual sins lie not in being too sexual, but in not being sexual enough in the way God has intended us to be" ("Reuniting Sexuality and Spirituality," by James B. Nelson, *The Christian Century,* February 25, 1987).

God created human beings with an ability to make a choice for good or evil. This divinely created freedom is a freedom to be cherished, as are all gifts from God.

We face a massive public health problem based on people's choosing violence. In 1977, the Centers for Disease Control (CDC) initiated a program to study the nature of violence in our society. In 1985, violence was declared a major health problem.

Violence takes many forms, and many different weapons are being used. Many people use their bodies as weapons to abuse children, their spouses, and the elderly, or to commit rape and other forms of violent battery. Deprivation of many kinds are forms of violence. Discrimination and poverty are forms of social violence. Indeed, Ghandi once said that poverty is the worst form of violence. And the threat of nuclear war constitutes a violent cloud over all of us.

The causes of violence and the escalation of violence in the U.S. are varied. However, public attitudes toward violence play a major factor in the cause and acceptance of violence in our society. In the United States, there is a large-scale tolerance of interpersonal violence. This society is permeated with images and myths about violence, from the old cowboy movies where justice and violence became synonymous, to the new type of stalk-and-slash movies that combine sexual exploitation with violence.

New technology has made sexually violent and pornographic films more available to more people regardless of age, location, or level of moral understanding. Now, persons of all ages can go to their own video stores and secure a wide variety of tapes for play on their videotape recorders, or telephone dial-a-porn from the privacy of their own home.

These new phenomena are especially dangerous, for several reasons:

1. A wide variety of videos is easily available at low cost;

2. Violent or sexually explicit scenes can be played over and over again, teaching through powerful visual images and repetition;

3. The highly erotic stimulation of dial-a-porn is particularly damaging to children and youth;

4. Videos and dial-a-porn are used without parental knowledge, consent, or interaction.

As a result, the sex education of our children is shifting dramatically from parents and the responsible institutions of our society to the powerful mass media of film, television, cable TV, and videocassettes. Carefully documented research has found false messages that predominate in many media images of sexuality:

- violence is a normal part of sexual relationships;
- women "enjoy" being forced into sex;
- women "invite" men to violate them;
- sex is something you "do to" rather than share with someone else.

The repeated viewing of sexually violent material by men:

- desensitizes men to violence on the screen;
- decreases their empathy with victims of sexual violence;
- increases their belief in the "rape myths" that women ultimately enjoy being raped, that "no" doesn't mean no, and that women are responsible for their own rape.

As Christians and as citizens, we recognize the need to differentiate between sex-education materials, erotica, sexually explicit material, and obscenity. The lines are neither self-evident nor clear and will differ among persons and groups. The Supreme Court has not defined pornography while finding "obscenity" not protected under the free speech provisions of the First Amendment.

We affirm the need for sex education in our schools, community youth organizations, and churches. Our young people need to know the biological facts, the health risks, the emotional impact and consequences of their choices, and the moral basis of their faith. We recognize the appropriateness and the need for explicit sexual information, both verbally and visually. In all instances, information should be used with restraint, and a clear attempt should be made to minimize erotic qualities.

Child pornography uses children alone, in sexual relationships with other children, or in sexual relationships with adults. Children are psychologically or physically coerced into participation by older children or by adults. Child pornography victimizes children and harms them physically, emotionally, and spiritually. Child pornographers and distributors should be prosecuted to the full extent of the law.

The Supreme Court declares that obscenity is not protected by the free speech provisions of the First Amendment. Material to be judged illegal must be offensive to community standards, must appeal to prurient interests, and must lack serious scientific, educational, literary, political, or artistic value. We believe that sexually violent material should be judged "obscene" within the context of the Supreme Court's decision.

In order to discuss issues related to sexually explicit material more clearly and precisely, we propose the following definitions:

Erotic material is sexually explicit and arousing but does not use coercion, inflict pain, or use violence in any way, and it rarely depicts sexual intercourse. Some of the world's greatest masterpieces are erotic.

Soft pornography may show persons in sexual intercourse, but it does not use coercion, inflict pain, or use violence. However, we believe that soft-core pornography usually is harmful, and erotica may be harmful to disturbed or immature persons.

Hard-core pornography may show persons in intercourse using coercion, or using violence and inflicting pain. It generally presents women in subordinate situations and degrades both men and women.

Sexual exploitation is a form of social violence that, when communicated to a large number of people, can create both tolerance of sexual violence and increase the incidence of such violence. The National Council of Churches conducted a study of "Violence and Sexual Violence in Film, Television, Cable and Home Video." Some key points that are relevant to this issue relate to this message: Violence, in all of its forms—whether social, as in the cases of discrimination and sexual exploitation, or physical, as in the cases of battery or sexual abuse—is a major public health problem in this nation. Therefore, a combined Christian and public health approach to resolving the problem needs to be applied.

As Christians, we need to examine those materials with which we interact to determine their social or physical violence characteristics. We must ensure that we do not communicate myths that perpetrate violence or allow images of violence, victimization, or exploitation to become a part of institutional communications.

A public health approach instructs our secular institutions to imitate educational and communication strategies that enable people to learn alternatives to violence, as well as other violence-prevention measures. People must be encouraged to seek help when victimized.

Institutions such as family counseling centers, drop-in crisis nurseries, battered women shelters, and runaway shelters need to be provided by both church and community.

In examining both our own media and secular media, the following points adopted by the National Council of Churches are helpful:

1. Our media environment is more complex than ever before. As entertainment forms increasingly include excessive portrayals of violence, parents and other concerned citizens often feel helpless before a media system that is seemingly out of control.

2. Christians are called to a ministry of concern and constructive response so that moral values that have emanated from families of faith can be preserved, perpetuated, and shared with others in our society. Christians also are called upon to bring prophetic judgment to bear on threats to public welfare through what is seen as a moral pollution of our media environment.

3. Only a genuinely open marketplace of ideas can guarantee the search for truth. For this reason, we are determined to defend the First Amendment guarantees of freedom of religion, of speech, and of the press. Society should seek to maximize the diversity of sources and ideas and to minimize the power of government or individuals to block or constrict this diversity of sources.

4. However, prior control of the content of media does exist in our society, as exercised by the government, by business, by education, and by the power of money and monopoly. With respect to any program, someone must decide what shall be included and what shall be left out. The issue is not whether there should be prior control, but rather who should exercise it, and how should it be exercised.

5. As Christians, we affirm our adherence to the principles of freedom of expression as a right of every person, both individually and corporately. We oppose any law that attempts to abridge the freedom of expression guaranteed by the First Amendment. At the same time, as Christians we affirm that the exercise of this freedom must take place within a framework of social responsibility.

6. Children are especially threatened by the pervasiveness of violence and sexual violence in media. Both ethically and constitutionally, it is the responsibility of the entire society to protect the interests of children and to provide for their education and welfare. We support the 1968 Supreme Court ruling that children may legally be barred from

theater showings of films deemed unsuitable for them. Parents should be helped to avoid the showing of that same material in their homes via television, cable, and videocassette.

7. The airwaves are held in trust for the public by radio and television broadcasters with licenses regulated by the government. The broadcaster is therefore responsible for the content of programming. However, this right does not abridge the public's "right to know" and to be fairly represented.

8. Federal regulation should require broadcast licensees and cable operators to make available regularly scheduled constructive programming to enlighten and entertain children.

9. We support criminal obscenity laws that do not embody prior restraint but that punish after-the-fact certain kinds of speech that the Supreme Court has determined are not protected by the First Amendment.

10. In any competitive business environment, some rules are necessary to bring about positive change. Laws and governmental regulation are essential in dealing with reform in the communications industry, because they can place all competitors on an equal basis and thus not disturb the working of the economic marketplace.

11. All mass media are educational. Whether they deal with information, opinion, entertainment, escape, explicit behavior models, or subtle suggestion, the mass media always, directly or indirectly, shape values.

12. In all broadcast and film media, advance information about the products offered should be made available by the industry to parents so they can guide their children's viewing.

13. It is important for research into the effect of media to continue, under a variety of auspices, so that society will have increasingly accurate information as the basis for remedial action to the problems presented by violence and sexual violence in the media. The Church has a special role for congregational education and public policy relative to pornography, violence, and sexual exploitation. The NCCC developed action strategies for churches on local, annual conference, and national levels:

(a) Communication agencies within the denominations and through the National Council of Churches' Communication Commission should monitor programs in order to assess danger levels of violence and sexual violence. Findings should be published for the guidance of parents, educators, and others;

(b) Theologians should examine the moral and spiritual implications of the violence phenomenon in media;

(c) Clergy, parents, and teachers within Christian communions should be trained and equipped to prepare children and youth to survive with integrity in a complex media environment;

(d) Churches and their agencies should join forces with other groups in society who share the same concern over the extent of violence in media in order to plan concerted counteraction;

(e) Religious communities should establish dialogue with creative media professionals. Their objective should be to support and encourage those producers, directors, writers, and actors who are willing to seek ways within the industry to provide viable alternatives to programming that exploits violence and sexual violence;

(f) Churches and church agencies should assist in funding and promoting general distribution programming that presents positive messages and does not contain exploitative sex and gratuitous violence;

(g) Opinions, both positive and negative, should be solicited from members of Christian churches and their leaders, to be presented to those responsible for media productions. Affirmation and encouragement should be sent to those responsible for quality presentations that lift the human spirit, while complaints and protests should go to those responsible for programs that exploit, demean, or desensitize audiences through excessive applications of violence and sexual violence.

Since United Methodists represent a broad spectrum of American society, and since pornography is no respecter of age, social, economic, or even religious condition, there are undoubtedly those among our constituency who are afflicted and are dependent on the habit of sexually violent material. There are persons within our congregations who need help. There are young people who need guidance. There are children who are being sexually abused and women who are being physically abused.

Therefore, we encourage our congregations to:

1. Use United Methodist sex-education curriculum;

2. Study the issues surrounding pornography;

3. Undertake training programs to learn to hear the "cries of help" from abused children and women and to develop a plan of referral of these persons to appropriate community-service organizations;

4. Support shelters for battered women and children; and

5. Join with other community groups in taking appropriate steps to curb distribution of sexually violent material and child pornography in our communities.

Further, we request that The United Methodist Church should, through all its agencies that manage investments, monitor such investments to ensure that no Church funds are invested in companies that are involved in the production, distribution, or sale of pornographic material, and *further,* if such investments are found, should move to divest holdings in such companies.

The misuse of our human sexuality through violence and coercion separates us from one another by making women and children fearful of men, and it separates us from our creator God.

ADOPTED 1988

See Social Principles, ¶¶ 65H, I, 66F, P; "Violence in Electronic Media and Film."

Understanding Living and Dying as Faithful Christians

I. Theological and Ethical Affirmation

A. Divine Creation of Human Life

All human life is the gift of God. Distinct from other creatures, we are created male and female in God's image with intellect and free will. Thus endowed with the capacities for knowledge, freedom, responsibility, and personal relationship, we are called in community to realize the divine purpose of living, which is to love God and one another. As Christians, we believe that God reaffirms the value of all human life through the incarnation of Jesus Christ and through the empowering presence of the Holy Spirit.

B. The Human Condition

Humanity is subject to disease and the inevitability of death. Death as well as life is a part of human existence. Given this relationship, we should be free from either denying or exalting death. Our propensity, however, to distrust God leads us to distort the ordered place and meaning of death. When we do, our fears and anxieties become exaggerated, and we are led into despair, believing God has forsaken us.

Our human situation is further exacerbated by our sins of indifference, greed, exploitation, and violence, and by the moral failure engen-
dered by stupidity and narrow-mindedness. As a result, we have
rendered our earthly environment unhealthy and have produced unjust social structures, perpetuating poverty and waste. This deprives
much of the human family of health, robs persons of dignity, and
hastens death.

C. *The Healing Christ*

Through Jesus Christ, God has entered human suffering even to the
point of dying on the cross. In the healing ministry and sacrificial death
of Jesus Christ, God transforms suffering and death into wholeness and
life. These realities call us to witness to God's presence in the midst of
suffering by sharing compassionately in the tasks of healing the sick
and comforting the dying.

D. *Stewardship of Life*

Life is given to us in trust: not that we "might be as gods" in absolute
autonomy, but that we might exercise stewardship over life while
seeking the purposes for which God made us. In this life we are called
by God to develop and use the arts, sciences, technologies, and other
resources within ethical limits defined by respect for human dignity,
the creation of community, and the realization of love.

The care of the dying must always be informed by the principle of
the loving stewardship of life. The direct, intentional termination of
human life, either by oneself or by another, generally has been treated
in the history of Christian thought as contradictory in such stewardship
because it is a claim to absolute dominion over human life.

Such stewardship, however, allows for the offering of one's life when
a greater measure of love shall be realized through such action than
otherwise would be possible, as in the case of sacrificing one's life for
others or choosing martyrdom in the face of evil. When a person's
suffering is unbearable and irreversible or when the burdens of living
outweigh the benefits for a person suffering from a terminal or fatal
illness, the cessation of life may be considered a relative good.

Christian theological and ethical reflection shows that the obligations
to use life-sustaining treatments cease when the physical, emotional,
financial, or social burdens exceed the benefits for the dying patient and
the caregivers.

E. Christian Hope

In the face of the ultimate mystery of why humans suffer and die, our hope rests in the God who brought again Jesus from the dead. God offers us, in the midst of our struggle and pain, the promise of wholeness within the unending community of the risen Christ. Nothing, neither life nor death, can separate us from the love of God in Jesus Christ.

II. Pastoral Care

A. Healing Ministry

Pastoral care should be an expression of the healing ministry of Christ, empowering persons in the experience of suffering and dying. Those who give pastoral care create a relationship wherein signs of God's presence are revealed. Pastoral care may come from the church and wider community of family, friends, neighbors, other patients, and the health-care team. Suffering and dying persons remain autonomous and have a right to choose their relationships with pastoral caregivers.

Persons offering pastoral care empathize with suffering patients and share in the wounds of their lives. In providing comfort, they point beyond pain to sources of strength, hope, and wholeness. They may join in prayer with a person who is facing death. Such prayer should focus on healing that points in wholeness of personhood, even in death. Healing implies affirmation of the goodness of life, while recognizing that death is not always an enemy.

B. Reconciliation

In both the healing ministry and the death of Jesus Christ, God enters into our suffering, sustains us, and provides the resources for reconciliation and wholeness. This means assisting a person in reactivating broken or idle relationships with God and with others, and being at peace with oneself.

C. Relationships and Care

Pastoral care provides families and friends an opportunity to share their emotions, including hurt and anger as well as grief, and it provides help for complex questions that frequently require difficult decisions.

Religious, cultural, and personal differences among family and friends must be considered with special sensitivity. Grieving persons need to be reminded that their feelings are normal human responses. Such feelings need not cause embarrassment or guilt. Families at the bedside usually act according to long-established patterns of relationships. Attention to the entire family as a unit must be incorporated into pastoral care.

Health-care workers also need pastoral care. Doctors and, especially, support staff have intimate contact with dying persons in ways experienced by few others. They live in the tension of giving compassionate care to patients while maintaining professional detachment. Pastoral care for health-care workers means helping them to take loving care of themselves as well as their patients.

D. Specific Pastoral Concerns

1. Communications with the dying person and family

Pastoral-care persons are trained to help patients understand their illness. While they usually do not communicate medical information to patients, they can assist in assimilating information provided by medical personnel. Pastoral-care persons are especially needed when illness is terminal and neither patients nor family members are able to discuss this reality freely.

The complexity of treatment options and requests by physicians for patient and family involvement in life-prolonging decisions require good communication. Pastoral-care persons can bring the insights of Christian values and Christian hope into the decision-making process. If advance directives for treatment, often called "living wills," are contemplated or are being interpreted, the pastoral-care persons can offer support and guidance to those involved in decision-making. They can facilitate discussion of treatment options, including home and hospice care.

2. Suicide

Some persons, confronted with a terminal illness that promises prolonged suffering and anguish for themselves and for loved ones, may consider suicide as a means to hasten death. When the natural process of dying is extended by application of medical technology, the emotional, economic, and relationship consequences for self and for others may lead a responsible person seriously to question whether continued living is faithful stewardship of the gift of life. Some may ask caregivers for assistance in taking their lives. Churches need to provide preparation in dealing with these complex issues.

Among the issues of stewardship to be considered in such a decision are: (a) God's sacred gift of life and the characteristics or boundaries of meaningful life; (b) the rights and responsibilities of the person in relationship to the community; (c) the exercise and limits of human freedom; and (d) the burdens and benefits for both the person and the community. Engagement with these issues is necessary for persons considering suicide.

When possible, others who are related to and care about the dying person should be included in discussion. The loving presence of Christ as manifested in the church community should surround those contemplating suicide and the survivors of those who take their own lives. An important pastoral concern is the guilt and stigma often felt by survivors, particularly when they have not been included in prior considerations.

3. Donation of organs for transplantation, or of one's body after death, to medical research

The gift of life in organ donation allows patients and survivors to experience positive meaning in the midst of their grief. Donation is to be encouraged, assuming appropriate safeguards against hastening death and with determination of death by reliable criteria. Pastoral-care persons should be willing to explore these options as a normal part of conversation with patients and their families.

4. Holy Living

A major concern of pastors and chaplains is the sustaining ministry to and spiritual growth of patients, families, and health-care personnel.

Pastoral-care persons bear witness to God's grace with words of comfort and salvation. In our United Methodist tradition, spiritual growth is nurtured by persons who offer prayers and read the Scriptures with patients and loved ones; by Holy Communion; by the laying on of hands; and by prayers of repentance, reconciliation, and intercession. A ritual of prayer or anointing with oil after miscarriage, or after a death in a hospital, nursing home, or hospice, are examples of means to bring comfort and grace to the participants. Rituals developed in connection with a diagnosis of terminal illness, of welcome to a hospice or nursing home, or of return to a local congregation by persons who have been absent for treatment or in the care of a loved one may also enhance spiritual growth. Preparation of these rituals with and by the persons involved is strongly encouraged.

Pastoral-care givers and the community of faith are called to be open to God's presence in the midst of pain and suffering, to engender hope, and to enable the people of God to live and die in faith and in holiness.

III. The Social Dimension

Ethical decisions about death and dying are always made in a social context that includes policies and practice of legislative bodies, public agencies and institutions, and the social consensus that supports them. Therefore, it is important for Christians to be attentive to the social situations and policies that affect the dying. The social context of dying decisively affects individual decisions to continue or forego treatment or to accept death. Social policies and practices must protect the fundamental values of respect for persons, self-determination, and patient benefit of treatment.

A. Respect for Persons: Holy Dying

Dying with dignity calls for care that puts emphasis on compassion, personal interaction between patient and caregivers, and respect for the patient as a whole person with social as well as medical needs.

To the extent that medical technology is used to sustain, support, and compensate for human functions, it supports the preservation of human dignity. Indeed, medical technology is a gift of our age, supported by the will and resources of a society that values life and is willing to apply the measures necessary for extending life when possible. When technology becomes an end in itself, however, unduly prolonging the dying process, it creates a paradox in which human dignity may be undermined and the goals of treatment distorted in the interest of technology.

When a person is dying and medical intervention can at best prolong a minimal level of life at great cost to human dignity, the objective of medical care should be to give comfort and maximize the individual's capacity for awareness, feeling, and relationships with others. In some cases of patients who are without any doubt in an irreversibly comatose state, where cognitive functions and conscious relationships are no longer possible, decisions to withhold or withdraw mechanical devices that continue respiration and circulation may justly be made by family members or guardians, physicians, hospital ethics committees, and chaplains.

B. Justice for All

All persons deserve to be able to die with dignity, regardless of age, race, social status, lifestyle, communicability of disease, or ability to pay for adequate care. The biblical witness of God's concern for justice, particularly for those most marginalized and powerless in society, demands such commitments. Equitable allocation of economic resources is necessary to ensure the protection of individuals in their dying from neglect, social isolation, unnecessary pain, and unreasonable expense.

C. Self-Determination

The right of persons to accept or reject treatment is protected in a just society by norms and procedures that involve the patient as an active participant in medical decisions. In order to safeguard the right of self-determination at a time when one may lack decision-making capacity due to dementia or unconsciousness, individuals are encouraged to designate a proxy or execute a durable power of attorney and to stipulate, in written advance directives, guidelines for their treatment in terminal illness.

All persons are endowed with the gift of freedom and are accountable to God and their covenant community for their decisions. Congregations and other church groups can play a particularly important role helping their members provide written guidance for their treatment in terminal illness and find support for implementing their own directives or those of others.

D. Pain and Dying

In spite of the belief held by some that euthanasia and suicide may be the humane solution for the problem of excruciating pain experienced by the terminally ill, use of these options is minimized by effective medical management of pain. Presently, the proper application of medical science, as demonstrated by hospice care, can in most cases enable patients to live and die without extreme physical suffering. Such methods of controlling pain, even when they risk or shorten life, can be used for terminally ill patients, provided the intention is to relieve pain and not to kill. The law should facilitate the use of drugs to relieve pain in such cases.

If adequate support by community, family, and competent pastoral-care givers is provided, the mental suffering of loneliness, fear, and anguish, which is often more painful than physical suffering, can be alleviated. This support is particularly important for those patients who are without any physical pain but who suffer emotional trauma in knowing that they are in the early stages of certain diseases currently considered incurable, such as Alzheimer's disease, amyotrophic laterial sclerosis, Huntington's disease, and HIV-related diseases.

E. Social Constraints

Certain social constraints militate against the ideals of holy dying.

1. Attitudes toward dying

The attempt to deny death frequently results both in reluctance by individuals to plan ahead for their dying and unwillingness in professionals to "let go" even when a patient is beyond medical help or benefit. This denial is intensified by negative attitudes toward old age, poverty, and disability.

2. Ethos of the medical profession

The emphasis on curing, healing, and restoration can contribute to uneasiness among physicians in making the transition from cure to care when possibilities of cure are exhausted. Members of the medical profession are to be commended when they accept the legitimacy of medicine oriented toward relief of suffering rather than extension of the inevitable process of dying. This is not easily done; institutional pressure encourages the use of sophisticated technology even when it can only prolong a patient's dying. This is heightened by the fear of physicians concerning legal liability for failing to use all available technologies.

3. Failures in distributive justice

Budget allocations and reimbursement policies for medical care by both private and government health plans give priority in finding technologically sophisticated diagnoses and treatments. At the same time, they often deny or minimize payments for less costly services that are critical for humane dying.

In addition, medical professionals are often constrained in their efforts to implement health-care plans that have patient benefit as their goal by payment policies of government and insurance companies that dictate the length and modalities of treatment. A society committed to helping every person realize a humane death will reverse these policies and give highest priorities to such services as hospice and home care, social services, and pastoral resources. This will include an adequately funded national health plan that assures all persons access to these resources.

4. Use of the legal system

Persons increasingly have sought to redress perceived injustices in medical treatment or to resolve difficult cases in the adversarial setting of the courtroom. As a result, the courts have become the site of medical decisions. The failure of society to provide effective support systems in health-care facilities, including the use of ethics committees, leaves individuals and institutions vulnerable to outside interference. The resulting practice of defensive medicine has frequently increased the use of futile diagnostic and treatment procedures by physicians and added to the cost of patient care.

F. United Methodist Response

Churches need to work together to overcome these social constraints. It is recommended that United Methodists:

1. Acknowledge dying as part of human existence, without romanticizing it. In dying, as in living, mercy and justice must shape corporate response to human need and vulnerability;

2. Accept relief of suffering as a goal for care of dying persons rather than focusing primarily on prolongation of life. It is within human and financial means, if made a priority, to provide pain control and comfort-giving measures in a setting of communal affection and support, such as a hospice;

3. Advocate equitable access for all persons to resources, including a national health-care plan, needed to relieve the dying and their loved ones of financial crises created by extended terminal illness;

4. Promote effective personal support systems, such as pastoral care teams, ethics committees in hospitals and nursing facilities, and church groups, for medical personnel who must implement difficult decisions on behalf of dying persons and their families;

5. Participate in congregational, ecumenical, and community-wide dialogue to help shape consensus on treatment of dying persons; and

6. Encourage persons to use advance directives for their treatment in terminal illness and dying. Congregations can be supportive by providing information, opportunities for considering alternatives, and assistance in implementing the directives.

Holy dying, with loving pastoral care and without efforts to prolong terminal illness, will be enhanced to the extent that the Church and the human community embody mercy and justice for all persons.

ADOPTED 1992

See Social Principles, ¶ 65L; "Suicide: A Challenge to Ministry"; "Organ and Tissue Donation"; "Universal Access to Health Care in the United States and Related Territories."

Use of Church Studies on Homosexuality

WHEREAS, our Social Principles state: "We recognize that sexuality is God's good gift to all persons. We believe persons may be fully human only when that gift is acknowledged and affirmed by themselves, the church, and society. We call all persons to the disciplined, responsible fulfillment of themselves, others, and society in the stewardship of this gift. We also recognize our limited understanding of this complex gift and encourage the medical, theological, and social science disciplines to combine in a determined effort to understand human sexuality more completely. We call the Church to take the leadership role in bringing together these disciplines to address this most complex issue. Further, within the context of our understanding of this gift of God, we recognize that God challenges us to find responsible, committed, and loving forms of expression" (¶ 65G); and

WHEREAS, the Committee to Study Homosexuality provided a meaningful model and process of study, prayer, reflection, and action on a complex and significant issue facing United Methodists; and

WHEREAS, the study resource includes stories of individuals struggling and growing, sharing their understanding of faithfulness to the mind of Christ; and

WHEREAS, the use of these materials expands our spiritual growth in understanding God's good gift of human sexuality; and

WHEREAS, perceptions and perspectives of individuals continue to benefit from open and informed discussion about homosexuality;

Therefore, be it resolved, that the annual conferences are urged to support the use of this study; and

Be it resolved, that the Council of Bishops is encouraged to use the study; and

Be it further resolved, that the Board of Discipleship facilitate the use of the study in church school, retreat, district council on ministries, and other settings.

ADOPTED 1996

See Social Principles, ¶¶ 65G, 66H.

World AIDS Day Observance

Each year, World AIDS Day is observed on December 1. It is a time for special programs on HIV/AIDS education and religious worship services that focus on intercessory and healing prayer, hope in God, and love and compassion in the midst of the HIV/AIDS pandemic.

We recommend that United Methodists be encouraged to observe World AIDS Day on or around December 1. We further recommend that voluntary offerings may be channeled through the Advance Special for HIV/AIDS Ministries (#982215-6). We ask that the Advance Committee include information in a mailing about World AIDS Day (December 1), which may be used as a vehicle for raising United Methodist awareness of ministries addressing this issue.

Materials for World AIDS Day are available each year from the World Health Organization, the General Board of Church and Society, and the General Board of Global Ministries of The United Methodist Church.

ADOPTED 1996

See Social Principles, ¶ 65; "AIDS and the Healing Ministry of the Church"; "Recognizing and Responding to the Many Faces of HIV/AIDS in the U.S.A."

THE SOCIAL COMMUNITY

Abusive Treatment Methods for Persons with Mental Disabilities

A large part of the ministry of our Lord focused on persons with mental disabilities. Such persons are children of God and, therefore, our brothers and sisters within God's family. The full and equal rights of persons with mental disabilities are enshrined in the Social Principles of The United Methodist Church.

Yet the use of abusive treatment methods as "therapy" for persons with mental disabilities still occurs. Such abusive treatment methods are used both on adults and children, and programs that rely on such abusive treatment methods are often funded by tax revenues. A number of organizations that advocate for persons with mental disabilities have already taken a stand against abusive treatment methods.

The United Methodist Church joins in affirming the right of persons with disabilities to freedom from abusive treatment methods. We oppose the use of any form of punishment for children or adults with mental disabilities in any case where such punishment would be considered illegal, abusive, or unconscionable if applied to a child or adult who is not disabled. In particular, we condemn as unacceptable the following practices:

1. treatment methods that result in physical injury or tissue damage to the person;

2. verbal abuse or insult, humiliation, or degradation;

3. prolonged isolation from others;

4. denial of food, warmth, hygiene, contact with other human beings, or other necessities of life;

5. the use of electric shock or noxious substances as a form of punishment;

6. the use of any punishment on a child with a mental disability that would be considered child abuse if used on a child with no disabilities;

7. neglect;

8. the misuse of physical or chemical restraint; and

9. the threat of any of the above treatments.

Any therapy used in the treatment of persons with mental disabilities must be potentially beneficial to the person. As an alternative to abusive treatment methods, we support the use of positive approaches in the treatment of persons with mental disabilities. Positive approaches affirm the humanity of these persons and recognize that the needs and desires of such persons are not significantly different from those of other persons. Our obligation to persons with mental disabilities is to support and assist them in their efforts to live lives as rich and rewarding as possible.

We call upon all public and private agencies and service providers involved in treating persons with mental disabilities to adopt and uphold the standards set forth in this resolution.

We call upon United Methodist church-related institutions and agencies, including hospitals, homes, schools, and universities, to adopt and uphold the standards set forth in this resolution and to support research on positive treatment methods.

We call upon governments at all levels to end immediately the expenditure of public revenues on any agency or program that fails to adopt and uphold the standards set forth in this resolution.

The United Methodist Church declares itself to be open to persons with mental disabilities and their families, and the Church commits itself to support such persons and families and to accommodate their needs within our community. We further pledge our support to help persons with mental disabilities and their families find appropriate services, programs, and supports, and to protect them from abusive treatment methods.

ADOPTED 1996

See Social Principles, ¶ 66Q; "Health in Mind and Body"; "Ministries in Mental Illness."

Act of Covenanting Between Other Christian Churches and The United Methodist Church

The United Methodist Church must always be open to the leading of God's Spirit. Today there is an expressed need for new relationship in the body of Christ. We believe that an Act of Covenanting between consenting churches may be one response to the need and to the witness of the Holy Spirit. In such an act, the participating churches will continue independence in their structures, traditions, styles of implementation of ministry, existing partnerships, agreements and explorations, forms of worship, and programs. The United Methodist Church will continue to see itself as an international Church.

The focus of an Act of Covenanting is the larger body of Christ, and thus it is open to potential covenanting churches of all Christian heritages. It is rooted both in the apostolic faith and in our contemporary experience of God's love and will.

The following sample elements of an Act of Covenanting with other Christian churches were adopted by the 1988 General Conference of The United Methodist Church for implementation and negotiation as indicated in the text:

Elements of an Act of Covenanting

1. *Introduction.* Covenants have been integral in the history of God's relationships with the People of God. Indeed, as the General Conference of 1968 stated (in *On the Ecumenical Road,* A Statement on the Cause of Christian Unity): "The profoundest imperative to Christian unity springs from God's own design and providence for his covenant people." In the Preamble to the Constitution of The United Methodist Church, we are alerted to the dangers of all dividedness: "The Church of Jesus Christ exists in and for the world, and its very dividedness is a hindrance to its mission in that world." In recent decades, we have received clearer understanding of the relationship between Christian unity and our covenant with God. At the same time, we have new insight into the nature of the Christian church and new sense of common global mission. Geographical and political boundaries do not limit the body of Christ.

The United Methodist Church has a stake in the faithful discipleship of other communions. Other communions have a stake in the faithful discipleship of The United Methodist Church. Thus, The United Methodist Church now seeks a new form of acceptance of God's gift of unity. We seek to engage in covenant with other Christian churches wherever more visible Christian unity can increase effective mission in the modern world. This covenant is a symbol of the search for deeper relationships with churches that are a part of the whole Covenant People of God.

2. *Possible Definition and Commitments.* In this Act of Covenanting, the emphasis is on our roots in the apostolic faith and in our contemporary experience of God's love and will. It is aimed at encouraging a new sense of global common cause, mutual support, mutual spiritual growth, common study of Scripture and culture, creative interaction as ministers in the mission of God's church, cross-fertilization of ideas about ways to be in that mission, sharing of resources, and exploring new forms of service directed at old and emerging needs.

In this covenant, the _____ Church and The United Methodist Church acknowledge the centrality of the sovereignty of Jesus Christ as basic to all relationships. Our links with the apostolic faith through Scripture, Tradition, Experience, and Reason lead us now solemnly to affirm to each other that "all who are baptized into Christ are members of Christ's ministry through the people of the one God, Father, Son and Holy Spirit" (COCU Digest, 1974, page 335; *Official Record*, XII, 1974).

(a) We therefore recognize our respective baptisms as different facets of the one baptism and mutually recognize that the members of the _____ Church and of The United Methodist Church are members one of the other.

(b) We therefore recognize each other as authentic expressions of the One, Holy, Catholic, and Apostolic Church of Jesus Christ.

(c) We therefore recognize the ordained ministries of our churches and pledge our mutual efforts at effecting forms of reconciliation of those ministries, including the exchange or transfer of ordained ministers between properly constituted bodies where the approval and consent of the appropriate authorities involved is given. The assumption of pastoral care of members visiting or residing in one another's countries is another instance of this aspect of the Act of Covenanting.

(d) We are committed to systematic participation in full Eucharistic fellowship as a symbol of transcendence over manifestations of human divisions.

(e) We expect that the various agencies of our own churches will function in new ways of partnership in mission and evangelism, in education and implementation of the gospel. Mutual sharing of principles and methods can improve our functioning in our separate contexts and especially in continuance or new development of joint projects in mission between the _____ Church and The United Methodist Church.

(f) We expect that an expanded and focused international linkage of visitations and partnerships will take place. The bishops or presidents of the churches will arrange for mutually agreeable visitations and exchanges that will provide contact with and some knowledge of the social, political, economic, moral, and religious context in which the people of the world struggle for existence, meaning, and purpose. Mutual visitations may include occasional presence at each other's appropriate assemblies.

(g) Extended partnerships might be possible between, for example, a covenanting church or its parts and a particular congregation, annual conference, or episcopal area of The United Methodist Church. Such participation in this covenant would be by special action subsequent to adoption of the covenant. Such an extended partnership, perhaps in consultation with specific United Methodist agencies as well, might be for a defined period to enable a mutual flow of persons, interest, and commitment. The partnership can be extended or ended by mutual agreement. Such extended partnerships would make palpable the global stake we have in each other in various parts of the world. These focused partnerships would be integrated with visitations by leaders and the sharing by agencies of time, ability, and funding resources.

(h) Our covenant assumes the continuing independence and autonomy of the covenanting churches in their structures, traditions, styles of implementation of ministry, existing partnerships, agreements and explorations, forms of worship, and program. But we look forward to knowing each other in love, to losing our fear of difference and our fear of differences for the mission of God's church. We make bold to anticipate that out of our experience we will be led by the Spirit to new forms of covenant and to new relationships for the global Christian community.

3. *Oversight of Covenant Projects and Participation.* For The United Methodist Church, oversight of the covenantal relationships is the responsibility of the Council of Bishops with the assistance of the General Commission on Christian Unity and Interreligious Concerns, while participation in specific projects is the responsibility of the appropriate general agency or agencies.

4. *Authorization.* The Council of Bishops shall represent The United Methodist Church in developing an Act of Covenanting with a prospective partner church. The Council of Bishops shall make recommendations to General Conference on such specific covenanting agreements. The Act of Covenanting becomes effective immediately upon approval by the General Conference and by the chief legislative body of the partner church, signed by the president of the Council of Bishops and

the secretary of the General Conference of The United Methodist Church and by the authorized persons in the covenanting church.

5. *Enabling Legislation.* Submitted separately for adoption and publishing in the *Book of Discipline* are several items of enabling legislation related to an Act of Covenanting.

6. *Liturgical Celebration.* A brief liturgical celebration of the Act of Covenanting shall be prepared by representatives of our two churches and shall be celebrated at the chief legislative bodies of both covenanting churches.

ADOPTED 1992

See Social Principles, ¶ 66; "Continuing Membership in the Consultation on Church Union"; "Toward an Ecumenical Future"; "COCU Consensus: In Quest of a Church of Christ Uniting."

Affirm the Purpose of United Methodist Women and Continue Giving Through Proper Channels

We, the executive committee of the Memphis Conference United Methodist Women, reaffirm the reasons for which we came into existence over one hundred years ago: to spread the gospel of Jesus Christ through mission outreach of the Church, especially to women and children, throughout the world.

This is emphasized in our purpose, which states: "The organized unit of the United Methodist Women shall be a community of women whose purpose is to know God and to experience freedom as whole persons through Jesus Christ; to develop a creative, supportive fellowship; and to expand concepts of mission through participation in the global ministries of the church."

We are therefore committed as United Methodists and as United Methodist Women to continue our giving through the proper channels of our organization.

Acting upon our purpose, United Methodist Women do not deviate from the *Discipline* or the Social Principles of The United Methodist Church.

ADOPTED 1996

See Social Principles, ¶ 66F; "The Status of Women."

An Affirmation of Basic Rural Worth

Rural people, rural communities, and rural congregations are of great value in God's creation.

While only 2 percent of people in the United States are directly involved in farming, approximately 30 percent live in rural areas.

Many rural communities are growing. Families and individuals are moving back to rural communities because of the quality of life there.

Recent developments in communications technology and improved transportation systems have done much to eliminate problems of isolation and distance.

Approximately 50 percent of United Methodist churches are located in rural areas with a population of 2,500 or less.

Rural people and rural churches have many gifts and strengths to share with the Church of the future.

Rural peoples are employed in farming, ranching, and other agricultural endeavors, trucking, migrant work, timbering, recreation, fishing and river work, rural factories, and small businesses of numerous kinds.

Therefore, be it resolved, that The United Methodist Church affirms that:

1. Persons who live in rural places, like other persons, are persons of sacred human worth for whom God's grace is available and operative;

2. Each rural church, regardless of size or location, is valuable to The United Methodist Church;

3. Rural communities are significant and valuable places of ministry, where new congregational development and congregational redevelopment should be, can be, and is happening;

4. Rural residents deserve the option of living and prospering in the communities where they live, and the goals and policies of the governments that relate to rural places should provide this option;

5. Rural peoples deserve equitable and continuing spiritual care, recreational opportunities, security for the elderly and those whose abilities are challenged, nurture and protection for children and youth, satisfying economic opportunity, and a sense of purpose and hope; and

6. As stewards of creation, rural people have a right to determination of how land, water, air, and other resources within their communities, especially in areas of limited population, are to be used, with particular attention given to land use and control being exercised by all who live within an area.

ADOPTED 1996

See Social Principles, ¶ 66; "Appointment of Clergy to Rural Ministry"; "Rural Chaplaincy as a Ministry of Laity and Clergy."

Affirmation of Support for the Ecumenical Decade of the Churches in Solidarity with Women

WHEREAS, The United Methodist Church at many levels has been an active participant in the World Council of Churches' program called Ecumenical Decade: Churches in Solidarity with Women, 1988–1998; and

WHEREAS, many members of The United Methodist Church have, through study and involvement, grown in understanding and in faith as a result of engaging the Decade's main goals:

1. To empower women to challenge oppressive structures in the global community, their country, and their church;

2. To affirm—in shared leadership and decision-making, theology, and spirituality—the decisive contributions women are making in churches and communities;

3. To give visibility to women's perspectives and actions in the struggle for peace, justice, and the integrity of creation;

4. To enable churches to free themselves from racism, sexism, and classism, and from teaching and practices that discriminate against women; and

5. To encourage churches to take actions in solidarity with women; and

WHEREAS, the Council of Bishops has contributed significantly to current theological reflection and has helped clarify the role of women's theological reflection and scholarship in their document entitled *Council of Bishops Report: Task Force on the Study of Wisdom;* and

WHEREAS, United Methodists have participated in WCC Team Visits to member churches worldwide in consultations regarding the goals of the Decade as "Living Letters" from the churches to one another, and through such visits have been challenged to deeper commitment, faithfulness, and witness; and

WHEREAS, from these visits emerge four areas of concern from women all around the world:

1. women's full and creative participation in the life of the Church;

2. violence against women in all its forms and dimensions;

3. the global economic crisis and its effects on women; and

4. racism and xenophobia and its specific impact on women; and

WHEREAS, the Fourth International Conference on Women in Beijing, in which United Methodists participated, has addressed vital, ongoing concerns regarding economic justice for women, access to health care

157

and family planning, participation of women in social and policy planning, violence against women, rights of women in inheritance, and women's roles in creating and promoting peace; and

WHEREAS, The United Methodist Church is currently growing in the richness and fullness of its own global nature and is therefore called to greater solidarity with women of the Church worldwide; and

WHEREAS, the search for Christian unity calls the Church to unity with wholeness at every level of its life together;

Therefore, we call upon The United Methodist Church to:

1. Reaffirm its commitment to the Ecumenical Decade: Churches in Solidarity with Women, 1988–1998;

2. Recommit itself to addressing the spiritual and social brokenness that condemns women to lives defined by poverty, powerlessness, and violence; and

3. Continue in study, spiritual reflection, and advocacy related to full voice and participation of women at every level of Church and society, in accordance with United Methodist doctrinal standards.

ADOPTED 1996

See Social Principles, ¶ 66F; "Ecumenical Decade: Churches in Solidarity with Women."

Affirmative Action

The United Methodist Church has long been committed to the principle of social inclusiveness. That is, in keeping with the spirit of the gospel, we affirm that all persons—whatever their racial or ethnic identity, whatever their gender or national origin, whatever their physical state or condition—are full-fledged members of the human community with every one of the rights and privileges that such membership entails.

In light of that commitment, the Church has, in years past, adopted a strong stand supportive of the concept of "affirmative action." Recently, this concept has been subjected to intense opposition. While some of the particular policies adopted under that rubric may be in need of revision—given developments that have occurred over the course of time—we would, at this moment, reconfirm our support for the basic concept.

The concept of affirmative action emerged in response to the civil rights movements of the 1960s as one of a set of public policies designed to overcome a tragic history of racist and sexist practices throughout this nation and to create a more equitable social system in keeping with the spirit of the gospel and in keeping with the proclaimed democratic ideals of the American people.

The specific intent of affirmative action, given its origins, was to bring the prestige and power of government to bear on economic and educational institutions, requiring them to put into effect carefully conceived plans to admit qualified persons who traditionally had been excluded from participating in them—women, ethnic and racial minorities, and, at a later time, persons with disabilities.

Over the past three decades, programs of affirmative action have had a significant effect in the employment patterns of corporations and public agencies and in the character of the professional staff and student bodies of educational institutions, private and public. Proportionately, more women, racial and ethnic minorities, and people with disabilities have found their talents and training recognized than before such programs were instituted.

At the same time, however, many women, racial and ethnic minorities, and persons with disabilities, though fully competent, have confronted obstacles in these settings, stifling their advancement in education and in employment. Unemployment of racial and ethnic minorities remains appreciably higher than the national average. Women workers continue to earn less than male workers in the same or similar positions, and they continue to confront limitations in promotion to a more prestigious and responsible level of jobs. Persons with disabilities are bypassed regardless of their motivations.

Despite these persistent inequities, the concept of affirmative action is currently under severe attack. In some locations, it has been abolished as a public policy on several (somewhat different and not altogether compatible) grounds:

- that it promotes the hiring (in business) or admission (to institutions of higher education) of unqualified persons;
- that it discriminates unduly against white males;
- that it has a negative impact on the self-esteem of affirmative action candidates; and
- that its goals have been at this time fully realized and therefore it is no longer necessary.

In light of the evidence, however, (except in those cases where policies of affirmative action have been badly or improperly administered) all of these alleged grounds seem specious. However persuasive they seem on the surface, they tend to slough off or to ignore the persistence of significant and widespread inequalities of opportunity affecting women, ethnic and racial minorities, and persons with disabilities throughout our social system.

From the perspective represented by The United Methodist Church, the most fundamental premise underlying the concept of affirmative action is both moral and spiritual. Concern for the disadvantaged and the oppressed is a major feature of the message of the Hebraic prophets and of Jesus. According to biblical teaching, we are mandated, in the face of inhumane discrimination—whether that discrimination is intended or unintended—to do what we can to redress legitimate grievances and to create a society in which the lives of each and all will flourish.

For this fundamental reason, we reconfirm our commitment to the concept of affirmative action. The use of numerical goals and timetables are a legitimate and necessary tool of effective affirmative action programs. This concept retains its pertinence as a means of attaining a more inclusive society in our educational systems, in our businesses and industries, and in religious and other institutions. No persons—whatever their gender, their ethnic or racial heritage, their physical condition—should be deprived of pursuing their educational or employment aspirations to the full extent of their talents and abilities.

Fairness is the rule for affirmative action guaranteeing more opportunities for all to compete for jobs. Indeed, the purpose of affirmative action has always been to create an environment where merit can prevail.

Rather than curtail or abolish programs in affirmative action, we should instead move toward the reallocation of the resources of our society to ensure such opportunities for all.

At the same time, given the tenacity of many forms of racism, sexism, and ableism—both blatant and subtle—the concept of affirmative action retains its relevance as part of an overall effort to create a more just and equitable social system.

Therefore, be it resolved, that the 1996 General Conference of The United Methodist Church calls upon all its members to:

1. Affirm our Judeo-Christian heritage of justice and inclusiveness as a foundation for the concept of affirmative action;

2. Constitute a model for others in society by practicing and strengthening our own affirmative action policies, whatever our station in life;

3. Declare our support of efforts throughout the society to sustain and, where needed, strengthen affirmative action legislation and programs;

4. Collaborate with movements and initiatives seeking to ensure effective participation of ethnic and racial minorities, women, and persons with disabilities in all sectors of our society; and

5. Interpret the genuine meaning of affirmative action, dispelling the myths and responding to the specious appeals that would undercut and vilify affirmative action policies and programs.

Be it further resolved, that the 1996 General Conference reaffirm its mandate to implement affirmative action programs in all general Church boards and agencies, annual conferences, church-related institutions, districts, and local churches.

Be it further resolved, that the General Commissions on Religion and Race and the Status and Role of Women continue to monitor The United Methodist Church and related institutions and to provide assistance in helping them move toward greater conformity with the principle of inclusiveness.

ADOPTED 1996

See Social Principles, ¶ 66; "A Charter for Racial Justice Policies in an Interdependent Global Community"; "Ethnic Membership on Boards and Agencies."

Affirming a Diversity of Language Usage in the United States and Opposing a Constitutional Amendment Making English the Official Language

The United States is a land whose inhabitants are enriched by diverse traditions, languages, and cultures. While English is the most commonly used or "primary" language of the country, there have always been other languages present throughout the history of the nation. Native American languages and Spanish were already spoken when the first English colonists arrived at Plymouth. Throughout that same history, there have been various efforts to prescribe the use of English and to proscribe the use of other languages. These efforts sometimes resulted in legislation that had the effect of legalizing discrimination against various language minority groups. However, such legislation was eventually overcome by the constitutional principles of equal rights for all. The acknowledgment of English as the primary language of the United States does not deny the right and contribution of other languages or the inherent right of people to retain and speak their mother tongues.

In recent years, there have been renewed efforts in different parts of the country to make English the official language of the nation. We are concerned that the movement to declare constitutionally English as the official language of the nation is not based upon any real need but, in fact, may be motivated by an effort to deny the pluralistic foundation of the country and to deny the dignity and wholeness of persons from different racial and ethnic groups who rightly considered their languages an integral part of their cultures. We fear the real purpose of some may be not so much to make English the *official* language of the U.S. as to make English the *exclusive* language of the nation.

For example, there is an English-only "movement" that has, within the last year, gained more national recognition. Organizations such as "U.S. English" and "English First" continue gaining support through active national activities and local English-only campaigns. In addition to promotion of their principles through the media, they are also involved in various legislative and lobbying activities. These include efforts to pass a constitutional amendment making English the official language of the United States, opposition to federal legislation for bilingual education, voting-rights bills, and the FCC licensing applications for Spanish-language broadcasts.

These efforts and their implications are another manifestation of the systemic racism that has infected this country for generations. The English-only movement blames the deterioration of the American fabric on immigration and the use of languages other than English. It contends that the nation's unity rests upon the use of an official language. It defines multiculturalism and multilingualism as "anti-unity." Consequently, the movement, if successful, could further discriminate and segregate the racial and ethnic minority population of the United States. Essential information such as the 911 emergency telephone number, hospital emergency rooms, police, firefighters, language services, bilingual education, and interpreters in the judicial system might be denied.

As Christians, we believe that we are children of God, created in God's image, and members of the family of God;

We believe that diversity is a gift of the creative genius of God and that languages are an expression of the wisdom of God;

162

We believe that competence in the English language is important to participate fully in the life of the United States, but that we also live in a global context, the global family of God, where people and nations experience interdependency at all levels;

We believe that our nation needs to take advantage of the rich contributions that the ethnic/language groups bring to this country by preserving those languages and encouraging North Americans to learn other languages;

We believe that it is the will of God that each human being is affirmed as a whole person and that it is in the acceptance and interchange of our uniqueness that we find oneness—total wholeness—*shalom;*

We oppose the attempt to rob a person of his or her language as dehumanizing and as a denial of that person's wholeness; and

We oppose the English-only movement as a manifestation of the sin of racism.

Therefore, the General Conference shall:

1. Express in writing to the President of the United States its support for practices and policies that permit provision of information in languages appropriate to the residents of communities and its opposition to the movement that seeks to make English the only language of the United States, which movement is discriminatory and racist;

2. Forward this resolution to members of Congress, governors, and the legislatures of the fifty states and territories;

3. Commend this resolution to all annual conferences for promotion and interpretation within the annual conferences; and

4. Ask the General Board of Church and Society to make this resolution an urgent item in their agenda for lobbying, constituency education, and advocacy.

ADOPTED 1988

See Social Principles, ¶ 66A; "A Charter for Racial Justice Policies in an Interdependent Global Community"; "Bilingual Education."

Affirming Rural Chaplaincy

WHEREAS, rural communities continue to suffer from the loss of leadership; economic resources; jobs in agriculture, mining, timber, processing, and textiles; small, family-owned businesses; opportunities for youth; human service institutions; environmental quality; political strength; and viable churches; and

WHEREAS, God continues to call both laity and clergy along with congregations and cooperative ministries to be responsive to the hurts of people who suffer from oppression, exploitation, and marginalization; and

WHEREAS, the General Board of Global Ministries' Office of Town and Country Ministries has facilitated a grassroots effort to enable local rural community and church leaders to address the issues and concerns of the rural crisis; and

WHEREAS, over one hundred persons representing the diversity of The United Methodist Church have become certified rural chaplains related to the General Board of Global Ministries; and

WHEREAS, rural chaplains have received enthusiastic affirmation of the whole Church and have extended fellowship to include ecumenical and international partners in ministry;

Therefore, be it resolved, that The United Methodist Church celebrate and affirm God's continued call of persons committed to serving as rural chaplains in difficult times and places; and

Be it further resolved, that The United Methodist Church reaffirm its commitment to rural community/church development and vigorously pursue rural chaplaincy as a significant part of resourcing renewal in rural churches/communities throughout the world.

ADOPTED 1996

See Social Principles, ¶ 66N; "Appointment of Clergy to Rural Ministry"; "The Church's Response to Changing Rural Issues"; "Rural Chaplaincy as a Ministry of Clergy and Laity."

African American Clergywomen

WHEREAS, African American clergywomen are subjected to sexism and racism within The United Methodist Church with respect to appointments; compensation; and election to chair, convene, and serve on various boards and agencies of the general Church; and

WHEREAS, these discriminatory practices have caused a significant number of African American clergywomen to suffer stress-related illnesses; and

WHEREAS, the salaries for African American clergy are substantially less than those of white female and male clergy;

Therefore, be it resolved, that the General Conference enact the following:

1. Commission the General Board of Higher Education and Ministry, Division of Ordained Ministry, to do a comprehensive study to docu-

ment the disparities affecting African American clergywomen with regard to:

(a) appointments, compensations, and elections to chair, convene, and serve on various boards and agencies of the general Church; and

(b) the nature and extent of stress-related illnesses suffered by African American clergywomen related to these disparities; and

2. Submit a report of these findings no later than the 2000 General Conference.

ADOPTED 1996

See Social Principles, ¶ 66A, F; "Eradication of Racism in The United Methodist Church."

African American Family Life

WHEREAS, our Social Principles state that "we believe the family to be the basic human community through which persons are nurtured and sustained in mutual love, responsibility, respect, and fidelity" (¶ 65A); and

WHEREAS, families of all types in the United States are vulnerable to social and economic change; and

WHEREAS, research shows that strong African American families are highly religious, but that the local church has limited resources to assist them in resolution of problems and crises; and

WHEREAS, African American families today face problems of epidemic proportions from violence within the geographical community, new and virulent health problems, a high rate of cardiovascular illness, economic stress, and so forth;

Therefore, be it resolved, that the General Board of Discipleship identify or create resources and materials to assist local churches in developing a program of mentoring, counseling, and referral that includes strategies to strengthen African American family life.

ADOPTED 1992

See Social Principles, ¶¶ 65A, 66A; "Putting Children and Their Families First"; "Protecting and Sustaining Children."

Aging in the United States of America

I. Preamble

The elderly in the United States of America occupy a new frontier in a rapidly changing industrial society. A frontier has two aspects: (1) its hazards, uncharted ways, unknowns, and anxieties; and (2) its promises, hopes, visions, and fulfillments. A frontier becomes a promised land when guides chart the way, pioneers settle, and builders develop the land. But this new frontier is yet to be charted for the aged. Existing institutions have not been able to adapt fast enough, nor have new institutions been created to meet the new conditions. Some research, however, has recently begun to topple some myths and stereotypes about the aging process and older persons.

This statement is for study, discussion, and implementation and action by The United Methodist Church in the United States. It contains brief sections on the current situation of the older population, on a theological response, and on calls to the society and to the Church. There has, however, been no attempt to set priorities for ministries in this new frontier described within this statement; it is hoped that appropriate Church agencies and units will set their own priorities.

II. The Situation

During the past 100 years, life expectancy in the United States has increased by about 27 years, a fact to be celebrated. The number of persons 65 years of age and older has grown from 3.1 million in 1900 (4.1 percent of the total population) to 28 million in 1984 (11.9 percent of the total population). This number is expected to increase from 34.9 million in the year 2000 (13.0 percent) to 65 million in the year 2030 (21.1 percent). The older population includes a disproportionate number of women (148 women to 100 men) and persons with a wide range of capacities, from active and employed to fragile, frail, and chronically disabled. The fastest growing age group in the population is those 85 years of age and over, and the second fastest growing is the 75 to 84 age group.[1]

The trend in recent years has been for older persons to live alone rather than with family members or in a formal care setting, primarily in nursing homes. In 1984, only 2 percent of those persons 65–74 years old were in nursing homes, while 7 percent of the 75- to 84-year-olds and 23 percent of those 85 years and over were living in long-term care facilities. Social security provides some benefits to about 92 percent of the older adult population.[2] However, about 12.4 percent, or 3.3 mil-

---

[1] A Profile of Older Americans, 1985 (AARP brochure).

[2] Social Security Administration, 1986. (Figure includes recipients of Railroad Retirement and Social Security benefits; it does not include SSI, or other disability related payments that are based on need and/or condition.)

lion persons 65 and older, had incomes below a subsistence poverty level in 1984.[3] The median annual income for older men in 1984 was $10,000, and for women, about $6,000—only $1,000 above the official poverty level[4] ($4,979 for individuals living alone, and $6,282 for older couples households in 1984).[5] It is not surprising that 72 percent of the elderly poor are women, and 28.1 percent of the total elderly minority population are considered marginally poor.[6]

Clearly, the elderly are not a homogenous group. These data point out that not all subgroups fit into the normative situation of the larger population of the elderly. In addition, middle-class persons with much higher incomes often find themselves reduced to poverty by the cost of health treatment and long-term care. The increased probability of widowhood and divorce also may produce economic instability for older women. For example, in the case of pensions, about 28 percent of men and 10 percent of women receive pensions.[7] "Currently, only one woman in five receives any type of pension, public or private, to supplement her Social Security payments. The median income for women from pensions in 1984 was $233 per month, about half of what men received. And only half as many women received pensions, whether as retired workers or as spouses of retired workers."[8]

The current health system is more adequate for persons who are younger and have excellent insurance plans. Even though aging itself is not a disease, older people have more illness for a longer period of time than younger people do. Adequate health insurance coverage for millions of uninsured women has been identified as the most pressing health issue faced by older women today. Older women under sixty-five who are neither married nor in the workforce often find health insurance so expensive that it is unaffordable or impossible to buy because of the exclusions for "existing conditions." This problem is made worse because they have no claim on employer-based group policies in which their husbands participated if divorce or death occurs, and they have fewer job options with good insurance plans if they choose to work outside the home.

---

[3] *A Profile of Older Americans.*

[4] *The O.W.L. Observer: National Newspaper of the Older Women's League,* Special Edition: Women and Pensions, November 1985; page 1.

[5] *A Profile of Older Americans.*

[6] 1985 *Bureau of Census, Poverty Report.*

[7] *Tomorrow's Elderly: A Report Prepared by The Congressional Clearinghouse of the Future,* U.S. House of Representatives, Ninety-Eighth Congress, October 1984; page 8.

[8] *The O.W.L. Observer.*

Medicare is a health insurance program primarily for persons over the age of sixty-five. Medicaid provides a supplement to Medicare as well as coverage for younger persons in poverty. Out-of-pocket health costs for older Americans rose to an average of $1,666 per person in 1985.[9] Medicare only covers about 40 percent of most older adults' individual medical expenses.[10]

In 1984, 78 percent of older men were married, while 50 percent of older women were widowed. There are about five times as many widows as widowers. Women are likely to live six more years as widows,[11] and 68 percent of them will live alone. A number of factors signal problems. For instance, because of traditional sex-role socialization, older men are psychologically ill-prepared for living alone, and older women are often inadequately prepared for assertiveness in financial and other management decisions when they find themselves alone. Since most people have been socialized to live in families, they are not prepared to live alone in old age. We need to develop adequate responses to single persons in a society that is oriented toward family living.

Although most older persons live in urban places, they also comprise a large proportion of rural populations where facilities and resources for them are extremely limited. This condition is complicated further by a disproportionately low allocation of federal funds to meet the needs of the rural elderly.

Race and ethnicity are important determinants of the residential patterns of elderly people. While about one third of all older persons live in central cities, one half of all African Americans and Hispanics over sixty-five is heavily concentrated in urban areas. The popular shifts in housing patterns brought about by urban renewal and gentrification (higher-income persons buying property in formerly poor neighborhoods) and the resultant increase in homeowner taxes have a major impact on the elderly, especially minorities. Houses that have been paid for are lost because of the tax increases, or low rents rise astronomically.

We need to dispel the common misunderstanding that aging is senility and that older persons are unable or unmotivated to learn, grow, and achieve. Opportunities for continuing education and growth have long been unmet by a system geared to the needs of the young.

---

[9] *Cut the Cost: Keep the Care: New Action Steps for 1986* (AARP brochure); page 5.

[10] *The Prudent Patient: How to Get the Most for Your Health Care Dollar* (AARP booklet); page 3.

[11] *Mortality Report, Division of Vital Statistics* (National Center for Health Statistics).

This demand for continuing education will become acute as better educated, younger generations grow older. We need to counteract the impact of racism and sexism on later life because of underemployment, no employment, inequitable access to education, and language or nationality barriers.

Some problems that beset older persons are the result of the social and physical process of aging. These include changes in work, family, and community roles; the reduction of energy; and the increase in chronic illness and impairments. These conditions can lead to increased dependence on others for life's necessities. Other problems faced by the elderly are the result of social and political institutions that sometimes victimize the elderly through various techniques of both subtle and overt discrimination. Being old today is not easy, in either the church or society. If the situation of older persons is to be improved, the Church must act.

III. The Technological Response

Aging is a process involving the whole life span from birth to death. A theological understanding of aging, therefore, must be concerned with the whole life process rather than with only its final stages. The meaning of life, rather than death, is the central point from which to theologize about aging. In our pluralistic Church, there is a certain legitimacy for several traditional, biblical, and theological understandings of the meaning of life in its progression from birth to death. The position presented here is one attempt to express this meaning.

A. All of creation is God's work (Genesis 1). Human beings are only a small part of the totality of life forms. The aging process is universal in all life forms. Birth, aging, and death are all part of divine providence and are to be regarded and taught as positive values. This does not in any way mean that such things as birth defects, disease, or deaths at an early stage in life are the will of God.

B. As Christians, the mystery of God's involvement in the person of Jesus Christ provides us with a unique source of divine help (grace) in our passage through life's successive stages. This is especially significant in the later stages, when spiritual maturation and well-being can be experienced even in times of physical decline. The power of the cross is a special revelation of how suffering can be reconciling and redemptive. Faith in the Resurrection provides us with an assurance of the abiding presence of the Risen Lord (Matthew 28:20) and the Holy Spirit (John 14:16-19; 2 Corinthians 3:17-18; Romans 8:9-11), and the permanence of our relationship with God beyond the mystery of death. In this spiritual presence we also find the source of the potential of all persons for self-transcendence. God's act in Christ was for life abundant (John 10:10) in all stages of life. Christ also gives us our traditional Wesleyan vision of the goal of ultimate perfection (Matthew 5:48). The grace of God in Christ is therefore important throughout life, including its last stages.

C. In response to this saving grace, we believe in the inevitable need to walk in the ways of obedience that God has enabled (Ephesians 2:8-10). These ways are defined by love for God and neighbor (Mark 12:28-31; Romans 13:8-9). It is therefore the privilege of Christians to serve all persons in love, including older persons with their special needs. Furthermore, since God's grace is not conditioned by any human standards of worthiness or usefulness (2 Corinthians 5:19), we should regard all persons as valuable to God (Matthew 6:25-30). In the larger pattern of human needs and rights, those of elderly persons must be consciously and intentionally included.

D. Older persons are not simply to be served but are also to serve; they are of special importance in the total mission of the church. Since the Christian vocation has no retirement age, the special contributions of elderly persons need conscious recognition and employment. The experience of all older persons, and the wisdom of many, are special resources for the whole church.

E. The church as the body of Christ in the world today (1 Corinthians 12:27) is God's method for realizing the reconciliation accomplished by Christ (Colossians 1:16-20). As such, it intentionally sponsors institutional forms that help reconcile persons of all ages to one another and to God. This especially includes those institutions designed to meet the needs of elderly persons and to keep them fully incorporated into the body of Christ. The church also is charged with an abiding concern for justice for all. It should work tirelessly for the freedom of all persons to meet their own fullest potential and to liberate those who are captive to discrimination, neglect, exploitation, abuse, or poverty.

IV. The Call

A. To society at all levels

United Methodist people are called upon to engage in sustained advocacy for the elimination of age discrimination in personal attitudes and institutional structures. We should pursue this advocacy vigor-ously and in cooperation with appropriate private and public groups, including all levels of government. We recognize that there needs to be creativity in developing the proper cooperative mix of private and public programs to serve the elderly, but all our efforts should be based on the following assumptions:

1. Religious institutions can make a unique and significant contri-bution to the context of care provided for persons. Secular society involves ethical issues and value decisions; therefore, a religious pres-ence in neighborhoods and institutions is important to the quality of total community life.

2. Government should play a critical role in ensuring that all benefits are available to all elderly persons to improve their quality of life. Christians should support governmental policies that promote sharing with those who are less fortunate. This does not absolve either the institutional church or individual Christians from responsibility for persons in need.

3. A standard of basic and necessary survival support systems should be accepted and established in our society and made available to all persons. These should include at minimum: health care, transpor-tation, housing, and income maintenance. Church people need to iden-tify and promote those facilities and services that ensure opportunities for prolonged well-being. These services should be provided at a cost within the financial means of the elderly, with appropriate public subsidy when necessary. They include the following:

(a) health-resources systems special to the needs of the elderly that are comprehensive, accessible, and feasible within available resources (these include long-term care, hospice care, home health care, and health maintenance organizations);

(b) health-education systems that emphasize proper nutrition, proper drug use, preventive health care, and immunization as well as information about the availability of health resources within the com-munity;

(c) training for medical and social service personnel concerning the special cultural, physical, psychosocial, and spiritual aspects and needs of the elderly;

(d) adequate housing that is both affordable and secure, with pro-tections that massive tax and rental increases will not create displace-ment, and transportation systems that meet the special needs of the elderly;

(e) a basic governmental income-maintenance system adequate to sustain an adequate standard of living affording personal dignity (This system should be supplemented when necessary by private pension programs. Both public and private pension systems must be financed in a manner that will ensure their ability to meet all future obligations as well as guarantee equitable consideration of the needs of women and minorities.);

(f) when basic pension systems benefit levels are not adequate to meet economic needs at least equal to the defined poverty level, supplementation by benefits from public funds;

(g) continuing educational and counseling opportunities for the elderly in preretirement planning, in work-related training, in interpersonal retirement relationships, and in personal enrichment;

(h) formal and informal community associations such as public and private centers that foster social, recreational, artistic, intellectual, and spiritual activities to help persons overcome loneliness and social isolation;

(i) continuing employment opportunities for those who desire them in flexible, appropriate work settings related to varying lifestyles; and

(j) opportunities for volunteer work and paid employment that best utilize the skills and experiences of the elderly.

Finally, our society is called upon to respond to a basic human right of the elderly: the right to die with dignity and to have personal wishes respected concerning the number and type of life-sustaining measures that should be used to prolong life. Living wills, requests that no heroic measures be used, and other such efforts to die with dignity should be supported.

B. *To the Church at all levels*

1. Each local church is called upon to:

(a) Become aware of the needs and interests of older people in the congregation and in the community and to express Christian love through person-to-person understanding and caring;

(b) Affirm the cultural and historical contributions and gifts of ethnic minority elderly;

(c) Acknowledge that ministry to older persons is needed in both small and large churches;

(d) Ensure a barrier-free environment in which the elderly can function in spite of impairments;

(e) Motivate, equip, and train lay volunteers with a dedication for this important ministry;

(f) Develop an intentional ministry with older adults that:

i. ensures each person health service, mobility, personal security, and other personal services;

ii. offers opportunities for life enrichment including intellectual stimulation, social involvement, spiritual cultivation, and artistic pursuits;

iii. encourages life reconstruction when necessary, including motivation and guidance in making new friends, serving new roles in the community, and enriching marriage; and

iv. affirms life transcendence, including celebration of the meaning and purpose of life through worship, Bible study, personal reflection, and small-group life;

(g) Recognize that older persons represent a creative resource bank available to the church and to involve them in service to the community as persons of insight and wisdom (this could include not only ministry to one another, but also to the larger mission of the Church for redemption of the world, including reaching the unchurched);

(h) Foster intergenerational experiences in the congregation and community including educating all age groups about how to grow old with dignity and satisfaction;

(i) Ensure that the frail are not separated from the life of the congregation but retain access to the sacraments and are given assistance as needed by the caring community;

(j) Provide guidance for adults coping with aging parents;

(k) Cooperate with other churches and community agencies for more comprehensive and effective ministries with older persons, including radio and television ministries;

(l) Accept responsibility for an advocacy role in behalf of the elderly; and

(m) Develop an older-adult ministry responsible to the council on ministries involving an adult coordinator or older-adult coordinator, volunteer or employed. (An older-adult council may be organized to facilitate the ministry with older adults.)

2. Each annual conference is called upon to:

(a) Provide leadership and support through its council on ministries for an intentional ministry to older persons in its local churches, with special attention to the needs of women and minorities;

173

(b) Develop a program of job counseling and retirement planning for clergy and lay employees;

(c) Share creative models of ministry and a data bank of resources with the local churches and other agencies;

(d) Define the relationship between the annual conference and United Methodist-related residential and nonresidential facilities for the elderly, so that the relationships can be clearly understood and mutually supportive;

(e) Relate to secular retirement communities within its boundaries;

(f) Recruit persons for professional and volunteer leadership in working with the elderly;

(g) Serve as both a partner and critic to local church and public programs with the elderly, promoting ecumenical linkages where possible;

(h) Support financially, if needed, retired clergy and lay church workers and their spouses who reside in United Methodist long-term care settings;

(i) Promote Golden Cross Sunday and other special offerings for ministries by, for, and with the elderly; and

(j) Recognize that other persons within the conference, both lay and clergy, represent a significant and experienced resource that should be utilized in both the organization and mission of the conference.

3. General boards and agencies are called upon to:

(a) Examine the pension policies of the general Church and their impact related to the needs of those who are single (retired, divorced, or surviving dependents of pensioners);

(b) Create specific guidance materials for ministry by, for, and with the elderly;

(c) Prepare intergenerational and age-specific materials for church school and for other special studies in the local church;

(d) Promote advocacy in behalf of all the elderly, but especially those who do not have access to needed services because of isolation, low income, or disability (this might include advocacy for health care, income maintenance, and other social legislation);

(e) Assist institutions for the elderly to maintain quality care and to develop resource centers for ministry with and by the elderly;

(f) Create a variety of nonresidential ministries for the elderly, such as Shepherd's Centers;

(g) Coordinate general Church training in ministry with the elderly;

(h) Provide for formal coordination on aging issues;

(i) Advocate the special concerns and needs of older women and minorities; and

(j) Utilize older persons as a creative resource bank in the design and implementation of these objectives.

4. Retirement and long-term care facilities related to the Church are called upon to:

(a) Develop a covenant relationship with the Church to reinforce a sense of joint mission in services with the elderly;

(b) Encourage the provision of charitable support and provide a channel for the assistance of the whole Church; and

(c) Encourage both residential and nonresidential institutional settings that emphasize the spiritual, personal, physical, and social needs of the elderly.

5. Seminaries and colleges are called upon to:

(a) Provide seminarians instruction on aging and experiences with older persons in the curriculum;

(b) Prepare persons for careers in the field of aging;

(c) Develop special professorships to teach gerontology, and to provide continuing education for those who work with the elderly;

(d) Stimulate research on the problems of aging, special concerns of minorities, the status of the elderly, and ministries with the elderly, the majority of whom are women; and

(e) Enable the elderly to enroll in courses and degree programs and to participate generally in the life of educational institutions.

6. Finally, all levels of the Church are called upon to:

(a) Include ministries for, with, and by the elderly as an essential component of the Church and its mission;

(b) Promote flexible retirement and eliminate mandatory retirement based solely on age;

(c) Develop theological statements on death and dying that recognize the basic human right to die with dignity;

(d) Develop ethical guidelines for dealing with difficult medical decisions that involve the use of limited resources for health and life insurance;

(e) Authorize appropriate research, including a demographic study of members of The United Methodist Church, to provide greatly needed information on the socioreligious aspects of aging; and

(f) Establish a properly funded pension system with an adequate minimum standard for all clergy and Church-employed laypersons and their spouses, including the divorced spouse.

V. Summary

Life in the later years has caused older persons to ask two questions: How can my life be maintained? What gives meaning and purpose to my life in these years? Both questions have religious implications.

Concern for older persons in the church is theologically grounded in the doctrine of Creation, in the meaning of God's work in Christ, in the response to grace that leads us into service, in the continuing value of older persons in the larger mission, and in the nature of the church as an agent of redemption and defender of justice for all.

Older adults in the United States deserve respect, dignity, and equal opportunity. The United Methodist Church is called to be an advocate for the elderly, for their sense of personal identity and dignity, for utilization of experience, wisdom, and skills, for health maintenance, adequate income, educational opportunities, and vocational and avocational experiences in cooperation with the public and private sectors of society.

The graying of America implies also the graying of The United Methodist Church. The Church, however, is called to be concerned, not only for its own, but also for all older people in our society.

As the aging process is part of God's plan of creation, with the good news of Christ's redemption giving hope and purpose to life, United Methodist people are called upon to help translate this message through words and deeds in the Church and in society.

ADOPTED 1988

See Social Principles, ¶ 66E.

American Indian Religious Freedom Act

WHEREAS, tribal people have gone into the high places, lakes, and isolated sanctuaries to pray, receive guidance from God, and train younger people in the ceremonies that constitute the spiritual life of Native American communities; and

WHEREAS, when tribes were forcibly removed from their homelands and forced to live on restricted reservations, many of the ceremonies were prohibited; and

WHEREAS, most Indians do not see any conflict between their old beliefs and the new religion of the Christian church; and

WHEREAS, during this century the expanding national population and the introduction of corporate farming and more extensive mining and timber industry activities reduced the isolation of rural America, making it difficult for small parties of Native Americans to go into the mountains or to remote lakes and buttes to conduct ceremonies without interference from non-Indians; and

WHEREAS, federal agencies began to restrict Indian access to sacred sites by establishing increasingly narrow rules and regulations for managing public lands; and

WHEREAS, in 1978, in an effort to clarify the status of traditional Native American religious practices and practitioners, Congress passed a Joint Resolution entitled "The American Indian Religious Freedom Act," which declared that it was the policy of Congress to protect and preserve the inherent right of American Indians to believe, express, and practice their traditional religions; and

WHEREAS, today a major crisis exists in that there is no real protection for the practice of traditional Indian religions within the framework of American constitutional or statutory law, and courts usually automatically dismiss Indian petitions without evidentiary hearings; and

WHEREAS, while Congress has passed many laws that are designed to protect certain kinds of lands and resources for environmental and historic preservation, none of these laws is designed to protect the practice of Indian religion on sacred sites; and

WHEREAS, the only existing law directly addressing this issue, the American Indian Religious Freedom Act, is simply a policy that provides limited legal relief to aggrieved American Indian religious practitioners;

Therefore, be it resolved, that the General Board of Global Ministries and the General Board of Church and Society make available to the Church information on the American Indian Religious Freedom Act; and

Be it further resolved, that the General Board of Church and Society support legislation that will provide for a legal cause of action when sacred sites may be affected by governmental action; proposed legislation should also provide for more extensive notice to and consultation with tribes and affected parties; and

Be it further resolved, that the General Board of Church and Society may enter and support court cases relating to the American Indian Religious Freedom Act; and

Be it further resolved, that the General Board of Church and Society communicate with the Senate Select Committee on Indian Affairs, declaring that the position of The United Methodist Church, expressed through the 1992 General Conference, is to strengthen the American Indian Religious Freedom Act of 1978 and preserve the God-given and constitutional rights of religious freedom for American Indians.

ADOPTED 1992

See Social Principles, ¶ 66; "Confession to Native Americans"; "Rights of Native People of the Americas"; "The United Methodist Church and America's Native People."

The United Methodist Church and America's Native People

Most white Americans are isolated from the issues of justice for the United States' native people by the lapse of time, the remoteness of reservations or native territories and the comparative invisibility of natives in the urban setting, the distortions in historical accounts, and the accumulation of prejudices. Now is the time for a new beginning, and The United Methodist Church calls its members to pray and work for that new day in relationship between native peoples, other minorities, and white Americans.

The United States has been forced to become more sharply aware and keenly conscious of the destructive impact of the unjust acts and injurious policies of the United States government upon the lives and culture of U.S. American Indians, Alaskan natives, and Hawaiian natives. In the past, the white majority population was allowed to forget or excuse the wrongs that were done to the indigenous peoples of this land. Today, U.S. American Indians and Alaskan and Hawaiian natives are speaking with a new and more unified voice, causing both the government and the American people to reexamine the actions of the past and to assume responsibility for the conditions of the present.

A clear appeal is being made for a fresh and reliable expression of justice. The call is being made for a new recognition of the unique rights that were guaranteed in perpetuity of U.S. American Indians by the treaties and legal agreements that were solemnly signed by official representatives of the United States government. A plea is being raised regarding the disruption of Alaskan and Hawaiian natives who were not granted the legal agreements protecting their culture and land base.

The time has come for the American people to be delivered from beliefs that gave support to the false promises and faulty policies that prevailed in the relations of the United States government with the United States of America's native peoples. These beliefs asserted that:

1. White Europeans who came to this continent were ordained by God to possess its land and utilize its resources;

2. Natives were not good stewards of the environment, permitting nature to lie in waste as they roamed from place to place, living off the land;

3. The growing white population tamed nature and subdued the natives and thus gave truth to the assumption that the white race is superior;

4. The forceful displacement of the natives was a necessary and justifiable step in the development of a free land and a new country;

5. The white explorers and pioneers brought civilization to the natives and generously bestowed upon them a higher and better way of life.

Rarely are these beliefs now so blatantly set forth, yet they are subtly assumed and furnish the continuing foundation upon which unjust and injurious policies of the government are based.

These beliefs, in former times, permitted the government, on the one hand, to seize lands, uproot families, break up tribal communities, and undermine the authority of traditional chiefs. On the other hand, the beliefs enabled the government to readily make and easily break treaties, give military protection to those who encroached on native lands, distribute as "free" land millions of acres of native holdings that the government designated as being "surplus," and systematically slay those natives who resisted such policies and practices.

In our own time, these beliefs have encouraged the government to:

1. Generally assume the incompetence of natives in the management and investment of their own resources;

2. Give highly favorable leasing arrangements to white mining companies, grain farmers, and cattle ranchers for the use of native lands held in trust by the federal government or historically used as supportive land base;

3. Use job training and other government programs to encourage the relocation of natives from reservations or native territories to urban areas;

4. Utilize government funds in projects that are divisive to the tribal or native membership and through procedures that co-opt native leadership;

5. Extend the control of state government over native nations that are guaranteed federal protection;

6. Terminate federal services and protection to selected native nations and further deny federal recognition to others;

7. Engage in extensive and expensive litigation as a means of delaying and thus nullifying treaty rights and aboriginal land claims;

8. Pay minimal monetary claims for past illegal confiscation of land and other native resources;

9. Lump together United States natives with other racial minorities as a tactic for minimizing the unique rights of native peoples; and

10. Punitively prosecute the native leaders who vigorously challenge the policies of the federal government.

The Church is called to repentance, for it bears a heavy responsibility for spreading false beliefs and for unjust governmental policies and practices. The preaching of the gospel to America's natives was often a preparation for assimilation into white culture. The evangelizing of the native nations often effected the policies of the government.

The Church has frequently benefited from the distribution of native lands and other resources. The Church often saw the injustices inflicted upon native peoples but gave assent or remained silent, believing that its task was to "convert" the heathen.

The Church is called through the mercy of almighty God to become a channel of the reconciling Spirit of Jesus Christ and an instrument of love and justice in the development of new relations between native nations, other minorities, and whites, in pursuit of the protection of their rights.

The United Methodist Church recognizes that a new national commitment is needed to respect and effect the rights of American Indians and Alaskan and Hawaiian natives to claim their own identities, maintain their cultures, live their lives, and use their resources.

The United Methodist Church expresses its desire and declares its intention to participate in the renewal of the national responsibility to the United States of America's native people.

The United Methodist Church calls its congregations to study the issues concerning American Indian and Alaskan and Hawaiian native relations with the government of the United States; to develop an understanding of the distinctive cultures and the unique rights of the native people of the United States; to establish close contacts wherever possible with native persons, tribes, and nations; and to furnish support for:

1. The right of native people to live as native people in this country;

2. The right of native people to be self-determining and to make their own decisions related to the use of their lands and the natural resources found on and under them;

3. The right of native people to plan for a future in this nation and to expect a fulfillment of the commitments that have been made previously by the government, as well as equitable treatment of those who were not afforded legal protection for their culture and lands;

4. The right of American Indian nations to exercise the sovereignty of nationhood, consistent with treaty provisions;

5. The right of Alaskan natives to maintain a subsistence land base and aboriginal rights to its natural resources; and

6. The right of native Hawaiians to a just and amicable settlement with the United States through federal legislation related to aboriginal title to Hawaiian lands and their natural resources.

The United Methodist Church especially calls its congregations to support the needs and aspirations of America's native peoples as they struggle for their survival and the maintenance of the integrity of their culture in a world intent upon their assimilation, Westernization, and absorption of their lands and the termination of their traditional ways of life.

Moreover, we call upon our nation, in recognition of the significant cultural attainments of the native peoples in ecology, conservation, human relations, and other areas of human endeavor, to receive their cultural gifts as part of the emerging new life and culture of our nation.

In directing specific attention to the problems of native peoples in the United States, we do not wish to ignore the plight of native people in many other countries of the world.

ADOPTED 1980

See Social Principles, ¶ 66A; "Confession to Native Americans"; "Toward a New Beginning Beyond 1992"; "American Indian Religious Freedom Act"; "Native American Representation in The United Methodist Church"; "Rights of Native People of the Americas."

Anna Howard Shaw Day

WHEREAS, The United Methodist Church, a union of several branches sharing a common historical and spiritual heritage, affirms "the importance of women in decision-making positions at all levels of Church life" (¶ 66F); and

WHEREAS, Barbara Heck and a slave girl named Betty helped form a Methodist society in New York in the fall of 1766; and

WHEREAS, although women class leaders and "exhorters" were part of Methodism from the beginning, it was not until 1847 that the United Brethren in Christ gave Charity Opheral a "vote of commendation" to engage in public speaking and then licensed Lydia Sexton to preach in 1851, and it was not until 1869 that Margaret (Maggie) Newton Van Cott became the first woman officially to be licensed to preach in the Methodist Protestant Church; and

WHEREAS, the Woman's Foreign Missionary Society of The Methodist Episcopal Church was formed in Boston in 1869, and beginning with Isabella Thoburn and Dr. Clara Swain, who went to India in 1870 as the first missionaries, a stream of women from all branches of United Methodism have ministered throughout the world; and

WHEREAS, Anna Snow Den Oliver and Anna Howard Shaw, the first women graduates of Boston University School of Theology, were not able to be ordained under the provisions of the 1876 *Discipline* of The Methodist Episcopal Church, but Anna Howard Shaw was ordained in The Methodist Protestant Church in 1880; and

WHEREAS, the 1880 General Conference of The Methodist Episcopal Church withdrew approval of the licensing of women as local preachers, not to be granted again until 1920; and

WHEREAS, Frances E. Willard and four other women were elected as delegates to the 1888 General Conference of The Methodist Episcopal Church but were denied seats; and

WHEREAS, in 1889 the General Conference approved the ordination of women, and at the 1890 Michigan Annual Conference, Mrs. I. J. Batdorf and Mrs. S. A. Lane were ordained and admitted to the itinerant ministry; and

WHEREAS, in 1895 a Mrs. Hartman from Oregon was acclaimed as "the first female member of an Evangelical Annual Conference"; and

WHEREAS, Bell Harris Bennett, educator and missionary advocate, worked diligently in The Methodist Episcopal Church, South, to gain full lay rights for women, approved in 1922; and

WHEREAS, Georgia Harkness, recognized in 1947 as "one of the ten most outstanding Methodists in America" and the first woman to be a professor of theology at a Methodist seminary, was one of the major champions of equal clergy rights for women; and

WHEREAS, the 1956 General Conference of The Methodist Church did approve equal rights and privileges so that today "both men and women are included in all provisions of the *Discipline* that refer to the ordained ministry" (¶ 412.2, 1996 *Book of Discipline*), and Maud Keister Jensen of Northern New Jersey became the first woman to become a clergy member of an annual conference under the new provision; and

WHEREAS, it was not until 1967 that a woman was appointed a district superintendent of the Maine Annual Conference; and

WHEREAS, The United Methodist Church did establish new professional standards for ordained ministry in 1968 that made it possible for the eventual 1980 election of the first woman bishop, Marjorie Swank Matthews, to be followed in 1984 by Leontine T. Kelly and Judith Craig, and in 1988 by Susan Murch Morrison and Sharon A. Brown Christopher; and

WHEREAS, during her lifetime, Anna Howard Shaw, S.T.B., M.D., ministered to the physical, emotional, and spiritual need of disadvantaged mothers and children, organized and lectured for the causes of temperance and women's suffrage, and sought for political solutions for the problems of women throughout the world; and

WHEREAS, Anna Howard Shaw was the best-known clergywoman in the world at the turn of the century, so that at the time of her death in 1919, *The New York Times* would say that she was "an American with the measureless patience, the deep and gentle humor, the whimsical and tolerant philosophy, and the dauntless courage, physical as well as moral, which we find most satisfyingly displayed in Lincoln, of all our heroes";

Therefore, because Methodism has been in the forefront against discrimination of any kind, and Anna Howard Shaw has become a role model for women in mission and ministry;

1. Each local United Methodist church around the world may set aside an Anna Howard Shaw Day annually as a time to remember the continuing struggles of "women and men to be equal in every aspect of their common life" (¶ 66F);

2. This shall be communicated each year through United Methodist publications; and

3. Appropriate agencies shall plan for the 150th anniversary of Anna Howard Shaw's birth on February 14, 1997.

ADOPTED 1992

See Social Principles, ¶ 66F; "Equal Rights of Women"; "Goals and Recommendations on Participation of Women"; "The Status of Women."

Annual Accessibility Audit

WHEREAS, our Social Principles state, "We affirm the responsibility of the Church and society to be in ministry with children, youth, and adults with mental, physical, developmental, and/or psychological disabilities" (¶ 66G); and

WHEREAS, the Americans with Disabilities Act calls for all public buildings to be made accessible to people with disabilities;

Therefore, be it resolved, that all United Methodist churches shall conduct an annual audit of their facilities to discover what barriers impede full participation of people with disabilities. Plans shall be made and priorities determined for the elimination of all barriers, including architectural, communication, and attitudinal barriers. The Accessibility Audit for Churches, available from the Service Center, shall be used in filling out the annual church/charge conference reports.

ADOPTED 1992

See Social Principles, ¶ 66G; "The Church and People with Mental, Physical, and/or Psychological Disabilities."

Appointment of Clergy to Rural Ministry

WHEREAS, The United Methodist Church seeks to affirm individuals in the exercise of their God-given gifts and areas of expertise; and

WHEREAS, there are unique differences in the needs, struggles, and strengths of urban, suburban, and rural communities; and

WHEREAS, primary emphasis in the form of funding and the appointment of experienced and well-trained pastors tends to focus on urban and suburban settings; and

WHEREAS, the 1988 *Book of Discipline* (¶ 532) states that "appointments shall take into account the unique needs of a charge in a particular setting and also the gifts and evidences of God's grace of a particular pastor";

Therefore, be it resolved, that pastors who have the unique gifts, training, experience, and interests needed to serve rural churches and communities creatively and effectively shall be appointed to rural assignments; and

Be it further resolved, that pastors assigned to rural appointments shall be equitably and adequately compensated for their work of ministry.

ADOPTED 1992

See Social Principles, ¶ 66N; "An Affirmation of Basic Rural Worth"; "Rural Chaplaincy as a Ministry of Laity and Clergy."

Available and Affordable Housing

The lack of available and affordable housing leads not only to economic hardship and instability but also to a sense of hopelessness among families and individuals who must live without the security and well-being that comes with a home to call their own.

The Church's interest in housing has been linked historically with its concern for alleviating poverty. One part of the United Methodists' efforts to eradicate poverty and to provide a decent standard of living for all persons has focused on better housing in both rural and urban settings.

All persons are equally valuable in God's sight. When persons are denied access to or opportunity for decent housing, their humanity is diminished. The Bible, in the Old and New Testaments, correlates the term *house* with identity, security, protection, power, and authority. House becomes more than a dwelling place; it is a space where rootage can take hold and where personal history begins and ends.

Therefore, God's vision of the new creation for human beings includes the affirmations to the effect that [all persons] shall live in the houses they build (Isaiah 65:21), and even the birds and foxes have places that they call their own (Matthew 8:20).

A dwelling place becomes an inherent part of God's design for the creation in which human beings are an important part. Housing may be understood to be the means of preserving and protecting the human body, which is characterized by the apostle Paul as the temple of God.

The need for adequate housing at affordable costs is critical. Millions of families around the world huddle together in densely overcrowded apartments, rural shacks, ancient house trailers, converted warehouses, and condemned or abandoned buildings. Because the remainder of us fail to recognize their plight or simply do not care enough, millions, through no fault of their own, live in inadequate housing that lacks such necessities as running water or plumbing. Still others, many of whom are children, have no shelter at all. While The United Methodist Church affirms the pervasive powers of families as "creators of persons, proclaimers of faith perspectives and shapers of both present and future society," it must continue its condemnation of policies that ignore the causal relationship between shortages of low-income housing and the lack of political will to ensure that safe and affordable housing is available to all.

Whatever the form of community organization, housing protection, management, or ownership of a housing project, every effort should be made at each developmental step to ensure that those who are being aided are afforded the opportunity, and indeed, are required, to take every action necessary to direct the undertaking. Recognizing housing conditions and needs over time has brought about trends that cannot be ignored. Only through concrete actions and a commitment to the goal of fit, livable, and affordable housing will we begin to see the demise of unfit conditions and increased rates of home ownership. The time has come to take steps to promote the more equitable distribution of wealth and resources so that a decent place for a family to live becomes the foundation for dignity and self-respect.

The religious community has a vital role to play in offering hope to those who see no reason for hope in their future. The United Methodist Church has been actively involved in social issues since its beginnings. As a significant presence in local communities, churches can make an impact in the area of affordable housing in the following ways:

1. Using volunteers who have technical expertise in the building and renovation of physical structures. Such volunteers must be committed to the hours of hard work and paperwork that housing ministries demand;

2. Funding projects and pooling resources to create, maintain, and improve affordable housing while improving the community. Members with experience in finance, construction, and advocacy work can be especially helpful in tackling the issue of affordable housing; and

3. Providing the widest possible range of supportive assistance to individuals, congregations, districts, conferences, and all forms of interfaith and cooperative groups sharing similar goals and policies so that our fellow citizens may achieve—as their right—safe, sanitary, and affordable housing as soon as possible.

Within the United States, we urge:

1. *Community organizing.* Church members are urged to contact national religious and secular organizations dealing with affordable hous-

ing to become familiar with opportunities for specific ministries and to advocate adequate affordable housing. Newsletters, fact sheets, and other resources are available from religious and secular agencies and organizations, including every level of government, business, and housing producers.

2. *Advocacy.* On the basis of sound facts and ethical concerns, individual members or church groups in the United States should write to government leaders in support of programs that would guarantee fair housing practices, provide more low-cost housing units, include units for rural residents and farm workers, prevent activities that would eliminate low-cost housing, and urge adequate funding for provisions under the National Affordable Housing Act of 1990 to provide more low-cost housing units such as by modular construction techniques.

3. *Prophetic role-denouncing.* Of great importance for providing nongovernmental funding are provisions of the Community Reinvestment Act as they affect banks and savings and loan institutions in the local community. Lending institutions that continue to discriminate against certain neighborhoods and communities in lending and financing should be challenged by churches and neighborhood organizations regarding practices that mirror past racial and geographical redlining procedures.

4. *Sensitizing.* Churches can take a lead in raising consciousness around the issues of affordable housing and homelessness. Many local agencies are in need of volunteers to conduct testing for fair housing. Opportunities are available for forming community trust funds and cooperative housing agreements that can provide financing and organizational opportunities for individuals or communities in need.

5. *Creating alternatives.* Congregations can even take on individual building or renovation projects. We offer praise to the Salkehatchie Summer Service sponsored by the South Carolina Conference Board of Missions. This program, which includes high school and college-age youth, and adult community leaders, is engaged in upgrading housing and motivating people to help themselves. The Kentucky Mountain Housing Corporation of Morefield, Kentucky, and Camp Hope of First United Methodist Church, Frostburg, Maryland, are other innovative housing ministries congregations can emulate.

Hundreds of local church volunteers and millions of dollars in financial aid are needed annually to construct affordable housing in many countries around the world.

In response to the housing needs of our world community we urge that United Methodists use resources such as:

1. General Advance Specials that provide an appropriate way to channel financial resources;

2. The General Board of Global Ministries Volunteers in Mission Program, which provides appropriate opportunities for volunteers to work side-by-side with people as they seek to achieve improved living conditions;

3. Habitat for Humanity and the Cooperative Housing Foundation, which have proven records of success. Both provide many opportunities in more than twenty-five developing countries for sharing in similar self-help partnership efforts to develop quality, affordable housing with those who need it desperately; and

4. We also urge that government, labor, and economic resources that are too often directed toward involvement in efforts of war and other destructive endeavors be utilized instead to build communities, assist in development, and bring modern technologies to destitute situations around the world.

Adequate human shelter is a primary goal for ministry of all who accept John Wesley's challenge that the world is our parish.

ADOPTED 1992

See Social Principles, ¶ 66; "Housing."

Black Leadership

Be it resolved, that The United Methodist Church in all of its annual conferences will actively seek to identify Black clergy and laity for leadership positions at the local, district, annual conference, jurisdictional, and general Church levels. Such active identification may be accomplished through:

- the conducting of district leadership training seminars, to which at least three members of each predominantly Black church has been invited;
- the establishment of a "mentor system" in which an effective Black leader would become a mentor to a potential Black leader and would encourage and assist that person in the full development of his or her leadership skills;
- the frequent fellowshipping of racial and ethnic congregations, leading to an understanding and knowledge of racial differences; and

- bishops' and district superintendents' actively choosing Black United Methodists to fill appointive positions in the district, annual conference, jurisdictional, and general Church levels.

ADOPTED 1992

See Social Principles, ¶ 66A; "Strengthening the Black Church for the Twenty-First Century"; "Resourcing Black Churches in Urban Communities."

Building New Bridges in Hope

"God whom Christians have come to know in Jesus Christ, has created all human beings in the divine image and . . . God desires that all people live in love and righteousness. . . .

"While we are committed to the promotion of mutual respect and understanding among people of all living faiths, we as Christians recognize a special relationship between Christians and Jews because of our shared roots in biblical revelation."[1]

A Quest for New Understanding

What is the relationship that God intends between Christianity and Judaism, between Christians and Jews? In The United Methodist Church, a search for understanding and appropriate response to this important theological and relational question has been under way for some time. A significant step in the development of United Methodist understanding of and intention for Christian-Jewish relations was taken in 1972, when the General Conference adopted a position statement under the title *Bridge in Hope*. This denominational statement urged church members and congregations to undertake "serious new conversations" with Jews in order to promote "growth in mutual understanding."[2] As it has been studied and used, *Bridge in Hope* has served as a strong foundation for United Methodist-Jewish dialogue in many settings.

Since 1972, other Christian denominations, as well as ecumenical bodies in which The United Methodist Church participates, such as the World Council of Churches, have also made statements on Christian-

---

[1] "The Churches and the Jewish People, Towards a New Understanding," adopted at Sigtuna, Sweden, by the Consultation on the Church and the Jewish People, sponsored by the World Council of Churches, 1988.

[2] *Bridge in Hope, Jewish-Christian Dialogue*, adopted by the General Conference of The United Methodist Church, 1972.

Jewish relations. Those voices have contributed to our further knowledge, reflection, and understanding. At the same time, we have learned much from the many relationships and dialogues that have flourished between Jews and Christians locally, nationally, and internationally.

Especially crucial for Christians in our quest for understanding has been the struggle to recognize the horror of the Holocaust as the catastrophic culmination of a long history of anti-Jewish attitudes and actions in which Christians, and sometimes the church itself, have been deeply implicated. Dialogues with Jewish partners have been central for Christians in our process of learning of the scope of the Holocaust atrocities, acknowledgment of complicity and responsibility, repentance, and commitment to work against anti-Semitism in all its forms in the future.

We are aware, however, that the Christian-Jewish bridge of understanding has only begun to be constructed. The United Methodist Church is committed to continuing clarification and expansion of our knowledge of Judaism and to strengthening our relationships with Jewish people. We seek mutual exploration of the common ground underlying Christianity and Judaism as well as that which makes each faith unique. This statement is an expression of the principles of that commitment.

Foundation for United Methodist Understandings of Christian-Jewish Relations

As expressed in its Constitution, The United Methodist Church has long been strongly committed to the unity of the church: "As part of the church universal, The United Methodist Church believes that the Lord of the church is calling Christians everywhere to strive toward unity. . . ."[3] For many years, The United Methodist Church has devoted itself at all levels of church life to building partnerships with other Christian denominations in striving to reveal the reality of the one Body, the whole church of Jesus Christ. "We see the Holy Spirit at work in making the unity among us more visible."[4]

By its *Book of Discipline*, The United Methodist Church is also dedicated to "serious interfaith encounters and explorations between Christians and adherents of other living faiths in the world." We believe that

---

[3] *The Book of Discipline of The United Methodist Church, 1992*, Constitution, Division One, Article 5; page 22.

[4] *The Book of Discipline of The United Methodist Church, 1992*, Doctrinal Standards, Our Theological Task; page 84.

"Scripture calls us to be both neighbors and witnesses to all peoples. . . . In these encounters, our aim is not to reduce doctrinal differences to some lowest common denominator of religious agreement, but to raise all such relationships to the highest possible level of human fellowship and understanding."[5] In an interdependent world of increasing awareness of the vitality and challenges of religious pluralism, we are called to "labor together with the help of God toward the salvation, health, and peace of all people."[6]

As with all theological questions, United Methodists approach the issues of interfaith relationships, including Christian-Jewish dialogue, by seeking understanding of God's will in Scripture in the context of tradition, reason, and experience. In that spirit and with that intention, we affirm the following principles for continued study, discussion, and action within The United Methodist Church, with other Christians, and especially with Jews.

United Methodist Guiding Principles for Christian-Jewish Relations

In order to increase our understanding of and with peoples of other living faith traditions, of ourselves as followers of Jesus Christ, and of God and God's truth, The United Methodist Church encourages dialogue and experiences with those of other faiths. For important and unique reasons, including a treasury of shared Scripture and an ancient heritage that belong to us in common but which also contain our dividedness, we look particularly for such opportunities with Jews. United Methodist participation in Christian-Jewish dialogue and relationships is based on the following understandings:

1. There is one living God, in whom both Jews and Christians believe.

While the Jewish and Christian traditions understand and express their faith in the same God in significantly different ways, we believe with Paul that God, who was in Christ reconciling the world to God's own self (2 Corinthians 5:18-19), is none other than the God of Israel, maker of heaven and earth. Above all else, Christians and Jews are bonded in our joyful and faithful response to the one God, living our faith as each understands God's call.

---

[5] Ibid.
[6] Ibid.

2. Jesus was a devout Jew, as were many of his first followers.

We know that understanding our Christian faith begins by recognizing and appreciating this seminal fact. Neither the ministry of Jesus and his apostles nor the worship and thought of the early church can be understood apart from the Jewish tradition, culture, and worship of the first century. Further, we believe that God's revelation in Jesus Christ is unintelligible apart from the story of what God did in the life of the people of Israel.

Because Christianity is firmly rooted in biblical Judaism, we understand that knowledge of these roots is essential to our faith. As expressed in a statement from the Consultation on the Church and Jewish People of the World Council of Churches: "We give thanks to God for the spiritual treasure we share with the Jewish people: faith in the living God of Abraham, Isaac, and Jacob; knowledge of the name of God and of the commandments; the prophetic proclamation of judgment and grace; the Hebrew Scriptures; and the hope of the coming Kingdom. In all these, we find common roots in biblical revelation and see spiritual ties that bind us to the Jewish people."[7]

3. Judaism and Christianity are living and dynamic religious movements that have continued to evolve since the time of Jesus, often in interaction with each other and with God's continual self-disclosure in the world.

Christians often have little understanding of the history of Judaism as it has developed since the lifetime of Jesus. As a World Council of Churches publication points out: "Bible-reading and worshiping Christians often believe that they 'know Judaism' since they have the Old Testament, the records of Jesus' debates with Jewish teachers and the early Christian reflections on the Judaism of their times. . . . This attitude is often reinforced by lack of knowledge about the history of Jewish life and thought through the 1,900 years since the parting of the ways of Judaism and Christianity."[8]

As Christians, it is important for us to recognize that Judaism went on to develop vital new traditions of its own after the time of Jesus, including the Rabbinic Judaism that is still vibrant today in shaping Jewish religious life. This evolving tradition has given the Jewish people profound spiritual resources for creative life through the centuries. We

---

[7] "The Churches and the Jewish People. . . . "

[8] "Ecumenical Considerations on Jewish-Christian Dialogue, 1993," World Council of Churches, paragraph 1.6.

increase our understanding when we learn about the rich variety of contemporary Jewish faith practice, theological interpretation, and worship, and discover directly through dialogue how Jews understand their own history, tradition, and faithful living.

4. Christians and Jews are bound to God though biblical covenants that are eternally valid.

As Christians, we stand firm in our belief that Jesus was sent by God as the Christ to redeem all people, and that in Christ the biblical covenant has been made radically new. While church tradition has taught that Judaism has been superseded by Christianity as the "new Israel," we do not believe that earlier covenantal relationships have been invalidated or that God has abandoned Jewish partners in covenant.

We believe that just as God is steadfastly faithful to the biblical covenant in Jesus Christ, likewise God is steadfastly faithful to the biblical covenant with the Jewish people. The covenant God established with the Jewish people through Abraham, Moses, and others continues because it is an eternal covenant. Paul proclaims that the gift and call of God to the Jews is irrevocable (Romans 11:29). Thus, we believe that the Jewish people continue in covenantal relationship with God.

Both Jews and Christians are bound to God in covenant, with no covenantal relationship invalidated by any other. Though Christians and Jews have different understandings of the covenant of faith, we are mysteriously bound to one another through our covenantal relationships with the one God and Creator of us all.

5. As Christians, we are clearly called to witness to the gospel of Jesus Christ in every age and place. At the same time, we believe that God has continued, and continues today, to work through Judaism and the Jewish people.

Essential to the Christian faith is the call to proclaim the good news of Jesus Christ to all people. Through the announcement of the gospel in word and work comes the opportunity for others to glimpse the glory of God, which we have found through Jesus Christ. Yet we also understand that the issues of the evangelization of persons of other faiths, and of Jews in particular, are often sensitive and difficult. These issues call for continuing serious and respectful reflection and dialogue among Christians and with Jews.

While we as Christians respond faithfully to the call to proclaim the gospel in all places, we can never presume to know the full extent of

God's work in the world, and we recognize the reality of God's activity outside the Christian church. It is central to our faith that salvation is accomplished not by human beings, but by God. We know that judgment as to the ultimate salvation of persons from any faith community, including Christianity and Judaism, belongs to God alone.

It is our belief that Jews and Christians are coworkers and companion pilgrims who have made the God of Israel known throughout the world. Through common service and action, we jointly proclaim the God we know. Together through study and prayer, we can learn how the God we believe to be the same God speaks and calls us continually into closer relationship with one another, as well as with God.

6. As Christians, we are called into dialogue with our Jewish neighbors.

Christians and Jews hold a great deal of Scripture, history, and culture in common. And yet, we also share 2,000 painful years of anti-Semitism and the persecution of Jews by Christians. These two apparently discordant facts move Christians to seek common experiences with Jews, and especially to invite them into dialogue to explore the meaning of our kinship and our differences. Our intention is to learn about the faith of one another and to build bridges of understanding.

While for Christians, dialogue will always include testimony to God's saving acts in Jesus Christ, it will include in equal measure listening to and respecting the understanding of Jews as they strive to live in obedience and faithfulness to God and as they understand the conditions of their faith.

Productive interfaith dialogue requires focused, sustained conversation based on willingness to recognize and probe genuine differences while also seeking that which is held in common. We are called to openness so that we may learn how God is speaking through our dialogue partners. As stated in the World Council of Churches' *Guidelines on Dialogue*, "One of the functions of dialogue is to allow participants to describe and witness to their faith on their own terms. . . . Participants seek to hear each other in order to better understand each other's faith, hopes, insights, and concerns."[9] Fruitful and respectful dialogue is centered in a mutual spirit of humility, trust, openness to new understanding, and commitment to reconciliation and the healing of the painful wounds of our history.

---

[9] "Guidelines on Dialogue," adopted at London Colney, England, by the Consultation on the Church and the Jewish People of the Unit on Dialogue and People of Living Faiths and Ideologies, World Council of Churches, 1981, paragraph 3.4.

7. As followers of Jesus Christ, we deeply repent of the complicity of the church and the participation of many Christians in the long history of persecution of the Jewish people. The Christian church has a profound obligation to correct historical and theological teachings that have led to false and pejorative perceptions of Judaism and contributed to persecution and hatred of Jews. It is our responsibility as Christians to oppose anti-Semitism whenever and wherever it occurs.

We recognize with profound sorrow that repeatedly and often in the last 2,000 years, the worship, preaching, and teaching of the Christian church has allowed and sometimes even incited and directed persecution against Jews.

The church today carries grave responsibility to counter the evil done by Christians to Jews in the Crusades, the Inquisition, and the pogroms of Eastern Europe and elsewhere, carried out in the name of Jesus Christ. In the twentieth century there is the particular shame in the failure of most of the church to challenge the policies of governments that were responsible for the unspeakable atrocities of the Holocaust.

Historically and today, both the selective use and the misuse of Scripture have fostered negative attitudes toward and actions against Jews. Use of New Testament passages that blame "the Jews" for the crucifixion of Jesus have throughout history been the basis of many acts of discrimination against Jews, frequently involving physical violence. There is no doubt that traditional and often officially sanctioned and promulgated Christian teachings, including the uncritical use of anti-Jewish New Testament writings, have caused untold misery and form the basis of modern anti-Semitism.

Misinterpretations and misunderstanding of historical and contemporary Judaism continue, including the mistaken belief that Judaism is a religion solely of law and judgment while Christianity is a religion of love and grace. The characterizations of God in the Hebrew Bible (called the Old Testament by Christians) are rich and diverse; strong images of a caring, compassionate, and loving deity are dominant for Jews as well as for Christians. Further, there are parallels between New Testament Christian understandings of the "spirit of the law" and contemporaneous theological developments in first-century Jewish theology.

The church has an obligation to correct erroneous and harmful past teachings and to ensure that the use of Scripture, as well as the preparation, selection, and use of liturgical and educational resources, does not perpetuate misleading interpretations and misunderstanding of Judaism.

It is also essential for Christians to oppose forcefully anti-Jewish acts and rhetoric that persist in the present time in many places. We must be zealous in challenging overt and subtle anti-Semitic stereotypes and bigoted attitudes that ultimately made the Holocaust possible, and which stubbornly and insidiously continue today. These lingering patterns are a call to Christians for ever-new educational efforts and continued vigilance, so that we, remembering and honoring the cries of the tortured and the dead, can claim with Jews around the world to be faithful to the post-Holocaust cry of "Never Again."

8. As Christians, we share a call with Jews to work for justice, compassion, and peace in the world in anticipation of the fulfillment of God's reign.

Together, Jews and Christians honor the commandment to love God with all our heart, soul, and might. It is our task to join in common opposition to those forces—nation, race, power, money—that clamor for ultimate allegiance. Together, we honor the commandment to love neighbor as self. It is our task to work in common for those things that are part of God's work of reconciliation. Together, we affirm the sacredness of all persons and the obligation of stewardship for all God has created.

Jews still await the messianic reign of God foretold by the prophets. Christians proclaim the good news that in Jesus Christ, "the kingdom of God is at hand"; yet we, as Christians, also wait in hope for the consummation of God's redemptive work. Together, Jews and Christians long for and anticipate the fulfillment of God's reign. Together, we are "partners in waiting." In our waiting, we are called to witness and to work for God's reign together.

9. As United Methodist Christians, we are deeply affected by the anguish and suffering that continue for many people who live in the Middle East region that includes modern Israel. We commit ourselves through prayer and advocacy to bring about justice and peace for those of every faith.

Within The United Methodist Church, we struggle with our understanding of the complexity and the painfulness of the controversies in which Christians, Jews, and Muslims are involved in the Middle East. The issues include disputed political questions of sovereignty and control, and concerns over human rights and justice. We recognize the theological significance of the Holy Land as central to the worship, historical traditions, hope, and identity of the Jewish people. We are mindful of this land's historic and contemporary importance for Christians and Muslims. We are committed to the security, safety, and well-being of Jews and Palestinians in the Middle East, to respect for the legitimacy of the state of Israel, to justice and sovereignty for the Palestinian people, and to peace for all who live in the region.

As we join with others of many religious communities in wrestling with these issues and searching for solutions, we seek to work together with other Christians, Jews, and Muslims to honor the religious significance of this land and to bring about healthy, sustainable life, justice, and peace for all.

New Bridges to Christian-Jewish Understanding

The above statements of principle and affirmation offer a foundation for theological reflection within The United Methodist Church and with other Christians on our understanding of our relationships with the Jewish people. They are meant to be the basis of study, discussion, and action as we strive for greater discernment within the Church.

Further, we hope that the statements of guiding principle will be important as bases of cooperative efforts, and especially for dialogue between United Methodists (sometimes in the company of other Christians) and Jewish communities, as we mutually explore the meaning of our kinship and our differences.

Using the foregoing foundation and principles, The United Methodist Church encourages dialogue with Jews at all levels of the Church, including and especially local congregations. It is also hoped that there will be many other concrete expressions of Jewish-Christian relationships, such as participating in special occasions of interfaith observance, and joint acts of common service and programs of social transformation. These offer great opportunity to Christians and Jews to build relationships and together work for justice and peace (*shalom*) in our communities and in the world, serving humanity as God intends.

We dare to believe that such conversations and acts will build new bridges in hope between Christians and Jews, and that they will be among the signs and first fruits of our sibling relationship under our parent God. Together, we await and strive for the fulfillment of God's reign.

ADOPTED 1996

See Social Principles, ¶ 66B; "Guidelines for Interreligious Relationships."

Call to the Bishops to Undergird Cooperative Parish Ministry

WHEREAS, cooperative parish ministry is a style of ministry by which laity can participate in and take ownership of ministry and mission and is also a way for pastors to give and receive support from colleagues in ministry; and

WHEREAS, cooperative parish ministry is a way through which groups of churches, with the guidance of the Holy Spirit, intentionally and intensively witness to the unity of the Church in Christ through more-effective responses to both local and global issues and needs; and

WHEREAS, cooperative parish ministry is a way for churches, especially small membership churches, in rural and urban settings, to remain viable and to develop what can be done better together than alone; and

WHEREAS, the bishops, laity, and clergy present at the Third National Consultation on Cooperative Parish Ministries, which met in November of 1991, affirmed cooperative ministry as one of the primary forms of ministry for United Methodism at the present time and in the future; and

WHEREAS, those present at the consultation emphasized the need for all bishops to provide specific leadership for cooperative ministries within their episcopal areas; and

WHEREAS, those present at the consultation also stressed the need for the development of recommendations as to how connectional agencies of the Church can undergird cooperative ministries;

Therefore, be it resolved, that the Council of Bishops be called on to develop recommendations to enable the implementation of United Methodist and ecumenical cooperative ministries and to urge the implementation of their recommendations by annual conference and general Church boards and agencies; and

Be it further resolved, that the Council of Bishops be called on to create a continuing process for the training and regular updating of bishops and district superintendents regarding the cooperative parish ministry paradigm; and

Also, be it further resolved, that all bishops be called on to give attention within their cabinets to developing organizational structures and processes that will facilitate more-effective appointment-making to cooperative ministries.

ADOPTED 1992

See Social Principles, ¶ 66; "Considering Community Contexts in the Appointment-Making Process."

Care of the Elderly

WHEREAS, the total number and percentage of the elderly of the population in many countries will continue to increase into the next century; and

WHEREAS, the health-care needs in the form of basic care for some of these elderly citizens will likewise expand; and

WHEREAS, all elderly persons, no matter how frail in body or mind, are persons of sacred worth to whom we owe a duty of care and respect; and

WHEREAS, individuals, families, and governmental bodies all incur a great and growing expense for this basic care; and the continuing ability to provide such care cannot be taken for granted; and

WHEREAS, the ongoing expense for this type of care could potentially bankrupt individuals, families, and the nation as a whole; and

WHEREAS, there is potential for conflict in providing for the health-care needs of the elderly and the available workers whose tax dollars will be used to pay for such services; and

WHEREAS, present cost-cutting proposals and measures could mean fewer services and poor quality of care for the elderly population; and

WHEREAS, the people providing direct care in institutional settings such as long-term care facilities are very low-paid; and

WHEREAS, the profit margins of some institutions are razor thin; and the needs of elderly residents compete with the needs of investors for a profit; and

WHEREAS, many so-called long-term care facilities are no more than warehouses for large numbers of crippled bodies; and

WHEREAS, in many instances the elderly resident of such an institution has survived most family members and has only a church body to visit or to express concern on his or her behalf; and

WHEREAS, Jesus has called his church to action on behalf of the weakest members of society (Matthew 25:34-40); and

WHEREAS, faith without works is dead (James 2:14-18); and

WHEREAS, there are potential curses for a church body for not responding to a need that is within our ability to alleviate (Matthew 25:41-46; Revelation 3:15-16);

Therefore, be it resolved, that The United Methodist Church will endeavor to:

• Pray for God's guidance in this and all areas of ministry;

• Undertake a timely, thorough study of the need for and provision of health- and social-care services to the growing elderly population;

• Identify and publicize programs and institutions that seem to be successfully meeting the needs of elderly individuals and groups, with the idea that such successful approaches can be copied by others in their communities;

• Focus locally upon the spiritual, physical, and emotional needs of long-term care facilities' residents and the homebound elderly, encouraging new or expanded services at the local church level;

• Explore the need for and development of new approaches in health- and social-care delivery that provide quality care and fullness of life at affordable cost for the elderly, their families and friends, and society as a whole;

• Research the potential for and promote the development of new technologies to help debilitated elderly individuals meet their basic needs for cleanliness, safety, and comfort at a reasonable cost while promoting job security and enhanced status for the health-care workers directly helping the elderly; and

• Mobilize the appropriate financial and personal resources of the boards, agencies, and institutions of the Church to address this pressing concern.

ADOPTED 1996

See Social Principles, ¶ 66E; "Aging in the United States of America."

Caring Communities—The United Methodist Mental Illness Network

The mission to bring all persons into a community of love is central to the teachings of Christ. We gather as congregations in witness to that mission, welcoming and nurturing those who assemble with us.

Yet we confess that in our humanity we have sometimes failed to minister in love to persons and families with mental illness. We have allowed barriers of ignorance, fear, and pride to separate us from those who most need our love and the nurturing support of community.

To support United Methodist congregations in their goal to reach out to persons and families with mental illness, the General Board of Church and Society established the United Methodist Mental Illness Network. It is a network of "Caring Communities," congregations and communities in covenant relationship with persons and families with mental illness.

United Methodist congregations, annual conferences, jurisdictions, and boards are called to join the United Methodist Mental Illness Network:

• To educate their members about mental illness; and

• To enter into a covenant relationship of understanding and love with persons and families with mental illness, in order to nurture them; and to reach out to the larger community.

ADOPTED 1996

See Social Principles, ¶ 66; "Ministries in Mental Illness."

The Church's Response to Changing Rural Issues

Be it resolved, that The United Methodist Church, through its boards and agencies at all levels of organization, encourage and assist urban, suburban, and rural churches to address and respond to the following issues, which while present in rural society, often are not recognized or acknowledged by the larger society:

• poor self-esteem and mental health;

• the abandonment of the elderly;

• homelessness and poor housing;

• the changing role of the family;

• deterioration of the family;

• the incidence of alcohol and substance abuse;

• inadequate physical and psychological health care, public transportation, children's services, and legal assistance;

• crime;

• the effects of regional consolidations;

• stewardship of the environment, including the care of the soil, air, and water;

• ownership and control of land; and

• the changing role of the Church.

ADOPTED 1992
AMENDED & READOPTED 1996

See Social Principles, ¶ 66N; "U.S. Agriculture and Rural Communities in Crisis"; "An Affirmation of Basic Rural Worth."

A Charter for Racial Justice Policies in an Interdependent Global Community

Racism is the belief that one race is innately superior to all other races. In the United States, this belief has justified the conquest, enslavement, and evangelizing of non-Europeans. During the early history of this country, Europeans assumed that their civilization and religion were innately superior to those of both the original inhabitants of the United States and the Africans who were forcibly brought to these shores to be slaves. The myth of European superiority persisted and persists. Other people who came and who are still coming to the United States, by choice or by force, encountered and encounter racism. Some of these people are the Chinese who built the railroads as indentured workers; the Mexicans whose lands were annexed; the Puerto Ricans, the Cubans, the Hawaiians, and the Eskimos who were colonized; and the Filipinos, the Jamaicans, and the Haitians who lived on starvation wages as farm workers.

In principle, the United States has outlawed racial discrimination; but in practice, little has changed. Social, economic, and political institutions still discriminate, although some institutions have amended their behavior by eliminating obvious discriminatory practices and choosing their language carefully. The institutional church, despite sporadic attempts to the contrary, also still discriminates.

The damage of years of exploitation has not been erased. A system designed to meet the needs of one segment of the population cannot be the means to the development of a just society for all. The racist system in the United States today perpetuates the power and control of those of European ancestry. It is often called "white racism." The fruits of racism are prejudice, bigotry, discrimination, and dehumanization. Consistently, African Americans, Hispanics, Asians, Native Americans, and Pacific Islanders have been humiliated by being given inferior jobs, housing, education, medical services, transportation, and public accommodation. With hopes deferred and rights still denied, the deprived and oppressed fall prey to a colonial mentality that acquiesces to the inequities, occasionally with religious rationalization.

Racist presuppositions have been implicit in U.S. attitudes and policies toward Asia, Africa, the Middle East, and Latin America. While proclaiming democracy, freedom, and independence, the U.S. has been an ally and an accomplice to perpetuating inequality of the races and colonialism throughout the world. The history of The United Methodist

Church and the history of the United States are intertwined. The "mission enterprise" of the churches in the United States and "Westernization" went hand in hand, sustaining a belief in their superiority.

We are conscious that "we have sinned as our ancestors did;/we have been wicked and evil" (Psalm 106:6, Today's English Version). We are called for a renewed commitment to the elimination of institutional racism. We affirm the 1976 General Conference Statement on The United Methodist Church and Race, which states unequivocally: "By biblical and theological precept, by the law of the Church, by General Conference pronouncement, and by Episcopal expression, the matter is clear. With respect to race, the aim of The United Methodist Church is nothing less than an inclusive church in an inclusive society. The United Methodist Church, therefore, calls upon all its people to perform those faithful deeds of love and justice in both the church and community that will bring this aim into reality."

Because we believe:

1. that God is the Creator of all people and all are God's children in one family;

2. that racism is a rejection of the teachings of Jesus Christ;

3. that racism denies the redemption and reconciliation of Jesus Christ;

4. that racism robs all human beings of their wholeness and is used as a justification for social, economic, and political exploitation;

5. that we must declare before God and before one another that we have sinned against our sisters and brothers of other races in thought, in word, and in deed;

6. that in our common humanity in creation all women and men are made in God's image and all persons are equally valuable in the sight of God;

7. that our strength lies in our racial and cultural diversity and that we must work toward a world in which each person's value is respected and nurtured; and

8. that our struggle for justice must be based on new attitudes, new understandings, and new relationships and must be reflected in the laws, policies, structures, and practices of both church and state.

We commit ourselves as individuals and as a community to follow Jesus Christ in word and in deed and to struggle for the rights and the self-determination of every person and group of persons. Therefore, as United Methodists in every place across the land, we will unite our efforts within The United Methodist Church:

1. To eliminate all forms of institutional racism in the total ministry of the Church, giving special attention to those institutions that we support, beginning with their employment policies, purchasing practices, and availability of services and facilities;

2. To create opportunities in local churches to deal honestly with the existing racist attitudes and social distance between members, deepening the Christian commitment to be the Church where all racial groups and economic classes come together;

3. To increase efforts to recruit people of all races into the membership of The United Methodist Church and provide leadership-development opportunities without discrimination;

4. To create workshops and seminars in local churches to study, understand, and appreciate the historical and cultural contributions of each race to the Church and community;

5. To increase local churches' awareness of the continuing needs for equal education, housing, employment, and medical care for all members of the community and to create opportunities to work for these things across racial lines;

6. To work for the development and implementation of national and international policies to protect the civil, political, economic, social, and cultural rights of all people such as through support for the ratification of United Nations covenants on human rights;

7. To support and participate in the worldwide struggle for liberation in church and community; and

8. To support nomination and election processes that include all racial groups employing a quota system until the time that our voluntary performance makes such practice unnecessary.

ADOPTED 1980

See Social Principles, ¶ 66A; "Global Racism" ; "Elimination of Racism in The United Methodist Church" ; "Racial Harassment" ; and a number of other resolutions in "The Social Community" dealing with aspects of racial justice.

Church and Community Workers, 1988

WHEREAS, during the past quadrennium, the National Division of the General Board of Global Ministries has shown commendable progress in financially supporting and in deploying additional church and community workers to serve as national missionaries of the Church; and

WHEREAS, for many years, Church and Community Ministry has proven itself to be an effective response of national missionary outreach for The United Methodist Church in rural areas that have needed caring and creative leadership; and

WHEREAS, church and community workers as "national" missionaries have numerous skills that have enriched Christian ministry in town and country communities where personal, family, and community crises have existed; and

WHEREAS, rural America continues to be in great transition due to crises being faced by family farmers, the loss of industrial employment opportunities, and the breakup of rural communities;

Therefore, be it resolved, that the General Conference direct the National Division through the General Board of Global Ministries to increase the number of church and community workers; and

Be it further resolved, that special attention be given to assigning church and community workers to work closely with cooperative parish ministries and districts in order to provide leadership, ministering skills, and other supports to:

- local churches located in rural communities that are experiencing high levels of transition;
- the "new" poor in rural communities; and
- the initiation of economic development alternatives; and

Be it further resolved, that the National Division make every effort to raise the salary of the church and community workers to a more commensurate level.

ADOPTED 1988

See Social Principles, ¶ 66N; "Church and Community Workers, 1992."

Church and Community Workers, 1992

Be it resolved, that the 1992 General Conference of The United Methodist Church commend the National Program Division of the General Board of Global Ministries for its continuing support of Church and Community Ministry, and offer grateful recognition to these church and community workers; and

Be it further resolved, that congregations be encouraged to enter covenant relationship agreements in support of these national mission workers as Mission Link partners; and

Be it further resolved, that the National Program Division be requested to enlarge the number and expand the deployment of church and community workers, giving special consideration to cooperative parishes of various types, community development opportunities, relief of human need, ministries seeking human justice, and economic development efforts; and

Be it further resolved, that the National Program Division be urged to increase support for church and community workers to a level more commensurate with their valuable contributions to the ministry of the Church.

ADOPTED 1992

See Social Principles, ¶ 66N; "Church and Community Workers, 1988."

The Church and People with Mental, Physical, and/or Psychological Disabilities

We call United Methodists to a new birth of awareness of the need to accept, include, receive the gifts of, and respond to the concerns of those persons with mental, physical, and/or psychological disabilities, including their families.

Because the experience of disabilities is included in all racial, social, sexual, and age groupings, and this experience is common to every family and at some time in every life;

And because a large part of the ministry of our Lord focused on persons with mental, physical, and/or psychological disabilities;

And because the body of Christ is not complete without people of all areas of life;

And because we cannot afford to deny ourselves fellowship with these persons and must intentionally develop more healthy attitudes and behavioral responses to people with disabilities;

And because there exist inadequacies in the Church and in society with regard to concerns for the rights of people with disabilities, utilization of talents, and their full participation within the life of the Church and society;

And because of more suffering and exclusion from the fellowship of the Church of persons with mental, physical, and/or psychological disabilities;

And believing that the Church is most faithful to the teachings and example of Jesus when it expresses love in concrete ways in a mutual ministry with those who are outcasts, neglected, avoided, or persecuted by society;

And believing in the legacy of John Wesley, Phillip Otterbein, and Jacob Albright, who held that vital piety flows into compassionate ministry;

And knowing that prevailing societal norms unduly glorify the conditions of youthful beauty, mental alertness, and material affluence to the exclusion and avoidance of those whose disabilities put them outside these norms;

Therefore, we pledge ourselves to:

Accessibility:

1. Renew and increase our commitments as a Church to the development of a barrier-free society, especially in the many facilities of the Church and parsonages. To indicate the seriousness of our intent, we must set time limits to ensure the greatest physical accessibility in the shortest feasible periods and extend our policy of not providing funding through or approval by United Methodist agencies unless minimum guidelines are met, which include but are not limited to:

(a) providing adequate access to sanctuary pews, altars, chancel areas and pulpit, classrooms, and restrooms;

(b) providing curb cuts, ramps with at least a 1:12 inclination or platform lifts; and

(c) providing facilities with equipment and supplies to meet the needs of persons with seen and unseen disabilities, including persons with vision and/or hearing impairments.

2. All meetings of The United Methodist Church, beyond the local church, be accessible to people with disabilities. As general Church agencies, jurisdictions, annual conferences, and districts nominate people with disabilities to their boards and committees, it is necessary for these boards and committees to accommodate these persons.

3. All United Methodist churches are asked to conduct an audit of their facilities to discover what barriers impede the full participation of people with disabilities. Steps should then be taken to remove those barriers. The accessibility audit for churches is a recommended resource available from the General Board of Global Ministries.

Awareness:

1. Sensitize and train local church pastors to the needs and opportunities for those who have a disability and their families to better minister to and with them.

2. Lead the local churches in attitudinal change studies, to the end that the people called United Methodists are sensitized to the gifts, needs, and interests of people with disabilities, including their families.

3. Take advantage of the great opportunities for our Church to work cooperatively with other denominations who also are addressing these issues and extend an active invitation to work jointly where possible.

4. Suggest one Sunday each year as Access Sunday to sensitize people to our accessibility concerns.

Adequate Resources:

1. Provide resources through the Church at all levels, including curricula, for persons with various disabilities, such as those who are blind, deaf, para- or quadriplegic, mentally retarded, psychologically or neurologically disabled, and so forth, so that each individual has full opportunity for growth and self-realization with the community of faith and the society at large.

2. Strongly recommend that all curriculum material be so designed that it can be adapted to meet the needs of people with disabilities; that curriculum material portray people with disabilities in leadership roles within church and society; that curriculum material reflect the Guidelines for the Elimination of Handicappist Language as produced by the General Council on Ministries.

Affirmative Action:

1. Include in all our efforts of affirmative action the concerns and interests of people with disabilities, particularly in the active recruitment and encouragement of these persons for leadership roles, both clergy and lay, within the Church and its agencies, in hiring practices, job security, housing, and transportation.

2. Urge the General Board of Higher Education and Ministry to monitor annual conference boards of ordained ministry so that people with disabilities are given equal treatment in the steps to ordained ministry.

3. Strongly urge that our schools of higher education and theological training provide specialized courses for faculty and students in the awareness and appreciation of gifts, needs, and interests of people with disabilities. This must include the emphasis of accessibility and equal employment in these institutions, as well as those in the larger society. Accreditation by the University Senate should be withdrawn where

persons who are disabled are excluded, either from attendance, services, or employment.

4. Strongly urge local churches to conduct needs-assessment surveys. Such a survey would suggest to a local church what particular actions must be taken to fully include people with disabilities within the life of the church.

Advocacy Within the Church:

Implement within each annual conference methods of recruiting, sensitizing, and training persons as advocates to work with and on behalf of people with disabilities on a one-to-one basis and to enable them to achieve their human and civil rights as well as to assume their rightful place in the life of the Church and community. Each annual conference should also develop the larger concern of advocacy for people with disabilities to enable them to achieve appropriate housing, employment, transportation, education, and leisure-time development.

Advocacy Within the Society:

While there is much to be done within the Church to make real the gospel of inclusiveness with regard to people with disabilities, there is a world society that also must be made aware of the concerns and needs of these persons. We admonish the Church and its people to stand alongside people with disabilities and to speak out on their rights in society. These rights include access to jobs, public transportation and other reliable forms of transportation, adequate housing, and education. We are people under orders to minister to and with all God's children. We are all a people in pilgrimage! We have too often overlooked those of God's children who experience life in different ways from ourselves. We pledge ourselves to an inclusive, compassionate, and creative response to the needs and gifts of people with mental, physical, and/or psychological disabilities.

Barrier-Free Construction for People with Disabilities:

Be it resolved, that Church monies from agencies of The United Methodist Church beyond the local church be granted, loaned, or otherwise provided only for the construction of church sanctuaries, educational buildings, parsonages, camps, colleges, or other Church-related agencies or facilities that meet minimum guidelines in their plans for barrier-free construction;

That local churches utilizing their own funds or funds secured through lending agencies and institutions beyond The United Methodist Church be urged to make adequate provision in their plans to ensure that all new church buildings shall be of barrier-free construction;

That local churches be urged to adapt existing facilities through such programs as widening doorways, installing ramps and elevators, eliminating stairs where possible, providing handrails, adequate parking facilities, and rest rooms so that people with disabilities may take their appropriate place in the fellowship of the church; and

That the appropriate national agencies provide technical information for local churches to assist in providing barrier-free facilities.

ADOPTED 1984
AMENDED & READOPTED 1996

See Social Principles, ¶ 66G; "Compliance with the Americans with Disabilities Act for Employers"; "Communications Access for People Who Have Hearing and Sight Impairment."

The Church's Response to Ethnic and Religious Conflict

Would that you knew the things that make for peace.
-Jesus of Nazareth (Luke 19:42)

The tragic conflicts in such places as Bosnia, the Middle East, Rwanda, Northern Ireland, and Sri Lanka, as well as interethnic conflict in the United States, reveal the deep potential for hatred and violence in humankind. These conflicts pose a great challenge to the Christian church as the mediator of Jesus' gospel of love and reconciliation in the world, as well as to the wider religious community. The church's pain is only made greater by the fact that so many of these violent conflicts pit one religious group against another: Protestant against Catholic; Muslim against Jew; Hindu against Buddhist; or Orthodox, Catholic, and Muslim against one another.

The rising tide of violence in the world threatens to engulf communities, nations, and world civilizations. As we approach the year of our Lord 2000, it is time for the Church to become proactive in resolving conflict and developing alternatives to violence. Specifically:

We call upon the General Board of Global Ministries to enter into discussions with Christian Peacemakers, a group that provides a Christian presence in situations of international, interreligious, and interethnic conflict, to explore the possibility of including United Methodists on the teams that are sent to areas of conflict;

We call upon the General Board of Global Ministries to incorporate the principles of nonviolent conflict resolution and interethnic and interreligious dialogue in the Shalom Zone Program;

We call upon the General Board of Church and Society, together with the General Commission on Religion and Race, to hold a series of interreligious dialogues to develop new approaches to mutual understanding, respect, and cooperation, and to develop, for use in local church and community settings, guidelines on how to set up local dialogues and how to develop and implement alternatives to violence;

We call upon our seminaries and United Methodist-related colleges and universities to offer courses on alternatives to violence and to sponsor local community initiatives to diffuse ethnic and religious conflict. We also call on our seminaries to encourage the study of the theological roots of violence and of Jesus' teachings on nonresistance and resisting evil; and

We call upon the U.S. government, working with the United Nations, to give leadership in retraining the military for the tasks of peacemaking, peacekeeping, reconstruction, and rehabilitation. This means reallocating funds from building weapons to building communities, from teaching to kill to teaching to protect life. Modest beginnings in such an effort can be seen in community policing initiatives in many of our cities, in the peacekeeping force in Bosnia, and in the nonviolent transition to democracy in South Africa.

ADOPTED 1996

See Social Principles, ¶¶ 66*A, B*, 69*C*; "The United Methodist Church and Peace"; "Communities of Shalom."

COCU Consensus: In Quest of a Church of Christ Uniting

WHEREAS, The United Methodist Church believes that Christ wills for the church to be visibly one; and

WHEREAS, the 1984 *Book of Discipline* (¶ 69) affirms that "along with all other Christians, [we] are a pilgrim people under the Lordship of Christ"; and

WHEREAS, throughout the church of Jesus Christ, significant ecumenical proposals continue to emerge that envision the achievement of visible unity through a series of covenants that unite our memberships, ministries, observances of the sacraments, and mission, rather than a single act of merger of structures; and

WHEREAS, The Evangelical United Brethren Church and The Methodist Church were founding members of the Consultation on Church Union, and in successive General Conferences The United Methodist Church has affirmed its strong participation and has adopted specific aspects related to mutual recognition of memberships and theological agreements; and

WHEREAS, The United Methodist Church (in the Preamble to the Constitution) recognizes that "the Church of Jesus Christ exists in and for the world, and its very dividedness is a hindrance to its mission in that world"; and

WHEREAS, United Methodists diligently have participated in the development of the Consultation Consensus as a way of reducing dividedness among Christians:

Therefore, be it resolved, that the 1988 General Conference claims the 1984 Consultation Consensus on these three points:

1. The United Methodist Church recognizes in the Consensus an expression in the matters with which it deals of the apostolic faith, order, worship, and witness of the Church;

2. The United Methodist Church recognizes in the Consensus an anticipation of the Church Uniting, which the participating bodies, by the power of the Holy Spirit, wish to become; and

3. The United Methodist Church recognizes in the Consensus a sufficient theological basis for the covenanting acts to be proposed by the Consultation that we expect to be recommended to the General Conference of 1992.

Therefore, The United Methodist Church requests that the Council of Bishops transmit this action to the Consultation on Church Union.

ADOPTED 1988

See Social Principles, ¶ 66B; "Continuing Membership in the Consultation on Church Union"; "Act of Covenanting Between Other Christian Churches and The United Methodist Church."

Comity Agreements Affecting Development of Native American Ministries by The United Methodist Church

WHEREAS, certain annual conferences of The United Methodist Church have used the alleged Comity Agreement as the basis for their functional relationship among Native Americans, limiting their capability to develop Native American ministries in certain geographical areas; and

WHEREAS, the effects of practicing the concept of a Comity Agreement by The United Methodist Church have resulted in the failure of the Church to follow through with the biblical mandate of propagating the gospel to all nations and, further, have caused the failure of the Church to create the climate for leadership development of Native Americans; and

WHEREAS, such a Comity Agreement would be discriminatory in that it would violate the right of Native Americans to associate with the denomination of their choice;

Therefore, be it resolved, that The United Methodist Church states, as a matter of policy, that it is not a party to any interdenominational agreement that limits the ability of any annual conference in any jurisdiction to develop and resource programs of ministry of any kind among Native Americans, including the organization of local churches where necessary.

ADOPTED 1980

See Social Principles, ¶ 66A; "The United Methodist Church and America's Native People"; "Confession to Native Americans."

Communications Access for People Who Have Hearing and Sight Impairment

Because The United Methodist Church believes that all United Methodists are full members of the Church and is committed to ministry by and with people with disabilities; and

Public accommodations such as restaurants, hotels, theaters, doctors' offices, pharmacies, retail stores, museums, libraries, parks, private schools, and daycare centers may not discriminate on the basis of disability, effective January 26, 1992

Auxiliary aids and services must be provided to individuals with vision or hearing impairments or other individuals with disabilities so that they can have an equal opportunity to benefit, unless an undue burden would result. (from a synopsis prepared by the Civil Rights Division, U.S. Department of Justice)

And because, despite sincere efforts on the part of the Church, people with disabilities are still confronted by barriers to communications within the Church;

We call upon the Church to:

1. Increase its awareness; and

2. Use appropriate technologies to make essential communications accessible to people who are deaf and hearing impaired, including:

(a) considering production of alternative versions of Church-produced video, films, or other audiovisuals at meetings for people who are deaf or hearing impaired, and people who are blind or partially sighted; and

(b) considering the use of assistive technologies in telephone communications for persons who are deaf or hearing impaired.

ADOPTED 1992
AMENDED & READOPTED 1996

See Social Principles, ¶ 66G; "The Church and People with Mental, Physical, and/or Psychological Disabilities."

Communities of Shalom

WHEREAS, the General Conference responded to the Los Angeles crisis of 1992 by creating a new strategy called Communities of Shalom, which incorporates evangelism and community action by focusing on spiritual renewal, congregational development, community economic development, health, and strengthening race and class relationships;

The Communities of Shalom concept was piloted in seven communities in Greater Los Angeles and through struggle and determination enabled a new and comprehensive paradigm for ministry. The Communities of Shalom strategy has spread throughout the Church and in early 1996 engaged more than 250 urban and rural churches and community organizations in the United States, and one in Africa;

The United Methodist Church, through the General Board of Global Ministries in consultation with the National Shalom Committee, designed and carried out a successful training and technical-assistance program for those developing Communities of Shalom. These new resources are enabling churches and communities to develop and renew community life. The training has been utilized in sixteen annual conferences and stimulates new enthusiasm and plans for creative ministry;

The need for Communities of Shalom within urban and rural areas continues to grow. Additional communities and churches in Los Angeles, the nation, and the world are seeking effective ministry models that transform congregations, communities, and individuals for God's ministry of *shalom*.

Therefore, be it resolved, that The United Methodist Church:

1. Commend the ministry of churches and communities in Greater Los Angeles that pioneered the Communities of Shalom strategy;

2. Strongly urge the continual expansion of Shalom ministries throughout the United States and the world for churches in urban and rural communities in crisis and transition;

3. Through the General Board of Global Ministries, resource Communities of Shalom in the United States and around the world through training and technical assistance;

4. Affirm the Shalom Committee and its continued work with the General Board of Global Ministries and other general Church agencies. The committee shall be composed of twelve (12) members and two (2) ex officio members. There shall be six (6) members selected by the Council of Bishops, three (3) by the General Board of Global Ministries, and three (3) selected by the Shalom Committee for their expertise. The general secretary of the General Board of Global Ministries and a staff person of the General Board of Pensions shall serve as the ex officio members with vote;

5. Mandate that The United Methodist Church, at its general and local levels, continue to collaborate with other denominations, businesses, and community organizations to transform congregations and communities through the Shalom strategy;

6. Charge all general Church agencies in the next quadrennium to explore and develop opportunities to work collaboratively to assist local churches with the Communities of Shalom strategy; and

7. Endorse the solicitation of Shalom resources from foundations, corporations, government sources, individuals, and churches utilizing the Advance, a foundation structure, and other necessary strategies.

ADOPTED 1996

See Social Principles, ¶ 660; "Holy Boldness: A National Plan for Urban Ministry."

Compliance with the Americans with Disabilities Act for Employers

WHEREAS, the General Board of Global Ministries, on October 16, 1979, called "United Methodists to a new birth of awareness of the need to include, assimilate, receive the gifts, and respond to the needs, of those persons with mental, physical, and/or psychologically handicapping conditions, including their families"; and

WHEREAS, the General Conference resolved in 1980 to take major steps in adapting facilities, new and existing, such as "church sanctuaries, educational buildings, parsonages, camps, colleges, or other church-related agencies or facilities" so that they meet minimum guidelines for "barrier-free construction" (*see* "Barrier-Free Construction for People with Disabilities"); and

WHEREAS, President Bush signed into law the Americans with Disabilities Act (ADA); and

WHEREAS, love without justice is empty and meaningless, and it is unjust to deny anyone employment based solely on human-created obstacles; and

WHEREAS, it is fitting that Christians be a "cloud of witnesses" for the secular world;

Therefore, be it resolved, that all United Methodist churches investigate and attempt to comply with Title I of the ADA, which states that employers "may not discriminate against qualified individuals with disabilities" and will "reasonably accommodate the disabilities of qualified applicants or employees unless undue hardship would result."

ADOPTED 1992
AMENDED & READOPTED 1996

See Social Principles, ¶ 66G; "The Church and People with Mental, Physical, and/or Psychological Disabilities."

Comprehensive Health Care

WHEREAS, the role of the Church includes concern for the whole person, including the physical body; and

WHEREAS, the Church has a long and glorious history of being involved in matters that affect the life of the community; and

WHEREAS, the health of many citizens is being invaded by illnesses that can be prevented with a change of lifestyle; and

WHEREAS, the ability of citizens to receive quality health care is directly related to income level; and

WHEREAS, certain illnesses present themselves at an alarming rate in some minority communities, especially in the Black community; and

WHEREAS, the Church often enjoys a presence in the minority community that makes it a prophetic catalyst for change; and

WHEREAS, it is incumbent upon the body of Christ to be about the work of Christ in bringing healing to the people;

Therefore, be it resolved, that The United Methodist Church support all movement toward the provision of quality health care, regardless of race, gender, ethnicity, and economic status; and

Be it further resolved, that The United Methodist Church initiate discussions with other denominations regarding serving as catalysts for becoming the fiscal intermediary for new and progressive methods of providing health insurance to the otherwise uninsured; and

Be it further resolved, that The United Methodist Church explore the possibility of creating parish staff positions that would address the physical health needs of congregations.

ADOPTED 1996

See Social Principles, ¶ 66Q; "Health and Wholeness"; "Health in Mind and Body"; "Universal Access to Health Care in the United States and Related Territories."

Concerning Demeaning Names to Native Americans

In our society today, there is a growing debate and discussion about the appropriateness of using Native American names as nicknames for professional sports teams and university mascots. As the publication *Words That Hurt, Words That Heal,* produced by The United Methodist Church, highlights, the use of names and language is a powerful instrument for good and destructive purposes. It is demeaning to Native Americans and other members of our society to depict Native Americans as violent and aggressive people by calling a sports team the "Braves" or the "Warriors." The implication is that all Native Americans are aggressive and violent people. This use of nicknames is not conducive to the development of a society committed to the common good of its citizenry.

In "The United Methodist Church and America's Native People" (*The Book of Resolutions, 1992;* page 178), The United Methodist Church has issued a call for repentance for the Church's role in the dehumanization and colonization of our Native American sisters and brothers. In light of this stand and the fact that we strongly believe the continued use of Native American names as nicknames is demeaning and racist, we urge all United Methodist-related universities, colleges, and schools to set an example by replacing any nicknames that demean and offend our Native American sisters and brothers; and we support efforts throughout our society to replace such nicknames, mascots, and symbols.

ADOPTED 1996

See Social Principles, ¶ 66A; "The United Methodist Church and America's Native People"; "Confession to Native Americans."

Confession to Native Americans

WHEREAS, the gospel calls us to celebrate and protect the worth and dignity of all peoples; and

WHEREAS, the Christian churches, including The United Methodist Church and its predecessors, have participated in the destruction of Native American people, culture, and religious practices; and

WHEREAS, the churches of this country have not sufficiently confessed their complicity in this evil; and

WHEREAS, the churches have been blessed by having members who are Native Americans as well as by engaging in dialogue with Native Americans who practice their traditional religions; and

WHEREAS, confession of our guilt is a first step toward the wholeness that the churches seek through the ecumenical movement;

Therefore, be it resolved, that the United Methodist General Conference confesses that The United Methodist Church (and its predecessor bodies) has sinned and continues to sin against its Native American brothers and sisters and offers this formal apology for its participation, intended and unintended, in the violent colonization of their land; and

Be it further resolved, that The United Methodist Church pledges its support and assistance in upholding the American Indian Religious Freedom Acts (P.L. 95-134, 1978) and within that legal precedent affirms the following:

1. the rights of the native peoples to practice and participate in traditional ceremonies and rituals with the same protection offered all religions under the Constitution of the United States of America;

2. access to and protection of sacred sites and public lands for ceremonial purposes; and

3. the use of religious symbols (feathers, tobacco, sweet grass, bones, and so forth) for use in traditional ceremonies and rituals.

Be it further resolved, that the General Conference recommends that local churches develop similar statements of confession as a way of fostering a deep sense of community with Native Americans and encourages the members of our Church to stand in solidarity on these important religious issues and to provide mediation when appropriate for ongoing negotiations with state and federal agencies regarding these matters.

ADOPTED 1992

See Social Principles, ¶ 66; "American Indian Religious Freedom Act"; "Native American History and Contemporary Culture as Related to Effective Church Participation"; "Comity Agreements Affecting Development of Native American Ministries by The United Methodist Church"; "The United Methodist Church and America's Native People."

Considering Community Contexts in the Appointment-Making Process

WHEREAS, congregations of all sizes need to understand and respond to the dynamics of their contexts in order to become "a strategic base from which Christians move out to the structures of society"; and

WHEREAS, The United Methodist Church has responsibility for enabling every church to fulfill the holistic "expectations of an authentic church, through community outreach as a key for Christian witness"; and

WHEREAS, church profiles developed by the pastor, the pastor-parish relations committee, and the district superintendent for use with appointment-making are to include information on the church's size, finances, lay leadership, spiritual life, and the church's ministry for the sake of its community;

Therefore, be it resolved, that our episcopal and other United Methodist leaders challenge and guide the churches toward an increased understanding that the contextual communities where their congregations are located are as important to their ministries as are the needs of their members; and

Be it further resolved, that the bishops of the Church and their appointive cabinets be open to making intentional appointments to communities as well as to congregations so that Christian responses can be made through ministries of service, through organizing, through advocacy, and through economic development relevant to specific and diverse community contexts.

ADOPTED 1992

See Social Principles, ¶ 66.

Continuance of Funding to the Evangelical Seminary of Puerto Rico

WHEREAS, The Methodist Episcopal Church, one of the predecessors of The United Methodist Church, was one of the founders of the Evangelical Seminary of Puerto Rico through the Board of Home Missions and Church Extension in 1919; and

WHEREAS, close to thirty graduates of the Evangelical Seminary of Puerto Rico are serving The United Methodist Church in the United States, and it is expected that the flow of pastors coming from Puerto Rico to serve in The United Methodist Church will continue;

Therefore, be it resolved, that the General Conference of The United Methodist Church mandates the General Board of Global Ministries and the General Board of Higher Education and Ministry to consult with the Evangelical Seminary of Puerto Rico, to study the impact of any reduction of funds in the aforementioned institution, and to continue the funding up to 1996. Both agencies should consider the continuation of the present financial support at the current level through the year 2000, and what financial assistance is possible beyond the beforementioned period in the light of our ecumenical and moral responsibilities as founders. Both agencies shall report their findings and recommendations to the 1996 General Conference.

ADOPTED 1992

See Social Principles, ¶ 66B; "Puerto Rico and Vieques."

Continuing Membership
in the Consultation on Church Union

WHEREAS, the Constitution of The United Methodist Church states that the dividedness of the Church is a "hindrance to its mission" in the world and has committed us to ecumenical involvement; and

WHEREAS, the predecessor churches of The United Methodist Church were founding members of the Consultation on Church Union, and The United Methodist Church has been an active supporter of COCU for almost twenty-five years; and

WHEREAS, the 1988 General Conference of The United Methodist Church affirmed *The COCU Consensus* as an authentic expression of the apostolic faith and a sufficient theological foundation for covenanting; and

WHEREAS, the United Methodist Council of Bishops stated in May 1992, "We celebrate God's call to the concept of covenant relationships expressed at *Churches in Covenant Communion* . . . [and] long for the day when the covenant may be realized among us, and acknowledge with joy our eagerness to enter into covenant";

Therefore, be it resolved, that the General Conference directs:

1. The Council of Bishops and the General Commission on Christian Unity and Interreligious Concerns to continue in dialogue with covenanting partners, clarifying questions, and developing the covenanting process; and

2. The Council of Bishops and the General Commission on Christian Unity and Interreligious Concerns to lead The United Methodist Church in continuing prayer and study as we move toward a vote on *Churches in Covenant Communion* at the 1996 General Conference.

ADOPTED 1992

See Social Principles, ¶ 66; "Toward an Ecumenical Future."

Continuing Membership in the National Council of Churches

WHEREAS, the Constitution of The United Methodist Church states that the dividedness in the church of Jesus Christ "is a hindrance to its mission in [the] world" and has committed us to ecumenical involvement; and

WHEREAS, The United Methodist Church and its predecessor churches have been charter members of the National Council of the Churches of Christ in the U.S.A.; and

WHEREAS, the NCCC/USA is a "community through which the churches are seeking to make visible their unity given in Christ"; and

WHEREAS, the NCCC/USA is "an instrument of the churches' ecumenical witness to live responsibly in mutual accountability and service"; and

WHEREAS, the NCCC/USA provides a unique opportunity for denominational representatives to share divergent traditions in matters of faith and practice; and

WHEREAS, the NCCC/USA provides a channel for denominational cooperation in Christian education, mission and justice issues, communications, interfaith matters, evangelism, and relationships with local ecumenical expressions; and

WHEREAS, the United Methodist delegates from each of the jurisdictions have offered distinguished leadership to the NCCC/USA, and successive General Conferences have supported the continuing membership in the NCCC/USA since its founding in 1950; and

WHEREAS, we congratulate Bishop Melvin G. Talbert on his election as president of the NCCC/USA for a two-year term, to be served during the coming quadrennium;

Therefore, be it resolved, that the 1996 General Conference of The United Methodist Church reaffirms its membership in and support of the National Council of the Churches of Christ in the U.S.A., in accordance with the 1992 *Book of Discipline* (¶ 2402.2).

ADOPTED 1992
AMENDED & READOPTED 1996

See Social Principles, ¶ 66; "Toward an Ecumenical Future."

Continuing Membership in the World Council of Churches

WHEREAS, The United Methodist Church and its predecessor churches have been founding members of the World Council of Churches (WCC); and

WHEREAS, United Methodist delegates in leadership positions among the 330 member churches continue to make significant contributions to this worldwide body, and the General Conference and Council of Bishops have continued to offer strong commitment for the WCC; and

WHEREAS, we eagerly look forward to the 1998 VIII Assembly of the World Council of Churches, which will celebrate the fiftieth anniversary of its founding, in Harare, Zimbabwe, on September 10–22, 1998, with the theme "Turn to God: Rejoice in Hope," in which United Methodists will participate;

Therefore, be it resolved, that the 1996 General Conference of The United Methodist Church reaffirms its membership in and support of the World Council of Churches, in accordance with the 1996 *Book of Discipline* (¶ 2402.3).

ADOPTED 1992
AMENDED & READOPTED 1996

See Social Principles, ¶ 66B.

Dependent Care

The Problem

Almost all families at one time or another need assistance from persons outside the immediate family structure. Increasing numbers of families require some degree of help in the day-to-day care of family members who, because of age or disability, need constant supervision. With a growing number of women entering the paid labor force and with the increased mobility of families away from communities where elderly parents and relatives reside, more and more families need some kind of support care.

1. *Need for a Safe Environment for Children.* Children are often victims at an age when they should be developing trust and confidence in persons and in life itself. Children determine neither what food they will eat nor who will care for them in the absence of parents. Adults make these and other life-affecting decisions for them.

The church has a special responsibility to children and their families to demonstrate concern for and responsiveness to human need. The Christian faith proclaims that children are to be valued not as potential adults, but as persons in their own right—persons deserving of dignity, joy, and a protected environment. Because of their vulnerability, children need defenders and guardians, both within the family circle and in the larger extended family of the community. They must be protected from prejudices that may victimize them because of their racial, ethnic, and socioeconomic backgrounds.

In many communities are large numbers of latchkey children—children who are unsupervised during parts of the day or night because their parents are at work and no one is available to care for them. Unfortunately, these children are often victimized by persons who prey on the unprotected. To avert potential problems, the U.S. Department of Agriculture and the 4-H community clubs have initiated a nationwide program to teach latchkey children various techniques for survival and self-protection. But these children also need to have someone reach out to them, sharing love, care, and security.

2. *Need for Long-Term Dependent Care.* The ability of families to remain intact is severely strained when a child, a spouse, or an older relative is disabled and needs constant health-monitoring or supervised care. Families often need help with these situations in the form of in-home health care or custodial care. In many cases, a small amount of assistance could enable these families to function well and maintain healthy relationships with minimal stress. But without aid, stress related to these circumstances can result in divorce, separation, or institutionalization of loved ones—eventualities neither wanted nor necessary.

The need for long-term dependent care frequently arises from several trends in modern society. Among them, the increased mobility of persons worldwide and the movement from rural to urban areas often result in the isolation of family units from their network of relatives. Older relatives then find themselves separated by long distances from other family members.

Too, the need of many families to rely on the cash economy has moved more women—traditionally the caregivers for family members with long-term needs—into the paid workforce, rendering them no longer available to provide free care. Recent statistics show that in the United States:

• Eighty percent of home health care is provided by female relatives whose average age is 55. Forty-four percent of these caregivers are also in the paid workforce;

• Two thirds of the women in the paid workforce are either sole providers or have husbands who earn less than $15,000;

• Forty-six percent of all preschool children and 46 percent of all school-age children have mothers in the paid workforce.

A myriad of problems—ranging from inadequate facilities to the high cost of securing persons who can provide care—is placing an unnecessary strain on many modern families who have limited resources and nowhere to turn for help.

The Call

The Christian faith mandates us to recognize and respond to the value of each human person. Our task as the Church is to minister to the needs of all persons and to ensure for them a caring community where all may be nurtured in a dignified and loving manner. This mandate is to be seen not as a burden, but rather as an opportunity. We are called to participate in the creative, redemptive work of God. Jesus, who provides our example, said: "The Spirit of the Lord is upon me,/because he has anointed me/to preach good news to the poor./He has sent me to proclaim release to the captives/and recovering of sight to the blind,/to set at liberty those who are oppressed,/to proclaim the acceptable year of the Lord" (Luke 4:18-19, Revised Standard Version).

Christians who take their commission seriously will accept the challenge to become responsive to the needs of families for external support systems. God has given each person an element of sacredness by the very nature of having been born into the world. This blessing carries the need for a commitment by families, church, and community to help enable persons to live life in the fullness that Jesus proclaimed.

We have answered the call in the past by building hospitals, homes for the elderly, and institutional settings for children who need them. This has been done on a worldwide basis. Now, we must take seriously the opportunity to create and support responsive systems of childcare and long-term care for those persons who are elderly or who have disabilities (in independent living situations or within family settings).

The Task

In matters of public concern, the Church has a responsibility to make its voice heard. Since dependent care (such as child daycare, senior daycare, home health handicaps) is important to the present and future well-being of various segments of our society, the Church's position on the system of dependent care delivery constitutes an appropriate public policy concern. The role of dependent care in its various forms should be seen as a support system for families. Such services enable, rather than usurp, the traditional role of families.

A national survey of church-based childcare discovered that in the United States, churches are the major providers of out-of-home childcare. These childcare workers listed as a priority task the provision of care that benefits the emotional, social, and learning needs of children. Within this context, persons sponsoring or overseeing church-based programs and churches with special ministries to families have a responsibility to be involved in policy discussions on the form and function of dependent care.

It becomes the obligation of churches to urge and promote coherent, inclusive, and equitable policies that affect families. There is a temptation to separate dependent care from the various programs designed to support and aid families in their life in the church and community, but it must be recognized that most families, at some time or another, rely on formal or informal support systems relative to the care of children, the elderly, or people with disabilities.

As it approaches public advocacy for dependent care, the Church must be guided by the variety of forms of its ministry. The Church must acknowledge the importance and implement the provision of affordable and high-quality family support systems that are equitably distributed to those who need them.

Toward this end, the Church on all levels is called to advocate the following policies:

1. Public policies that enhance the availability of dependent care in its varied forms to meet the needs of families by providing:

(a) adequate financial aid (such as private foundation grants, tax credits, tax reimbursement, and sliding fees) to allow families to care for loved ones at home, rather than having these persons institutionalized when that option is not desired, needed, or economically possible; and

(b) sufficient information on the availability of dependent-care services as well as on methods of evaluating the care provided;

2. Church policies and ministries that enhance the spiritual and psychological needs of families who care for dependent members; and

3. Community services that help families/individuals who are under psychological and psycho-social pressures resulting from the responsibilities of caring for dependent family members.

ADOPTED 1984

See Social Principles, ¶ 66C; "Putting Children and Their Families First."

Domestic Violence and Sexual Abuse

The deafening and disabling silence that has surrounded the abuse of women and children must be broken. Overwhelming numbers of women and children in our churches and communities are being battered, raped, emotionally and psychologically abused, physically and sexually assaulted. The abuse occurs in similar percentages in communities of every racial composition and every economic status, in rural areas as well as cities, in families adhering to every religion and to no religion. Silence shields us from our complicity in the violence as well as our failure to overcome it. The facts are grim:

One out of three girls and one out of seven boys in the United States will be sexually abused before the age of eighteen.[1] Fifteen million U.S. adults alive today were incest victims as children.[2] Forty-nine percent of reported rape cases in Malaysia involve children under fifteen years of age, with the majority of abusers being fathers, stepfathers, or other relatives.[3] In 80 percent of wife assault cases in Canada, children are present.[4] One out of every two U.S. women is battered by her spouse

---

[1] Sexual Assault Center, Harborview Medical Center, Seattle, Washington.
[2] ABC network documentary on incest.
[3] Women's International Network, Lexington, Massachusetts.
[4] Ibid.

or intimate partner sometime during her lifetime.[5] Fourteen percent of married women report being raped by their husband.[6] In Peru, 70 percent of all crimes reported to the police are women beaten by their partners.[7] Dowry deaths in India (a wife killed by her husband for failing to produce requested monies from her family) increased by 100 percent in two years during the 1980s.[8] Two million children in the U.S. are victims of physical abuse and neglect, and between two thousand and five thousand children die each year as the result of child abuse.[9] Fifty-four percent of all murders in Austria are committed within the family, with children and women constituting 90 percent of the victims.[10] One third of all U.S. women are raped during their lifetime; approximately 70 percent of those rapes are by persons known to the victims. Only one in ten rapes is ever reported; only 40 percent of reported rapes result in arrest; about 1 percent of rapists are convicted.[11] International attention to the prevalence of rape is increasing: The 1991 murder of 19 girls and the rape of 71 others at a rural boarding school in Kenya was described in a statement by two leading Kenyan women's organizations as "a mirror of the kind of abuse and violence that women and girls are going through at home, in the workplace and in public places."[12] Children in one out of ten U.S. families hit, beat, stab, or shoot their parents. More than one million parents over sixty years of age will be abused by their own children this year.[13]

We must acknowledge the ways in which misinterpretation and misuse of Christian Scriptures and traditions have contributed to violence against women and children, to the guilt, self-blame, and suffering that victims experience to the rationalizations used by those who abuse. A reexamination of those misused passages can help us reclaim traditions in a way that supports victims and challenges abuse in the family.

Stories of violence against women and children are so common that we scarcely notice them, even in the Bible. Yet they atre there. Women, only a few of them even named, are abused, rejected, and raped by brothers, husbands, and strangers. Daughters are traded and sacrificed.

---

[5] Fund for the Feminist Majority, Washington, D.C.

[6] Ibid.

[7] Worldwatch Institute.

[8] *New York Times*, January 15, 1989.

[9] Clearinghouse on Child Abuse and Neglect Information.

[10] Worldwatch Institute.

[11] Winters, *Laws Against Sexual and Domestic Violence*.

[12] Fund for the Feminist Majority.

[13] *New York Times*, August 4, 1991.

A concubine wife is sliced into pieces by the master who had traded her body for his own safety.[14] Yet even this last, most violent story, in Judges 19, cannot be used to justify abuse, for it ends with this command: "Consider it, take counsel, and speak" (verse 30). It is the silence, the unwillingness to acknowledge the horror, that leaves victims isolated, protects perpetrators, and thwarts healing. We are commanded to break the silence, to give credence to the stories, to be agents of wholeness and justice.

Jesus' concern for the victims is seen in the story of the good Samaritan (Luke 10:25-37). By concluding this parable with the words "Go and do likewise," Jesus indicates that we are to receive all people who have been violated or abused, who are weak or vulnerable, with compassion and caring. It is significant that those who failed to come to the aid of the assault victim in the parable were religious leaders. Jesus made it clear that meeting a legalistic obligation is not enough; we must go beyond the letter of the law in reaching out to comfort and assist those who have been harmed.

The Church must reexamine the theological messages it communicates in light of the experiences of victims of domestic violence and sexual abuse. We must treat with extreme care the concepts of suffering, forgiveness, and the nature of marriage and the family.

The Social Principles of The United Methodist Church affirm the family as "the basic human community through which persons are nurtured and sustained in mutual love, responsibility, respect, and fidelity" (¶ 65A). Clearly, violence and abuse cannot be tolerated within such an understanding. The Social Principles "reject social norms that assume different standards for women than for men in marriage" (¶ 65C), thus eliminating most of the tacit rationalizations that undergird spouse battering. The Social Principles also call for the protection of children from all forms of exploitation and abuse.

Situations of violence and abuse exist in families in virtually every congregation; tragically, no church or community is exempt. Numerous pastors have been asked, after asserting their conviction that there were no families experiencing violence or abuse in their congregations, to mention the issues from the pulpit, using words like *battering, rape, incest, child abuse*. Virtually without exception, they have reported that members have subsequently come to them with current stories of abuse in their families. Clearly, church families are not immune, and many are

---

[14] Phyllis Tribble, *Texts of Terror* (Fortress Press, 1984).

waiting for a signal that these concerns are appropriate ones to share and struggle with within a Christian community.

The Church is being challenged to listen to the stories of victims and survivors and to obtain information and guidance that will lead to wiser and more effective ways of ministry with persons who experience domestic violence and sexual abuse. The church must be a refuge for people who are hurting, and it is an entirely appropriate place for these issues to be addressed. We must find ways to demonstrate that the church is a place where people can feel confident in turning first, not last, for comfort and healing.

People of faith should take the lead in calling for a just response by the community in the face of domestic violence and sexual abuse. A just response involves several steps: righteous anger; compassion for the victim; advocacy for the victim; holding the offender legally and spiritually accountable for his or her sin against the victim and the community; treatment for the offender; and prevention of further abuse by addressing the societal roots and not merely the symptoms of violence and abuse.

Policy Statements and Actions

The United Methodist Church affirms the sacredness of all persons and their right to safety, nurture, and care. It names domestic violence and sexual abuse as sins and pledges to work for their eradication. The Church commits itself to listen to the stories of battered spouses, rape victims, abused children, adult survivors of child sexual abuse, and all others who are violated and victimized. The Church further commits itself to provide leadership in responding with justice and compassion to the presence of domestic violence and sexual abuse among its membership and within the community at large.

The following actions are commended to general agencies, seminaries, and annual conferences:

1. Provide to clergy and laity education and training that address domestic violence and sexual abuse. Seminaries are urged to include mandatory courses in their curriculum, and annual conferences are urged to offer courses in their continuing education programs for clergy;

2. Support policies, programs, and services that protect victims, hold offenders accountable for the offense, provide appropriate incar-

ceration and treatment for offenders, and provide support for other family members;

3. Provide training in abuse prevention, detection, and intervention to church school teachers, youth leaders, and pastors, and encourage them to use abuse-protection curriculum. Urge churches to sponsor marriage enrichment and parenting classes;

4. Develop and implement clear policies to deal with sexual abuse by clergy; and

5. Encourage governments to ratify the United Nations Conventions on the Elimination of all Forms of Discrimination Against Women and on the Rights of the Child.

The following actions are commended to local congregations:

1. Create a church climate of openness, acceptance, and safety that encourages victims to speak their pain and seek relief;

2. Encourage all clergy and lay leaders to work with specialized community agencies on prevention strategies and to provide for the physical, emotional, and spiritual needs of victims, offenders, and other family members;

3. Assess currently available prevention and response resources in the community and, where indicated and appropriate, initiate new programs and services. Wherever possible, undertake new programs ecumenically or as part of a community coalition;

4. Set up peer support groups for battered spouses, for adults who were sexually abused as children, and for rape victims. A trained resource person or professional counselor should be consulted for assistance in setting up peer support groups;

5. Encourage church members to volunteer their services to existing shelters, crisis centers, and other community services. Insist upon training for volunteers;

6. Reexamine and change scriptural and theological messages, cultures, and traditions that validate violence or abuse or that support a view of women as subordinate to men or children as property of adults;

7. Maintain a library of printed and video resources on domestic violence, sexual abuse, and the role of the Church. Develop a utilization plan;

8. Participate in Domestic Violence Awareness Month each October and Child Abuse Prevention Month each April in the United States, or similar emphases in other countries. Clergy are urged to preach on domestic violence and sexual abuse topics; congregations are urged to

host or cooperate in community education events and to highlight opportunities for involvement in prevention and service activities.

ADOPTED 1992

See Social Principles, ¶ 65*I* ; "Putting Children and Their Families First."

Drug and Alcohol Concerns

As God's children and participants in the gift of abundant life, we recognize the need to respond to those who know brokenness from the widespread abuse of alcohol and other drugs in our world. The experience of God's saving grace offers wholeness to each individual. In light of the reality of alcohol and other drug abuse, the Church has a responsibility to recognize brokenness and to be an instrument of education, healing, and restoration. First, we must be committed to confronting the denial within ourselves that keeps individuals and nations from overcoming their struggle with alcohol and other drug abuse. Second, the alcohol and other drug problem must be understood as a social, economic, spiritual, and health problem. Third, the Church has a fundamental role in reorienting the public debate on alcohol and other drugs by shifting the focus from punishment to prevention and treatment. This is rooted in the Christian belief in the ongoing possibilities for transformation in the life of each individual and in our world.

The alcohol and other drug crisis has reached global proportions. More alcohol and other drugs are produced and consumed than ever before. In consuming countries, with their attendant problems of poverty, racism, domestic violence, hopelessness, and material despair, alcohol and other drug abuse is a part of a continuing cycle of economic and spiritual turmoil.

Abuse of legal drugs (alcohol, tobacco, and pharmaceuticals) remains a leading cause of disease and death around the world. While recreational use of illegal drugs in the United States has declined, the use of drugs remains socially acceptable as levels of addiction and abuse continue to rise.

Growing numbers of cities, small towns, and rural areas around the world are caught in a web of escalating alcohol and other drug-related violence. As the findings of the regional hearings in the United States stressed: "Drug addiction crosses all ethnic, cultural, and economic backgrounds." Social systems are dangerously strained under the heavy weight of alcohol and other drug-related health and social problems. Meanwhile, the supply of drugs from developing countries continues to grow in response to high demand from the developed countries.

The United States policy response to the drug crisis has focused almost exclusively on law enforcement and military solutions. This policy, in some cases, has led to the erosion of precious civil liberties and human rights, especially for poor and minority communities.

International strategies should reflect the need for balanced, equitable economic growth and stable democratic governments in drug-producing developing countries. Most importantly, any alternative strategy must be rooted in local communities. The most creative and effective approaches to the present crisis begin at the local level.

The United Methodist Church has long opposed abuse of alcohol and other drugs. In 1916, the General Conference authorized the formation of a Board of Temperance, Prohibition, and Public Morals "to make more effectual the efforts of the church to create public sentiment and crystallize the same into successful opposition to the organized traffic in intoxicating liquors."

During the 1988–92 quadrennium, The United Methodist Church launched a comprehensive Bishops' Initiative on Drugs and Drug Violence, which, through regional hearings across the United States, deepened the denomination's awareness of alcohol and other drug problems. The report of these hearings concluded: "Therefore, The United Methodist Church must play a key role in confronting drug and alcohol addiction. . . ." Today, The United Methodist Church remains committed to curbing drug traffic and the abuse of alcohol and other drugs.

In response to the alcohol and other drug crisis, The United Methodist Church commits itself to a holistic approach, which emphasizes prevention, intervention, treatment, community organization, public advocacy, and abstinence. Out of love for God and our neighbors, the Church must have a positive role by offering a renewed spiritual perspective on this crisis. We commend local congregations, annual conferences, and general agencies and seminaries to take action in the areas of alcohol, tobacco, and other drugs.

I. Alcohol

Alcohol is a *drug*, which presents special problems because of its widespread social acceptance. We affirm our long-standing conviction and recommendation that abstinence from alcoholic beverages is a faithful witness to God's liberating and redeeming love.

This witness is especially relevant because excessive, harmful, and dangerous drinking patterns are uncritically accepted and practiced. Society glamorizes drinking, and youthful immaturity can be exploited for personal gain. The costs associated with alcohol use/abuse are more than the costs associated with all illegal drugs combined. Worldwide, millions of individuals and their families suffer as a result of alcoholism. The medical consequences of alcohol abuse include fetal alcohol syndrome—which is a preventable cause of mental retardation—cardiac defects, and pre- and postnatal growth retardation. Chronic alcohol consumption can have a damaging effect on every body organ, including brain, liver, heart, stomach, intestines, and mouth. Alcohol is a factor in many other social problems such as crime, poverty, and family disorder. The societal costs of alcohol abuse include lost productivity, increased health-care costs, loss of lives in vehicular accidents, and criminal activity.

Thus, The United Methodist Church bases its recommendation of abstinence on critical appraisal of the personal and societal costs in the use of alcohol. The Church recognizes the freedom of the Christian to make responsible decisions and calls upon each member to consider seriously and prayerfully the witness of abstinence as part of his or her Christian commitment. Persons who practice abstinence should avoid attitudes of self-righteousness that express moral superiority and condemnatory attitudes toward those who do not choose to abstain. Because Christian love in human relationships is primary, abstinence is an instrument of love and sacrifice and always subject to the requirements of love.

Our love for our neighbor obligates us to seek healing, justice, and the alleviation of the social conditions that create and perpetuate alcohol abuse. *Therefore:*

1. We urge individuals and local congregations to demonstrate active concern for alcohol abusers and their families. We encourage churches to support the care, treatment, and rehabilitation of problem drinkers;

2. We urge churches to include the problems of alcohol and the value of abstinence as a part of Christian education;

3. We encourage individuals and local congregations to develop prevention education for family, church, and community. We encourage sound empirical research on the social effects of alcohol;

4. We oppose the sale and consumption of alcoholic beverages within the confines of United Methodist Church facilities and recommend that it be prohibited;

5. We ask individuals and local congregations to study and discuss the problem of driving while intoxicated and impaired by alcohol or other drugs, and we support legislation to reduce such activity;

6. We direct the General Board of Discipleship and The United Methodist Publishing House to incorporate educational material on alcohol and other drug problems, including the material on prevention, intervention, treatment, and the value of abstinence throughout its graded literature;

7. We expect United Methodist-related hospitals to treat the alcoholic person with the attention and consideration all patients deserve. We urge the worldwide health-care delivery system to follow this example;

8. We urge all legislative bodies and health-care systems to focus on and implement measures to help meet the special needs of particular groups disproportionately affected by alcohol use;

9. We favor laws to eliminate all advertising and promoting of alcoholic beverages. We urge the General Board of Church and Society and local churches to increase efforts to remove all advertising of alcoholic beverages from the media. We urge special attention to curbing promotions of alcoholic beverages on college campuses as well as racial minority communities;

10. We urge the Federal Trade Commission to continue developing better health hazard warning statements concerning the use of alcohol; and

11. We ask the United States government to improve interagency coordination of drug and alcohol abuse efforts so that there are uniform policies and regulations, and we look forward to the cooperation of all governments in these areas.

II. Tobacco

The use of tobacco is another form of drug abuse, even though it is legal. Overwhelming evidence links cigarette-smoking with lung cancer, cardiovascular diseases, emphysema, and chronic bronchitis. In addition, cigarette-smoking can negatively affect a developing fetus, and secondary smoke is a known carcinogen. The United Methodist Church discourages all persons, particularly youths and young adults, from using any form of tobacco.

We commend the suspension of cigarette advertising on radio and television. We are concerned about other advertisements that associate smoking with physical and social maturity, attractiveness, and success, especially those targeted at youth, racial minorities, and women. We support the Federal Trade Commission's rules requiring health warning statements in cigarette packaging. We are also concerned that the tobacco industry is marketing tobacco in developing countries. *Therefore:*

1. We recommend that tobacco use be banned in all church facilities;

2. We recommend a tobacco-free environment in all public areas;

3. We recommend the prohibition of all commercial advertising of tobacco products;

4. We support expanded research to discover the specific mechanisms of addiction to nicotine. We urge the development of educational methods that effectively discourage the use of tobacco and methods to assist those who wish to stop using tobacco;

5. We urge the Department of Agriculture and other government agencies to plan for and assist the orderly economic transition of the tobacco industry—tobacco growers, processors, and distributors—into industries more compatible with the general welfare of the people.

III. Drugs

The United Methodist Church recognizes the widespread use and misuse of drugs that alter mood, perception, consciousness, and behavior of persons among all ages, classes, and segments of our society. Pharmacologically, a drug is any substance that by its chemical nature alters the structure or function of any living organism. This broad definition encompasses a wide range of substances, many of which are psychoactive and have the potential for abuse. These include marijuana, narcotics, sedatives and stimulants, psychedelics, and hallucinogens. Additionally, commonly used products such as glue, paint thinners, and gasoline have the potential to be abused as inhalants.

A. Marijuana

Like alcohol and tobacco, marijuana is frequently a precursor to the use of other drugs. The active ingredient is THC, which affects the user by temporarily producing feelings of euphoria or relaxation. An altered sense of body image and bouts of exaggerated laughter are commonly reported. However, studies reveal that marijuana impairs short-term memory, altering sense of time and reducing the ability to perform tasks requiring concentration, swift reactions, and coordination.[1]

B. Sedatives and Stimulants

Sedatives, which include barbiturates and tranquilizers, are prescribed appropriately for treatment of anxiety. These legally prescribed drugs need to be taken only under appropriate medical supervision. The use of this class of drugs can result in dependence.

Severe physical dependence on barbiturates can develop at doses higher than therapeutic doses, and withdrawal is severe and dangerous. The combination of alcohol and barbiturates is potentially lethal.

Stimulants range from amphetamines to mild stimulants such as caffeine and nicotine. Prescribed for obesity, sleep disorders, hyperactivity, fatigue, and depression, stimulants produce a temporary sense of vitality, alertness, and energy.

Unlike other stimulants, cocaine has limited medical uses. When the powder form is inhaled, cocaine is a highly addictive central nervous system stimulant that heightens the body's natural response to pleasure and creates a euphoric high, and has the potential to be extremely lethal.

"Crack," a crystallized form of cocaine, is readily available because of its lesser cost. Addiction often comes from one use of the substance.

C. Psychedelics or Hallucinogens

Psychedelics or hallucinogens, which include LSD, psilocybin, mescaline, PCP, and DMT, produce changes in perception and altered states of consciousness. Not only is there limited medical use, the use of these drugs may result in permanent psychiatric problems.

D. Narcotics

Narcotics are prescribed for the relief of pain, but the risk of physical and psychological dependencies is well documented. Derived from the opium plant, natural narcotics include heroin, morphine, codeine, and percodan, while synthetic narcotics include methadone and meperidine.

Therefore, as The United Methodist Church:

---

[1] Performance Resource Press, Inc., Troy, Michigan.

1. We oppose the use of all drugs, except in cases of appropriate medical supervision;

2. We encourage the Church to develop honest, objective, and factual drug education for children, youths, and adults as part of a comprehensive prevention education program;

3. We urge the Church to coordinate its efforts with ecumenical, interfaith, and community groups in prevention, rehabilitation, and policy statements;

4. We encourage the annual conferences to recognize the unique impact of drugs and its related violence upon urban and rural areas and provide appropriate ministries and resources;

5. We strongly encourage annual conferences to develop leadership training opportunities and resources for local church pastors and laity to help them with counseling individuals and families who have alcohol and other drug-related problems; counseling those bereaved by alcohol and other drug-related deaths and violence; and teaching stress management to church workers in communities with high alcohol and other drug activity;

6. We encourage all educational systems at every level to develop comprehensive drug-education programs and courses;

7. We urge redevelopment of more effective methods of treatment of drug abuse and addiction;

8. We support government policies concerning drugs that are compatible with our Christian beliefs about the potential transformation of all individuals;

9. We urge all United Methodist churches in the United States to work for a minimum legal drinking age of twenty-one years in their respective states; and

10. We support strong, humane law-enforcement efforts against the illegal sale of all drugs, and we urge that those arrested for possession and use of illegally procured drugs be subject to education and rehabilitation.

ADOPTED 1996

See Social Principles, ¶ 66J; "Oxford House Model for Treatment of Drug and Alcohol Abuse."

Ecumenical Decade: Churches in Solidarity with Women

When we look at women across the world, we discover millions who are still on the margin of their societies. Some are there largely because they were born female instead of male. Others are on the fringe because they are old in societies that want women to be eternally young. Young women who are single parents with families and have few marketable skills cannot support their children. Women may find themselves on the fringes of society because of age, caste, class, color, ethnic or national origin, or marital status.

The margin of society is dangerous. Women are forced to live there by reason of poverty, famine, war, illiteracy, ageism, disabilities, refugee or illegal alien status, homelessness, or incarceration. Women are not the only ones to suffer. When women suffer, there is a ripple effect. So central are the well-being and economic security of a woman to the lives of others that her marginalization adversely impacts not only the quality of her development but that of her family and her community as a whole. The well-being of women is central to the well-being of all.

Signs of hope are emerging across the world as women are making the journey away from the fringes of society, empowering one another through care and struggle for life.

The United Nations Decade for Women (1975–1985) has pointed the way to what can be done. Much is still before us. The United Nations "End of the Decade Conference" held in Nairobi, Kenya, in 1985 was a milestone. It was the starting point for the sustained hard work required for the decades to come.

The "Forward Looking Strategies for the Advancement of Women by the Year 2000," which emerged from the 1985 End of the Decade Conference, should be implemented. But in the churches, there is need for another decade. The World Council of Churches, on Easter 1988, launched a new focus called "An Ecumenical Decade." It builds on the momentum of the United Nations Decade for Women and gives the churches a new opportunity to respond to God's call for inclusiveness and solidarity and sharing of power. Some of the obstacles women face were cited in the World Council of Churches report to the national conference:

• In time of economic recession, women are among the first to be thrown out of work;

• Women in rural areas receive the least attention in development plans and are not consulted about their basic needs;

• The effects of famine are hardest on women, who bear the heaviest responsibility for the family;

• As socioeconomic situations deteriorate, the frustration of jobless men often leads to increased sexual abuse and violence against women;

- Growing poverty, the spread of military bases, and the promotion of sex-tourism have greatly increased the plague of prostitution, involving even younger women and children;
- Among the victims of nuclear testing are women, such as in the Pacific, who bear the burden of increased miscarriages and deformed children;
- Women industrial workers are often without protection and receive the lowest wages from local and multinational industries, exploiting women's vulnerable positions;
- Apartheid and other forms of racism oppress women in a specific way and make them suffer often double and triple oppression as women, as poor people, and as racial or ethnic people.

Men of the Church and in society are joining women in acts of reformation and even re-creation in working to transform old orders of relationships and systems to better serve the needs of women and men and whole communities.

When we strive together to end the physical and emotional abuse of women, their economic insecurity and political powerlessness, and their exclusion from decision-making processes, we ensure that women will be able to make their full contribution to every aspect of society. We work out of a faith commitment that proclaims that through Christ a new humanity can be established for all persons in all places.

The World Council of Churches directs us to the biblical and theological roots for the ecumenical decade. Rooted in the biblical accounts of the genesis of the world and the human family is the declaration that all persons, female and male, are created in the image of God, the giver of life. Human relationships have failed to mirror this imagery of creation in God's image, but women's experiences, their struggles for life and for nurturing life, are crucial perspectives for safeguarding and liberating the creation.

In calling for an ecumenical decade for women, the World Council of Churches reminds us that the prophetic tradition calls the people of God to take on the task of living and working in solidarity with the oppressed to bring oppression to an end. We are also reminded of the affirmation that through our baptism, we are incorporated into the body of Christ, the new community in which old patterns of relationships among classes, races, and genders have been ended and new patterns are embodied that reflect the caring of the new age. The Call reminds us of the diversity of gifts that the Spirit imparts upon persons in the human family and the challenge to enable all persons to use those gifts for the building up of the community for justice and reconciliation in the world.

In the words of the 1981 World Council of Churches Consultation on the Community of Women and Men in the Church, "We receive a foretaste of a global community of women and men vulnerable to the pain of all forms of oppression and united in struggle against them."

We call upon The United Methodist Church to:

1. Participate fully in "The Ecumenical Decade—Churches in Solidarity with Women" (1988–1998) launched by the World Council of Churches (WCC), including support for:

(a) Women's full participation: includes the question of power, power sharing, and empowerment; women's presence on decision-making bodies and in bodies where ideas (e.g., theology, public policy) and plans are developed;

(b) Women's visions and perspectives, concerns and commitments related to the ecumenical study "Justice, Peace and the Integrity of Creation"; and

(c) Women doing theology and sharing spirituality: How can we enable an integrated process of study, sharing, acting, and celebrating?

2. Produce educational resources and programs on the marginalization and oppression of women, their struggle for human dignity and a better life, and their creative contribution in theology, spirituality, and ministry.

3. Encourage all levels of the Church—general, jurisdictional annual conference, district, and local church—to participate in the Ecumenical Decade by studying the root causes of sexism, exploring ways to increase participation of women in all aspects of Church life, and being open to ways of addressing injustices toward women through the Church and society.

4. Urge all commissions and program agencies to study and implement as appropriate the priorities of the "Forward Looking Strategies";

5. Increase the involvement of racial, ethnic, and national minority women as well as other oppressed women;

6. Improve relationships with women suffering under sexism, racism, and casteism, and support the World Council of Churches' Women Under Racism Programme;

7. Continue efforts that both the Church and the society accomplished during the United Nations Decade for Women toward the goals of equality, development, and peace;

8. Work for women to participate equally with men in the decisions of the Church and the society concerning justice and peace;

9. Urge United Methodists to encourage governments to commit themselves to appropriate action for the implementation of the strategies within the framework of their national development plans and programs;

10. Monitor and be supportive of the continual emphasis on women by the United Nations, and participate in all the United Nations arenas where nongovernmental organizations have potential for influence;

11. Support the "United Nations Convention on the Elimination of All Forms of Discrimination Against Women," and urge United Methodists to work through local and national organizations to encourage their governments not only to ratify but also to implement the Convention.

ADOPTED 1988

See Social Principles, ¶ 66F; "Affirmation of Support for the Ecumenical Decade of the Churches in Solidarity with Women."

Ecumenical Interpretations of Doctrinal Standards

WHEREAS, the 1970 General Conference passed a "Resolution of Intent"concerning the ecumenical interpretation of the Thirty-Nine Articles, which was mistakenly deleted from the 1970 *Book of Resolutions;* and

WHEREAS, it is common knowledge that the context of the original Thirty-Nine Articles (1563)—and specifically Articles XIV, XIX, XXI, XXII, XXIV, XXV, XXVIII, XXX, XXXI, and XXXIV—were bitterly polemical, it is of prime importance that they should be reconsidered and reassessed in the contemporary context. They were aimed, deliberately, at the Roman Catholic Church in a time of strife and were a mix of the theological and nontheological convictions of embattled schismatics, fighting as they believed for national survival and evangelical truth. John Wesley's hasty abridgment (1784) of the original Thirty-Nine Articles (down to twenty-four) retained seven out of ten of these anti-Roman references—XIV, XV, XVI, XVII, XIX, XX, XXI—in his enumeration. This reflects his conviction as to their applicability to the Roman Catholic Church as he perceived it. This much must be recognized and acknowledged as belonging to our inheritance from our Anglican-Wesleyan past. It is, however, one of the virtues of historical insight that it enables those in a later age to recognize the circumstances of earlier events and documents without being bound to their historical evaluation, especially in a subsequent epoch when relationships have been radically altered; and

WHEREAS, we rejoice in the positive relationships developed between The United Methodist Church and the Roman Catholic Church, at levels both official and unofficial;

Therefore, be it resolved, that we declare it our official intent to interpret these Articles in consonance with our best ecumenical insights and judgment.

Be it further resolved, that this resolution be printed in its entirety in the 1992 *Book of Resolutions* and that appropriate reference be noted in the *Book of Discipline* to correct the inaccuracies found in page 30, footnote #3, and page 64, footnote #5.

ADOPTED 1992

See Social Principles, ¶ *66B;* "Toward an Ecumenical Future."

Education: The Gift of Hope

WHEREAS, the United Methodist heritage is rich with concern for the education of all God's children; and

WHEREAS, that heritage is filled with vivid examples of Christlike concern for training the mind as well as nurturing the faith; and

WHEREAS, John Wesley was "a unique and remarkable educator (who) gave to the whole Methodist movement throughout the world a permanent passion for education"[1]; and

WHEREAS, the current educational environment in the United States is one of challenge and transition; and

WHEREAS, contemporary educational issues include concerns for quality control, choice, and opportunity; and

WHEREAS, the Church has a positive and constructive role to play in the discussion of education in our society and must become involved in ways that provide assistance to the community and support for educational leaders; and

---

[1] *The Story of Methodism,* Halford E. Luccock, Paul Hutchinson, Robert W. Goodloe (Abingdon Press, 1926; page 361).

WHEREAS, the General Board of Higher Education and Ministry has developed a study paper, *Education: The Gift of Hope*, reminding the Church of its Wesleyan commitment, challenging the Church to understanding, and calling the Church to involvement in local education;

Therefore, be it resolved, that the 1996 General Conference receive *Education: The Gift of Hope* and affirm the challenge by the General Board of Higher Education and Ministry;

Be it further resolved, that the 1996 General Conference urge every local congregation to study *Education: The Gift of Hope* to learn of our heritage, the current situation and concerns, and the hopes for education;

Be it further resolved, that the Church join hands with educators in seeking more effective ways to prepare our children for a future in which they will both find personal fulfillment and make a significant contribution to the world;

Be it further resolved, that each local congregation develop a plan for concrete involvement in the educational activity of its community, seeking to improve the system, and becoming involved with students;

To the end that John Wesley's concern for education will be manifest among United Methodists and bring with it the gift of hope.

ADOPTED 1996

See Social Principles, ¶¶ 66C, 68D; "Church-Government Relations."

Elimination of Racism in The United Methodist Church

WHEREAS, the General Commission on Religion and Race has identified the persistent presence of racism within our lives and within local churches, annual conferences, jurisdictional structures, general agencies, seminaries, and other institutions as one of the underlying causes for the inability of the denomination to become the true community of *shalom*; and

WHEREAS, we profess an understanding of the will of God and a willingness to surrender our lives to Jesus Christ; and

WHEREAS, we realize the necessity to engage regularly in events/activities that will enable us to grow toward Christlike perfection;

Therefore, the General Commission on Religion and Race petitions:

1. That the 1996 General Conference call on all local churches, districts, annual conferences, jurisdictional structures, seminaries, general agencies, institutions, and the Council of Bishops to make the eradication of racism a priority in all of their agendas and to commit themselves

to the eradication of racism—attitudinal, behavioral, cultural, and institutional;

2. That all local churches, districts, annual conferences, jurisdictional structures, seminaries, general agencies, and institutions develop a clear affirmative action policy with goals and timelines, so as to ensure and reflect the rich racial and ethnic diversity of The United Methodist Church;

3. That all local congregations, districts, annual conferences, jurisdictional structures, general agencies, seminaries, and institutions examine and rewrite as needed policies, practices, and procedures in order to ensure the full participation and contribution of racial and ethnic minority persons within the life of the denomination;

4. That all local congregations, districts, and annual conferences through the work areas on religion and race; district directors of religion and race; and conference commissions on religion and race provide ongoing opportunities for cross-racial and interethnic dialogue;

5. That the annual conferences, colleges of Bishops, and seminaries of the North Central Jurisdiction, Northeastern Jurisdiction, and South Central Jurisdiction participate in the General Commission's Anti-Racism Training Program during the 1997–2000 quadrennium;

6. That the district boards, annual conference boards and agencies, jurisdictional boards and agencies, general agencies, seminaries, denomination-related institutions, and the Council of Bishops provide for their staff and members of their policy-making organizations skills training in interpersonal communication and intercultural communication; and

7. That on or before August 1, 1999, annual conferences, jurisdictional structures, general agencies, seminaries, and denomination-related institutions report to the General Commission on Religion and Race the status of their efforts to eradicate the sin of racism.

ADOPTED 1996

See Social Principles, ¶ 66A; "Racism: The Church's Unfinished Agenda"; "Charter for Racial Justice Policies in an Interdependent Global Community"; "Global Racism: A Violation of Human Rights."

Equal Rights of Women

The Gospel makes it clear that Jesus regarded women and men as being of equal worth. Nowhere is it recorded that Jesus treated women in a different manner than he did men. Although the Gospel writers recorded little in the way of verbal statements of Jesus *about women*, they have preserved for us many incidents in the life of Jesus that indicated that he understood the equality of all people, male and female alike, to be a significant element of his message.

While Jesus called only males to be part of the Twelve, biblical evidence indicates that others, including women, were considered disciples or followers of Jesus. In open defiance of the customs of his society, Jesus taught women, spoke to them in public, and refused to confine women to the traditionally accepted roles. Moreover, women were the first witnesses to the Resurrection and were directed to go and tell their brothers.

While both the Old and New Testaments came out of male-centered cultures and necessarily reflect that culture, interpretations of the Scriptures by the church have unduly emphasized male "superiority." For example, popular interpretations of the two Creation stories often assume the women as "help mate" or "helper," which implies female inferiority or subordination. In the original Hebrew, however, the word translated *helper* described a person of at least equal status to the one helped. Indeed, in the majority of times this word appears in the Old Testament it is speaking of God as "helper." Rather than defining women as secondary to men, each Creation story points to the equality of the male and female, both of whom are made "in the image of God."

A number of statements attributed to Paul have frequently been cited to support the idea of feminine subordination and submission. However, when these statements are taken in context and balanced against the rest of the New Testament, especially against the message of Jesus, there can be no doubt that women are of equal value with men and should enjoy the same rights, privileges, and obligations as men.

The support of The United Methodist Church for equal rights of women derives from our traditional concern for justice, human dignity, and equality of all persons.

Examples of courageous action throughout our history inspire us as we move into our third century. Grounded in our biblical understanding, experience, and tradition, equal rights for women in church life, public institutions, and personal relationships have been, and will continue to be, fundamental in our call to be faithful as United Methodists.

Since 1972, this commitment was focused through our denomination's effort to support ratification of the Equal Rights Amendment to the United States Constitution. Three successive General Conferences, with practically unanimous votes, supported involvement in the ratification effort for the proposed 26th amendment, which would have guaranteed equity in the formation and implementation of the legal statutes in the United States. Yet the deadline for ratification occurred in 1982, with only three states lacking the necessary approval. Thus, in the United States, citizens continue to live in a situation where the laws at the local, state, and federal levels discriminate against persons. Social policies that view women as dependents continue to the extent that many women reach mature adulthood and their senior years to find themselves in poverty. Trends indicate that women, children, and other dependents living in families headed by women will compose almost all the persons living in poverty in the United States by the year 2000 if current social policies continue. These social conditions include social services cutbacks, unemployment, salary discrimination, inequality of opportunity, and the weakening of affirmative action and Equal Employment Opportunity regulations. For women of racial or language minority groups or women who are older, the burden of these conditions is the most extreme.

Therefore, be it resolved, that we, as United Methodists, will continue:

1. To lift up our historic concern for the equality of women and men, to confess those times when we have failed to confront discrimination, and to rejoice in efforts to support human dignity;

2. To work through local churches, councils of churches, conference committees, general agencies, and appropriate coalitions to research laws and policies that discriminate on the basis of gender, and to advocate changes that enable equality of rights and opportunities (this work will continue to require strategic focus and coordination on every level);

3. To support the passage of the Equal Rights Amendment to the U.S. Constitution; to educate United Methodists and others to its history, meaning, and purpose; and to work through all appropriate channels for its passage;

4. To monitor those public policies and practices that affect unemployment; pay inequity; inequality of opportunity; and, in the United States, the weakening of affirmative action (with special concern for the interlocking impact of discrimination on the basis of gender, race, and age); to support those public policies and practices that create new jobs, that encourage women to move into nontraditional jobs, and that alleviate competition between women and minorities for jobs; and

5. To encourage United Methodist general program agencies and annual conferences to develop creative approaches for the development of governmental social policies that will eliminate the burden of poverty on women and children; to offer opportunities for service and action to United Methodists who want to be involved in eradicating those conditions; and to work for economic justice.

ADOPTED 1984

See Social Principles, ¶ 66F; "The Status of Women"; "Ecumenical Decade: Churches in Solidarity with Women."

Eradicating Abusive Child Labor

In the Gospels, the disciples' attitude toward God was measured by their attitude toward children and their ability to "become as a little child." The protection of childhood and the nurture of children are, therefore, among our most sacred human responsibilities. Reflecting this, the Social Principles of The United Methodist Church upholds the rights of children to growth and development, adequate nutrition, health services, housing, education, recreation, protection against all forms of racial discrimination, cruelty, neglect, and exploitation.

However, throughout the world, childhood itself is under assault by new as well as historic forces. Today's child, in too many parts of the world, must not only cope with warfare, famine, and pestilence at an early age, but is too often denied childhood itself by being forced into labor under abusive and destructive conditions. Many millions of children around the world labor in work that is coerced, forced, bonded, enslaved or otherwise unfair in wages, injurious to health and safety, and/or obstructive of educational or moral development.[1]

WHEREAS, the majority of child labor is found in informal sectors of the world's poorest economies, a growing element in global competition is the employment of children in developing-country export industries making products such as glass, garments, brassware, leather goods, and hand-knotted carpets for sale on the international market. The oriental carpet industry employs one of the most abusive forms of bonded child labor, involving perhaps as many as one million children in South Asia.[2]

---

[1] A. Bequele and W.E. Myers, *First Things First in Child Labour: Eliminating Work Detrimental to Children*, ILO and UNICEF, 1995; pages 1–27.

[2] U.S. Department of Labor, *By the Sweat and Toil of Children*, 1994.

The United Nations and the International Labor Organization (ILO) have established universal principles to protect children from such abuse, including the International Covenant on the Rights of the Child and the ILO Convention No. 138 for Minimum Age for Admission to Work. These international conventions have been ratified by many countries, not including the United States.

There is growing awareness in international-development agencies that child labor is not a byproduct of generalized poverty, but is rooted in specific policies that disproportionately neglect or disadvantage certain populations—ethnic, caste, or gender groups—and that unbalanced development policies have contributed to the exacerbation of child labor.[3]

We therefore call on The United Methodist Church:

1. To support public policies that include the ratification and enforcement of international labor conventions regarding child labor, affirmed by The United Methodist Church in the resolution on the "Rights of Workers" (adopted 1988), and the Convention on the Rights of the Child, affirmed by The United Methodist Church in the resolution on the "Ratification of Human Rights Covenants and Conventions";

2. To work to eradicate the evils of child labor through encouraging the appropriate agencies and units to join the Child Labor Coalition, a broad-based coalition of medical, welfare, religious, consumer, labor, and human-rights organizations in the United States, and to support such consumer initiatives as the RUGMARK campaign, initiated in India by UNICEF, the South-Asian Coalition on Child Servitude, and others to label and market oriental carpets made without exploited child labor;

3. To support legislative and administrative measures to ban the international trafficking in goods made by child labor; and

4. To support unilateral and multilateral aid and development policies that attack the root causes of child labor, such as lack of basic education, gender and caste prejudice, and unbalanced development schemes that disadvantage certain populations.

ADOPTED 1996

See Social Principles, ¶ 66C; "Putting Children and Their Families First."

---

[3] Pharis J. Harvey, "Where Children Work: Child Servitude in the Global Economy," *The Christian Century*, April 5, 1995; pages 362–65.

Eradication of Racism in The United Methodist Church

WHEREAS, The United Methodist Church, through its principles, its policies, and its affirmation of equality as a biblical principle, has sought to place racism as unacceptable in God's eyes and the Church's ministry; and

WHEREAS, ethnic churches of color and clergy of color continue to suffer the injustices that grow out of acceptance of racism as a fact of life; and

WHEREAS, we, who are striving for perfection but realize we have not attained perfection in the case of our corporate sins of racism, call upon The United Methodist Church to move farther down the Emmaus road with Jesus that our eyes may be fully opened to the beauty and gifts that all of God's children bring in the table of Christian service;

Therefore, be it resolved, that the General Conference of The United Methodist Church reaffirm its commitment to the following:

1. The placement of clergy shall be based on gifts and graces, not race;

2. The churches of color within The United Methodist Church shall be looked upon and included as equals in programming and staffing of general Church agencies, annual regional conferences, and the conference council on ministries; and

3. The General Commission on Religion and Race or other appropriate bodies shall maintain data and evidence of these activities to be reported through general Church channels or publications on a quadrennial basis.

ADOPTED 1996

See Social Principles, ¶ 66A; "Elimination of Racism in The United Methodist Church"; "Charter for Racial Justice Policies in an Interdependent Community."

Eradication of Sexism in the Church

WHEREAS, sexism continues to be a pervasive and systematic force within our Church and our society; and

WHEREAS, sexism deprives the Church and society of the opportunity to use the skills and talents that women have; and

WHEREAS, the study showing the pervasiveness of sexual harassment throughout The United Methodist Church raised many concerns about changing this trend; and

WHEREAS, the recent Judicial Council decision ruling against the mandatory inclusion of women at all levels of the Church seems to be a sign that women are losing ground; and

WHEREAS, sexism, when not monitored, rears its ugly head and denies the majority of women in The United Methodist Church the opportunity to participate fully and equally in all areas of the Church;

Therefore, be it resolved, that the General Conference affirm the work and the necessity for the continuance of the General Commission on the Status and Role of Women and of the annual conference commissions on the status and role of women; and

Be it further resolved, that each annual conference commission be given the financial backing to pursue projects that are aimed at educating the members of the local churches about the issues of sexism and at sponsoring the leadership events that enable the annual conference commission members to be better advocates for all who seek equity and inclusiveness; and

Be it further resolved, that the General Conference make it mandatory for each annual conference, United Methodist seminary, and all United Methodist-related institutions to have policies on sexual harassment in force by General Conference 2000; and

Be it further resolved, that the General Conference support the General Commission on the Status and Role of Women as the advocacy and monitoring agency of women's issues for increasing opportunities for females in leadership, promoting equality in filling decision-making posts, and fostering inclusiveness in all facets of The United Methodist Church.

ADOPTED 1996

See Social Principles, ¶ 66F; "Sexual Abuse Within the Ministerial Relationship and Sexual Harassment Within The United Methodist Church"; "Ecumenical Decade: Churches in Solidarity with Women."

Ethnic Membership on Boards and Agencies

Be it resolved, that the delegates at the various jurisdictional conferences be urged to be intentional in their nominations to the various general boards and agencies to ensure that ethnic minorities are elected to these boards and agencies in representative numbers; and

Be it further resolved, that the nominating committees of each annual conference include in their nomination and election process an equitable number of ethnic minorities on every board and agency.

ADOPTED 1992

See Social Principles, ¶ 66; "Affirmative Action."

Federal Funds for Indian Health Services

WHEREAS, Native Americans are the most socioeconomically deprived minority group in the United States; and

WHEREAS, the United States government is bound by treaty to provide health care for all Native Americans and their descendants; and

WHEREAS, the United States government now provides these medical services through Indian Health Services, United States Public Health Service, Department of Health and Human Services; and

WHEREAS, medical services currently provided by the Indian Health Services for health education and prenatal care have contributed to an even more rapid decline in infant mortality among Native Americans than among more affluent whites; and

WHEREAS, similar successes of these health programs are likely to have occurred for all Native Americans living in the United States; and

WHEREAS, despite these successes, the current administration proposes substantial funding cuts for the Indian Health Services; and

WHEREAS, any funding cuts could severely curtail or cancel health care for a large number of eligible Native Americans; and

WHEREAS, a small number of Native Americans have private health insurance, and an even larger number cannot afford to buy such insurance.

Therefore, be it resolved, that all Native Americans have access to adequate medical services to ensure a balance of physical, mental, and spiritual well-being for the "Journey Toward Wholeness"; and that the current appropriation committee allow no decrease in federal funds to operate Indian health facilities.

Be it further resolved, that the General Board of Church and Society submit this resolution, on behalf of the General Conference, to all United States senators and legislators who have Indian Health Services within their respective state.

ADOPTED 1988

See Social Principles, ¶66F; "The United Methodist Church and America's Native People"; "Rights of Native People of the Americas."

Global Racism: A Violation of Human Rights

There is no longer Jew or Greek, there is no longer slave or free, there is no longer male and female; for all of you are one in Christ Jesus.

(Galatians 3:28)

251

The Social Principles of The United Methodist Church affirm that all persons are equally valuable in the sight of God. "The rights and privileges a society bestows upon or withholds from those who comprise it indicate the relative esteem in which that society holds particular persons and groups of persons" (¶ 66, the *Book of Discipline*).

At the World Summit for Social Development held in Copenhagen, Denmark, in 1995, nations of the world agreed that

> an inclusive society must be based on respect for all human rights and fundamental freedoms, cultural and religious diversity, social justice and the special needs of vulnerable and disadvantaged groups, democratic participation and the rule of law. The pluralistic nature of most societies has at times resulted in problems for the different groups to achieve and maintain harmony and cooperation, and to have equal access to all resources in society.

"*Racism* is the combination of the power to dominate by one race over other races and a value system that assumes that the dominant race is innately superior to the others. Racism includes both personal and institutional racism. Personal racism is manifested through the individual expressions, attitudes, and/or behaviors that accept the assumptions of a racist value system and that maintain the benefits of this system. Institutional racism is the established social pattern that supports implicitly or explicitly the racist value system" (Social Principles, ¶ 66).

The plague of racism is manifested all over the world, intensifying discrimination and marginalization of people based on their race, ethnicity, nationality, language, or caste, and that of indigenous peoples. It creates environments where the marginalized internalize that culture, are dehumanized, and are denied their own identities, values, and perspectives. Polarization between dominant groups and marginalized groups and intolerance of "outsiders"—migrants, immigrants, refugees, and the internally displaced—is increasing in many societies. Civil unrest is not uncommon, often leading to violence, xenophobia, organization of hate groups and private militia, and ethnic conflict.

The media and educational systems have often served to validate, rather than dispel, negative racial stereotypes. If unchallenged, exposure to these images and concepts from early childhood can contribute to racist attitudes and behaviors or self-hatred in adulthood.

The resurgence of questionable scientific practices based on theories that postulate that racial or ethnic persons are inherently inferior to those of the dominant race has global implications. Such scientific research and tests that predict behavior and rationalize the lack of educational and social achievement have been used to establish policies and procedures that further institutionalize racism.

Racism and racial discrimination continually assume new forms, intensified by conflict over economic resources in developed as well as in developing countries. The commitment and investment of societies in the health and welfare of individuals and groups is increasingly disparate. This can be seen in, among other things, the decreasing incomes, scarcity of meaningful work, lack of proper nutrition and access to physical and mental health care, poor education, increasing illiteracy, disproportionate incarceration rates and death sentences, dislocation of families, unemployment, homelessness, landlessness, denial of effective participation in the political process, and social exclusion and isolation of minority and indigenous groups in society.

Environmental racism has endangered the quality of life in communities where large minority and low-income populations live. In industrialized countries and in developing countries, companies often use the lack of government controls to pollute these communities, exposing the people to poisonous chemicals. Health and safety of peoples are also jeopardized by toxic contamination due to the disposal process and placement of facilities for the production, storage, and treatment of hazardous materials and wastes in their communities.

The impact of militarism continues to affect developing nations and minority communities in many ways. Lands of developing nations, lands sacred to indigenous peoples, and colonized lands are often used as testing grounds for nuclear weapons and emerging technologies. The worldwide dependence on armaments for security has sustained the expanding arms industry and intensified conflicts and wars, many involving one ethnic or national group against another.

The colonial and imperial subjugation of peoples throughout the world represses, sometimes violently, movements for self-determination of peoples, as seen in East Timor, Hawaii, and other islands in the Pacific, Western Sahara, Puerto Rico, Northern Ireland, and countries in eastern and central Europe.

Women of color in many nations suffer the compounding effects of discrimination, oppression, marginalization, and exclusion. Women of color are all too often confronted with hostility and subjugated by race, gender, class/status, and caste. They are particularly victimized and relegated to lower-paying jobs, inadequate social resources, unjust laws, sexual abuse, and prostitution because of historical patterns of racism, sexism, and classism.

The "Charter for Racial Justice Policies" calls United Methodists to recognize racism as a rejection of the teachings of Jesus Christ. Racism used as a justification for social, economic, cultural, legal, and political exploitation robs all human beings of their wholeness. The Charter also reminds United Methodists that racial and cultural diversity strengthen the Church's work toward a world in which each person's value is respected and nurtured. The struggle for justice is based on the belief that new attitudes, new understandings, and new relationships must be reflected in the laws, policies, structures, and practices of both church and state.

The United Methodist Church confesses that it has not accepted the struggle against racism as central to the Church's mission in the world. The Church has failed to proclaim and live out the gospel message of love toward all God's people no matter their race, nationality, ethnicity, or caste. Within the United Methodist community, institutional racism continues to deny the full involvement and leadership of members throughout the life of the Church. In society, the Church has not been a strong, prophetic voice calling people to right relationships and to protect the human rights of all.

Therefore, United Methodists will:

1. Continue to work toward the elimination of personal racism and all forms of institutional racism within the total ministry of the Church; empower the General Commission on Religion and Race to carefully monitor local churches, annual conferences, and the general boards and agencies; and urge all boards, agencies, commissions, and institutions to continue to include an internal mechanism for monitoring within their respective structures;

2. Urge their governments to implement the United Nations Convention on the Elimination of Racial Discrimination, which guarantees the right to equal treatment before the law, security of person (protection from violence), right to participate in the political process, and equal access to public service, as well as protection and remedy from racial discrimination; urge the United Methodist Office for the United Nations to monitor reports from nations on their progress in implementing the Convention and to publicize the findings; and support agencies and human-rights groups such as Amnesty International and Human Rights Watch in their efforts to identify and address issues of global racism;

3. Urge that the General Board of Global Ministries, the General Board of Discipleship, seminaries, and denomination-related institu-

tions develop and disseminate resources, educational opportunities, and programs that encourage and support antiracist leanings and behaviors; examine the contributions of multicultural and bilingual skills and experience in eradicating global racism; and train Church leadership, including all mission volunteers and personnel, in antiracism strategies;

4. Support the United Nations Decade for Indigenous Peoples (1995–2005), which includes, among other things, the protection of land rights, the elimination of environmental racism, and respect for their cultural identities and their self-determination; and urge the General Board of Global Ministries and the General Board of Church and Society to develop programs of advocacy in solidarity with indigenous peoples;

5. Advocate for a moratorium on the dumping of toxic and hazardous materials and wastes and the siting of hazardous waste treatment, storage, and disposal facilities in large minority and low-income communities in industrialized countries and in developing countries;

6. Oppose and ameliorate xenophobic and racist reactions against migrants, immigrants, refugees, and the internally displaced and work toward developing hospitable communities and humane policies that are nonexclusionary; and urge the United Methodist Committee on Relief to provide resources and ministries to enable local churches and annual conferences to become involved in the development of such communities;

7. Facilitate the full participation of groups marginalized because of their race in all aspects of the political, economic, social, religious, and cultural life of our societies and in the economic progress and social development of our countries; recognize and respect people of different racial, ethnic, linguistic, national, and caste backgrounds and protect the rights of those persons and groups; and urge general boards, agencies, commissions, and the Council of Bishops to continue to engage United Methodists in ministries that promote the above;

8. Support the World Council of Churches Programme to Combat Racism and consider financial support for its Special Fund to Combat Racism; and urge all general boards and agencies to support the World Council of Churches Programme to Combat Racism and its "Special Fund to Combat Racism";

9. Advocate for the elimination of stereotyping of racial, ethnic, and indigenous groups in print and mass media; affirm the right of all people to originate information about themselves, their own

cultures, and their own perceptions; affirm the right of all peoples to access to the means of communications; and urge United Methodist Communications to monitor their own productions and engage producers of mass media in dialogue to encourage the elimination of stereotypes and the inclusion of multicultural perspectives in their products;

10. Use the full resources of United Methodist structures to support public and corporate policies designed to eliminate racism and to redress its past and present effects; and

11. Work in coalition with secular groups to monitor and actively combat the activities of hate groups, extremist groups, and militia groups in the United States and other parts of the world.

ADOPTED 1996

See Social Principles, ¶ 66A; "A Charter for Racial Justice Policies in an Interdependent Global Community"; "Racism: The Church's Unfinished Agenda"; and a number of other resolutions in "The Social Community" that address the issue.

Goals and Recommendations on Participation of Women

Goals

The United Methodist Church, in serious consideration of the issue of the role of women in the Christian community and their participation in the life and work of The United Methodist Church, believes that it should direct its energies and resources:

1. To move toward the liberation of all persons so that all may achieve full humanity;

2. To bring about attitudinal changes in relation to: (a) theological, philosophical, and biblical interpretations and understandings of the role of women; and (b) expectations for achievement and contributions of women;

3. To make all United Methodists sensitive to the issues involved in the rights of women;

4. To overcome rigid sex-role distinctions that have traditionally characterized church structures and society;

5. To eliminate all discriminatory language, images, and practices in the life and work of The United Methodist Church;

6. To create an openness and receptivity for women in the professional ministry of The United Methodist Church;

7. To utilize the full potential of both men and women in elections and appointments at all levels in The United Methodist Church; and

8. To establish a process for evaluation of the performance of The United Methodist Church regarding the role and participation of women in its life and work.

Recommendations for the Enhancement of the Participation of Women

1. That every programming agency in the denomination give serious attention to developing new avenues of participation for younger adult members of the denomination, particularly women in the twenty to thirty-five age range; and further, that this attention be in the form of staff time and financial resources needed to explore varied styles of family life, that alternative lifestyles be considered, and that new styles (e.g., single women, employed women) be made more acceptable in the overall Church population;

2. That inasmuch as the Study Commission has been preoccupied with the study of the problems of women's roles in general to the exclusion of the particular problems of women in racial and ethnic groups, the study should be continued with special attention given to the roles of women of minority racial groups and ethnic groups within The United Methodist Church;

3. That experimental ministries be developed for and by women, in order to increase awareness of roles and potential of women through consciousness raising, counseling, education, and political action;

4. That the media-development agencies of the Church produce and disseminate materials that would aid a sensitization process concerning the role of women, with consideration being given to all forms of media presentation;

5. That there be a development of curriculum that would help United Methodists avoid sustaining an inadequate image of male and female roles and understand how our rigidly held sexual roles deprive us of our full humanity, and that also would assist in the exploration and development of new and alternative lifestyles;

6. That careful consideration be given to the professional ministry, beginning with the traditional practices of entering the profession, continuing through recruitment and acceptance at the schools of theology, educational programs for women in the schools of theology, the processes and attitudes of annual conference boards of ministry, and the attitudes of local congregations toward women clergy;

7. That the Theological Study Commission on Doctrine and Doctrinal Standards be requested to study and report on the role of women from a theological and doctrinal perspective;

8. That all nominating committees in local churches and annual, jurisdictional, and General conferences give attention to the nomination of women for membership on committees, commissions, boards, councils, and other organizations, so that women are included in all of these units in significant numbers (bearing in mind that at least 50 percent of the membership of The United Methodist Church is made up of women); and

9. That the General Conference take whatever action is necessary to

(a) ensure an increased proportion of women in all levels of professional staff in general boards and agencies;

(b) create a more favorable setting for the recruitment, education, and appointment of women clergy; and

(c) encourage local churches to be open to the acceptance of women as clergy (senior ministers, associate ministers, and ministers in special appointments) and as lay employees; and

10. That the General Conference establish a Commission on the Role of Women in The United Methodist Church to foster an ongoing awareness of the problems and issues relating to the status of women and to stimulate progress reports on these issues from the various boards and agencies. (The legislation for the organization and work of the commission is in the *Discipline*.)

ADOPTED 1972

See Social Principles, ¶ 66F; "Equal Rights of Women"; "The Status of Women"; "Ecumenical Decade: Churches in Solidarity with Women."

Guidelines for Interreligious Relationships: "Called to Be Neighbors and Witnesses"

Nations of the world are growing increasingly interdependent politically and economically, and the various world religious communities are also encountering one another in new ways. Religions of Asia and Africa are showing new life and power within their homelands and are spreading to other continents, creating new multireligious societies, especially in Western nations. New sects, cults, and ideologies merge and seek converts to their faith.

The emergence of these religiously diverse societies and the new dynamics in old religious communities have forced many faiths to reconsider how they relate to one another and to secular ideologies. There is danger that religious tensions will lead to oppression of religious minorities and curtailment of religious freedom with real potential for armed conflict. Worldwide problems of human suffering due to poverty, wars, and political oppression are so vast and pervasive that no one faith group can solve them, yet tensions between religious groups often prevent cooperation in solving these urgent human problems. As ancient religions demonstrate new life and power to speak to the deepest human concerns, questions are raised for Christians regarding their understanding of these faiths and regarding their claims to a global mission to all people.

What are the implications of this religiously diverse situation for Christian theology? What does it mean to be a faithful follower of and witness to Jesus Christ? Can we of different faiths live together as neighbors, or will diverse religious loyalties result in mutual antagonism and destruction? What are the resources of United Methodist Christians for building constructive relationships between persons of different faiths?

The United Methodist Church provides this statement as guidance to its members and congregations in facing these questions in their relations with persons of other faiths.

Called to Be Neighbors

For some Christians, it seems strange even to refer to "persons of other faiths." We are accustomed to calling them "non-Christians" or "nonbelievers." These attitudes have developed out of confidence in the ultimate truth of our own faith, and from ignorance of and insensitivity to other faiths, to the truth they contain, and to the profound meaning and purpose they give to the lives of people.

In conversation with a lawyer (cf. Luke 10:25), Jesus reminded him that his neighbor, the one to whom he should show love and compassion, included a stranger, a Samaritan. Today, our Lord's call to neighborliness (cf. Luke 10:27) includes the "strangers" of other faiths who have moved into our towns and cities. It is not just that historical events have forced us together. The Christian faith itself impels us to love our neighbors of other faiths and to seek to live in contact and mutually beneficial relationships—in community—with them.

What does it mean to be a neighbor? It means to meet other persons, to know them, to relate to them, to respect them, and to learn about their ways, which may be quite different from our own. It means to create a sense of community in our neighborhoods, towns, and cities and to make them places in which the unique customs of each group of people can be expressed and their values protected. It means to create social structures in which there is justice for all and in which everyone can participate in shaping their life together "in community." Each race or group of people is not only allowed to be who they are, but their way of life is valued and given full expression.

Christians distinguish several meanings of "community." One definition expresses their relationships as members of one another in the body of Christ, the church, a people called together by Christ, a "communion of saints" who look to the reign of God. A broader definition points to the relationship that is shared with others in the wider human community, where Christians are concerned for peace, justice, and reconciliation for all people. Other faiths also have their understanding of "community." The vision of a "worldwide community of communities" commends itself to many Christians as a way of being together with persons of different faiths in a pluralistic world. That suggests that we United Methodist Christians—not just individually, but corporately—are called to be neighbors with communities of other faiths (Buddhist, Jewish, Muslim, Hindu, and others) and to work with them to create a human community, a set of relationships between people at once interdependent and free, in which there is love, mutual respect, and justice.

Within this religiously diverse community, Christians, trusting in Jesus Christ for their salvation, are called to witness to him as Lord to all people (cf. Acts 1:8). We witness to our Lord through words that tell of his grace, through deeds of service and social change that demonstrate his love, and through our life together in the Christian community, exhibiting God's power to heal, reconcile, and unite.

As relationships with persons of other faiths deepen, Christians discover how often their witness has been unneighborly, how much we have talked and how little we have listened, and how often insensitive and unappreciative approaches have alienated sincere truth seekers and persons who already have strong faith commitments. We become aware that we frequently communicate attitudes of superiority regarding our own faith and inferiority toward that of others, and that in so doing, we perpetuate walls and hostilities between us as human beings that lessen the chances that our witness will be received.

As we United Methodist Christians reflect anew on our faith and seek guidance in our witness to and encounter with our new neighbors, we rediscover that God, who has acted in Jesus Christ for the salvation of the whole world, is also Creator of all humankind, the "one God and Father of all men, who is Lord of all, works through all, and is in all" (Ephesians 4:6, Today's English Version). The God to whom we point in Jesus Christ is the God who is at work in every society in ways we do not fully understand and who has not left himself without witness in any human community. Here, Christians confront a profound mystery, the awareness of God who is related to all creation and at work in the whole of it, and the experience of God who has acted redemptively for the whole creation in Jesus Christ. Christians witness to God in Jesus Christ in the confidence that here all people find salvation and in the trust that because of what we know of God in Jesus, God deals graciously and lovingly with all people everywhere.

Dialogue: A Way to Be Neighbors and Witnesses

Dialogue is the word that has come to signify a different approach to persons of other faiths, one that takes seriously both the call to witness and the command to love and be neighbors, and sees witnessing and neighborliness as interrelated activities. Rather than a one-sided address, dialogue combines witnessing with listening. It is the intentional engagement with persons of other faiths for mutual understanding, cooperation, and learning.

"Dialogue" may be as informal as a conversation in the marketplace, or as formal as the leader of one religious group explaining to others its philosophy or worship life. Dialogue is more than an individual or academic enterprise. It also involves groups or communities of people holding different faiths who reach out to one another. This community orientation gives a practical bent to interreligious dialogue.

In dialogue, one individual or group may seek a relationship with another in order to expose misunderstandings and stereotypes and to break down barriers that separate and create hostility and conflict. Ethnic or religious communities may approach one another in dialogue in order to resolve particular problems or to foster cooperation in dealing with a local, national, or even global situation of human suffering. At its deepest level, dialogue is both learning about and sharing our respective faiths. Each partner learns from the rich store of wisdom of the other, and each expresses his or her own deepest conviction in the faith that it has a truth worth sharing with the other.

Through dialogue with persons of other faiths, new insights are received regarding God's activity in the world today and the divine purpose for humankind as a whole, and the place of the Christian community within these purposes. It is also a common experience for Christians to feel the need to express their own faith with greater clarity. We can expect the Holy Spirit to make known new and different insights through our encounter with persons of other faiths.

Because the Jewish community is the largest community of another faith in the United States, Jews will be a major partner in dialogue for the United Methodists. Christians need Judaism, lest their faith in God be compromised and truncated in a rootless Christianity. For many United Methodists, especially those in Asia, Buddhists, Hindus, or Muslims will be their natural partners in dialogue. Dialogue with persons in these faith groups is increasingly important for United States Christians as well, since their numbers there are increasing. Muslims and Christians also share a close but often unrecognized relationship, since both have roots that go back to Abraham. In many nations, long histories of separation between Buddhist, Hindu, and Christian communities have yet to be bridged, while in the United States, many youth have been attracted to the deep spirituality of Buddhist and Hindu adherents. Dialogue offers the possibility of sharing mutually beneficial insights, as well as overcoming past hostilities.

Dialogue frequently has been misunderstood. Some see it as limited to the commonalities between persons and communities of different faiths. It is important to discern and explore those commonalities and to utilize them to strengthen relationships. But there is more! Dialogue offers to both partners the opportunity of enriching their own faith through the wisdom of the other. In the process, it helps overcome the deep mistrust, hatred, hostility, and conflict that characterize so many intercultural and interreligious relations. Each religious community asserts that its faith offers a way to resolve conflict in positive ways and has resources for building community among diverse peoples. Dialogue seeks to provide an environment that allows space for differences and to build on the positive affirmations of each faith and bring them into relationship with one another.

The only precondition for dialogue is a willingness to enter a relationship of mutual acceptance, openness, and respect. Effective dialogue requires that both partners have deep convictions about life, faith, and salvation. True dialogue requires that Christians *not* suspend their fundamental convictions concerning the truth of the gospel but enter into dialogue with personal commitment to Jesus Christ and with the desire to witness to that faith. Effective dialogue also requires that Christians be open to persons of other faiths, to their convictions about life, truth, and salvation, and to their witness, as others also feel called to witness to their faith and teachings about the meaning of life.

Dialogue: An Exchange of Witness

Is not this urge to witness an obstacle to interreligious dialogue? It often has been, but it need not be. Where there is listening as well as speaking, openness and respect as well as concern to influence, there is dialogue *and* witness. Indeed, dialogue at its most profound level is an *exchange of witness*. Participants share with one another their perceptions of the meaning of life, of ultimate reality, salvation, hope, and the resources of their faith for enabling community. In genuine "dialogue," we "witness and are witnessed to." The most effective dialogue takes place when both sides really do care that the other hears, understands, and receives their wisdom. Part of our witness is our openness to hearing the witness of the other.

Dialogue at these depths holds great promise. Long-cherished convictions may be modified by the encounter with others. Misunderstandings may be clarified, potential hostilities reconciled, and new insights regarding one's own faith may emerge in contrast to that of another. The depths of another's faith may be so disclosed that its power and attractiveness are experienced. Dialogue is a demanding process, requiring thorough understanding of one's own faith and clear articulation of it to the other person.

Dialogue is *not* a betrayal of witness. Dialogue and witness are wrongly placed in opposition to each other. They need each other. Dialogue creates relationships of mutual understanding, openness, and respect. Witness presses dialogue to the deepest convictions about life, death, and hope.

Many persons of other faiths are suspicious that dialogue is a new and more subtle tool for conversion. In some ways this is inevitable, since Christians do want others to learn of and receive the truth and grace we know in Jesus Christ. The difference between dialogue and other forms of witness is that it is a context for learning from the other the truth and wisdom of the other faith as well as sharing with the other the truth and wisdom of our own. We leave to the Holy Spirit the outcome of our mutual openness. Our concern is to be obedient to our own call to witness and to the imperative to be loving and neighborly to persons of other faiths. In dialogue, these deeply held truths encounter one another in witness and love, so that larger wisdom and larger understanding of truth may emerge that benefit all parties in the dialogue. As we exhibit courtesy, reverence, and respect and become neighbors, our fears of one another are allayed, and the Holy Spirit works within these relationships.

Neighbors and Witnesses

The command to love one's neighbors and the call to witness to Jesus Christ to all people are inseparably linked. The profound challenge that this represents for United Methodist Christians can be seen most sharply in the new religious movements that have arisen in recent years. These movements have become a source of concern for many Christians. Some groups seem to use methods that are manipulative and coercive. However, many people have found new vision, meaning, and hope in some of these new faiths. These new religious movements are very diverse, and they should not be lumped together indiscriminately, condemned, and dismissed. Neither should they automatically be embraced as valid expressions of human dignity and freedom.

Careful study and contact will enable Christians to distinguish those that are manipulative and coercive and those that are to be challenged for reasons of faith. Questions of basic human rights are raised both by tactics sometimes employed by some religious movements and by acts of opposition against them. In particular, enforced deprogramming represents a violation of the personality of individuals and their rights of free choice. The question of what means are justified in trying to win back persons who have joined cults is a difficult one, and one to which Christians will respond differently. Where children of church members are involved, the parents are in special need of pastoral counseling and support. The best preparation for meeting these groups is the development within families and through the educational program of the Church of a deeper understanding of and commitment to Jesus Christ and his claims, especially the costliness of following our "suffering servant" Lord. This commitment is deepened through the experience of acceptance and personal relationship within the fellowship of the Christian community.

As we take seriously this calling to be witnesses and neighbors to people of all faiths, old and new, we become aware of the biblical caution not to bear false witness (cf. Matthew 19:18) and the admonition to live at peace with all people (cf. Hebrews 12:14). How are we to avoid bearing false witness unless we know our neighbors and understand their faith commitments? How can one truly love a neighbor and hold back what to Christians is the greatest of all gifts—God becoming present to people in Jesus Christ? How can we live peacefully together unless we are willing to be neighborly? How can we say we love our neighbor if we are unwilling to be attentive to the message and the gifts that God has given him or her? Love of neighbor and witness to Christ are the two primary attitudes of United Methodist Christians in their relationship with persons of other faiths. And when we become this kind of neighbor, we discover that God has given us another gift—people of different faiths.

Guidelines for Interreligious Relationships

The following guidelines will assist United Methodists to be faithful to their call to witness and to the call to be neighbors with persons of other faiths.

1. *Discover and find out about the persons of other faiths in your town or city and educate your congregation about them.*

(a) Plan experiences that bring Christians into contact with persons of other faiths. Whenever possible, initiate these experiences ecumenically. In the absence of cooperative efforts to develop relationships and explore tensions and difficulties, United Methodist initiative is encouraged.

(b) Visit the services and meeting places of other faiths, but respect their sacred times and places and do not treat them as "tourist" attractions.

(c) Study the new religious movements carefully and develop attitudes of courtesy toward them.

Support efforts in the community to ensure that their human rights are not violated. Seek assistance both in cases where efforts are being made to ensure the human rights of members of a group by testing their freedom to leave it and in developing perspectives on Christian witness to these new religious movements.

2. *Initiate dialogues with other faith communities.*

(a) Seek relationships with Jews, Muslims, Buddhists, and Hindus and their respective organizations. Initiate conversations, programs, and dialogues leading to understanding of each faith, appreciation of their particular gifts, discovery of commonalities and differences, and areas of mutual cooperation.

(b) With the Jewish community, seek an awareness of both our common roots and the tragic interlocking of our histories, sensitivity to anti-Semitism among Christians, and an understanding of the significance of the Holocaust and the importance of Israel for Jews.

(c) With the Muslim community, explore the negative stereotypes that perpetuate misunderstanding and continue to hinder the establishment of positive relationships, and seek an understanding of the role of the Islamic faith in various Middle Eastern societies.

(d) With the Buddhist and Hindu communities, explore their spiritual practices and understandings, which have attracted many people in the West.

Prepare for dialogue through reflection on the following:

(1) Clarity regarding your understanding of and commitment to your own faith is absolutely essential.

(2) Each partner must believe that the other is speaking in good faith.

(3) Each partner must strive for a clear understanding of the faith of the other and be willing to interpret it in its best light rather than its worst.

(4) Each partner must forthrightly face the issues that cause separation as well as those that create unity.

3. *Share in common enterprises with persons of other faiths in practical ways.*

(a) Work together to resolve economic, social, cultural, and political problems in the community. Together, become sensitive to infringements of the human rights of groups within the community and threats to their cultural values and heritage, and initiate steps to protect them.

(b) Jointly plan community celebrations with an interreligious perspective.

(c) Participate in interreligious associations.

(d) Seek to generate interreligious educational efforts in the community. This could include enlisting the aid of school authorities in the examination of texts used in schools to see that the various religious groups are depicted fairly and accurately. Other educational ventures might include providing courses in adult schools and for people who are planning trips abroad or developing special programs for media such as television and radio to reach a wider audience.

4. *Prepare carefully before sharing in celebrations, rituals, worship, and meditation with persons of other faiths.*

It will not be possible for Christians to participate fully in another faith's rituals and worship, nor should they expect it. However, it is appropriate, where invited, to share in such occasions. Some may wish to share in joint prayer services. On such occasions, care should be taken not to relativize all religious symbols and practices to make religious differences unimportant. It is unwise to juxtapose symbols of different religions. Each partner must approach such occasions out of the integrity of his or her own faith.

Intent

The intent in developing interreligious relationships is not to amalgamate all faiths into one religion. We Christians have no interest in such syncretism. To engage in interreligious dialogue is not to say that any religion is all right, just as long as you have one. Far from requiring a lessening of commitment to Christ, effective dialogue is only possible when one's own faith is strong.

We Christians are seeking to be neighbors with persons of other faiths whose religious commitments are different from our own and to engage one another about the deepest convictions of our lives. In our assurance of and trust in God's grace in Jesus Christ, we open ourselves to dialogue and engagement with persons of other faiths and to other Christians whose understandings may be different from our own.

This interreligious engagement challenges United Methodist Christians to think in new ways about our life in the broader human community, about our mission, our evangelism, our service, and our life together within the Christian church. We seek to promote peace and harmony with persons of other faiths in our various towns, cities, and neighborhoods.

Yet we do not hide our differences, nor avoid conflicts, but seek to make them constructive. In each place we share our lives with one another, we witness and are witnessed to, we invite others into the Christian community, and we are invited into theirs. Our prayer is that the lives of all in each place will be enriched by the differences of others, that a new sense of community may emerge, and that others may receive the gift of God in Christ, while we receive the gifts that have been given them.

ADOPTED 1980

See Social Principles, ¶ 66*B;* "Our Muslim Neighbors"; "Building New Bridges in Hope."

Healing the Wounds of Genocidal Acts Toward Native American and African American People

The General Conference shall direct the General Board of Church and Society and the General Commission on Religion and Race to work with governmental and other secular and religious agencies to enhance or develop museums that acknowledge acts of genocide toward Native Americans and African Americans and other racial or ethnic groups to commemorate the work by people of all colors to redress these wrongs.

ADOPTED 1996

See Social Principles, ¶ 66*A;* "A Charter for Racial Justice Policies in an Interdependent Global Community."

Health for All by the Year 2000

WHEREAS, The United Methodist Church is global in its outreach and has a strong commitment to work with other churches and secular organizations that are concerned about the health of the world's people; and

WHEREAS, The United Methodist Church has had a long history of medical missions, training of health personnel, support of health facilities, involvement of local churches in health education and direct service programs; and

WHEREAS, The United Methodist Church affirms health as a condition of physical, mental, social, and spiritual well-being to be desired and worked for by all persons; and that all persons are entitled to basic health care, while at the same time having a responsibility to care for their own health and to protect the health of others; and

WHEREAS, it is recognized that more than anything else, people's health is affected by the circumstances of their lives, including living and environmental conditions, education and employment opportunities, resources and lifestyle, political and socioeconomic realities, spiritual nurture, and supportive relationships; and

WHEREAS, it has been a part of the prophetic, redemptive, and healing ministry of The United Methodist Church to identify always with those persons whose needs are not being met; to focus clearly on those factors that impede individuals and communities in their search for health and wholeness; and to point to what must be done if people are to be freed from those powers and practices that stand in the way of healthy development—physically, mentally, socially, and spiritually; and

WHEREAS, the member states of the World Health Organization, including the United States, affirmed in 1977 at the thirtieth World Health Assembly that one of the most important social goals of the world community in the coming decades should be the attainment by all people of the world by the year 2000 of a level of health that will permit them to lead a socially and economically productive life; and

WHEREAS, the Director General of the World Health Organization has affirmed that cooperation between sectors of society, with an emphasis on religious as well as secular bodies, is essential toward the goal of health for all by the year 2000; and

WHEREAS, The United Methodist Church, through its seven central conferences, 73 annual conferences, 38,000 local churches, 9,500,000 members, and its involvement with health ministries around the world, has a unique opportunity to protect and promote health; minister with persons who have illnesses of body, mind, and/or spirit; create opportunities for individuals and communities to participate in determining local health priorities and methods for delivery of needed services, identifying unmet needs, and advocating that those needs be met; and address those political, economic, and social factors that contribute to ill health and the unequal distribution of those opportunities, goods, and services that are essential to attaining and maintaining health;

Therefore, be it resolved, that The United Methodist Church:

1. *Joins* with the international community in affirming health for all by the year 2000 as one of the most important social goals of the twentieth century;

2. *Asks* its annual conferences, central conferences, their related institutions, local churches, and all church members to be informed about the goal of health for all by the year 2000, and to work with other groups to develop means of promoting and protecting health, giving particular attention wherever possible to the needs of mothers and infants; children, youth, and families; older persons; people with disabilities; and immigrants and refugees, being aware of how ageism,

sexism, racism, handicappism, poverty, and other forms of discrimination impede persons and communities in their achievement of health and wholeness;

3. *Encourages* each annual conference and central conference to focus on health for all by the year 2000 through its health and welfare unit or other most appropriate unit; and

4. *Assigns* responsibility to the Health and Welfare Ministries Program Department of the General Board of Global Ministries to develop and make available interpretive material about health for all by the year 2000 and to suggest ways in which the various units of The United Methodist Church can be involved in this goal.

ADOPTED 1984

See Social Principles, ¶ 66Q; "Health and Wholeness"; "Health in Mind and Body"; "Universal Access to Health Care in the U.S. and Related Territories."

Health in Mind and Body

Mental health is intimately linked with the fundamental purpose of the church—the love of God, others, and self. Mental, physical, social, emotional, and spiritual health are intricately interwoven. How persons think about themselves, about life, and about the future has an impact on other areas of health. A healthy mind is necessary to get the most out of living. Positive mental health results in constructive activities and enables persons to use both good and bad experiences as opportunities for personal growth.

These concepts are consistent with biblical themes in which God reassures the people of God to have faith and hope, and not to fear. Wisdom literature refers again and again to the grounding of integrity and character in wisdom, insight, and a heart of purity (Job 42:1-6; Psalm 51:6-12; Proverbs 4:7; 28:6). In the New Testament, Jesus reshapes these traditions to the teaching that real obedience to God begins in the heart (Matthew 5:8, 21-32; 15:1-20). Paul, too, expresses his confident hope in the face of suffering: "We are troubled on every side yet not distressed; we are perplexed, but not in despair" (2 Corinthians 4:8, King James Version).

There are clear indications and opportunities for the Church to harness and use its worship, preaching, church school, group life, and evangelism as strategic educative, preventive, and therapeutic resources to bring hope and healing. The 1990 World Summit on Children addressed the fact that the world's children are living in conditions without hope. The National Institute on Mental Health, in its annual report, shared that "in the last three decades mood disorders will afflict more than 20 million Americans at some point in their lifetime."

I. Reasons for Actions

Mental health and those factors that affect it can be seen in global, national, community, and individual contexts.

A. Children and youth across the world suffer from war, regional conflicts, and national resources spent on the military rather than on human services such as education, housing, clean air and water, and health care. Children are often exploited for economic gain. As a result, many see the world as hostile and violent. They respond out of fear, anxiety, anger, and aggression.

B. National daily news reports about killings, family violence, gang violence, suicide, racial attacks, child abuse and neglect, and random street shootings all contribute to individuals' and communities' feeling insecure, anxious, and afraid.

C. The changing forms of the family in the United States—from an extended, close-knit one to a two-parent nuclear one to an ever-increasingly younger, female-headed single-parent family—have left children and adults with fewer supportive, nurturing family members. Families are facing more stressful and episodic crises than previous generations. Some of these stresses are a result of inadequate wages to support families and the lack of health insurance, all of which affect the overall emotional well-being of families.

D. Substance abuse has become a national crisis, especially the use of crack cocaine and its related violence. Children born to parents who abuse drugs are increasing in number, and too many children no longer feel safe or secure at home, in school, or within the community. Families and communities are becoming dysfunctional units because of this crisis.

E. People of color face the ordinary demands of life in addition to the vicissitudes of racism, sexism, and classism. The constant emotional and psychic energies used to thwart daily social pressures of inequality prevent people of color from reaching their full potential. The increasing incidence of racial violence in neighborhoods adds to the emotional toll of alienation, isolation, and lack of acceptance of people of color in God's global community.

F. Clergy also are under stress. Today's clergy are expected to meet their traditional duties of pastoral care, teaching, preaching, and worship while simultaneously addressing the daily adversities that affect members of their congregations and communities. Ministry is increasingly more complex. The personal and vocational expectations and demands of ministry may drain clergy, their families, and congregations of healthy coping skills.

G. Laity in the life of the Church may find themselves alone and without emotional support as they cope with the loss of a loved one because of suicide, murder, or traumatic circumstances such as terrorism; as their lives are touched by AIDS; as they care for the chronically ill parent or child; as they are confronted with physical, sexual, and emotional abuse; and as they face unemployment and other life-shattering experiences.

II. Policy Statement

The Church's concern for mental health lies at the center of its mission to enable persons to develop and maintain peace and strength of mind.

We affirm the need for the Church to avoid policies that harm mental health, such as those emphasizing status and power rather than Christlike service to God in daily vocation. We affirm the need for the Church to receive all persons as children of God, so that none are considered more holy than others. Likewise, we affirm the need for the Church to consider the effect on human dignity of every sermon that is preached, every lesson that is taught, and every program that is planned and developed. We affirm the development of mental health ministries at all levels of the Church through seminars, model sharing, skill-building opportunities, and direct services that bring healing and wholeness.

III. Action

· The Christian faith encourages people to become whole with sound minds. This faith enables persons to care for their physical bodies, to live in harmony with the environment, and to face adversities with balance. It urges one to care about one's mental outlook toward life, living in peace and acceptance of oneself, with respect, fair play, justice, and acceptance of others as children of God.

• We urge all United Methodists to use the resources of the Church to affirm positive mental health as an essential part of the gospel of Jesus

Christ and to make this affirmation a reality by planning appropriate programs and events through the local church's health and welfare ministries representative.

• We urge local churches to be in mission within the congregation and community through support groups, advocacy, public policy education, information sharing, and direct-service ministries with individuals and families.

• We urge United Methodist-related institutions of higher education to make mental health a part of the educational process by shaping a vision of human community that is inclusive of all persons, hopeful about the future, and confident of God's sustaining presence through holding convocations and special educational events and including in the curriculum the concept of cultural diversity, the responsibility of Christians to participate in public life, and ethical practices stemming from the Christian belief that material resources are to be used in service to alleviate human suffering.

• We urge United Methodist schools of theology to continue to develop practical theology that instills in students the need for the mental health aspects of preaching, pastoral care, administration, and Church polity. Seminary education should provide opportunities for prospective clergy to become involved in multidisciplinary settings and with challenges from other professionals to help congregations develop and maintain good mental health.

We ask the General Board of Global Ministries to:

• Develop models for mental health that relate to the local church;

• Provide research on mental health to other general agencies for their work on policy development, curriculum development, and programs;

• Provide to annual conferences specific plans on how conferences can develop programs that develop and promote good mental health within congregations and communities; and

• Develop resources for local churches' and annual conferences' health and welfare representatives of specific actions they can take that will affirm good mental health.

ADOPTED 1992

See Social Principles, ¶ 66Q; "Health and Wholeness"; "Health for All by the Year 2000"; "Ministries in Mental Illness"; "Universal Access to Health Care in the U.S. and Related Territories."

273

Health and Wholeness

Introduction

All human beings have been created in the image of God and are called to the abundant life. In the biblical story of the woman with the hemorrhage, Jesus provides an example of his healing ministry that includes the spiritual as well as the physical status of the person.

> And behold, a woman who had suffered from a hemorrhage for twelve years came up behind him and touched the fringe of his garment; for she said to herself, "If I only touch his garment, I shall be made well." Jesus turned, and seeing her he said, "Take heart, daughter; your faith has made you well." And instantly the woman was made well.
> (Matthew 9:20-22, Revised Standard Version)

The United Methodist Church, as an entity, believes that its mission is to continue the redemptive ministry of Christ, including teaching, preaching, and healing. Christ's healing was not peripheral but central in his ministry. The Church, therefore, understands itself as called by the Lord to the holistic ministry of healing: spiritual, mental and emotional, and physical.

Health in this sense is something beyond, but not exclusive of, biological well-being. In this view, health care is inadequate when it fixes its attention solely on the body and its physiological functions, as is any religion that focuses its interest entirely on the spirit. Taking the Gospel mandates seriously, United Methodists are called to work toward a healthy society of whole persons. Part of our task is to enable people to care for themselves and to take responsibility for their own health. Another part of our task is to ensure that people who are ill, whether from illness of spirit, mind, or body, are not turned aside or ignored but are given care that allows them to live a full life. We see this task as demanding concern for spiritual, political, ethical, economic, social, and medical decisions that maintain the highest concern for the condition of society, the environment, and the total life of each person.

Human suffering is caused by a variety of factors—the environmental, social, and personal factors mentioned, as well as others that remain unknown to us.

Environmental Factors. Clean air, pure water, effective sanitary systems for the disposal of wastes, nutritious foods, adequate housing, and hazard-free workplaces are essential to health. The best medical system cannot preserve or maintain health when the environment is disease-producing.

274

Social Factors. Inadequate education, poverty, unemployment, lack of access to food, stress-producing conditions, and social pressures reinforced by marketing and advertising strategies that encourage the use of tobacco, alcohol, and other drugs are detrimental to good health.

Personal Habits. Overeating or eating non-nutritious foods, substance abuse (including alcohol, tobacco, barbiturates, sedatives, and so forth) are clearly destructive of health. Failure to exercise or to rest and relax adequately are also injurious to health.

Although medical care represents a very important part of health care, it does not include the whole. More medical care does not always equal better health.

Medical care in much of the world has evolved too much as disease care rather than health care. Disease prevention, public health programs, and health education appropriate to every age level and social setting are needed globally. Services should be provided in a compassionate and skillful manner on the basis of need, without discrimination as to economic status, mental or physical disability, race, color, religion, sex, age, national origin, or language.

A Just Health System

Within a just society, every person has a right to:

1. basic health services that are accessible and affordable in each geographic and cultural setting;

2. an environment that promotes health;

3. active involvement in the formulation of health-care activities that meet local needs and priorities;

4. information about his or her illness, and to be an active participant in treatment and rehabilitation;

5. receive compassionate and skilled care;

6. a health-care system sensitive to cultural needs; and

7. access to funding sources where necessary for basic health services.

Health Insurance

For all persons to have adequate access to needed health-care services, public financing must be a significant part of an overall health insurance plan. Public funding is necessary to pay for insuring those who cannot pay part or all of the necessary premiums required.

Health Maintenance

Many health problems and illnesses are preventable if we accept the fact that health maintenance requires understanding of the unity of the human body, mind, and spirit. The whole person needs proper nutrition, exercise, the challenge to learn and grow, and an acknowledgement that this is a lifelong process. We recognize that these needs are difficult to meet when environmental factors contribute to ill health. But we must acknowledge the fact that we have separated spiritual health from physical health. In Western Protestant interpretation of health and healing, the union of the body and spirit are often dismissed. Cultures that respect and revere that union are often disregarded or looked upon in a condescending manner. The early church did not make these distinctions, nor did Jesus in his healing ministry. We must, if we are to obtain good health, unite the body and spirit in our thinking and actions.

Therefore, as Christians we accept responsibility for modeling this holistic, preventive style of health maintenance. We commit ourselves to examining the value systems at work in our society as they impact the health of our people and to working for programs and policies that enable people to breathe clean air, drink clean water, eat wholesome food, and have access to adequate education and freedom that enable mind and spirit to develop.

Medical Services

We support the following principles of access to health services:

1. In a just society, all people are entitled to basic maintenance and health-care services. We reject as contrary to our understanding of the Gospel the notion of differing standards of health care for various segments of the population;

2. Health care should be comprehensive, including preventive, therapeutic, and rehabilitative services;

3. Religious and other appropriate forms of counseling should be available to all patients and families when they are called upon to make difficult medical choices, so that responsible decisions, within the context of the Christian faith, may be made concerning organ transplants, use of extreme measures to prolong life, abortion, sterilization, genetic counseling, institutionalization, and death with dignity;

4. We encourage development of community support systems that permit alternatives to institutional care for such groups as the aging, the terminally ill and mentally ill, and other persons with special needs;

5. Professional health-care personnel should be recruited and appropriately educated to meet the health-care needs of all persons. Especially urgent is the need for physicians trained in geriatric medicine. Special priorities should be established to secure among the professional group at least proportional representation of women and minorities who are now seriously underrepresented;

6. In areas where medical services are not available or are undersupplied, we urge private or public funding to provide the full range of needed services. To meet these goals, we recommend the reallocation of funds from armaments to human services, both nationally and internationally (Social Principles, ¶ 69C);

7. Regional planning processes should coordinate the services rendered by all health-care institutions, including those funded by governments, to create a more effective system of health services in every area. Priorities should be established for the provision of health services, such as preventive care, mental-health services, home care, and health education;

8. Corrective measures should be taken where there is maldistribution or unavailability of hospital beds, intermediate care and nursing home care, home-delivered care, neighborhood health centers, community mental-health centers, and emergency care networks;

9. We encourage medical education for laypersons that will enable them to effectively evaluate medical care they need and are receiving; and

10. We support the medical community in its effort to uphold ethical standards and to promote quality assurance.

Health and Wholeness Ministry

As United Methodists, we are called to a ministry of health and wholeness. Therefore, we challenge our membership to:

1. Make health concerns a priority in the Church, with special emphases that include but are not limited to women's health concerns; appropriate, unbiased, informed diagnosis and treatment of older adults; preventive care (including health education); special health concerns and needs of children and youth; and establishment of networks for information sharing and action suggestions;

2. Support the provision of direct-health services where needed and to provide, as we are able, such services in hospitals and homes, clinics, and health centers;

3. Accept responsibility for educating and motivating members to follow a healthy lifestyle reflecting our affirmation of life as God's gift;

4. Become actively involved at all levels in the development of support systems for health care in the community, including: dependent care (respite and twenty-four-hour care, in-home and short-term out-of-home care), meals, programs for women in crisis, halfway houses, support systems for independent living, and family support systems;

5. Become advocates for a healthful environment; accessible, affordable health care; continued public support for health care of persons unable to provide for themselves; continued support for health-related research; and provision of church facilities to enable health-related ministries;

6. Become involved in a search for Christian understanding of health, healing, and wholeness and the dimensions of spiritual healing in our congregations and seminaries;

7. Encourage colleges, universities, hospitals, and seminaries related to The United Methodist Church connectional units to gain an added awareness of health issues and the need for recruitment and education of persons for health-related ministries who would approach such ministries out of a Christian understanding and commitment; and

8. Support public policies and programs that will ensure comprehensive health-care services of high quality to all persons on the principle of equal access.

In the United States, we affirm the findings of the president's Committee on Medical Ethics of 1983. While noting the importance of cost containment, the committee wrote: "Measures designed to contain health care costs that exacerbate existing inadequacies or impede the achievement of equity are unacceptable from a moral standpoint."

A positive response to these challenges within the Christian context will help assure to all persons an abundant mental, emotional, and spiritual life.

ADOPTED 1984

See Social Principles, ¶ 66Q; "Health for All by the Year 2000"; "Health in Mind and Body"; "Universal Access to Health Care in the U.S. and Related Territories."

Higher Education Training and Scholarships

WHEREAS, The United Methodist Church supports the public education system in America and realizes that in an ever-changing society, "Excellence in Education" can be achieved with proper nourishing; and

WHEREAS, church, community, and federal government involvement is imperative if the current trend in public education is to be reversed; and

WHEREAS, The United Methodist Church believes that every person has a right to an education and that it is society's responsibility to enable every person to obtain this right; and

WHEREAS, The United Methodist Church believes in universal public education and supports public educational institutions; and

WHEREAS, individuals have the right and freedom to inquire, discuss, and teach, regulated by self-discipline of scholarship and good judgment;

Therefore, be it resolved, that the General Conference:

1. Encourages all local churches to establish learning enrichment centers with tutors who can provide supplementary instruction for students to ensure academic excellence according to each one's potential;

2. Supports the training and recruitment of qualified ethnic minority teachers who will serve as positive role models for ethnic minority students; and

3. Directs the General Board of Higher Education and Ministry to seek additional funding for scholarships for ethnic minority persons.

ADOPTED 1992

See Social Principles, ¶ 66A; "A Charter for Racial Justice Policies in an Interdependent Global Community."

History of Blacks in The United Methodist Church

WHEREAS, an examination and assessment of the Methodist legacy in America reveals that Black persons and their contributions continue to receive inadequate credits; and

WHEREAS, at the present time there are more written resources available about Blacks in the history of Methodism; and

WHEREAS, literature about Black persons in the Methodist history and/or literature written from the perspective of the Black ethos is perceived as resources primarily for Black persons; and

WHEREAS, an important element in the interrelationship of the different groups within the Church family is to respect thoroughly and understand the uniqueness and contributions of Black persons in the evolving history of Methodism and the U.S.A.;

Therefore, be it resolved, that the General Commission on Archives and History and The United Methodist Publishing House, in joint consultation with the General Commission on Religion and Race, determine the most effective means to identify additional Black literary and historical records that have not been acknowledged and/or published; promote the use of these and other such resources among whites and other racial and ethnic minorities; and encourage training sessions led by Blacks using these resources that acknowledge the contributions of Black persons to the legacy and heritage of Methodism in the United States of America and the world.

ADOPTED 1992

See Social Principles, ¶ 66A; "History of Racial/Ethnic United Methodists."

History of Racial/Ethnic United Methodists

WHEREAS, persons of Pacific Island, Asian, African, Hispanic, and Native American descent have made significant contributions to the history of The United Methodist Church and its predecessors; and

WHEREAS, these contributions have received scant attention and acknowledgement by the Church and its historians; and

WHEREAS, this lack has begun to be addressed with the publication in 1991 of four histories of Asian Americans, African Americans, Native Americans, and Hispanic Americans within the United Methodist tradition and with four accompanying bibliographies;

Therefore, be it resolved, that the General Commission on Archives and History commends these histories and bibliographies to the United Methodist denomination and urges that archivists and historians at all levels of the Church continue to collect, document, research, and disseminate sources and publications of racial and ethnic persons within United Methodism.

ADOPTED 1992

See Social Principles, ¶ 66A; "Elimination of Racism in The United Methodist Church."

Holy Boldness: A National Plan for Urban Ministry

WHEREAS, change is inevitable but transformation is optional. As United Methodists, our biblical and Wesleyan heritage calls us to transform urban churches and communities with *holy boldness*. We are called to provide prophetic vision for the future as well as identify goals and strategies to mobilize resources and people for the transformation of urban congregations and communities. A new comprehensive urban-ministry plan called *Holy Boldness* was developed for this purpose.

The Holy Boldness National Urban Ministry Plan was developed by more than 1,000 United Methodists representing urban, suburban, and rural communities and congregations, as well as annual conferences and national leadership. The plan sets forth a vision, goal areas, and outcomes to organize and resource congregations and church-based community organizations for transforming urban congregations and communities through the gospel of Jesus Christ.

It is a grassroots movement that will empower congregations and church-based organizations to develop local strategies for urban ministry. The objective is not to create new national structures or priorities, but to work within present structures and existing resources to leverage new opportunities for urban ministry.

Therefore, be it resolved, that The United Methodist Church:

1. Commend the ministry of urban churches and church-based organizations that share the gospel of Jesus Christ through prophetic vision and proclaiming God's Word;

2. Urge congregations and church-based organizations to become covenanting sponsors of the Holy Boldness Urban Ministry Plan and work toward developing and carrying out local strategies that address Holy Boldness goal areas: contextual urban theology, urban evangelism, leadership development, community economic development, eradication of racism, strengthening multicultural collaboration, and health and healing;

3. Mandate the general Church agencies' staff having responsibility for urban concerns and/or the general secretary's designee(s) from Religion and Race, Discipleship, Global Ministries, Communications, Higher Education and Ministry, Council on Ministries, and Church and Society, and a representative from the Council of Bishops to work together to develop collaborative agency strategies for resourcing as well as to review existing resources that may be channeled for the Holy Boldness Urban Ministry Plan;

4. Charge the designated representative staff of the previously mentioned general Church agencies to work with the National Urban Strategy Council to report to the 2000 General Conference on the effectiveness of the Holy Boldness Urban Ministry Plan's ability to: (a) organize and mobilize congregations and church-based organizations to accomplish local church and community transformation, and (b) evaluate how well the general Church agencies collaborated to resource and enable the plan to be carried out in local urban contexts; and

5. Affirm the Holy Boldness effort and plan as a movement and plan for United Methodist urban ministry.

Holy Boldness: A National Urban Ministry Plan

Change is inevitable, but transformation is optional. As The United Methodist Church, we have the opportunity to transform urban churches and communities with *holy boldness*. The Holy Boldness plan is not a perfect plan, but a dynamic tool for organizing and mobilizing people for urban transformation. It recognizes that there are regional and local differences and invites churches and church-based community organizations to develop local strategies to carry out the goals.

The material in the Urban Ministry Plan was identified by the more than 650 participants at the 1995 National Urban Ministry Convocation. The material developed by the participants over a three-day period was further refined through more than fifty focus groups across the country. The goal of the process and plan is to provide a vision for the future, identify areas of focus, and organize and mobilize resources and people to carry out the plan. Ultimately, the Holy Boldness plan will be effective if local churches and church-related community organizations and agencies develop strategies and carry out the agreed-upon goals. It is also critical for the whole Church (congregations in and outside urban areas, annual conferences, and general Church agencies) to work in collaboration to support those working locally to transform urban congregations and communities.

Goal Areas

The goal areas identified for this plan were determined through a national survey of laity, pastors, church-related community-organization staff, conference staff, and bishops. The plan does not claim to meet every urban church and community need, but it is a first step toward

organizing and mobilizing United Methodists to work locally on goals
for church and community transformation. The goal areas are:
1. Urban theology;
2. Evangelism and congregational development;
3. Eradication of racism;
4. Strengthening of multicultural relationships;
5. Leadership development;
6. Community economic development; and
7. Health and healing.

Asset-Based

While there are serious urban problems inside and outside the
Church, transformation is possible through the resources and strengths
of the Church and community. The Holy Boldness plan calls for
churches and communities to identify their assets and build on these
assets as people are mobilized for transformation. *Some* of the assets
identified by the 650 planners who helped to prepare this document
are:
1. God's transforming power through Jesus Christ;
2. The local church and church-based community organizations;
3. The people of our churches and cities who represent a wide variety
of racial and ethnic traditions and have the talents for transformation;
4. United Methodist general agencies and schools; and
5. Ecumenical and interfaith partners.

Congregation-Based

As a Church, we are blessed with congregations, church-related
community organizations, and institutions that seek to transform urban
communities. All are important to the life of urban communities and
will be challenged to work toward the goals of the Urban Plan. The plan
calls for a significant focus on local urban congregations that, because
they are strategically located, have the opportunity to share God's love
in word and deed and are in need of development. If the Church is to
transform communities, the local church is critical.

Collaborative Effort

Urban transformation will require a collaborative effort by local
churches working in cooperation with other denominations, commu-

nity organizations, businesses, and governmental institutions. Collaboration will need to occur beyond city limits by collaborating with rural churches that share similar problems and with suburban churches that have committed volunteers and resources and relational roots in urban neighborhoods, all which strengthen ministry.

Collaboration will also need to occur at the national level. General Church agencies will need to work together to identify common strategies that they can mutually accomplish. The national strategies should link with local strategies and needs. National collaboration must also involve other ecumenical and interfaith bodies and national urban resources.

Covenant-Inspired

The Urban Plan invites people, churches, church-based community organizations, and church agencies to covenant to work toward the established goals. Churches and organizations will review the plan and make a commitment to work toward the goals in their setting. Covenanting churches and groups will become part of a nationwide network for support, idea development, and resourcing. Three thousand churches and church-related organizations/agencies will be invited to covenant to work toward the plan's goals.

Local Strategies

This plan does not identify how the goals will be implemented. It is believed that strategies and action plans for these goals are best developed at the local level and by others who commit to carry out the strategies.

Holy Boldness

Churches and church-related community organizations are encouraged to take *authority and responsibility* in being *bold* and *holy* to accomplish the Urban Ministry Plan goals. This will require local strategies and local ownership. With God's help, transformation of urban congregations and communities is possible.

United Methodist Urban Ministry Vision

We will become a Church that practices "holy boldness" in urban areas as evidenced by the Church:

1. Risking all we have to share God's transforming love as experienced through Jesus Christ in both word and deed;

2. Ministering with and among the poor;

3. Transforming and developing urban congregations;

4. Celebrating and honoring diversity within the congregation, church-related organizations, agencies, and the community;

5. Living and proclaiming God's justice and equality in every situation without fear of being isolated and ridiculed;

6. Being an agent for healing in the midst of broken lives and communities; and

7. Effectively developing the spiritual, social, and physical well-being of individuals and communities.

Goals

Urban Theology:

1. Teach within churches and church-related organizations, and be a living example in the community that urban ministry is based in the person, ministry, and stories of Jesus Christ, who provided an example of meeting the physical needs of others and proclaiming the saving power of God;

2. Develop an urban academy with a strong urban theology component, as well as practical components for carrying out our theology in the world through community development, eliminating racism, developing multicultural collaboration, urban evangelism, and leadership development; and

3. Encourage congregations to model a theology that serves all people and focuses on the poor and marginalized.

Urban Theology Outcomes Anticipated by the Year 2000:

1. An urban theology academy will train and re-train 400 people for urban ministry who will resource other churches for urban ministry;

2. Fifty United Methodist congregations and congregations from other denominations who effectively minister to the poor and marginalized will be identified as models for other urban churches;

3. Seventy congregations (at least one in each annual conference) will covenant to focus their ministry with the poor and marginalized and incorporate the worshiping congregation;

4. A video and discussion guide will be produced and utilized in 500 urban churches to help congregations explore and begin to identify God's vision for their church and community; and

5. Three thousand churches will covenant to base their ministry in the life and teaching of Jesus Christ and to develop ministries that respond to urban spiritual, physical, and social needs.

Urban Evangelism and Congregational Development:

1. Develop the necessary support and systems to enable longer pastoral appointments;

2. Design resources and training to help congregations communicate the gospel of Jesus Christ effectively in a diverse and changing urban environment;

3. Use existing resources and develop new resources for urban congregational Bible study to deepen people's faith and challenge them to live the gospel;

4. Develop a prayer network that links churches in partnerships (this can include urban churches with other urban, rural, or suburban churches); and

5. Increase the number of worshipers in urban congregations through evangelism and outreach to the neighborhood in which the church is located and other community networks.

Urban Evangelism and Congregational Development Outcomes
Anticipated by the Year 2000:

1. A printed resource will be developed to assist bishops/district superintendents with ideas for supporting urban pastors;

2. Fifty bishops/district superintendents will covenant to use the resource with urban pastors;

3. Five hundred urban congregations will covenant to explore and identify strategies for urban evangelism and congregational development;

4. One thousand congregations and church-based community organizations will develop at least one new Bible study that will disciple people in the faith and strengthen people to work in the community;

5. Five hundred congregations will be linked in a prayer network; and

6. The development of a voluntary clergy salary-equalization program will be explored.

Eradicating Racism and Other Forms of Oppression:

1. Organize a local and national support system for those willing to risk pursuing the vision and agenda of eliminating racism;

2. Highlight model programs that are challenging and working toward eradicating racism and other forms of oppression in the congregation and the community so that other congregations can develop similar efforts; and

3. Be sensitive to racism in all urban training experiences.

Eradicating Racism Outcomes Anticipated by the Year 2000:

1. Identify and link 500 people and churches/organizations;

2. Identify and produce a resource guide on twenty effective models that challenge racism in churches and communities and use the resource in 200 churches; and

3. Design a resource that will help address racism in urban training sessions and distribute to 400 urban trainers.

Developing and Strengthening Multicultural Collaboration:

1. Develop the resources for, and encourage congregations to participate in, cultural immersion and cross-cultural experiences; and

2. Design new and use existing church resources for the arts, music, worship, and Bible study that model, encourage, and strengthen multiculturalism.

Developing and Strengthening Multicultural Collaboration Outcomes Anticipated by the Year 2000:

1. Identify/develop ten models and supporting resources for ministry in cross-cultural experiences. At least two of the models will be youth-focused. The models and supporting resources will be utilized in 200 churches.

2. Solicit 1,000 churches to participate in cross-cultural experiences; and

3. Invite the 1,000 covenanting churches to commit to an intentional program that broadens multicultural understanding and enables congregations to collaborate multiculturally.

Leadership Development:

1. Extend the Hispanic Plan model of lay missioner for urban leadership;

2. Empower laity and clergy for ministry and mission by freeing them from unnecessary bureaucracy within the Church;

3. Assertively train lay and clergy leadership for urban ministry, including advocating and effecting change in public and private life; and

4. Intentionally recruit more clergy and laity for urban ministry and offer them opportunities to be involved in hands-on experiences.

Leadership Development Outcomes Anticipated by the Year 2000:

1. Adapt the lay missioner model for use in 200 urban situations;

2. Identify 300 churches that will analyze their structures for unnecessary bureaucracy and develop methods for freedom for urban mission and ministry;

3. Conduct ten regional and two national opportunities for training in urban ministry; and

4. Identify and work with 100 sites where children and youth can be introduced to urban ministry.

Community Economic Development:

1. Create a national United Methodist community-development loan fund that helps United Methodist congregations and individuals invest money for community development through churches;

2. Continue and further develop the Communities of Shalom Initiative as a holistic strategy for developing communities and strengthening congregations;

3. Provide training and technical assistance to help churches engage in systemic change and community economic development by working with an existing community-development corporation or by starting a community-development corporation when necessary;

4. Assist churches in learning how they can raise additional dollars for community development from sources outside the church; and

5. Assist congregations in utilizing their buildings for community economic development and outreach.

Community Economic Development Outcomes Anticipated by the Year 2000:

1. Establish a United Methodist Community Economic Development Loan Fund that will have a $50 million revolving loan fund;

2. Establish 300 Communities of Shalom as a strategy for developing communities and strengthening congregations;

3. Identify training and technical assistance models to help 500 churches engage in systemic change and community development;

4. Identify twenty-five financial consultants to assist the five jurisdictions in training to raise money and package resources to develop communities and strengthen local congregations; and

5. Identify twenty models that exemplify how churches have creatively utilized their church buildings to be in expanded and extended ministry for community economic development.

Wholeness, Healing, and Health:

1. Increase the understanding of how people are marginalized and what can be done to develop wholeness, healing, and health;

2. Assist congregations in developing a comprehensive understanding of how they can be healing agents in their neighborhoods and bring about a healthy community;

3. Challenge congregations and agencies to develop ways to improve the spiritual, social, and physical well-being of individuals and communities;

4. Communicate through the Holy Boldness network models of ministry with homeless, the hungry, people who are HIV-positive, individuals who are physically and mentally ill, victims of violence, and people with addictions; and

5. Publicize successful models where spiritual development by congregations and/or community organizations has brought about wholeness, healing, and health in urban settings.

Wholeness, Healing, and Health Outcomes Anticipated by the Year 2000:

1. Identify forty models that demonstrate the spiritual as well as the social aspects in developing wholeness, healing, and health;

2. Provide technical assistance to 100 congregations and agencies that are seeking to develop effective social ministries;

3. Establish a national network for United Methodist churches addressing key health and healing concerns; and

4. Identify forty models of collaboration through which barriers to mission and ministry have been removed.

Immediate Actions:

1. Establish a telephone technical-assistance program by using experienced volunteer urban-ministry practitioners from around the country;

2. Publish a newsletter listing urban-ministry resources and accomplishments toward the established goals;

3. Develop an urban covenant that can be used by covenanting churches and organizations;

4. Hold a November 6–9, 1997, Urban Ministry Convocation in the Western Jurisdiction; and

5. Publish an occasional journal on urban ministry issues.

ADOPTED 1996

See Social Principles, ¶ 66; "Resourcing Black Churches in Urban Communities"; "Special Emphasis on Reclaiming the Cities."

Homelessness in the United States

Homelessness is a scourge upon the nation's conscience. In the most materially rich nation in the world, the homeless are people who sleep 300 to a room in an old tire factory in San Diego. They are the lonely who pass their time talking to themselves in every big city and small town in the nation. They are rural families without the economic means to travel long distances to shelters and other public services. The homeless are people who have been displaced and discarded. Their numbers alone make them a nation of strangers, highly mobile and rootless, surrounded by wealth, glamor, and excess of all of that which they so desperately lack. On any given night in the United States, it is estimated that at least 735,000 individuals are without shelter. As many as two to three million people are without shelter one or more nights during the course of the year.

They are people with past histories and future hopes. They are young and old. They are from rural areas and big cities. They are black, brown, and white. They are Native Americans and recent Asian immigrants. They are women and men, families and children. The homeless are people who shiver in doorways and cower in subway tunnels. They are migrants who live in the back seats of cars and mothers with children who wait daily in soup lines for something to eat. They are multiple families crammed together in small apartments, and mothers with children living in dilapidated chicken coops. They are farmers evicted from the land. Homelessness is a crisis that strikes at the soul of the nation and at the heart of the church. As Christians and as the church, we must come to know the homeless and know these facts:

- Between 25 and 33 percent of homeless people are families with children.
- In some rural areas of the nation, 65 percent of the homeless are families.
- Approximately one fourth of homeless people suffer from chronic mental illness or personality disorders.
- Veterans (especially Vietnam-era veterans) make up 22 to 46 percent of the homeless population.
- Around 4 percent of homeless people are unaccompanied youths.
- Migrant workers and migrant worker families are increasingly among the homeless.
- The homeless are disproportionately African Americans and other peoples of color.
- A substantial percentage (22 percent) of the homeless are employed full- or part-time, albeit in low-paying jobs.
- Males make up the majority of homeless people (66 percent).
- The median age for homeless people is around 35 years.
- Only about one third of the homeless receive public assistance.
- More than 50 percent have been homeless for less than one year.

But the homeless are most assuredly the people of God—the people of God who call the church to both repentance and action. They are the hungry we are asked to feed, the strangers we are to welcome, the naked whom we are to clothe. They are the sick and imprisoned we are commanded to visit (Matthew 25:31-36). The homeless are our neighbors, living in closer proximity to our church buildings than many of our members.

The 1990 annual report of the U.S. Conference of Mayors reports a hardening of attitudes and a growing callousness among the larger population to the plight of the homeless. Yet the Church cannot turn its face from the poor. It must continue to respond to those who have been left out and shunted aside. Few biblical mandates are clearer than those charging us to care for the poor. In Isaiah 58:6-7, God says, "Is not this the fast that I choose/. . . to share your bread with the hungry,/and bring the homeless poor into your house;/[and] when you see the naked, to cover them?" Theologian Walter Brueggemann says, "The Bible itself is primarily concerned with the issue of being displaced and yearning for a place." What we must seek as a nation for all of our people is safe, sanitary, and affordable housing. But as Christians and as the Church, we must seek more than just shelter. We must do more than house the homeless and feed the hungry. We must build community. We must strive to make the kingdom of God evident upon the earth. We must seek solutions that both ease the pain and ultimately heal the wound. We must seek justice—the kind of justice that calls evil to task and then redeems or destroys it. The Church must be the voice that calls us all to account for what we have done and to covenant around what we must do. The Church must ever promise that the broken will be made whole and that which is rent will be sewn together again. Home as a promise to the homeless must be the ongoing commitment of the Church.

Homelessness has many faces and many causes, but its root is in the failure of the nation to commit itself through public policies and programs to eradicate poverty. In the United States today, more people are living in poverty than at any time since 1965. Homelessness has increased each year since 1980 and shows no sign of lessening or leveling off. In fact, indications are that if something is not done, by the year 2000 more than 15 million citizens will be homeless, and the majority of these will be women and children. A poor child born in the United States in 1990 has a better chance of being homeless sometime in his or her growing up than he or she has of being a high school graduate. "Today families with children make up one third of the nation's homeless population." In some parts of the country, they make up the majority. Nationwide, one in every five homeless people is a child. Every night, 100,000 children go to sleep without homes.

A comprehensive, all-out attack on poverty must be waged. Poverty must be eliminated in order for homelessness to be eradicated. This nation proved during the 1960s that poverty can be drastically reduced by a combination of public response and private commitment. Investments by the government in its citizenry through job training, aid to education, community economic development, childcare, family support services, low-income housing initiatives, income maintenance, and public/private partnership covering a broad spectrum of creative responses to the crisis of poverty *can* and *will* work. The cost of eliminating poverty in the United States is less than one might think. Outlays of $53.8 billion or the equivalent of one percent of our 1990 gross national product could do the job. This cost to eliminate poverty pales in comparison to what it will cost the nation to bail out the bankrupt savings and loan industry, estimates of which now exceed $200 billion. Homelessness and poverty cannot be separated. One is a child of the other, and the two must be confronted together.

Many factors contribute to the growing ranks of the homeless: lack of community support for deinstitutionalized people with chronic mental illness; discontinuance or reduction of public benefits to significant numbers of elderly and disabled people; a minimum-wage structure that locks the working poor into poverty; loss of family farms; closure of plants and businesses; an economy increasingly built on low-paying temporary and seasonal jobs with few or no benefits; the increasing number of single-parent households with associated low incomes; lack of housing for people with AIDS; and displacement of inner-city residents by urban renewal.

But the biggest factor contributing to today's alarming homelessness crisis is the acute and growing shortage of affordable housing for low-income persons. Since 1980, the total number of low-income housing units has decreased by 2.5 million units nationally. In particular, this country has seen a dramatic loss of single-room units, the number of which fell from 126,000 units in 1974 to less than 50,000 units in 1988. All types of affordable housing continue to be lost to abandonment, foreclosure, gentrification, and destruction. The rate of replacement falls far short of the rate of loss.

Low incomes, economic shifts, and the growing numbers of people who live in poverty, coupled with the loss of affordable housing, mean that people must pay more and more of their income for shelter. A 1990 study shows that 63 percent of U.S. citizens are paying more than 50 percent of their income for housing. Forty-five percent of citizens pay 70 percent or more of their income for housing. Thirty-two million people live below the poverty line, and the numbers continue to increase.

Homelessness is both a rural and an urban problem. In some areas of the northwestern United States, the percentage of homeless people in rural areas exceeds the percentage of those found in cities. The rural homeless tend to be young, white, and female. Rural shelters are scarce, so homeless people often double up with friends and relatives. The

Housing Assistance Council has found that rural homeless people are migrant workers, displaced renters, bankrupt farmers, and laid-off workers. Native Americans and other residents on Indian reservations are increasingly found among the rural homeless. Extremely high unemployment, coupled with the increased numbers of Native American people returning to live on reservations, has placed undue burdens on an already overtaxed and inadequate social service system. Rural homeless people often migrate to cities, thus contributing to urban homelessness.

The tragedy of the homeless in the United States, however, cannot be told in statistics alone. Homelessness often has a hidden face. Homeless persons are hidden due to the fact that they might be living with friends or relatives, camping in public recreation areas, or seeking cover in barns or in other inappropriate shelters. They are hidden because they are often too proud to ask for help. The homeless are people with no place to go and little to call their own.

The United Methodist Church and all people of faith must seize the moment and demand an end to homelessness in the United States. It must raise an outcry against the injustice of such suffering toward homeless persons as individuals while advocating with others for just societal responses that address the root causes of homelessness. Piecemeal solutions are not enough. The people of this nation must insist that a safe, affordable, and sanitary place to live is a basic human right to be enjoyed by all citizens.

Policy Statement and Actions

The United Methodist Church affirms the right of all persons to live without deprivation in safe, sanitary, and affordable housing. The United Methodist Church asserts that inequitable public policies and unfair and discriminatory private-sector practices have deprived many of that right. The Church views homelessness as a violation of human dignity and an affront to the biblical mandate to do justice. It pledges to do all in its power to eliminate the causes of homelessness and to work along with others to eradicate it. The Church commits itself to welcoming the stranger into its midst and to seeing all people as belonging to the family of God. The Church recognizes homeless people as its neighbors, seeking to learn their names and speaking out on their behalf in the councils of government, in their own congregational settings, and in the larger community. The Church further commits itself to stand with homeless people as they organize to speak out on their own behalf. The United Methodist Church, through its prayers, policies, and actions, will make its voice heard in the land, affirming that all human beings are bound by sacred trust to God and that God, in faithfulness to that trust, will never abandon God's people.

The following actions are commended to general agencies, annual conferences, and local churches:

1. General Agency Recommendations:

(a) Provide to clergy and laity educational and training resources and opportunities that address the root causes of homelessness and provide models for addressing the problem. Urge seminaries to include courses in their curriculum that help prepare clergy for effective leadership around systemic contradictions in our society that create poverty and homelessness. Encourage annual conferences to include courses in their plans for continuing education for clergy at least once a quadrennium;

(b) Continue to support and work with national, regional, and local housing advocacy groups to implement this resolution. Endorse a National Interfaith Conference on the Church and Homelessness as soon as possible after the 1992 General Conference to build a base for impacting Congress to pass comprehensive national housing legislation;

(c) Join with other communions to promote affordable housing for low-income persons through the National Low-Income Housing Coalition and other appropriate networks;

(d) Document and affirm the work of local churches and service providers who provide needed ministries of compassion to homeless persons through church-based soup kitchens, transitional housing programs, shelters, food pantries, clothes closets, and rent and utility assistance programs. Promote their efforts throughout the local church by soliciting financial contributions and volunteer support, and by encouraging members to contribute specialized skills and technical assistance; and

(e) Identify effective existing models and provide new models for local congregations and clergy who wish to undertake Bible study/theological reflection around the root causes of homelessness. Provide outlines for both study and action on the local level.

2. Annual Conference Recommendations:

(a) Adopt the "One Church—One Home" campaign of the Churches' Conference on Shelter and Housing, and push for implementation of the campaign through the districts and their local congregations. This program encourages each United Methodist church throughout the world to reach out in a people-to-people action to adopt at least one of the world's millions of homeless persons or families, to ensure that these people's basic needs for food, housing, health care, education, and employment are met and to enable them, warmed in body and soul, to face the future with hope;

(b) Inform clergy and laity about avenues available to churches seeking to become involved in housing developing through creative ventures such as cooperating housing with other area congregations, development of unused or underutilized church land or building space for housing, development of affordable rental units, or renting apartments for subleasing at a subsidized rate;

(c) Adopt a resolution on homelessness encouraging actions at the congregational level to address the homeless crisis in local communities;

(d) Encourage local churches to conduct a survey on homelessness in their areas to determine what services are currently being provided and to discover gaps in services toward which the church should direct its efforts; and

(e) Undergird cooperative parishes as a major strategy for responding to the problem of homelessness.

3. Local Church Recommendations:

(a) Involve clergy and laity in local church volunteer networks, direct-service programs, and ecumenical coalitions for the homeless. Provide directories of local service providers, speaking opportunities for groups such as Habitat for Humanity, and workshops led by local homeless advocates and the homeless themselves; and

(b) Promote local church-based community organizing efforts to empower neighborhoods and influence government at every level.

4. All Levels of Church:

Call upon Congress to pass comprehensive National Housing Legislation, as outlined in the General Conference resolution on housing.

ADOPTED 1992

See Social Principles, ¶ 66; "Available and Affordable Housing"; "Housing."

Housing

The Scriptures look ahead to that ideal day when all persons will enjoy pleasant, peaceful, and secure shelter under their own vines and fig trees and "no one shall make them afraid" (Micah 4:4).

In many portions of the Gospel, we find Jesus seeking out homes for retreat and renewal, for fellowship and hospitality. Similarly, all persons are entitled to dwelling places that provide for privacy and recreation.

The Social Principles statement of The United Methodist Church declares: "We hold governments responsible for . . . guarantee of the rights to adequate . . . shelter" (¶ 68A). We reaffirm this right as well as the assertion of the 1972 General Conference that "housing for low income persons should be given top priority. . . ."

There are approximately 88 million occupied housing units in the United States. Of these, 7.5 million are seriously substandard; another 25 to 30 million are marginal for human habitation. Nationally, it has been estimated by the Low Income Housing Coalition that by 1985, there were twice as many low-income households as there were low-cost housing units. In California, the ratio of low-income households to low-cost housing units in 1985 was four to one. Between 1970 and 1980, available housing in Detroit decreased by 11 percent, more than any other U.S. city. Furthermore, 6.33 million U.S. citizens (almost half of all low-income households) are paying more than 40 percent of their incomes for housing. The need for adequate housing at affordable costs is critical (Congressional Research Service).

Love for neighbor demands that Christians care about how adequately their neighbors are sheltered. Christians should identify with those who suffer daily from a shortage of available, decent, safe, and sanitary housing. There are many levels and forms of deprivation. Nearly every American town and city has its "homeless," those who exist literally without any form of shelter, living under bridges, in cars and abandoned buses, carrying their entire possessions with them in a few shopping bags.

Millions of families huddle together in densely overcrowded apartments, rural shacks, ancient house trailers, converted warehouses, and condemned or abandoned buildings. At least 7 million of our fellow citizens live in housing that lacks such necessities as running water or plumbing, and an additional estimated 1 to 3 million have no permanent housing (the homeless) because the remainder of us fail to recognize their plight or simply do not care enough.

Since December of 1986, families with children have become the fastest growing homeless group and now comprise an estimated 38 percent of all homeless persons in the United States. The National Housing Law Center estimates that 2.5 million people lose their homes each year to condominium conversion, redevelopment, and building abandonment. Ninety-two percent of cities in the United States surveyed show an increase in the number of homeless families. While The United Methodist Church affirms the pervasive powers of families as "creators of persons, proclaimers of faith perspectives and shapers of both present and future society," it must continue its condemnation of policies that ignore the causal relationship between shortages of low-income housing and the lack of initiative or political will to ensure that safe and affordable housing is available to all citizens.

The deinstitutionalization of persons diagnosed as mentally ill or recovering, or who could live full lives with minimal supervision, is a concept of worth. However, a lack of regional and community planning has allowed many people to be released from a variety of institutions with no place to go, no affordable housing on the budgets allotted to persons through federal or state funds, and no supervised environment for those who need it. Few services exist to maintain supervised, semi-independent, safe, affordable housing. The National Institute of Mental Health estimates that one third of the homeless have mental health problems. Some are persons who were deinstitutionalized with no support; others became ill because of the environment of homelessness.

"Am I my brother's keeper?" (Genesis 4:9) becomes a challenging alternative when concerned United Methodists begin to address the phenomenon of increased homeless families in our country. We must grapple with ways to meet the needs of the homeless. We must be more open to using church buildings that are outmoded and excess land in urban and rural areas. We must examine needs and services in our communities and develop a better understanding of our role in local, state, and federal policy development. We commend United Methodists who are engaged in the effort to change such intolerable housing conditions. We commend every such individual, local church, interfaith group, nonprofit, for-profit, and government effort. We endorse with gratitude and appreciation the thousands of dollars and untold hours of voluntary service that United Methodists dedicate to this battle to improve human shelter in our country. We urge local churches, districts, and annual conferences to strengthen every housing ministry taking place within their communities by providing additional financial, technical, counseling, and spiritual resources.

Many specific activities deserve greater United Methodist support.

A. At the local level

Local churches, individually or in cooperation with other churches, can identify specific housing needs existing in their communities. Often, bringing to public consciousness the plight of people in need of shelter is the first step toward alleviating such need. Sometimes the use of existing church buildings can graphically demonstrate both the need and a solution that then can be developed more fully through the use of other facilities and financial resources.

Formation of nonprofit and limited-divided housing corporations or housing cooperatives is a viable approach in many situations. There are excellent opportunities for establishing housing construction, management, and advocacy programs. However, expert consultative and technical services generally are needed from the earliest conception. We urge the use of the services provided by the General Board of Global Ministries, National Division, Housing Consultant Services and Economic Development Programs. We urge landowners, apartment and housing managers, and policy boards to allow federally subsidized tenants to inhabit their dwellings. This is a serious problem at this time, because U.S. government policy recommends selling up to 30 percent of public housing units for private development. The net result is displacement of the poor. Availability of housing for them is limited because of discrimination and a reluctance on the part of the government to maintain federally subsidized housing monies for privately owned housing.

B. At the regional level

The atmosphere of conflict infects the relationship between cities, towns, suburban areas, counties, and states throughout our nation. Too often, competition for use of land cloaks subtle racism. Economic profit, likewise, often is used to justify a lack of concern for the impact of taxation measures. Uncoordinated planning and development results in jobs being located beyond the reach of those most in need of work. The "trickle-down theory" of housing occupancy masks a selfish motivation and results in the maintenance and expansion of existing ghettos, causes the formation of new ghettos, and enforces negative attitudes that support class and racial segregation. We urge United Methodists to challenge all such practices and to engage in every activity to eliminate such vestiges of discrimination from our nation.

Every urbanized area in our country is required to have some form of a regional planning agency. Most rural areas have some similar agency, such as an area development district. Generally these political structures have considerable influence upon housing patterns, planning, production, and usage. Most can have citizens' advisory groups that develop strategy proposals and monitor private and governmental housing activities. We urge United Methodists to become knowledgeable of and involved in such planning agencies.

C. At the national level

Since the enactment of the National Housing Act of 1949, the United States has set a goal that every citizen be housed in "decent, safe and sanitary housing." Yet the reality is that we are farther from that goal today than ever before. In part, this is due to growth of population and the ever-increasing gap between those who are economically well off and those who are not. But in large measure, the disparity is due to an unwillingness of our elected representatives to use general tax revenues to achieve the goals more fully. Generally, legislators feel they represent the views of their electorate and receive very little support for using tax dollars to build more housing for low- and moderate-income families. The moral commitment first stated in 1949 and restated in every subsequent Housing Act by Congress (1959, 1968, 1974, 1978) has gone greatly unheeded. If "decent, safe and sanitary housing" is to be a citizen's right, a much greater moral outcry must be raised.

Therefore, we call upon United Methodists to undertake a concerted effort to impress upon their elected representatives a profound concern over the continuing housing deficiencies existing in our cities, towns, and rural areas. Much more effort needs to be made to influence the legislative processes that affect housing, including improving existing laws, developing more imaginative approaches where possible, and providing adequate funding for housing designated to meet the needs of the ill-sheltered.

1. Subsidized rental housing (Section 8) and public housing

Under the Section 8 Housing Assistance Payments Program, renters normally pay a percentage of their income for rent, and the federal government makes up the difference between that and the HUD-(Department of Housing and Urban Development) established Fair Market Rent. We support this program for subsidizing rents as one way of opening up more housing units to low-income families and yet expecting such families, when possible, to provide their fair share of costs. However, the reality is that there are just not enough units of housing available at a cost that can be afforded by the poor, even with payment assistance. There is a great need for developing more housing units. In 1985, more than 8 million low-income renters were in the market for the only 4.2 million units available at an affordable (minimum of 25 percent of income) price.

Aid to Families with Dependent Children (AFDC) is the primary source of income for many people who now find themselves homeless. The amount of money that many families with children receive is lower than the average cost of housing in many states.

We are greatly concerned over the rapidly increasing trend toward converting rental housing to condominiums for sale. Too often in practice this means pushing people out of housing they can afford to rent but can't afford to buy. We therefore recommend that the rate of condominium conversion of rental units be slowed, or that percentages of the units be set aside with affordable rental rates. Further, we urge local housing authorities to offset this trend by encouraging increased housing stock of subsidized rental units.

We support use of a wide variety of subsidized housing approaches in order to meet a greater demand to house needy people. However, the development of a "voucher" program with no ceiling on the actual rent that can be charged and no local community guarantee of housing set aside for the poor will not alleviate the present situation.

Public housing continues to be a vital necessity in both urban and rural areas. Every incorporated city, town, and county can and should provide public, well-constructed and well-managed rental housing for those who cannot obtain it on the open market. Nearly 50 percent of all housing is now occupied by the elderly. Since the Church has traditionally expressed concern and provided care of the aging, it is especially crucial that this program is continued, expanded, and adequately funded.

We must at all times critically examine the setting at the local, state, and federal levels, because governmental policies affect the funding improvement and provision of housing resources for any given community. The Federal Administration between 1981 and 1988 tried to eliminate or reduce the main federal programs used by states and local governments to help the poor and the homeless. The Community Development Block Grant Program, General Revenue Sharing, and the Temporary Emergency Food Assistance Program have all been affected. The Community Development Block Grant Program budget has been cut almost yearly. General Revenue Sharing was eliminated. The Administration has targeted for elimination the Temporary Emergency Food Assistance Program. Congress has repeatedly come to the rescue of these programs and in 1986 passed a law allowing the homeless to receive Aid to Families with Dependent Children, social security, and Medicaid.

2. Fair Housing

Fair housing in our nation has regressed in the past decade. Because housing remains segregated in most places in the United States, schools tend to be segregated and jobs tend to be located at inconvenient distances from ethnic minority neighborhoods.

We therefore call upon the U.S. Congress to provide the Department of Housing and Urban development with "cease and desist" enforcement powers, and we encourage HUD to apply these powers evenly and with relentless determination to ensure equal access to affordable housing in all markets. We support state and local legislation that would strengthen fair housing enforcement across the country; we also support HUD and Farmers Home Administration funding for states with laws that are substantially equivalent to federal law. We also call for the expansion of coverage in the Fair Housing Act to provide protection for people with disabilities.

Equal access to housing not available represents an unrealizable right. Therefore, to fulfill equal opportunity objectives we urge that more housing be built and offered at prices most persons can afford to pay.

A. Redlining

We deplore the practice of "redlining" as it occurs in many urban areas. This generally means that financial institutions, insurance companies, and mortgage brokers collectively make it difficult for home-owners to secure adequate financing and insurance at reasonable rates in a certain neighborhood of a given urban community. We ask that all necessary steps be taken, through negotiation and legislation, to eliminate this immoral practice, and that churches take the lead in encouraging financial support arrangements that rejuvenate instead of destroy our neighborhoods. Vigilant monitoring by the religious community can forestall such unhealthy practices.

We support existing laws such as the Home Mortgage Disclosure Act, which provides information to the public on where banks and savings and loans make their loans, and the enlarged Community Reinvestment Act, which mandates that banks and savings and loans have the responsibility to serve the credit needs of moderate and lower-income communities.

We urge compliance of the institutions in which the Church deposits funds with the Home Mortgage Act; and we support such additional regulations and laws that will ensure reinvestment in currently red-lined communities, in a way that will not result in unjust displacement of elderly, poor, ethnic minority, and other persons.

B. *Housing for Older Adults*
 and People with Disabilities

The Section 202 federal program is a bright spot in an otherwise dismal picture of housing for older adults and people with disabilities of any age. Restricted to sponsorship by nonprofit groups (the majority of which are related to religious groups), the 202 continues to offer a direct ministry opportunity. Since it is a loan guarantee program with lower-than-market interest rates, it needs to be funded at much more realistic levels than in the past. There is also a need for expanding the congregate housing services project for semi-independent older adults or people with disabilities. The steady increase in age of our population is evidence for the need to expand the 202 program until the need for this type of rental housing for the elderly has been met. This program provides support services for persons using 202 housing and is cost effective because it allows people who might have to be institutionalized to live in much lower-cost housing.

3. Housing for Native Americans

Housing policy, as in other aspects of national policy and practices toward Native American tribes, is grossly inadequate. We call for a substantial increase in programs at the federal level and for the implementation of state and local housing programs in every possible way, so that the shocking condition of substandard reservation housing can be quickly improved. Special efforts through programs of United Methodist general agencies, in partnership with ethnic conferences and funds for ethnic minority ministry, should be supportive of actions to improve housing for Native Americans.

4. Financing of Housing

Traditionally, the vast majority of housing in our country has been financed through the private money-lending industry. There is little likelihood that this would need to change if the traditional principles against usury are followed. But more attention needs to be given to developing ways mortgage money can be made available to low-income persons for home ownership, and to provide rental housing for low-income people. Federal and state programs aid the moderate- and upper-income segments of our population quite well, but similarly helpful programs for the lower-income sector of the population do not exist. The 1980s have seen the greatest benefit go not to the neediest families, but to those who are sufficiently well off to purchase homes. In 1985, tax immunities relief to homeowners totalled $30.4 billion (up from $8.2 billion in 1970) in the form of federal income-tax immunities deductions for mortgage interest rates. An additional $8.6 billion in relief came through state and local property tax immunities deductions.

The higher the family income, the more these tax immunities breaks help. Three fourths of these tax immunities breaks go to homeowners in the top 15 percent of the income bracket. Poor or lower-middle class homeowners (with incomes of $15,000 or less) get only 3 percent of the tax immunities breaks. Government-subsidized mortgage programs need to be developed that can also aid the lower-middle class and poor individuals and families.

In contrast to the rapid growth in federal aid to more well-to-do homeowners through the code, use of federal budget authority for low-income housing programs declined from an annual average of $24.3 billion during the 1977–1981 years to $8.4 billion per year between 1982 and 1986.

New methods of private financing need to be developed so that traditional money sources are not withdrawn from the housing industry in favor of other, more profitable forms of investment.

Recommendations

A number of federal programs as well as some state programs exist today to make possible the meaningful participation of church groups in providing adequate housing in a wholesome environment. We encourage churches to join in such programs that require minimal capital investment but substantial commitment of time and energy. Churches should be aware that these programs are available in both urban and rural areas. More church groups ought to:

1. Be concerned about the conditions of housing in their communities;

2. Use the tools available (e.g., National Division, General Board of Global Ministries Housing Consultant Services) to provide better housing;

3. Dedicate a special day or Sunday as a Day of Prayer and Action for Shelter, as has been developed by Habitat for Humanity (contact the General Board of Church and Society for special resources); and

4. Develop a sense of mission and assume responsibility as stewards to meet these needs without expectation of monetary reward.

In implementing any housing ministry, church people must maintain great sensitivity to community needs and work to achieve community participation and control. Tenants' need for adequate, reasonably priced and energy-efficient housing should be recognized. Care must always be exercised to ensure our Christian involvement as "enablers" rather than "controllers." Our goal must always be to enable those we help to be in control of their own lives, futures, and destinies. Whatever the form of community organization, housing production, management, or ownership of a housing project, every effort should be made at each developmental step to ensure that those who are being aided are afforded the opportunity, and indeed, are required, to take every action necessary to direct the undertaking. Wherever possible, we must train rather than service, transfer power rather than decide, empower rather than control. In this as in all other aspects of housing ministries, United Methodists should seek the best technical guidance and ensure the greatest professional competence for such a ministry. Let us equip ourselves and provide the widest possible range of supportive assistance to individuals, congregations, districts, conferences, and all forms of cooperative groups sharing similar goals and policies so that our fellow citizens may achieve, as their right, "decent, safe and sanitary housing" as soon as possible.

ADOPTED 1988

See Social Principles, ¶ ¶ 66, 68A; "Available and Affordable Housing"; "Homelessness in the United States."

In Support of Reparations for African Americans

WHEREAS, at the conclusion of the Civil War, the plan for the economic redistribution of land and resources on behalf of the former slaves of the Confederacy was never enacted; and

WHEREAS, the failure to distribute land prevented newly freed Blacks from achieving true autonomy and made their civil and political rights all but meaningless; and

WHEREAS, conditions comparable to "economic depression" continue for millions of African Americans in communities where unemployment often exceeds 50 percent; and

WHEREAS, unabated narcotics trafficking and gang killings as a result of these economic realities can be traced to the broken promise that each slave would receive "forty acres, fifty dollars, and a mule"; and

WHEREAS, the economic gains that were temporarily experienced by the Black middle class following the passage of the Civil Rights Bill of 1964 and President Lyndon B. Johnson's Executive Order 11246 have been seriously eroded by the failure to enforce the same and by the Supreme Court's attack and the U.S. House of Representatives' attack on affirmative action; and

WHEREAS, Supreme Court Justice Clarence Thomas and conservative scholar Dr. Shelby Steele have both contended that the danger facing civil rights in America is not the absence of law, but failure to enforce existing laws; and

WHEREAS, January 5, 1993, Congressman John Conyers Jr. (D-Mich.) introduced H.R. 40 to the House of Representatives, calling for the establishment of the Commission to Study Reparation Proposals for African Americans, "acknowledging the fundamental injustice, cruelty, brutality and inhumanity of slavery in the United States from 1619 to the present day," for the purpose of submitting a report to Congress for further action and consideration with respect to slavery's effects on African American lives, economics, and politics;

Therefore, be it resolved:

1. That we support the discussion and study of reparation for African Americans;

2. That we petition President Bill Clinton, Vice President Al Gore, and the United States House of Representatives to support the passage and signing of H.R. 40;

3. That the General Commission on Religion and Race and the General Board of Church and Society develop a strategy for interpreting and promoting the issue of economic reparations for African Americans; and

4. That a written copy of this petition be delivered to the President and Vice President of the United States, United States Senate Majority Leader Bob Dole, House Speaker Newt Gingrich, and House member John Conyers Jr.

ADOPTED 1996

See Social Principles, ¶ 66A; "Racism: The Church's Unfinished Agenda"; "Racism"; "Racism Today."

In Support of the Rio Grande Conference

WHEREAS, November 20, 1995, was the 142nd anniversary date that Benigno Cárdenas, under the auspices of The Methodist Episcopal Church, preached the first sermon in Spanish in what is now the state of New Mexico and became the first Hispanic clergy in that church and a pioneer in what is now the Rio Grande Conference of The United Methodist Church; and

WHEREAS, the Rio Grande Conference has recently celebrated its 80th anniversary of being organized as an annual conference to reach and serve Hispanics in Texas and New Mexico; and

WHEREAS, the Rio Grande Conference, as the only Spanish-speaking conference in The United Methodist Church in the United States, continues to be a viable mission structure to reach Hispanics for Christ and his church in those two states, continues to develop significant ministries in the communities it serves, continues to develop leadership for this ministry in spite of limited resources, and has welcomed other sister conferences beginning to respond to the overwhelming Hispanic population growth in the area (over 1.4 million in one decade); and

WHEREAS, the Rio Grande Conference, through the years to the present time, has developed and shared its leadership—lay and clergy—with other conferences, general agencies, and the whole Church; and

WHEREAS, the Rio Grande Conference continues to play an important and vital role in the implementation of the National Plan for Hispanic Ministries; and

WHEREAS, the Rio Grande Conference in its last annual conference session affirmed its desire to determine its own future and has established a process of self-study, visioning, and planning to accomplish this goal as it has done before in past self-studies; and

WHEREAS, the Rio Grande Conference at its last session declared its commitment and resolve to pray and to continue to work to strengthen and expand its ministry and outreach; to deepen its spiritual life; and to dedicate itself to grow in all aspects of its ministry, including its stewardship, membership, participation in various ministries, and so forth; and

WHEREAS, the South Central Jurisdiction College of Bishops, and perhaps others, have had conversations regarding the future structure of the Rio Grande Conference;

Therefore, be it resolved, that the General Conference continue to affirm and support the Rio Grande Conference, its ministry, and its leadership as a viable missional structure.

ADOPTED 1996

See Social Principles, ¶ 66A; "History of Racial/Ethnic United Methodists."

In Support of Women, Infants, and Children's Supplemental Food and Nutrition Education Program (WIC Program)

WHEREAS, the Women, Infants, and Children's Supplemental Food and Nutrition Education (WIC) Program provides nutrition education and food coupons for needy high-risk pregnant women, lactating women, and children under five years of age; and

WHEREAS, the WIC food coupons are available to high-risk needy pregnant women such as those who are anemic, overweight or underweight, teenage or over thirty-five, or those who have had problems with a previous pregnancy; and

WHEREAS, the WIC coupons, costing an average of twenty-seven dollars per month per person on the program, can be used only for milk, cheese, eggs, juices high in Vitamin C, iron-fortified cereal, and iron-fortified formula and not for high-caloric junk foods that are low in certain essential nutrients; and

WHEREAS, malnutrition is a primary cause of low-birth-weight babies; and

WHEREAS, low-birth-weight babies get off to a slow start in life at great emotional expense to the parents and financial hardship to families, insurance companies, and the taxpayers; and

WHEREAS, the cost of putting weight on a newborn baby in a "premie nursery" is about $600 per day and about $5,000 per pound of weight gain; and

WHEREAS, inadequate diet in the formative years is a major cause of some types of mental retardation; and

WHEREAS, 60 percent of the total number of brain cells are already developed at the time of birth, the other 40 percent are developed by the age of three, and from age three to age five the brain cells increase in size but not in number; and

WHEREAS, the cost of institutional care of a mentally retarded child is $1,400 per month or more, and that of a mentally retarded adult is $700 to $1,400 per month for life;

Therefore, be it resolved, that The United Methodist General Conference go on record as supporting the Women, Infants, and Children Supplemental Food and Nutrition Education Program, Public Law 95627 of the Child Nutrition Act, as a positive, cost-effective malnutrition preventive measure.

ADOPTED 1980

See Social Principles, ¶ 66C, F; "A Call for Increased Commitment to End World Hunger and Poverty"; "Putting Children and Their Families First"; "Protecting and Sustaining Children."

Inclusive History

WHEREAS, The United Methodist Church celebrates regularly the growth and development of the Methodist legacy in America; and

WHEREAS, the influence of the literary records has shaped the images, values, and perceptions of racial and ethnic minority groups toward one another; and

WHEREAS, the most positive images and dominant contributions in the Methodist legacies are credited and related to Caucasian persons; and

WHEREAS, nominal historical recognition is given to Asians, Blacks, Hispanics, Native Americans, and Pacific Islanders and their contributions to the Methodist legacy in America; and

WHEREAS, The United Methodist Church proclaims a commitment to the goal of realizing racial and ethnic minority inclusiveness;

Therefore, be it resolved, that the General Commission on Archives and History and The United Methodist Publishing House, in joint consultation with the General Commission on Religion and Race, determine the most effective means to identify all Asian, Black, Hispanic, Native American, and Pacific Islander literary and historical records that have not been acknowledged and/or published; promote the use of these resources among whites and racial and ethnic minorities; and encourage training sessions led by Asians, Blacks, Hispanics, Native Americans, and Pacific Islanders using these resources that acknowledge the contributions of these racial and ethnic minorities to the legacy and heritage of Methodism in the United States of America and the world.

ADOPTED 1992

See Social Principles, ¶ 66A; "History of Racial/Ethnic United Methodists"; "History of Blacks in The United Methodist Church"; "Native American History and Contemporary Culture as Related to Effective Church Participation."

Increased Support for Programs Impacting the Higher Education of Native Americans

WHEREAS, the National United Methodist Native American Center, Inc., supports and endorses the goal of optimum educational achievement for all United Methodist Church members; and

WHEREAS, the concept of illiteracy is unacceptable in a time when society projects a formal demeanor of progress and opportunity for all members; and

WHEREAS, past support for The United Methodist Church for the participation of Native Americans in higher education has been minimal, productive, and appreciated; and

WHEREAS, a trend of decreasing Native American participation in higher education is beginning to appear at the national and regional levels; and

WHEREAS, the consistently rising costs of higher education contribute considerably to the decrease of Native American participation in higher education; and

WHEREAS, recent statistics suggest an upward trend of academic success for Native Americans currently participating in higher education; and

WHEREAS, the National United Methodist Native American Center, Inc., supports the philosophy that every person has a right to an education and it is society's responsibility to enable every person to obtain this right; and

WHEREAS, the foundation to Native American growth and progress in society lies within the domain of formal education;

Therefore, be it resolved, that the General Conference encourage the General Board of Higher Education and Ministry, if monies are available, to sponsor a Native American Higher Education Forum in the fall of 1993 to:

1. Collect data about the causes for higher dropout rates among Native American students;

2. Identify self-help trends among Native Americans who feel isolated from mainstream society on college and university campuses; and

3. Develop practical strategies that will appropriately address these causes within the Native American community.

Be it further resolved, that the General Conference endorse and support the funding, development, implementation, and assessment of a higher education recruitment/retention forum, sponsored by The United Methodist Church for Native Americans throughout the denomination's regions, to be organized and managed by the National United Methodist Native American Center, Inc., in cooperation with local churches reflecting a significant population of Native Americans.

Be it further resolved, that the General Conference encourage The United Methodist Church to utilize the information and materials generated as a result of the forum for sensitizing and familiarizing non-Indian membership about Native Americans in their respective communities.

ADOPTED 1992

See Social Principles, ¶ 66A; "Shared Financial Support for the Native American Center"; "The United Methodist Church and America's Native People."

Institutional Racism in General Church Processes

The General Conference directs the general agencies of The United Methodist Church to refrain from any practice of institutional racism in relating to racial ethnic groups, such as pitting them against one another or against different organizations within a given group or making them compete for the same funds or any other kind of resources.

ADOPTED 1996

See Social Principles, ¶ 66A; "Racism: The Church's Unfinished Agenda"; "Elimination of Racism in The United Methodist Church."

Ku Klux Klan and Other Hate Groups in the United States

The Charter for Racial Justice Policies holds us accountable as United Methodists in the United States to be conscious that "we have sinned as our ancestors did; we have been wicked and evil" (Psalm 106:6, Today's English Bible). We are called to a renewed commitment to the elimination of institutional racism. We affirm the 1976 General Conference statement on "The United Methodist Church and Race," which states unequivocally:

> By biblical and theological precept, by the law of the Church, by General Conference pronouncement, and by episcopal expression, the matter is clear. With respect to race, the aim of The United Methodist Church is nothing less than an inclusive church in an inclusive society. The United Methodist Church therefore calls upon all its people to perform those faithful deeds of love and justice in both the church and community that will bring this aim into full reality.

The United Methodist Church has expressed its opposition to all forms of racism and anti-Semitism in the past. Racism replaces faith in the God who made all people with a belief in the superiority of one race over another.

Nevertheless, racism still exists in the United States, congealed in its most violent, antidemocratic form—the white supremacist movement.

The white supremacist movement has developed into two distinct trends. One is the clandestine and semi-clandestine movement committed to terror and violence to popularize its aims and achieve its goals. The other trend has specialized in developing an elaborate facade, designed to win new supporters who would otherwise be repelled by an open appeal to violence and neo-Nazism. Together these groups form a fascist movement with a stable core and expanding spheres of influence, despite the temporary fortunes or misfortunes of its constituent groups.

An underground composed of members of different Klan factions, the Aryan Nations (which include the Church of Jesus Christ-Christian, the Mountain Kirk, and other nonchurch organizations), and other neo-Nazi formations continue to exist. The underground was typified by The Order, a basic philosophy of the Ku Klux Klan. Activities carried out under this philosophy include murder, theft, vandalizing synagogues, counterfeiting, bombing churches and public buildings, and bank robbery.

The racist movement has already entered the twenty-first century with an increasingly sophisticated technical apparatus. The Aryan Nations organization operates five different "Liberty Net" computer bulletin boards that relay messages among white supremacists, which allows them a wider public audience for their ideas.

Ku Klux Klan and neo-Nazi groups engage in open paramilitary activity. Training bases of groups are located in all sections of the country. From the White Aryan Resistance in the West, to the Christian-Patriots Defense League in the Midwest, to the Ku Klux Klan in the South, hate groups are trained with highly sophisticated weaponry.

On the other hand, Posse Comitatus-type groups have recruited farm and rural whites throughout the depressed agricultural sections of the country. They have used clever schemes based on providing fraudulent legal assistance and grassroots organizing to win new recruits. Although organizers of groups such as National Agricultural Press Association (NAPA), Farmer Liberation Army, and the Iowa Society of Educated Citizens don't openly identify themselves as neo-Nazi, they do place the blame for the crisis in agriculture on a mythical international Jewish conspiracy. Some of the members of the Posse Comitatus-like groups have been involved in violent altercations with the law.

In addition to the paramilitary, economic, and political organizing of the fascist movement, a powerful religious movement called Christian Identity has developed. Christian Identity is derived from a century-old religious doctrine known as British Israelism. It provides theological unity to disparate sections of the white supremacist movement and an attraction to the racist movement for those whose beginning interests are primarily religious. Christian Identity functions in the religious sphere much like fraudulent legal schemes do among economically distressed farmers. Christian Identity theology teaches that people of color are "pre-Adamic," lower forms of species than white people; that Jews are children of Satan; and that the white people of northern Europe are the Lost Tribes of Israel.

Therefore, be it resolved, that the General Conference, in solidarity with victims of recent outbreaks of racial violence:

1. Calls upon the appropriate boards and agencies of The United Methodist Church to:

(a) Educate clergy and laity to the insidiousness of the Christian Identity movement, the Ku Klux Klan, and other hate groups who claim their values and practices are based in Christianity. Education should include courses in seminaries as well as education for children, youth, and adults in church programs;

(b) Develop special programs to support churches and persons harassed by hate groups, particularly in rural areas where the social institutions that mediate conflict are weak and hate group activity is prevalent;

(c) Support coalitions that oppose bigotry and hate groups; and

(d) Oppose the involvement of minors in paramilitary training sponsored by the Ku Klux Klan and other racist groups; and

2. Calls upon government and its agencies to:

(a) Ensure that law-enforcement personnel take the necessary steps to maintain accurate records on racist violence and bring to justice the perpetrators of such violence and intimidation; and

(b) Hold hearings on racist violence, particularly in those states where statistics reveal an increase in the activity of the Ku Klux Klan and other hate groups. Congressional hearings should be held when there are allegations of government involvement or negligence exacerbating such violence.

ADOPTED 1988

See Social Principles, ¶ 66A; "Support Legislation Prohibiting Malicious Harassments"; "Racial Harassment"; "Prejudice Against Muslims and Arabs in the U.S.A."

Medical Rights for Children and Youth

Out of long tradition, our society has valued the family as its fundamental social institution. The family is seen as the primary locus for the nurture and protection of children and youth. To preserve, protect, and defend the family as a social unit, the family's right to privacy has been protected in almost absolute fashion by law and custom. The rights of parents to determine the conditions and circumstances of their children have known little limitation.

When children are abused or maltreated, therefore, the tragic facts are often hidden or little known. We must awaken now to the reality that some of our children, at some times and places, have been battered and beaten within their own families. It has been estimated that "10,000 children are severely battered every year, at least 50,000 to 75,000 are sexually abused, 100,000 are emotionally neglected, and another 100,000 are physically, morally, and educationally neglected."

In light of these tragic facts, we, as church people, should particularly bear witness to our conviction that parental rights over children are limited, that all children are gifts of God and belong to God, and that parents do not own their children. Children have fundamental rights as persons—rights that are to be protected by the community at large when the family system fails any particular child.

Medical care represents a particularly crucial area of the rights of children. We therefore call particular attention to the following statement of the medical rights due children and youth, and we commend its principles for adoption:

The Pediatric Bill of Rights Preamble

Every child, regardless of race, religion, ethnic background, or economic standing, has the right to be regarded as a person and shall have the right to receive appropriate medical care and treatment. The Pediatric Bill of Rights shall not be construed as a bypassing of the family's right to personal privacy, but shall become operative when parental rights and the child's rights are in direct conflict and it becomes necessary to act in the best interests of the child. Provision shall be made for adequate counseling of the child as to his right to receive and deny medical care. To the extent that a child cannot demand his rights as a person, those involved in his health care shall move to protect that child's medical interests to the best of their ability.

Canon I. Every person, regardless of age, shall have the right of timely access to continuing and competent health care.

Canon II. Every person, regardless of age, shall have the right to seek out and receive information concerning medically accepted contraceptive devices and birth-control services in doctor-patient confidentiality. Every person, regardless of age, shall have the right to receive medically prescribed contraceptive devices in doctor-patient confidentiality.

Canon III. Every person, regardless of age, shall have the right to seek out and receive information concerning venereal disease, and every person, regardless of age, shall have the right to consent to and receive any medically accepted treatment necessary to combat venereal disease in doctor-patient confidentiality.

Canon IV. Every person, regardless of age, shall have the right to seek out and accept in doctor-patient confidentiality the diagnosis and treatment of any medical condition related to pregnancy. Every person, regardless of age, shall have the right to adequate and objective counseling relating to pregnancy and abortion in doctor-patient confidentiality; and every person, regardless of age, shall have the right to request and receive medically accepted treatment that will result in abortion in doctor-patient confidentiality.

Canon V. Every person, regardless of age, shall have the right to seek out and receive psychiatric care and counseling in doctor-patient confidentiality.

Canon VI. Every person, regardless of age, shall have the right to seek out and receive medically accepted counseling and treatment for drug or alcohol dependency in doctor-patient confidentiality.

Canon VII. Every person, regardless of age, shall have the right of immediate medical care when the life of such person is in imminent danger. The decision of imminent danger to the life of such person is a decision to be made solely by the attending physician; and the attending physician shall decide what treatment is medically indicated under the circumstances.

Canon VIII. Any person, regardless of age, who is of sufficient intelligence to appreciate the nature and consequences of the proposed medical care and if such medical care is for his own benefit, may effectively consent to such medical care in doctor-patient confidentiality. The same shall not apply to Canons II through VIII, which are deemed to be absolute rights.

Canon IX. In every case in which a child is being examined by, treated by, or is under the medical care of a qualified medical practitioner, and where, in the opinion of that qualified medical practitioner, the child is in need of immediate medical care, and where the parent or the legal guardian of said child refuses to consent to such needed, immediate medical treatment, said medical practitioner shall notify the juvenile court or the district court with juvenile jurisdiction immediately. The juvenile court or the district court with juvenile jurisdiction shall immediately appoint a guardian *ad litem,* who shall represent the child's interests in all subsequent legal proceedings. The juvenile court or the district court with juvenile jurisdiction shall immediately set a date for hearing, not to exceed ninety-six hours from the receipt of the initial report. The court shall determine at the hearing, based upon medical and other relevant testimony and the best interests of the child, whether or not said medical treatment should be so ordered by the court.

Canon X. Every person, regardless of age, shall have the right to considered and respectful care. During examinations, every attempt shall be made to ensure the privacy of every patient, regardless of age; and every person, regardless of age, has the right to know, if observers are present, what role the observer may have in regard to the patient's treatment and shall have the right to request that observers remove themselves from the immediate examining area.

Canon XI. Every person, regardless of age, shall have the right to know which physician is responsible for his care. Every person, regardless of age, shall have the right to be informed concerning his diagnosis, his treatment, and his prognosis in language that is readily understandable to him. Every person, regardless of age, shall have the right to ask pertinent questions concerning the diagnosis, the treatment, and the tests and surgery done, on a day-to-day basis in a hospital setting; and every person, regardless of age, shall have the right to immediate response to the best of the attending physician's knowledge and in language that the patient clearly understands.

ADOPTED 1976

See Social Principles, ¶ 66C, Q; "Health and Wholeness"; "Universal Access to Health Care in the U.S. and Related Territories."

Membership in Clubs or Organizations that Practice Exclusivity

WHEREAS, membership held in any club or organization that practices exclusivity based on gender, race, or socioeconomic condition is clearly in violation of the stance of the United Methodist Social Principles;

Therefore, it is recommended, that United Methodists who hold memberships in clubs or organizations that practice exclusivity based on gender, race, or socioeconomic condition prayerfully consider whether they should work for change within these groups or resign their membership. If one decides to resign, we urge that the decision and reasons be made public. This reflects the intent and purpose of the Social Principles of The United Methodist Church.

ADOPTED 1992

See Social Principles, ¶ 66A; "Racial Harassment"; "Racism Today"; "Racism: The Church's Unfinished Agenda."

Ministries in Mental Illness

Mental illness is a group of brain disorders that cause severe disturbances of thinking, feeling, and acting. Treatment should recognize the importance of a nonstressful environment, good nutrition, and an accepting community—as well as medical and psychiatric care—in regaining and maintaining health. Churches in every community are called to participate actively in expanding care for the mentally ill and their families and communities.

John Wesley's ministry was grounded in the redemptive ministry of Christ with its focus on healing that involved spiritual, mental, emotional, and physical aspects. His concern for the health of those to whom he ministered led him to create medical services at no cost to those who were poor and in deep need, refusing no one for any reason. He saw health as going beyond a simple biological well-being to wellness of the whole person. His witness of love to those in need of healing is our model for ministry to those who are suffering from mental illness.

All aspects of health—physical, mental, and spiritual—were of equal concern to Jesus Christ, whose healing touch reached out to mend broken bodies, minds, and spirits with one common purpose: the restoration of well-being and renewed communion with God and neighbor. But those whose illness brought social stigma and isolation, such as the man of Gadara, whose troubled spirit caused fearsome and self-destructive behavior, were embraced and healed with special compassion (Mark 5:1-34). When the man of Gadara said his name was "Legion; for we are many" (verse 9), his comment was suggestive of the countless individuals, in our time as well as his, whose mental dysfunction—whether genetically, environmentally, chemically, socially, or psychologically induced—causes fear, rejection, or shame, and to which we tend to respond with the same few measures no more adequate for our time than for his: stigmatization, isolation, incarceration, and restraint.

We confess that our Christian concepts of sin and forgiveness, at the root of our understanding of the human condition and of divine grace,

318

are sometimes inappropriately applied in ways that heighten paranoia or clinical depression. Great care must be exercised in ministering to those whose brain disorders result in exaggerated self-negation, for while all persons stand in need of forgiveness and reconciliation, God's love cannot be communicated through the medium of forgiveness for uncommitted or delusional sins.

We reaffirm our confidence that God's unqualified love for all persons beckons us to reach out with fully accepting love to all, but particularly to those with disabling inability to relate to themselves or others due to mental illness.

Research published since 1987 has underscored the physical and genetic basis for the more serious mental illnesses, such as schizophrenia, manic-depression, and other affective disorders.

Public discussion and education about mental illness are needed so that persons who suffer from brain disorders, and their families, can be free to ask for help. This includes freedom from the stigma attached to mental illness that derives from a false understanding that it is primarily an adjustment problem caused by psychologically dysfunctional families. Communities need to develop more adequate programs to meet the needs of their mentally ill members. This includes the need to implement state and local programs that monitor and prevent abuses of mentally ill persons, as well as those programs that are intended to replace long-term hospitalization with community-based services.

The process followed in recent years of deinstitutionalizing mental patients has corrected a longstanding problem of "warehousing" mentally ill persons. However, without adequate community-based mental-health programs to care for the dehospitalized, the streets, for too many, have become a substitute for a hospital ward. Consequently, often the responsibility, including the costs of mental-health care, have simply been transferred to individuals and families or to shelters for the homeless that are already overloaded and ill-equipped to provide more than the most basic care. Furthermore, the pressure to deinstitutionalize patients rapidly has caused some mental-health systems to rely unduly upon short-term chemical therapy to control patients rather than upon more complex programs that require longer-term hospitalization or other forms of treatments where research provides successful outcomes achieved. Such stopgap treatment leads to repeated short-term hospitalizations, with little or no long-term improvement in a person's ability to function.

The Church, as the body of Christ, is called to the ministry of reconciliation, of healing, and of salvation, which means to be made whole. We call upon the Church to affirm ministries related to mental illness that embrace the role of community, family, and the healing professions in healing the physical, social, environmental, and spiritual impediments to wholeness for those afflicted with brain disorders and for their families.

1. We call upon all local churches, districts, and annual conferences to support the following community and congressional programs:

(a) adequate public funding to enable mental-health systems to provide appropriate therapy;

(b) expanded counseling and crisis intervention services;

(c) workshops and public awareness campaigns to combat stigmas;

(d) housing and employment for deinstitutionalized persons;

(e) improved training for judges, police, and other community officials in dealing with mentally ill persons;

(f) community and congregational involvement with patients in psychiatric hospitals and other mental-health-care facilities;

(g) community, pastoral, and congregational support for individuals and families caring for mentally ill family members;

(h) more effective interaction among different systems involved in the care of mentally ill persons, including courts, police, employment, housing, welfare, religious, and family systems;

(i) education of their members in a responsible and comprehensive manner about the nature of the problems of mental illness facing society today, and the public-policy advocacy needed to change policies and keep funding levels high;

(j) active participation in helping their communities meet both preventive and therapeutic needs related to mental illness; and

(k) the work of the National Alliance for the Mentally Ill (NAMI), Washington, D.C., a self-help organization of mentally ill persons, their families, and friends, providing mutual support, education, and advocacy for those persons with severe mental illness and urging the churches to connect with NAMI's religious outreach network. We also commend to the churches Pathways to Promise: Interfaith Ministries and Prolonged Mental Illnesses, St. Louis, Missouri, as a necessary link in our ministry on this critical issue.

2. We call upon seminaries to provide:

(a) technical training, including experience in mental-health units, as a regular part of the preparation for the ministry, in order to help congregations become more knowledgeable about and involved in mental-health needs of their communities.

3. We call upon the general agencies to:

(a) advocate systemic reform of the health-care system to provide more adequately for persons and families confronting the catastrophic expense and pain of caring for mentally ill family members;

(b) support universal access to health care, insisting that public and private funding mechanisms be developed to ensure the availability of services to all in need, including adequate coverage for mental-health services in all health programs;

(c) advocate community mental-health systems, including public clinics, hospitals, and other tax-supported facilities, being especially sensitive to the mental-health needs of culturally or racially diverse groups in the population;

(d) support adequate research by public and private institutions into the causes of mental illness, including, as high priority, further development of therapeutic applications of newly discovered information on the genetic causation for several types of severe brain disorders;

(e) support adequate public funding to enable mental-health-care systems to provide appropriate therapy; and

(f) build a United Methodist Church mental illness network at the General Board of Church and Society to coordinate mental-illness ministries in The United Methodist Church.

ADOPTED 1992

See Social Principles, ¶ 66Q; "Health in Mind and Body"; "Ministries in Mental Illness"; "Caring Communities—The United Methodist Mental Illness Network."

Ministry to Runaway Children

The United Methodist Church calls its members to follow Jesus Christ in his mission to bring all persons into a community of love. The Social Principles uphold the potential of the community for nurturing human beings into the fullness of their humanity through its basic unit, the family. We as United Methodists acknowledge children as beings to whom adults and society in general have obligations: the rights to food, shelter, clothing, health care, and emotional well-being. We also recognize youth and young adults as those who frequently find full participation in society difficult.

The United Methodist Church, having accepted its commission to manifest the life of the gospel in the world within the context of hope and expectation, deplores the fact that in this nation, 1,000,000 children are reported missing every year, that countless thousands are forced out or "thrown away," and that homicide is one of the five leading causes of death among children between the ages of one and seventeen. We recognize the prevalence of physical, sexual, or emotional abuse as the underlying cause for almost half of the behaviors classified as running away.

Running away is not unique to any social class. The average age for runaways is dropping, and the majority are girls. We are alarmed that a whole new category of children known as "street children" are living degrading and dangerous lives in the streets of our towns and cities.

We believe these runaways should neither be a police problem nor processed through the legal system where they are usually incarcerated rather than protected, and adjudicated rather than enlightened. Most such youths require temporary shelter and supervision instead of secure detention.

We commend those congregations and annual conferences already engaged in outreach to runaway youth, providing food, shelter, and protection from personal exploitation as well as referral to sources of help. We feel that the runaway crisis offers a further opportunity to help families when they want and are receptive to such help. Therefore, we support immediate crisis intervention and counseling for youth and their families, with the primary objective of returning the youth to his or her home. When there is no possibility of its becoming a healthy environment, we support the development of alternate living arrangements that provide a nurturing environment.

We further urge that United Methodist agencies join in efforts to develop innovative ministries of support and protection for street children who would not usually come to a runaway shelter.

We encourage local church efforts toward prevention by programming to strengthen and support families within their congregations. We call Christians everywhere into service wherever God and a loving heart may call them; into the schools where poor school performance is often the precipitating crisis to running; into their own neighborhoods and community where there are countless opportunities to help troubled youth; into supporting programs in the community that deal compassionately with abusing parents.

"And the King will answer them, 'Truly, I say to you, as you did it to one of the least of my brethren, you did it to me' " (Matthew 25:40, Revised Standard Version).

ADOPTED 1984

See Social Principles, ¶66C; "Protecting and Sustaining Children."

Mission Personnel in the United States

WHEREAS, mission personnel in the United States, which includes church and community workers, US-2s, mission interns, summer interns, community developers, rural chaplains, lay missioners, and others, have faithfully and effectively enabled The United Methodist Church to facilitate mission and ministry across the United States in settings often neglected and overlooked by others; and

WHEREAS, for many people in the United States, life is becoming increasingly difficult, with the basic necessities of food, shelter, health care, job and educational opportunities, childcare, and transportation required for daily survival often being beyond reach; and

WHEREAS, God continues to hear the cries of the oppressed, impoverished, and neglected people; and

WHEREAS, God continues to call persons to offer themselves for service with the poor to provide both compassionate care and personal empowerment; and

WHEREAS, The United Methodist Church, with its unique Wesleyan traditions of identity and advocacy with the poor and its historical focus on social issues and human development, is challenged by God to be radically attentive and responsive to marginalized and dispossessed people and to bear responsibility for keeping their plight before the total church and world community; and

WHEREAS, mission personnel in the United States provide vital leadership required to initiate and maintain cooperative ministries, shalom zones/communities, and so forth that focus attention on the needs of women, children, youth, racial and ethnic populations, the aging, and people with disabilities in both rural and urban areas;

Therefore, be it resolved, that The United Methodist Church reaffirm its commitment to impoverished people and oppressed communities in the United States by creating and maintaining among its highest levels of priority the recruitment, training, and placement of mission personnel in the United States who can enable people, churches, and communities to move beyond their present circumstances to participate in healthy, whole communities;

Be it further resolved, that new and innovative means of providing financial support for mission personnel in the United States be developed as The United Methodist Church at all levels confronts the challenge to deal with limited available resources.

ADOPTED 1996

See Social Principles, ¶ 67E; "Economic Justice"; "Call for a Rebirth of Compassion."

Mutual Recognition of Members

Introduction

The General Conferences of 1976 and 1980 adopted affirmations of the basic Consultation on Church Union (COCU) principle of mutual recognition of memberships based on baptism. All other member churches have done the same. Now, as the Consultation is moving forward on further implications of theological consensus, mutual recognition, covenanting together, and eventual reconciliation, The United Methodist Church wishes to join with other churches in moving from affirmation to action.

The plenary of the Consultation on Church Union in November 1984 will focus on the new theological statement of consensus, the implications of a developing covenant toward unity (that is expected to be before the General Conference of 1988), and liturgical expressions of both. These emphases are related to the new World Council of Churches statement on "Baptism, Eucharist, and Ministry" currently being reviewed and responded to by United Methodists.

We have a stake in the faithful discipleship of other communions. Other churches have a stake in the faithful discipleship of The United Methodist Church. For it is the church of Jesus Christ that is called to share in mission and ministry for the world. God's covenant is with the whole people of God. A concurrent expression of United Methodist seriousness in the cause of Christian unity is needed. Clear, visible evidence that we understand ourselves to be part of the body of Christ is needed.

Therefore, be it resolved, that participation with voice in United Methodist governing bodies and agencies and the joining in our liturgical celebrations by representatives from other communions are both symbols of the oneness of the church of which we are a part and signs to others of our ecumenical seriousness.

To manifest our integrity as part of the church of Jesus Christ, several items of legislation are proposed to the General Conference, including the permissive inclusion (outside of quota requirements) of representatives from other communions in General Conference, annual conferences, general and conference boards, and other agencies. This resolution supplements that legislation with specific recommendations that relate to annual conferences and local churches, namely:

1. That United Methodist annual conferences be empowered, encouraged, and enabled to invite official representatives from other denominations, especially from member churches of the Consultation on Church Union, to their sessions and committees with voice, and that United Methodist judicatory leaders nominate representatives to the official church bodies of other denominations where invited to do so;

2. That representatives of other denominations be invited to participate in the laying on of hands in annual conference ordination ceremonies, symbolizing the catholicity of our ministry;

3. That annual conference commissions on Christian unity and interreligious concerns and conference councils on ministry be alert to and consider carefully the development by the Consultation on Church Union of 1984 of: (a) the principles and the text of an "Act of Covenanting"; (b) development by them of enabling acts related to possible representation on "Councils of Oversight" that may be formed at middle judicatory levels of the COCU member churches; and (c) encourage responsiveness to liturgical formulations developed by COCU, which will be based on theological consensus and the covenanting processes;

4. That United Methodist local churches be encouraged to invite representatives from other denominations to participate in celebrations such as World Communion Sunday, baptism, and confirmation, and in special commemorative occasions in the congregation's life;

5. That local churches be urged to take initiatives in cooperation with congregations of other denominations in issues of racial and social justice, in mission and evangelism, and in occasions of special study and celebration (such as Advent, Lent, Easter, and Pentecost); and that special efforts be made to share persons with special skills, talents, and imagination between denominations in order to strengthen the whole body of Christ in its nature and witness; and

6. That local churches and annual conferences, aided by the General Commission on Christian Unity and Interreligious Concerns

(GCCUIC), study the COCU publication of a seven-chapter consensus on *In Quest of a Church of Christ Uniting* and respond to the GCCUIC.

ADOPTED 1984

See Social Principles, ¶ 66B; "Continuing Membership in the Consultation on Church Union"; "Guidelines for Interreligious Relationships"; "Toward an Ecumenical Future"; "COCU Consensus: In Quest of a Church of Christ Uniting."

National Observance of Children's Sabbaths

More than 14.6 million American children live in poverty. Today, 100,000 children are homeless each night, and 9.3 million are not covered by insurance at any time. Only 55.3 percent of U.S. two-year-olds were immunized against preventable diseases in 1992, and 5,356 children and teenagers died in 1991 as a result of firearm injuries, including homicide, suicides, and accidents. Between 1979 and 1991, nearly 50,000 American children were killed by guns. Four million low-income children under age twelve are hungry in this country. According to UNICEF, about 1 million children die of measles every year, approximately 3 million children die of diarrhea every year, and about 30 million children will die of pneumonia during the 1990s.

The National Observance of Children's Sabbath was born out of the concern for children's conditions in the U.S. and the world. A growing religious and social movement for children's well-being, across a range of denominations, coalesced their concern for poor and neglected children in a united moral witness.

This effort has been supported and led by the Children's Defense Fund (CDF), a nonprofit, nonpartisan organization that provides a strong and effective voice for the children of our nation who cannot vote, lobby, or speak out for themselves.

Since 1981, CDF has worked in partnership with the religious community to mobilize congregations across the U.S. to increase their awareness on the conditions of children. In 1993, CDF distributed more than 30,000 Children's Sabbath kits in response to requests from clergy, laypersons, and religious organizations.

Our biblical tradition beseeches us to make children one of our major concerns for ministry (Matthew 18:1-7, 10). We are called to protect our children and to guide them in the way of righteousness (Proverbs 22:6; Ephesians 6:4; 2 Timothy 3:14-15).

The Social Principles of The United Methodist Church state that "children *have the rights* to food, shelter, clothing, health care, and emotional well-being as do adults, and these rights we affirm as theirs *regardless of actions or inactions* of their parents or guardians" (¶ 66C, emphasis added).

The United Methodist resolution on "Protecting and Sustaining Children" states that "the future of the human race is in our children, but in decision-making they are voiceless and powerless. Children cannot speak for themselves. They depend on us to speak for them and to be their advocates. They suffer most when resources are misappropriated. They need us to bring their very special needs to the notice of societies and those in power." That resolution calls all levels of the Church to "engage in denominational and ecumenical efforts to end child poverty."

The United Methodist Church is one of more than 150 denominations and religious organizations that cooperate in the National Observance of Children's Sabbath.

The religious affairs division of the Children's Defense Fund has collaborated extensively with the General Board of Church and Society, the United Methodist Women's Campaign for Children, and the Conference Schools of Christian Mission.

The United Methodist Church is one of the Children's Sabbaths' greatest supporters, with nearly 700 churches receiving materials to assist them in planning for the observation.

We strongly urge all United Methodist churches to celebrate the National Observance of the Children's Sabbath annually, for as long as our children are at risk.

ADOPTED 1996

See Social Principles, ¶ 66C; "Putting Children and Their Families First"; "Protecting and Sustaining Children."

Native American History and Contemporary Culture as Related to Effective Church Participation

WHEREAS, current literature and research suggest a substantial "communication gap" between Native Americans and non-Indian United Methodist Church entities, specifically as it relates to non-Indian entities comprehending the concept of Native American life, culture, language, spirit, values, and such; and

WHEREAS, this vague communication has been a consistent problem over history, with minimal effort from non-Indian entities to change their attitudes toward Native Americans until recent trends; and

WHEREAS, such attitude of society reflects a growing trend toward developing and implementing a system accommodating, to a high degree, cultural diversity; generally speaking, society is beginning to demonstrate comprehension of the term *multicultural education* as related to the year 2000 and is making efforts to become even more informed; services that once perpetuated Eurocentric society only are now examining the values of the ever-growing ethnic populations and attempting to integrate these values into their service activities (education, government, health, business, and such); and

WHEREAS, there are substantial numbers of ethnic professionals capable of providing effective instruction in cultural diversity as related to The United Methodist Church's current and future thrusts; and

WHEREAS, there still is a critical need for The United Methodist Church to become concretely familiar with its Native American membership in order to ensure their religious, denominational, spiritual, and emotional well-being; and

WHEREAS, there is an expressed concern from The United Methodist Church's Native American membership that racism and prejudice are significant contributors to the absence of Native American representation in the Church's hierarchy; and

WHEREAS, the formal means of eliminating this condition is through the formal instruction in Native American history, culture, and contemporary affairs of non-Indian entities of The United Methodist Church;

Therefore, be it resolved, that General Conference advocate the development and implementation of a training policy whereby Native American history, culture, and contemporary affairs will be an integral part of ministry and administrative training for all aspects of The United Methodist Church;

Be it further resolved, that General Conference designate the National United Methodist Native American Center, Inc., as the center for the research, development, and training components of the requested curriculum;

Be it further resolved, that General Conference support a policy that the concept of "Indian preference" be utilized in the selection of instructors and speakers for the proposed training components.

ADOPTED 1992

See Social Principles, ¶ 66A; "The United Methodist Church and America's Native People"; "Native American Social Witness Program"; "Native American Representation in The United Methodist Church."

Native American Representation in The United Methodist Church

WHEREAS, the population of Native Americans has grown dramatically during the past two decades; and

WHEREAS, this trend of population growth is accompanied by a substantial positive interest in Native American culture and history in regard to The United Methodist Church participation among traditionally noninterested individuals; and

WHEREAS, leadership of The United Methodist Church has recently demonstrated a sincere desire to "include" Native Americans in the decision-making activity of the Church; and

WHEREAS, there is a significant need to recruit Native Americans into "role model" positions within the Church as a means to enhance church membership, ministry numbers, and an overall understanding of contemporary Native American life as related to racial communication; and

WHEREAS, current attitudes among Native Americans reflect a critical desire to present and communicate accurate Native American perspectives to, and for, decision-making bodies of The United Methodist Church; and

WHEREAS, there is currently a minute number of Native Americans serving on the national United Methodist Church policy-making boards, management committees, education boards, finance committees, information areas, and such; and

WHEREAS, current trends suggest a decrease in church membership and attendance among Native American citizenry;

Therefore, be it resolved, that General Conference strongly support the following tasks as related to accurate Native American representation and participation on local, regional, and national policy-making, managerial, and implementation/evaluation boards/committees of The United Methodist Church:

1. Establish a policy of defining Native American identity as "any individual who can provide verification of membership in a tribe of the United States";

2. Develop a policy that will ensure that Native Americans will be identified, selected, and placed on pertinent boards and/or committees as previously stated; and

3. Urge national, regional, and annual conference activities to select Native American representation from Native American individuals

who have a background of relevant Native American history, cultural sensitivity, and contemporary affairs.

Be it further resolved, that The United Methodist Church supports the integration of a policy on Native American definition within the *Book of Discipline*, specific to the current and future regard of Native American representation on such national, regional, and local efforts.

ADOPTED 1992

See Social Principles, ¶ 66A; "Native American Young Adults in Mission"; "Native American Social Witness Program"; "Promote the Observance of Native American Awareness Sunday."

Native American Social Witness Program

WHEREAS, Native American churches have historically been seen as being on the receiving end of mission and ministry; and

WHEREAS, yet many social concerns are presently being addressed by Native American communities; and

WHEREAS, the potential and need for social justice ministries among Native Americans is tremendous, and Native American congregations have been put into the role of recipient rather than being empowered;

Therefore, be it resolved, that the General Board of Church and Society make available, on request, to every Native American United Methodist church, ministry training and consultation on social witness during the 1992–1996 quadrennium. Such program will be designed and patterned after the gospel of Jesus Christ, which will empower congregations to engage in social witness to their respective Native American communities.

ADOPTED 1992

See Social Principles, ¶ 66A; "Native American Representation in The United Methodist Church"; "The United Methodist Church and America's Native People."

Native American Young Adults in Mission

WHEREAS, by treaty obligation many Native American tribes are recognized as "nations" within the territorial boundaries of the United States; and

WHEREAS, the National and World Divisions and the Mission Personnel Resources Program Department of the General Board of Global

Ministries of The United Methodist Church sponsor the Mission Intern Program, the World Division assigns young adults overseas to develop leadership skills, and the National Division assigns young adults within the boundaries of the United States to develop leadership skills; and

WHEREAS, opportunities for mission and evangelism exist within Native American nations and tribes within the territorial boundaries of the United States;

Therefore, be it resolved, that the Mission Personnel Resources Program Department, World and National Divisions, be directed to assign Native American young adults in "Native American Nations and Tribes" within the boundaries of the United States and in overseas assignments.

ADOPTED 1992

See Social Principles, ¶ 66A; "Native American Social Witness Program"; "Native American Representation in The United Methodist Church."

New Developments in Genetic Science

I. Foreword

The 1988 General Conference approved a statement affirming the positive prospects and warning of the potential dangers of genetic technologies. The General Conference authorized the establishment of a representative task force to:

1. Review and assess scientific developments in genetics and their implications for all life;

2. Take initiatives with industrial, governmental, and educational institutions involved in genetic engineering to discuss further projections and possible impact;

3. Convey to industry and government the sense of urgency to protect the environment as well as animal and human life;

4. Support a moratorium on animal patenting until the task force has explored the ethical issues involved;

5. Cooperate with other churches, faith groups, and ecumenical bodies sharing similar concerns;

6. Explore the effects of the concentration of genetic engineering research tasks and applications in a few crops; and

7. Recommend to the 1992 General Conference such further responses and actions as may be deemed appropriate. The term *genetic science*

was adopted to identify collectively the aforementioned issues, and the task force was thus named the Genetic Science Task Force.

The task force was appointed in March 1989. Task force members include scientists, educators, health professionals, ethicists, theologians, a social worker, a lawyer, and a farmer. Informational hearings in the following areas provided basic data on the issues: Houston and College Station, Texas; Boston, Massachusetts; Washington, D.C.; San Leandro, California; Ames, Iowa; Durham, North Carolina; and Oak Ridge, Tennessee.

Testimony was received from geneticists, physicians, theologians, ethicists, social workers, attorneys, officers of biotechnology companies, journalists, insurance executives, governmental regulatory agency representatives, educators, and persons with genetic disorders and the family members of such persons. The hearing process formed the basis of the recommendations contained in this resolution. A more complete discussion of issues can be found in the complete report of the task force to General Conference.

II. Our Theological Grounding

The United Methodist doctrinal/theological statement affirms that "new issues continually arise that summon us to fresh theological inquiry. Daily we are presented with an array of concerns that challenge our proclamation of God's reign over all of human existence" (1988 *Book of Discipline*, ¶ 69).

One of the concerns that merits critique in light of theological understandings is genetic science. The urgent task of interpreting the faith in light of the biotechnology revolution and evaluating the rapidly emerging genetic science and technology has only begun. The issues demand continuing dialogue at all levels of the Church as persons from diverse perspectives seek to discern and live out God's vision for creation.

The following affirmations provide the theological/doctrinal foundation of the task force's work and recommendations. These historic affirmations represent criteria by which developments and potential developments in biotechnology are evaluated by the community of faith, the Church. The task force urges the whole Church to join in the urgent task of theological inquiry in what has been called the genetic age.

A. All Creation Belongs to God the Creator

Creation has its origin, existence, value, and destiny in God. Creation belongs to God, whose power and grace brings the cosmos out of nothingness, order out of chaos, and life out of death. Creation is a realm of divine activity as God continually seeks to bring healing, wholeness, and peace. All creation is accountable to God; therefore, all existence is contingent, finite, and limited. Creation has been declared "good" by the Creator, and its goodness inheres in its fulfillment of the divine purpose. The goodness of our genetic diversity is grounded in our creation by God.

B. Human Beings Are Stewards of Creation

While human beings share with other species the limitations of finite creatures who owe their existence to God, their special creation "in the image of God" gives them the freedom and authority to exercise stewardship responsibly. This includes the knowledge of human life and behavior as it is being expanded by genetic science. The biblical imperative is that human beings are to nurture, cultivate, and serve God's creation so that it might be sustained. Humans are to participate in, manage, nurture, justly distribute, employ, develop, and enhance creation's resources in accordance with their finite discernment of God's purposes. Their divinely conferred dominion over nature does not sanction exploitation and waste; neither does responsible stewardship imply refusal to act creatively with intelligence, skill, and foresight.

The image of God, in which humanity is created, confers both power and responsibility to use power as God does: neither by coercion nor tyranny, but by love. Failure to accept limits by rejecting or ignoring accountability to God and interdependency with the whole of creation is the essence of sin. Therefore, the question is not Can we perform all prodigious work of research and technology? but, Should we? The notion that the ability to do something is permission to do it ignores the fundamental biblical understanding of human beings as stewards accountable to the Creator and as contingent, interdependent creatures. Although the pursuit of knowledge is a divine gift, it must be used appropriately with the principle of accountability to God and to the human community and the sustainability of all creation.

C. Technology in Service to Humanity and God

God has given human beings the capacity for research and technological invention, but the worship of science is idolatry. Genetic techniques have enormous potential for enhancing creation and human life when they are applied to environmental, agricultural, and medical problems. When wisely used, they often provide positive—though limited and imperfect—solutions to such perplexing social problems as insufficient food supply, spread of disease, ecological deterioration, overpopulation, and human suffering. When used recklessly, for greedy profit, or for calculated improvement of the human race (eugenics), genetic technology becomes corrupted by sin. Moreover, we recognize that even the careful use of genetic technologies for good ends may lead to unintended consequences. We confess that even our intended consequences may not be in the best interest of all.

D. From Creation to Redemption and Salvation

Redemption and salvation become realities by divine grace as we respond in faith to God's action in Jesus Christ to defeat the powers of sin that enslave the human spirit and thwart the realization of God's purposes for creation. Jesus Christ is the incarnation of God's eternal Word and wisdom. His redemptive life, ministry, death, resurrection, and sending of the Spirit reveal God's vision for humanity. Having distorted God's good intention for us in creation, we now are called to be conformed to God's true image in Jesus Christ.

Through the affirmation of the goodness of creation and the saving work of Christ, God has claimed all persons as beloved sons and daughters with inherent worth and dignity. Therefore, we understand that our worth as children of God is irrespective of genetic qualities, personal attributes, or achievements. Barriers and prejudices based on biological characteristics fracture the human family and distort God's goal for humanity. The community of Christ bears witness to the truth that all persons have unity by virtue of having been redeemed by Christ. Such unity respects and embraces genetic diversity, which accounts for many differences among people. Love and justice, which the Scriptures uplift and which Jesus Christ supremely expresses, require that the worth and dignity of the defenseless be preserved and protected. As the community of Christ, the Church seeks to embody love and justice and to give of itself on behalf of the powerless and voiceless.

E. God's Reign is for All Creation

The coming of God's reign is the guiding hope for all creation. Hebrew Scripture and the life, teaching, death, and resurrection of Jesus Christ affirm that God's reign is characterized by liberation from all forms of oppression, justice in all relationships, peace and good will among all peoples, and the healing of all creation. It is both the vision of God's new heaven and new earth and the recognition of our limits that must inform and shape our role as stewards of earth and life in the emerging age of genetics. It is in the context of God's sovereignty over all existence, our hope for the coming of God's reign, our awareness of our own finitude, and our responsibility as stewards that we consider these issues and the following recommendations.

III. Issues in the Development of Genetic Research and Technology

A. Why the Church is Addressing These Issues

God's sovereignty over all creation, our status as stewards of creation's resources, and the Church's nature as a nurturing and prophetic community living toward God's reign over all existence propel us to consider the theological/ethical implications of genetic science. As genetic science probes the very structure of biological life and develops means to alter the nature of life itself, the potential for relief of suffering and the healing of creation is enormous. But the potential for added physical and emotional suffering and social and economic injustice also exists. Developments in genetic science compel our reevaluation of accepted theological/ethical issues, including determinism versus free will, the nature of sin, just distribution of resources, the status of human beings in relation to other forms of life, and the meaning of personhood.

B. Genetic Science Affects Every Area of Our Lives

The food we eat, the health care we receive, our biological traits, and the environment in which we live are all affected by research and developments in genetic science. As stewards of and participants in life and its resources, we seek to understand, to evaluate, and to utilize responsibly the emerging genetic technologies in accordance with our finite understanding of God's purposes for creation. The divine purpose includes justice, health, and peace for all persons, and the integrity and ecological balance of creation. The uses of genetic science have the potential for promoting as well as thwarting these aspects of the divine purpose.

Genetic issues are much more pressing than is generally recognized. Every community contains individuals and families who daily face genetic concerns in the workplace or as result of their own genetic makeup. The rapid growth of genetic science has increased our awareness of these concerns, has created new concerns, and has accelerated the theological, ethical, and pastoral challenges that genetics poses to persons of faith.

C. Scientific Change Now Leads Societal Change

The rise in importance of science and technology has been one of the most significant developments in the last 400 years. Beginning with the industrial revolution, we have witnessed a succession of revolutions: the technological, the atomic, and the biological. Each of these revolutions has presented society with a host of religious challenges and threats that have taken enormous and ongoing efforts to resolve constructively. The very nature of work, perceptions of the world, international relations, and family life has changed in part because of these revolutions.

A major dimension of the biological revolution is genetic science. Less than fifty years ago, the actual genetic substance of living cells, DNA, was firmly identified. Now, altering DNA in plants and animals, even humans, in order to correct disorders or to introduce more desirable characteristics is being done. Genetic developments in medicine and agriculture promise to alter the very nature of society, the natural environment, and even human nature. Christians must evaluate these developments in light of our basic understanding of God as creator and of humans as stewards of creation, including technology.

D. Genetic Science Challenges Society

Biotechnology based on genetic research is already upon us. Thousands of people and millions of dollars are devoted to genetic science. Gene therapy has already been introduced as an experimental medical treatment. Extensive research is being conducted in plant and animal genetics, with significant implications for the food supply, farm policy, agricultural economics, and ecological balance. The efforts to identify the estimated one hundred thousand human genes (the Human Genome Project) are well underway with funding from both the National Institutes of Health and the U.S. Department of Energy.

In spite of the rapid growth in genetic research, many people tend to see genetics merely as an extension of the changes in medical, agricultural, and other technologies. In fact, genetic science crosses new frontiers as it explores the essence of life. The implications of genetic research and development are so far-reaching that society must consider the effect of these developments on persons, animal and plant life, the environment, agriculture, the food supply, patent policies, and medicine. Delays in commercializing some of the technologies may afford society and the Church additional time to address the implications, but the time available for serious reflection on the consequences of these technologies prior to their implementation is brief.

IV. Questions About Biotechnology

New developments in technology always challenge society's imagination and understanding. Technology is often viewed either with awe or with fear. The popular view of the geneticist alternates between a saint who cures all disease and a mad scientist who creates monsters or perverts life. The extreme image must be avoided as society raises questions about the technologies themselves and questions how they should be properly developed and controlled. Although genetic technologies are similar to other technologies, genetic science and technology force us to examine, as never before, the meaning of life, our understanding of ourselves as humans, and our proper role in God's creation.

Several basic questions can provide a framework within which to evaluate the effect of genetics (or any other new technology) on any segment of society. The questions revolve around issues of appropriateness, availability, efficacy, and accessibility.

V. The Patenting of Life Forms

The patenting of life forms is a crucial issue in the debate over access to genetic technologies. Some claim that patenting of life will give complete control to the owner and so limit access. Others insist that the scientists and funding agencies or institutions must have some return on their investment. A compromise that many societies have worked out in order to provide economic returns for those who have developed a technology while providing access, eventually, to the entire society is the patent, or exclusive control of a technological invention for a period of years. But should exclusive ownership rights apply to the gene pool?

In 1984, the General Conference of The United Methodist Church declared genes to be a part of the common heritage of all peoples. The position taken by the Church in 1984 is consistent with our understanding of the sanctity of God's creation and God's ownership of life. Therefore, exclusive ownership rights of genes as a means of making genetic technologies accessible raises serious theological concerns. While patents on organisms themselves are opposed, process patents— wherein the method for engineering a new organism is patented— provide a means of economic return on investment while avoiding exclusive ownership of the organism and can be supported.

VI. Affirmations/Recommendations/Conclusions

A. General

1. We affirm that knowledge of genetics is a resource over which we are to exercise stewardship responsibly in accordance with God's reign over creation. The use of genetic knowledge in ways that destabilize and fragment creation is resisted as a violation of God's vision of justice, peace, and wholeness.

2. We caution that the prevalent principle in research that what *can* be done *should* be done is insufficient rationale for genetic science. This principle should be subject to legal and ethical oversight in research design and should not be the prevalent principle guiding the development of new technologies. Applications of research to technologies need moral and ethical guidance.

3. We urge adequate public funding of genetic research so that projects not likely to be funded by private grants will receive adequate support and so that there will be greater accountability to the public by those involved in setting the direction of genetic research.

4. We urge that genes and genetically modified organisms (human, plant, animal) be held as common resources and not be exclusively controlled, or patented. We support improvements in the procedures for granting patents on processes and techniques as a way to reward new developments in this area.

B. Medical Recommendations

1. Testing and Treatment

(a) We support the right of all persons to health care and health-care resources regardless of their genetic or medical conditions.

(b) We support equal access to medical resources, including genetic testing and genetic counseling by appropriately educated and trained health-care professionals. We affirm that responsible stewardship of God's gift of human life implies access of all persons to genetic counseling throughout their reproductive life.

(c) We support human gene therapies that produce changes that cannot be passed on to offspring (somatic) but believe that they should be limited to the alleviation of suffering caused by disease. We urge that guidelines and government regulations be developed for the use of all gene therapies. We oppose therapy that results in changes that can be passed to offspring (germ-line therapy) until its safety and the certainty of its effects can be demonstrated and until risks to human life can be demonstrated to be minimal.

(d) We support the use of recombinant DNA for the purposes of genetic therapy and the prevention of genetic disorders. However, we oppose its use for eugenic purposes or genetic enhancements designed merely for cosmetic purposes or social advantage.

2. Privacy and Confidentiality of Genetic Information

(a) We support the privacy of genetic information. Genetic data of individuals and their families shall be kept secret and held in strict confidence unless confidentiality is waived by the individual or his or her family, or unless the collection and use of genetic identification data are supported by an appropriate court order.

(b) We support increased study of the social, moral, and ethical implications of the Human Genome Project. We support wide public access to genetic data that do not identify particular individuals.

(c) We oppose the discriminatory or manipulative use of genetic information, such as the limitation, termination, or denial of insurance or employment.

C. Agriculture

1. We support public involvement in initiating, evaluating, regulating, and funding of agricultural genetic research.

(a) We believe the public has an important policy and financial role in ensuring the continuation of research that furthers the goal of a safe, nutritious, and affordable food supply.

(b) We believe that the public should have input into whether a research effort, or its products, will serve an unmet need in food and fiber production and processing. We urge United Methodists to be active participants in achieving this accountability in all areas of the world.

(c) We believe that the benefits of research applications should accrue to the broadest possible public, including farmers and consumers.

2. We support the sustainability of family farms, natural resources, and rural communities and urge that genetic research in agriculture and food products promote these goals.

D. Environment

1. As stewards of the planet Earth, we should strive to perpetuate all of God's living creations as long as possible. We should be concerned not only with the well-being of humans, but also with the wholeness of the rest of creation. We should try to maintain ecological balance as God intended. Technologies such as genetic engineering can affect ecological balance. Genetic technologies must be used carefully to help sustain the planet.

2. We caution that genetically engineered organisms be released into the environment only after careful testing in a controlled setting that stimulates each environment in which the organisms are to be used.

3. We urge the development of criteria and methodologies to anticipate and assess possible adverse environmental responses to the release of genetically engineered organisms.

4. We urge that prior to the release of each organism, plans and procedures be developed to destroy genetically engineered organisms that may cause adverse environmental responses.

E. What the Church Can Do

1. Expand education and dialogue around ethical issues in the development of genetic science and technology.

(a) We request that The United Methodist Church and its appropriate boards and agencies educate laity and clergy on the issues of genetic science, theology, and ethics by conducting workshops and seminars, producing resource materials, and training pastors and laypersons to deal constructively with these issues. Sessions on the ethical implications of genetics technology should be included as part of seminary training, continuing education requirements for clergy, Christian educators' training events, adult and youth Sunday school curriculum, schools of mission and schools of church and society, and campus ministry programs.

(b) We request that clergy be trained to provide pastoral counseling for persons with genetic disorders and their families as well as those facing difficult choices as a result of genetic testing. These choices might include decisions such as those related to reproduction, employment, and living wills. Churches are encouraged to provide support groups for individuals and families affected by genetic disorders.

(c) We call on the Church to support persons who, because of the likelihood of severe genetic disorders, must make difficult decisions regarding reproduction. We reaffirm the 1988 General Conference (1988 *Book of Discipline,* ¶ 71G) position opposing the termination of pregnancy solely for the purpose of gender selection.

(d) We urge theological seminaries to offer courses and continuing education events that equip clergy to address theological and ethical issues raised by scientific research and technology.

(e) We urge the Church to establish and maintain dialogue with those persons working to develop or promote genetics-based technologies.

The complexity and multifaceted implications of genetic science require continuing interaction among scientists, technologists, theologians, ethicists, industrial and corporate leaders, government officials, and the general public. The Church can facilitate dialogue on the emerging issues. The Genetic Science Task Force hearings revealed a strong interest on the part of persons from various perspectives, experiences, and interests in exploring the ethical, theological, and societal implications of developments in genetics. Providing a forum for informed discussion will enable the Church to inform the public, raise relevant theological/ethical concerns, expand and deepen theological exploration in light of contemporary developments, and more adequately support scientists and technologists who seek to live out their faith in their vocations.

The ethical concerns of the Church need to be interjected into the laboratory, the factory, and the halls of government in an ongoing manner. Local churches, districts, annual conferences, and appropriate general agencies should participate in dialogues with university, industry, and government bodies.

2. Produce resources to educate on genetics issues. General agencies of the Church should develop additional interpretive resources on genetics issues.

(a) United Methodist Communications is urged to cooperate with the General Board of Church and Society to develop an episode of "Catch the Spirit" highlighting persons who testified to the Genetics Science Task Force.

(b) The Board of Discipleship is urged to develop curriculum materials stressing the ethical dimensions of the widespread use of genetic technologies in health, agriculture, and other industries.

(c) The Division of Health and Welfare Ministries of the General Board of Global Ministries is urged to develop materials in cooperation with United Methodist-affiliated hospitals on the ethical issues families may face regarding the use of new diagnostic tests and other procedures.

(d) The General Board of Higher Education and Ministry is urged to survey seminaries and United Methodist-affiliated schools for academic courses related to genetic science and to make this listing available through its publications.

(e) The General Council on Ministries Research Section is urged to survey United Methodist general agencies and annual conferences requesting the names of informed speakers in the following categories:

(1) families affected by genetic disorders;

(2) clergy with experience in the fields of genetics research or genetics counseling;

(3) genetic counselors, social workers, psychologists, and other counseling professionals who work with individuals and families with genetic disorders;

(4) social and physical scientists researching the effect of genetics technologies on society;

(5) environmental, agricultural, and biomedical scientists;

(6) theologians and ethicists;

(7) farmers and others concerned about agricultural and environmental effects of these technologies;

(8) technologists and representatives of industry;

(9) physicians knowledgeable in genetic issues, especially obstetrician-gynecologists and pediatricians; and

(10) educators.

3. Continue and increase The United Methodist Church's work in the area of genetics.

(a) The General Council on Ministries is urged to convene a meeting of general agency staff in early 1993 to review the work each agency plans in the 1993–1996 quadrennium relative to the ethics of genetic science technologies.

(b) The General Board of Church and Society is urged to continue its work in these areas, to publish a summary of the hearings it conducted on genetic science, and to monitor legislative and governmental actions related to genetic technologies.

(c) All general agencies are urged to cooperate with ecumenical groups as they seek to coordinate actions regarding the use of knowledge gained from genetic science. Concern for justice for persons and the integrity of all life should form the basis of our ecumenical witness.

(d) Local churches are urged to study the issues raised in this statement and to act on the recommendations.

ADOPTED 1992

See Social Principles, ¶ 66*M;* "U.S. Agriculture and Rural Communities in Crisis."

Observance of Dr. Martin Luther King Jr. Day

WHEREAS, the observance of Dr. Martin Luther King Jr. Day is in keeping with the spirit of the Social Principles of The United Methodist Church and the inclusiveness of the denomination;

Therefore, be it resolved, that each annual conference observe Martin Luther King Jr. Day with appropriate services of commemoration in recognition of Dr. King; and

On that day we recommend that we close the bishop's office, all conference offices, all district offices, all local church offices, and, where feasible, business offices of Church-related institutions; and

Support local activities surrounding the celebration of Dr. King's life and ministry; and

Encourage local school districts not to hold classes on Dr. Martin Luther King Jr. Day; or

If local school districts hold classes, encourage them to use Dr. Martin Luther King Jr. Day to celebrate Dr. King's work and address the need for the continuing struggle for justice.

ADOPTED 1992

See Social Principles, ¶ 66*A;* "A Charter for Racial Justice Policies in an Interdependent Global Community."

Observance of Health Care Sabbaths

In 1994, the Interreligious Health Care Access Campaign inaugurated the observance of a Health Care Sabbath by persons of faith as a symbol of their faithfulness to the goal of health care for all. Rather than specifying a particular date for this observance, the Campaign encouraged communions and congregations to select a Sabbath date that reflected their individual commitment to issues of health and wholeness. In support of this interfaith effort and in faithful witness to the beliefs articulated in the United Methodist resolutions on "Health and Wholeness," "Universal Access to Health Care in the United States and Related Territories," and "Health for All by the Year 2000," The United Methodist Church calls congregations to designate one Sunday during the calendar year for the observance of a Health Care Sabbath.

The Health Care Sabbath is a day of rejoicing and reflection. It is a time for thanksgiving for the health and well-being enjoyed by many in our world community and thanksgiving for the diverse caregivers who minister to our needs. It is a time to reflect on those who are sick, who struggle with chronic illnesses, who lack access to the health-care services they need, and who are denied those basic elements essential to achieving health. It is a time to focus on our belief that health care is a right and a responsibility, public and private. It is a time to challenge our communities of faith to seek their role in making "Health Care for All" a reality.

To assist congregations in their observance of a Health Care Sabbath, resources will be made available by the General Board of Church and Society.

ADOPTED 1996

See Social Principles, ¶ 66Q; "Health in Mind and Body"; "Health and Wholeness"; "Universal Access to Health Care in the U.S. and Related Territories."

Opposition to Abusive Treatment of Persons with Mental Disabilities

WHEREAS, a large part of the ministry of our Lord focused on persons with mental disabilities; and

WHEREAS, persons with mental disabilities are children of God and are therefore our brothers and sisters within the human family; and

WHEREAS, the full and equal rights of persons with mental disabilities are enshrined in the Social Principles of The United Methodist Church, as well as in the Constitution and laws of the United States of America;

Therefore, be it resolved, that The United Methodist Church affirms the right of persons with disabilities to freedom from abusive treatment;

Be it further resolved, that The United Methodist Church opposes the use of any form of punishment for children or adults with mental disabilities in any case where such punishment would be considered illegal, abusive, or unconscionable if applied to a child or adult who is not disabled. In particular, we condemn as unacceptable the following practices:

1. treatments that result in physical injury or tissue damage to the person;

2. verbal abuse or insult, humiliation, or degradation;

3. denial of food, warmth, hygiene, contact with other human beings, or other necessities of life;

4. the use of electric shock or noxious substances as a form of punishment;

5. the use of any punishment on a child with mental disabilities that would be considered child abuse if used on a child with no disabilities;

6. neglect;

7. the use of physical or chemical restraint when the individual or others are not in danger of physical harm; and

8. the threat of any of the above treatments.

Any therapy used in the treatment of persons with mental disabilities must be potentially beneficial to the person. As an alternative to abusive treatments, we support the use of positive approaches in the treatment of persons with mental disabilities. Positive approaches affirm the humanity of persons with mental disabilities and recognize that the needs and desires of such persons are not significantly different from those of other persons. Our obligation to persons with mental disabilities is to support and assist them in their efforts to live lives as rich and rewarding as possible.

Be it further resolved, that we call upon all public and private agencies and service providers involved in providing services to persons with mental disabilities to adopt and uphold the standards set forth in this resolution.

Be it further resolved, that we call upon all federal, state, and local governments to end immediately the expenditure of public revenues on any agency or program that fails to adopt and uphold the standards set forth in this resolution.

Be it further resolved, that The United Methodist Church declares itself to be open to persons with mental disabilities and their families, and it commits itself to support such persons and families and to accommodate their needs within our community. We further pledge our support to help persons with mental disabilities and their families find appropriate services, programs, and supports, and to protect them from abusive treatments.

ADOPTED 1996

See Social Principles, ¶ 66Q; "Health in Mind and Body"; "Ministries in Mental Illness"; "Caring Communities—The United Methodist Mental Illness Network."

The Oxford House Model for Treatment of Drug and Alcohol Abuse

WHEREAS, 12.1 million U.S. citizens have one or more symptoms of alcoholism[1]; and

WHEREAS, Oxford Houses are self-run, self-supporting, nonsubsidized shared-residence programs utilizing ordinary rental housing in order to provide effective peer support (rather than governmentally, or institutionally, or staff-dependent support) for persons in recovery; and

WHEREAS, a 1988 poll of some 1,200 persons who had lived in Oxford Houses for some period during the previous twelve years showed that some 80 percent had maintained sobriety (as contrasted with the 20 percent rate of the abuse-free maintenance that is customarily reported for those who have completed rehabilitation programs without subsequent residence in Oxford House); and

WHEREAS, a 1991 survey of forty-five residents of six newly formed Oxford Houses by Dr. William Spillane of the Catholic University of America, Washington, D.C., indicated a relapse rate of only 9.3 percent;

Therefore, be it resolved, that General Conference hereby encourages each of its member congregations to become knowledgeable about the Oxford House model so that these congregations might provide all feasible support and assistance in the creation and maintenance of such recovery houses in their respective local communities.

Be it further resolved, that the General Conference direct the Health and Welfare Department of the General Board of Global Ministries to provide appropriate informational assistance in this effort, within the constraints of the current budgetary allotments.

ADOPTED 1992

See Social Principles, ¶ 66J; "Drug and Alcohol Concerns."

---

[1] "National Institute on Alcohol Abuse and Alcoholism, a Working Paper: Projections of Alcohol Abusers," January 1985.

Pan-Methodist Approach

WHEREAS, the Constitution of The United Methodist Church calls for our church to "seek, and work for, unity at all levels of church life" (¶ 5); and

WHEREAS, The United Methodist Church has a historical relationship and shared tradition with The African Methodist Episcopal Church, The African Methodist Episcopal Zion Church, and The Christian Methodist Episcopal Church; and

WHEREAS, the General Conference of 1984 authorized involvement in a Commission on Pan-Methodist Cooperation "to define, determine, plan, and, in cooperation with established agencies of the several denominations, execute activities to foster meaningful cooperation" (¶ 2403); and

WHEREAS, events and activities planned and held Pan-Methodistically can work for the unity we seek; and

WHEREAS, the general agencies need to be sensitive to this commitment to Pan-Methodist cooperation;

Therefore, be it resolved, that a Pan-Methodist approach be given to any major event planned by a general agency of The United Methodist Church, by the agency's notifying early in the planning stage: (1) the corresponding agency in the other Pan-Methodist denominations, and (2) the six members of the United Methodist delegation on the Commission on Pan-Methodist Cooperation; and

Be it further resolved, that the General Council on Ministries establish a Pan-Methodist approach to its coordinating responsibilities as given in ¶¶ 904; 905.2, .4; and 906.5–.6.

ADOPTED 1996

See Social Principles, ¶ 66A; "Pan Methodist Unity"; "History of Blacks in The United Methodist Church."

Pan Methodist Unity

WHEREAS, the Constitution of The United Methodist Church calls for our church to "seek, and work for, unity at all levels of church life . . . through plans of union with churches of Methodist or other denominational traditions" (Constitution, ¶ 5); and

WHEREAS, on March 22, 1991, the Fifth Consultation of Methodist Bishops, consisting of bishops of The African Methodist Episcopal, The

African Methodist Episcopal Zion, The Christian Methodist Episcopal, and The United Methodist churches passed the following resolution:

> In the Fifth Consultation of Methodist Bishops at St. Simon's Island, as an outgrowth of presentation of papers dealing with the global and national witness of the Christian faith in our world of the present day and accepting the challenge for the church to begin to set its house in order as it relates to the absence of unity within the Body of Christ, this Consultation of Methodist Bishops responds by supporting the following:

WHEREAS, a consensus developed among those bishops attending the Consultation that the mission of the Church compels us to reexamine the relationships and cooperative structures of The African Methodist Episcopal Church, The African Methodist Episcopal Zion Church, The Christian Methodist Episcopal Church, and The United Methodist Church; and

WHEREAS, these four denominations share a common history and heritage, with similar polity, episcopal form of leadership, itineracy, and Wesleyan priorities; and

WHEREAS, new forms of relationships, missional structures, and possible merger would make a powerful witness to Christ in a world torn by such evils as injustice and racism;

Therefore, be it resolved, that the bishops of each of our four churches petition their respective General Conferences to authorize a Study Commission for the purpose of exploring possible merger. Each such petition should request that:

1. Each respective General Conference provide for five representatives to this commission reflecting the wholeness of the Church, and provide needed financial support;

2. The commission be authorized to seek such staff support from existing denominational staff as it shall deem needful;

3. Progress reports be made regularly to each body of bishops, and that a final report should be prepared for each General Conference no later than 1996;

4. The task of the commission shall include, but not be limited to, the following:

(a) Keeping clear the missional reasons for this exploration and ensuring that such a mission focus be written into any proposal or plan;

(b) Ensuring that all proposals provide recognition of each denomination's heritage and appropriate representation of persons in any future structures;

(c) Developing a plan of merger that includes a proposed constitution, organizational plan, and continuation of the episcopacy and itineracy; and

(d) Recognizing the global nature, polity, and mission of our churches;

5. The chairperson of the commission shall rotate among the participating denominations in alphabetical order, with each denomination choosing its chairperson from among its representatives;

6. We hold open the possibility of other Methodist denominations joining us in this quest for unity and wholeness; and

7. This proposal does not discourage the continuation of any existing merger conversations.

Be it further resolved, that the General Conference of The United Methodist Church authorizes participation of The United Methodist Church in the Study Commission proposed in the Bishops Consultation resolution, with five members reflecting the wholeness of the Church to be appointed by the Council of Bishops. Funding will be provided by the General Council on Finance and Administration.

Be it further resolved, that the work of the commission proceed according to the guidelines of the Bishops Consultation resolution of March 22, 1991, except that the report to the 1996 General Conference shall not necessarily be a final report.

ADOPTED 1992

See Social Principles, ¶ 66A; "Pan-Methodist Approach"; "History of Blacks in The United Methodist Church."

Population

The creation of the world out of chaos into order is the initial biblical witness. In this witness is the affirmation of the freedom and responsibility of humankind. We affirm God to be the Creator, the one who grants us freedom, and the one to whom we are responsible.

God's ongoing creative and re-creative concern for the universe was expressed through Jesus Christ, who has called us to find the meaning of our lives in dual love of God and neighbor. In this context, we live responsibly before God, writing history by the actions of our lives. The imperative upon the individual Christian and the Christian community is to seek patterns of life, shape the structures of society, and foster those values which will dignify human life for all.

In this quest we must not "quench the Spirit," but allow the Spirit to lead us into God's new day for all people, a new day that calls for the compassionate and passionate desire to see a new birth out of justice.

We believe that history is not finished, but that we are engaged in a history. This is an age of possibility, in which we are called under God to serve the future with hope and confidence. Christians have no alternative to involvement in seeking solutions for the great and complex set of problems that face the world today. All these issues are closely interrelated: hunger, poverty, denial of human rights, economic exploitation, overconsumption by the rich, technologies that are inadequate or inappropriate, depletion of resources, and rapid population growth.

Hunger and poverty, injustice and violence in the world, cannot simplistically be blamed on population growth, yet the rapidly swelling numbers of humankind are making it increasingly difficult to solve the other interconnected problems. There is much we do not yet know about the relationship between population size and the sustaining environment, but clearly we do know there can be too many people.

Programs aimed at reducing population growth should not be ends in themselves, not substitutes for other measures necessary to eliminate hunger and poverty. The Church supports population programs as needed to move toward its goal of a just and humane world order.

The population situation is different in different societies, and therefore nations must be free to develop policies in keeping with their own needs and cultures. These global and regional aspects affect all humankind and can only be solved by international cooperation.

At the individual level, our Church has long recognized the basic human right to have the education and means to plan one's family. For women, particularly, the ability to control fertility is a liberating force, making it possible to assume other roles and responsibilities in society. Men and women alike bear responsibility for family planning and contraceptives practices.

Today, there are those who claim that some nations are beyond help because of their rapid population growth. The Christian church cannot accept these voices of despair. Even as just means for achieving stabilization are urgently sought, the Christian church must reaffirm the sacredness of each individual and stand fast against attitudes and practices that treat people as mere numbers or masses.

We welcome the growing understanding of what just and desirable means for lowering fertility rates may encompass, and we affirm that the use of such means must take into consideration the critical importance and interrelated nature of these aspects: better education and the opportunity for people to participate in decisions that shape their lives; the provision of basic economic security, including old-age security; upgrading the status of women; improved maternal and child health care; and finally, a strong birth-control program.

The Church should take the lead in actions that can help focus on the problems caused by rapid population growth and to support measures to deal with them. We therefore call on the people and agencies of the Church to:

1. Recognize rapid population growth to be a matter of great religious and moral concern, to develop education and action programs on the issues raised, and to increase understanding of the interrelationships between population growth and other world problems. Education must include sensitivity toward the existence of varying sociological patterns and religious philosophies;

2. Develop programs to increase understanding of the meaning in today's world of responsible parenthood. Churches can encourage acceptance of the idea that not everyone needs to be a parent and that those who choose to have children should accept the small family norm as responsible practice in today's world;

3. Help the affluent realize the devastating impact on the world and its people of wasteful consumption patterns and exploitative economic systems, and to develop resources and curriculum that encourage change in overly materialistic lifestyles;

4. Urge that United Methodist medical and mission facilities and programs provide a full range of fertility-related and family planning information and services. The Church should exert leadership in making possible the safe and legal availability of sterilization procedures for both men and women, and of abortion where appropriate.

The Church should offer informed counseling and support to both men and women on all options regarding childbearing. The Church bears a particular responsibility to stand guard against coercive use of birth-control practices aimed at the poor and powerless;

5. Take the lead in measures to upgrade the status of women in societies and to include them in all development planning and processes, and give increased support to policies that will further the goal of equal rights for women, such as the Equal Rights Amendment in the United States;

6. Call on all governments to give priority to implementing the provisions of the World Population Plan of Action that the United Nations approved in 1974, which called for population policies in a context of total social and economic development planning. We especially call on the United States government to develop a national population policy that would include the goal of stabilizing the United States population, and recommendations on population distribution and land and resource use;

7. Call on the United States Congress and legislative bodies of the affluent nations to recognize the crucial nature of population growth, and to give maximum feasible funding to programs of population, health, agriculture, and other technological-assistance programs for the poor nations. International assistance programs should be based on mutual cooperation, should recognize the diversities of culture, should encourage self-development and not dependency, and should not attempt to require "effective population programs"as a prerequisite for other developmental assistance; and

8. Call for government and private agencies to place a higher priority on research aimed at developing a range of safe, inexpensive contraceptives that can be used in a variety of societies and medical situations.

A high priority should also be given to research aimed at gaining greater understanding of attitudes, motivations, and social and economic factors affecting childbearing.

Even as we urge individuals and governments to intensify efforts immediately to achieve population stability as soon as possible, the churches need to keep before people the moral reasons why we need to be concerned with the population problem. Our goal in history is that everyone may have the conditions of existence necessary for the fulfillment of God's intentions for humanity. Our context in history is the preciousness of life and the love of God and all creation.

ADOPTED 1980
AMENDED & READOPTED 1992

See Social Principles, ¶ 66I; "A Call for Increased Commitment to End World Hunger and Poverty"; "Justice, Peace, and the Integrity of Creation."

Prejudice Against Muslims and Arabs in the U.S.A.

Today in the United States of America there are approximately 3 million persons who are adherents of Islam. Arab Americans, both

Christian and Muslim, constitute an ever-larger number of persons in the American population. These persons are suffering the effects of a particularly virulent prejudice too often aided and abetted by statements and images in the media and by rhetoric from some of the highest political leadership.

As part of the fabric of racism in the U.S.A., in which both subtle and violent acts continue against ethnic minority groups and persons, so too have such acts been perpetuated against the Arab and Muslim communities in the U.S.A.

Arab American organization offices, mosques, and Islamic centers have been bombed and torched. Leaders of the community have been murdered. Questionable uses of law have been utilized to stifle the rights of association and freedom of expression. Though discriminatory acts against Arabs and Muslims do not stand in isolation from similar acts perpetuated against other racial and ethnic minority persons in the U.S.A., their existence and effects upon Arabs and Muslims has been little acknowledged in U.S. society, with concomitant deleterious effect on U.S. perceptions, internationally, as they touch upon relations with predominantly Arab and Muslim nations and organizations.

Therefore, The United Methodist Church, in the knowledge that Jesus calls us to the blessings of peacemaking and reminds us that the highest law is to love God and neighbor, calls its members:

1. To oppose demagoguery, manipulation, and image making that seeks to label Arabs and Muslims in a negative way;

2. To counter stereotypical and bigoted statements made against Muslims and Islam, Arabs and Arabic culture;

3. To increase knowledge of neighbor by study and personal contact that yield a greater appreciation of the Muslim and Arabic contributions to society;

4. To act decisively to include Arabs and Muslims in interfaith and community organizations; and

5. To pray for the perfection of community among us and to participate fully in the process of bringing it into being.

In order to aid United Methodists to respond to this call, all boards, agencies, and institutions of The United Methodist Church are requested to provide resources and program and, where appropriate, to act in advocacy.

ADOPTED 1988

See Social Principles, ¶ 66B; "A Charter for Racial Justice Policies in an Interdependent Global Community"; "Our Muslim Neighbors."

Principles of Welfare Reform

As people of faith and religious commitment, we are called to stand with and seek justice for people who are poor. Central to our religious traditions, sacred texts, and teachings is a divine mandate to side with and protect the poor. We share a conviction, therefore, that welfare reforms must not focus on eliminating programs but on eliminating poverty and the damage it inflicts on children (who are two thirds of all welfare recipients), on their parents, and on the rest of society.

We recognize the benefit to the entire community of helping people move from welfare into the job market when possible and appropriate. We fear, however, that reform will fail if it ignores labor-market issues such as unemployment and an inadequate minimum wage, and important family issues such as the affordability of childcare and the economic value of care-giving in the home. Successful welfare reform will depend on addressing these concerns as well as related issues, such as pay equity, affordable housing, and the access to health care.

We believe that people are more important than the sum of their economic activities. Successful welfare reform demands more than economic incentives and disincentives; it depends on overcoming both biased assumptions about race, gender, and class that feed hostile social stereotypes about people living in poverty and suspicions that people with perspectives other than our own are either indifferent or insincere. Successful welfare reform will depend ultimately upon finding not only a common ground of policies but a common spirit about the need to pursue them for all.

The following principles neither exhaust our concerns nor resolve all issues raised, but these principles will serve as our guide in assessing proposed legislation. We hope they may also serve as a rallying point for a common effort with others throughout the nation.

We call upon the 1996 General Conference of The United Methodist Church to adopt the following statement, "Principles of Welfare Reform," and to have it sent to the President of the United States, the Speaker of the House of Representatives, and the United States Senate Majority Leader. In addition, annual conferences are asked to send this statement to appropriate state officials.

A Statement of Shared Principles of Welfare Reform

An acceptable welfare program must result in lifting people out of poverty, not merely in reducing welfare roles.

1. The federal government should define minimum benefit levels of programs serving low-income people, below which states will not be permitted to fall. These benefits must be adequate to provide a decent standard of living.

2. Welfare reform efforts designed to move people into the workforce must create jobs that pay a livable wage (at least 150 percent of the poverty level, plus full benefits) and do not displace present workers. Programs should eliminate barriers to employment and provide training and education necessary, including post-high school education such as vocational school and college, for inexperienced and young workers to get and hold jobs. Such programs must provide childcare, transportation, and other ancillary services that will make participation both possible and reasonable. If the government becomes the employer-of-last-resort, the jobs provided must pay a family-sustaining wage.

3. Disincentives to work should be removed by allowing welfare recipients to retain a larger portion of wage earnings and assets before losing cash, housing, health, childcare, or other benefits.

4. Work-based programs must not impose arbitrary time limits. If mandated, limits must not be imposed without availability of viable jobs at a family-sustaining wage. Exemptions should be offered for people with physical or mental illness, disabling conditions, responsibilities as caregivers for incapacitated family members, and for those primary caregivers who have responsibility for young children.

5. Welfare reform should result in a program that brings together and simplifies the many efforts of federal, state, and municipal governments to assist persons and families in need. "One-stop shopping centers" should provide information, counseling, and legal assistance regarding such issues as child support, job training and placement, medical care, affordable housing, food programs, and education.

6. Welfare reform should acknowledge the responsibility of both government and parents in seeking the well-being of children. No child should be excluded from receiving benefits available to other siblings because of having been born while the mother was on welfare. No child should be completely removed from the safety net because of a parent's failure to fulfill agreements with the government. Efforts are needed to increase the level of child-support assistance from noncustodial parents.

7. Programs designed to replace current welfare programs must be adequately funded. It must be recognized and accepted that more will be invested in the short-term than the present Aid to Families with

Dependent Children Program. However, if welfare reform programs are successfully implemented, they will cost less as the number of families in need of assistance diminishes over the long term. In financing this effort, funding should not be taken from other programs that successfully serve the poor.

ADOPTED 1996

See Social Principles, ¶¶ 67E, 68A; "The United Methodist Church and Church-Government Relations."

A Program to Emphasize Inclusiveness in All Dimensions of the Church

A door of opportunity has been opened to The United Methodist Church—the opportunity to consolidate endeavors to discern the barriers to racial and cultural inclusiveness. Many annual conferences responded to the action of the 1992 General Conference calling upon annual conferences to develop "programs to emphasize inclusiveness in all dimensions of the Church." However, many annual conferences have not yet responded to that call.

In recognition of the need to plan in order to implement intentions to be inclusive, the 1996 General Conference reaffirms the commitment that each annual conference, led by the bishop and cabinet, develop comprehensive programs that place fresh emphasis upon inclusiveness—cultural, racial, lingual, gender—throughout the life and ministry of The United Methodist Church.

These plans should provide that strategies similar to those outlined in the resolution adopted in 1992 continue:

1. That this program include a conference-wide enlistment and recruitment program that seeks clergy and laity who will give themselves to cross-racial and cross-cultural appointments, to begin new Sunday schools and congregations among poor people and people of color;

2. That the program include a determined effort to enlist and recruit some of the most competent, experienced pastors for such cross-racial and cross-cultural appointments rather than simply enlisting the newest clergy;

3. That the General Conference make it possible for the bishop to appoint "tentmaker" clergy who will not obligate the conference in salary or pension to be appointed to start new congregations or to strengthen existing congregations;

4. That this "inclusive" emphasis include asking and actively encouraging all multistaff congregations to deliberately make their staffs inclusive in terms of gender, race, and ethnicity;

5. That goals and strategies be established in each conference so that cross-racial and cross-cultural appointments become normative for the conference and one of the essential ways in which the conference engages in the mission of Christ;

6. That the program include experiences for the conference lay and clergy leadership that increase their knowledge and understanding of all the people and cultures who reside within the borders of the conference;

7. That this conference program include programs for children and youth, such as multicultural camps, human-relations conferences/ seminars, and various kinds of work camps;

8. That the conference program include the enlisting and recruitment of young adults to become "people in mission" who work on a subsistence basis or pay their own way;

9. That this program enable the establishment of new congregations—rural, suburban, and urban—in town and country;

10. That this program will encourage diversity in styles and kinds of ministries, in worship styles, and in language and thought forms in order to enable the gospel and The United Methodist Church to again have impact on working-class people, the poor, people of color, and other target groups of people;

11. That this program make appointments of tentmaker clergy to ministries of justice and peace, to ministries of prevention and rehabilitation in drug abuse, and to children and young people caught in the spiraling crisis of drugs, violence, racism, and poverty;

12. That each conference program will include assisting local congregations and pastors in sharing-facilities situations to develop an "inclusive" model for the congregation, even though worship services occur in several languages, and in eliminating the "landlord-tenant" model of relationships;

13. That the program include a provision that we will no longer sell church buildings in the urban areas to churches of other denominations but will instead place tentmaker clergy and laity in those situations, assisting them in finding the way to create a new people in that place for mission to the people in that community;

14. That the conference program will include a major training and additional skills strategy, using pastors' schools, annual conference

sessions, and United Methodist theological schools (where a United Methodist seminary is not within the bounds of the conference or area, the conference should enlist schools of other denominations) to create resources for the inclusive ministry and to empower conference clergy and laity; and

15. That this conference program also include an effort to develop what Black Methodists for Church Renewal calls "outrageous ministries," innovative ministries in urban, suburban, and rural areas, so that an unfettered gospel can do the work of the Crucified and Risen One.

Further, that as annual conferences continue to revise and perfect their inclusiveness programs, that special attention be given to the following points of concentration:

1. That Comprehensive Plans for Racial Ethnic Ministries be reviewed, revised, and implemented. Further, that the Comprehensive Plans incorporate the two national plans adopted by the 1992 General Conference, the National Plan for Hispanic Ministries and the Native American Comprehensive Plan, and other plans for racial and ethnic ministries that may be approved by the 1996 General Conference;

2. That bishops and cabinets design specific strategies with timelines to make cross-racial and cross-cultural appointments the norm rather than the exception. That these strategies include preparation of pastors, congregations, and pastor-parish relations committees before an appointment is made, and provisions for support for pastors and congregations in cross-racial and cross-cultural appointments;

3. That annual conference leaders at all levels—local church, district, conference, bishops, and cabinets—seek ways to enhance their skills in the areas of interpersonal communication, cross-cultural communication, and conflict management and resolution. The General Commission on Religion and Race may be consulted for resources;

4. That councils on ministries provide opportunities for ongoing dialogue—cross-racial, cross-cultural, interethnic, cross-gender—at all levels of the conference about what it means to be the inclusive Church;

5. That annual conferences, seminaries, and United Methodist-related colleges and universities participate in the general commission's National Convocation on the Inclusive Church to be held during the 1997–2000 quadrennium, the concept of which is under consideration by the Council of Bishops;

6. That each annual conference report to the General Commission on Religion and Race on its progress by July 1, 1998; and

7. That each annual conference report to the General Conference in 2000 on its program and progress; that these reports come through the report of the General Commission on Religion and Race.

ADOPTED 1996

See Social Principles, ¶ 66A–H; "Eradication of Racism in The United Methodist Church"; "Racism: The Church's Unfinished Agenda"; "Eradication of Sexism in the Church."

Project Equality

In consideration of long-established support, by The United Methodist Church, for fair employment practices; and

In consideration of national policy for fair employment practices in the United States, which policy embraces legislation against unemployment discrimination; and

In recognition of The United Methodist Church's responsibility to make ethical use of its own financial resources; through effective use of equal employment opportunity as one of its purchasing criteria; and

In recognition that Project Equality provides a technical-assistance resource to agencies and institutions of The United Methodist Church in the development of equal employment and affirmative action programs; and

In the conviction that Project Equality, a voluntary cooperative inter-denominational enterprise of churches, synagogues, and related institutions, provides a responsible, consistent, ethical, practical, effective, and positive means whereby The United Methodist Church and other churches can support fair employment practices in the United States;

Therefore, be it resolved, that The United Methodist Church endorses Project Equality and recommends cooperation, both through participation and financial support, on the part of all United Methodist annual conferences, local churches, local or national institutions, agencies, and organizations.

ADOPTED 1968
AMENDED & READOPTED 1988

See Social Principles, ¶66A; "A Charter for Racial Justice Policies in an Interdependent Global Community"; "Economic Justice."

Promote the Observance
of Native American Awareness Sunday

WHEREAS, the Native American population continues to shift in larger numbers from the rural areas to the urban population centers; and

WHEREAS, the human conditions of numerous Native Americans in the rural and urban environments reflect a legacy of poverty and socioeconomic denial; and

WHEREAS, there is a serious shortage of Native American pastors and trained professionals to respond to the human conditions in the Native American communities; and

WHEREAS, there is a National United Methodist Native American Center, which has been created to recruit, train, and deploy Native American leadership; and

WHEREAS, the financial support that is required to sustain the center is beyond the capability of the Native American communities; and

WHEREAS, the 1988 General Conference approved Native American Awareness Sunday as a means for providing opportunities for the denomination to support Native American ministries;

Therefore, be it resolved, that all annual conferences promote the observance of the Native American Awareness Sunday and encourage local churches to support the Sunday with programming and offerings.

Be it further resolved, that the agencies that develop and provide resources for this special day report to the General Commission on Religion and Race their plans, strategies, and timelines for addressing the goals and objectives related to Native American Awareness Sunday.

ADOPTED 1992

See Social Principles, ¶ 66A; "The United Methodist Church and America's Native People"; "Shared Financial Support for the Native American Center."

Proposal for the Adoption
of Church in Covenant Communion

WHEREAS, the Scriptures call us to one hope; "one Lord, one faith, one baptism, one God and Father of [us] all, who is above all and through all and in all" (Ephesians 4:4-6); and

WHEREAS, Jesus prayed for the church, "that they may all be one" (John 17:21); and

WHEREAS, despite the brokenness of the church, the Holy Spirit works among us to break down the dividing walls between Christians; and

WHEREAS, the diversity of gifts among Christians is for building up and strengthening the body of Christ; and

WHEREAS, The United Methodist Church has pursued and supported the unity of the church through prayer, study, and leadership in the ecumenical movement; and

WHEREAS, The United Methodist Church has been a member of the Consultation on Church Union (COCU) from its beginnings, giving leadership to the work of the nine churches in the U.S.A. as they have sought to make visible the unity of the body of Christ; and

WHEREAS, *The COCU Consensus: In Quest of a Church of Christ Uniting* was given overwhelming support by the 1988 General Conference as an expression of the apostolic faith and "a sufficient theological basis for the covenanting acts to be proposed by the Consultation" (1992 *Book of Resolutions;* page 206); and

WHEREAS, the COCU covenanting proposal, *Churches in Covenant Communion,* has been developed by the representatives of the nine member churches of the Consultation and studied by The United Methodist Church over the past eight years; and

WHEREAS, The United Methodist Church Council of Bishops stated in May 1992, "'We celebrate God's call to the concept of covenant relationships expressed in *Churches in Covenant Communion . . .* [and] long for the day when the covenant may be realized among us, and acknowledge with joy our eagerness to enter into covenant'" (1992 *Book of Resolutions;* page 217); and

WHEREAS, this covenanting proposal offers to open doors to greater unity in theology, worship, sacraments, ministry, and mission among Christians in the U.S.A.;

Therefore, be it resolved, that the following changes be made in the *Book of Discipline* on the issue of the covenanting proposal:

1. Article 5, Division 1 of the Constitution, after the word *Union,* insert the words *and covenantal relationships.*

2. ¶ 2402, in the heading, after the word *Churches,* add *and Covenantal Relationships.*

3. ¶ 2402.1, in the heading, after the word *Union,* add *and the Church of Christ Uniting.*

4. Add a new ¶ 2402.1*b: The United Methodist Church is in covenantal relationship with other churches in the Church of Christ Uniting.* Present ¶ 402.1*b* becomes ¶ 2402.1*c.*

5. ¶ 918.2, after *Church Union,* add *and the Church of Christ Uniting.*

Be it further resolved, that the 1996 General Conference of The United Methodist Church adopt the covenanting proposal of the Consultation on Church Union and approve the text *Churches in Covenant Communion: The Church of Christ Uniting* as the basis for agreement to join with other participating churches in covenant communion, including the acts sufficient to enable it; and

Be it further resolved, that The United Methodist Church declares its willingness to enter into a relationship of Covenant Communion with the member churches of the Consultation on Church Union and other churches that similarly approve this agreement and *The COCU Consensus,* which is its theological basis, sealed by the proposed inaugural liturgies; and

Be it further resolved, that The United Methodist Church will begin to identify for itself such steps and procedures as may be necessary to prepare for the reconciliation of ordained ministries and for entering into Covenant Communion as set forth in this document; and

Be it further resolved, that the Council of Bishops shall oversee The United Methodist Church's participation in the Church of Christ Uniting and shall develop and present to future General Conferences such changes in the *Book of Discipline* as may become necessary as we live into this covenant; and

Be it further resolved, that the 1996 General Conference of The United Methodist Church entrusts to the Council of Bishops, in cooperation with the General Commission on Christian Unity and Interreligious Concerns, the guidance of The United Methodist Church at national, regional, and local levels into the covenanting acts and relationships described in *Churches in Covenant Communion,* including the steps and procedures necessary to prepare for the recognition and reconciliation of ordained ministries; and

Be it further resolved, that the 1996 General Conference of The United Methodist Church send greetings of grace and peace in Christ to the other member churches of the Consultation, offering prayers that we "may all be one . . . so that the world may believe" (John 17:21).

ADOPTED 1996

See Social Principles, ¶ 66B; "COCU Consensus: In Quest of a Church of Christ Uniting"; "Continuing Membership in the Consultation on Church Union"; "Support the Consultation on Church Union Proposal."

Protecting and Sustaining Children

"And they were bringing children to him, that he might touch them. . . . 'Let the children come to me, do not hinder them; for to such belongs the kingdom of God. Truly, I say to you, whoever does not receive the kingdom of God like a child shall not enter it.' And he took them in his arms and blessed them, laying his hands upon them" (Mark 10:13-16, Revised Standard Version).

"Fear not, O Jacob my servant,/Jeshurun whom I have chosen./For I will pour water on the thirsty land,/and streams on the dry ground;/I will pour my spirit upon your descendants,/and my blessing on your offspring./They shall spring up like grass amid waters,/like willows by flowing streams" (Isaiah 44:2-4, RSV).

"We are guilty of many errors and many faults, but our worst crime is abandoning the children, neglecting the foundation of life. Many of the things we need can wait. The child cannot. Right now is the time its bones are being formed, blood is being made and senses are being developed. To this child we cannot answer, 'Tomorrow.' This child's name is 'Today'" (Gabriela Mistral, Nobel Prize-winning poet from Chile).

Introduction

Children are powerless. The future of the human race is in our children, but in decision-making they are voiceless and powerless. Children cannot speak for themselves. They depend on us to speak for them and to be their advocates. They suffer most when resources are misappropriated. They need us to bring their very special needs to the notice of societies and those in power.

Who will survive? And how has the world protected its children? By killing and maiming millions of them through war and an unjust global economic system. "The children of the world are already living in the rubble of World War III," Dr. Bernard Lowe, co-president of the International Physicians for the Prevention of Nuclear War, stated in 1986: "Every three days, 120,000 children die unnecessarily—the very toll of casualties following the atomic bombing of Hiroshima." United Nations Children's Fund's (UNICEF) 1987 "State of the World's Children" says that 14 million innocent children under five die each year from preventable undernutrition and infection, twenty-seven every minute of the day and night.

An escalating arms race and misdirected priorities doubly threaten children's survival: A single hour's global military expenditure could save 3.5 million children otherwise destined to die annually from preventable infectious diseases. Yet every minute of the day, 1.9 million dollars is spent by leaders of nations around the world—not only superpowers—on an arms race that assumes the existence of a political issue worth destroying all the children in the world.

Survival Often Means a Lifetime of Suffering and Neglect

Those children who do survive often grow up under a blanket of poverty and despair. In Asia, Africa, and Latin America, many children go hungry, remain poor, suffer from preventable diseases, lack education, lack fuel and clean water.

Causes and Extent of Child Poverty and Neglect

Poverty is the cause of early deaths, ill health, and poor physical and intellectual growth among many of the world's children. In the 1980s, progress against that poverty has been slowed—and in many nations thrown into reverse—by the effects of long-running world recession.

Governments, almost universally, have responded to the recession by decreasing the share of social expenditures as a proportion of total government spending, either by stopping the expansion of services or by dropping the quality of existing services.

There is a clear correlation between reductions in government spending and a deterioration in children's welfare. While the richer people manage to remain relatively isolated from the effects of the world economic recession, the children of the poor (and in some countries, the children of the lower-middle class) have borne the brunt of a significant and global cutback in services. This has resulted in a loss of the civil, political, social, and economic rights of the world's children, and it is manifested by:

- Frequent infection and widespread undernutrition kills over a quarter of a million children every week. These children do not die of exotic diseases requiring sophisticated cures. They die in the long, drawn-out process of frequent illness and poor nutrition that gradually loosens their grip on life.
- Millions of children are forced into prostitution, pornography, and other forms of abuse and exploitation. More than 100 million children are employed under hazardous and often fatal working conditions.

- The use and manipulation of children as soldiers, targets for assassination, torture, and imprisonment without trial has increased as armed conflict and civil unrest rises. The situation in South Africa is a prime example of a deliberate policy by the government to terrorize and subjugate Black children and youth, with thousands detained without trial.
- The manipulation and institutionalized control of children's minds and values by the media, war toys, the education system, and sometimes, subconsciously, the family and church, lead to false stereotypes and the perpetuation of systems of injustice and violence.
- Armed conflict, civil unrest and famine displace children and separate them from their families. Children make up more than 70 percent of the population in many refugee camps, while 80 million children are homeless worldwide.
- The availability of formal education has decreased. In 1970, if all the world's children who did not have access to school held hands, they would go around the world three times. In 1985, they would go around the world four times.
- Youth unemployment is now at epidemic proportions. Youth have been forced into a critical situation where they lack basic skills and training in societies with high unemployment and underemployment.
- Urban unemployment and underemployment, low wages, loss of rural profits, and decreases in services for the poor have been partly responsible for detrimental changes in child rearing and protection practices.

Children and Poverty in the United States

And it is not just in Bangladesh, Sri Lanka, or El Salvador that children are dying unnecessarily. In the United States, in 1987, poverty killed 10,000 children—one every fifty-three minutes. In fact, the United States has slipped from sixth to a tie for last place among twenty industrialized nations in keeping babies alive in the first year of life.

In the United States, children are the largest single age group living in poverty. For the more than 13 million who are poor, childhood can be a time of privation and violence, loneliness and hunger—a time when they and their families must focus on a vision of basic survival. In the most affluent nation in the world in 1987, one out of three children did not see a dentist, two out of three poor children had no regular health insurance, and 6.5 million children lived in families with annual incomes less than $5,000. But statistics alone cannot measure the prevailing sense of hopelessness and lack of life options faced by poor children in the United States.

The cultural and educational impact of poverty upon children is immeasurable. Eighty-seven percent of U.S. children from all income groups are educated in the public school system; yet the public schools are failing to educate many, especially those from economically disadvantaged backgrounds.

The failure of our educational system to provide all children with a solid base of academic skills hurts young people and society in the long run. When compared to those with above-average skills, youths reaching age eighteen with the weakest reading and math skills are:

- eight times more likely to have children out of wedlock;
- eight times more likely to drop out of school before graduation;
- four times more likely to be both out of work and out of school; and
- four times more likely to be forced to turn to public assistance for basic income support.

Racial Injustice and Children in the United States

Poverty disproportionately affects children of color; therefore, child poverty cannot be fully understood without addressing the issue of racism. According to the resolution "Children and Their Welfare and Health Care" (1972 *Book of Resolutions*): "Racism does its most serious damage to children who already have much against them—poverty, broken homes, hunger, crowded living conditions." In order to diminish child poverty in the world, we must work toward societies in which each person's value is recognized, maintained, and strengthened. In more concrete terms, as stated in the Social Principles, "We assert the obligation of society and groups within society to implement compensatory programs that redress long-standing, systemic social deprivation of racial and ethnic people" (¶ 66A).

Prevention of Child Poverty Is Cost Effective

Budget cuts that affect children, made as a result of recession and budget deficits, are inhuman and shortsighted. Nations must invest in their children, because children are the future of the world.

Research substantiates that children's programs providing services such as prenatal care, immunizations, and primary health care save more money than they cost. For example, in the U.S. it costs about ten dollars to provide a baby with a series of immunizations, compared with hundreds of thousands of dollars for a lifetime of care for a disabled child. Every dollar spent on comprehensive prenatal care saves more than three dollars in health care in just the first year of an infant's life. UNICEF estimates that a five-dollar course of immunizations per child could save as many as five million children each year.

The federal budget deficit and world economic recession are the most frequently heard political excuses for neglecting children. Our response is five-fold: (1) children did not cause the deficit, nor the world economic crisis, and hurting them more will not cure it; (2) children and their families have sacrificed proportionately more than any other group as nations cut back on their government programs; (3) investing in children now saves money later—to fail to prevent sickness, malnutrition, and illiteracy is to perpetuate the very dependence cycle and high remediation costs so many currently decry; (4) investing in children is feasible: We know how to do it and how to achieve positive results for relatively modest investment; and (5) children are dying right now unnecessarily—one every fifty-three minutes in the United States, one every two seconds in the world. How can we dare not save them if we believe God exists?

Statement of Christian Conviction

It is not only sensible, but right and just to protect our children, who are the least among us. "The death of one child, when that death could have been avoided," United Nations Secretary General Javier Perez de Cuellar said in 1986, "is a rebuke to all humanity." The death of millions of children from preventable poverty and disease at home and abroad is a rebuke to the God who saved Isaac and Ishmael, the sons of Abraham, and the God who sent Christ in the form of a child as the messenger to bring good news to the poor. Christ rebuked those who sought to push children aside, saying, "Whoever receives this child in my name receives me; and among you all, he is the greatest" (Matthew 18:4-5, adapted).

Children are our gift of hope for a future time when our broken and injured world is healed and our relationship with God becomes whole and just. Adults are called to protect and advocate for the world's children as a thankful response to the covenant that God has made with us and that has been extended to us down through the ages. How do we protect and nurture our children? What gifts do we give them to enable them to survive in wholeness and justice? Do we pass on our brokenness, or do we find ways to strengthen and share in the light and freshness that they bring to the task of mending this world?

As we look at poverty through the eyes of children, we see the hope, faithfulness, and courage that children bring to the world—and we observe the barriers and obstacles that are placed in the way of their special contributions. We remind ourselves that as Christians we are called to dissolve those obstacles and to pursue public policies at the local, national, and international levels that nurture and celebrate the hope that rests in children.

Summary

There are many issues adversely affecting children in the United States and the world that cannot be covered in one resolution; however, most fall under the themes of child survival and preventive investment in children. Therefore, The United Methodist Church encourages all general boards, conferences, their related institutions and committees, and congregations to become involved in the following related topics of concern:
- teenage pregnancy
- abuse of children (physical and sexual)
- children of South Africa
- children who have never known peace
- children who are imprisoned
- disappeared children
- refugee children
- abandoned children
- pedophilia
- sex tourism
- torture
- children without education
- children and labor
- substance abuse

The Challenge

The overall message is that the methods of alleviating child death and poverty are now proven and tested, available and affordable. We know the way; we need the will.

A principal challenge of the next decade is the protection of the world's children from lifelong poverty and death. Between now and the year 2000, the nations of the world must mount a carefully conceived, comprehensive human-investment effort to ensure that every child has basic health, nutrition, shelter, education, and training. Surely the time has come to put the massive deaths and suffering of children alongside slavery, racism, and apartheid on the shelf reserved for those things which are simply no longer acceptable.

The long-term solution lies in implementing structural changes within nations—including land reform, the redistribution of income-earning opportunities, and economic policies designed to empower women and poor people. Similarly, structural changes between nations—including fairer and more stable commodity prices, more market access for the manufactured good of the developing world, a reform of the international monetary system, and an increase in both official aid and low-interest loans—are also fundamental to the creation of the conditions in which the vast majority of the world's families can earn enough, through their own efforts, to improve the quality of life for themselves and their families.

Recommendations to The United Methodist Church

The Rights of Children:

WHEREAS, The Social Principles uphold the rights of children to growth and development, adequate nutrition, health services, housing, education, recreation, protection against all forms of racial discrimination, cruelty, neglect, and exploitation;

Therefore, be it resolved, that The United Methodist Church shall uphold the rights of children, speak out when abuses occur, and advocate for the strengthening and strict enforcement of these rights.

Racial Justice:

WHEREAS, racism robs and deprives children of their basic rights and diminishes their opportunities; and

WHEREAS, the "aim of The United Methodist Church is nothing less than an inclusive church in an inclusive society";

Therefore, be it resolved, that The United Methodist Church calls upon all its people to perform those faithful deeds of love and justice in both the Church and the community that will bring this aim into reality by actively implementing the Charter for Racial Justice Policies.

Outside Our Own Community:

WHEREAS, The United Methodist Church affirms that child advocacy begins at home;

Therefore, be it resolved, that The United Methodist Church urges:

1. Local congregations to give ample opportunity to children to share in the central worship life of the congregation as full participants;

2. Local congregations and the United Methodist general agencies to enable adequate provision for Christian education for children within the life of the congregation. Children should also be included in the mission life of the congregation in age-appropriate ways; and

3. Conferences, their related institutions and committees, congregations, and the United Methodist Women to give heightened attention and focus to public education, direct involvement, and legislative advocacy on behalf of children.

The Child Survival Revolution

This program promotes breast-feeding, immunizations, growth monitoring, and oral rehydration therapy (ORT). In several nations, including Bangladesh and Nicaragua, these low-cost child-protection strategies have gone into action on a large scale.

WHEREAS, the same kind of public support and momentum that has been mobilized against famine and starvation is now needed for the global implementation of the Child Survival Revolution;

Therefore, be it resolved, that The United Methodist Church calls upon all general boards, conferences, their related institutions and committees, and congregations to:

1. Educate Church members and society at large about the revolution in child health and survival;

2. Encourage financial contributions to and volunteer participation in UNICEF's Child Survival Campaign;

3. Support the United Methodist Committee on Relief (UMCOR) in its efforts to enhance child heath and survival;

4. Support the effort of Women's Division and World Division, General Board of Global Ministries, to work with Methodist women's

organizations around the world in strengthening ministry with and advocacy for women and children; and

5. Support the efforts of the General Board of Church and Society in advocating for federal policies that significantly increase United States support for United Nations Children's Fund (UNICEF) and funding for the U.S. Agency for International Development's "Child Survival Fund."

Preventive Investment in Children in the United States

WHEREAS, one out of five children in the United States lives in poverty, and it is time to begin the hard but necessary task of readjusting our national priorities;

Therefore, be it resolved, that The United Methodist Church calls upon all general boards, conferences, their related institutions and committees, and congregations to:

1. Educate all Church members and society at large about the needs of children in the United States and encourage preventive investment in children before they get sick, drop out of school, or get into trouble;

2. Support United Methodist agencies, including the Institutional Ministries of the National Division of the General Board of Global Ministries, that work to alleviate child poverty and neglect in local communities and states;

3. Advocate for federal and state policies that provide preventive programs for children, ensuring basic health, nutrition, and early childhood services. These include prenatal and maternity-care programs (including Medicaid), job training programs, childcare, and protective services;

4. Support educational proposals to help children with special needs, including expanding successful federal programs as well as supporting promising new efforts. These include: Chapter I, Head Start, bilingual education, desegregation assistance, education for children with disabilities, dropout prevention, and "community learning centers." In addition, encourage parental and guardian involvement in their children's education;

5. Engage in denominational and ecumenical efforts to end child poverty;

6. Be aware and supportive of the United Methodist Women's "Campaign for Children in the United States," the purpose of which is to focus on the critical needs of children in poverty in local communities; and

7. Continue to advocate for systemic changes affecting children and their families, such as welfare reform, increase in the minimum wage, national health insurance, and job creation.

ADOPTED 1988

See Social Principles, ¶ 66C; "Ministry to Runaway Children"; "Medical Rights for Children and Youth"; "Putting Children and Their Families First."

Racial Harassment

The first two chapters of the Book of Genesis describe the creative genius of God. The writers tell us that God created heavens and earth and gave life to woman and man. Animals, vegetation, and the entire universe were the product of God's grace and work. The psalmist of Psalm 24 reaffirms the relationship between all of God's creation and the divinity of God.

Yet in spite of humanity's common legacy as God's descendants, we have consistently established differences among God's children because of their race. We have continuously engaged in verbal exchanges and behavioral demonstrations that have rejected the sacredness of all persons. The belief that one race is superior to others has permeated our lives, thus creating the perception of inferiority of some persons because of their skin color, features, language, and their racial and ethnic heritage.

When this prejudicial and/or racist attitude is expressed in a behavior that is focused specifically in the abuse, humiliation, and defamation of persons because of their race or ethnicity, it has become racial harassment.

Racial harassment is in reality an act of covert or overt racism. The United Methodist Church, committed to the elimination of racism, cannot tolerate this racist manifestation. Because of the many definitions of racial harassment currently found in society that are too general and even confusing, precise guidelines are needed from the denomination that will enable local churches, conferences, agencies, and church organizations to identify conditions or for situations of racial harassment.

Therefore, be it resolved, that the General Conference of 1992 defines the following conditions as racial harassment:

1. abusive and/or derogatory language that in a subtle or overt manner belittles, humiliates, impugns, or defames a person or a group of persons based on racial and ethnic traits, heritage, and characteristics;

2. a behavior (individual, group, or institutional) that abuses, belittles, humiliates, defames, or demeans a person or a group of persons based on racial and ethnic traits, heritage, and characteristics; and

3. documentation, printed or visual, that abuses, humiliates, defames, or demeans a person or groups of persons based on racial and ethnic heritage and traits, heritage, and characteristics.

Be it further resolved, that The United Methodist Church and all its agencies:

1. Encourage law-enforcement personnel to maintain accurate records on hate crimes and to bring to justice the perpetrators of such violence and intimidation;

2. Support hearings on hate crimes, particularly in those states where statistics reveal an increase in the activity of the Ku Klux Klan and other hate groups; and

3. Support congressional hearings when there are allegations of government involvement or negligence exacerbating such violence.

ADOPTED 1992

See Social Principles, ¶ 66A; "A Charter for Racial Justice Policies in an Interdependent Global Community"; "Global Racism: A Violation of Human Rights"; "Eradication of Racism in The United Methodist Church."

Racism

WHEREAS, racism continues to be a pervasive and systemic force within our Church and our society; and

WHEREAS, racism has the effect of diminishing self-worth and denying equal opportunity; and

WHEREAS, racism deprives the Church and society of the opportunity to utilize some of the best minds, skills, and talents they have; and

WHEREAS, racist attitudes and practices in this country and in the Church do not abate without intensive effort on the part of those who seek to ensure justice and equality;

Therefore, be it resolved, that the General Conference continues the General Commission on Religion and Race and its mandate that there be a Commission on Religion and Race in every annual conference; and

Be it further resolved, that each annual conference be urged, through its commission, to design programs specifically aimed at eradicating racism and achieving equality and inclusiveness; and

Be it further resolved, that each annual conference be encouraged to urge its local churches to develop programs and activities that are directed at promoting inclusiveness within the local congregation.

ADOPTED 1996

See Social Principles, ¶ 66A; "Global Racism: A Violation of Human Rights"; "A Charter for Racial Justice Policies in an Interdependent Global Community"; "Racism Today"; "Black Leadership."

Racism: The Church's Unfinished Agenda

WHEREAS, racism is the Church's unfinished agenda;

WHEREAS, for twenty-five years the General Commission on Religion and Race has been an effective tool in the struggle to overcome the racism endemic within our fellowship;

But WHEREAS, current politically popular social thinking dismisses the evils of racism as a thing of the past despite the increase of racially motivated hate crimes; the increase of racial/ethnic children living in poverty; the consistently higher percentage of racial/ethnic teenagers who cannot find work and racial/ethnic adults who have been out of work so long they have given up; the collapse of our urban public school systems because of antiquated and racially biased funding methods;

WHEREAS, if the Church is not to be a cruel reflection of the worst in society, it must be continually vigilant both of the world and of itself;

And WHEREAS, the monitoring tasks of the General Commission on Religion and Race have proven to be effective tools in the continuing work to end the evil of racism;

Now, *therefore, be it resolved,* that the 1996 General Conference of The United Methodist Church:

1. Renew our Church's stand against racism in any form and in every place;

2. Reaffirm our commitment to work against racism by strengthening the General Commission on Religion and Race; and

3. Make this the quadrennium in which every annual conference and every local congregation is asked to develop specific programs to combat racism within their institution and to witness against the racism in the society about them.

ADOPTED 1996

See Social Principles, ¶ 66A; "Eradication of Racism in The United Methodist Church"; "A Charter for Racial Justice Policies in an Interdependent Global Community"; "Global Racism: A Violation of Human Rights."

Support "Racism in Rural Areas" Task Force Report

WHEREAS, the Racism in Rural Areas Task Force, created by the 1992 General Conference, through comprehensive study, has indeed determined that racism is "alive and active in our society and in the church" in rural areas; and

WHEREAS, racism is sin, separating us from God and one another; and

WHEREAS, a manifestation of sin is injustice, abuse, and violence; and

WHEREAS, the task force found personal and institutional racism and interethnic conflict in rural areas throughout the United States;

Therefore, be it resolved, that the 1996 General Conference of The United Methodist Church affirms the work of the Racism in Rural Areas Task Force, accepts the report, and approves the adoption and implementation of the recommendations contained in the report.

Be it also resolved, that the 1996 General Conference of the United Methodist Church designates The Elimination of Racism in its Many Forms as a special emphasis of the Church, to be addressed by every level of the Church, and to be included by every general board and agency as one of the continuing priorities for the quadrennium 1997–2000.

ADOPTED 1996

See Social Principles, ¶ *66A;* "Racism in Rural Areas of the United States and the Church's Response."

Racism in Rural Areas of the United States and the Church's Response

WHEREAS, racism is sin; sin separates us from God and one another; and

WHEREAS, a manifestation of sin is injustice, abuse, and violence; and

WHEREAS, racism diminishes self-worth and denies equal opportunity; and

WHEREAS, the 1992–1996 quadrennium has been marked by a new upsurge of racially motivated bigotry and violence across the United States; and

WHEREAS, there have been hundreds of incidents in which racial and ethnic persons have suffered violence through intimidation, shootings, assaults, and murder; and

WHEREAS, white supremacist groups such as, but not limited to, the Ku Klux Klan (KKK), Christian Identity, Neo-Nazi, Possé Comitatus, and Skinheads have spread north, south, east, and west in the United States, especially in rural areas; and

WHEREAS, some of these groups have adopted nonphysical tactics that are equally as "deadly," such as producing and distributing cable-television programs to promote racist ideology and establishing home pages on the Internet; and

WHEREAS, the racial demographic changes of the United States are reaching more and more rural areas; and

WHEREAS, interracial relationships in America are marked by four different but related characteristics, where white persons, generally, as a group:

1. Retain most, if not all, positions of important decision-making power;

2. Maintain informal (and sometimes formal) policies and practices that discourage racial and ethnic minority access to many societal benefits;

3. Assume the superiority of their cultural norms and values and, therefore, tend to be insensitive to alternative lifestyles and values; and

4. Misplace the problem by focusing critically or paternalistically on racial and ethnic minority persons and not on themselves; and

WHEREAS, racism is both the conscious and unconscious perpetuation of a disproportionate distribution of power between races, the denial of access to resources on the basis of race, color, ethnicity, and rationalization of racial superiority by "blaming the victims"; and

WHEREAS, prejudice is any attitude formed without adequate facts, while racism is prejudice plus power; and

WHEREAS, understanding that the historical dimensions of racism are important; and

WHEREAS, true multiculturalism and diversity require an increase in personal awareness; the learning of new behaviors; removal of bias and barriers; changes in policies, practices, and structure; and the creation of new rules; and

WHEREAS, creating a multicultural and diverse Church means moving beyond recovering from the past toward shaping the future in community, a future of God's shalom that recognizes, values, and celebrates the unique qualities, gifts, and God's grace in all persons; and

WHEREAS, the Racism in Rural Areas Task Force affirms efforts by concerned persons, congregations, groups, and annual conferences in rural areas who are confronting racism in their individual and corporate lives, the Task Force concludes that racism continues to be a pervasive and systemic force within the rural church and community and must continue to be understood as the entire Church's unfinished agenda;

Therefore, be it resolved, that the 1996 General Conference accept and move to implement the following recommendations of the Racism in Rural Areas Task Force:

General Church

It is recommended that:

1. The Rural Chaplains Association, a network of clergy and laypersons, be affirmed in its work with individuals, rural churches, and communities in *shalom* ministries, and that the General Board of Global Ministries continue to resource the rural chaplains;

2. Training be made available by the General Commission on Religion and Race to enable each annual conference commission on religion and race to serve as a resource and support group for promoting cross-cultural understanding in rural areas;

3. New rural-oriented resources on racism and interethnic conflict be developed by the General Board of Discipleship, in consultation with the General Commission on Religion and Race. These resources should be developed for all age-level educational work of the Church:

(a) cross-cultural resources for local churches and annual conferences in rural areas should be developed by the General Board of Discipleship in consultation with United Methodist Rural Fellowship;

(b) resources on racism, interethnic conflict, and cross-cultural material should be listed on pages or sections within the existing catalogs produced by the general program agencies in consultation with the General Commission on Religion and Race; and

(c) in each level of the Course of Study, material on racism and interethnic conflict in rural settings should be developed and included by the Division of Ordained Ministry of the General Board of Higher Education and Ministry, in consultation with the General Commission on Religion and Race;

4. Recommendations for course work and "field experience" to understand racism and interethnic conflict in rural settings be developed

by the Division of Diaconal Ministry, General Board of Higher Education and Ministry, in consultation with the General Commission on Religion and Race;

(a) cross-cultural rural experiences should be reflected in all dated curriculum for children/youth church school material developed by the General Board of Discipleship;

5. Training for all national mission personnel related to the General Board of Global Ministries include a rural component on rural racism and multiculturalism;

6. The development and nurturing of shalom ministries in rural areas be a priority of the General Board of Global Ministries, such as Upper Sand Mountain Cooperative Parish;

7. Cooperative parish ministry as a viable style of nurture, outreach, and witness be undergirded and resourced by the General Board of Global Ministries and the General Board of Discipleship;

8. Efforts of African American, Native American, and other farmers of color to preserve and increase land ownership be supported by all general program agencies;

9. All general program agencies advocate to end discrimination against racial and ethnic minority farmers and rural organizations by local, state, and federal officials;

10. Advocacy supports be provided by the General Board of Global Ministries and the General Board of Church and Society to organizations that are led by racial and ethnic minority persons, such as the Federation of Southern Cooperatives and the Intertribal Agricultural Council;

11. The General Board of Church and Society and the General Board of Global Ministries work cooperatively to help local congregations, cooperative parish ministries, and annual conferences establish ministries with farm workers;

12. The General Board of Church and Society and the General Board of Global Ministries provide resources for local congregations and annual conferences to assist in combating rural racism;

13. The General Board of Church and Society and the General Board of Global Ministries join national efforts to promote farm worker justice;

14. The General Board of Church and Society and the General Board of Global Ministries take legislative (political) action—ecumenically, if possible—to direct the United States Department of Agriculture to decrease agricultural subsidies that are given mostly to huge corporate farmers; further, that at least 15–25 percent of the subsidy money should

be directed to racial and ethnic minority farmers and farm organizations to improve farming methods, try new crops, and provide loans to purchase needed farm supplies and equipment; and

15. The General Commission on Religion and Race monitor the implementation of the recommendations to general agencies.

Annual Conference/District

It is recommended that:

1. Support group(s) be developed for persons active in anti-racism strategies and for persons ministering to victims of hate crimes;

2. An immediate response-support task group be formed by the bishop and cabinet to respond to bigotry and violence in the Church and/or society;

3. Cross-racial appointment orientation workshop(s) for local churches and pastors be incorporated and conducted by the bishop and cabinet in their operational policies;

4. Cooperative ministries be initiated and undergirded in rural areas that include diverse racial and ethnic minority congregations and encourage cross-cultural/racial cooperation and ministry;

5. Those applying to be probationary members in the annual conference be expected by the board of ordained ministry to participate in a cross-cultural rural experience;

6. Individuals and congregations consult the conference commission on religion and race and the conference committee with responsibilities for rural ministries for suggestions on places within the annual conference for cross-cultural rural experiences;

7. Training in each district/subdistrict/cluster/ministirium to promote rural cross-cultural understanding be made available by the conference commission on religion and race;

8. A working plan to provide for cross-cultural experiences in rural areas be developed and implemented by the conference committee on ethnic local church concerns;

9. A response team to deal with hate crime and violence, in church and society, especially in rural areas, be established by cabinets and bishops (compare with Eastern Pennsylvania model);

10. Congregations in rural areas be prepared by annual conference and/or district leadership for the new influx of diverse populations so

that the Church will model the new community of inclusiveness and shalom;

11. Concern and support for pastors in cross-racial appointments be demonstrated by the bishop and cabinet; the conference commission on religion and race train persons to be listener-advocates as part of a support team;

12. Listening posts be provided that allow racial and ethnic minority persons a safe place to tell their stories, thereby helping to confront the white Church with its culture of racism;

13. The identification and development of rural shalom ministries be a part of a conference comprehensive plan for strengthening racial and ethnic minority churches and communities;

14. Each annual conference advocate to end discrimination against racial and ethnic minority farmers and rural organizations by local, state, and federal officials;

15. Advocacy support be provided by annual conferences to organizations that are led by racial and ethnic minority persons, such as the Federation of Southern Cooperatives and the Intertribal Agricultural Council;

16. Annual conferences and local congregations equally assume responsibility to:

(a) establish a farm worker ministry to sensitize members of the concerns of farm workers and to advocate for farm worker justice;

(b) join the Farm Worker Action Network of the National Farm Worker Ministry;

(c) observe a Farm Worker Sabbath/Farm Worker Sunday to raise awareness of farm worker issues, possibly being a part of Rural Life Sunday observance; and

(d) become informed about and advocate for support of organizations, such as the National Farm Worker Ministry, that focus on improving working conditions, housing, wages, and health care of farm workers.

Local Church

It is recommended that:

1. Congregations be prepared to support open itineracy and experience workshops/seminars on inclusiveness, racism, and cultural awareness by local pastor-parish relations committees;

2. Opportunities for the congregation to deal with the issues of racism and to experience varied styles and forms of worship be provided by

the council on ministries/administrative council/church council, through appropriate work area or ministry group committees;

3. When a pastor of a different racial or ethnic minority group is appointed, the pastor and the congregation together develop a covenant that enables the fulfillment of the new opportunity for ministry;

4. Planning and programming that include awareness of the surrounding community and its racial and ethnic minority composition be on the agenda of the council on ministries/administrative council/church council so that the ministry of the congregation is enhanced and relevant;

5. Use of curriculum resources such as *The Language of Hospitality, Creating a New Community: God's People Overcoming Racism,* and *Building a New Community: God's Children Overcoming Racism* be encouraged;

6. Congregations work ecumenically and with secular agencies on issues of rural racism;

7. Intentionally inclusive mission statements be written by local churches;

8. Advocacy supports be provided by the local church to organizations that are led by racial and ethnic minority persons, such as the Federation of Southern Cooperatives and the Intertribal Agricultural Council;

9. Local churches support efforts of African Americans, Native Americans, and other farmers of color to preserve and increase land ownership;

10. Local churches develop a model counseling course to help rural pastors become confident and skilled to counsel parents of children who commit hate crimes or who are victims of hate crimes; and

11. Local churches encourage ways to provide more inclusive mental-health services in rural areas and offer additional courses on crisis counseling to rural pastors.

Individual

It is recommended that:

1. Persons not be silent. If you are subject to an act of bigotry or racial violence, tell someone. Tell your family, your friends, neighbors, the church; seek support for yourself. Report the incident to police. Insist that the crime be reported as a "hate crime";

2. Support be given to the victim, and encourage him or her to report the incident to the police. Enlist aid and support from the church and

community. Witness to the law of love as exemplified in Christ's teaching of the good Samaritan; and

3. Persons teach children about other cultures and countries, opening minds that the church is global.

Institutions of Higher Education

It is recommended that:

1. The General Commission on Religion and Race and the Office of Town and Country Ministries of the National Division of the General Board of Global Ministries be invited by schools of theology to design and implement rural cross-cultural experiences for seminary students preparing to serve as diaconal or ordained ministers;

2. Boards of trustees be reviewed by all of the two- and four-year colleges with a relationship to The United Methodist Church, except historically Black colleges, for racial, ethnic, and gender inclusiveness, and, where necessary, begin to be reflective of all United Methodists of the annual conference in which it is located;

3. All conference-elected trustees of two- and four-year colleges related to The United Methodist Church, except historically Black colleges, ask for admission statistics that include racial and ethnic minority makeup and encourage the college to reflect at least the racial and ethnic minority makeup of all high school students from which their student body is drawn geographically;

4. Training on racism appropriate for college trustees, administration, faculty, staff, and students be designed and made available by the General Commission on Religion and Race to all two- and four-year colleges related to The United Methodist Church; and

5. Faculties be reviewed by all two- and four-year colleges with a relationship to The United Methodist Church, except historically Black colleges, for racial, ethnic, and gender inclusiveness and, where necessary, begin to be reflective of all United Methodists from which their student body is drawn geographically.

ADOPTED 1996

See Social Principles, ¶ 66A; "Church's Response to Changing Rural Issues"; "Racism Today."

Racism Today

The United Methodist Church made a prophetic witness against racism during the civil rights revolution, and we are committed to becoming a truly inclusive Church. However, the face of racism in America has changed from the crudeness of segregation to more sophisticated but equally oppressive forms. If our Church is to maintain a strong witness against racism and for an inclusive Church, we need an analysis in keeping with the times.

Because of past inequality of opportunity and because of continuing discrimination against racial and ethnic minorities, it is Pan-Africans, Latinos, and Native Americans who are hardest hit by rising unemployment. Because they have been kept at the bottom of the economic ladder in numbers disproportionate to their percentage of the general population, they are the first and the hardest hit by cuts in welfare, health care, education, and by harsher prison conditions and parole policies. These policies, seemingly racially neutral on their face, are harshly racist in their effect and implementation. One of the most blatant forms of this new sanitized racism is the rising clamor for imposition of the death penalty. Over 85 percent of the men on death row in United States prisons are Pan-African and Latino. This is due in large measure to their economic inability to afford high-priced legal representation, but this is never mentioned openly by those who cry the modern equivalent of "Crucify him!"

The new face of racism requires new remedies. To this end, we call for:

1. the General Commission on Religion and Race to develop new programs to unmask and eliminate racism in its new guises;

2. every annual conference to conduct anti-racism training programs, with a list of organizations and groups who provide such training to be provided by GCORR;

3. continued United Methodist opposition to the death penalty, emphasizing its disproportionate impact upon racial and ethnic persons; and

4. local churches to become intentionally multicultural and to share power with those they seek to include.

It is a simple issue of justice that we must ensure that racial and ethnic and women clergy who serve churches in economically depressed and/or blighted communities receive fair and equitable compensation. We strongly recommend that all annual and missionary conferences take appropriate steps to meet minimum salary and housing standards for pastors who serve in these circumstances.

In addition, we call for local, state, and national governments to place greater emphasis on education, job creation, drug rehabilitation, and community development than on building prisons, hiring police, and the imposition of the death penalty.

ADOPTED 1996

See Social Principles, ¶ 66A; "Global Racism: A Violation of Human Rights"; "A Charter for Racial Justice Policies in The United Methodist Church."

Reducing the Risk of Child Sexual Abuse in the Church

Jesus said, "Whoever welcomes [a] child . . . welcomes me" (Matthew 18:5). Children are our present and our future, our hope, our teachers, our inspiration. They are full participants in the life of the church and in the realm of God.

Jesus also said, "If any of you put a stumbling block before one of these little ones . . . it would be better for you if a great millstone were fastened around your neck and you were drowned in the depth of the sea" (Matthew 18:6). Our Christian faith calls us to offer both hospitality and protection to the little ones, the children. The Social Principles of The United Methodist Church state that "children must be protected from economic, physical, and sexual exploitation and abuse" (¶ 66C).

Tragically, churches have not always been safe places for children. Child sexual abuse, exploitation, and ritual abuse[1] occur in churches, both large and small, urban and rural. The problem cuts across all economic, cultural, and racial lines. It is real, and it appears to be increasing. Most annual conferences can cite specific incidents of child sexual abuse and exploitation within churches. Virtually every congregation has among its members adult survivors of early sexual trauma.

Such incidents are devastating to all who are involved: the child, the family, the local church, and its leaders. Increasingly, churches are torn apart by the legal, emotional, and monetary consequences of litigation following allegations of abuse.

God calls us to make our churches safe places, protecting children and other vulnerable persons from sexual and ritual abuse. God calls us to create communities of faith where children and adults grow safe

---

[1] "Ritual abuse" refers to abusive acts committed as part of ceremonies or rites; ritual abusers are often related to cults, or pretend to be.

384

and strong. In response to this churchwide challenge, the following steps should be taken to reduce the risk of child sexual abuse:

A. *Local churches should:*

1. Develop and implement an ongoing education plan for the congregation and its leaders on the reality of child abuse, risk factors leading to child abuse, and strategies for prevention;

2. Adopt screening procedures (use of application forms, interviews, reference checks, background clearance, and so forth) for workers (paid and unpaid) directly or indirectly involved in the care of children and youth;

3. Develop and implement safety procedures for church activities such as having two or more nonrelated adults present in classroom or activity; leaving doors open and installing half-doors or windows in doors or halls; providing hall monitors; instituting sign-in and sign-out procedures for children ages ten or younger; and so forth;

4. Advise children and young persons of an agency or a person outside as well as within the local church whom they can contact for advice and help if they have suffered abuse;

5. Carry liability insurance that includes sexual abuse coverage;

6. Assist the development of awareness and self-protection skills for children and youth through special curriculum and activities; and

7. Be familiar with annual conference and other Church policies regarding clergy sexual misconduct.

B. *Annual conferences should:*

1. Develop safety and risk-reducing policies and procedures for conference-sponsored events such as camps, retreats, youth gatherings, childcare at conference events, mission trips, and so forth; and

2. Develop guidelines and training processes for use by Church leaders who carry responsibility for prevention of child abuse in local churches. Both sets of policies shall be developed by a task force appointed by the cabinet in cooperation with appropriate conference agencies. These policies shall be approved by the annual conference and assigned to a conference agency for implementation. It is suggested that the policies be circulated in conference publications and shared with lay professionals and clergy at district or conference seminars.

C. *The General Board of Discipleship and the General Board of Global Ministries should cooperatively develop and/or identify and promote the following resources:*

1. Sample policies, procedures, forms, and so forth for reducing the risk of sexual abuse and exploitation of children and youth in local churches, both in relation to their own sponsored programs and to any outreach ministries or other programs for children or youth that use church space;

2. Child abuse prevention curriculum for use in local churches;

3. Training opportunities and other educational resources on child sexual abuse and exploitation and on ritual abuse; and

4. Resources on healing for those who have experienced childhood sexual trauma.

ADOPTED 1996

See Social Principles, ¶ 66C; "Putting Children and Their Families First"; "Sexual Abuse Within the Ministerial Relationship and Sexual Harassment Within The United Methodist Church."

Relationship Between The United Methodist Church and the New Affiliated Autonomous Methodist Church of Puerto Rico

[*Note: Paragraph references in the text of this resolution refer to the 1988* Book of Discipline.]

This is to petition the General Conference to establish the foundations to govern the relationship between The United Methodist Church and The Methodist Church of Puerto Rico during the interim period before the formal signing of an Act of covenanting in accordance with the 1988 *Book of Discipline*, ¶¶ 648 and 650. The unique character of this process is acknowledged due to the close relationship between both churches, as well as the unique link between the United States and Puerto Rico.

1. The advent of the new Methodist Church in Puerto Rico is celebrated and supported as part of a growth process and self-determination. The United Methodist Church in its global vision of the church affirms that the new Methodist Church of Puerto Rico must be viewed as a powerful ally in meeting the needs of and challenges to Hispanics

on the United States mainland. It will also be a link between the United States, the Caribbean, and Latin America.

2. As a means for the empowerment of the new Methodist Church in Puerto Rico throughout its formation period of two quadrennia (1992–2000), the following principles are established:

(a) The Methodist Church of Puerto Rico constitutes a unique case and shall be considered in the most favorable manner by the general agencies of The United Methodist Church;

(b) the general agencies will give equal access and consideration to petitions and requests for resources from The Methodist Church of Puerto Rico for the transition period, in the manner provided to any other United Methodist annual conference;

(c) all of the agreements between the general agencies and the Puerto Rico Annual Conference entered into the records of the general agencies and the Puerto Rico Annual Conference for the transition period will be honored by the general agencies and The Methodist Church of Puerto Rico;

(d) all decisions that affect The Methodist Church of Puerto Rico shall be made in consultation with The Methodist Church of Puerto Rico; no unilateral decisions are to be made that in any way will weaken the local mission as it has developed during the last ninety-two years;

(e) in order that no action shall be taken that can be constituted as having vestiges of racism or discrimination, the General Commission on Religion and Race will retain jurisdiction on this matter through the 1992–2000 time period;

(f) The Methodist Church of Puerto Rico will continue providing significant pastoral leadership for Hispanic ministries in The United Methodist Church. The Evangelical Seminary of Puerto Rico will continue as a center for the theological education of Hispanic ministers, both for the United States and for Puerto Rico; and

(g) the above-mentioned principles shall govern all agreements with the general agencies of The United Methodist Church.

3. To facilitate the coordination of mission efforts between The Methodist Church of Puerto Rico and The United Methodist Church, a provision is made in order that the bishop of The Methodist Church of Puerto Rico will sit with voice but no vote in The United Methodist Council of Bishops. Periodic episcopal visitation from The United Methodist Church will be welcomed by The Methodist Church of Puerto Rico (¶ 646.4).

4. The Methodist Church of Puerto Rico shall be entitled to continue to send two delegates, one clergy and one lay, to the General Conference of The United Methodist Church, with all rights and privileges (¶ 602.18 and ¶ 12.2 of the Constitution).

5. In order to provide adequate coordination and programmatic support during the 1992–2000 period, The Methodist Church of Puerto Rico will continue its membership in the boards of directors of the following agencies: General Council on Ministries, General Board of Global Ministries, General Board of Church and Society, General Board of Discipleship, Board of Global Higher Education and Ministry, General Commission on the Status and Role of Women, and General Commission on Religion and Race (¶ 805.1, .2).

6. The Methodist Church of Puerto Rico is committed to contribute at least at the present level to the general benevolence fund of The United Methodist Church for the 1992–2000 period. The Methodist Church of Puerto Rico is also committed to continue purchasing and using printed and other resources produced by The United Methodist Church.

ADOPTED 1992

See Social Principles, ¶¶ 66, 69; "Puerto Rico and Vieques."

Resourcing Black Churches in Urban Communities

WHEREAS, the struggle for social, economic, and political survival of Black people in the United States is manifested in their historical migration to urban centers; and

WHEREAS, the problems that have evolved through the decade now face this population of people, isolated from access to the material resources needed to unleash its power and creativity in a manner that will build rather than destroy communities; and

WHEREAS, the Black United Methodist churches in urban communities have historically been centers of spiritual nurture and social and political action that have cared for the youth and offered viable alternatives to the negative aspects of decaying urban centers; and

WHEREAS, there is a demonstrated need in all urban communities in this country for strong, vital Black congregations to reach into the hurts and pains of the community and provide the spiritual revival that is needed in order to reclaim individuals and communities and manifest the healing power of God to combat drugs, violence, and a growing sense of hopelessness; and

WHEREAS, the gospel mandates that we "seek the welfare of the city where I have sent you into exile, and pray to the LORD on its behalf, for in its welfare you will find your welfare" (Jeremiah 29:7); and

WHEREAS, Black United Methodist congregations in urban communities are called, as are all churches, to minister to the needs of persons in the communities where the church is located; and

WHEREAS, the conditions in urban communities for Black persons continue to worsen, and the need for grounding in a faith and reliance on the power of God for the strength and vision to reclaim and rebuild strong, proud, faith-centered communities grows daily while the resources and persons in Black urban congregations decrease;

Therefore, be it resolved, that the General Conference direct the General Board of Discipleship to develop programs and strategies that will enable the development of Black leadership, and specific programs and strategies that will foster financial self-sufficiency, such as launching a stewardship education program.

Be it further resolved, that the General Board of Global Ministries, National Division, work with existing Black churches in urban communities to develop and maintain vital congregations providing practical ministries that address the spiritual, social, and economic decline in these communities.

Be it further resolved, that the National Division coordinate its work in strengthening Black urban congregations with the General Board of Discipleship, the annual conferences and urban ministry units of annual conferences, the General Board of Global Ministries, and the General Board of Discipleship, and provide a comprehensive progress report—including activities, human resources, and funds that have been committed to this effort—to the General Council on Ministries by December 31, 1994.

ADOPTED 1992

See Social Principles, ¶ 66A; "Church and Community Workers, 1988"; "Church and Community Workers, 1992"; "Holy Boldness: A National Plan for Urban Ministry."

Support Restitution to the Cheyenne and Arapaho Tribes of Oklahoma for the Sand Creek Massacre

WHEREAS, in 1851 the Cheyenne and Arapaho tribes signed a treaty with the U.S. government called the Fort Laramie Treaty; and

WHEREAS, the Cheyenne and Arapaho tribes were given 51.2 million acres covering three U.S. territories, including the Territory of Colorado; and

WHEREAS, in 1859 gold was discovered at Pike's Peak, Colorado, which was part of the land given to the Cheyenne and Arapaho tribes through the Fort Laramie Treaty; and

WHEREAS, the U.S. government was powerless to stop the thousands of greedy miners who wantonly violated the provisions of the Fort Laramie Treaty and began to enter onto the Cheyenne and Arapaho lands to establish numerous mining towns such as Denver, Pueblo, and Colorado City; and

WHEREAS, the Territory of Colorado made it a public policy to "rid itself" of any tribe(s) of Native Americans through whatever means expedient; and coupled with rampant rumors of Indian uprisings, attacks were made on Indian villages, where women were raped and food and other possessions taken; and

WHEREAS, one of the peace chiefs, Black Kettle, had met with the governor and with Colonel John Chivington to stop the attacks against one another and was assured by Governor Evans that hostilities would cease; and giving him a U.S. flag to fly over his village, Governor Evans asked Black Kettle and his people to camp for the winter at Sand Creek in Southern Colorado; and

WHEREAS, on November 29, 1864, Colonel John Chivington, a Methodist lay preacher, did lead the Third Regiment of the First Colorado Volunteers into a pre-dawn attack upon Black Kettle and his peaceful village at Sand Creek, killing over 200 people, most of whom were women and children; and

WHEREAS, horrible acts of inhumanity were committed upon the dead in the Cheyenne village, with bodies mutilated and dismembered, and then taken to display in a parade through downtown Denver; and

WHEREAS, the history of the hostilities of the whites against the Indians of Colorado was fought purely for gold and riches, which the Indians had no use for, as their values were different from those of the white man; and

WHEREAS, this wrong against humanity was acknowledged by the U.S. government, resulting in the Thirty-ninth Congress's awarding the descendants of the survivors of this massacre millions of dollars; but to this date not one descendant has received any money award;

Therefore, be it resolved, that the 1996 General Conference of The United Methodist Church hereby declare that this wrong has gone unrectified long enough and support the efforts of the Cheyenne and Arapaho tribes of Oklahoma in having the actions of the Thirty-ninth Congress fulfilled; and

Be it further resolved, that the 1996 General Conference of The United Methodist Church, through the Council of Bishops and the General Board of Church and Society, urge all members of Congress to respond to the efforts of the Cheyenne and Arapaho tribes in having this money award appropriated and disbursed to the Cheyenne and Arapaho people, posthaste.

ADOPTED 1996

See Social Principles, ¶ 66A; "The Sand Creek Apology"; "The United Methodist Church and America's Native People."

Support the Return of the Fort Reno, Oklahoma, Lands to the Cheyenne and Arapaho Tribes

WHEREAS, in 1869 the southern Cheyenne and Arapaho tribes settled on five million acres of land in what is today northwest Oklahoma, designated as a reservation for the two tribes; and

WHEREAS, in 1883 Fort Reno was carved out of this reservation by executive order of President Chester A. Arthur for "military purposes exclusively," with the understanding that the tribes would get the land back when and if it was no longer needed for military purposes; and

WHEREAS, in 1890 the Dawes Act disbanded the Cheyenne and Arapaho Reservation and opened millions of acres to white settlement, but Fort Reno remained a military reserve; and

WHEREAS, in 1949 the army ceased any further military use of the Fort Reno property, and for forty-seven years now, the tribes have been seeking return of the Fort Reno lands; and

WHEREAS, the 103rd Congress stated in 1995 that the United States Department of Agriculture research station now located on the Fort Reno property be defunded and closed as a part of Congress's plan to reduce the federal budget; and

WHEREAS, this USDA research station no longer serves a purpose other than providing subsidies to selected local farmers and is being advocated to remain open by Congressman Frank Lucas (R) of Cheyenne, Oklahoma; and

WHEREAS, according to the Federal Surplus Property and Administrative Services Act of 1976, property declared "excess" within the original reservation boundary of the tribe where the property was situated was to be returned to the Department of Interior for the tribes in trust;

Therefore, be it resolved, that the 1996 General Conference of The United Methodist Church hereby supports the efforts of the Cheyenne and Arapaho tribes of Oklahoma in having the Fort Reno, Oklahoma, lands returned to them either through executive order of the President or through the provisions of the Federal Surplus Property and Administrative Services Act.

Be it further resolved, that the 1996 General Conference of The United Methodist Church, through the Council of Bishops and the General Board of Church and Society, urge members of Congress to declare the USDA station closed and the Fort Reno property declared "excess" and to authorize the return of the Fort Reno lands to the Cheyenne and Arapaho tribes of Oklahoma through the provisions of the Federal Surplus Property and Administrative Services Act.

Be it also resolved, that if it is more expedient for an executive order to be issued by the President of the United States in order to return these lands to the Cheyenne and Arapaho tribes of Oklahoma, that this route be pursued.

ADOPTED 1996

See Social Principles, ¶ 66A; "The United Methodist Church and America's Native People."

Rights of All Persons

Around the world, political and religious groups attempt to mandate discrimination against gay and lesbian persons through local and national legislative initiatives. We feel called as Christians to reconfirm our resistance to the strategies and intent of such groups. These groups falsely portray the basic human rights of equal opportunity, access to redress for harm, and justice as "special rights" in the case of gay and lesbian persons.

This legal systemic attack results in persecution and suffering. The legislative initiatives effectively limit freedom of speech, freedom of inquiry, and access to health care for persons with HIV/AIDS. This endeavor to isolate and discriminate against gay, lesbian, and bisexual persons as a group within our society hurts them and diminishes the rights of all. It must be stopped now.

It is particularly disturbing when religious values are used as a foundation for persecution of select groups of people. It is crucially important that Christians insist that all people are God's children who deserve the protection of their human and civil rights.

The Social Principles statement of the United Methodist *Book of Discipline* gives us clear direction in the matter:

> We insist that all persons, regardless of age, gender, marital status, or sexual orientation, are entitled to have their human and civil rights ensured. (¶ 65G)

> The rights and privileges a society bestows upon or withholds from those who comprise it indicate the relative esteem in which that society holds particular persons and groups of persons. We affirm all persons as equally valuable in the sight of God. We therefore work toward societies in which each person's value is recognized, maintained, and strengthened. (¶ 66)

Therefore, all United Methodists are called upon:

1. To refrain from signing petitions and to vote against measures that advocate the denial of basic human and civil rights to anyone;

2. To educate congregation and community alike about the position of the United Methodist *Discipline* on civil rights and its broad applications; and

3. To stand against any political or physical acts that deny human and civil rights and the sacred worth of all persons.

We do this as part of our Christian witness and ministry. Never let it be said that United Methodists were silent during this attack on the rights of all.

ADOPTED 1996

See Social Principles, ¶¶ 66A, H, 68A, 69D; "Human Rights."

Rights of Native People of the Americas

WHEREAS, many of the native people living in the Americas are held captive by policies that violate their rights as human beings; and

WHEREAS, these policies deny the worth and God-given right of every human being to live free of injustice, discrimination, and fear; and

WHEREAS, the human rights of native people of the Americas have been and continue to be grossly violated by various governments that suppress freedom; and

WHEREAS, native people of the Americas are in countries experiencing civil war, and their lives are continually threatened and endangered; and

WHEREAS, our religious faith calls us to affirm the dignity and worth of every human being and to struggle with our oppressed brothers and sisters for justice; we are called to "proclaim release to the captives/. . . to set at liberty those who are oppressed" (Luke 4:18, RSV);

Therefore, be it resolved, that we petition the 1988 General Conference to direct the General Board of Church and Society to design, coordinate, and facilitate—in consultation with the Native American International Caucus, the Oklahoma Indian Missionary Conference, and all other appropriate United Methodist Native American organizations—a strategy that will bring the power of moral and religious influence to bear upon the struggles of the oppressed native people of the Americas.

ADOPTED 1988

See Social Principles, ¶ 66A; "The United Methodist Church and America's Native People"; "American Indian Religious Freedom Act"; "Toward a New Beginning Beyond 1992."

Rural Chaplaincy as a Ministry of Laity and Clergy

WHEREAS, continued decline of rural America constitutes an ongoing struggle that holds rural communities in long-term crisis; and

WHEREAS, the need for specialized and caring ministries in rural communities has become critical; and

WHEREAS, the Rural Chaplains Association is providing training for the certification of laity and clergy as rural chaplains; and

WHEREAS, rural chaplains are persons called by God whose gifts and graces are uniquely suited for mission and ministry with town and rural persons, families, communities, and churches; and

WHEREAS, rural chaplains respond to spiritual dimensions of life when rural peoples who relate to farming, mining, timbering, fishing, rural industries, businesses, and so forth experience harmful, social, technological, and economic changes; and

WHEREAS, rural chaplains advocate the provision of human services that respond to the needs of persons, families, and communities; and

WHEREAS, rural chaplains are interpreters of town and rural issues to denominational, local, and denominational forms of the Church, and also to local communities and society at all levels; and

WHEREAS, rural chaplains provide encouragement to persons who choose to integrate their theological and ethical understandings of society and creation in a lifestyle that calls for a just, participatory, and sustainable economy, and also challenge secular perceptions of environmental and ecological issues; and

WHEREAS, rural chaplains have long-term commitments to serve in communities where they have been appointed or called by the Church, and to use their skills for the purposes given above by participating in a network for fellowship, encouragement, and sharing; and

WHEREAS, forty rural chaplains, including seven laypersons and nine women, from twenty-two annual conferences and five jurisdictions now have been certified;

Therefore, be it resolved, that The United Methodist Church affirm rural chaplaincy as a viable and specialized ministry for town, country, and rural settings; and

Be it further resolved, that The United Methodist Church affirm rural chaplaincy as a ministry of both laity and clergy.

ADOPTED 1992

See Social Principles, ¶ 66; "An Affirmation of Basic Rural Worth"; "Appointment of Clergy to Rural Ministry"; "The Church's Response to Changing Rural Issues."

The Sand Creek Apology

WHEREAS, the Cheyenne and Arapaho tribes of Oklahoma have suffered extreme transgressions against them throughout history in America's great westward expansion; and

WHEREAS, one of the blights on America's past was an event that happened on November 29, 1864, when a Cheyenne village was camped on the banks of the Sand Creek in Colorado. The Cheyenne were led by a chief named Black Kettle, who, during a treaty signing ceremony with the Territory of Colorado, had been given an American flag to fly over his teepee; and

WHEREAS, Chief Black Kettle had been told that if he flew this flag, his village would be protected from any American aggression because Americans would not fire on anyone under the protection of the U.S. flag; and

WHEREAS, the First Colorado Cavalry, a unit of Colorado volunteers under the command of Colonel John Chivington, a Methodist lay preacher, led a pre-dawn attack on Black Kettle's village, killing and then mutilating many Cheyenne, mostly helpless, unarmed women and children; and

WHEREAS, this atrocity, had it been committed in 1995, would have been condemned by all the nations of the world, and those responsible would have been branded and tried as war criminals; and

WHEREAS, Colonel Chivington not only received commendations for this crime against the Cheyenne people but was honored at his death in October, 1894, as a hero and pioneer who both Coloradans and Methodists looked up to; and

WHEREAS, Colonel Chivington's funeral, conducted by the Reverend Robert McIntyre, pastor of the Trinity Methodist Church, was attended by over 600 Masons and several hundred members of the Grand Army of the Republic, the Colorado Pioneers Association, and the Pioneer Ladies Society, in addition to survivors of the First Colorado Cavalry; and

WHEREAS, Colonel Chivington, who had held various pastoral appointments, including a district superintendency, is buried in a cemetery in downtown Denver, Colorado, just minutes from the 1996 General Conference of The United Methodist Church; and

WHEREAS, The United Methodist Church has held itself up as a champion of ethnic minority causes and prides itself in its ethnically diverse membership; and

WHEREAS, the United Methodists began their missionary work among the Native American people early in the 1700s and established many Native American mission churches in Oklahoma as early as the 1830s; and

WHEREAS, The United Methodist Church has established Native American congregations in the Cheyenne and Arapaho tribal areas of Clinton, Thomas, Kingfisher, and El Reno, Oklahoma; and

WHEREAS, the people called Methodists have never apologized to the Cheyenne and Arapaho people for the atrocities committed at Sand Creek, Colorado, by one of their own clergy members, who, although commissioned as an officer of war, was commissioned by the Church as an officer to bring peace and reconciliation to all of God's people; and

WHEREAS, the Cheyenne and Arapaho still carry deep scars from this genocidal act, which manifest themselves, even today, both socially and spiritually; and

WHEREAS, we, the United Methodist people, who believe in the ministry of reconciliation for all people, must now after 132 years offer a sincere apology to those who have been wronged and further offer a healing service to our Cheyenne and Arapaho brothers and sisters; and

WHEREAS, this 1996 General Conference will be in session during the Native American Awareness Sunday of April 21, 1996; and

WHEREAS, to not make ourselves aware of the pain still carried by our Native American brothers and sisters is to diminish the opportunities that Native American Awareness Sunday offers to all of us;

Therefore, be it resolved, that this body of the 1996 General Conference extend to all Cheyenne and Arapaho a hand of reconciliation and ask forgiveness for the death of over 200 persons, mostly women and children, who died in this state where this great conference is being held; and

Be it further resolved, that The United Methodist Church offer at this General Conference a healing service of reconciliation, asking that tribal leaders, elders, and spiritual leaders come and sit with us, pray with us, and bless us; and let us heal the past and offer to one another the gifts with which God (Ma-Hay-O) has blessed each of us, acknowledging that racism is a sin, but also seeing one another as whole people who need one another, as we acknowledge that we also need God.

ADOPTED 1996

See Social Principles, ¶ 66A; "The United Methodist Church and America's Native People"; "Rights of Native People of the Americas."

School Busing

WHEREAS, the Supreme Court in 1954 ruled that segregated public schools are inherently unequal and that de jure segregation in such schools is unconstitutional; and

WHEREAS, integrated schools provide the best means for reducing racial bias and may be useful in providing beneficial learning experiences; and

WHEREAS, the busing of pupils is often the only method available to achieve racial integration and quality education in the public schools;

Therefore, be it resolved, that we call upon The United Methodist Church to support the use of busing where appropriate for school integration and to oppose legislative action or constitutional amendments prohibiting such busing.

ADOPTED 1972

See Social Principles, ¶ 66A; "Church-Government Relations"; "The United Methodist Church and Church-Government Relations."

Shared Financial Support for the Native American Center

WHEREAS, the National United Methodist Native American Center, Inc. (NUMNAC) has functioned as one of four national centers focused on ethnic enlistment, training, and assistance in the deployment of ordained and diaconal ministry and other professional leaders in their respective communities; and

WHEREAS, NUMNAC has operated admirably with a limited staff of the executive director, associate director, and an administrative assistant; and

WHEREAS, NUMNAC's previous funding was authorized by the General Conference with linkage responsibilities resting on the General Board of Higher Education and Ministry (GBHEM); and

WHEREAS, NUMNAC's service record over the past eight years has been extremely contributory to active Native American recruitment into the ordained ministry, higher education opportunities for United Methodist Native American students, Native American youth involvement in The United Methodist Church, pastoral care and training for current ministry, spiritual reinforcement in Native American congregations, communication between Native American and non-Indian churches, and research relating to the growing cultural diversity within The United Methodist Church; and

WHEREAS, there exists a continuous need for Native American understanding, sensitivity, input, and participation among and within the Church administration and general community; and

WHEREAS, NUMNAC's past funding of approximately $160,000 per year from the General Board of Higher Education and Ministry has been insufficient for carrying out assigned goals, and the current level of proposed funding is less than one half of last year's budget;

Therefore, be it resolved, that in 1992, the General Conference endorse the quadrennium funding, 1993–1996, of NUMNAC through a "shared focus" among the General Board of Higher Education and Ministry (GBHEM), General Board of Global Ministries (GBGM), General Board of Discipleship (GBOD), and General Board of Church and Society (GBCS), and that the General Council on Finance and Administration (GCFA) appropriate money for this purpose. NUMNAC board and staff will raise any additional funds needed to fulfill program goals and needs.

Be it further resolved, that the General Conference endorse NUMNAC's current functions and roles as related to its initial goals and objectives, its proposed activities for the next quadrennium, and that it be supported by related entities of The United Methodist Church as a center for Native American cultural, spiritual, and contemporary training for United Methodist lay people.

GCFA recommends that the General Council on Ministries, prior to the end of the 1989–1992 quadrennium, convene representatives of the General Board of Higher Education and Ministry, the General Board of Global Ministries, and the center to recommend to GCFA the amount and source of additional funding for the center from their budgets or other sources. The center is also encouraged to seek approval for funding through general Advance Special Gifts.

ADOPTED 1992

See Social Principles, ¶ 66A; "The United Methodist Church and America's Native People"; "Native American Representation in The United Methodist Church."

Special Emphasis on Reclaiming the Cities

WHEREAS, the Christian church—and the Methodist Church in particular—originated in the city; and

WHEREAS, the fastest-growing populations in the United States are among the Asian, Hispanic, and African American people; and

WHEREAS, The United Methodist Church has had its greatest growth among the poor and "underclass," and our inner cities have become the home of the masses; and

WHEREAS, the Bishops' Initiative has shown that a great deal of human deprivation and desolation are concentrated in our cities—and especially among African American and Hispanic males;

Therefore, be it resolved, that there be a United Methodist Church special emphasis on "Reclaiming the Cities" by:

1. Evangelizing the poor and oppressed;

2. Giving special leadership and more quality time to the cities;

3. Putting more of our human, financial, and other material resources in the cities;

4. Uniting our Methodist families—The African Methodist Episcopal Church, The African Methodist Episcopal Zion Church, The Christian Methodist Episcopal Church, and The United Methodist Church—to make one powerful Methodist voice and presence in our cities; and

5. Leading the way for an ecumenical thrust to save the cities of our nation.

Be it further resolved, that this special emphasis be implemented, as appropriate, by each program board and agency and coordinated by the General Council on Ministries.

ADOPTED 1992

See Social Principles, ¶ 66O; "Holy Boldness: A National Plan for Urban Ministry."

Spiritual Unity in Human Diversity

WHEREAS, The United Methodist Church is experiencing conflicting expressions of faith and biblical theology; and

WHEREAS, The United Methodist Church incorporates confessional traditions (i.e., the Articles of Religion and the Confession of Faith from *The Book of Discipline, 1992*) and inclusive tradition ("The Catholic Spirit" sermon by John Wesley); and

WHEREAS, *The Book of Discipline, 1992* (Part II: "Doctrinal Standards and Our Theological Task") "preserves the inherent tension between doctrinal standards and theological exploration . . . [and] involves dialogue, debate, and some conflict" ("Biblical Wisdom and Current Theological Ferment," Council of Bishops, October 31–November 4, 1994); and

WHEREAS, maintaining an inclusive spirit about doctrinal, theological, and language issues serves the greater purpose of helping people to affirm faith in Jesus Christ and to appropriate the historic confessions of the Church; and

WHEREAS, confessing faith in scriptural truth honors rich diversity in the biblical witness and informs a deeper understanding of diversity among people of faith; and

WHEREAS, "indeed, the body does not consist of one member but of many. . . . [and] God arranged the members in the body, each one of them, as he chose. . . . The eye cannot say to the hand, 'I have no need of you,' nor again the head to the feet, 'I have no need of you.' On the contrary, the members of the body that seem to be weaker are indispensable, and those members of the body that we think less honorable we clothe with greater honor, and our less respectable members are treated with greater respect; whereas, our more respectable members do not need this. But God has so arranged the body, giving the greater honor to the inferior member, that there may be no dissension within the body, but the members may have the same care for one another" (1 Corinthians 12:14-25);

Therefore, be it resolved, that The United Methodist Church reject any spirit that seeks to divide the body of Christ (and especially The United Methodist Church) and that cuts off the confessing and inclusive heritages by which United Methodists know themselves to be people of God; and

Be it further resolved, that we affirm our biblical faith in Jesus Christ and the spiritual gift of unity in human diversity.

ADOPTED 1996

See Social Principles, Preamble; "Make Evangelism the Number One Priority for the Next Quadrennium"; "Prayer in the Local Church."

Strongly Urge the General Board of Church and Society to Create a Standing Committee on Drug and Alcohol Abuse

It is time for The United Methodist Church to fully reclaim its historic position in leading efforts to confront drug and alcohol abuse and to promote abstinence in modern society.

In 1990, the Council of Bishops, through its Special Initiative on Drugs and Violence, captured the attention of the world when it showed that the church can have an impact on communities and families torn apart by drug and alcohol abuse and violence. This special ministry resulted in the grassroots focus of the Special Program on Substance Abuse and Related Violence created by the 1992 General Conference and supported by the generous contributions to the Mission Initiatives Fund.

While the Special Program has been highly successful in its initial efforts to overcome denial and to raise the issue of drug and alcohol abuse and violence throughout the Church, we believe that it must be followed by a deeper commitment on the part of all areas of the Church. Simple words printed in a book of resolutions are not enough. It is a sin to mouth words without following them with the appropriate actions, especially when millions of lives are at stake.

We strongly urge the General Board of Church and Society to form a Standing Committee on Drug and Alcohol Abuse during the 1996 quadrennium. We would pray that the committee's advocacy would be supported by appropriate financial resources and staffing that befits the crisis in our midst. We would encourage the board to strengthen its efforts assisting churches to become involved in ministries with persons in recovery.

We believe there is no other issue that the board must confront that puts more lives at risk every day, every month, every year. Such an action would be in keeping with the board's historic role as an advocate for holy living and calling our governmental leaders into accountability for their actions.

ADOPTED 1996

See Social Principles, ¶ 66J; "Drug and Alcohol Concerns."

The Status of Women

I.

Christianity was born in a world of male preference and dominance. Practices, traditions, and attitudes in almost all societies viewed women as inferior to men, as having few talents and contributions to make to the general well-being of society aside from their biological roles. This was true of the Judaic society of which Jesus was a part.

But the life of Jesus, the Redeemer of human life, stood as a witness against such cultural patterns and prejudices. Consistently, he related to women as persons of intelligence and capabilities. He charged women as well as men to use their talents significantly in the cause of God's kingdom. His acts of healing and ministry were extended without distinction to women and men.

The central theme of Jesus' teaching is love for God and neighbor. Jesus embodied this message in his life, and, in the early church, women held prominent positions of leadership. Christian love as exemplified in the New Testament requires that we relate to others as persons of worth. To regard another as an inferior is to break the covenant of love; denying equality demeans, perpetuates injustice, and falls short of the example of Jesus and the early church.

II.

The movement to improve the status of women is one of the most profoundly hopeful of our times. The United Methodist Church in various ways has sought to support that movement. Although change is taking place, in most societies women are still not accorded equal rights and responsibilities.

There is increasing awareness that we cannot solve world problems of hunger, population growth, poverty, and peace so long as the talents and potential of half the world's people are disregarded and even repressed. There are strong interrelationships between all these problems and the status of women.

The years from 1975 to 1985 have been designated the Decade for Women, a time for correcting these ancient injustices. For Christians, it is a time for repentance and for new dedication to Christ's ideal of equality. It is a time for examining specific areas that need to be addressed in societies:

Economics. Often the productive labor of women is ignored in economic statistics, reinforcing the impression that work done by women is peripheral, of secondary importance, even dispensable. For that reason, few studies have actually evaluated the importance of contributions by women. As one example, when women grow food to feed their families, they are "just" tending kitchen gardens, but when men grow cash crops such as tobacco and coffee, they are engaged in agricultural and commercial enterprises. In more industrialized societies, the enormous amount of volunteer work done by women is not counted as adding to the nation's wealth.

In the United States, nearly half of all women are working outside the home in the paid labor force, and there are well-publicized professional successes, yet actually, the earning gap between men and women is greater than it was in the 1950s. Everywhere, women tend to be clustered in the lower-paying jobs and in certain stereotyped job fields.

Legal Rights. In 1945, only 31 countries allowed women to vote; today women have the right in more than 125 nations. Only eight countries exclude women entirely from political processes open to men. Still, many areas of legal discrimination remain. In some nations, women are still considered the chattels of their husbands, with few rights in family law, landholding, inheritance, and guardianship of children.

In the United States, some of the more glaring inequities are being corrected step by step. Nonetheless, a 1978 report of the Civil Rights Commission noted continuing discrimination on the basis of sex in the federal statutes.[1]

Cultural Factors. The perception of women as inferior and dependent is perpetuated through many institutions in society—the media, school textbooks and curricula, political structures, and, often, religious organizations. Education is one of the principal ways of opening doors to

---

[1] Statement on Equal Rights Amendment, U.S. Commission on Civil Rights Clearinghouse Publication 56, December 1978; page 5.

wider participation in society. Thus, it is distressing that, while the percentage of literate women is at an all-time high, the absolute number of illiterate women is greater than at any time in the past. The fact that two thirds of the world's illiterates are female is evidence of continuing disparity in importance given to the education of boys and girls.

Traditional perceptions of female qualities also are a factor in the widespread domestic violence against women, now coming to be recognized as a tragically widespread occurrence.

Human Rights in Fertility Decisions. Throughout the centuries, women have been little consulted or involved in the decisions regarding fertility-related laws or practices. For women, particularly, the ability to make choices concerning fertility is a liberating force, helping to safeguard their health and that of their children, to plan for the future, to assume wider roles and responsibilities in society.

The United Nations has declared that education and access to means for determining the number and spacing of children is a human right, yet this is an ideal far from realization.

Coercion is still common, sometimes aimed at increasing births, sometimes at limiting them. Evidence now clearly shows that many poor, particularly ethnic, women have been sterilized without their understanding of what was being done to them and without their informed consent. In many places, safe and legal abortion is denied, in some cases even to save the life of the pregnant woman. In other cases, women are threatened that welfare payments or aid programs will be cut if the pregnancy continues. Such inconsistency reflects lack of value-centered decision-making, as well as insensitivity to the personhood of the woman involved.

While societal needs should be considered more and more in fertility matters, this should never be at the price of demeaning the individual or applying restrictive measures only to the poor. Women should be fully informed and fully involved in the decision-making.

Development Programs. National and international development programs now often stress the need to "integrate" women into the development process. Full recognition is seldom given to the contributions women already make to economic and social progress. For example, women make up 60–80 percent of the agricultural workers of the world; in some parts of Africa, women manage one third of the farms. Yet few programs of agricultural development seek to upgrade the skills of women, provide easier access to credit, assure them the right to land titles in their own names, and so forth. In some cases, modernization actually degrades the already low status of women.

III.

Across the nations of the world, new movements are growing that address the serious handicaps and harsh realities of the lives of many women. In the context of this increasing momentum for a more just society, we call on local congregations and the agencies of the Church:

1. To exert leadership in working, wherever possible, for legal recognition of equal rights for women. In the United States, this means a strengthened determination to secure passage for the Equal Rights Amendment,[2] in line with the United Methodist Conference affirmations of 1972 and 1976. We need to recognize that this measure has become a symbol of the drive for equality. It has meaning far beyond the borders of one nation in the search for equal rights in other societies;

2. To urge governments to ratify the Convention on the Elimination of Discrimination Against Women, which was adopted by the United Nations in December 1979;

3. To encourage support of studies by scientific and governmental bodies of the economic contributions made by women outside the formal economic sector, and to include this information in the gross national product of nations or compilations of national wealth;

4. To examine governmental policies and practices, including development assistance, as to their impact on women's lives; to work to ensure that policies upgrade the status of women and that women are included in decision-making regarding development goals and programs. The key roles of women as workers and consumers and as transmitters of culture must be given adequate weight in national development activities;

5. To examine the impact of transnational corporations on women's lives, and to work to eradicate exploitative practices where identified. One such area is the promotion and selling of inappropriate products and technologies;

---

[2] Proposed 27th Amendment:

Section 1. Equality of rights under the law shall not be denied or abridged by the United States or by any State on account of sex.

Section 2. The Congress shall have the power to enforce, by appropriate legislation, the provisions of this article.

Section 3. This amendment shall take effect two years after the date of ratification.

6. To encourage private charitable organizations, including churches, to initiate and support more programs of leadership education for women and other educational programs that upgrade the status of women;

7. To monitor printed and audio/visual media and other means of communication on their portrayals of the roles and nature of women and men, and to seek ways to eradicate narrow stereotypes that limit the possibilities of useful contributions by both sexes. The Church should encourage study of the impact of Western—particularly U.S.—television, radio, and other media on cultural patterns and national development around the world, and it should draw public attention to cases where such influence is destructive to other cultures;

8. To support programs providing knowledge of the access to resources in the area of family planning and contraception, including that which is Christian based, to encourage abstinence outside of marriage as a method of birth control, and to involve women in the preparation and distribution of these resources. Attention should particularly be given to ensuring access to safe, legal, and noncoercive contraception; well-informed choice regarding abortion and its alternatives (adoptions and so forth); informed consent for sterilization procedures; and safe women's health-care facilities. We also oppose profit-making referral agencies, which charge fees for providing information freely available elsewhere; and

9. To examine the impact of judicial decisions at all levels upon the daily lives of women in such areas as child custody, employment, civil rights, racial and sexual discrimination, credit practices, estate settlements, reproduction and education, and socioeconomic status.

ADOPTED 1992
AMENDED & READOPTED 1996

See Social Principles, ¶ 66F; "Equal Rights of Women"; "Ecumenical Decade: Churches in Solidarity with Women"; "Eradication of Sexism in the Church"; "Sexual Harassment in Church and Society in the U.S.A."

Strengthening the Black Church for the Twenty-First Century

WHEREAS, African Americans have been present and active in The United Methodist Church from the inception of Methodism in the United States; and

WHEREAS, this involvement for African Americans continued in spite of the fact that we were placed in missionary conferences within annual conferences in a segregated Central Jurisdiction; and

WHEREAS, in 1968 the Black Methodists for Church Renewal, Inc. (BMCR), was formed to "help The United Methodist Church become inclusive of African Americans"; and

WHEREAS, from the beginning, BMCR has been concerned with recruitment and itineracy of Black pastors, supporting, empowering, and informing Black pastors and congregations; and

WHEREAS, BMCR has suggested new forms for the life of local congregations and precipitated creative motives for the kind of unity among Black Methodists that can mean a vigorous, faithful witness in Methodism and toward the gospel of Jesus Christ; and

WHEREAS, the following 1992 statistical report indicates the racial composition in The United Methodist Church population as

- Hispanic Americans   0.63%
- Native Americans   0.26%
- Asian Americans   0.71%
- Pacific Islanders   0.12%
- African Americans   4.27%*

* the largest percentage of any other racial/ethnic constituency

Therefore, be it resolved, that the 1996 General Conference give its endorsement to "Strengthening the Black Church for the Twenty-First Century"; and

Be it further resolved, that the General Conference direct the General Council on Ministries to include within its regular evaluation process with the general program agencies a review of each agency's effectiveness in strengthening the Black church from the period 1997–2000, including the 2000 General Conference; and

Be it further resolved, that GCOM consult with the general program agencies for encouragement to build program initiatives and budgets around program projections for strengthening the Black church.

ADOPTED 1996

See Social Principles, ¶ 66A; "African American Clergywomen"; "History of Blacks in The United Methodist Church"; "Resourcing Black Churches in Urban Communities"; "Black Leadership."

Suicide: A Challenge to Ministry

The apostle Paul, rooted in his experience of the resurrected Christ, affirms the power of divine love to overcome the divisive realities of human life, including suicide:

> For I am convinced that neither death, nor life, nor angels, nor rulers, nor things present, nor things to come, nor powers, nor height, nor depth, nor anything else in all creation will be able to separate us from the love of God in Christ Jesus our Lord. (Romans 8:38-39)

Paul's words are indeed sources of hope and renewal for persons who contemplate suicide, as well as for those who grieve the death of friends and family members who have committed suicide. These words affirm that in those human moments when all seems lost, all may yet be found through full faith.

A Christian perspective on suicide thus begins with an affirmation of faith: Suicide does not separate us from the love of God.

Unfortunately, the church throughout much of its history has taught just the opposite, that suicide is an unforgivable sin. As a result, Christians, acting out of a sincere concern to prevent suicide, often have contradicted Christ's call to compassion.

For example, victims have been denounced and presumed to be in hell, and families have been stigmatized with guilt and inflicted with economic and social penalties.

This statement is intended to be a guide and a challenge for United Methodist ministry as it relates to suicide in light of such attitudes and actions by the Church. Its purpose is to encourage the sharing of God's grace in circumstances involving suicide and to offer a word of faith and hope to all who are affected by the tragedy of suicide.

Demography of Suicide

Although suicide rates in the United States have remained steady over the past few decades, new phenomena have arisen. Suicide victims in the past were most typically older white males who had suffered loss of family or material security and who may have first turned to the use of alcohol or drugs as a means of escape.

The picture is quite different in the 1980s. The rate of suicide among teens and young adults has increased dramatically. There is also a small but noticeable increase in suicide among women and ethnic minorities, as well as a rapid increase among white, male youth.

According to data from the National Center for Health Statistics, the annual suicide rate among 15- to 24-year-olds increased 129 percent from 1960 to 1983, from 5.2 to 11.9 suicides per 100,000 youth. During 1983, 28,295 Americans took their lives. That's an average of 14 suicides per day, and of these, 5,050 were between the ages of 5 and 24 years old.

These official, well-researched reports document circumstances in which there is little doubt about the intent of the victim. The actual number of deaths due to suicide may be twice as high as the reported incidence.

Many coroners and medical examiners are reluctant to list suicide as the cause of death because of the stigma attached to it. Listing suicide as the cause of death is further complicated because (1) there is no commonly recognized definition of suicide (one that specifies factors that identify a suicide-caused death—for example, the existence of a note); and (2) families feel the need to mask the death as a traffic fatality, a mixing of lethal combinations of drugs (i.e., alcohol and barbiturates), or other "accidents."

Causes of Suicide

The Centers for Disease Control (CDC) of the U.S. Public Health Service has been able to identify causes of many suicides. Specific groups in society appear more *vulnerable* to suicide than others. People in such groups are at special risk of committing suicide, especially if they experience certain precipitants (events in their lives such as disease, loss of family, friends, job, and so forth) and have access to a method for ending their lives, that is, an *enabling environment*. These factors—vulnerability, precipitating events, enabling environment—must be recognized and addressed if there is to be any reduction in the suicide rate.

The problem of suicide and suicide attempts is extremely serious in this country. One in five women fall into the vulnerable group, and the female to male rate of suicide completion is about 3.5 to 1. In the past, women have used passive methods to attempt suicide. However, now the enabling environment, in terms of both attitude and access to weaponry, has changed, and the ratios are changing.

Youth experience alienation and rejection by society, family, and the church when dealing with sexual-identity issues, including homosexuality. For many youth, the only perceived way out is suicide.

Societal Attitudes

The prevailing attitudes of society, both secular and religious, have been to condemn the victim and ignore the victim's family and friends, and survivors.

> There are always two parties to a death; the person who dies and the survivors who are bereaved . . . the sting of death is less sharp for the person who dies than it is for the bereaved survivor. This, as I see it, is the capital fact about the relation between the living and the dying. There are two parties to the suffering that death inflicts; and in the apportionment of the suffering the survivor takes the brunt.
> —Arnold Toynbee, from *Man's Concern with Death*

Churches sometimes have denied funerals and memorial services to bereaved families. Victim's remains have been banned from cemeteries. Medical examiners have falsified records for families so they can receive economic aid. The U.S. Office of the Inspector General conducted a national survey on societal attitudes related to suicide when the teen suicide crisis became evident. The findings of that study, quoted below, provide a picture of these observations and factors related to suicide:

- "Youth at risk of suicide come from various walks of life and personal experiences. They come from dysfunctional families, as well as loving, supportive families. However, health, educational and social service agencies describe increasing trends in (a) the number of very young (aged ten and under) attempters, (b) suicide ideation (ideas, concern with, sometimes obsession with suicide) among youth of all ages, (c) multiple forms of self-destructive behavior, and (d) a sense of futility among youth.
- "Suicide is the ultimate form of self-destructive behavior. It is a symptom and should not be dealt with in isolation from other self-destructive behaviors or from social, health and educational problems.
- "Community response to suicide ranges from fear, denial and resistance to widespread support for suicide prevention.
- "Many youth who eventually kill themselves never enter the health service system and those who do often drop out prior to completing treatment. This is due, in part, to a stigma associated with mental health problems and suicide.
- "Lack of financial resources or private insurance limits access to mental health treatment.
- "More than half the study respondents cited family problems as contributing factors to suicidal risk. Family support is key to (a) getting youth into treatment, (b) assuring they do not drop out of treatment, and (c) effecting a successful outcome.

410

- "The most significant gaps in the service system include (a) too few inpatient psychiatric adolescent beds, particularly for public pay patients who, if admitted, are discharged prematurely, (b) limited subacute (non-critical) and alternative living arrangements, including residential treatment, day treatment, group homes and foster care, (c) limited outpatient treatment in community mental health centers where demand is greater than supply, and (d) scarce crisis intervention programs and hotlines with a special focus for youth.
- "Suicide prevention must be community based. School programs are key and should be developed in coordination with existing community resources, including mental health and crisis intervention programs. Networking is crucial to keeping youth from falling through the cracks."

The Church's Response

Recognizing that the church's historical response to suicide includes punitive measures intended to prevent suicide and that there is no clear biblical stance on suicide, the General Conference of The United Methodist Church strongly urges the employment of major initiatives to prevent suicide. Additionally, the General Conference recommends to the boards, agencies, institutions, and local churches of The United Methodist Church that the ministry of suicide prevention should receive urgent attention. The families of victims should also receive priority concern in the overall ministry of the Church. Harsh and punitive measures (such as denial of funeral or memorial services, or ministerial visits) imposed upon families of suicide victims should be denounced and abandoned. The Church should participate in and urge others to participate in a full, community-based effort to address the needs of potential suicide victims and their families. Each annual conference and local church should respond to issues of ministry related to suicide prevention and family-support services.

It must be emphasized that suicide increases in an environment or society that does not demonstrate a caring attitude toward all persons. The Church has a special role in changing societal attitudes and the social environment of individuals and families. To promote this effort, the Church should do the following:

1. The General Board of Discipleship shall develop curriculum for biblical and theological study of suicide and related mental and environmental health problems and promote the programs recommended

411

by the American Association of Pastoral Counseling and the use of the scientific research of the Centers for Disease Control and the American Association of Suicidology;

2. The General Board of Higher Education and Ministry shall develop materials for United Methodist-related seminaries to train church professionals to recognize treatable mental illness associated with suicide (e.g., depression) and to realize when and how to refer persons for treatment; it shall ensure that all pastoral counseling programs include such training and strategies for ministry to families of suicide victims;

3. The General Board of Church and Society shall support public policies that: (a) promote access to mental-health services for all persons regardless of age, (b) remove the stigma associated with mental illness, and (c) encourage "help-seeking" behavior;

4. Embrace all persons affected by suicide in loving community through support groups and responsive social institutions, call upon society through the media to reinforce the importance of human life and to advocate that public policies include all persons' welfare, and work against policies that devalue human life (i.e., nuclear armaments, war, and so forth);

5. Affirm that we can destroy our physical bodies but not our being in God, and affirm that a person stands in relationship to others. The loss of every person is a loss in community;

6. Support the United Methodist childcare institutions that provide treatment for emotionally disturbed children, youth, and their families; and

7. Strengthen the youth ministries of the local church, helping the young people experience the saving grace of Jesus Christ and participate in the caring fellowship of the church.

Conclusion:

"The church is called to proclaim the gospel of grace and, in its own life, to embody that gospel. It embodies that gospel when it is particularly solicitous of those within its number who are most troubled, and when it reaches beyond its own membership to such people who stand alone" (Dr. Philip Wogaman, Professor of Christian Social Ethics, Wesley Theological Seminary).

ADOPTED 1988
AMENDED & READOPTED 1996

See Social Principles, ¶¶ 65L, 66; "Understanding Living and Dying as Faithful Christians."

Support the Consultation on Church Union Proposal

WHEREAS, the principles and procedures of the Church of Christ Uniting and the Consultation on Church Union (COCU) are a viable format for continuing discussion of the unity of the church; and

WHEREAS, through the Covenanting Proposal, meaningful dialogue is maintained with eight Christian communities besides our own; and

WHEREAS, that meaningful dialogue is extended to include advisory consultants from four other Christian communities; and

WHEREAS, by this effort we are also witness to many other Christian communities; and

WHEREAS, this covenant parallels the ecumenical discussion of *Baptism, Eucharist and Ministry* (Faith and Order Paper Number 111 of the World Council of Churches); and

WHEREAS, there is currently a COCU staff person holding discussion meetings in urban areas at which non-COCU communities have not only willingly participated, but in some cases have asked to be included; and

WHEREAS, there is a need to increase awareness of the Covenanting Proposal; and

WHEREAS, the unity of the church was the prayer of our Lord;

Therefore, be it resolved, that the General Conference of The United Methodist Church reaffirm support for the Consultation on Church Union and its covenanting proposals;

Be it further resolved, that the General Commission on Christian Unity and Interreligious Concerns be directed, within the framework of the existing budget, to promote interest in the Covenanting Proposal and to develop for use by the fall of 1993 a "user-friendly" curriculum to study the document;

Be it further resolved, that the Council of Bishops encourage and support, within the financial limitations of their existing budget, the Covenanting Proposal of the consultation both through our continued denomination representation and through directions to local churches.

ADOPTED 1992

See Social Principles, ¶ 66; "Continuing Membership in the Consultation on Church Union"; "Toward an Ecumenical Future."

413

Teens at Risk

WHEREAS, we recognize that teens dealing with questions about sexual orientation are at a greater risk of suicide; and

WHEREAS, an individual of any age confronting his or her own homosexual orientation and/or that of a close family member, friend, or associate often experiences isolation, confusion, and fear when he or she needs information, guidance, and support; and

WHEREAS, United Methodist Women have many effective channels for disseminating information and are known for providing a supportive community; and

WHEREAS, the concerns and action embodied in this resolution were originally proposed by the Troy Annual Conference United Methodist Women Mission Team;

Therefore, be it resolved, that the Women's Division is directed to use its available channels (such as the *Response* magazine, reading program, program book, spiritual growth study, and others) to provide factual information, program ideas, and resources on this topic for use by individuals and groups. These materials could include books, guides for developing support groups, suggestions for ways to find counselors/therapists, supportive clergy and/or congregations, and organizations in a particular area.

ADOPTED 1996

See Social Principles, ¶ 66D, H; "Ministry to Runaway Children"; "Putting Children and Their Families First"; "Suicide: A Challenge to Ministry."

Tent-Building Ministries

WHEREAS, many small churches/congregations are facing increasingly difficult financial situations; and

WHEREAS, pastoral support is the largest single item in the budgets of these churches; and

WHEREAS, many other denominations function successfully with pastors with secular jobs as their primary income;

Therefore, be it resolved, that we support encouraging more tent-building ministries as a help to these small churches/congregations.

ADOPTED 1992

See Social Principles, ¶ 66.

Toward an Ecumenical Future

WHEREAS, the Constitution of The United Methodist Church affirms that Jesus Christ is "calling Christians everywhere to strive toward unity . . . at all levels of church life" (Division One, Article V); and

WHEREAS, the Council of Bishops has consistently upheld the commitment of The United Methodist Church to ecumenism, especially in the Report of the Conciliar Review Committee of the Council of Bishops in 1984; and

WHEREAS, The United Methodist Church or its predecessors have been founding members of ecumenical organizations such as the World Council of Churches, the National Council of the Churches of Christ in the U.S.A., the Consultation on Church Union (COCU), and the World Methodist Council; and

WHEREAS, three general conferences have affirmed the Consultation on Church Union's "Mutual Recognition of Members," and the 1988 General Conference adopted *The COCU Consensus: In Quest of a Church of Christ Uniting* as a sufficient theological basis for covenanting among the member churches; and

WHEREAS, the full United Methodist Church delegation appointed by the Council of Bishops and other member delegations voted unanimously at the 1988 COCU plenaries to send *Covenanting* to the churches for appropriate action;

Be it resolved, that the General Conference direct the Council of Bishops and the General Commission on Christian Unity and Interreligious Concerns to develop a comprehensive policy for United Methodism's ecumenical involvement into the twenty-first century for action at the 1996 General Conference, utilizing:

• the COCU proposal, *Churches in Covenant Communion,* including the concrete steps and procedures to prepare for a recognition of churches and reconciliation of ministries that would lead toward unity in Eucharistic celebration and engaging in common mission;

• the contributions that dialogue among communions can make toward increased understanding and ecumenical hospitality;

• national and international expressions and relationships of Christian unity wherever The United Methodist Church exists, including relationships with conciliar organizations and Christian world communions; and

• the Preamble of our Constitution, which states that "the church of Jesus Christ exists in and for the world, and its very dividedness is a hindrance to its mission in that world."

ADOPTED 1992

See Social Principles, ¶ 66*B*; "Ecumenical Interpretations of Doctrinal Standards"; "Guidelines for Interreligious Relationships: 'Called to Be Neighbors and Witnesses'"; "Support the Consultation on Church Union Proposal."

Toward a New Beginning Beyond 1992

The 1988 General Conference, in adopting petition number 1295, "A New Beginning," called United Methodists to declare 1992 "The Year of a New Beginning" through appropriate resolutions and legislation. It urged the 1992 General Conference to "take the necessary measures so that The United Methodist Church will place itself at the vanguard of the efforts to undo and correct the injustices and the misunderstandings of the last 500 years in this hemisphere."

For a "new beginning" to take place, new learnings resulting from the 1992 activities must shape perspectives, programs, and advocacy initiatives across the denomination for many years after 1992. This resolution recommends ways for individual local churches and the general Church to respond and incorporate these concerns into their life and ministry.

The 1992 "celebration" in the Western Hemisphere and Europe has brought renewed attention to the consequences of the European colonial ventures in the Americas. The very use of the term *discovery* revealed the blindness of the "discoverers," who did not even acknowledge the humanity of the native inhabitants. It also "justified" the shameful stealing of the natives' land and other goods and the cruel destruction of their culture, arts, religion, the environment, and other living things on which their lives depended.

Eventually, oppression, exploitation, brutality, and enslavement led to the partial—and in some places, complete—extermination of the land's original inhabitants. The tragedy was compounded when African and Caribbean people were forced into slavery as a way to alleviate the problem. This only added countless new innocent people to the toll of those who suffered injustices, dispossession, and uprootedness.

A fair retelling of history, which is one of the goals of the Church regarding quincentennary events, does not require us to assume that the native peoples were perfect. Yet, although humanly flawed (but not more so than their oppressors), history clearly demonstrates that their friendliness and good nature, as well as their initial goodwill, made them extremely vulnerable to those who were more aggressive, those armed with more deadly weapons.

While Spain was the greatest offender 500 years ago, it was not only Spaniards or Roman Catholics who oppressed and exploited their colonial subjects. Other European powers proved equally inhuman and unjust. The sanitized version of the encounter of Indians and colonizers celebrated in the United States as Thanksgiving is very far from the Indian experience of oppression, exploitation, massacres, mass exclusion from their own lands, and an endless string of broken treaties and promises.

Unfortunately, the role of the churches in these events was ambiguous at best. Evangelization provided the excuse for the domination of indigenous peoples and Africans and for the destruction of their culture and religion. Nevertheless, evangelization did take place, in spite of the manipulation of religion for their own purposes by the colonizers. The power of the gospel of Christ to transcend human sinfulness was able to raise prophetic voices who denounced injustice and worked to alleviate the conditions of the oppressed. Still, centuries later, Protestant denominations divided the tribes among themselves, just as the colonial powers had earlier divided the land.

While it is difficult to judge past events in light of contemporary moral sensibilities, Christians have the responsibility to understand them and to face up to their contemporary consequences. Oppression, exploitation of people and their land, and cultural depreciation of people of color, minorities, and others suffering under structures of domination are still widely practiced, even if old-style colonialism has been defeated almost everywhere. Intolerance, racism, and greed are still the dominant value systems in many public and private centers of power in the world.

As people of faith, we confess that God is the creator of all that exists and that all humans are created equal in dignity, rights, and responsibilities. Therefore, we must challenge all value systems and structures that in theory and/or practice devalue human beings and rob them of their dignity and their relationship to the rest of God's creation, which sustains us all. The Scriptures teach us that the earth is indeed the Lord's, and therefore we must oppose individual and corporate greed that seeks to take land away from the poor and often use it in ways that disregard ecological consequences.

When we today seek the face of our crucified and risen Lord, we hear the words that he can be found when we seek and serve "the least of these." We are, therefore, compelled to go beyond intellectual awareness of suffering and take concrete steps to walk in love and solidarity with those who today suffer the consequences of our past sins. Indeed, the resurrection of Jesus Christ is the greatest "new beginning." It inspires and empowers us to overcome the paralysis of guilt and move on to new opportunities for seeking peace with justice in every corner of the world.

The Social Principles call us to be "faithful stewards of all that has been committed to us by God the Creator" (*Book of Discipline*, Preamble to ¶ 64), while denying to "any person or group of persons exclusive and arbitrary control of any other part of the created universe" (¶ 67A). The Social Principles also "denounce as immoral an ordering of life that perpetuates injustice" (¶ 69D).

Because of our biblical faith and our Social Principles, United Methodists cannot ignore the fact that the events that started 500 years ago were not a "discovery," but a conquest; not so much an exchange of cultures, as an invasion by an occupying force; not so much a bringing of civilization, as an imposition by force of a foreign culture and values on peoples who already had their own civilizations, history, culture, languages, and values. Again, because of our faith and principles, we cannot ignore that the five centuries since Columbus's arrival have left a legacy of violence and unjust sociopolitical and economic/ecological systems in the Western Hemisphere that has oppressed especially women, children, indigenous peoples, and people of African descent. The United Methodist "Charter for Racial Justice Policies" states that "during the early history of this country, Europeans assumed that their civilization and religion were innately superior to those of both the original inhabitants of the United States and the Africans who were forcibly brought to these shores to be slaves. The myth of European superiority persisted and persists" (1988 *Book of Resolutions;* page 167). A basic step toward a new beginning requires us to abandon this Eurocentric myth that continues to operate in both church and society in most parts of the world.

United Methodists stand ready to accept the call to a "new beginning." Accepting this call means turning away from past practices and habits based on exploitation, racism, and injustice. It means affirming, respecting, celebrating, and seeking reconciliation with cultures other than those that are dominant in our societies, with particular attention to indigenous groups. In order to make this possible and to effect significant personal and institutional growth in the life of the Church, several recommendations are proposed for the Church in general, and then for each specific level.

General recommendations:

All levels of the Church are urged to provide leadership and resources to support United Methodist efforts toward a "new beginning" beyond 1992. The Council of Bishops is specially requested to lead the Church by education and example on the issues raised by this resolution.

A first step in these efforts is to heed the call from the Seventh Assembly of the World Council of Churches that all member churches move beyond words to action, in these areas:

1. To negotiate with indigenous people to ascertain how lands taken unjustly by churches from indigenous people can be returned to them;

2. To recognize, acknowledge, and vigorously support self-determination and sovereignty of indigenous people, as defined by them, in church and society; and

3. To oppose the continuing and now increasing exploration of indigenous peoples' land and mineral resources.

Local church recommendations:

In the spirit of a new beginning, each local church, starting with its pastor and lay leaders, is to seek changes in the following areas:

1. *Nurture.* In preaching and Christian education, churches will seek to study and reflect on how the exploitation and genocide of natives and other racial and ethnic minority peoples started with the colonial conquerors 500 years ago, how it was continued by their successors, and how it persists to this day. Special attention is to be given to Bible study and to local resources. Important also is to observe worship opportunities such as Native American Awareness Sunday, Human Relations Day, and Peace with Justice Sunday, where the congregation may find ways to meet with local people from racial and ethnic minority communities in their own setting to hear ways to work with them.

2. *Outreach.* Identify discriminated, oppressed, or dominated groups in their community. Seek a new beginning with them through church programs. Provide resources for programs that promote empowerment, self-determination, and care for creation.

3. *Witness.* Accept the challenge of a new beginning in the approach of witnessing to new groups. The new approach would involve knowing the life of the people from inside; living, learning, and sharing with the people; believing that God is already present with the people; and calling the people into service. Witnessing also includes analysis of public policy formation and advocacy actions that lead to peace with justice in the name of Jesus Christ.

Annual conference recommendations:

In order to support the work of local churches, annual conferences will:

1. Stimulate and support local churches in implementing new beginning-inspired programs by developing appropriate programs and resources. Whenever resources are prepared, they should be explicit on how the issue discussed will affect people of color;

2. Provide training and educational opportunities for clergy and lay leadership to be held within an ethnic community in order to begin to hear, understand, and respect their culture and tradition and the issues related to this resolution. Special attention should be given to training in the dynamics of institutional racism and ways to eliminate it;

3. Use the guidelines and resources developed by Project Equality, and make them available to local churches and all conference bodies;

4. Use publications and all other types of media available to keep issues before the people. Make sure writers/producers include people of color in the annual conference. Strengthen racial and ethnic minority ministries, and support significant programs such as the Hispanic and Native American comprehensive plans;

5. Identify, celebrate, and include racial and ethnic minority cultures and traditions within the life of the conference; and

6. Support and be an advocate for the struggle for self-determination and other rights of indigenous people.

General agency recommendations:

1. The General Board of Discipleship is to develop appropriate curriculum and worship resources to support local churches in these efforts, while making sure that all curriculum and worship materials include racial and ethnic culture and traditions;

2. The General Board of Higher Education and Ministry is to request that United Methodist theological seminaries incorporate these concerns into the basic theological education curriculum. This is to be done also for the Course of Study programs for local pastors;

3. The General Board of Global Ministries is to develop ways to implement in its programs of mission and evangelism the perspectives advanced by this resolution. This includes the reviewing of all existing policies and procedures to make sure that funding, mission personnel, and other resources are fully available to racial and ethnic communities. Future mission studies, both ecumenical and United Methodist, should provide opportunities for studying the issues raised in this resolution and their mission implications. In line with our denominational affirmation of "the contributions that United Methodists of varying ethnic, language, cultural, and national groups make to one another and to our Church as a whole" ("The Present Challenge to Theology in the Church," the 1996 *Book of Discipline,* ¶ 63), this board is asked to take the initiative to enable the exploration of indigenous theologies in the Americas, including ecumenical and interfaith perspectives; and

4. The General Board of Church and Society is to support and be an advocate for self-determination and empowerment of indigenous people and the just observance of international treaties with indigenous nations.

ADOPTED 1992

See Social Principles, ¶ 66; "A Charter for Racial Justice Policies in an Interdependent Global Community"; "Rights of Native People of the Americas"; "The United Methodist Church and America's Native People."

The Treatment of Women in the United States Under Social Security

The Old and New Testaments share prophetic-messianic traditions in which God stands with the oppressed against a dehumanizing and destructive social order. The emphasis on the protection of those in deepest need was a theme of the events of Exodus. And Jesus, drawing on intimate knowledge of the Hebrew Scriptures, inaugurated his ministry with a quotation from Isaiah: "The Spirit of the Lord . . . has anointed me to preach good news to the poor . . . to set at liberty those who are oppressed" (Luke 4:18-19, RSV; cf. Isaiah 61:1-2).

The early Christian church in Jerusalem, following this tradition, established a community in which all things were held in common. Special attention was given to those who were the neediest—widows, the elderly, the disabled. Israel and the early church exemplify the role that a community of faith is called upon to play—concern for the welfare of the poor and establishment of a just social system.

In the United States, millions of aged and disabled persons, especially women, depend on the social security system for the necessities of life. For most Americans, especially older women, the social security system is often the one program that stands between them and poverty.

Inequities in the system, however, also make it a program that tends to keep many women in poverty. Because of the important role of social security, people of faith have a special interest in ensuring that it is operated fairly and securely. Its benefits must be designed to overcome disadvantages of age, race, sex, or disability. And it must be regularly reviewed to ensure that it is flexible enough to adjust to the changing needs of our society.

The social security system in the United States has historically functioned as a basic insurance program to provide income and medical expenses for those persons who are retired or disabled. It has helped to hold families together by maintaining income in times of personal hardship. It has relieved younger people of the necessity of total care for aging parents while also allowing retired persons the independence and dignity of their own income by providing basic benefits. Since its enactment in the 1930s, the program has been a cornerstone of the social policy of the United States. However, U.S. society has radically changed in the intervening years, and modifications in the social security system are now required to meet those social changes.

When the social security system was first established, only 17 percent of the paid workforce was female. Today, over half of all women in the United States work outside the home. However, the wage differential between women and men has been deteriorating during the last twenty-five years. It is now about sixty cents to one dollar. Changes in the labor force, participation of women, and the inequality of pay, combined with an increased divorce and remarriage rate and extended life-expectancy of women, have resulted in an oppressive situation for many women under social security.

In 1980, approximately 52 percent of all social security recipients were women, either as workers or dependents. Thirteen percent were children, and the remaining 35 percent were men. The average monthly social security benefit in 1982 for adult women was $308, compared to $430 for men. Retired female workers averaged $335, compared to $438 for men. Spouses of retired or disabled husbands averaged $196, and widows $351. The median annual income for all women over sixty-five from all sources was only $4,757, as compared to $8,173 for men in 1981. The figures for minority persons are painfully lower.

Clearly, the system needs attention. Widowed, divorced, and never-married women account for 72 percent of all older adults living in poverty. Changes in the social security system are desperately needed in order to achieve equal and adequate treatment of all persons. Benefits are clearly inadequate for divorced women, widowed women, ethnic minority women, women who have never married, and women who are not citizens. The current benefit structure penalizes women who work regularly but who spend time out of the labor force to bear and raise children. Further, couples with one wage earner receive larger benefits than do two-earner couples with the same total earnings. Structural unemployment results in increased numbers of unemployed American women and, therefore, less social security coverage. Also, the growing issue of undocumented workers who pay into the social security system but receive no benefits from their payments needs to be addressed.

The 1983 report of the National Commission on Social Security Reform did not deal with basic systemic change in the gender-based system. However, after the report was released, a majority of the commissioners declared in favor of "earnings sharing," a concept that affirms marriage as a partnership, dividing equally any earnings by either spouse for social security purposes. Following that report, the General Boards of Global Ministries and Church and Society affirmed "earnings sharing" as a way of bringing greater equality to the social security system.

The United Methodist Church, in its Social Principles, urges social policies and programs that ensure to the aging the respect and dignity that is their right as senior members of society; affirms the need to support those in distress; and calls for the equal treatment of men and women in every aspect of their common life.

Therefore, be it resolved:

1. That the 1984 General Conference supports the effort to address the many inequities suffered by women in the social security system and urges that the governmental body established to consider these inequities should consult with older women, ethnic minority women, and representatives of organizations dealing with older women's issues. Such a body should give special attention to:

(a) the concept of "earnings sharing" with a "hold harmless" provision that would prevent persons now receiving benefits from being cut;

(b) social security credits for the homemaker; and

(c) an allowance for more "childcare" years spent out of the workforce;

2. That the secretary of the General Conference shall communicate this support to the appropriate officials in the executive and legislative branches of the U.S. government;

3. That the General Boards of Church and Society and Global Ministries shall continue to document social security issues and shall inform their constituencies about the needs for reform; and

4. That The United Methodist Church shall educate its constituencies so that churches and individual United Methodists can encourage their legislators to support needed reform;

ADOPTED 1984

See Social Principles, ¶ 66F; "Equal Rights of Women"; "The Status of Women."

Universal Access to Health Care in the United States and Related Territories

The health care system in the United States is in need of serious systemic change. We call for legislation that will provide universal access to quality health care with effective cost controls.

John Wesley was always deeply concerned about health care, providing medical services at no cost to the poor in London and emphasizing preventive care. The first Methodist Social Creed (adopted in 1908) urged working conditions to safeguard the health of workers and community.

Through its many hospitals and health-care facilities around the world, as well as public-policy advocacy for health, The United Methodist Church continues to declare its commitment to quality and affordable health care as a right of all people.

The concern of The United Methodist Church for health is rooted in our biblical understanding that salvation embraces wholeness of mind, body, and spirit. Jesus revealed the meaning of divine love in his acts of healing for all and the meaning of justice in his inclusion of all persons in the healing and saving power of God. The redemptive ministry of Christ, which focused on healing and wholeness—spiritual, mental, physical, and emotional—is our model for health ministry.

Persons in the United States have been conditioned to expect quality health care. The United States has one of the lowest overall mortality rates compared with other countries. Its medical technology expertise is evident in the many success stories of curing severe illness and prolonging life. The quality of medical training in the United States has also been very high, benefiting those who have access to the services of doctors and other health professionals.

Unfortunately, the excesses of the present system are beginning to erode many of these achievements. Nearly 37 million Americans are denied appropriate health care simply because of their economic status and/or disability. Within this group are some of the most vulnerable members of society, particularly 11 to 13 million children. Even those adults who are working are not spared: Two thirds of those without insurance belong to families with steadily employed workers. Many working people also belong to another large group in danger—more than 60 million with underinsurance.

Not surprisingly, the poor, the aging, women, children, people with disabilities, and persons of color are most at risk in this system. The infant mortality rate in the United States is the worst among the "developed" countries. Black women die from cervical cancer at three times the rate of white women. Black Americans have a significantly lower life-span than white Americans—an average of six years less—and Hispanics have the least access to the health care system of any group. Native Americans, besides suffering greatly from alcoholism, have a tuberculosis rate 600 times higher than average U.S. rates. Recent immigrants who experience health problems find the health care system poorly equipped to meet their needs.

Even persons with middle income have difficulty finding affordable, quality care. Families in which a member suffers from catastrophic illness find their health insurance premiums priced so high they can no longer afford them, or in some cases, insurance is canceled. Businesses are overwhelmed with the cost of health insurance, a problem The United Methodist Church is also facing. The dissatisfaction with the U.S. health system ranks highest among the middle class in many surveys.

Despite these inadequacies, the health care system is extremely costly, consuming 12 percent of the gross national product in 1990, while Canadian health-care costs still hold at 8 percent.

Finally, the providers of health care and corporate America both are unhappy with the present system. Doctors object to excessive paperwork, malpractice suits, and inadequate government programs. Hospitals can no longer stay financially sound under existing policies. Corporate America has called for radical change because our economic position in the world is being eroded by rising health costs. Unions, as well, are unhappy, and a large number of strikes in recent years have stemmed from disputes over health care.

We therefore seek legislation that incorporates the following principles:

Principle 1

We seek a national health-care plan that serves and is sensitive to the diversity of all people in the United States and its territories.

Principle 2

We seek a national health-care plan that will provide comprehensive benefits to everyone, including preventive services, health promotion, primary and acute care, mental-health care, and extended care.

Principle 3

We seek a national health-care plan with an equitable and efficient financing system drawn from the broadest possible resource base.

Principle 4

We seek a national health-care plan that provides services based on equity, efficiency, and quality, with payments to providers that are equitable, cost-efficient, and easy to administer and understand.

Principle 5

We seek a national health-care plan that reduces the current rapid inflation in costs through cost-containment measures.

Principle 6

We seek a national health-care plan that is sensitive to the needs of persons working in the various components of the health care system and gives special attention to providing not only for affirmative action in the recruitment, training, and employment of workers, but also for just compensation for all workers at all levels and for retraining and placement of those displaced by changes in the health care system.

Principle 7

We seek a national health-care plan that promotes effective and safe innovation and research for women and men in medical techniques, the delivery of health services, and health practices.

Principle 8

We seek a national health-care plan that assesses the health impacts of environmental and occupational safety, environmental pollution, sanitation, physical fitness, and standard-of-living issues such as housing and nutrition.

We, in The United Methodist Church, are called to a ministry of healing. *Therefore,* we challenge our Church to:

1. Support the Interreligious Healthcare Access Campaign and its public-policy advocacy to provide access to universal health care for all;

2. Educate and motivate persons to pursue a healthy lifestyle, thus avoiding health problems by practicing preventive medicine;

3. Affirm the role of Christlike care in institutions that provide direct health services by units of The United Methodist Church;

4. Develop a curriculum model on universal health-care advocacy suitable for United Methodist Church seminaries; and

5. Ensure that persons representative of the groups most directly affected by inaccessibility to quality health care participate in all levels of efforts by The United Methodist Church directed toward the implementation of a national health-care policy.

ADOPTED 1992

See Social Principles, ¶ 66Q; "Health for All by the Year 2000"; "Health in Mind and Body"; "Health and Wholeness"; "Medical Rights for Children and Youth."

The Use of Alcohol and Drugs on Campuses

WHEREAS, United Methodist colleges should provide an environment suitable for pursuing a higher education in a Christian atmosphere;

Therefore, be it resolved, that The United Methodist Church addresses this issue by (1) promoting an alternative lifestyle that encourages "wellness" without drugs and alcohol, (2) seeking authentic advocates for this alternative lifestyle, and (3) having these advocates promote this image on United Methodist campuses across the nation.

ADOPTED 1984

See Social Principles, ¶ 66J; "Drug and Alcohol Concerns."

Use of Church Facilities by Community Groups

Encouragement shall be given for the use of local church facilities by community groups and agencies that serve social and service needs of the total community.

ADOPTED 1970

See Social Principles, ¶ 66; "Church and Community Workers, 1988"; "Church and Community Workers, 1992."

THE ECONOMIC COMMUNITY

Appalachia: God's Face Toward the Mountains

WHEREAS, The United Methodist Church continues its mission and ministry denominationally, as directed by the General Conference of 1968, through the coordination of the United Methodist Appalachian Development Committee, and ecumenically through the Commission on Religion in Appalachia; and

WHEREAS, The United Methodist Church has engaged in ministry and mission in the Appalachian region for over two centuries. Even though many resources have been committed through ministries such as Red Bird Missionary Conference (Kentucky), Hinton Rural Life Center (North Carolina), Upper Sand Mountain Cooprtive Parish (Alabama), Jackson Area Ministries (Ohio), Heart and Hand House (West Virginia), Connellsville Cooperative Ministry (Pennsylvania), Jubilee Project (Tennessee), and in many other local and community ministries, conditions among many people in this region continue to worsen; and

WHEREAS, the plight of the Appalachian region, with the exploitation of its people and natural resources, continues to manifest a striking similarity to conditions in developing colonized nations of the world; and

WHEREAS, focused efforts on the part of private, church, and governmental agencies over the past three decades, aimed at stimulating appropriate development and at restoring health and dignity to the people and to the mountains, have fallen far short of projected goals; and

WHEREAS, the United Methodist bishops of Appalachia, along with other religious leaders, have joined the Roman Catholic bishops of the region in producing their pastoral letter, "God's Face Toward the

Mountains," calling attention to the continued exploitation of the people of Appalachia and of the land; and

WHEREAS, a study guide has been produced to challenge The United Methodist Church to revisit Appalachia with all of its beauty and strength alongside the need for renewed commitment to ministries of compassion and hope;

Therefore, be it resolved, that The United Methodist Church reaffirm its commitments denominationally and ecumenically to be present with and supportive of the people and churches of Appalachia as they struggle toward the realization of the vision set forth in the Appalachian bishops' pastoral; and

Further, be it resolved, that The United Methodist Church, through all of its boards and agencies, examine ways it might be participating in the ongoing plight and exploitation of the people and land of Appalachia.

ADOPTED 1996

See Social Principles, ¶ 67E; "The Appalachian Mission."

The Appalachian Mission

WHEREAS, The United Methodist Church has engaged in ministry and mission in the Appalachian region since the beginnings of the denomination; and

WHEREAS, conditions among people in this region are actually worsening, according to numerous social, economic, and religious indicators; and

WHEREAS, according to the latest census figures, the Appalachian region (in the eastern mountainous section of the United States, northern Alabama to lower New York—398 counties in 13 states) is home to 20.5 million people, of which 9 percent are United Methodists—more than double the proportion in the nation as a whole—although membership has declined over the past decades; and

WHEREAS, per capita income in Appalachia is 69.96 percent of the U.S. average, a decline of 5.35 percent during the past ten years; 25 percent of the region's children live in poverty; unemployment is above 20 percent in many portions of the region; and opportunities continue to decline with the exodus of industry and the growing mechanization of coal mining and timbering; and

WHEREAS, in many counties, only 20 percent of the land is owned and controlled by indigenous people, with large holdings of the federal government and multinational corporations being operated for the benefit of outsiders, and vast areas of the region becoming a dumping ground for the entire eastern seaboard; and

WHEREAS, reduction of federal assistance programs and inequitable taxation mean that the suffering of people here increases in terms of health care, education, housing, transportation, and economic opportunity; and

WHEREAS, for many years there have been numerous creative outreach programs by the twenty-four annual conferences serving here and by the general Church program boards, supported in large measure by people from the entire Church; and

WHEREAS, among the all-too-few signs of hope in the region are the ministries of the Church, many of which are the result of ecumenical cooperation and joint action, and in partnership with broad-based community organizations controlled by Appalachian people;

Therefore, be it resolved, that The United Methodist Church reaffirm its commitment to mission and ministry here denominationally through the coordination of the Appalachian Development Committee, and ecumenically through the Commission on Religion in Appalachia; and

Be it further resolved, that all levels of the Church be called upon to consider the worsening conditions in Appalachia, to reexamine mission and ministry and the priorities set, and to work with other groups ecumenically and in conjunction with government and community organizations to respond to the hurts and needs of Appalachian people and communities through a comprehensive program of spiritual renewal, social recovery, empowerment, economic transformation, and political responsibility and compassion.

ADOPTED 1992

See Social Principles, ¶ 67E; "Appalachia: God's Face Toward the Mountains."

Closing of Military Installations

Be it resolved, that the 1996 General Conference work for economic and environmental justice throughout the global community by encouraging all nations to work for the:

1. Reduction in military spending;
2. Development of detailed and broad-based community planning for the downsizing or closing of military installations; and

3. In the U.S., supporting of Restoration Advisory Boards, technical Review Committees, BRAC re-Use Committees, and other official bodies overseeing environmental cleanup and conversion planning at Department of Defense or Department of Energy sites, and through parallel instruments in other nations.

ADOPTED 1996

See Social Principles, ¶¶ 67, 69C; "The United Methodist Church and Peace"; "Nuclear Abolition: Saying No to Nuclear Deterrence."

Support Efforts to Provide Economic Development for Native Americans

WHEREAS, The United Methodist Church recognizes and supports the sovereignty of Native American nations; and

WHEREAS, sovereign nations have within their power the ability to influence lives and spiritual values; and

WHEREAS, many Native American sovereignties have chosen to use and promote gambling as a means of economic development; and

WHEREAS, The United Methodist Church has historically and strongly deplored gambling;

Therefore, be it resolved, that sovereign Native American nations are urged to explore and implement means of economic development not dependent upon gambling; and

Be it further resolved, that United Methodists everywhere be urged to reaffirm the historical United Methodist stand against gambling and to support the efforts of sovereign Native American nations to provide means and methods of economic development that do not depend upon gambling.

ADOPTED 1996

See Social Principles, ¶ 66A, ¶ 67; "The United Methodist Church and America's Native People"; "Toward a New Beginning Beyond 1992"; "Rights of Native People of the Americas."

Economic Justice

I. Introduction

The results of rapid consolidation of wealth and power by fewer individuals, corporations and banks, the shift in government priorities from social to military expenditures, and the growing interconnections between national economies have led to increases in poverty, hunger, and despair in the human family. Materialism and selfishness are undermining the values of community and mutual sharing. Within this situation, The United Methodist Church, following its traditional commitment, is called to analyze international economics and work for biblical justice.

II. Biblical/Theological Background

God has created us for wholeness (*shalom*) and interdependence. God's creation is such that our well-being is dependent upon the well-being of all creation. Created in the image of God (Genesis 1:27), we are accountable to God, the Creator, in caring for the earth in ways that will bring wholeness to all of creation.

Within the universal gift of God's creation, we are called into the particular tradition and mission of being a covenant people. In response to God's gift of grace, centered in the biblical experiences of exodus and resurrection, we are to live in relationship to God as communities of witness in the midst of the world (Exodus 19:4-6). In covenant we are committed to the welfare of our neighbors, and this must include our economic and political relationships. Covenant people are committed to equitable distribution of resources to meet basic human needs and to social systems that provide ongoing access to those resources. Covenant people are equally committed to decision-making and the use of power in a social order that is characterized by justice. The biblical mandate is to uphold the right of all persons to fullness of life and to confront all people and systems that would deny this right to others.

Covenant relationship to God and neighbors was expressed in concrete social structures as seen in Israel's law codes. The Ten Commandments (Exodus 20:2-17) emphasize that loyalty to God alone is tied to responsible life in human relationships of respect and equity. Law codes in Exodus, Leviticus, and Deuteronomy show a special concern for the resources necessary to meet human needs and guarantee basic rights such as food (Leviticus 19:9-10; Deuteronomy 23:21-22; 24:19-22), clothing (Exodus 26–27), just business dealings (Deuteronomy 25:13-16), and access to just juridical process (Exodus 23:6-8). Special concern is expressed for those who are marginal in society: the poor (Exodus 23:6; Deuteronomy 15:7-11), the stranger (Exodus 21:21-24), the sojourner (Deuteronomy 10:19), the widow and the orphan (Deuteronomy 24:19-22). To periodically rebalance economic inequities, the covenant community was called to observe sabbatical years in which the land was not worked and its produce was available to the poor (Exodus 23:10-11), and slaves were set free (Exodus 21:2). In the fiftieth year, the Jubilee is to be celebrated (Leviticus 25:8-55) as the year of God's release when prisoners are set free, debts are canceled, and land is returned to families.

Israel again broke its covenant with God during the period of the kings when the people began to turn away from Yahweh to patterns of idolatry, greed, privilege, materialism, and oppressive power. The economic system of the community was no longer based on equality and concern for those who were powerless in the community but on economic privilege to the benefit of the rich and powerful. The prophets warned again and again that an economic system based on greed, economic exploitation, and indifference to the needs of the poor was contrary to God's will (Amos 8:4-6; Jeremiah 22:13-17).

Like the Hebrew prophets who took their stand with the poor, Jesus embodied the messianic promise to the poor and alienated. As indicated in Luke 4:18-19, Jesus began his public ministry with these words:

> The Spirit of the Lord is upon me,/because God has anointed me/to preach good news to the poor./God has sent me to proclaim release to the captives/and recovery of sight to the blind,/to set at liberty those who are oppressed,/to proclaim the acceptable year of the Lord. (Revised Standard Version, adapted)

Jesus Christ is proclaimed as new creation and new covenant. In him, dividing walls of hostility are broken down, the far-off are brought near, those divided are made one (Ephesians 2). Those who follow Christ as the center of their faith must take notice of his concern for both physical and spiritual wholeness, and his care for the poor and the oppressed. Jesus' frequent teachings on economic matters reveal his concern that faith brings forth efforts for social, as well as spiritual, well-being. This was evident in the early church, as it shared all that it had and especially cared for the widows and the orphans (Acts 2:44-45; 2 Corinthians 8:13-15).

Today, we are called to patterns of community that take seriously our roots in biblical faith, as well as a sensitivity to what God is doing in our own time. Acknowledging that we are part of God's creation, called into covenant community and empowered by the model of Jesus Christ, we must analyze economic systems and their impact on justice and peace. We approach this responsibility as the Church, a community transcending narrow interests of nation, race, or class in obedience to the call to be God's people. We seek to express a love of God that can only be pursued by taking seriously the concern for our neighbor's well-being as our own.

III. Tradition of The United Methodist Church Witness for Economic Justice

The United Methodist Church and its predecessor bodies have a long history of public witness on matters of economic justice. John Wesley set the example in his famous sermon on "The Use of Money," his public stand against slavery, and his witness among England's working class. The 1908 "Social Creed" committed The Methodist Episcopal Church to work for the protection and rights of people disadvantaged by society. And The Evangelical United Brethren Church made a comparable commitment to personal, social, and international justice in its *Discipline* statement, "Moral Standards of The Evangelical United Brethren Church" (Section IX).

As United Methodists, we are guided by the Social Principles, as adopted in the 1984 *Book of Discipline* (¶¶ 70–76; in the 1996 *Book of Discipline*, ¶¶ 64–70). "The Economic Community" section begins with these words: "We claim all economic systems to be under the judgment of God no less than other facets of the created order." The Social Principles contain basic principles that are useful in an analysis of contemporary economics.

IV. Structures of Injustice in the Global Economy

A. Concentration of Wealth and Power

"We support measures that would reduce the concentration of wealth in the hands of a few" (¶ 67, 1996 *Book of Discipline*).

The world economy has changed markedly over the past decades. Transnational corporations and banks have extended their ownership and control of agriculture, industry, land, finances, and communications. As this process has taken place, two consequences have emerged:

1. The separation between the rich and the poor has become greater; and
2. Many corporations have become increasingly unaccountable to their employees, to the communities in which they operate, and to governments.

B. Production and Work

"Every person has the right and responsibility to work for the benefit of himself or herself and the enhancement of human life and community to receive adequate remuneration. . . . We support the rights of workers to refuse to work in situations that endanger health and/or life, without jeopardy to their jobs" (¶ 73C, 1984 *Book of Discipline*; ¶ 67C, with different language, 1996 *Discipline*).

Transnational corporations have transferred much of the manufacturing base of industrial countries to developing countries, seeking cheaper labor and less stringent regulation of environmental practices, consumer protection, and occupational safety and health. They have also taken advantage of favorable tax treatment for overseas investment. In many cases, this has resulted in a "global assembly line" made up of workers who receive low wages, have few rights, and are forbidden to join democratic labor unions. Many of the workers on the global assembly line are women, particularly young women, who toil under difficult and unsafe conditions.

In the United States, the decline in industrial jobs has coincided with a rise in high-technology jobs, low-paying jobs and part-time service jobs, information jobs, and nonunion jobs with minimal job security and benefits (i.e., fast food, retail, health care, maintenance, and computer). A growing number of the new jobs involve women, many of whom do subcontract work in their homes—again, under conditions of low pay and no benefits.

C. Export-Led Development

"We affirm the right and duty of the people of developing nations to determine their own destiny. We urge the major political, social, and economic self-determination of developing nations rather than to further their own special interests" (¶ 75B, 1984 *Discipline*; ¶ 69B, with different language, 1996 *Discipline*).

The global economic system and external debts continue to force developing countries to allocate major resources to produce goods with heavy emphasis on production for export rather than for domestic use. Many developing nations are locked into exporting primary commodities at prices that fluctuate widely. Even those few developing nations that do export manufactured goods face uncertain markets due to growing protectionism. They commit their natural resources, environment, and land to competition for world markets, while they sacrifice their domestic economy, social welfare, and human lives.

D. Debt Crisis/Financial Crisis

"We applaud international efforts to develop a more just international economic order in which the limited resources of the earth will be used to the maximum benefit of all nations and peoples. We urge Christians in every society to encourage the governments under which they live and the economic entities within their societies to aid and work for the development of more just economic orders" (¶ 69B, 1996 *Discipline*).

After more than a decade of heavy borrowing encouraged by Western banks, many developing countries found that by the early 1980s (when interest rates rose and raw material prices collapsed), they could no longer meet the service payments on their debts. The creditor banks and governments turned to the International Monetary Fund (IMF), which makes new loans contingent on strict austerity programs. The IMF remedies have placed the burden of debt-repayment squarely on the shoulders of poor and working people by devaluing currencies, freezing wages, curbing government price subsidies (on rice, cooking oil, beans, and other essential items), and cutting subsidized credits in rural areas.

Simultaneously, the United States is having debt problems of its own. The federal budget is chronically in deficit; the foreign (trade) debt has become monumental; and consumers continue their heavy dependence on credit, while foreclosures of farms and small businesses assume record proportions. The actual result of the pressing debt in both the Third World and the United States is that the poor, with and without employment, carry the burden.

E. Military Spending

"Human values must outweigh military claims as governments determine their priorities; . . . the militarization of society must be challenged and stopped; . . . the manufacture, sale, and deployment of armaments must be reduced and controlled" (¶ 69C, 1996 *Discipline*).

Many governments, in shifting major resources to the military, have hurt the most vulnerable people in their societies. Some economies, such as that of the United States, increasingly depend on the military for jobs, exports, and economic growth. Among developing countries, some produce weapons to pay their foreign debt, while others import military equipment to control their own populations.

V. The Effects of the Global Economic System

Injustices are imposed on the people of the world by economies characterized by a concentration of wealth and power, an export-based development, heavy indebtedness, and reliance on a militarized national security system. The following are some reminders:

A. Poverty and hunger have increased, especially among women and children. In developing countries, this has been most marked in the growing shanty-towns that surround major cities as people leave rural areas. In the United States, it is estimated that as much as 20 percent of the population may be living in poverty. African Americans and Hispanics make up a disproportionate share of that group. Homelessness is rampant in cities, while rural communities are in rapid decline as farms go bankrupt in record numbers.

B. Unemployment and underemployment are unacceptably high; education and job training opportunities are inadequate; and increasingly meaningful work is difficult to secure. In some communities, the situation is so severe that employment is virtually nonexistent.

C. The increasing ability of large corporations to shift their resources around the globe has contributed to an erosion of worker rights everywhere. Third world governments compete to offer the lowest labor costs to the transnational corporations while at the same time, in the United States, these same corporations win major concessions from workers and communities by threatening to move to lower-wage areas. As wages and benefits decline, the number of full-time employees living in poverty increases.

D. The environment and fragile natural resource base of many countries are deteriorating. Developing countries desperate for employment and capital try to attract transnational corporations with weaker environmental regulations than those in much of the industrialized world. The effect is destruction of fragile topsoil and rain forests, and a shift in agricultural production into chemically dependent cash crops.

E. A strong belief that competition results in greater economic growth underlies much of the international economic order. In the production and consumption of goods, corporations are to compete with corporations; individuals with one another; and societies with other societies. The central value is "more." The corporate culture of materialism, of "more is better," has spread throughout the world by sophisticated advertising of Western images. It is a culture that has little use for those who lack the means to consume.

Churches and social-service agencies have struggled to meet the spiritual and psychological needs these economic effects create in persons, families, and communities. In communities under economic stress, there is a rising incidence of suicides, child and spouse abuse, family breakdown, drug and substance abuse, and other forms of antisocial behavior.

VI. Actions for The United Methodist Church

The United Methodist Church, as a covenant community committed to justice, must work toward a just global economy. Our Social Principles remind us that "in spite of general affluence in the industrialized nations, the majority of persons in the world live in poverty. In order to provide basic needs such as food, clothing, shelter, education, health care, and other necessities, ways must be found to share more equitably the resources of the world" (¶ 67E, 1996 *Discipline*).

Faced with this task, we specifically call upon The United Methodist Church to:

A. Challenge each local congregation to study global economic justice issues, using this resolution as a basic resource. To assist this process:

1. The General Board of Discipleship, in cooperation with the General Board of Church and Society and the General Board of Global Ministries, shall prepare appropriate curriculum, including Bible study, and study materials for all ages. These resources would help local congregations to understand the impact of global economics on individuals, communities, and nations and suggest appropriate tasks for Christian mission;

2. United Methodist Communications shall develop media resources on global economic justice issues to accompany this churchwide study; and

3. The General Board of Higher Education and Ministry shall work with United Methodist theological seminaries to include Christian responsibility for economic justice as a necessary part of education for ministry;

B. Commit the General Board of Church and Society and the General Board of Global Ministries to engage in an ongoing search for and study of alternative systems of economic order, for the purpose of addressing the needs of an increasingly interdependent global economy;

C. Urge the General Board of Church and Society and the General Board of Global Ministries to work with annual conferences to initiate and support legislative efforts at the local, state, and national levels that will address "The Structure of Injustice in the Global Economy" (Section IV). Priority attention should focus on the accountability of transnational corporations and banks, the need for land reform, and the increasing dependency of national economies on the military;

D. Challenge all bodies related to the Church to be more energetic in using their investment portfolios to strengthen developing national economies and global economic justice; and

E. Challenge annual conferences, local churches, and individuals to a simpler, more modest lifestyle; and bring church and community people together to identify specific economic issues that affect individuals, families, and communities, such as plant closing and relocation, deterioration of public education, homelessness, and lack of affordable housing; and to respond to these issues through the strategies of study, service, advocacy, and community economic development.

Finally, as delegates to the 1988 General Conference, we resolve and covenant with others to do the following:

1. Lift up the concerns of people affected by global economic injustice in personal and corporate prayer; and

2. Initiate study and action programs for global economic justice in our local congregations and annual conferences.

ADOPTED 1988

See Social Principles, ¶ 67; "Pay Equity in the U.S.A."; "Extension of the Right to Organize and Bargain Collectively"; "Global Debt Crisis"; "Rights of Workers."

Emphasis of Concern for Workers

Be it resolved, that the 1996 General Conference authorize an Emphasis of Concern of the Worker, to be conducted in the 1997–2000 quadrennium and reported to the 2000 General Conference. The Emphasis of Concern will provide opportunities for our denomination, annual conferences, districts, and local congregations to explore the history of our Church and its relationship to workers in their struggles for workplace peace and justice. This Emphasis of Concern will explore:

- ways United Methodists can celebrate workers, their economic importance to our community, and their many and diverse contributions to a free and just society;
- the new challenges that confront us in an international economy, finding ways we can stand together in continuing struggles; and
- ways to implement the actions called for in the resolution entitled "The Rights of Workers" passed at the 1988 General Conference (*The Book of Resolutions, 1988;* pages 369–70).

The Emphasis of Concern may, for example, organize a nationwide Conference on The United Methodist Church and Working People.

The General Conference shall direct the General Board of Global Ministries and the General Board of Church and Society to appoint a task force to coordinate the activities of the Emphasis of Concern. This task force will be composed of both clergy and laity. The General Board of Global Ministries and the General Board of Church and Society will each appoint one third of the task force. Those appointed will then nominate the final one third of the task force to represent the Church at large. All appointees will be persons who are informed about the issues and/or presently engaged in ministry to working people, the unemployed, and the underemployed. The task force will be gender, race, and class inclusive.

Be it further resolved, the General Conference shall encourage each annual conference, district, and local congregation to explore and develop their own ministries to working people, the unemployed, and the underemployed. The General Board of Global Ministries and the General Board of Church and Society will assist these efforts to:

- Identify working people, the unemployed, and the underemployed who worship in our local congregations and, in the best tradition of Wesleyan inclusiveness, design settings in which to hear their stories, survey their needs, affirm their diverse gifts, and nurture their leadership skills;
- Encourage regular dialogue with local organized labor communities and reach out to unorganized workers;
- Advocate for the economic, social, political, and spiritual interests of working people, the unemployed, and the underemployed within annual conferences, districts, and local congregations;
- Be in special community with all who are affected during grievances, organizing efforts, contract negotiations, strikes, lockouts, or plant closings;

- Participate in ecumenical, interfaith, and other community-centered efforts to serve working people, the unemployed, and the underemployed; and
- Help to find funds both within and without the Church to undergird ministries of support and advocacy for the unemployed and the underemployed.

Our denomination, its annual conferences, districts, and local congregations, its boards, commissions, agencies, hospitals, nursing homes, seminaries, and other higher education institutions employ many workers. We lift up the standards of being model employers, including:

- Listening to the concerns of our employees and responding to their suggestions and grievances;
- Supporting, not impeding, their efforts to organize for the purpose of collective bargaining; and
- Developing written guidelines based on the Social Principles for use within the denomination, its annual conferences, districts, local congregations, agencies and affiliated institutions that affirm the rights of workers to organize for the purpose of collective bargaining.

The General Conference recognizes that an Emphasis of Concern alone will not solve the workplace crisis. Each United Methodist must make a personal commitment to join the struggle. We worship the Carpenter and embrace the wisdom of John Wesley. Both served working people. United Methodists are well-positioned to serve working people. We are workers, bosses, farmers, shoppers, preachers, educators, missionaries, administrators, corporate officers, landlords, doctors, bankers, stockholders, and consumers. Embracing the Spirit and implementing the call of the 1988 resolution, United Methodists can help working people realize their full potential and find justice, peace, and wholeness within their workplaces. By our actions, we seek to proclaim the sacredness of the workplace and the dignity of its workers.

ADOPTED 1996

See Social Principles, ¶ 67B, C; "Rights of Workers"; "Extension of the Right to Organize and Bargain Collectively."

Extension of the Right to Organize and Bargain Collectively

Historically, The United Methodist Church has recognized and supported the right of workers to organize into unions of their own choosing and to bargain collectively over wages, hours, and conditions of employment. National policy since 1935 has codified procedures for the election of labor unions by industrial workers, for the recognition of those unions by management, and for collective bargaining, with the result of lessened conflict in the private industrial sector of the economy.

However, a major category of employees was excluded from the coverage of the National Labor Relations Act. These are the employees working for the federal government and employees of any political subdivision such as a state or school district.

Unfortunately, social strife in the occupational markets of public employees has led to high social costs such as the interruption of vital community services and even the tragedy of death. In view of this continued unresolved strain and many attendant injustices, The United Methodist Church requests the Congress to amend the National Labor Relations Act to include under its coverage government employees—federal, state, and local—and to institute methods—for example, various forms of arbitration—for resolving disputes that significantly affect the health and safety of the public.

ADOPTED 1976

See Social Principles, ¶ 67B; "Economic Justice"; "Emphasis of Concern for Workers"; "Rights of Workers."

Gambling

The Social Principles state that, "Gambling is a menace to society, deadly to the best interests of moral, social, economic, and spiritual life, and destructive of good government. As an act of faith and concern, Christians should abstain from gambling and should strive to minister to those victimized by the practice. Where gambling has become addictive, the Church will encourage such individuals to receive therapeutic assistance so that the individual's energies may be redirected into positive and constructive ends. The Church should promote standards and personal lifestyles that would make unnecessary and undesirable the resort to commercial gambling—including public lotteries—as a recreation, as an escape, or as a means of producing public revenue or funds for support of charities or government" (¶ 67G).

When asked which commandment is first of all, Jesus answered, "Hear, O Israel: the Lord our God, the Lord is one; you shall love the Lord your God with all your heart, and with all your soul, and with all your mind, and with all your strength" (Mark 12:29-30). Gambling feeds on human greed and invites persons to place their trust in possessions rather than in God. It represents a form of idolatry that contradicts the first commandment. Jesus continued: "The second is this, ' You shall love your neighbor as yourself ' " (Mark 12:31). In relating with compassion to our sisters and brothers, we are called to resist those practices and systems that exploit them and leave them impoverished and demeaned.

Gambling, as a means of acquiring material gain by chance and at the neighbor's expense, is a menace to personal character and social morality. Gambling fosters greed and stimulates the fatalistic faith in chance. Organized and commercial gambling is a threat to business, breeds crime and poverty, and is destructive to the interests of good government. It encourages the belief that work is unimportant, that money can solve all our problems, and that greed is the norm for achievement. It serves as a "regressive tax" on those with lower income. In summary, gambling is bad economics; gambling is bad public policy; and gambling does not improve the quality of life.

We oppose the growing legalization and state promotion of gambling.

Dependence on gambling revenue has led many states to exploit the weakness of their own citizens, neglect the development of more equitable forms of taxation, and thereby further erode the citizens' confidence in government.

We oppose the legalization of pari-mutuel betting, for it has been the opening wedge in the legalization of other forms of gambling within the states and has stimulated illegal bookmaking. We deplore the establishment of state lotteries and their use as a means of raising public revenues. The constant promotion and the wide advertising of lotteries have encouraged large numbers of persons to gamble for the first time.

We express an even more serious concern for the increasing development of the casino enterprise in the United States, for it has taken captive entire communities and has infiltrated many levels of government with its fiscal and political power.

Public apathy and a lack of awareness that petty gambling feeds organized crime have opened the door to the spread of numerous forms of legal and illegal gambling.

We support the strong enforcement of anti-gambling laws, the repeal of all laws that give gambling an acceptable and even advantageous place in our society, and the rehabilitation of compulsive gamblers.

The Church has a key role in fostering responsible government and in developing health and moral maturity that free persons from dependence on damaging social customs. It is expected that United Methodist churches abstain from the use of raffles, lotteries, bingo, door prizes, other drawing schemes, and games of chance for the purpose of gambling or fundraising. United Methodists should refrain from all forms of gambling practices carried on in our communities and should work to influence community organizations to develop forms of funding that do not depend upon gambling.

The General Board of Church and Society in cooperation with other general agencies shall provide materials to local churches and annual conferences for study and action to combat gambling and to aid persons addicted to gambling. The general agencies, annual conferences, and local churches should work with the National Coalition Against Legalized Gambling, a grassroots organization of religious and community persons working to stop and reverse legalized gambling.

ADOPTED 1980
AMENDED & READOPTED 1996

See Social Principles, ¶ 67G; "Economic Justice"; "The United Methodist Church's Position on Gambling."

The United Methodist Church's Position on Gambling

WHEREAS, the Social Principles state, in part: "Gambling is a menace to society, deadly to the best interests of moral, social, economic, and spiritual life, and destructive of good government. As an act of faith and concern, Christians should abstain from gambling.... The Church should promote standards and personal lifestyles that would make unnecessary and undesirable the resort to commercial gambling—including public lotteries—as a recreation, as an escape, or as a means or producing public revenue or funds for support of charities or government" (¶ 67G); and

WHEREAS, the number of organizations and governments using lotteries, raffles, and bingo as a revenue resource has dramatically increased recently; and

WHEREAS, high-stakes gambling has led to tragedy and the disruption of community life; and

WHEREAS, raffles and other types of gambling methods are used in some United Methodist churches; and

WHEREAS, many other Christian denominations rely heavily upon the proceeds from raffles, lotteries, and other gambling devices as means of fundraising;

Therefore, be it resolved, that The United Methodist Church reaffirm its position on gambling; and

Be it further resolved, that the appropriate general agencies continue to provide material to the local churches for study and action to combat gambling and aid persons addicted to gambling.

ADOPTED 1992

See Social Principles, ¶ 67G; "Gambling."

Global Debt Crisis

I. Introduction

The growth of the global debt has precipitated a crisis for business and industry, church and schools, and, above all, children, women, and men. Countries in Africa, Asia, the Pacific, Latin America, and the Caribbean now owe more than one trillion dollars to Western banks, governments, and international financial institutions. The burden of repayment and current strategies for managing the crisis have contributed to a decline in living standards, employment, and health, as well as rising death rates. Farmers and workers in industrialized countries also have suffered losses as exports of the goods they produce to debt-ridden developing nations have fallen. It is urgent that United Methodists everywhere strengthen their advocacy for the poor, the farmers, and the workers so severely affected by the debt crisis.

II. Causes of the Debt Crisis

The causes of the debt crisis are complex. One of the roots of the crisis lies in the legacy of colonialism, which enriched colonizing countries and exploited the land, resources, and people of the colonies. In the post-colonial era, the nations of Africa, Asia, the Pacific, Latin America, and the Caribbean struggled to gain full control of their land and resources. But the trading system gave former colonial powers an advantage in controlling international markets.

Although most of the former colonies gained their political independence from the late 1800s through the 1960s, economic independence still eludes most of them. Most developing countries continue to export (sell) raw materials and import (buy) manufactured goods. The international trading system continues to favor exporters of manufactured goods, as prices of raw material exports tend to rise less rapidly than manufactured imports. This inequality has grown even worse in the last decades. In 1986 alone, the United Nations estimated that the developing world lost $44 billion to the developed world due to these unfavorable price movements.

This debt crisis escalated in the late 1960s and 1970s as a result of trade imbalances. The oil-producing nations deposited billions of dollars in Western commercial banks. In turn, many banks aggressively marketed their loans to developing countries who were short on cash, facing high oil costs, and eager to borrow. Banks' normal loan-review procedures were often abandoned in the rush to lend large amounts of money quickly.

Some of the loans to developing countries went to productive uses, such as water purification and sewage systems, education and health programs, and subsidies for basic food staples. Many, however, went for purposes that had little to do with the needs of the majority. For example, loans went toward large projects such as nuclear power plants and dams, many of which were never finished or had dramatic human and environmental costs. Other loans ended up with rich individuals who, with the assistance of the banks, quietly transferred the money out of their country. In case after case, the vast majority of the people knew nothing about nor benefited from the borrowing.

The lending bonanza ended abruptly in the early 1980s when the Western countries decided to clamp down on inflation and contracted their economies. This led to a worldwide recession, lowering the demand for and prices of third world exports. Meanwhile, interest rates skyrocketed, adding dramatically to debt service costs for debtors. In August 1982, Mexico launched what is known as the debt crisis by announcing it could no longer service its debt. Debt services payments became so high that many developing nations found themselves borrowing money just to cover interest payments on their loans.

When debtor nations run into serious trouble paying either their debt or at least the interest on their debt, they have few options but to turn to the International Monetary Fund (IMF), the lender of last resort. In return for emergency loans, the IMF has required debtor governments to adopt certain policies often referred to as an "austerity package." In such packages, debtor governments are usually required to cut wages, increase exports and cut imports, cut subsidies for farmers, eliminate low prices for vital foodstuffs, and reduce government spending on items such as health and education. While such measures are designed to restore a country's creditworthiness in the future, the immediate impact is to disproportionately hurt the poor. The burden of repayment has forced debtor nations to gear their economics further toward exports since the debt has to be repaid in hard currencies, such as the dollar. This tends to divert resources from production to meet local needs, and it benefits foreign and local elites who dominate export industries.

As developing-country economies stagnate due to the austerity programs, most U.S. banks have turned to new growth areas: U.S. consumers—especially through credit card and home-equity borrowing—and U.S. businesses, which are taking over other companies in record numbers.

Recently, the U.S. government has become the world's largest debtor to foreign creditors. In October 1987, the U.S. foreign debt was $450 billion and growing weekly as the interest rates climbed. As the U.S. has joined the ranks of the debtor world, it becomes increasingly vulnerable to shifts in the international economy.

III. Consequences of the Global Debt Crisis

The costs of the debt crisis have been staggering. For example, national development policies, poor people, and United Methodist Mission partners have felt the impact in the following ways:

Impact on National Development Policies:

• The World Bank estimates that the combination of debt repayments and the reduction of new lending has resulted in a negative transfer of nearly $30 billion from poor countries to the industrialized countries in 1986 alone, in addition to money loss due to unfavorable prices. This negative transfer deprives the developing countries of needed capital investment and economic growth.

• The export drive to earn foreign exchange in order to repay the banks has pushed several developing countries into the production and export of military equipment. Other governments, in response to the growing unrest of their impoverished populations, have imported more military hardware in order to control their own people.

• The combination of IMF austerity programs and the use of foreign exchange to service developing countries' debts has prevented developing countries from purchasing goods and services from industrialized countries and has undercut prices of agricultural and manufactured goods. Over one million U.S. workers lost their jobs as U.S. exports to Brazil, Mexico, and other debtor nations were cut.

Impact on People:

• Trends of migration from impoverished rural areas to even more impoverished urban areas have grown, as have unemployment, poverty, social unrest, and destruction of democratic institutions.

• Outside lending to developing countries for projects such as water, sewage, health facilities, housing, education, and nutrition has diminished, while at the same time these countries have had to divert local funds from these projects to service their foreign debts.

• Poor people in developing countries have been dramatically affected by the austerity programs because they have no cushion in their living standards. They have been among the first to lose their jobs or have their wages reduced. Because they do not receive benefits, such as unemployment insurance, they have been profoundly affected by the elimination of subsidies that once kept basic staples within reach. Food prices have doubled or tripled overnight in some countries when the local currency has been devalued.

• According to the United Nations Children's Fund (UNICEF), the wrenching economic adjustments taking place this decade, particularly in Africa and Latin America, have led not only to more people living in absolute poverty, but also to increasing inequity among social groups. In its 1987 publication "Adjustment With a Human Face," UNICEF points to the prospect of a lost generation of children due to deteriorating nutritional status, increasing infant mortality rates in some countries, and declining access to and quality of health and educational services thus far in the 1980s. For example, UNICEF found that in Jamaica, public schools and health clinics were closed due to budget cuts. In Ghana, diseases presumed to be eradicated, such as yaws and yellow fever, have reemerged, and in Peru and the Philippines, deaths from tuberculosis and the incidence of other communicable diseases were on the rise. In Chile, cases of typhoid fever and hepatitis have increased following cuts in government spending on drinking water and sanitation. In many parts of the developing world, UNICEF concludes: "Permanent damage has already been done to the physical and mental capacity of much of the future labor force." According to the Children's Defense Fund, the incidence of infectious mortality rates has increased among infants in the first twenty-eight days of life.

• Even in industrialized nations, many family farmers and industrial workers have lost their means of livelihood. Many have lost jobs; many others have experienced reduction in wages and benefits, including

449

denial of unemployment insurance. Whole communities have been threatened economically. Individuals have suffered psychologically, spiritually, and physically.

Impact on Mission Partners:

• In the early 1980s, the economic crisis impacted the churches so that many had to cut back mission outreach programs, freeze or in some cases cut back the salaries of pastors and lay workers. Some churches had to totally put aside general maintenance and upkeep of church buildings and property.

• In 1983, inflation in Zaire resulted in a 480 percent devaluation of its currency. The government drastically reduced its subsidies to medical and educational institutions overnight, and personnel for support services were fired. Within the past three years, the government has virtually assigned the support and operation of schools and hospitals to the Church in Zaire.

• Inflation in Bolivia at one point passed 2,000 percent. Salaries of pastors dwindled from 150 U.S. dollars per month to 10 U.S. dollars. This is in a country where a family of five needs at least $125 per month for food alone.

• The General Board of Global Ministries has received requests from Mozambique, Kenya, and several other African countries for emergency grants to keep hospitals open that would have shut their doors due to lack of salaries for medical personnel, medical supplies, and upkeep and maintenance of equipment and buildings. Even though Asia is not frequently in the international news for eternal debt problems, many Asian countries are in serious economic trouble. The deteriorating economic conditions of these Asian countries are impacting the mission and ministry of our partner churches. The churches in India, Malaysia, Indonesia, and the Philippines have sought assistance from the General Board of Global Ministries to cope with their financial hardship in underwriting their programs and workers' salaries. These stories are being replicated throughout the third world.

IV. Biblical/Theological Background

As Christians, we believe that all creation is a gift from God, that all people are created in God's image. We believe that every human being has personal worth and basic rights, including the right to affirm his or her dignity. We believe that when one of God's creatures is diminished, we all are diminished and thus our covenant with God is broken. We find many biblical references to indebtedness, especially in the Old Testament. The wealthy landowners of Israel lent money to the peasants who needed it due to their misfortune through drought, fire, floods, and for taxes. Because of the high interest rates and because the drought continued, they could not pay the debt or the interest. The peasants' first step was to sell their house and belongings, and later their animals and land, and finally themselves and their families. They had to work as slaves. The landowners added this money to the capital already invested in other projects, and thus continued to purchase land and to lend money. This pattern of accumulation of land and wealth was seen in the early biblical times and eventually led to the centralization of economic power and eventually enslaved even the Israelites.

Later, the prophets, such as Isaiah, admonished the Israelites' behavior as they became selfish, more greedy, and forgot the poor: "You are doomed! You buy more houses and fields to add to those you already have. Soon there will be no place for anyone else to live, and you alone will live in the land" (Isaiah 5:8, Today's English Version).

Jesus Christ is proclaimed a new creation and a new covenant. In him, dividing walls of hostility are broken down and those who are divided are made one (Ephesians 2). Jesus taught about the covenant relationship when he told the parable of the servant whose debt is generously forgiven, but he deals harshly with those who owe him debts (Matthew 18:23-35). Such behavior is a violation of the Kingdom and fails to show an understanding of Jesus' message that God's love is always tied to the love of neighbor (Mark 12:29-32).

The early church was committed to a covenant community as they shared their resources so that no one would be in need. Their concern about the use of wealth was that it not be used selfishly, but to build community (Acts 2:44-47).

The problem of the global debt crisis today, as in the biblical communities, is that the debtors not only pay with their lives, but also with the lives of future generations. Part of God's creation has been diminished, the covenant broken. The covenant relationship demands justice.

V. Principles to Guide Debt-Crisis Solutions

As Christians, our love of God and neighbor must be reflected by our actions within the global family. Thus, we affirm the following policies and principles as needed in a just resolution to the debt crisis:

• As disciples of Christ, we need to examine patterns of greed that may cause us as individuals and nations to become debtors and lenders. We encourage the development of patterns of giving our material wealth and our knowledge so that others are benefited.

• The poor should not bear the burden of adjustment. Living standards of those least responsible and most vulnerable should not be sacrificed in order to meet external obligations. Developing countries should have the right to choose their own development paths with no military or economic interference from outside.

• The burden should be shared equitably among credit institutions and the debtor governments, corporations, and elites that incurred the debt.

• Factors adding to and perpetuating the debt problem but beyond the control of debtor countries—such as U.S. budget deficits, high interest rates, unfair commodity prices, and trade barriers—should be alleviated.

• Developing nations should not be forced to surrender their right to political or economic self-determination in exchange for relief.

• Debt relief should be fashioned in a way that benefits the poor and helps move debtors beyond debt repayment to development.

• Long-term solutions should promote a more just international economic system in order to prevent such crisis from recurring.

• Strong efforts should be made to encourage the easing of East-West tensions in order that military spending may be channeled to debt relief and humanitarian purposes.

VI. Recommended Actions for The United Methodist Church Through Its General Agencies and Local Congregations

The United Methodist Church, as a covenant community committed to Christian discipleship and advocacy for the poor, must work toward "measures that would reduce the concentration of wealth in the hands of a few" (¶ 67, preface). Thus, we specifically call upon The United Methodist Church, through its general agencies and local congregations, to:

A. Continue to undergird mission partner churches and agencies through understanding their reality and responding to their needs as expressed in the programs of the General Board of Global Ministries;

B. Urge the General Board of Church and Society and the General Board of Global Ministries to work with annual conferences to become advocates for equitable resolutions of the global debt crisis that will protect the poor through public policy and corporate responsibility;

C. Challenge each local congregation to study the global debt crisis, using this resolution as the basic resource. To assist this process:

1. The General Board of Global Ministries shall facilitate speaking tours of Persons in Mission and other international guests to talk about the human side of the debt crisis and should develop audiovisual resources to help interpret the crisis;

2. The General Board of Global Ministries shall encourage study tours aimed at in-depth study of the effect of the debt crisis and solutions coming from those affected;

3. The General Board of Discipleship, in cooperation with the General Boards of Church and Society and Global Ministries, shall prepare appropriate curriculum and study materials for all ages on the causes and effects of the global debt crisis; and

4. United Methodist theological seminaries shall include Christian responsibility for economic justice, including the debt crisis, as a necessary part of education for ministry;

D. Challenge the General Boards of Church and Society and Global Ministries to conduct a study, reflection, and action process on the effects of international speculation on the growing debt crises;

E. Strengthen public policy advocacy for reform of the international banking, trade, and corporate systems to ensure their accountability to the community as well as to shareholders;

F. Strengthen ecumenical and coalition work already being done on the debt crisis and economics;

G. Request the Council of Bishops, with the cooperation and participation of the General Board of Global Ministries and other general agencies of the Church, to conduct hearings and to create major study documentation on the current global debt crisis and the international economic system; and

H. Develop tours, curriculum, study materials, seminary courses, ecumenical and coalition work, hearings, and major study documentation.

These recommended actions shall represent extensive research and include the benefits of borrowing and lending on individual, corporate, and national levels, as well as the disadvantages and risks. They shall include reports on the standards of living in developing countries before and after the inceptions of international trade. Where appropriate, Western systems of international economic relationships shall be compared with Asian systems. The preparation process shall include extensive consultation with United Methodist laity involved in international trade, banking, economic education, and the poor.

ADOPTED 1988

See Social Principles, ¶ 67; "Economic Justice"; "The United Methodist Church and Peace."

God's Vision of Abundant Living

All creation has been brought into being by God, who "saw everything that [God] had made, and indeed, it was very good" (Genesis 1:31). All creation declares God's handiwork; everything exists in an intricate web of interdependence, and all this is given value and blessed by God (Genesis 1).

The initial and foundational value of all creation comes from its being the handiwork of God. God seeks the salvation, healing, and reconciliation of all creation: "God so loved the world that he gave his only Son" (John 3:16). In Jesus Christ, "God was pleased to reconcile to himself all things, whether on earth or in heaven, by making peace through the blood of his cross" (Colossians 1:20).

Through the divine Creation and Incarnation of God in Christ, we see the world as a loving creation—a creation intimate with its Creator. It is through this intimacy with God through Jesus Christ that we find our value and our worth.

The whole of creation contains all that is necessary to sustain itself and is an indication of God's affection and desire for re-creation.

We are people called to live toward God's vision of reconciliation through Christ Jesus. This reconciled world, or "new heaven and a new earth" (Revelation 21:1), includes creation healed—a creation where diversity is celebrated as a gift, rather than resisted and destroyed; where loving relationships are supremely valued and the resources of the world are shared equitably and justly; where all persons know their worth and value as children of God who seek the well-being of God's creation above their own greed.

It is a world where we live out of a theology of "enough," a theology based in knowledge that we are grounded in Christ; that our sense of personal value and esteem grow from our Christ-centered life. It is a theology that allows us to move away from worshiping the gods of consumption and material need.

In living out a theology of "enough," we will no longer expend our physical resources in consumption and our emotional resources in worrying over status. Our security and sense of well-being will be defined in relationship to God, not by our possessions. We will center our lives around God.

We hear a reminder of this style of living throughout Jesus' teachings: "Do not worry, saying, 'What will we eat?' or 'What will we drink?' or 'What will we wear?' For it is the Gentiles who strive for all these things; and indeed [God] knows that you need all these things. But strive first for the kingdom of God and [God's] righteousness, and all these things will be given to you as well" (Matthew 6:31-33). While Christ does not seek for any of us to be without basic necessities, a simplified life will move us away from the expectations and injustices of affluent living. abundant living is a life of greater simplicity, of a more responsible use of resources, and of a deeper faith.

Jesus discusses the foolishness of the rich and the greed that builds treasures on the earth. He admonishes us to build treasures in heaven, so that we might keep ourselves pure in heart and faithful to God (Luke 12).

In the "new heaven and new earth," we will choose a just lifestyle and share our wealth with the poor because we no longer need "things" to give us worth. With a theology of "enough," we will find gracious and fulfilled living in meeting our own basic needs and those of others. We will truly be "keepers" and "doers" of God's Word.

A Corrupted Vision of Abundant Living

There is a conflict between what abundant living means for a Christian and what it has come to mean in secular society. In secular society, abundant living is defined by one's aspiration to purchase an endless number of things, far more than is needed. Secular abundant living is experienced when one desires to live in luxury with every whim satisfied. This type of abundant living creates a system where the wealthy consume a disproportionate amount of resources and produce a disproportionate amount of waste. This living is rooted in a consumerism that exploits natural resources, exacerbates global resource crises, and causes cycles of global poverty that often lead to local and international violence.

Hearing these facts often raises feelings of guilt, anger, and denial. The false hope that technology will find fixes for all problems leads us to believe that change is not necessary. We who live in a culture of consumerism believe we have earned and deserved all of what we have; we do not want to give up anything. Our "things" give us a misguided status, a false sense of security, and a distorted sense of self-worth.

If we fail to believe in our hearts that our worth comes from our relationship to Christ and that we are called to bring God's redeeming love to creation through our actions and lifestyles, then all the arguments and information on the global crisis will be ignored. We will care about our impact on creation when we each recognize that creation is a gift given by a loving God for the benefit of all life. Only then will we assess how our lifestyles (what we do, use, buy, wear, eat, live in, and travel in) affect all present and future life.

We have a choice: We can be sustainers, or exploiters, of creation.

Visions of Faithful Abundant Living on Earth

Abundant living is when all people have their basic needs met for food, shelter, and good health.

Abundant living occurs when all have meaningful and fulfilling work that contributes to the common good of all others.

Abundant living is providing not only for the needs of this generation, but also for generations to come.

Abundant living is found in having time for family and community life.

Abundant living produces an environment where children are valued, cared for, and nurtured in families and communities.

Abundant living is a lifestyle that protects the diversity of all creation.

Abundant living is based on spiritual principles, which results in unity, sharing, mutual respect, and appreciation.

Abundant living is found in a church that nurtures growth and a deepening relationship with God through Christ.

Abundant Living Toward Redemption and Renewal

The United Methodist Church is called to help find opportunities for individuals to reevaluate their sense of value and to center their lives and lifestyles around God, rather than around consumption of material things.

The following are steps to assist The United Methodist Church in responding to its call:

United Methodist Congregations

Local congregations will reclaim the Spirit of sacrificial discipleship through networks and abundant-living communities. These will nurture the conversion of people in local communities through study, lifestyle assessment, and nurture of spiritual life. (The General Board of Church and Society can suggest resources.)

General Board of Church and Society

The General Board of Church and Society, working with the General Council on Ministries, will assist general agencies, boards, councils, and annual conferences to assess their patterns of consumption (including but not limited to facility use, travel, compensation packages, and purchase of reusable materials).

General Board of Discipleship

The General Board of Discipleship, with support of the General Board of Church and Society, will develop ways of assisting persons (especially those who have experienced programs such as the DISCIPLE Bible study or other Bible-study programs) to reassess personal lifestyles, with the goal of a conversion to a more simple, less-consumptive lifestyle and to a greater sensitivity to each person's decision-making responsibility in relation to national, global, social, environmental, and economic problems.

General Board of Global Ministries

The General Board of Global Ministries will look at the models of development taught to and by World and National Division partners and assess these models' roots in the culture of consumerism. The Women's Division shall include the focus of abundant living in the Schools of Christian Mission.

Council of Bishops

The General Board of Church and Society will work with episcopal leaders to increase their awareness and modeling of abundant living and support their commitment to ministries to and with the poor of the world.

General Board of Higher Education and Ministry

The General Board of Higher Education and Ministry will work with United Methodist seminaries and schools to provide education to promote individual conversion to a simplified lifestyle.

ADOPTED 1996

See Social Principles, ¶ 67; "Economic Justice"; "Call for a Rebirth of Compassion"; "A Call for Increased Commitment to End World Hunger and Poverty."

Guidelines for Initiating or Joining an Economic Boycott

Preamble

An economic boycott is understood to be a combined effort to abstain from the purchase or use of products or services provided by a targeted firm, government, or other agency. The purpose of a boycott is to persuade the targeted body to cease from certain practices judged to be unjust, and/or to perform certain practices deemed to be just.

Acknowledging the boycott as a legitimate Christian response to an identified social or economic injustice, we recommend the following criteria as a process for guiding the Church and its agencies in decisions regarding boycott. This process includes the following steps:

- preparation
- decision-making
- monitoring
- suspension/termination

The decision-making body shall designate those persons who will perform the tasks of each step.

The twelve criteria are the minimal concerns to be addressed as a decision-making body secures information and data upon which to determine its action.

The questions following the criteria statements are not part of the criteria but are given to help a decision-making body address specific areas of concern and secure information that will assist in its decision.

The gathered information and data are to be written and distributed to the decision-making body.

Clarifying Who May Call

Any local church, district, annual conference, or general Church board or agency shall be empowered to initiate, participate in, monitor, and terminate a boycott in its own name. Such decision shall be made consistent with criteria established by General Conference.

Any of the above may request the General Conference to join it in the boycott in the names of The United Methodist Church. Only the General Conference shall be empowered to initiate a boycott in the name of The United Methodist Church. It shall designate responsibility for monitoring and suspending and/or terminating such a boycott.

Preparation

I. Identify in writing the biblical and theological imperatives that address the issues involved in this particular conflict. How are the issues involved related to the purposes and mission of the decision-making body?

II. Document the social-justice issues in the dispute through on-site investigation, interviews, and hearings and study of literature, including input from:

A. Each of the major parties in the dispute;

B. United Methodist sources, including the presiding bishop(s), leadership of the annual conferences, superintendent(s), and local church leadership (laity and clergy) in the region where the dispute or alleged injustice is occurring; and

C. Objective third parties.

1. How do the social justice issues affect various segments of society and the communities in the area?

2. What sources of political, economic, or social power does each party in the dispute or alleged injustice have?

3. How will a boycott affect a potential resolution of the situation?

4. Are the leaders in the dispute or grievance supported by the persons for whom they speak, and are they committed to nonviolent action?

5. What denominational reviews have been made on this issue?

6. What groups, agencies, or governmental bodies have been seeking resolution in the conflict?

III.   Evaluate the conflict described by the gathered information in rela-
       tion to the theological, ethical, and social principles of Christian
       tradition and The United Methodist Church.
       1. Is intervention needed, and what magnitude of response is
       appropriate to the scope of the injustice?
       2. Is the desired end clearly specified?
IV.   Generate a list of potential public and private means of interven-
       tion in the situation, and evaluate the probable results of each.
       1. What methods of mediation, dialogue, and negotiations have
       been attempted and evaluated?
       2. Have these means of intervention been publicized and shared
       with connectional leadership in the region of the conflict and
       other constituencies?
       3. Is the injustice of sufficient scope to warrant the mobilization
       of a boycott?
       4. Is a boycott a more constructive and effective means of
       achieving justice than more coercive means?
       5. What are likely to be the positive and negative consequences
       of a boycott?
       6. What will the effects likely be in the local community?
       7. Are the issues adequately clarified so as to provide support
       for a boycott?
       8. How can negative stereotyping of contending parties be
       avoided?
V.   Clearly state in writing the objectives the potential boycott is in-
       tended to achieve.
       1. How will these objectives be shared with the disputing
       parties?
       2. Is it clear as to how the objectives of the potential boycott
       relate to other strategies being used by this or other church
       bodies?
       3. Are these objectives in harmony with the theological, ethical,
       and social principles? (*See* criteria I and III.)
VI.   Develop a plan and identify resources for carrying out a potential
       boycott, including mechanisms for:
       A. Communicating to Church constituencies the objectives of the
          boycott; the issues as seen by the various parties; and the
          biblical, theological, and ethical imperatives for involvement;
       B. Informing disputing parties of an intention to call or participate
          in a boycott;

C. Coordinating efforts with other United Methodist bodies, inter-faith coalitions, and groups dealing with the issues;

D. Monitoring the progress of the boycott (*see* VIII);

E. Suspending/terminating the boycott when objectives are met (*see* IX, X, XI); and

F. Developing ministries of reconciliation between aggrieved parties, during and following the boycott action.

1. What resources and plans have been made to ensure that the potential boycott will be carried out effectively and responsibly?

2. Have the presiding bishop(s), council director(s), superintendent(s), pastors, and membership in the region been afforded opportunity for participation in the development of this plan?

Decision

VII. On the basis of the information obtained in I and II above, decide whether a boycott action is merited.

1. What opportunity has been or will be provided for thorough consideration and debate of the issues?

2. Why is this the best time for this decision-making body to enter the boycott?

3. Is the boycott likely to achieve the stated objectives and assist in resolution of the dispute?

Monitoring

VIII. Designate a group of persons, including church representatives from the local area affected, who will monitor the boycott. Monitoring shall include:

A. Regular evaluation and reporting of progress toward the stated objective;

B. Regular written reporting of such progress to the local area affected and to the constituencies of the decision-making bodies through appropriate denominational channels;

C. Reporting substantial changes in the conditions under which the boycott is being carried out;

D. A process for issuing public statements; and

E. Coordination with designated coalitions and interfaith groups.

Suspension/Termination

IX.   In those cases where circumstances have changed, making it unclear whether the objectives of the boycott are being met, in consultation with the designated coalition and/or participating groups that are coordinating the boycott action, the decision-making body, or its designate, may call for suspension of the boycott while monitoring and evaluation continues.

X.   When the clearly stated written objectives of the boycott have been met, in consultation with the designated coalition and/or participating groups that are coordinating boycott action, the decision-making body or its designate shall terminate boycott participation.

XI.   Notification of suspension/termination shall be made in writing to all parties in the dispute and to all constituencies of the decision-making body.

XII.   Following this notification, monitoring of compliance with objectives and ministries of reconciliation shall be continued by the decision-making body for a responsible period of time.

ADOPTED 1988

See Social Principles, ¶ 67; "Economic Justice"; "Infant Formula Abuse."

Investment Ethics

The United Methodist Church and its predecessor denominations have a long history of witness for justice in the economic order. John Wesley and early Methodists, for instance, were staunchly opposed to the slave trade, to smuggling, and to conspicuous consumption. In fact, John Wesley refused to drink tea because of its relationship to the slave trade. Social creeds adopted by our predecessor churches, beginning in 1908, stressed social justice in the economic world, with special attention to the exploitation of child labor and inhumanely long working hours.

Throughout this century our Church has promoted decent working conditions and the right to organize and bargain collectively, and it has opposed discrimination in the workplace on the basis of race, ethnic background, gender, age, or disability. Historically our tradition has opposed Church investments in companies manufacturing liquor or tobacco products or promoting gambling.

Since the 1960s, our denomination and its predecessors have built a solid record expressing our ethics in our investment decisions. United Methodist agencies and conferences fought against the manufacture of napalm and were involved in the social-justice issues raised by religious shareholders. In the mid-1970s, the General Council on Finance and Administration (GCFA) began official social responsibility guidelines for general Church investments.

While the issue of economic sanction against *apartheid* in South Africa has engaged us more than any other, United Methodist agencies, affiliated institutions, conferences, congregations, and individual members have brought the Church's Christian witness to business in relation to numerous issues, including employment discrimination, environmental preservation, militarism, nuclear weapons production, and infant formula abuse.

We affirm that all financial resources of the Church and its members are God-given resources, to be held in trust for use or investment in ways that promote the reign of God on earth.

Further, we recognize that every investment has ethical dimensions. Financial investments have consequences that are both fiscal and social. We believe social justice and social usefulness must be given consideration together with financial security and financial yield in the investment of funds by United Methodist Church agencies and affiliated institutions, and by congregations as well as individual United Methodists. Socially responsible investing by Christian institutions and individuals must take account of both sets of considerations.

Our Church's witness through investments has taken three forms, each of which may be employed with the others. They are:

1. *Avoidance by Divestment.* This policy prohibits investment in enterprises that have policies or practices that are so morally reprehensible that investment in these companies is not tolerated by the Church. Our denomination traditionally has avoided investments in liquor, tobacco, and gambling. Many Church investors have refused to invest in major military contractors, companies with nuclear weapons contracts, or companies doing business in South Africa under *apartheid*. In some cases, they have divested of such companies, making public their action as a moral statement.

2. *Affirmative Choice.* This strategy is to choose intentionally enterprises for investment based on careful consideration of return, both in social values and in social justice, as well as financial security and monetary profit. For United Methodist investors, the Social Principles

and the *Book of Resolutions* delineate the social goals to which we expect all our investments to make a positive contribution. But with certain affirmative investments we may seek a very specific social outcome, such as the construction of affordable housing, the renewal of a particular neighborhood, or the expansion of business ownership to those traditionally excluded.

3. *Shareholder Advocacy*. The practices of corporations in which the Church invests may fall short of the moral standards expressed in the Social Principles and the *Book of Resolutions*. Responsible Christian investing includes seeking to change company policies for the better. Church investors have, as shareholders of corporations, engaged corporate management in a great variety of ways—from gentle persuasion to public pressure, from dialogue to voting proxies to filing shareholder resolutions. In many cases, corporate policies have changed as a result.

Policy and Implementation of Policy

1. The policy goals of the General Conference of The United Methodist Church, its general agencies, and entities under its control shall be:

A. To invest as much as possible in entities that are making a positive contribution to the communities, societies, and world on which they have impact and to the realization of the goals outlined in the Social Principles and the *Book of Resolutions* of our Church.

B. To employ this combination of socially responsible approaches that contribute to economic justice and corporate responsibility:

1. Avoidance by nonpurchase or divestment of holdings in companies that:

(a) Produce tobacco products or alcoholic beverages, or manage or own gambling establishments, or have as their primary business the production, distribution, or sale of pornographic material;

(b) Rank among the top 100 Department of Defense (DOD) contractors (those receiving the largest volume of prime contract awards) for the past three years; and have DOD contracts larger than 10 percent of sales for voting securities and 5 percent of sales for nonvoting securities; the GCFA shall publish the listing of the top 100 DOD contractors annually;

(c) Make components for nuclear explosive devices; or

(d) Manufacture chemical or biological warfare materials.

2. Affirmative investing in companies, banks, funds, or ventures that are seeing specific targeted social goals upon which the Church places high value, such as those that:

(a) Encourage recycling and use recycled products;

(b) Work within legally imposed discharge limits for toxic chemicals, noise, and water temperature;

(c) Do not sell chemicals that would be banned in the company's country of origin;

(d) Invest in low-income housing;

(e) Invest in companies that have positive records in hiring and promoting women and racial and ethnic persons; and

(f) Are companies owned by women and by racial and ethnic persons.

3. Shareholder advocacy through which the agency exercises its rights as shareholder to persuade corporations to end irresponsible behavior or live up to high moral standards by using any combination of the following approaches:

• letter of inquiry or expression of its position to management
• dialogue with management
• voting proxies
• soliciting votes for a particular reason
• soliciting or cosponsoring resolutions for votes at stockholder meetings
• speaking at stockholder meetings
• legal action
• publicity
• working in coalitions with other concerned shareholders
• petitioning the SEC or Congress for changes in the proxy rules

C. To maintain and promote economic pressure against South Africa by both divestment and shareholder advocacy until such time as *apartheid* is abolished and the vote is given to persons of all races, or those on the forefront of the struggle have concluded that the time has come to normalize relations with a new South Africa.

D. To seek opportunities to commend corporations publicly for socially responsible behavior and for excellence on social issues that are major concerns of The United Methodist Church.

E. To consider using investment-portfolio managers and funds that specialize in corporate social responsibility screening.

1. The General Council on Finance and Administration is assigned responsibility by the *Book of Discipline* for preparing and distributing the

Investment Guidelines that must be used by all general agencies receiving general Church funds, including social responsibility guidelines. The council shall periodically review and update these guidelines as needed, inviting the counsel of the agencies and other interested sectors of the Church. The council encourages the active involvement of investing agencies in the overview of socially responsible investing described in this policy.

2. All general agencies receiving general Church funds shall file a copy of their investment policy with the General Council of Finance and Administration. It shall be available upon request to any interested member of the Church.

3. These policy goals are strongly recommended to all the institutions affiliated with The United Methodist Church and any of their entities, and to the annual conferences and local churches and any funds of foundations related to them. It is also recommended that a copy of their social responsibility investment guidelines be available upon request by any United Methodist Church member.

4. Where financial considerations preclude immediate divestment of securities held in violation of the above policy goals, boards, agencies, and institutions of The United Methodist Church shall develop a plan for meeting the criteria that will bring them into compliance no later than the 1996 General Conference.

5. These policy goals are also strongly recommended to all individual United Methodist investors and users of financial services.

ADOPTED 1992

See Social Principles, ¶ 67.

National Incomes Policy

Many Americans live today under economic conditions that do not permit them to meet their basic needs. This situation is deplorable because it is not necessary. The economic productivity of our society, instead of meeting the needs of all its people, serves the interest of special groups. The present programs for increasing employment are inadequate to meet the need. Likewise, various income transfer programs, such as public welfare, unemployment insurance, and even Social Security itself, have failed to make possible an adequate minimum standard of existence. While a national program of income maintenance is not a substitute for a full-employment policy, neither is a full-employment policy a substitute for an incomes policy. Both programs are needed, and if one or both are missing, we shall continue to block the development of the maximum productive skills of a tragically large number of citizens. Wage standards are needed that provide a living wage for all workers. It is also necessary to broaden and improve social welfare services.

Our present economic system functions imperfectly. It is the responsibility of society to develop new institutions that more adequately fulfill human rights—jobs, food, clothing, housing, education, and health care. As Christians, we have the obligation to work with others to develop the moral foundation for public policies that will provide every family with the minimum income needed to participate as responsible and productive members of society.

We, as Christians, also recognize our obligation to work with others to develop in each person an attitude of responsible stewardship of time, talent, and resources that will enable the maximum number of families to be self-reliant and economically independent to the greatest possible extent.

Some basic objectives of a strategy for economic justice are:

1. A return to a full-employment policy with the federal, state, and local government as the employers of the last resort;

2. A guaranteed minimum annual income sufficient for every family living in the United States based on the Bureau of Labor Statistics' lower budget;

3. Supportive social services in the fields of education; health; housing; job training; and particularly adequate, comprehensive child development and daycare services for all children, especially those of the poor and low-income groups; and

4. Improvement and expansion of the food stamp program, school breakfast and lunch programs, and the creation of new means to ensure that no person be hungry in this society of abundance.

We call upon our churches and the general boards and agencies:

1. To study the various methods for providing every individual and family an income capable of supporting human life in dignity and decency; and

2. To participate in the development and implementation of a national income policy that best fulfills the following criteria:

(a) designed to provide a means to an income adequate for living and available to all as a matter of right;

(b) adequate to maintain health and human well-being and adjusted to changes in the cost of living;

(c) administered so as to extend coverage to all persons in need;

(d) developed in a manner that will respect the freedom of persons to manage their own lives, increase their power to choose their own careers, and enable them to participate in meeting personal and community needs;

(e) designed to reward rather than penalize productive activity;

(f) designed in such a way that existing socially desirable programs and values are conserved and enhanced; and

(g) federally standardized, taking into consideration local and regional differences in cost of living.

ADOPTED 1976

See Social Principles, ¶ 67E, F; "Economic Justice"; "Pay Equity in the U.S.A."; "Special Needs of Farm Workers."

Pay Equity in the U.S.A.

I. Introduction

Pay equity , or *comparable worth* (the terms are used interchangeably), is a remedy for wage discrimination. Its goal is to eliminate sex and race discrimination from the wage-setting process. Pay equity ensures that compensation is based on relevant factors, such as skill, responsibility, and working conditions. Simply stated, the concept means that if the same amount of effort, skill, responsibility, experience, and education is required to do two different jobs, then the persons doing those jobs should be paid the same.

II. Biblical and Theological Background

Our biblical faith affirms the inherent value and equal worth in God's sight of every person; it requires the faithful to be advocates for those who have suffered oppression and discrimination. In his ministry, Jesus continually lifted up women, poor people, and social outcasts as deserving not only of special loving care but also of having the wrongs done them redressed by the community. When asked to read a passage from the prophet Isaiah in the synagogue, Jesus chose one that called the faithful to release prisoners, to restore sight to the blind, to set the oppressed at liberty and "to proclaim the acceptable year of the Lord"

(Luke 4:16-19, Revised Standard Version). This "acceptable year," or "year of the Lord's favor," is believed by scholars to refer to the year of Jubilee, a time when slaves were set free, debts were repaid, and land and wealth were equitably redistributed (Leviticus 25:10-17). It is significant that Jesus chose this passage to announce his ministry. An additional passage that speaks to the issue of workers' rights to fair compensation is 1 Timothy 5:18 (The Living Bible): "Those who work deserve their pay!"

United Methodists have tried to be faithful to this mandate to protect the powerless and to restore the oppressed to their rightful place of dignity and equality. We have understood this responsibility to extend into the economic life of the community. In our Social Principles, we "assert the right of members of racial and ethnic groups to equal opportunities in employment and promotion" (¶ 66A), and we "affirm the right of women to equal treatment in employment, responsibility, promotion, and compensation" (¶ 66F). A 1984 General Conference resolution on the "Equal Rights of Women" committed United Methodists to "monitor public policies and practices which affect unemployment, pay inequity, [and] inequality of opportunity. . . ." It also calls us to "research policies that discriminate on the basis of gender and to advocate changes that enable equality of rights and opportunities." Taking these commitments and responsibilities seriously leads us to embrace the concept of pay equity.

III. The Context

Most women and most persons of color in the United States are still concentrated in low-paying jobs with limited opportunities for advancement. These jobs have historically been underpaid and undervalued precisely because they have been held primarily by women and by persons of color.

Women's earnings are an indispensable share of the incomes of more and more families. Families headed by women are the fastest-growing segment of the poverty population and now represent 75 percent of all individuals in poverty. Many mothers must support their family on their income alone; a significant portion of these mothers are women of color. Thus, the elimination of wage-based sex and race discrimination in the labor force is an important element in ending the "feminization of poverty." Because men of color, as well as women, are at the lower end of the wage-earning scale, pay equity is not only a "women's issue" but a quality-of-life family issue as well.

Women's involvement in the workforce has increased dramatically during the last decade. In 1985, women accounted for nearly half of all full-time workers. It is projected that 67 percent of all new workforce entrants between 1987 and 2000 will be female. The average full-time woman worker earned 64 cents for every dollar earned by a man in 1985. The wage gap was even greater for African American and Hispanic women, who earned, respectively, 59 cents and 55 cents for every dollar earned by men. If the trend of low pay for jobs held primarily by women continues, it is estimated that by the year 2000 virtually all of the poverty population will be women and their children. While part of this gap can be attributed to differences in education, experience, and job tenure, most of these wage gaps are due exclusively to occupational segregation and sex discrimination in the labor force. The value of a job to society has little or no current correlation to remuneration; sanitation workers continue to earn far more than childcare workers.

Despite the fact that "equal pay for equal work" is the law (Equal Pay Act of 1963, Title VIII of the Civil Rights Act), the wage gap persists. This is due in large measure to the fact there are few white men in women-dominated jobs; women and men must work in the same job in order to determine if there is a violation of the Equal Pay Act. It is at this point that there is a breakdown in the argument that legal remedies for wage discrimination already exist.

Two other frequently cited arguments against the concept of pay equity are that it will interfere with the free market law of supply and demand, and that its cost will be prohibitive. In fact, most current wage discrepancies can hardly be attributed to impartial market forces. Two current examples are: (1) a large city that pays its police dispatchers (mostly Black women) several thousand dollars less than it pays its predominately white male fire dispatchers, and (2) the fact that secretaries, who are in short supply, are paid less than truck drivers, who are in considerable surplus. On the cost question, public and private employers who have voluntarily implemented pay equity policies consistently report that it has not been as expensive as predicted and that, in fact, they have avoided prolonged litigation and costly settlements. It is well to remember that similar predictions of economic chaos preceded the adoption of minimum wage and child labor laws.

Pay equity is a growing national movement; support for it is steadily increasing across the country through collective bargaining, legislation, voluntary initiatives and litigation. Pay equity initiatives are moving at a rapid pace at state levels, and significant gains have been made in the private sector as well. Well over one hundred governmental units, both state and local, have taken actions on pay equity. Over forty-seven states are doing or have already completed studies to find if there is sex and race discrimination in how they pay their employees, and twenty states have begun to implement pay adjustment. The national conferences both of governors and of mayors have adopted resolutions supporting pay equity. Some employers in the private sector have already voluntarily taken actions to remove wage discrimination from their workplace, thus avoiding the time, expense, and conflict resulting from lack of action. A 1984 survey by Marttila and Kiley of Boston revealed that a majority of U.S. workers think pay equity is necessary to remove sex and race bias in wages. There is a trend among private employers to support the elimination of wage discrimination between different jobs as "good business" and not inconsistent with remaining competitive in the marketplace.

Therefore, be it resolved, that we, as United Methodists, endorse the principle of pay equity, whereby wage structures in the Church and in the public and private sectors are based on unbiased evaluation of the jobs' requirements and value to the employer.

1. We call upon the General Council on Finance and Administration to evaluate internal wage structures and practices of general agencies in light of the principle of pay equity and to include this assessment in its regular monitoring of equal employment opportunity compliance (¶ 807.9*b*);

2. We call upon The United Methodist Church at all levels to:

(a) Evaluate all internal Church wage structures in light of the principle of pay equity and move with dispatch to correct any inequities;

(b) Provide educational resources that will assist the Church in understanding the issue of pay equity;

(c) Monitor relevant federal, state, and municipal legislation, and advocate policies that lead to adoption of pay equity as a national standard;

(d) Exercise shareholder rights by voting shares in favor of voluntary implementation of pay equity programs in companies that do not currently have them;

471

(e) Encourage individual United Methodists to work for voluntary implementation of pay equity in their places of business; and

(f) Monitor and advocate for the strengthening of affirmative action and antidiscrimination efforts at national, state, and local levels.

ADOPTED 1988

See Social Principles, ¶¶ 66F, 67; "Economic Justice"; "Rights of Workers"; "Equal Rights of Women"; "The Status of Women."

Call for a Rebirth of Compassion

The great strength of U.S. society has always been that its citizens believed that despite hardship, inequities, and injustice, the system has the capacity to be fundamentally fair and offers the possibility of a better life to all its citizens. This belief, despite segregation, led African Americans to work to reform and not overthrow the system. It led women, despite patriarchy and discrimination, to demand and work for full participation in the system. In the worst social crisis of this century, the Great Depression, widespread unrest and upheaval was avoided when the system moved quickly to assist the poor and the unemployed. In these times of crisis, the U.S. people have joined together for the common good, drawing upon a deep-seated sense of fairness and compassion rooted in their religious and ethical tradition.

Today, this "social contract," which has been the glue holding together a nation as diverse as any in the world, is being replaced by a new spirit of divisiveness and narrow self-interest. It is as though the challenge of John F. Kennedy, "Ask what you can do for your country," has been changed to "Ask only what's in it for you." This has led to a massive upward redistribution of wealth in U.S. society until today, the top 5 percent have more wealth than the bottom 40 percent combined. Conspicuous consumption and waste goes hand in hand with rising homelessness, children born into poverty, and the elderly forced into poverty. As this process continues, Middle America, for the first time since the Depression, has seen its standard of living decline and can no longer expect the next generation to have a better life.

The response of our political leadership to this crisis has been to point the finger of blame at those deemed responsible—the poor. In a "big lie" reminiscent of Nazi Germany, the problems of U.S. society are blamed on teenage mothers, welfare recipients, racial minorities, women's liberation, programs of social welfare, and homosexuals.

In a climate of anger, violence, and stridency, even Jesus would be derided were he to call in to one of the popular talk shows and call for a rebirth of compassion. There are few politicians in either major party who are willing to challenge the ethics of selfishness, greed, and scapegoating that characterize politics today. Too few voices challenge the culture of sex, violence, self-indulgence, and instant gratification spewed into millions of homes twenty-four hours a day.

We believe that it is to such a time and such a mission that God is calling the church 2000 years after the Savior's birth. It is the unique mission of the religious community to call this nation to a rebirth of compassion. How prophetic today are the words of Jesus, quoting Isaiah: "The Spirit of the Lord is upon me,/because he has anointed me to bring good news to the poor./He has sent me to proclaim release to the captives/and recovery of sight to the blind, to let the oppressed go free,/to proclaim the year of the Lord's favor" (Luke 4:18-19).

In this spirit, we call upon United Methodists throughout the land not only to feed the hungry and house the homeless, but also to work for policies that will end hunger and homelessness. We call upon our bishops to speak boldly for those who cannot speak for themselves— against economic policies that benefit the few at the expense of the many, against violence toward women and homosexuals, and against the continued militarization of a nation with no external threat.

We call on our people to support candidates for office who are committed to policies of full employment, universal health insurance, long-term health care, quality public education for all children, reduced military spending, and progressive taxation.

Finally, we call on our churches to reach out in love and compassion to all persons, regardless of race, economic condition, sexual preference, and religious persuasion, becoming beacons of love in a stormy sea of hatred, discrimination, and violence. Let us be signs of the coming reign of God in our midst—a reign marked by compassion and justice.

ADOPTED 1996

See Social Principles, ¶67; "Economic Justice"; "God's Vision of Abundant Living"; "Self-Help Efforts of Poor People."

Rights of Workers

I. Concern of the Church

The concern of The United Methodist Church for the dignity of workers and the rights of employees to act collectively has been stated in its Social Principles. Both employer and union are called to "bargain in good faith within the framework of the public interest" (¶ 67B). However, given the new international economic setting, it is necessary to reaffirm once again the Church's position.

Genesis teaches that human beings, as the image of God, have an innate dignity (1:27). It also declares that people are to work the land and replenish the world (1:28; 2:25). Work is one of the ways through which human beings exercise the self-creativity given by their Creator.

Based on the dignity of both work and the worker, the Church teaches that society should provide employment under safe and decent conditions so that the dignity of the workers can be elevated and their creativity exercised (1984 *Book of Resolutions;* pages 237, 431).

In Scripture, the emphasis on human dignity is complemented by a demand for justice. Justice, as taught by the Jubilee theme of Leviticus (chapter 25) and Deuteronomy (chapter 15) and in the cries of the prophets, cautions against concentrated economic power and demands that the poor be reinstated into the body of society as brother and sister. Jesus, in his parables of the rich man and Lazarus (Luke 16), the final judgment (Matthew 25), and the rich fool (Luke 12), affirms a similar message.

Scriptural teaching mandates that society and its institutions are to be structured so that the weaker and poorer groups can participate in the shaping of society and their own futures.

II. Characteristics of the International Economy

The economies of nations are becoming increasingly internationalized. Within that process, however, there are currents that pose serious threat to both the rights and the dignity of workers. Those currents include the following:

A. *International Corporate Competition.* The emerging world economy is dominated by transnational corporations and banks whose activities are often coordinated with their "home" governments. At times, these corporations compete vigorously around the globe. At other times, they conspire together to maintain shares of the market. Since they control a considerable portion of the world's resources, technologies, and investment capital, they are able to locate their facilities where an advantage of profit or market power can be gained. Other considerations, including the rights of labor and community, are made subservient to the corporation's drive for a more competitive profit.

B. *Transformation of Industries and Jobs.* New technologies are transforming the structures and the nature of businesses everywhere. Production technologies redefine jobs into widely disparate classes; some workers are upgraded to higher skills and professions while, at the same time, many are downgraded to levels of minimum skill, or their jobs are eliminated altogether.

C. *Increasing Centralization of Decision-Making.* The speed and accuracy by which information is transmitted around the globe have made data processing and information services the largest and fastest growing sector of some economies.

These technologies make it possible for corporate headquarters in one location to control an industrial-financial empire that extends across the nations of the world. The capacity of executives to swiftly transfer business out of one place and into another may deindustrialize Pittsburgh, Pennsylvania, for example, while at the same time industrializing a remote village like Pohang, Korea.

In both situations, the basic decisions are made by corporations and/or governments with little or no input from the workers or citizens in either place.

III. *Effects on Labor*

The combined effect of these characteristics on labor has been immense:

A. In economic systems, labor is considered primarily as a cost of production. Its human aspects are often ignored. Modern technologies make it feasible for industries constantly to relocate in search of cheaper labor, thus pitting workers of various countries against one another and depressing wages and benefits in richer and poorer nations. Together, corporate competition and skill-reducing technology tend to downgrade the humanity of labor.

B. The centralization of decision-making power under the control of a few corporate board members and executives usurps the rights of employees and communities to have a say in what determines their lives. In some countries, worker organizations are intentionally weakened and/or repressed altogether.

Some labor leaders have themselves adopted the thought patterns and values of big business, thus impeding the workers' ability to respond to the challenges of the corporation. Union support from the rank and file is weakened, and solidarity is eroded. Worker loyalty is transferred to the company or to themselves, rather than to fellow workers.

C. A third effect of the internationalizing economy is the fracturing of many jobs into temporary, part-time, subcontracted, and cottage-industry jobs that are claiming larger numbers of employees. The impacts are many:

1. Wages of regular, full-time jobs are pressured downward, or the jobs are eliminated altogether;

2. Benefits are reduced or eliminated;

3. Low-paying jobs keep people and families in poverty; and

4. Women and children are increasingly employed in these jobs, thus perpetuating a poverty class with sex and race characteristics.

D. As the internationalizing process has taken place, labor unions have at times failed to uphold solidarity among the world's workers. Some unions have adopted thought patterns and values that impede their ability to adjust to today's transformation in jobs and industrial organization. Consequently, established unionism is often irrelevant to workers in many new sectors of the world's economy, and even in traditionally organized sectors, rank-and-file members are at times alienated from their leadership.

E. In less industrialized countries, foreign businesses are induced to come by promises that there will be no labor union problems, workers being kept docile by threats of dismissal and/or police suppression.

IV. Policy Directions for the Church

Given the circumstances of an international economy and the principles taught by Scripture and by the Social Principles, The United Methodist Church should advocate for the following:

A. Support for internationally recognized worker rights based on ILO Conventions (places of employment should guarantee to the workers a safe work environment, fair compensation, just supervision, and the right to representation by a worker's organization of their own choosing);

B. Recognition of these rights of workers by international banks and corporations, and the obligation to practice them in their places of employment;

C. Acceptance of union responsibility to look beyond their own organizational benefit and be more active in organizing women, temporary employees, people of color, and others disadvantaged in the labor market;

D. Full participation of rank-and-file members in union decision-making; unions should defend the rights of the organized and unorganized and develop global solidarity across nations and industries; and

E. Government passage and enforcement of legislation that protects workers' rights and guarantees collective bargaining.

V. Actions by the Church

Given the above policies, The United Methodist Church should take the following actions:

A. All churches and Church agencies shall respect their employees' rights to good working conditions, fair compensation, and collective action.

B. The General Board of Church and Society and the General Board of Global Ministries, in cooperation with Methodist churches in other countries, shall communicate to domestic and international banks and corporations the Church's:

1. concern over low wages and inadequate benefits;

2. distress at unsafe and health-threatening working conditions;

3. expectation that employees have the freedom to organize unions of their own choosing without employer interference; and

4. call for collective bargaining to be carried out promptly and in good faith.

C. The General Board of Church and Society and the General Board of Global Ministries, in conjunction with annual conference and local church leaders, shall sponsor religion and labor programs that: (a) study the theological significance of work and employment, and (b) initiate cooperation with workers and labor unions about how best to protect and enhance the rights of all workers, especially those of women, children, and people of color.

D. The General Board of Church and Society and the General Board of Global Ministries, in conjunction with annual conference and local church leaders, shall support legislation that:

1. protects the health and safety of employees at their workplace;

2. guarantees workers the right to freely organize unions of their own choosing;

3. facilitates the negotiating process for the signing of collective contracts between management and union; and

4. controls and monitors plant relocations and closings.

ADOPTED 1988

See Social Principles, ¶ 67B, C; "Economic Justice"; "Emphasis of Concern for Workers."

Safety and Health in Workplace and Community

Just as biblical religion affirms that God is involved in the healing of individuals (Genesis 20:17; Matthew 8), so also does God's covenant with his people include the mandate to protect the community from dangers that threaten the health of the people (Leviticus 14:33–15:14). At the beginning of Methodism, John Wesley provided medicine and medical treatment at no cost to the poor in London and Bristol. In addition to pioneering free dispensaries in England, Wesley emphasized prevention of illness. In his book *Primitive Physic,* he dealt with nutrition and hygiene, as well as treatment of the sick.

The first Social Creeds, adopted by the 1908 General Conference of The Methodist Episcopal Church (North), declared that workers must be protected "from dangerous machinery, occupational disease, injuries, and mortality," and that working conditions must be regulated to safeguard the physical and moral health of the community. Today as well, the Church is called to declare that the health of every individual is part of community health, including safe and healthy conditions in places where people work. The Church has a responsibility to pronounce clearly the implications of God's law of love for human health. Where human life and health are at stake, economic gain must not take precedence.

A. Public Health Hazards

Public health hazards originate from a variety of sources, including organisms (e.g., bacteria, fungi, and viruses), physical conditions (e.g., hazardous machinery and excessive noise), toxic chemicals, and radiation. Some public health hazards, such as venereal disease and lead poisoning, were known to our biblical forbears and to other ancient civilizations. Other hazards such as toxic chemical wastes are products of the past century's rapid technological development. Such hazards can produce infectious diseases, disabling injuries, incapacitating illnesses, and death. Toxic substances and related hazards such as ionizing radiation threaten the exposed individual to additional hazards such as cancer and sterility, and they also threaten future generations with birth defects and gene mutations.

A single toxic substance may have wide-range usage, from the home to the workplace to the environment. It may persist for years in the form of dangerous wastes and residues. The human consequences of such public health hazards are vast. In 1977, work-related injuries claimed 5.3 million victims, 4,760 of whom died.[1] In 1976, compensation payments of $7.5 billion were made for work-related deaths, disease, and disability.[2] Environmental and occupational cancer are estimated to represent 20–38 percent of all cancer.[3] One substance alone, asbestos, is expected to claim the lives of 1.6 million of the 4 million individuals heavily exposed since World War II, including a substantial number of shipyard workers.[4] These deaths, diseases, and disabilities have an additional impact on the affected individuals and their families in terms of medical costs, lost earning capacity, pain, suffering, and grief. When long-term diseases such as cancer, birth defects, and gene mutations are involved, the human consequences extend far beyond the immediately perceived hazards of infection or injury.

B. Declaration

Public health is dependent on effective prevention and active protection before illness or injury have occurred. To fulfill God's commandment to love our neighbor as ourselves, we should support action to protect each individual's health and to preserve the health of the community. To this end, we declare:

1. Every individual, including those with disabilities, has a right to a safe and healthful environment unendangered by a polluted natural world, a hazardous workplace, an unsanitary community, dangerous household products, unsafe drugs, and contaminated food. This human right must take precedence over property rights. Moreover, the necessary preservation of human life and health must not be sacrificed or diminished for economic gain. It is unconscionable that anyone should profit from conditions that lead to the disease, disability, or death of another. Furthermore, the essential protection of the physical and moral quality of human life must not be compromised by

---

[1] *Statistical Abstract of the U.S., 1978*, U.S. Department of Commerce, 99th edition, paperback, 1057 pages; page 78, No. 112, 5,203 deaths from industrial-type accidents shown for 1976.

[2] Ibid., page 354, Table No. 558, "Workmen's Compensation Payments."

[3] "Estimates of the Fraction of Cancer in the United States Related to Occupational Factors," prepared by the National Cancer Institute, National Institute of Environmental Health Sciences, National Institute for Occupational Safety and Health, mimeographed report, September 14, 1978; page 24.

[4] "Estimates of the Fraction of Cancer in the United States Related to Occupational Factors" prepared by the National Cancer Institute, National Institute of Environmental Health Sciences, National Institute for Occupational Safety and Health, mimeographed report, September 15, 1978; page 9.

competing considerations of capital investment and return, or diminished by society's insistence on affluence, luxury, and convenience.

2. Public health hazards must be *prevented* in order to avoid the serious individual and community consequences of injury, illness, and untimely death, including disability, physical pain, mental anguish, lost human potential, family stress, and the diversion of scarce medical resources.

3. Public health hazards to future generations, such as toxic substances and wastes that produce birth defects and gene mutations, must be prevented in order to avoid a legacy of disease, disability, and untimely death. No generation has the right to assume risks that potentially endanger the viability of future life.

4. The public health risks of technological development must be fully and openly assessed before new technologies are introduced into the home, the workplace, the community, or the environment. Medical research should be required to give high priority to the identification of hazardous substances and processes.

5. The preservation and protection of human life from public health hazards is a fundamental responsibility of government that must be maintained by active public support and adequate public funds. Efficient administration and effective enforcement of public health laws, including those governing the use and disposal of toxic substances, should be supported at all levels of government.

6. Preventive health care should be taught in educational institutions to persons in every age group at every level of society. Health professionals in all branches of medicine and public health, and those in related fields, should be educated in practicing preventive medicine, implementing community preventive health strategies, and assisting patients in the adoption of healthy lifestyles. Programs should be implemented that educate and inform consumers and workers about physical, chemical, biological, and radiological hazards of products, services, working conditions, and environment contaminants.

ADOPTED 1988

See Social Principles, ¶¶ 66Q, 67B, C, F; "Universal Access to Health Care in the U.S. and Related Territories"; "Rights of Workers"; "Emphasis of Concern for Workers."

Self-Help Efforts of Poor People

We note with satisfaction the recent upsurge of community-based, cooperative self-help efforts on the part of groups of low-income rural people in all parts of the Untied States. However, we recognize that such efforts do not offer a total solution to the problem of rural poverty or obviate the necessity for massive efforts on the part of government and private sector to combat rural poverty in other ways.

The church of Jesus Christ is concerned with the fulfillment of whole persons in community. Economic development that produces human and community development is to be preferred over other forms of economic activity. In the cooperative and other community-based enterprise of poor people, we find a combination of economic gain, personal fulfillment, and community development.

We applaud and will support these indigenous and cooperative self-help efforts, because we see in them social and spiritual as well as economic values of great consequence.

We call upon our general boards, jurisdictions, area offices, annual conferences, districts, local churches, and members to seek ways to become acquainted with the self-help efforts of poor people in rural areas and to help them with grants, credit, technical assistance, and training facilities.

We call upon federal and state governments, private industry, banks, colleges and universities, foundations, and all other public and private agencies to provide massive resources, both financial and technical, to assist the valiant efforts of low-income rural people to solve their own problems through self-help.

ADOPTED 1976

See Social Principles, ¶ 67E, F; "Rights of Workers"; "Economic Justice"; "Emphasis of Concern for Workers."

Sexual Harassment in Church and Society in the U.S.A.

All human beings, both male and female, are created in the image of God, and thus have been made equal in Christ. From the beginning, God intended us to live out our equality in relation with one another. Yet in our human brokenness, we have given greater value and power to men than to women. Jesus was sent into this world that we might experience whole relationships with one another and with God. "There is neither Jew nor Greek, there is neither slave nor free, there is neither male nor female; for you are all one in Christ Jesus" (Galatians 3:28, Revised Standard Version). Still both the church and the society condone and ignore personal and institutional abuse of women.

Sexual harassment is an unwanted sexual advance or demand, either verbal or physical, that is perceived by the recipient as demeaning, intimidating, or coercive. Sexual harassment must be understood as an exploitation of a power relationship rather than as an exclusively sexual issue. Sexual harassment also includes the creation of a hostile or abusive working environment resulting from discrimination on the basis of gender. The successful 1986 Supreme Court case of *Meritor Savings Bank et al.* v. *Vinson* substantially broadened the legal definition of sexual harassment, holding that it is a violation of federal antidiscrimination laws and saying that companies may be liable for the misbehavior of one employee. This decision upheld the 1981 guidelines of the Equal Employment Opportunity Commission (EEOC), which holds employers liable for all forms of sexual harassment, including coworker harassment and harassment from clients and customers. From the EEOC guidelines it is clear that the employer bears an affirmative responsibility to maintain a workplace free from sexual harassment, to investigate quickly and impartially any charge of sexual harassment, and to take action against all offenders.

At the workplace, at one extreme, sexual harassment is the demand for sexual compliance coupled with the threat of firing if the person refuses. On the other, it is being forced to work in an environment in which, through various means, the person is subjected to stress or made to feel humiliated because of one's gender. Sexual harassment is behavior that becomes coercive because it occurs in the employment context, thus threatening both a person's job satisfaction and security. This critical problem affects all persons regardless of job category or description, age, race, economic or educational background.

It affects women who are church professionals as well as those who work in secular occupations. Sexual harassment has been documented in United Methodist churches, agencies, and institutions, including seminaries. It is becoming clear as statistics emerge that whatever their occupation, women share a common problem—the possibility of sexual harassment. Men can also be the victims of sexual harassment.

National surveys done by the Working Women's Institute, *Redbook* magazine, and an independent study in Illinois from 1975 through 1980 found that from 59 percent to 88 percent of all women surveyed responded that they had been made to feel humiliated or threatened by sexual harassment in their present place of employment. A 1981 survey of crises experienced by United Methodist women revealed that even without being provided a definition of sexual harassment, one out of every eight respondents reported that she had been harassed on her job.

It is clear from currently available data that the Church suffers from the sin of sexual harassment in ways that mirror the society. However, more current research is needed. The Christian community has a responsibility to deal resolutely with the issue of sexual harassment. It demeans and destroys the dignity of the victim. Rather than affirming women as whole persons as Jesus did, it reinforces the idea of women as sexual objects. It challenges women's humanity, undermining their self-esteem, job satisfaction, and self-confidence; and it keeps women at lower status in the workforce.

Therefore, be it resolved, that The United Methodist Church stands in opposition to the sin of sexual harassment in the Church and the society at large and calls upon the Church at all levels to:

1. Provide educational resources to assist United Methodists in understanding the issue of sexual harassment;

2. Develop clear policies and procedures related to sexual harassment establishing grievance procedures for victims and penalties for offenders;

3. Monitor federal, state, and local legislation, advocating for just laws that will help to eradicate sexual harassment; and

4. Model in its own life an environment of hospitality where there is not only an absence of harassment but the presence of welcome, respect, and equality.

Be it further resolved, that a United States survey be conducted by the General Council on Ministries to determine the extent of sexual harassment and the policies and procedures to deal with it inside our own Church structures, including all related agencies and institutions. The findings and recommendations of this survey will be reported to agencies, annual conferences, and local churches by December 1990.

ADOPTED 1988

See Social Principles, ¶¶ 65I, 66F; "Sexual Harassment and The United Methodist Church."

Sexual Harassment and The United Methodist Church

According to the 1988 resolution, "*Sexual harassment* is any unwanted sexual advance or demand, either verbal or physical, that is perceived by the recipient as demeaning, intimidating, or coercive. Sexual harassment must be understood as an exploitation of a power relationship rather than as an exclusively sexual issue. Sexual harassment also includes the creation of a hostile or abusive working environment resulting from discrimination on the basis of gender" (*see* previous resolution).

In this context, the 1988 General Conference directed the General Council on Ministries (GCOM) to conduct a survey of United Methodist clergy, laity, college and seminary students, and non-clergy Church employees. The General Council on Ministries reported its finding in 1990 to agencies, annual conferences, and local churches. The GCOM survey concluded: "The presence of sexual harassment in environments associated with The United Methodist Church interferes with the moral mission of the Church and disrupts the religious activity, career development, and academic progress of its participants. This study shows that unwanted sexual behavior takes place in variety of circumstances in the church and has a range of negative consequences for its victims.

"Sexual harassment creates improper, coercive, and abusive conditions wherever it occurs in society, and it undermines the social goal of equal opportunity and the climate of mutual respect between men and women. Unwanted sexual attention is wrong, discriminatory, and illegal. Its victims have formal recourse through public agencies and the courts, but they have hesitated to deal with their circumstances publicly. According to the results of this study, people in the Church who are subjected to unwanted sexual attention want most of all for it to cease through ignoring it and avoiding the person. Women especially have been socialized to be 'pleasant,' to avoid challenging men, and to adopt a wary attitude about the risks of resistance. Harassers then misuse their personal and organizational power by treating those in more vulnerable statuses as 'fair game.'

"The experience of sexual harassment can be devastating to its victims. Coerced relationships set up a climate of intimidation and humiliation. Unwanted behavior damages the moral environment where people worship, work, and learn. This study documented the large costs in the form of lowered self-esteem borne by respondents, especially students. Victims often suffer profound personal distress and cope alone with intolerable conditions. Also, sexist behavior wherever it occurs causes emotional and psychological pain not only to individuals but also to those they are responsible for: spouses and children. Family relationships undergo strain when victims are debilitated by anxiety and misplaced self-blame because of unwanted sexual advances and a hostile, offensive, and degrading social environment" (*see* "Sexual Harassment in The United Methodist Church," page 11).

The survey provided continuing documentation that sexual harassment is a significant problem in The United Methodist Church and that it detracts from the ministry and mission of Jesus Christ. Specific survey findings are available from the General Council on Ministries or the General Commission on the Status and Role of Women.

Therefore, The United Methodist Church shall undertake the following plan to begin to eliminate sexual harassment in the denomination and its institutions in the following three areas:

Education

1. The General Commission on the Status and Role of Women will work cooperatively with other Church bodies to explore ways to develop educational resources (workshops, print and audiovisual materials, and so forth) to assist United Methodists throughout the Church in understanding the issues of sexual harassment;

2. The General Commission on the Status and Role of Women will explore ways to develop relevant education resources on sexual harassment specific to those in the ordained and diaconal ministry; students, faculty, and administrators of United Methodist-related educational institutions; and laity, paid and volunteer, throughout The United Methodist Church; and

3. The General Commission on the Status and Role of Women will ensure that United Methodist Church-developed materials are made available to annual conference boards of ordained and diaconal ministry; United Methodist-related educational institutions; and other agencies, groups, and individuals throughout The United Methodist Church.

Policies and Procedures

1. Each annual conference, general agency, and United Methodist-related educational institution will have a sexual harassment policy in place, including grievance procedures for victims and penalties for offenders. A copy of these policies is to be forwarded to the General Commission on the Status and Role of Women by January 1, 1995, to be summarized and reported to the 1996 General Conference. The General Commission on the Status and Role of Women will be available to

provide resources and counsel on the components of effective policies; and

2. The General Board of Church and Society will continue to monitor federal legislation and compliance with EEOC regulations. The General Board of Church and Society will also continue to be an advocate for just laws that will help to eradicate sexual harassment. This information will be available upon request.

Continuing Self-Assessment

The General Commission on the Status and Role of Women will explore with the General Council on Ministries and other appropriate Church bodies ways to assess the effectiveness of the Church's efforts to eradicate sexual harassment.

ADOPTED 1992

See Social Principles, ¶¶ 65I, 66F; "Sexual Harassment in Church and Society in the U.S.A."

Special Needs of Farm Workers

Calling for special attention is the situation of farm workers in the United States. Traditionally, they have been among the most poorly paid, housed, educated, and poorly served by health, welfare, and other social agencies. They have been systematically excluded from all, or nearly all, the benefits of social legislation.

Specifically, they have been and are excluded from unemployment insurance and workmen's compensation. Their coverage by social security, minimum wage, and child labor laws has come belatedly and is still inferior to that of most workers in industry. We support legislation designed to correct these injustices and to handle the strain within the labor market at the agricultural sector so that public interest is protected.

For over fifty years, the churches have sought to improve the lot of seasonal farm workers through the Migrant Ministry, an ecumenical program to which The United Methodist Church has given significant support. The Migrant Ministry sincerely sought to meet some of the most acute needs of these oppressed people.

In recent days, the churches have come to recognize that the most fundamental of all the needs of farm workers is the need for dignity, for self-determination, and for self-organization. Benefits won by any other route are at best second-rate.

At last, the ten-year struggle of the farm workers in California has led to a major legislative breakthrough that is designed to ensure seasonal and year-round farm workers an opportunity to vote in secret-ballot elections for the unions of their choice. The California Agricultural Labor Relation Act of 1975 provides a better framework for the working out of justice in the fields, but it does not guarantee that justice will finally prevail. Farm workers in other states are struggling also to bargain as equals with their employers. We call upon the Congress to enact legislation that enables farm workers to organize into unions of their own choosing.

We commit The United Methodist Church to support state legislation similar to the California law in other states when farm workers are pressing for such legislation.

The United Methodist Church will continue to press for better educational opportunity, housing, and welfare services, more adequate minimum wages, and full coverage by all social legislation designed for the protection of workers.

We also call upon the federal government to allocate more attention and resources to the task of retraining and adjustment for those farm workers who are being progressively displaced by mechanization of agricultural operations.

We urge all United Methodists to monitor situations where farm workers have won elections but have not been able to negotiate effective agreements, and to use their personal and institutional resources to encourage bargaining in good faith.

We urge the California legislature, without further delay, to appropriate the funds that would allow the provisions of the Farm Labor Act to be carried out.

We urge the support of Farm Workers Week with special bulletin inserts and the invitation by local churches and/or districts to workers to inform the people of the week and of the aspirations of these persons.

The United Methodist Church affirms in principle the position of the recently formed National Farm Worker Ministry (a continuation of the Migrant Ministry) that the Church's most significant role must be as advocate and supporter of the efforts of farm workers toward their own responsible self-organization and self-determination.

ADOPTED 1976

See Social Principles, ¶¶ 66N, 67F; "Economic Justice"; "An Affirmation of Basic Rural Worth"; "Emphasis of Concern for Workers."

Taxation Fairness

WHEREAS, it has been well documented beyond question that the United States Tax Code penalizes couples for being legally married; and

WHEREAS, under current tax law, many married couples pay significantly more in income taxes each year than they would have paid if they were single; and

WHEREAS, tax credits and other provisions to reduce the "Marriage Penalty" have been proposed on numerous occasions to the United States Congress; and

WHEREAS, United States Treasury officials have acknowledged that the marriage penalties greatly exceed $2 billion a year; and

WHEREAS, our society's very existence is dependent upon stable family environments; and

WHEREAS, The United Methodist Church has consistently supported holy and legal marriage as one of the bedrocks of our civilization;

Therefore, be it resolved, that we, the General Conference of The United Methodist Church, call upon all members of Congress to support the immediate elimination of any and all tax provisions that penalize legally married couples and cause their income tax obligation to be greater than it would be if they were filing as single individuals.

ADOPTED 1996

See Social Principles; ¶ 67, Introduction; "Economic Justice."

Tobacco Marketing by Philip Morris and RJR Nabisco

The United Methodist Church and its predecessor denominations have a long history of witness against the use and marketing of tobacco products. There is overwhelming evidence linking cigarette smoking with lung cancer, cardiovascular diseases, emphysema, chronic bronchitis, and related illnesses.

We are outraged by the use of marketing techniques aimed at children by leading cigarette manufacturers. Two specific companies using marketing strategies aimed at children are Philip Morris, which sells Marlboro cigarettes, and RJR Nabisco, which sells Camel cigarettes.

Therefore, as people of faith who believe our bodies are temples of the living God (1 Corinthians 6:13-20), we:

1. Direct the General Board of Church and Society to maintain and publish a current list of consumer products produced by Philip Morris

and RJR Nabisco so that United Methodists are made aware of their indirect support of the tobacco industry;

2. Commend the General Board of Pensions and Health Benefits for its long-standing exclusion of tobacco manufacturers from its investment portfolio and ask it to challenge public media in its portfolio not to carry advertisements and promotion of tobacco products;

3. Ask all United Methodist agencies and related institutions to take into account the Church's Social Principles and tobacco concerns and, specifically, to consider the role of Philip Morris and RJR Nabisco in tobacco marketing as a factor in any decision concerning purchasing food products manufactured by them;

4. Request the United Methodist Association of Health and Welfare Ministries, the General Board of Global Ministries, and the General Board of Higher Education and Ministry to communicate, interpret, and advocate for this concern with their affiliated institutions;

5. Ask all local churches and annual conferences to educate their membership about the tobacco industry's marketing tactics aimed at children. It is equally important we understand the connection between our purchasing food products and our indirect support of the tobacco industry;

6. Request the General Board of Church and Society to explore productive measures aimed at stopping tobacco companies from marketing cigarettes and other tobacco products to children and, if necessary, organize a boycott; and

7. Direct the General Board of Church and Society to communicate this resolution to the tobacco companies, serve as continuing advocate of the United Methodist position within The United Methodist Church and with the companies, and monitor the implementation of this resolution for report at the next General Conference.

ADOPTED 1996

See Social Principles, ¶ 66K; "Drug and Alcohol Concerns"; "Health and Wholeness"; "Investment Ethics."

Unemployment

I. Historic Commitments

"Historically, The United Methodist Church has been concerned with the moral issues involved with the social problem of unemployment" (opening sentence, 1976 General Conference statement on "Unemployment").

Three key statements from the Social Principles provide the basis for the Church's approach to this critical social concern:

1. "Every person has the right to a job at a living wage" (¶ 67C, "Work and Leisure").

2. "We recognize the responsibility of governments to develop and implement sound fiscal and monetary policies that provide for the economic life of individuals and corporate entities and that ensure full employment and adequate incomes with a minimum of inflation" (¶ 67, introductory paragraph, "The Economic Community").

3. "We believe private and public economic enterprises are responsible for the social costs of doing business, such as employment . . . , and that they should be held accountable for these costs" (¶ 67, "The Economic Community").

The 1976 General Conference adopted the most recent statement on "Unemployment" (as part of a comprehensive resolution on "Human Relations"), which built on the historic concern for translating these basic principles into "governmental policies . . . that would ensure full employment in order that workers may fully participate in society with dignity, so that families may be economically secure, and so that the nation may achieve coherent high priority goals" (from introductory paragraph, 1976 General Conference statement on "Unemployment").

This 1984 resolution reaffirms and updates these historic commitments of our denomination.

II. Present Situation

In the intervening years since 1976, however, little has been done to resolve the issue of unemployment. In 1984, unemployment rates still remain at about 7.8 percent, underemployment results in large numbers of families living under the poverty level, and increasing numbers of people have become discouraged and have dropped out of the labor force altogether.

Furthermore, the levels of unemployment among African Americans, Native Americans, Hispanics, and some other minorities have become a national disaster.

III. Call to Action

Once more it is necessary for the Church to remind itself and the nation of this unhappy and unjust situation and to recommend, as it did in 1976, certain specific policy actions that will help move society toward full-employment.

A. The General Conference of The United Methodist Church calls upon the local, state, and federal governments in the United States to:

1. Develop policies and programs that will help achieve full employment.

2. Cooperate with private business and labor to institute comprehensive job-training programs. (These programs must be devised to meet the special needs of minorities and women who bear a disproportionate share of unemployment and underemployment.)

3. Cooperate with private business and labor to create the jobs needed to secure employment for all who wish to work. (It is to be remembered that government has the right responsibility to invest in the public service sectors of transportation, health, education, and environment, all of which create many jobs. Some funds presently going to production of military weapons converted to these public service purposes could supply the needed investment funds.)

4. Cooperate with private business and labor to provide the unemployed workers with an income adequate to meet their families' needs.

B. The General Conference also calls upon the churches to:

1. Prepare the moral climate understanding that would enable the nation to discover the resolving unemployment, by: (a) educating its own constituencies and the general public about the causes, effects, and victims of unemployment and underemployment in the current and emerging American and global economy; (b) undergirding this educational effort with the biblical-theological basis of Christian responsibility for helping to resolve these issues; and (c) incorporating in this education an emphasis on a biblical and social ethical analysis of the interrelationships between unemployment and racism, sexism, classism, militarism, and other forms of social violence.

2. Provide *direct services* to address unmet needs for employment, food, clothing, shelter, health care, and emergency financial assistance; and for counseling and support groups to meet the personal and family, economic and spiritual needs of the victims of unemployment.

3. Support *community-based economic development ventures* that provide local job opportunities and the recycling of money within local communities.

4. Encourage and support *local, state, regional, and national coalitions* that constructively address private- and public-sector policies that relate to the issues of unemployment and underemployment, plant closings, economic dislocation, and other ancillary concerns.

ADOPTED 1984

See Social Principles, ¶ 67; "Economic Justice"; "Rights of Workers"; "National Incomes Policy"; "Emphasis of Concern for Workers."

THE POLITICAL COMMUNITY

Against Political Mudslinging

WHEREAS, the use of character assassination and the misrepresentation of another candidate's position and record is deceptive and manipulative, preying on our worst human qualities instead of building on our best; and

WHEREAS, instead of distorting the truth for political gain we should "speak the truth to our neighbors" (Ephesians 4:25), and the General Rules of The Methodist Church condemn "uncharitable or unprofitable conversation; particularly speaking evil of magistrates or of ministers";

Therefore, be it resolved, that The United Methodist Church call upon all candidates for public office to focus their campaigns on the issues and on their own qualifications to serve in office; that they refrain from personal attacks and name-calling of opponents; that they do not distort an opponent's views by taking quotes out of context or misrepresenting the opponent's positions or voting record; and that they set an example of truthfulness and integrity for the public.

Be it further resolved, that The United Methodist Church call upon all candidates for the office of President of the United States to lead the country in this style of campaigning by conducting their campaigns with honesty and respect.

Be it further resolved, that the General Conference write a letter communicating this concern to the President of the United States, both houses of Congress, and to all the national political parties.

ADOPTED 1996

See Social Principles, ¶ 68B; "A Call for Truth, Fairness, and Accuracy."

Assistance and Sanctuary for Central American Refugees

WHEREAS, at various times in history the Christian church has been called upon to give concrete evidence of its commitment to love and justice even when it seems contrary to public opinion; and

WHEREAS, according to the terms of the Refugee Act of 1980, the United States accords refugee or asylum status to persons who cannot return to their countries of origin because of persecution or fear of persecution, for reasons of race, religion, nationality, membership in a particular social group, or political opinion; and

WHEREAS, refugees from Central America and other areas of Latin America and the Caribbean are fleeing to the United States to escape the persecution, torture, and murder of their civil-war-torn homelands; and

WHEREAS, many of these refugees have been tortured and murdered when forced to return to their homelands; and

WHEREAS, Scripture says not to mistreat foreigners who live in your land (Leviticus 19:33) because sojourners and strangers have a special place in the heart of God.

Therefore, be it resolved, that The United Methodist Church strongly:

1. Urges the President of the United States, the Department of State and the Department of Justice, and the Congress to grant "extended voluntary departure" legal status to refugees from El Salvador and Guatemala, and other areas of the Caribbean and Latin America;

2. Requests that annual conferences and local churches assist in ministries to Central American, Caribbean, and other Latin American refugees by providing them with legal assistance, bail bond funds, food, housing, and medical care;

3. Encourages congregations who take seriously the mandate to do justice and to resist the policy of the Immigration and Naturalization Service by declaring their churches to be "sanctuaries" for refugees from El Salvador, Guatemala, and other areas of the Caribbean and Latin America; and

4. Urges the United States to follow the United Nations definition of refugees.

ADOPTED 1984

See Social Principles, ¶¶ 68A, 69A; "Immigrants and Refugees: To Love the Sojourner"; "Immigrants in the United States: Ministries of Hospitality, Advocacy, and Justice"; "Encounter with Christ in Latin America and the Caribbean"; "Opposition to Deportation of Salvadoran Refugees from the United States"; "God's Shalom for the People of Central America."

Bilingual Education

The United States is a country based on the contributions of different races, ethnic groups, languages, and traditions. The fabric of the U.S. society thus is a mosaic of diversity that has enriched its history and its common life as a nation.

Education has played a very important role in the development of this nation. To have access to it and to receive a sound education are considered inalienable rights of all children. Bilingual education has been and is a critical tool to ensure these rights for non-English-speaking children living now in this country. It has been an instrument of education for children to make the transition from their native tongues to English while at the same time staying at the level correspondent to their age.

WHEREAS, we believe that these values are part of the trust of this nation; and

WHEREAS, most educators have confirmed that non-English-speaking children will make the transition from their native tongues to English more easily within the context of a good bilingual program; and

WHEREAS, the growth of the non-English-speaking population continues to increase through immigration, and it is estimated to be even larger in the next few decades; and

WHEREAS, the percentage of Hispanic dropouts from school is one of the largest in the country, thus challenging the nation to provide resources for this segment of the population more effectively in both elementary and high schools; and

WHEREAS, projections of the future envision a larger demand in the fields of mathematics and sciences, precisely where women, Hispanics, African Americans, and Native Americans are currently almost non-present; and

WHEREAS, more intentional efforts must be made to bring children and youth from these groups to the same level of the rest of the student population;

Therefore, be it resolved, that the 1992 General Conference proclaim bilingual education to be an educational program needed for this country that must be not only perpetuated but also strengthened; and

Be it further resolved, that the General Conference affirm in writing to the President of the United States, the United States Congress, and the Department of Education that bilingual education is a right for all children and that by strengthening such a program the nation will in reality be laying the foundations for a better future in this land; and

Be it further resolved, to commend this resolution to all annual conferences for promotion and interpretation, and to ask the General Board of Church and Society to make this resolution an important item in its program and work agenda.

ADOPTED 1992

See Social Principles, ¶ 68D; "Protecting and Sustaining Children"; "Immigrants in the United States: Ministries of Hospitality, Advocacy, and Justice."

A Call for Increased Commitment to End World Hunger and Poverty

I. Introduction

At the Last Judgment, the question is asked, "Lord, when was it that we saw you hungry and gave you food?" (Matthew 25:37). The answer follows, "As you did it to one of the least of these my brethren, you did it to me" (Matthew 25:40). Saint Paul, interpreting the new ethic of the Kingdom, instructed the early church to satisfy the hunger and thirst of enemies (Romans 12:20).

From the earliest times, the Christian community, in response to these teachings, has expressed compassion and care for those in need. In recent years, this has been expressed in the giving of millions of dollars for direct food distribution. More systemically, the church has deployed agricultural missionaries, supported demonstration farming and development programs, challenged unjust social and economic systems that condemn people to poverty, and witnessed for just public food policies at state and federal levels.

Scant progress has been made in meeting the food needs of the hungry on a continuing basis. Too often, the attention span of church leaders and those who follow is curtailed by institutional interests and program fads. Our involvement as the owners of lands and buildings, our identification with social, economic, and political establishments, and our approval of those values which limit productive and distributive justice work together to limit our ministries to "the least of these."

II. Analysis of Current Situation

Despite marked increases in food production throughout the world, poverty and subsequent hunger is increasing. Most of the world's underfed teenagers and most of the underfed mothers and fathers of hungry children help to grow and harvest the world's food supply. For example, men and women on the farms of Asia, Africa, and Latin America produce more than half of the world's supply of "coarse grains" such as maize, sorghum, and millet. Yet in the countries of Africa and Asia 80–90 percent and in Latin America 50 percent of the populations, representing a total of at least half a billion people, are at constant risk of hunger. The food missing from the daily lives of these people amounts to a very small part of the world's annual harvest. Nevertheless, they face hunger day after day, year after year. Unfortunately, many of the circumstances contributing to their hunger and the hunger of people worldwide are beyond their control and will remain so until the systems underlying those circumstances change.

Hunger is growing even in the United States. Since the early 1970s, the income gaps between rich and poor families have widened significantly. In 1988, the richest fifth of all families in the United States received 44 percent of the national family income, while the poorest fifth of families received 4.6 percent. Among those most likely to be poor in the United States are racial- and ethnic-minority families headed by single women, children, the elderly, and groups within geographic areas such as Appalachia and the Southwest border.[1] Economic changes in agriculture in the United States, particularly in continuing loss of family farm and the related rural crisis, have had a devastating effect. The rural U.S. poverty rate has increased even faster than that of urban centers.[2]

III. Causes of the World Food Crisis

Since 1980, the portion of the earth's population that is chronically malnourished (70 percent fewer calories than necessary for health) has grown from one ninth to one sixth. This has both precipitating causes and much deeper systemic causes.

A. *Precipitating Causes.* Among the many precipitating causes, these stand out: the weather, political decisions, war, economic problems, and

---

[1] Center on Budget and Policy Priorities, Washington, D.C.; April 1990.
[2] For a longer discussion, *see* "U.S. Agriculture and Rural Communities in Crisis."

wasteful consumerism. Hunger cannot be dissociated from systems that keep people in poverty, and therefore powerless. Politics draws the line between poverty and power. Poverty controls lives because it entails housing, water, heat, and other necessities of life. Working to alleviate the causes of hunger requires working against poverty. It also entails organizing the poor and building economic justice coalitions that can change or transform the power arrangements.

B. *Systemic Causes.* Beyond the immediate causes of malnourishment lie more fundamental structural constraints, of which hunger and poverty are but symptoms.

1. *Unjust economic systems, a legacy of colonialism.* Almost without exception, the poor countries were at one time colonies of imperial powers. Colonialism developed them primarily for the export of raw materials, mainly mining products and agricultural crops (coffee, tea, sugar, rubber, cocoa, and so forth). To achieve this, the colonial powers restructured traditional social and legal customs, land distribution and tenure, food production, political power, regional and international economic relations, and the economy. The colonial system depended upon depressed wages and local elites.

2. *Maldistribution of wealth.* Corrupt practices of entrenched politicians and neocolonial governments favor monopolistic policies of privileged families and corporations.

3. *Policies of lending institutions.* The stiff policies and conditions imposed on undeveloped and underdeveloped nations by lending institutions, such as the World Bank (IBRD) and the International Monetary Fund (IMF), have resulted, in many cases, as in the Philippines, in unjustly favoring the interest of the privileged few and further aggravating and perpetuating the sad state and the ill effects of poverty and dehumanization of peoples in weak and defenseless nations.

These lending practices are also widespread in disadvantaged communities in developed nations.

4. *Insufficient food production in developing nations.* A principal result from colonial policies has been the insufficient development of food production in many lower-income countries. This distortion occurs through market forces and tax policies that encourage the cultivation of a single crop for export rather than the balanced production of food for domestic use.

5. *Population growth.* Rapid population growth and inadequate food supply have a common origin and a joint explanation. They both are symptoms of structural poverty—those economic and political frame-

works in which poor people exist. The experience is worldwide. Wherever poverty gives way to a rising standard of living, the birth rate declines. Wherever the security of the family increases, the birth rate declines. Such family security depends on social and economic development, which is based on the values of justice and shared power.

6. *Maldevelopment in the rich nations.* While inadequate and unbalanced development exists in the low-income countries, acute maldevelopment exists in the rich nations. This maldevelopment is characterized by militarism, waste of resources by the production of unnecessary goods and services, degradation of the environment, increasing structural unemployment, institutionalized consumerism, persistence of poverty, rising nationalism, and a crisis in values felt especially in the lives of the young.

In 1980, the rich nations with 24 percent of the earth's population consumed 79 percent of the world's goods and services, leaving 21 percent for the developing nations with 76 percent of the population. In public health expenditures, the rich nations consumed 92 percent of the goods and services; the developing nations received 8 percent. Without significant change, the structural distortions will continue their toll on the human family.

IV. Theological Bases for Hope

As Christians, the central question we must ask ourselves in this situation is: What does God require and enable us individually and corporately to do? Some of our central affirmations of faith provide at least a partial answer.

God is Creator of all and loves and cares for all creation. Because every person is a creature loved of God, every person has a basic human right to food, a necessity for survival. Because all persons are creatures of God, equally subject to God's grace and claim, all are bound together in inseparable ties of solidarity. It is the task of God's people to show solidarity in support of adequate provision for basic human needs such as food.

In the incarnation, life, death, and resurrection of Jesus Christ, the promise and first fruits of redemption have been brought to our sinful and selfish humanity. Jesus' own concern for human need in his ministry is a model for the church's concern. His opposition to those who would ignore the needs of the neighbor make clear that we grossly misunderstand and fail to grasp God's grace if we imagine that God overlooks, condones, or easily tolerates our indifference to the plight of our neighbors, our greed and selfishness, or our systems of injustice and oppression.

As Holy Spirit, God is at work in history today, refashioning lives, tearing down unjust structures, restoring community, engendering faith, hope, and love. It is the work of the Holy Spirit that impels us to take action even when perfect solutions are not apparent. Thus, we engage in the struggle for bread and justice for all in the confidence that God goes before us and that God's cause will prevail.

V. Goals for Action by Christians

In faithfulness to our understanding of God's good intentions for all peoples, we can set for ourselves no lesser goals than repentance for the existence of human hunger and an increased commitment to end world hunger and poverty. Movement toward that ultimate goal of the abolition of hunger from the earth requires commitment to such immediate and instrumental goals as the following:

A. The transformation of persons and institutions such as the World Bank and the International Monetary Fund, which create and perpetuate strongholds of power and privilege for some at the expense of many, into new personal, social, economic, and political environments that are committed to ending hunger and poverty, and which are more conducive to justice, liberation, self-development, a stabilized population, and a sustainable environment.

B. The simplification of urgently needed "interim" measures and long-term distributive systems that, recognizing the unique status of food as a commodity essential for survival, assure to every human being access to food as a matter of right and recognizing that the self-reliant agriculture must be a part of ending hunger and poverty.

VI. Conclusion

1. We call upon all nations, but particularly the developed nations, to examine those values, attitudes, and institutions that are the basic causes of poverty and underdevelopment, the primary sources of world and domestic hunger.

2. We call for The United Methodist Church to engage in an educational effort that would provide information about the scale of world and domestic hunger and its causes, and to engage in study and effort

to integrate the Church's missional programs into a coherent policy with respect to a just, sustainable, and participatory development.

3. We specifically call upon each local church, cooperative parish, district, and conference to increase sharing resources through support of church and community agencies dedicated to eliminating hunger and poverty at home and abroad.

4. We call for The United Methodist Church through its appropriate agencies to develop effective public policy strategies that would enable Church members to participate in efforts to:

(a) Decrease mother/child mortality;

(b) Promote environmental justice and sustainable practices for using and restoring natural resources;

(c) Provide safe drinking water and sustainable water-management systems;

(d) Support community organizing to effect change in systems that keep people poor and powerless;

(e) Organize and work to retain programs such as Women, Infants, and Children (WIC), food stamps, and food co-ops;

(f) Develop and implement agricultural policies that increase food production on family farms, provide just wages and working conditions for farm workers, and provide incentives for farmers to produce crops using appropriate technology with equitable access to land by all;

(g) Become advocates for reduction of military spending and reallocation of resources to programs that provide human services, convert military facilities to provide for civilian needs, and protect and restore the environment (see 1988 Book of Resolutions, "Economic Justice," item E; page 336);

(h) Become advocates of trade policies that alleviate economic disparities between rich and poor countries while protecting labor and human rights; environmental, health, and safety standards; and respecting the need for agricultural and food security;

(i) Protect craftspeople and artisans from exploitative trade practices; and

(j) Support community-based economic development that provides jobs; recycles money within communities; provides low-cost, high-quality services to meet basic human needs; and combats unemployment and underemployment.

ADOPTED 1992

See Social Principles, ¶¶ 67E, 68A; "Call for a Rebirth of Compassion"; "Human Rights"; "God's Vision of Abundant Living."

Campaign Finance Reform in the United States

In the U.S.A., the pouring of tens of millions of dollars into political campaigns in order to buy special influence with legislators has become a national scandal. Citizens forsake participation in the political process because they believe policies are shaped by money from special interests—not by the national interest or the needs of the people.

The issue of campaign financing is far more than a political matter. It goes to the heart of the ethical and moral life of our nation.

The present system compels most members of Congress to continually court monied special interests in order to finance their next election campaign. It is time to free Congress from this corrupting pressure—through a system of public campaign financing that would take government away from special interests and return it to the people.

If the members of Congress are to focus on the well-being of the people and the nation, they must be able to depend on public financing rather than pursuing special-interest money.

We commend those politicians of both parties who are working to achieve real campaign financing reform.

We call upon all United Methodists who are citizens of the U.S.A. to work within their own states to build support for measures that would end the flood of special-interest monies to political campaigns and restore integrity to decision-making in Congress.

ADOPTED 1996

See Social Principles, ¶ 68A, B; "Church-Government Relations."

Capital Punishment

In spite of a common assumption to the contrary, "an eye for an eye and a tooth for a tooth" does not give justification for the imposing of the penalty of death. Jesus explicitly repudiated the *lex tallionis* (Matthew 5:38-39), and the Talmud denies its literal meaning and holds that it refers to financial indemnities.

When a woman was brought before Jesus having committed a crime for which the death penalty was commonly imposed, our Lord so persisted in questioning the moral authority of those who were ready to conduct the execution that they finally dismissed the charges (John 8:31 f.).

The Social Principles of The United Methodist Church condemn the "torture of persons by governments for any purpose" and assert that it violates Christian teachings. The Church, through its Social Principles, further declares, "We oppose capital punishment and urge its elimination from all criminal codes."

After a moratorium of a full decade, the use of the death penalty in the United States has resumed. Other Western nations have largely abolished it during the twentieth century. But a rapidly rising rate of crime and an even greater increase in the fear of crime has generated support within the American society for the institution of death as the punishment for certain forms of homicide. It is now being asserted, as it was often in the past, that capital punishment would deter criminals and would protect law-abiding citizens.

The United States Supreme Court, in *Gregg* v. *Georgia,* in permitting use of the death penalty, conceded the lack of evidence that it reduced violent crime, but permitted its use for purpose of sheer retribution.

The United Methodist Church cannot accept retribution or social vengeance as a reason for taking human life. It violates our deepest belief in God as the Creator and the Redeemer of humankind. In this respect, there can be no assertion that human life can be taken humanely by the state. Indeed, in the long run, the use of the death penalty by the state will increase the acceptance of revenge in our society and will give official sanction to a climate of violence.

The United Methodist Church is deeply concerned about the present high rate of crime in the United States and about the value of a life taken in murder or homicide. When another life is taken through capital punishment, the life of the victim is further devalued. Moreover, the Church is convinced that the use of the death penalty would result in neither a net reduction of crime in general nor a lessening of the particular kinds of crime against which it was directed. Homicide—the crime for which the death penalty has been used almost exclusively in recent decades—increased far less than other major crimes during the period of the moratorium. Progressively rigorous scientific studies, conducted over more than forty years, overwhelmingly failed to support the thesis that capital punishment deters homicide more effectively than does imprisonment. The most careful comparisons of homicide rates in similar states with and without use of the death penalty, and also of homicide rates in the same state in periods with and without it, have found as many or slightly more criminal homicides in states with use of the death penalty.

The death penalty also falls unfairly and unequally upon an outcast minority. Recent methods for selecting the few persons sentenced to die from among the larger number who are convicted of comparable offenses have not cured the arbitrariness and discrimination that have historically marked the administration of capital punishment in this country.

The United Methodist Church is convinced that the nation's leaders should give attention to the improvement of the total criminal justice system and to the elimination of social conditions that breed crime and cause disorder, rather than foster a false confidence in the effectiveness of the death penalty.

The United Methodist Church declares its opposition to the retention and use of capital punishment in any form or carried out by any means; the Church urges the abolition of capital punishment.

ADOPTED 1980

See Social Principles, ¶ 68F; "Criminal Justice."

Certification of Conscientious Objectors

The United Methodist Church today nurtures a substantial number of conscientious objectors among its members. Since 1936, The United Methodist Church or one of its predecessors has provided to those of its members who claim to be conscientious objectors the opportunity to register. Certified copies of such registration are supplied for use with the draft authorities.

We support this procedure and propose that The United Methodist Church further develop a churchwide process that certifies the decision of its members who seek to be identified as conscientious objectors. That process should be created by the General Board of Church and Society in cooperation with the General Board of Discipleship.

The process may begin in the local church, where the pastor, in cooperation with the pastor-parish relations committee and the council on ministries, could select a person or committee to implement the process developed by the general agencies.

The United Methodist theological statements, Social Principles, and historic statements on war, peace, and conscription should be primary points of reference. It is the responsibility of the Church at all levels to inform its members of the fact that conscientious objection, as well as conscientious participation, is a valid option for Christians and is recognized in many countries as a legal alternative for persons liable to military conscription.

The local committee's action does not express agreement or disagreement with the convictions of the applicant member. Rather, the committee's task is to record which of the church's members are opposed to participation in military service on grounds of conscience and to assist them in securing proper counsel. When a member has registered and his or her registration has been certified to the proper authorities, that action should be recorded with the conference and General Board of Church and Society.

ADOPTED 1980

See Social Principles, ¶ 68G; "The United Methodist Church and Peace"; "Support Conscientious Objectors to Registration."

Church-Government Relations

Introduction

In response to a question about paying taxes, Jesus said: "Render to Caesar the things that are Caesar's, and to God the things that are God's" (Luke 20:25). Although this statement refers specifically to taxation, its apparent implications are that there are separate obligations and responsibilities to government and to religion.

The Social Principles of The United Methodist Church assert: "We believe that the state should not attempt to control the church, nor should the church seek to dominate the state. 'Separation of church and state' means no organic union of the two, but it does permit interaction. The church should continually exert a strong ethical influence upon the state, supporting policies and programs deemed to be just and opposing policies and programs that are unjust" (¶ 68B).

As we consider the religious protections of the First Amendment—the free exercise and nonestablishment of religion—we are profoundly grateful for the major statement made by the 1968 General Conference on "Church/Government Relations." In recognizing that debt, we reaffirm much of the substance of that declaration prepared by two distinguished committees under the authority of the General Conference and operating over two quadrenniums of the life of the Church.

A Statement Concerning Church-Government Relations and Education

1

The fundamental purpose of universal public education at the elementary and secondary levels is to provide equal and adequate educational opportunities for all children and young people, and thereby ensure the nation an enlightened citizenry.

We believe in the principle of universal public education, and we reaffirm our support of public educational institutions. At the same time, we recognize and pledge our continued allegiance to the U.S. constitutional principle that citizens have a right to establish and maintain private schools from private resources so long as such schools meet public standards of quality. Such schools have made a genuine contribution to society. We do not support the expansion or the strengthening of private schools with public funds. Furthermore, we oppose the establishment or strengthening of private schools that jeopardize the public school system or thwart valid public policy.

We specifically oppose tuition tax credits or any other mechanism that directly or indirectly allows government funds to support religious schools at the primary and secondary level. Persons of one particular faith should be free to use their own funds to strengthen the belief system of their particular religious group. But they should not expect all taxpayers, including those who adhere to other religious belief systems, to provide funds to teach religious views with which they do not agree.

To fulfill the government's responsibility in education, sometimes it and nonpublic educational institutions need to enter a cooperative relationship. But public funds should be used only in the best interests of the whole society. Extreme caution must be exercised to ensure that religious institutions do not receive any aid directly or indirectly for the maintenance of their religious expression or the expansion of their institutional resources. Such funds must be used for the express purpose of fulfilling a strictly public responsibility, subject to public accountability.

Public schools have often been an important unifying force in modern pluralistic society by providing a setting for contact at an early age between children of vastly different backgrounds. We recognize in particular that persons of all religious backgrounds may have insight into the nature of ultimate reality, which will help to enrich the common life. It is therefore essential that the public schools take seriously the religious integrity of each child entrusted to their care. Public schools may not properly establish any preferred form of religion for common exercises of worship, religious observance, or study. At the same time, however, education should provide an opportunity for the examination of the various religious traditions of humankind.

2

We believe that every person has a right to an education, including higher education, commensurate with his or her ability. It is society's responsibility to enable every person to enjoy this right. Public and private institutions should cooperate to provide for these educational opportunities.

3

Freedom of inquiry poses a risk for established ideas, beliefs, programs, and institutions. We accept that risk in the faith that all truth is of God. Colleges and universities can best perform their vital tasks of adding to knowledge and to the perception of truth in an atmosphere of genuine academic freedom.

We affirm the principle that freedom to inquire, to discuss, and to teach should be regulated by the self-discipline of scholarship and the critical examination of ideas in the context of free public dialogue, rather than by supervision, censorship, or any control imposed by churches, governments, or other organizations. In the educational process, individuals have the right to appropriate freely for themselves what they believe is real, important, useful, and satisfying.

4

Experience has demonstrated that freedom to inquire, to discuss, and to teach is best preserved when colleges and universities are not dependent upon a single base or a few sources of support. When an educational institution relies upon multiple sources of financial support, and where those sources tend to balance one another, the institution is in a position to resist undue pressures toward control exerted from any one source of support. In the case of church-related colleges and universities, we believe that tuitions; scholarships; investment return; bequests; payments for services rendered; loans; government grants; and gifts from individuals, business corporations, foundations, and churches should be sought and accepted in as great a variety as possible. Care must be exercised to ensure that all support from any of these sources is free from conditions that hinder the college or university in the maintenance of freedom of inquiry and expression for its faculty and students.

We are very much aware of the dangers of church-sponsored colleges and universities being overly dependent upon government funding. However, we are also aware that given the independent thought of most college students today, there is little danger of using government funds to indoctrinate students with religious beliefs. Therefore, institutions of higher learning should feel free to receive government funds (except for religious teaching and structures for worship). At the same time, they should be eternally cognizant of the dangers of accompanying government oversight that might threaten the religious atmosphere or special independent character of church-sponsored educational institutions.

No church-sponsored higher education institution should become so dependent upon government grants, research projects, or support programs, that its academic freedom is jeopardized, its responsibility for social criticism (including criticism of governments) inhibited, or its spiritual values denied.

We recognize that the freedom necessary to the existence of a college or university in the classical sense may be threatened by forces other than those involved in the nature and source of the institution's financial support. Institutional freedom may be adversely affected by governmental requirements of loyalty oaths from teachers and students, by public interference with the free flow of information, or by accreditation and certification procedures and requirements aimed at dictating the content of college and university curricula.

With respect to church-related institutions of higher education, we deplore any ecclesiastical attempts to manipulate inquiry or the dissemination of knowledge, to use the academic community for the promotion of any particular point of view, to require ecclesiastical "loyalty oaths" designed to protect cherished truth claims, or to inhibit the social action activities of members of the academic community. We call upon all members of The United Methodist Church, in whatever capacity they may serve, to be especially sensitive to the need to protect individual and institutional freedom and responsibility in the context of the academic community.

5

We are persuaded that there may be circumstances or conditions in which the traditional forms of tax immunities granted to colleges and universities may be a necessary requirement for their freedom. Therefore, we urge a continuation of the public policy of granting reasonable and nondiscriminatory tax immunities to all private colleges and universities, including those that are related to churches.

We believe that colleges and universities should consider the benefits, services, and protections that they receive from the community and its governmental agencies and should examine their obligations to the community in the light of this support. We believe it is imperative that all church-related institutions of higher education determine on their own initiative what benefits, services, and opportunities they ought to provide for the community as a whole, as distinct from their usual campus constituencies.

A Statement Concerning Church-Government Relations and Governmental Chaplaincies

1

We recognize that military and public institutional chaplaincies represent efforts to provide for the religious needs of people for whom both churches and governments are responsible. We recognize that in such a broad and complex undertaking there are bound to exist real and serious tensions that produce genuine uneasiness on the part of government officials as well as church leaders. Great patience and skill are required to effect necessary accommodations with understanding and without compromising religious liberty.

2

We believe that there are both ethical and constitutional standards that must be observed by governments in the establishment and operation of public chaplaincies. At a minimum, those standards are as follows:

First, the only obligation that governments have is to ensure the provision of opportunities for military personnel, patients of hospitals, and inmates of correctional institutions to engage in religious worship or have access to religious nurture.

Second, participation in religious activities must be on a purely voluntary basis; there must be neither penalties for nonparticipation nor any rewards for participation.

Third, no preferential treatment should be given any particular church, denomination, or religious group in the establishment and administration of governmental chaplaincies.

Fourth, considerable care should be exercised in the role assignments of chaplains so they are not identified as the enforcers of morals. Precaution should also be taken to avoid chaplains' being given duties not clearly related to their primary tasks.

Standards should be maintained to protect the integrity of both churches and governments. The practice of staffing governmental chaplaincies with clergy personnel who have ecclesiastical endorsement should be continued. The practice of terminating the services of such personnel in any instance where it becomes necessary for ecclesiastical endorsement to be withdrawn should also be continued. Supervision of clergy personnel in the performance of their religious services in governmental chaplaincies should be clearly effected through ecclesiastical channels with the cooperation of the public agencies and institutions involved. In the performance of these administrative functions, churches and agencies of government have an obligation to be fair and responsible and to ensure that due process is observed in all proceedings.

3

The role of a governmental chaplain should be primarily pastoral but with important priestly, prophetic, and teaching roles. The chaplain has an obligation to perform these ministries in as broad an ecumenical context as possible. A chaplain is responsible for the spiritual welfare and religious life of all the personnel of the military unit or the public institution to which he or she is assigned.

There are many persons, and some groups, whose personal religious practices or whose church's rules make it impossible for them to accept the direct ministry of a particular chaplain. In such instances, the chaplain, to the full extent of his or her powers, has an obligation to make provision for worship by these persons or groups. A chaplain is expected to answer specific questions by members of faith groups other than his or her own. Chaplains must know the basic tenets of their denominations in order to protect such members in the expression and development of their faith. The absence of parochialism on the part of a chaplain is more than an attitude; it necessitates specific, detailed, and accurate knowledge regarding many religions.

4

The churches should strive to make public chaplaincies integral expressions of their ministry and to face the implications of this for supervision and budget. The chaplain represents the church by affirming the dignity of all persons in military service through the chaplain's function in upholding their freedom of religion and conscience. Every person exists within a broader set of values than those of the military, and within a broader spectrum of responsibilities than those created by military orders. The chaplain is a bearer of the gospel to affirm the freedom of the individual and represents The United Methodist Church at that point of tension. Whether the freedom of the gospel is compromised or limited may be a result of either external pressures or internal submission, or both. Failure to sustain the freedom of the gospel lies within any human system or any individual. It is the task of the Church to confront prophetically institutions or chaplains who compromise the gospel. The United Methodist Church provides presence, oversight, and support to chaplains who risk ministry in such a setting.

There are degrees of tension in present arrangements whereby a chaplain is a commissioned officer of the armed forces or an employee of a public institution. As such, he or she is a member of the staff of the military commander or of the director of the public institution involved. Government regulations and manuals describe him or her as "the advisor on religion, morals, morale, and welfare." Therefore, we believe it is the chaplain's duty in faithfulness to his or her religious commitments to act in accordance with his or her conscience and to make such viewpoints known in organizational matters affecting the total welfare of the people for whom the chaplain has any responsibility. The chaplain has the obligation and should have the opportunity to express his or her dissent within the structures in which the chaplain works, in instances where he or she feels this is necessary. With respect to such matters, it is the obligation of religious bodies to give the chaplain full support.

Churches must encourage chaplains who serve in the armed forces to resist the exaltation of power and its exercise for its own sake. They must also encourage chaplains who serve in public institutions to maintain sensitivity to human anguish. Churches and chaplains have an obligation to speak out conscientiously against the unforgiving and intransigent spirit in people and nations wherever and whenever it appears.

A Statement Concerning Church-Government Relations and Tax Exemption

1

We believe that governments recognize that unique category of religious institutions. To be in this unique category is not a privilege held by these institutions for their own benefit or self-glorification but is an acknowledgment of their special identity designed to protect their independence and to enable them to serve humankind in a way not expected of other types of institutions.

2

We urge churches to consider at least the following factors in determining their response to the granting of immunity from property taxes:

1. Responsibility to make appropriate contributions for essential services provided by government; and

2. The danger that churches become so dependent upon government that they compromise their integrity or fail to exert their critical influence upon public policy.

3

We support the abolition of all special privileges accorded to members of the clergy in U.S. tax laws and regulations and call upon the churches to deal with the consequent financial implications for their ministers. Conversely, we believe that all forms of discrimination against members of the clergy in U.S. tax legislation and administrative regulations should be discontinued. We believe that the status of an individual under ecclesiastical law or practice ought not to be the basis of governmental action either granting or withholding a special tax benefit.

A Statement Concerning Church Participation in Public Affairs

1

We recognize that churches exist within the body politic, along with numerous other forms of human association. Like other social groups, their existence affects, and is affected by, governments. We believe that churches have the right and the duty to speak and act corporately on those matters of public policy that involve basic moral or ethical issues and questions. Any concept of, or action regarding, church-government relations that denies churches this role in the body politic strikes at the very core of religious liberty.

The attempt to influence the formation and execution of public policy at all levels of government is often the most effective means available to churches to keep before humanity the ideal of a society in which power and order are made to serve the ends of justice and freedom for all people. Through such social action churches generate new ideas, challenge certain goals and methods, and help rearrange the emphasis on particular values in ways that facilitate the adoption and implementation of specific policies and programs that promote the goals of a responsible society.

We believe that any action that would deny the church the right to act corporately on public policy matters threatens religious liberty. We therefore oppose inclusion of churches in any lobby disclosure legislation.

This does not mean, in any way, that we wish to hide actions taken by the Church on public issues. On the contrary, we are usually proud of such actions. It does recognize, however, that the Church is already responding to members who request information with respect to Church action on public policy questions. In effect, in accordance with legislation enacted by the 1976 General Conference, The United Methodist Church already has its own lobby disclosure provisions in place.

It is quite another matter, however, for the government to insist that it must know everything about what a church is saying in its private communications with its own members.

When the U.S. Supreme Court acted in the 1971 landmark case of *Lemon* v. *Kartzman* (403 U.S. 602, 612–13), the Court applied a test to determine the constitutionality of legislation on First Amendment grounds as it deals with religion. Among its three criteria were these two: (1) its principle or primary effect must neither advance nor inhibit religion; (2) the statute must not foster an excessive government entanglement with religion.

Lobby disclosure legislation before the U.S. Congress over the last several years has required: (1) extremely burdensome recordkeeping and reporting of all legislative activity; (2) reporting of contributions of churches giving $3,000 or more annually to a national body if a part of this is used for legislative action; (3) criminal penalties with up to two years in jail for violations; and (4) unwarranted subpoena powers to investigate church records.

Legislation that passed the House in 1978 would have required detailed records of expenditures of twenty-two items. As such, it would have been burdensome and would "inhibit religion" in that The United Methodist Church would have been severely handicapped in implementing its Social Principles due to being neutralized by minutia.

Furthermore, if the government insists on knowing everything the church is doing on public policy questions over a five-year period (as was required) and imposes a criminal sentence for violations, this could "inhibit religion" to the extent that the church might be tempted to limit severely its activity to avoid noncompliance.

If the government is going to require that religious groups keep burdensome records and make voluminous reports, and there is some question as to whether the churches are complying, federal authorities would be authorized to step in and check church records and files. Such action would undoubtedly represent an unconstitutional "excessive government entanglement with religion."

The United Methodist Church would have great difficulty in complying with the provision that all organizational contributions of $3,000 annually be reported if some of these funds are used for lobbying. Since local churches contribute generously to the World Service Dollar, and a small portion of those funds are used for legislative action, this brings our Church under coverage of this provision. Such a requirement could mean that reports of contributions of some 30,000 United Methodist churches would have to be made to the government shortly after the close of each year. This could not be done, and we would be in violation, having "knowingly" omitted material facts "required to be disclosed." As a result, Church officials would be subject to criminal penalties of up to two years in prison.

For these reasons, we oppose lobby disclosure measures for the churches. In its most stringent form, this legislation would inhibit our free exercise of religion. It would be impossible for the Church to comply with certain provisions, thus subjecting our Church leaders to criminal penalties.

2

We believe that churches must behave responsibly in the arena of public affairs. Responsible behavior requires adherence to ethically sound substantive and procedural norms.

We live in a pluralistic society. In such a society, churches should not seek to use the authority of government to make the whole community conform to their particular moral codes. Rather, churches should seek to enlarge and clarify the ethical grounds of public discourse and to identify and define the foreseeable consequences of available choices of public policy.

In participating in the arena of public affairs, churches are not inherently superior to other participants, hence the stands that they take on particular issues of public policy are not above question or criticism.

Responsible behavior in the arena of public affairs requires churches to accept the fact that in dealing with complex issues of public policy, good intentions and high ideals need to be combined with as much practical and technical knowledge of politics and economics as possible.

Another norm of responsible behavior derives from the fact that no particular public policy that may be endorsed by churches at a given point in time should be regarded as an ultimate expression of Christian ethics in society. Churches should not assume that any particular social pattern, political order, or economic ideology represents a complete embodiment of the Christian ethic.

When churches speak to government, they also bear the responsibility to speak to their own memberships. Cultivation of ethically informed public opinion is particularly crucial in local congregations. It is essential to responsible behavior that procedures be established and maintained to ensure full, frank, and informed discussion by religious groups within the arena of public affairs. In the present period of human history, attention should be given to the dignity of every person, and appeal should be made to the consciences of all persons of good will. Churches must acknowledge and respect the role of the laity as well as the clergy in determining their behavior in the arena of public affairs.

Because of their commitment to unity, and in the interest of an effective strategy, churches should, to the maximum extent feasible, coordinate their own efforts and, where appropriate, cooperate with other organizations when they seek to influence properly the formation and execution of public policy at all levels of government.

Finally, churches should not seek to utilize the processes of public affairs to further their own institutional interests or to obtain special privileges for themselves.

3

United Methodism is a part of the universal church. In the formulation and expression of the United Methodist voice in public affairs, we must listen to the concerns and insights of church members and churches in all nations. It is imperative that our expressions and actions be informed by participation in the universal church.

4

With particular reference to The United Methodist Church and public affairs, we express the following convictions: Connectional units of the denomination (such as General Conference, jurisdictional conference, annual conference, local congregation, or general board or agency) should continue to exercise the right to advocate government policies that involve basic moral or ethical issues or questions. In exercising this right, each such connectional unit, or any other official group within The United Methodist Church, should always make explicit for whom or in whose name it speaks or acts in the arena of public affairs. Only the General Conference is competent to speak or act in the name of The United Methodist Church.

ADOPTED 1980

See Social Principles, ¶ 68; "The United Methodist Church and Church-Government Relations"; "Religious Liberty"; "Separation of Church and State."

The United Methodist Church and Church-Government Relations

A Statement Concerning Church-Government Relations and Social Welfare

1

The United Methodist Church is concerned about the health and well-being of all persons because it recognizes that physical health and social well-being are necessary preconditions to the complete fulfillment of man's personal and social possibilities in this world. Our Master himself cared for the sick and fed the multitudes in recognition that man's physical well-being cannot be divorced from his spiritual health.

Service to persons in need, along with social education and action to eliminate forces and structures that create or perpetuate conditions of need, is integral to the life and witness of Christians, both as individuals and as churches. However, there are no fixed institutional patterns for the rendering of such service. It may be rendered effectively as a Christian vocation or avocation, and through the channels of either a governmental or a private agency.

We recognize that churches are not the only institutions exercising a critical and prophetic role in the community and in society. They share that responsibility with many other institutions and agencies in such fields as law, education, social work, medicine, and the sciences. Yet churches cannot escape their special obligation to nurture and encourage a critical and prophetic quality in their own institutional life. That quality should be expressed also through their members—as they act as citizens, trustees of agencies, and persons with professional skills. It should be understood that the performance of such roles by church members will often involve them in revaluing the norms avowed by churches as well as using such norms as a basis for judgment.

2

We recognize that governments at all levels in the United States have increasingly assumed responsibility for the performance of social welfare functions. There is reason to believe that this trend will continue and, perhaps, be accelerated. We assume that governments will continue to use private nonprofit agencies as instrumentalities for the implementation of publicly formulated social welfare policies. This means that private agencies will continue to face unprecedented demand for their services and have unprecedented access to government resources.

It is now evident that a variety of contributions is required to achieve a comprehensive social welfare policy for the nation, for the states, and for each community. Such a policy includes identification of the range of human needs, transformation of needs into effective demands, and development of programs to meet those demands. We believe that all the organizations and resources of the private sector, as well as those of governments, should be taken into account in the formulation and execution of social welfare policies.

We recognize that appropriate government bodies have the right to prescribe minimum standards for all private social welfare agencies. We believe that no private agency, because of its religious affiliations, ought to be exempted from any of the requirements of such standards.

3

Governmental provision of material support for church-related agencies inevitably raises important questions of religious establishment. In recognition, however, that some health, education, and welfare agencies have been founded by churches without regard to religious proselytizing, we consider that such agencies may, under certain circumstances, be proper channels for public programs in these fields. When government provides support for programs administered by private agencies, it has the most serious obligation to establish and enforce standards guaranteeing the equitable administration of such programs and the accountability of such agencies to the public authority. In particular, we believe that no government resources should be provided to any church-related agency for such purposes unless:

1. The services to be provided by the agency shall meet a genuine community need;

2. The services of the agency shall be designed and administered in such a way as to avoid serving a sectarian purpose or interest;

3. The services to be provided by the agency shall be available to all persons without regard to race, color, national origin, creed, or political persuasion;

4. The services to be rendered by the agency shall be performed in accordance with accepted professional and administrative standards;

5. Skill, competence, and integrity in the performance of duties shall be the principal considerations in the employment of personnel and shall not be superseded by any requirement of religious affiliation;

6. The right to collective bargaining shall be recognized by the agency.

4

We recognize that all of the values involved in the sponsorship of a social welfare agency by a church may not be fully expressed if that agency has to rely permanently on access to government resources for its existence. We are also aware that under certain circumstances sponsorship of a social welfare agency by a church may inhibit the development of comprehensive welfare services in the community. Therefore, the church and the agency should choose which pattern of service to offer: (1) channeling standardized and conventional services supplied or supported by government, or (2) attempting experimental or unconventional ministries and criticizing government programs when they prove inadequate. We believe that these two patterns are difficult, if not impossible, to combine in the same agency, and that the choice between them should be made before dependence upon government resources makes commitment to the first pattern irreversible.

5

We believe that persons in both public and private institutions of social welfare should have adequate opportunities for religious services and ministries of their own choosing. Such services and ministries should be available to all, but they should not be compulsory. Under certain circumstances, failure to provide such services and ministries may have a serious adverse effect on the free exercise of religion. Where, for medical or legal reasons, the free movement of individuals is curtailed, the institutions of social welfare involved ought to provide opportunities for religious worship.

6

There is a new awareness of the need for welfare services to be complemented by action for social change. We believe that agencies of social welfare to churches have an obligation to provide data and insights concerning the causes of specific social problems. It should be recognized that both remedial and preventive programs may require legislation, changes in political structures, and cooperation in direct action and community organization.

In their efforts to meet human needs, churches should never allow their preoccupation with remedial programs under their own direction to divert them or the larger community from a common search for basic solutions. In dealing with conditions of poverty, churches should have no stake in programs that continue dependency or embody attitudes and practices that may be described as "welfare colonialism."

We believe that churches have a moral obligation to challenge violations of the civil rights of the poor. They ought to direct their efforts toward helping the poor overcome the powerlessness that makes such violations of civil rights possible. Specifically, churches ought to protest such policies and practices by welfare personnel as unwarranted invasions of privacy and requirement of attendance at church activities in order to qualify for social welfare services.

ADOPTED 1968

See Social Principles, ¶ 68; "Church-Government Relations"; "Religious Liberty"; "Separation of Church and State."

Community Life

At the heart of the Christian faith is an abiding concern for persons. This concern is evidenced by the Christian's sensitivity to all factors that affect a person's life. In our society, the community has become known as a gathering of people who nurture one another and create for all an atmosphere for general enhancement. The community should be characterized by good schools, adequate housing, spirit-filled churches, and creative community organizations.

The Church has always been interested in communities as arenas where people engage in the common experiences of life. It is in community that men, women, and youth discover and enhance their identity. And it is in community that all persons learn to appreciate social, religious, and ethical values.

Communities are undergoing serious changes. Perhaps the most serious of these changes are destructive to the forces that have built communities in the past. Integrated housing patterns are beginning to prevail in many sections all across America. The previous pattern was accentuated by massive flight of white residents to the suburbs and an entrenchment of African Americans in the inner city. This polarization along racial lines serves to destroy the idea of a democratic community and has brought into being hostile entities along political, social, and educational lines.

The development of federal and state housing authorities with a democratic pattern for housing development has restored the faith of many that the possibilities of a new community are there. We affirm the 1972 Statement on Housing.

The Local Church and the Local Public School

In innumerable and concrete ways, the local church serves as interpreter of and witness to the gospel in the life of its community. Therefore, it is the primary channel through which the demands of the gospel are made known in society. By virtue of the nature of the church, there is nothing in the community outside its concern or beyond its ability to affect.

The local public schools historically represent one of the fundamental focal points in American communities. This is as it should be, because the democratic approach to education is the bedrock of democratic, political, and economic systems. The local public schools also represent one of the largest financial outlays in any given community. In these days, many public school systems have been caught in the whirling social and educational changes of the times and have fallen victim to influences and powers that have not kept the fundamental purposes of the public schools as highest priorities.

Some of the many challenging issues confronting the schools are: financial inadequacies, historic racial attitudes, busing, curriculum, growing professionalism of teachers and administrators, and the lack of well-informed and sensitive school board members. Many times these issues are combined, making the problems that much more acute.

The issues confronting public schools may be different in the respective communities, as the Church is different in its respective communities. Yet by the virtue of its calling, the Church must lead the communities in exploring the issues and in identifying and seeking solutions to their particular problems.

In each community, the local United Methodist Church is responsible for being a catalyst in helping the entire community become sensitive to the issues of public education.

We encourage each local church to recognize the importance of the culture, history, and important contributions of ethnic minorities to the educational process and the resulting loss when these are omitted from the curriculum. Local churches should take the initiative to be certain that local school boards in their area or communities at every level of education include in the total curricula all contributions of all peoples to the growth and development of the United States.

The lack of opportunities to learn and understand the history and cultures of all races is reflected in our present problems in human relations.

Our Judeo-Christian tradition reveals clearly our personal accountability to almighty God in relation to our personal responsibility to and for our fellow human beings.

Where problems exist, it is especially important that the local United Methodist church support and work with existing community groups and organizations in bringing solutions. It is also recommended that each local United Methodist church develop a committee or an informal group of members to keep the congregation and community aware of public school issues and their obligation to assist in finding meaningful solutions.

ADOPTED 1976

See Social Principles, ¶ 68; "Church-Government Relations."

Criminal Justice

Justice is the basic principle upon which God's creation has been established. It is the necessary ingredient required for the achievement of humanity's ultimate purpose.

Justice is an integral and uncompromising part in God's redemptive process, which assures wholeness. It is a quality relationship based on God's love and the human response motivated by love.

Justice is the theme that permeates the history of God's people as participants in the ongoing human drama of their daily existence.

The gospel, through the example of Jesus Christ, conveys the message for Christians to be healers, peacemakers, and reconcilers when faced with brokenness, violence, and vengeance. Through love, caring, and forgiveness, Jesus Christ was able to transform lives and restore the dignity and purpose in those who were willing to abide by his principles.

Jesus Christ was opposed to vengeance as the way to administer justice (Matthew 5:38-44).

As Christians, we recognize that each person is unique and has great value before God. Human worth does not diminish when a person violates laws made by human beings, for human worth has been guaranteed even when God's law has been violated.

The Christian church as an institution is charged with the responsibility to ensure that a system of justice safeguards the inherent right that human beings possess as God's creatures and objects of the love and care that derive from that relationship.

The primary purpose of the criminal justice system and its administration is to protect individuals and society from any violation of their legal and constitutional rights.

The criminal justice system in this country has been adversely affected by economic and social conditions that have resulted in discrimination against the poor, minorities, and women.

Too often, prisons are places where dehumanizing conditions reinforce negative social behavior. This contributes to the high incidence of recidivism and perpetuates the cycle of violence, crime, and incarceration.

The administration of the criminal justice system has reached a level of saturation that leads to expediency rather than the even-handed application of justice and punishment.

As United Methodist Christians, we are called to sensitize those institutions that operate within the criminal justice system to be responsible, more humane and just, to ensure the full participation in society by those who have deviated from laws established as normative guidelines for behavior. *Therefore,* we will:

1. Minister to prisoners, offenders, ex-offenders, victims, and to the families involved (this includes working toward the goal of restoration and reconciliation of victims and offenders);

2. Develop and offer competent ministries of mediation and conflict resolution, within the criminal justice system;

3. Nurture members of The United Methodist Church and the general public in the insights of the faith as they provide guidance in expressing redemption and reconciliation for those persons embroiled in the criminal justice system;

4. Develop attitudes of acceptance in the community and opportunities for employment for those persons who are released from imprisonment or who are participating in programs that assist them to re-enter community life; and

5. Monitor governmental policies and programs in the field of criminal justice and respond to them from our faith perspective.

Law Enforcement and Courts

Because we believe in reconciliation and redemption, we will work for a criminal justice system that is just and humane and has as its goals restoration rather than vengeance. Toward this end, we will support the following:

1. Provision of safeguards to ensure that the poor, minorities, and the inexperienced have available the legal assistance and other advantages available to the rich, powerful, and the experienced;

2. Elimination of influences and practices of discrimination based on race, ethnic or cultural background, political identification, age, class, or sex;

3. Staffing of the criminal justice system at every level by persons who represent a diversity of backgrounds in our society and who meet high standards of training and experience, including cultural understanding and care about the persons who come under their jurisdiction; and

4. Separation of juvenile offenders from adult offenders, with correction given to them outside the traditional courts and correctional system;

With specific regard to law-enforcement officials and the courts, we as United Methodists:

1. Support efforts to develop alternative methods to the use of deadly force by law enforcement officials;

2. Insist that accused persons should have competent legal assistance and be ensured a speedy trial; and

3. Recognize that organized crime has corrupting power over the racial, political, and economic life of our nations and support efforts to oppose it through effective legislation, strong law enforcement, and the development of public awareness.

Sentences

The primary purpose of a sentence for a crime is to protect society from future crimes by the offender, the deterrence of offenders from committing a crime, restitution of the victim, and assistance to the offender to become a law-abiding citizen.

Believing in the love of Christ who came to save those who are lost and vulnerable, we urge the creation of a genuinely new system and programs for rehabilitation that will restore, preserve, and nurture the total humanity of the imprisoned. We believe that sentences should hold within them the possibilities of reconciliation and restoration.

Therefore, we assert that:

1. In the sentencing by the courts and in the implementation of the sentences, the criminal justice system should use all resources and knowledge available to ensure that sentencing embodies the possibility of rehabilitation and reconciliation;

2. Imprisonment should be imposed only when the continued freedom of the offender poses a direct threat to society and when no acceptable alternative exists;

3. Capital punishment should be eliminated, since it violates the concept of sacredness of human life and is contrary to our belief that sentences should hold within them the possibilities of reconciliation and restoration;

4. Sentences to restitution, community service, and other nonimprisonment alternatives provide economical, rational, and humane systems

of justice for nondangerous offenders and provide justice for the victim;

5. Community involvement and concern is needed to monitor the policies and practices of the criminal justice system;

6. The criminal justice system must be accessible to all persons;

7. Accused persons must not be prejudged for detention before trial on the basis of their character, race, culture, gender, or class; and

8. Percentage-of-sentence limitations on "good behavior" paroles violate the Christian mandates for redemption and reconciliation.

ADOPTED 1984

See Social Principles, ¶ 68F; "Equal Justice"; "Grand Jury Abuse"; "The Local Church and the Local Jail"; "Penal Reform"; "Police Firearms Policies"; "Victims of Crime."

Opposition to the Deportation of Salvadoran Refugees from the United States

The Old Testament directs us to care about the "foreigners" in our midst (Exodus 23:9, King James Version) and reminds us that we too are "sojourners" (Leviticus 25:23, Revised Standard Version). The New Testament recounts how Jesus and his family had to flee to Egypt to escape persecution (Matthew 2:13-15). We are told in Hebrews 13:2 (RSV), "Do not neglect to show hospitality to strangers for thereby some have entertained angels unawares."

The United Methodist Church has strongly and consistently expressed concern for Central American refugees and the peace process in that region, as stated in the 1992 *Book of Resolutions:* "Immigration" (pages 507–10); "Assistance and Sanctuary for Central American Refugees" (pages 463–64); "Central America: Peace and Justice with Freedom" (pages 557–61); and "Concern for El Salvador" (page 570).

Thousands of Salvadorans were forced to flee their homes in El Salvador to escape death and persecution because of civil war. Many came to the United States for refuge.

Now that the civil war in El Salvador has ceased, the U.S. government has ended the temporary protected status of the Salvadoran refugees. Deportation proceedings could legally begin; over 150,000 Salvadoran refugees could be affected.

Children of refugees born in the United States have no knowledge of El Salvador and will face great hardships there. Moreover, El Salvador still remains a place of danger for many of the Salvadorans who face deportation.

El Salvador is a country in turmoil. The return of thousands of refugees from the United States will have catastrophic consequences on this small and impoverished country, which is recovering from a bloody and debilitating war. Unemployment is rampant, and the Salvadoran economy depends heavily on remittances from Salvadorans living outside the country.

Therefore, be it resolved, that the General Conference of The United Methodist Church opposes the deportation of Salvadoran refugees from the United States and calls on the President of the United States and the United States attorney general to grant them permanent residency.

ADOPTED 1996

See Social Principles, ¶¶ 68A, 69; "Assistance and Sanctuary for Central American Refugees"; "Immigrants in the United States: Ministries of Hospitality, Advocacy, and Justice."

Domestic Surveillance

Openness is a redemptive gift of God, calling for trust and honesty between various segments of the community. Justice is the cornerstone of that trust we have come to expect in our elective and appointive representatives of the community. Communal wholeness is attained through the concerted use of these elements.

Domestic surveillance is an issue that, without adequate safeguards of civil rights, threatens the moral and legal fiber of our society.

Domestic surveillance is the gathering of information pertaining to the intent, capabilities, and activities of individuals and/or groups involved in criminal activities for a foreign agent or power. The intent is to root out elements that threaten or harm the national security of a country. Yet congressional hearings, over time, have revealed that intelligence agencies often misuse and abuse surveillance activities: "Domestic intelligence has threatened and undermined the constitutional rights of Americans to free speech, associations, and privacy. It has done so primarily because the constitutional system for checking abuse of power has not been applied" (Senator Church's Committee Report on Intelligence, 1976).

Examples of abuse include:

1. The use of grand jury investigations to harass American citizens and groups exercising their freedom of speech under the First Amendment. Those under subpoena to grand juries have been incarcerated after exercising their rights under the Fifth Amendment; and

2. The surveillance, disruption, infiltration, and harassment of and thefts from peace groups during the Vietnam era, and later, antinuclear, antiwar groups.

Governmental directives and policies have been formulated that provide the intelligence agencies with a wider latitude in initiating domestic investigations. Recent directives expand the role these agencies play in conducting surveillance, and use techniques that heretofore had been considered violent and extreme. These directives legitimize abuses by giving the intelligence agencies the power to:

1. Conduct warrantless searches and seizures, in direct violation of the Fourth Amendment of the Bill of Rights, including electronic surveillance, unconsented physical surveillance, and mail surveillance;

2. Direct intelligence techniques toward anyone who comes in contact with a foreign person or organization, i.e., "foreign" friends, members of the United Nations, church and related support agencies;

3. Infiltrate and influence the activities of law-abiding organizations in the United States, without valid reason to suspect or allege illegal activities;

4. Use journalists, missionaries, students, businesspersons, and teachers as undercover agents, oftentimes without their expressed knowledge; and

5. Conduct secret campus research, if authorized by undefined "appropriate officials."

As United Methodists, the issue of domestic surveillance and its misuse and abuse deserves a renewed focus. As stated in the Social Principles (¶ 68A, C):

We also strongly reject domestic surveillance and intimidation of political opponents by governments in power and all other misuse of elective and appointive offices. . . . Citizens of all countries should have access to all essential information regarding their government and its policies. Illegal and unconscionable activities directed against persons or groups by their own governments must not be justified or kept secret, even under the guise of national security.

We therefore call upon The United Methodist Church at all levels to:

1. Affirm the rights of individuals and groups to address governmental policies that reject the freedom to associate and the freedom of speech, especially to the beliefs that enhance the political, social, economic, and spiritual quality of life;

2. Recommend revocation of directives and policies that reduce public review of executive, judicial, and legislative procedures;

3. Support the continuing need for the present Freedom of Information Act (FOIA). Actions to weaken FOIA and to restrict public access to local, state, and federal documents violate the principles of trust and openness, elements that enhance human development;

4. Affirm the responsibility of governments to ensure the national security of their people. We reject the use of "national security" as a guise for illegal and unconstitutional actions of governments. Invocation of the term *national security* for unjust reasons undermines the credibility of governments and threatens the safety of its citizenry at home and abroad; and

5. Support local, state, and federal actions and policies that respond adequately to the needs of the citizenry and ensure their fundamental moral and legal rights. Local, state, and federal agencies should work together with community representatives in formulating policies that account for these needs.

ADOPTED 1984

See Social Principles, ¶ 68A and C; "Repression and the Right to Privacy."

Enabling Financial Support for Domestic Programs

The United Methodist Church has declared war to be "incompatible with the teachings of Jesus Christ"; and

Dr. Martin Luther King Jr. wrote that "racism and its perennial ally," economic exploitation, "provide the key to understanding most of the international complications of this generation"; and

General Colin Powell offered testimony to the Congressional Black Caucus that the military presently provided the only means whereby thousands of Black youth and young adults could obtain a decent standard of living and an education, going on to say that such opportunities should also be made available by the private and the rest of the public sectors; and

While there is unemployment among other minority groups, tens of thousands of African American male and female young adults have never been employed and are, therefore, not counted in current unemployment statistics; and

The majority of public school districts (especially those that serve the masses of urban Black, Hispanic, and poor people) find themselves facing severe financial shortfalls, staff cuts, the elimination of vital programs, and school closings; and

Those same communities are experiencing social trauma due to plant closings and the relocation of industry to countries where the wages are from fifty cents to one dollar an hour; and

The Free Trade Agreement, proposed by President George Bush, will facilitate further plant closings and create further hardships for Black, Hispanic, and other poor communities.

We petition the President and Congress of the United States to reduce the U.S. military presence by recognizing principles of sovereignty in every region of the world.

We petition the President and Congress of the United States to reapportion dollars, saved by reduced military spending and base closings, for domestic programs that will enable the financial support for an increase in quality educational offerings in the public school systems of the country, adequate health care, the creation of sufficient employment opportunities, and a new comprehensive employment training act, which will appropriate federal dollars into elements of the private sector that are currently in compliance with affirmative action guidelines, for the purpose of encouraging their participation in the retraining of U.S. workers, and redevelopment of plants within the continental United States.

ADOPTED 1992

See Social Principles, ¶ 68; "The United Methodist Church and Peace"; "Unemployment"; "Call for a Rebirth of Compassion."

Equal Justice

It must be remembered that the advice "Let every person be subject to the governing authorities" (Romans 13:1) is preceded by "Live in harmony with one another; do not be haughty, but associate with the lowly; never be conceited. Repay no one evil for evil, but take thought for what is noble in the sight of all" (Romans 12:16-17). The admonition is directed to the authorities who govern as well as those who may be subject.

The Social Principles of The United Methodist Church state (¶ 68B, F): "The church should continually exert a strong ethical influence upon the state, supporting policies and programs deemed to be just and opposing policies and programs that are unjust. . . . We support governmental measures designed to reduce and eliminate crime that are consistent with respect for the basic freedom of persons. We reject all misuse of these necessary mechanisms, including their use for the purpose of persecuting or intimidating those whose race, appearance, lifestyle, economic condition, or beliefs differ from those in authority; and we reject all careless, callous, or discriminatory enforcement of law."

The Police

In our democratic society, the police fill a position of extraordinary trust and power. Usually the decision of whether a citizen is to be taken into custody rests solely with the police. For these reasons, law enforcement officers must be persons who possess good judgment, sound discretion, proper temperament, and are physically and mentally alert.

Unusual care must be exercised in the selection of those persons to serve as police officers. We recommend psychological testing prior to employment of police officers and periodically thereafter. During the period of training and continually thereafter, police must be instilled with the knowledge that the rights of many will never be secured if the government, through its police powers, is permitted to prefer some of its citizens over others. The practice of citizen preference in the enforcement of our criminal laws must not be tolerated. Our laws must be fairly enforced and impartially administered. No one is immune from the requirements of the law because of power, position, or economic station in life. Further, the power of the police must never be used to harass and provoke the young, the poor, the unpopular, and the members of racial and cultural minorities.

Where there is heavy pressure upon police officers by police departments to regularly make a large number of arrests as a demonstration of their initiative and professional performance, we urge that such practice be discontinued.

In a democratic society, however, a large majority of police work encompasses peacekeeping and social services rather than crime control functions. Police routinely use more than 85 percent of their duty time in giving assistance to citizens and making referrals to other governmental agencies. It is important for police to be recognized and promoted for their effectiveness in such roles as diverting youths from disorderly activities, peacefully intervening in domestic quarrels, anticipating disturbances through the channeling of grievances, and the building of good community relationships.

The United Methodist Church recommends that police departments publicly establish standards of police conduct and policies for promotion. To this end, congregations should encourage the police to conduct public hearings among all classes of citizens, giving adequate weight to peacekeeping, life-protecting, and other service roles, as well as the bringing of criminal offenders to justice. The standards must include strict limits on the police use of guns.

We further recommend that police officers live within the jurisdiction in which they are employed.

We make these recommendations not only in concern about the frequent abuses of people by the police, but also because we are concerned for more effective control of crime. We observe that only about one half the victims of serious crime, and a far smaller proportion of witnesses, report to the police. If offenders are to be apprehended and convicted, police and law-abiding citizens must work closely together. Such cooperation can occur only when the police are fair and humane and when they are publicly known to be sensitive and considerate.

The United Methodist Church urges that communities establish adequate salary scales for police officers and develop high standards for recruiting both men and women, and members of all ethnic groups. Recruitment must be followed by adequate training in social relations and dispute settlement—as well as in law and the skills of crime detection investigation—and the apprehension of offenders. As police officers continue to meet those improved qualifications, we will recognize law enforcement as a profession with status and respect.

Criminal Laws and the Courts

Where the law recognizes and permits plea-bargaining, and in those instances where the ends of justice dictate that a renegotiated plea be considered, we recommend it should be permitted and approved only after full disclosure in open court of the terms and conditions of such plea-bargaining agreement. Equal justice requires that all trials and the sentencing of those convicted under our criminal laws must be conducted in the public courtroom.

Since at present 90 percent of all criminal convictions are by guilty pleas—an unknown but large proportion of those by plea-bargaining—this recommendation would mean a large increase in the work of the criminal courts. However, that work should be correspondingly eased by changes in the law, such as the moving of most traffic offenses out of criminal court to administrative procedures, and by relieving the court of great numbers of civil cases through the adoption of genuine no-fault motor-vehicle insurance laws. The courts must also organize their work efficiently, employing modern management procedures. Many improvements could be made by the use of administrative volunteers, including retirees who can furnish professional services to the court at minimal costs.

Other changes needed to obtain equal justice in the courts include:

1. The repeal of some criminal laws against certain personal conditions or individual misconduct. Examples are criminal prohibitions of vagrancy, personal gambling, public drunkenness, and prostitution. Together, these items alone account for more than half of all arrests in some jurisdictions. They result in little social good, but great evil in class discrimination, alienation, and waste of resources needed for other purposes. Some related laws such as those against drunken driving and those limiting and controlling the operation of gambling establishments need to be tightened;

2. The adoption of systematic new penal codes prescribing penalties proportionate to the predictable damage done by the various kinds of crime, without regard to the class of the offender;

3. The training of judges of juvenile and criminal courts in the use of nonincarcerating community sanctions wherever the offense does not involve persistent violence;

4. The adoption of systematic new penal codes prescribing a range of penalties without regard to the class of the offender, but utilizing nonincarceration community sanctions wherever possible; the provision for court-fixed sentences, rather than mandatory ones, in order to draw upon the skill and the training of qualified judges;

5. A statement by the sentencing judge of the reason or reasons why he or she is selecting from the range permitted by the law the particular sentence being pronounced;

6. The development of appropriate jury selection procedures that would ensure the most inclusive representation, including representatives of the socioeconomic class and ethnic group of the defendants;

7. The adoption by all courts of: (a) speedy trial provisions, which the Constitution guarantees; and (b) that degree of personal recognizance and supervision which each defendant's situation warrants, in place of the present, inherently discriminatory bail-bond, pretrial release process that exists in some courts;

8. When fines are assessed, they should be scaled to the magnitude of the crime and the ability of the offender to pay. In suitable cases, fines should be made payable in installments; and

9. Governmentally regulated programs of compensation for reimbursement of financial loss incurred by innocent victims of crime should be encouraged.

We recommend that local churches consider setting up court monitoring panels to observe the court operations and proceedings. Such panels may well adopt a role of "friends of the court" or of advocacy on behalf of accused persons. They may adopt other appropriate procedures in the interest of criminal justice, including close scrutiny of plea-bargaining and/or evidence of unequal imposition of sentences.

ADOPTED 1980

See Social Principles, ¶ 68F; "Criminal Justice"; "Grand Jury Abuse"; "Victims of Crime."

Free the Puerto Rican Political Prisoners

Today we have fourteen Puerto Rican political prisoners in the United States prison system. These men and women received sentences that are excessive and geared toward punishing political activity more than the stated crimes and for refusing to participate in the U.S. judicial system process based on their own conscientious objection. The average sentence among this group is 71.6 years for the men and 72.8 years for the women.

A total of thirty Puerto Rican prisoners refused to participate in the U.S. court system because of their belief that the U.S. government was the colonial and enemy power. They requested a war court trial and were denied. Some of these thirty have served their sentences; others were let go because no valid case could be brought against them.

The United Nations' resolutions on decolonization have clearly established that colonialism is a crime, and they recognize a colonized people's right to end colonialism. The United Nations also recognizes that these resolutions and laws apply to Puerto Rico. For many years, the United Nations Decolonization Committee has approved resolutions recognizing the inalienable right of Puerto Rico's people to independence and self-determination. The injustice suffered under Puerto Rico's colonial reality cannot be overlooked. President Bush admitted that the people of Puerto Rico have never been consulted as equals on their political status.

The call for the release of these prisoners enjoys wide support in the U.S., Puerto Rico, and internationally. Many civic, religious, and international organizations have also joined in the effort.

We, as Christians, have been called to identify with the prisoners and their needs. We have been called to bring justice to them when injustice has taken place (Luke 4:18; Matthew 25:36).

Therefore, be it resolved, that the General Conference of The United Methodist Church advocate for justice and freedom for the Puerto Rican political prisoners; *furthermore,* that a letter from the General Conference secretary be sent to the President of the United States asking him to grant pardon, because they have more than sufficiently served their sentences, to all fourteen Puerto Rican political prisoners who are presently found in federal and state prisons; and *in addition,* that a copy of the letter be forwarded to Dr. Luis Nieves Falcon, coordinator of the effort to free the Puerto Rican political prisoners.

ADOPTED 1996

See Social Principles, ¶ 68A, E; "Puerto Rico and Vieques."

Grand Jury Abuse

Jesus' words, "Do not judge, so that you may not be judged" (Matthew 7:1), surely imply that all judgments are judged in the light of God's truth. The Social Principles of The United Methodist Church state boldly that "governments, no less than individuals, are subject to the judgment of God" (¶ 68E). Such a social principle causes us, appropriately, to view with concern the government's use of the grand jury to control dissent and to harass those who act under the constraint of conscience.

The grand jury is envisioned in American law as a protector of citizens from unwarranted prosecutions. It is for this reason that its proceedings are secret and it has the power to subpoena witnesses.

Evidence indicates that in recent years, the extraordinary powers of the grand jury often have been used not for the *protection* of citizens, but in subjecting them to harassment and intimidation. Historically, political dissidents, antiwar activists, and leaders of minority groups and religious organizations have been particularly vulnerable to these abuses.

A government prosecutor can control the grand jury, thus distorting the grand jury's power to monitor and moderate the actions of the prosecution. The prosecutor can use the subpoena powers of the grand jury to conduct investigations that are the responsibility of law enforcement agencies. As an example, Congress has never given the Federal Bureau of Investigation subpoena powers, yet agents routinely threaten uncooperative persons with subpoenas from a grand jury. In fact, subpoenas are often served at the request of the Federal Bureau of Investigation.

The use of the powers of the grand jury to harass and pursue political dissidents is a departure from its proper constitutional function, and it is a threat to public order, lawful government, and true domestic security.

Witnesses called before a grand jury may be given little or no warning of their subpoenas, may be forced to travel to court at distances from their homes, may not know whether they are targets of prosecution, may have little understanding of their rights, and cannot have legal counsel in the chambers.

Comprehensive grand jury reform legislation is needed to restore the constitutional guarantees of protection for citizens. The Fifth Amendment right against self-incrimination and false accusation must be reestablished and reinforced.

The United Methodist Church, therefore, supports legislation designed to enhance the rights to due process of law, freedom of association, effective legal counsel, the presumption of innocence, and the privilege against self-incrimination of persons subpoenaed to testify before grand juries.

ADOPTED 1980

See Social Principles, ¶ 68F; "Equal Justice"; "Criminal Justice."

Gun Violence in the U.S.

With the mounting proliferation of firearms throughout the world, the safety of God's children cannot be guaranteed. Crime in city streets climbs, accidents abound, domestic violence erupts, and suicides soar. Christians concerned about reverence for life care about what is happening to many victims of gun murders and assaults. In the name of Christ, who came so that persons might know abundant life, we call upon the Church to affirm its faith through vigorous efforts to curb gun violence.

Gun violence around the world is a growing menace, particularly in the United States. Today, deaths and assaults involving guns of all kinds have reached devastatingly high levels. The Centers for Disease Control and the *New England Journal of Medicine* have declared this crisis one of "epidemic proportions." A severe health crisis is created in many communities as the physical and psychological health of innumerable urban and rural families is impacted by gun violence.

Gun violence is a deep concern to The United Methodist Church and the community of faith whose members are called to a vision of a peaceable kingdom, a society in which God's justice reigns, where reconciliation replaces alienation, where an open hand and a turned cheek replaces retaliation, where love of enemy is as important as love of neighbor. The religious community must also take seriously the risk of idolatry that could result from an unwarranted fascination with guns and that overlooks or ignores the social consequences of their misuse. The United Methodist Church regards effective gun control and regulation to be a spiritual concern and public responsibility.

Working as an instrument of reconciliation, The United Methodist Church is among those religious communions calling for social policies and personal lifestyles that bring an end to senseless gun violence. The United States might well learn from the experience of other societies where stringent gun-control laws are enforced. The gun murder rate per 100,000 population in the United States is 100 times greater than in England and Wales, where strict gun laws prevail; it is 200 times greater than in Japan, where it is impossible for the public to secure handguns legally. In the United States, more than 30,000 men, women, and children are shot to death in homicides, suicides, and accidents annually. This does not take into account the approximately 250,000 people suffering injuries costing the society over $24 billion each year. Over three quarters of these medical expenses are paid for with public tax dollars that could be used for community development and to aid those in need.

Behind the statistics often lies great tragedy: Children and teachers are being shot in school; depressed persons are taking their lives with guns; persons who purchase guns to protect their home often end up using them to kill a loved one; and police officers are being gunned down in increasing numbers in the course of duty.

As Christians who are deeply concerned about human life, we must do something about the unregulated and unnecessary access to guns.

Although there is vigorous debate over the meaning of the Second Amendment to the Constitution, which speaks to the right to keep and bear arms, the United States Supreme Court and lower federal courts have held that the private ownership of guns is not protected by the Second Amendment.

Most gun-related deaths and injuries in the United States are by handguns originally acquired for personal protection, target shooting, gun collections, and hunting. Some are by shotguns and rifles most often acquired for legitimate sporting or collecting. An increasing number of deaths and injuries are by semiautomatic and automatic guns, often referred to as assault weapons, developed for wartime purposes. The futility of these weapons far outweighs the utility.

In spite of the purpose for which guns are acquired, deaths and injuries resulting from their use contribute significantly to the atmosphere of violence, fear, and alienation that is a daily part of life in the United States today. There are over 65 million (estimated) handguns and 135 million rifles in the United States—nearly one gun for each man, woman, and child. While guns are not the sole cause of violence, their ready availability for purchase, easy accessibility to children, and convenient access to those contemplating criminal activity or suicide make gun violence a monumental social problem. We believe that the time has come for all nations to move toward a less violent and more civilized society.

As people of faith, we recognize the inherent goodness of all creation. We firmly believe in God as the giver and sustainer of all life. We also recognize that the ultimate purpose of creation is to reveal God's reign of justice and peace. The biblical admonition to choose life instead of death sets the tone for all human activity: "I call heaven and earth to witness against you today that I have set before you life and death, blessings and curses. Choose life so that you and your descendants may live" (Deuteronomy 30:19). Our focus must not lose the vision of transformation given to us in Micah to beat our swords into plowshares and our spears into pruning hooks (Micah 4:3). *Therefore,* The United Methodist Church:

1. Declares its support for meaningful and effective federal legislation to regulate the importation, manufacturing, sale, and possession of guns and ammunition by the general public. Such legislation should include provisions for the registration and licensing of gun purchasers and owners, appropriate background investigation and waiting periods prior to gun purchase, and regulation of subsequent sale;

2. Calls upon the United States government to establish a national ban on the importation, manufacture, sale, and possession of handguns and handgun ammunition, with reasonable limited exceptions. Such exceptions should be restricted to: the police, the military, licensed security guards, antique dealers who maintain guns in unfireable condition, and licensed pistol clubs where firearms are kept on the premises under secure conditions. Those who comply with the law and turn in their guns should be compensated at fair value through a cash payment or tax credit;

3. Opposes the licensing of individuals to carry concealed weapons. Special controls should be applied to the handgun, for it is the most deadly and least utilitarian weapon in American society. Because the handgun is concealable, it is the weapon of crime; because the handgun is available, it is the instrument used in suicides and crimes of passion;

4. Calls for the continuation and strengthening of the federal ban on the sale and possession of assault weapons;

5. Supports the outlawing of the production and sales of automatic weapon conversion kits, as well as the production of guns that cannot be detected by traditionally used metal-detection devices;

6. Calls upon the United States government to establish product protection laws and regulate guns through the Consumer Protection Agency;

7. Calls upon the print, broadcasting, and electronic media, as well as the entertainment industry, to refrain from promoting gun usage to children;

8. Discourages the graphic depiction and glorification of violence by the entertainment industry, which greatly influences our society, and recommends that these issues be addressed through education and consciousness raising;

9. Calls on all United Methodists who are members of gun clubs and associations to use their influence to help expand gun education and safety programs. These individuals should also enter into dialogue with their clubs and associations to establish responsible and safe gun regulations, and to build a safer and less violent society;

10. Calls for all church properties and facilities to be designated as "No Gun Zones" and to prohibit guns from being carried onto the premises;

11. Calls upon the federal and state governments to provide significant assistance to victims of gun violence and their families; and

12. Recommends that annual conferences make visible public witness to the sin of gun violence and to the hope of community healing.

ADOPTED 1996

See Social Principles, ¶ 68F, "Police Firearms Policies"; "Criminal Justice."

Human Rights

God created human beings,
in the image of God they were created;
male and female were created.
(Genesis 1:26-27, adapted)

We affirm that all persons are of equal worth in the sight of God, because all are created in the image of God. Biblical tradition demands that we live in an interdependent relationship with God and our neighbor. We must respond to human need at every community level.

As covenant people of God, we are called to responsibility rather than privilege.

God's vision for humanity as revealed in the life, death, and resurrection of Jesus Christ demands the total fulfillment of human rights in an interdependent global community. It is a vision of life where needs of the community have priority over individual fears and where redemption and reconciliation are available to all. Human rights are holistic in nature and therefore indivisible in their economic, social, cultural, civil, and political aspects. The omission of any of these aspects denies our God-given human dignity.

As Christians, we receive and carry a mandate to seek justice and liberation. Isaiah calls us to "loose the bonds of injustice,/to undo the thongs of the yoke,/to let the oppressed go free,/and to break every yoke" (Isaiah 58:6).

The United Methodist Church continues its commitment to human rights as grounded in God's covenant by critically assessing and safeguarding the following principles as defined in the Universal Declaration of Human Rights:

1. All persons are of equal worth and dignity;

2. All persons have the right to the basic necessities of life;

3. All persons have the right to self-determination, cultural identity, and minority distinction;

4. All persons have the right to religious expression and practice.

The United Nations has spoken strongly against racism as a human rights violation in the United Nations Declaration on the Elimination of All Forms of Racial Discrimination:

> Discrimination between human beings on the ground of race, colour or ethnic origin is an offence to human dignity and shall be condemned as a denial of the principles of the Charter of the United Nations, as a violation of the human rights and fundamental freedoms proclaimed in the Universal Declaration of Human Rights, as an obstacle to friendly and peaceful relations among nations and as a fact capable of disturbing peace and security among peoples.

In addition, the United Nations has also defined sexism as a violation of human rights in the Declaration on the Elimination of Discrimination Against Women:

> Discrimination against women, denying or limiting as it does their equality of rights with men, is fundamentally unjust and constitutes an offence against human dignity.

We call upon citizens within the Church and society to analyze critically trends and developments that adversely affect human rights. These include:

1. The increase of capital-intensive technology that destroys opportunities for productive and meaningful employment;

2. The intentional use of data banks to undermine rather than enhance abundant living;

3. The growing phenomenon of an "underclass" of persons domestically and internationally excluded from full participation in society due to educational, cultural, economic, and political conditions;

4. The possible economic and political scapegoating of such an underclass for technological and social displacement;

5. Increasing extrajudicial executions; torture; and disappearances of dissenters, their families, and communities;

6. The growth of militarism and the imposition of military-like control over civilians;

7. The increase of terrorism and the growth of white supremacist and racial hate groups, neo-Nazi groups, paramilitary units, and extreme ultranationalistic groups;

8. In many countries, the decreasing civilian control of domestic and international policing and intelligence units as well as increasing surveillance of their own citizenry, imposed under the guise of a potential threat to national security; and

9. The conflict between meeting the basic needs of developing countries and the disproportionate sharing of global resources.

We are increasingly aware that militarism and greed can overwhelm and undermine movements to secure human rights. The Church is called to be an advocate for the human rights of all persons in the political, social, and economic quest for justice and peace.

As people of faith and hope, we commend those trends that contribute positively to the human rights movement. Among them:

- the growing acceptance of universal standards for human rights;
- the establishment of organizations such as Amnesty International, which documents, verifies, and publicizes political imprisonment, torture, killings, and crimes against humanity;
- the increasing consensus against war as a viable solution to international conflicts;
- movement toward the inclusion of "basic human needs" criteria in international aid packages and financial aid programming;
- the growing importance of human rights offices in governments around the world; and
- the growing emphasis on technology appropriate to the cultural setting.

We uphold the requirements advocated by the National Council of Churches to preserve and protect human rights:

1. Human rights require world peace;
2. Human rights require a secure and sustainable environment;
3. Human rights require sustainable human development;
4. Human rights require the preservation of communities; and
5. Human rights require the preservation of religious liberty and freedom of conscience.

We call upon all governments to accept their obligation to uphold human rights by refraining from repression, torture, and violence against any person. We further call upon all governments to ratify and implement international conventions, covenants, and protocols addressing human rights in the context of justice and peace.

We call the Church to be a place of refuge for those who experience the violation of their human rights. It is the duty of Christians "to help create a worldwide community in which governments and people treat each other compassionately as members of one human family."

ADOPTED 1996

See Social Principles, ¶ 68A, "Domestic Surveillance"; "Repression and the Right to Privacy"; "Ratification of United Nations Covenants and Conventions by the United States."

Immigrants and Refugees: To Love the Sojourner

I. Biblical/Theological Basis

The Bible is full of stories of sojourners, strangers without homes, whom God called people to protect. The Israelites—God's chosen people—were themselves sojourners for forty years after the exodus from Egypt, as they sought the Promised Land. God did not let the Israelites forget that they had been without a homeland for such a long time; the ethic of welcoming the sojourner was woven into the very fabric of the Israelite confederacy. It was more than an ethic, it was a command of God. "Do not mistreat or oppress a stranger; you know how it feels to be a stranger, because you were sojourners in the land of Egypt" (Exodus 23:9, Revised Standard Version, adapted).

A *sojourn* implies uprootedness; sojourners are uprooted people. At times uprooted people in the Bible were looking for a home, but other times they were not. Often they were telling those who would listen that the real home was a spiritual home—with God providing accompaniment. Sojourners were messengers. The message they sent then as well as today is that the Spirit of God is with each of us as we sojourn through life. We are all on a journey, and God is with us. Such was the message of Moses and many of the prophets; such was the message of John the Baptist, a voice crying in the wilderness; and such was the message of Jesus Christ, whose own life was characterized by uprootedness. The infant Jesus and his family had to flee to Egypt to avoid persecution and death; they became refugees, sojourning in Egypt until they could come home. Jesus was a person on the move. Jesus' ministry occurred throughout the countryside of Judea, and his life was marked by uprootedness: "Foxes have holes, and birds of the air have nests; but the Son of Man has nowhere to lay his head" (Matthew 8:20). Jesus made a point of spending time with the poor, the powerless, the despised and rejected. Jesus did so while spreading the word of God's steadfast love, the same love spoken of in the Book of Hosea: "I will betroth you to me forever; yes, I will betroth you unto me in righteousness and justice, and in lovingkindness and mercy" (Hosea 2:19, New King James Version).

Jesus embodied the love of God to the world and modeled how we are to act with love and compassion for the sojourner. In fact, Jesus' most pointed description of how human beings should behave once they are aware of God's love is in the story of the good Samaritan, in which the love of God is expressed through the compassion of a stranger: "But a certain Samaritan, as he journeyed, came where he was: and when he saw him, he had compassion on him, and went to him, and bound up his wounds, pouring in oil and wine, and set him on his own beast, and brought him to an inn, and took care of him" (Luke 10:33-34, King James Version). This is the radical love of God as expressed by Jesus Christ. It transcends race, nationality, and religion and is a love that cries for justice and peace; it is a love that is sorely needed today.

II. Global Uprootedness

We live in a world where there are over 22 million people who are refugees, another 26 million who are internally displaced, and millions more who seek asylum or are migrants looking to find a way out of poverty. No nation can afford to turn a blind eye toward these realities. People who must flee their land because they have no choice are today's uprooted populations. They are given different labels depending on their circumstances: *refugees*—persons who have been officially recognized by the United Nations as having a well-founded fear of persecution because of their political affiliation, religion, race, nationality, or membership in a particular social group or opinion; *asylum seekers*—those who have left their homeland and are applying for political asylum in the country to which they have fled (in the United States, applying for asylum is a right that can be exercised); *internally displaced*—people who are displaced within the borders of their own lands because of civil strife but who cannot receive the protection of the international community because of the principle of national sovereignty; *economic migrants*—those who flee dire poverty in search of employment and a way to feed their families. No matter what label they are given, they are usually vulnerable people in need of compassion and protection. Most of them are women and children; often, the women are subjected to the brutality of sexual violence.

Even when refugees are allowed to return home, they face monumental problems, such as the possibility of being killed or maimed by land mines, millions of which have been left behind by former combatants. An example is Angola, a country that has more land mines than any other in the world. It is estimated that 20 million mines were laid during the twenty-year civil war there. Today, it is estimated that 70,000 Angolans have required amputations because of contact with mines. It is also estimated that there are between 150 and 200 land mine victims every week in Angola.

It is clear that the uprooted are vulnerable and need the protection of the international community. Their numbers are growing as more people worldwide become victims of wars, economic injustice, and environmental degradation. According to the United Nations High Commissioner for Refugees (UNHCR), it is estimated that one out of every 130 people worldwide has been forced into flight. Because of civil wars and ethnic-based conflict, political repression and gross human-rights violations, refugees are being produced at a rate of 10,000 per day. The 1990s is fast becoming the "decade of uprootedness."

Most refugees come from the South and remain in the South, often in countries of first asylum where conditions are barely humane. It is a myth that all people on the move wish to come to the nations of the North, but those who do come because it is their last hope for life. They have no choice. The nations of the industrialized North that are better equipped to provide safe haven to uprooted persons are currently lacking in the moral and political will to do so. Instead, the governments of these nations are reacting to a worldwide rise in xenophobia and racism by sharply curtailing existing programs that benefit newcomers and by instituting restrictive legislation designed to satisfy the nativists in their constituencies. Uprootedness is seen by the governments of the industrialized North as a problem to be dealt with by force rather than as a complex phenomenon needing coherent and humane solutions on a global scale. Uprooted people are looked upon as the cause of societal problems and are being blamed for increasing economic difficulties. Consequently, even refugees fleeing persecution are denied their human rights and the protection they need to save their lives, and they are summarily excluded and ostracized by governments. In Europe, many governments are implementing policies that are designed to prevent asylum seekers from successfully finding refuge within their borders. In Norway, for example, according to law, asylum seekers may not apply for asylum unless they have close ties with Norway. Such a law dispenses with equity in asylum procedures. The recent increase in the number of uprooted persons demonstrates that the international community, including the churches, must focus more attention on understanding and alleviating the causes of forced human uprootedness, as well as responding to the consequences.

III. Immigration and Asylum in the United States

Nearly all the citizens of the United States have ancestors who emigrated from other parts of the world. Since the seventeenth century, millions of immigrants have come to the United States, often to seek freedom from religious persecution and broader opportunities in a new land. No other nation has welcomed so many immigrants from so many parts of the world, and no other nation has taken such pride in its immigrant roots. Nevertheless, the history of immigration policy in the United States has been heavily influenced by economic and labor-force needs, as well as by systemic racism. The United States has at times encouraged the presence of immigrants who could provide the cheap hard labor to build canals and railroads, help with the harvesting of crops, and supply industry with needed workers. At other times, however, U.S. laws have systematically excluded immigrants because of racial, ethnic, religious, or other prejudicial reasons. Examples are the Chinese Exclusion Act of 1882, the Immigration Act of 1924, the Immigration Act of 1965, and the Immigration, Reform, and Control Act of 1986.

While the United States has a long history of immigration, its experience as a country of first asylum is relatively new and appears minor in comparison to that of many other countries of the world. Countries in Africa have opened their borders to millions of asylum seekers, while the United States has only had to work with asylum applications numbering in the hundreds of thousands.

The 1980s and early 1990s witnessed an influx of persons seeking asylum in the United States from Central America, including Haiti and Cuba. All of these groups fled a combination of dire poverty, government repression or persecution, and general strife in their homelands. This influx of refugees to the United States was unexpected, and many—particularly the Haitian, Salvadoran, and Guatemalan people— were denied the protection of asylum they so desperately needed.

In the United States, the federal government is proposing legislation to prevent further influxes of migrants and asylum seekers by reinforcing the borders and instituting restrictive measures. The United States has engaged in a policy of forced repatriation of unwanted Central American, Haitian, Cuban, and Chinese asylum seekers in violation of international law. It has also engaged in detention practices and forced repatriation of Chinese people and others without benefit of fair and equal protection under the law. Current legislative initiatives seek to reduce family immigration by 32 percent, slash refugee admissions by over 50 percent, introduce a national identification system, and bar legal immigrants' access to government assistance, leaving them vulnerable when they fall on hard times.

In California, the passage of Proposition 187, an initiative that would deny public education to the children of undocumented persons, would also deny them nonemergency health care and require government employees, private individuals, and providers to report to the authorities individuals whom they suspect are undocumented. The implementation of the initiative is currently pending in court. In the meantime, those who look or sound foreign already suffer from discrimination in both the workplace and in daily life.

Immigrant bashing, a particularly virulent form of anti-immigrant bias, seems stronger than ever in this atmosphere of misinformation, mistrust, and fear of economic instability. Unwilling to face the reality of their leaders' failure to deal expeditiously and honestly with their nation's adjustment to the new global society, many people in the United States have let themselves be vulnerable to the hysteria that says they are no longer in control of their borders or their destiny.

Therefore, we call upon The United Methodist Church, in collaboration with other ecumenical and interdenominational organizations, to urge the government of the United States:

1. To encourage and support international economic policies that promote sustainable development and that use capital, technology, labor, and land in a manner that gives priority to employment for all people and the production of basic human necessities, thereby reducing migration pressures;

2. To alleviate conditions of uprootedness by working toward the elimination of all forms of warfare and by supporting agrarian reform, social justice, and an adequate measure of economic security for all peoples;

3. To take decisive action to eliminate the sale and international trade in land mines and provide technical assistance to facilitate their removal from lands to which refugees are returning;

4. To withhold all support—diplomatic, military, and financial—to governments with a documented recent history of abuses and disregard for human rights, particularly the right of asylum;

5. To provide a fair and generous resettlement policy as one of the ways of ensuring meaningful protection and a durable solution for refugees;

6. To adopt reasonable standards for consideration as refugees for those seeking asylum and to eliminate within the Immigration and Naturalization Service (INS) all abuses of civil and human rights, including such practices as the violation of due process, denial of bond, and hasty deportation of people who are undocumented or overstayed; and to eliminate restrictive measures applied to asylum seekers at ports of entry, such as summary exclusion without benefit of adequate counseling;

7. To monitor all attempted reforms on immigration and refugee policy and practices in order to ensure fair and adequate process in regard to asylum petitions, judicial review, refugee resettlement priorities, and immigrant categories;

8. To review and reject all legislative measures that propose summary exclusion for *bona fide* asylum seekers, and to ensure access to counsel and meaningful review of asylum claims by an immigration judge; and

9. To ensure protection of the basic human rights of immigrants and refugees, such as the right to an education, adequate health care, due process and redress of law, protection against social and economic exploitation, the right to a cultural and social identity, and access to the social and economic life of the nation whether in documented or undocumented status.

As people of faith, we are called to do justice, love kindness, and walk humbly with God (Micah 6:8). We must work for justice and peace for all people and envision a world where institutions are transformed into true servants of the people, full of the compassion exemplified by Jesus Christ.

Therefore, in addition to advocating for the above measures, we call upon United Methodist churches and agencies:

1. To support international efforts to promote sustainable development policies designed to alleviate human suffering and counteract some of the root causes of forced migration;

2. To advocate for protection of uprooted women and children against all forms of violence and to call for full legal protection of uprooted children in the midst of armed conflict;

3. To provide assistance for projects of relief to refugees and displaced persons;

4. To provide assistance for projects of economic development for refugees and returnees;

5. To provide sponsorships for refugees through local congregations;

6. To denounce and oppose the rise of xenophobic and racist reactions against newcomers in the United States and elsewhere, and to support any and all efforts to build bridges between people of diverse ethnicities and cultures;

7. To continue to work with community-based organizations to provide forums for citizens to voice concerns, educate one another, and confront the problems of racism and xenophobia as obstacles to building community;

8. To work with civic and legal organizations to support communities that are now or will be affected by the destructive enactment of policies like California's Proposition 187;

9. To provide pastoral care and crisis intervention to individuals and families who are refugees and asylum seekers; and

10. To speak out, make declarations, and adopt resolutions to condemn and de-legitimize violence against foreigners.

We recommend that the General Board of Church and Society and the General Board of Global Ministries:

1. Monitor cases of possible human-rights violations in the area of immigration and give guidance to United Methodists in responding to such cases;

2. Advocate for human rights (including political, economic, and civil) for all people, and especially for the strangers who sojourn in the land;

3. Advocate against legislation that seeks to establish national identification systems;

4. Continue explorations of solutions to the problems of asylum seekers and undocumented people;

5. Lead United Methodists throughout the United States in the fight against nativism and continue to respond to the current threat against refugees and immigrants;

6. Lead the churches throughout the United States in recognizing the contributions newcomers have made that have culturally and economically enriched that nation;

7. Provide technical and financial assistance to local churches in active ministry with refugees and asylum seekers;

8. Continue the task of educating United Methodists about issues related to refugees, immigrants, and migrants;

9. Organize campaigns to counter and prevent racism, xenophobia, and hostility toward uprooted people;

10. Develop materials to educate the churches on immigration as well as on issues related to refugees and asylum seekers;

11. Assist the churches in advocating for fair and just immigration laws and practices; and

12. Support communities and congregations by prayer and action where such measures as Proposition 187 may be implemented at any time in the future, and develop strategies and action plans to counter similar initiatives in other states.

ADOPTED 1996

See Social Principles, ¶¶ 68A, 69A; "Immigrants in the United States: Ministries of Hospitality, Advocacy, and Justice."

Immigrants in the United States:
Ministries of Hospitality, Advocacy, and Justice

Our Christian roots are centered among people who were sojourners in the land. Throughout history, people have been uprooted under conditions similar to that of Mary and Joseph, who were forced to flee to save the life of their son. Most of our own forefathers and foremothers were immigrants to this country. The Bible is clear about how we should treat these wanderers:

> When strangers sojourn with you in your land, you shall not do them wrong. The strangers who sojourn with you shall be to you as the natives among you, and you shall love them as yourself; for you were strangers in the land of Egypt. . . .

> (Leviticus 19:33-34, Revised Standard Version)

Communities throughout our world are suffering from war, civil conflict, and persecution for political, religious, ethnic, or social reasons. The World Council of Churches reports that two out of every 100 human beings are fleeing their country, and many families are forcibly displaced within their own countries. For these reasons, we stand firmly opposed to legislative action such as that proposed in California's Proposition 187 or any similar legislation that may have the following effects:

• *Public Schools*: Districts are required to verify the legal status of students enrolling for the first time. The status of parents or guardians of students must also be verified;

• *Higher Education*: Undocumented immigrants are barred from community colleges and public institutions of higher learning;

• *Health:* Undocumented immigrants are ineligible for public health services, except for emergency care;

• *Welfare:* Undocumented immigrants are already ineligible for the major welfare programs. Most child-welfare and foster-care benefits are also eliminated;

• *Law Enforcement:* Service providers are required to report suspected undocumented immigrants. Law-enforcement agencies must verify the residency status of individuals arrested or suspected of being in the United States illegally. When legal residency cannot be proved, the person will be reported to the United States Immigration and Naturalization Service.

With grace and concern, the Church must address the legal, economic, social, and human rights conditions of people who are legal or undocumented immigrants, and it must oppose the introduction of legislation by any state that would cause human suffering and a denial of such individual's rights as interpreted through our biblical understanding of God's grace to all peoples, but especially to the sojourner. Our faith, grounded in Christ and in the Wesleyan call to work for prophetic justice, calls us to follow our Social Principles and respond in appropriate and direct ways to prevent harm to the sojourner.

Jesus teaches us to show special concern for the poor and oppressed who come to our land seeking survival and peace. We call upon United Methodists individually and through general boards and agencies throughout The United Methodist Church to do the following:

1. Actively oppose anti-immigrant legislative action and support legislative action that protects the poor and oppressed in their quest for survival and peace;

2. Urge stringent policing and penalties for coyotes (illegal transporters) and those individuals, businesses, or groups that fuel them and other exploiters of undocumented immigrants, since their activities may cause immigrants to suffer serious injury or death;

3. Urge that humane and fair treatment be extended to all immigrants by business and agricultural groups;

4. Advocate human rights (political, economic, and civil) for all people, including the strangers who sojourn in our land;

5. Support communities and congregations by prayer and action where anti-immigrant measures may be implemented;

6. Continue to work with community organizations to provide forums for citizens to voice concerns, educate one another, and confront the problems of racism as obstacles to building community;

7. Continue to work with civic and legal organizations to support communities who are now, or will be, affected by the destructive, deteriorating social issues raised by anti-immigrant measures.

Finally, we call upon United Methodists to practice hospitality and express our commitment to an inclusive Church and society through all our ministries in the spirit of our biblical tradition:

> Do not oppress an alien; you yourselves know how it feels to be aliens, because you were aliens in Egypt.
>
> (Exodus 23:9, New International Version)

ADOPTED 1996

See Social Principles, ¶¶ 68A, 69A; "Immigrants and Refugees: To Love the Sojourner."

The Local Church and the Local Jail

The writer of the Letter to the Hebrews, in suggesting conduct consistent with the new covenant brought through the mediation of Jesus, advises, "Remember those who are in prison, as though you were in prison with them" (Hebrews 13:3).

The Social Principles of The United Methodist Church urge that the love of Christ be translated into "new systems . . . for rehabilitation that will restore, preserve, and nurture the humanity of the imprisoned." This concern must be expressed in local communities by local congregations, for most of those imprisoned in the United States are in city and county jails.

Citizens pay millions of dollars for the support of jails in their local communities each year; yet for the individuals who are detained in them, jail life is a particularly dehumanizing experience accompanied by the loss of freedom, the loss of contact with family and friends, and the loss of self-determination.

According to recent studies, most local jails provide inadequate food services, minimal medical care, no libraries or recreational facilities, no educational programs, and only a limited religious ministry. These conditions are physically injurious, mentally deteriorating, and spiritually destructive to those who are confined.

Most of the persons detained in local jails are being held for trial and actually are serving sentences prior to their conviction.

Since incarceration is by its very nature dehumanizing and destructive, The United Methodist Church states its belief that every responsible means should be used to reduce the present jail population and to use methods (such as release on recognizance, bail, probation, and so forth) to keep persons out of jail.

All citizens have a fundamental right and obligation to know how the jails in their communities are being administered, how prisoners are being treated, and under what conditions they are being confined.

They should have further concern for the losses in human relationships and personal welfare that are suffered by those who are held in local jails.

The United Methodist Church urges its members to inform themselves about local jails through participation in citizen inspections; to establish programs of regular volunteer visitation with both individual staff members and confined residents of jails; to support chaplaincy programs within jails; and to diligently seek the alleviation of the present inhumane conditions while working for the eventual elimination of jails, except as necessary places of detention for dangerous criminals. Members of churches are further urged to support and fund organizations in their local communities that advocate the protection of the rights of all citizens. Where conditions are found to be substandard, United Methodist Church members are urged to request formal inquiry procedures.

ADOPTED 1980

See Social Principles, ¶ 68F; "Penal Reform"; "Criminal Justice."

The Church in a Mass Media Culture

Cyberspace, the information superhighway, and other technologies have moved the world from an agricultural and industrial dominance into the information and communication age. The primary communication method remains much the same as it has been throughout all human history—telling stories. Today, storytellers have techniques that have so improved the impact of visual images and so amplified their presence through broadcast, cable, satellite, and VCRs, and through video games, fiber-optics, interactive television, CD-ROMs, and global computer communications, that the traditional face-to-face storytellers—parents, pastors, and teachers—frequently are unheard.

Mass media have become so pervasive that people in the developing countries are affected as much as those in the developed countries. Yet the centers of control of these media rest in the developed countries, and many of the questions about the media relate to the bias of the people in these countries toward the rest of the world:

• The assumption in the developed countries is that free market forces are both necessary and desirable in bringing media to the public, but these materialistic forces have unfortunate historical and institutional ties to violence-driven and oppressive cultures.

• The term *mass media* implies that all persons have access to them and use of them, when in practice media have a narrow base of ownership among an elite group of affluent persons, mostly white Western men.

• The drive for mergers and consolidations among broadcasting companies, entertainment complexes, and electronic industries is basically a drive for profits, cloaked in the deceptive public relations language of consumer choice.

What has been called the "homogenization" of the media—that is, the tendency of mass media to imitate one another in producing programming that resembles the most successful formulas—ends in making highly biased cultural stereotypes the norm throughout the world.

Christian religious communities have sometimes been co-opted in a detrimental way by the claim of the mass media to be all-powerful, leading to passivity on the part of mainstream religions and an endorsement of the distorted values of the media by default.

United Methodist Traditions

As proclaimers of the good news of salvation in Jesus Christ, United Methodists have traditionally been concerned about communication. Both the individualistic tradition of pietism and the communitarian tradition of the social gospel have led United Methodists to raise concerns about the distorted images and values in mass media. The Social Principles speak to values in the media, decrying sensationalism and dehumanizing portrayals that "degrade humankind and violate the teachings of Christ and the Bible" (Social Principles, ¶ 72).

Thus, The United Methodist Church has a heritage of expressing its concern for the perceptions and images offered in the media, as well as the actual workings of new media technology. We have called, in the past, for inclusiveness in media institutions and for accountability of those who hold power in the media. This heritage justifies our making this public statement of concern and protest.

The goals of The United Methodist Church, based on our understanding of the gospel, are clear:

1. To challenge owners and operators of mass-media institutions to be more responsible in communicating truth and more humane values;

2. To advocate for access to the media and, where feasible, ownership of media institutions by marginalized groups;

3. To be more responsible as a community of faith by interacting with the media and using media creatively;

4. To become a model of communication by our own openness and wise use of the media; and

5. To empower people to tell their own story.

Affirmations

We invented these media, using the gifts of God's creation. We can also be a part of the solution. We continue to affirm:

• Freedom of expression—whether by spoken or printed word, or any visual or artistic medium—should be exercised within a framework of social responsibility. The church is opposed to censorship.

• The principle of freedom of the press must be maintained.

• The airwaves should be held in trust for the public by radio and television broadcasters and regulated in behalf of the public.

• Public broadcasting, as it continues to develop, should be supported by both public and private sectors of the society to help further the diversity of programming and information sources.

• As difficult as it may be to achieve, the goal is that all persons of every nation should have equal access to channels of communication so they can participate fully in the life of the world.

• No medium can be truly neutral. Each brings with it its own values, limitations, criteria, authoritarian or democratic structures, and selection processes.

Evaluation

We continue to oppose the practices of persons and systems that use media for purposes of exploitation, which comes in many forms:

• emphasizing violence;
• marketing pornography;
• appealing to self-indulgence;
• presenting consumerism as a desired way of life;

• favoring the mass audience at the expense of individuals and minorities;

• withholding significant information;

• treating news as entertainment;

• presenting events in isolation from a larger context that would make them understandable;

• stereotyping characters in terms of sex roles, ethnic or racial background, occupation, age, religion, nationality, disability, and economic status;

• dealing with significant political and social issues in biased and superficial ways;

• exhibiting an overriding concern for maximizing profit;

• discriminating in employment practices, particularly by failing to include women and racial or ethnic minorities in critical decision-making positions; and

• presenting misleading or dangerous product information or omitting essential information.

Questions

Because the media bring their own values with them, we as Christians must ask:

• How can the new media be used to proclaim the gospel of Jesus Christ?

• Who controls the media in a country? Who determines the structures of and the public's access to the mass media? Who controls international technologies of communication?

• Who determines message content and images and within what guidelines of responsibility?

• Who uses the media, and for what purposes?

• What is the appropriate response to the growing demands of developing countries for a more just world-information system?

• What rights do users have in determining media structure and content? How can the user bring critical appraisal to the messages received?

• If we are to be subjected to the information superhighway, how can users control the reception of undesired information?

• How can we introduce ethical and moral considerations into media programming without resorting to censorship?

Call to Action

We call upon the Church to respond to the mass media by:

• developing media literacy resources for church members;

• providing media literacy education to church members, thus equipping them to analyze and evaluate various forms of media rather than to be passive recipients;

• empowering church members to use media as a tool and to be makers of media themselves to share the gospel;

• participating in research on the effects of new technologies, media mergers, and globalization of media on communities in the developed and developing countries;

• advocating for those shut out of the media: the poor, the less powerful, and other marginalized people;

• advocating for socially responsible media and communication policies;

• working to ensure a public lane in the information superhighway;

• recognizing the close relationship between media and message, and using media as channels of education, witness, evangelism, information, social services, advocacy, and ministry; and

• affirming traditional modes of face-to-face communications, such as storytelling, dialogue, songs, and indigenous cultural modes of communication.

In our own communication structures and processes within the Church, we need to establish models of communication that are freeing, that respect the dignity of the recipient, and that are participatory and nonmanipulative. We need to democratize our own media to allow access and open dialogue. As a major institution within our society, we can demonstrate to other institutions the power of a connectional church that structures its communication patterns not by concentrating media power but by emphasizing the values of the gospel, which recognize the sanctity of every individual.

ADOPTED 1996

See Social Principles, ¶ 66*P*; "Sexual Violence and Pornography"; "Free Flow of Information Among All Peoples of the Earth"; "Violence in Electronic Media and Film."

Nuclear Abolition:
Saying No to Nuclear Deterrence

In 1986, the United Methodist Council of Bishops, after nearly two years of prayerful and penitent study, adopted a pastoral letter and foundation document entitled *In Defense of Creation: The Nuclear Crisis and a Just Peace*.[1]

The bishops' statement was deeply rooted in biblical faith. They wrote:

> At the heart of the Old Testament is the testimony of *shalom*, that marvelous Hebrew word that means peace. But the peace that is *shalom* is not negative or one dimensional. It is much more than the absence of war. *Shalom* is positive peace: harmony, wholeness, health, and well-being in all human relationships. It is the natural state of humanity as birthed by God. It is harmony between humanity and all of God's good creation. All of creation is interrelated. Every creature, every element, every force of nature participates in the whole of creation. If any person is denied *shalom*, all are thereby diminished. . . .[2]
>
> New Testament faith presupposes a radical break between the follies, or much so-called conventional wisdom about power and security, on the one hand, and the transcendent wisdom of shalom, on the other. Ultimately, New Testament faith is a message of hope about God's plan and purpose for human destiny. It is a redemptive vision that refuses to wallow in doom.[3]

Based upon this faith, the bishops in their pastoral letter stated unequivocally that "we say a clear and unconditional *No* to nuclear war and to any use of nuclear weapons. We conclude that nuclear deterrence is a position that cannot receive the church's blessing."[4]

The implication is clear. If nuclear weapons cannot be legitimately used for either deterrence or war fighting, no nation should possess them. Accordingly, in the foundation document the bishops indicated:

> We support the earliest possible negotiation of phased but rapid reduction of nuclear arsenals, while calling upon all other nuclear-weapon states to agree to parallel arms reductions, to the eventual goal of a mutual and verifiable dismantling of all nuclear armaments.[5]

In 1988, the United Methodist General Conference affirmed and supported the statements of the Council of Bishops contained in *In Defense of Creation*.[6] Four years later, in a resolution entitled "Nuclear Disarmament: The Zero Option," the 1992 General Conference stated that "now is the time to exercise the zero option: to eliminate all nuclear weapons throughout the globe,"[7] and the Conference offered a series of concrete actions for achieving this goal.

---

[1] *In Defense of Creation: The Nuclear Crisis and a Just Peace*, the United Methodist Council of Bishops (Nashville: Graded Press, 1986).

[2] Ibid., page 24.

[3] Ibid., page 28.

[4] Ibid., page 92.

[5] Ibid., page 76

[6] *The Book of Resolutions of The United Methodist Church, 1988*, page 503.

[7] Ibid., page 601.

Goals and Objectives

We reaffirm the goal of total abolition of all nuclear weapons throughout Earth and space. This can occur by achieving the following objectives:

1. Complete elimination of all nuclear weapons by all possessors;
2. Complete elimination of all delivery vehicles by all possessors;
3. Termination of all development, production, and testing of nuclear weapons by all nations and by all individuals and groups with nuclear ambition; and
4. Prevention of all nonpossessors from developing and otherwise acquiring nuclear weapons and their delivery vehicles.

These objectives should be achieved as soon as possible through a combination of international treaties and reciprocal national initiatives, carried out with adequate verification.

Progress and Prospects

The Cold War between the United States and the Soviet Union, which dominated world politics for more than four decades, has ended. The Berlin Wall has fallen. Eastern Europe is free from Soviet control. The Warsaw Pact has gone out of existence. The Soviet Union itself has dissolved. Most of the independent republics of the former U.S.S.R. are committed to democracy and a free-market economy.

Yet remaining is a large portion of the huge nuclear arsenal accumulated by the United States, the former Soviet Union, Great Britain, France, and China to apply the pernicious doctrine of mutually assured destruction. Moreover, Israel has developed a stockpile of nuclear weapons, India has attained the capability to produce nuclear weapons, and Pakistan is seeking to do likewise. Elsewhere, other nations, such as North Korea, Iran, Iraq, and Libya, seem interested in acquiring nuclear weapons.

On the positive side, the United States and the Soviet Union before its collapse agreed to eliminate all intermediate-range nuclear forces (INF) and to commence curtailment of long-range forces through provisions of the first Strategic Arms Reduction Treaty (START I). Subsequently, the United States and Russia have entered into START II to achieve further reductions. Belarus, Ukraine, and Kazakhstan have endorsed START II and have committed themselves to eliminating all nuclear weapons left on their territories when the Soviet Union disbanded.

International treaties have created nuclear weapon-free zones in South America, South Pacific, Antarctica, the seabed, and outer space. In 1995, the Non-Proliferation Treaty (NPT) was extended indefinitely, committing signatories not in possession of nuclear weapons to refrain from acquiring them and committing signatories possessing nuclear weapons to "systematic and progressive efforts to reduce nuclear weapons globally, with the ultimate goal of eliminating those weapons." And efforts are underway by the possessor nations to negotiate, adopt, and carry out a Comprehensive Test Ban (CTB) Treaty.

These are worthy efforts in the right direction. However, they are not proceeding far enough or fast enough toward the goal of nuclear abolition.

Further Initiatives Required

As a means of moving much more rapidly toward nuclear abolition, we recommend that the following initiatives be undertaken:

1. A global Comprehensive Test Ban should be agreed upon, honored, and enforced.

2. All nations possessing nuclear weapons should make an unconditional pledge of "no first use."

3. All nuclear weapon-free zones should be respected and further zones established.

4. START II should be fully carried out as quickly as possible.

5. As a prelude to further reductions, all possessor nations should immediately and concurrently move to zero alert by deactivating their entire strategic arsenal through removal of warheads or other vital components from delivery vehicles with safe storage under international inspection.

6. As a companion measure, all possessor nations should withdraw all tactical nuclear weapons from active deployment and store them safely under international inspection.

7. As rapidly as possible, all deactivated strategic and tactical nuclear weapons and all delivery vehicles should be dismantled under international inspection in an agreed sequence that is balanced so that at no stage could any nation gain an advantage.

8. All fissionable material removed from nuclear weapons should be carefully safeguarded with continuous international inspection.

9. All nations capable of producing nuclear weapons should immediately cease all production of fissionable material, testing of nuclear warheads, and manufacture of all delivery vehicles, including missiles, bombers, submarines, surface ships, and all other means of delivery.

10. All nuclear weapons production facilities should be closed, except as they might be used to disassemble nuclear warheads and convert nuclear material to nonweapon use.

11. All nations on Earth should become signatories of the Non-Proliferation Treaty and faithfully observe its requirements. To ensure universal compliance, the treaty should be vigorously enforced, with adequate financial and technical support to detect and halt covert nuclear activities.

12. All weapon-usable radioactive materials and nuclear facilities in all nations should be subject to international accounting, monitoring, and safeguards.

13. An international system should be instituted to prevent the development, production, and deployment of ballistic missiles capable of attacking an adversary's homeland. All existing ballistic missiles with such capability should be eliminated.

14. All efforts to develop and deploy strategic antimissile defense systems should be terminated as illusory, unnecessary, and wasteful.

Leadership for Study and Action

We call upon the Council of Bishops and the General Board of Church and Society to provide leadership, guidance, and educational material to United Methodists, congregations, and conferences in order to assist them in understanding and working for the goal and objectives of nuclear abolition.

Conclusion

We fervently believe that these recommendations will greatly enhance global security by eliminating the possibility of nuclear war. Furthermore, the resources of human talent, production capacity, and money released can become available to deal with urgent human problems around the globe. Nuclear abolition provides great hope for global peace and prosperity.

ADOPTED 1996

See Social Principles, ¶ 69C; "The United Methodist Church and Peace"; "Nuclear-Free Pacific"; "Justice, Peace, and the Integrity of Creation."

Opposition to a Call for a Constitutional Convention

As United Methodists, we are grateful that for almost 200 years the Constitution of the United States has provided a basis for cherished religious and civil liberties. The document drawn up by persons, including many descendants of those who fled to America because of persecution for their religious beliefs, has served as the cornerstone of our freedom. The Social Principles statement of The United Methodist Church "acknowledge[s] the vital function of government as a principal vehicle for the ordering of society." With the rules for governing, a constitutional convention would become a vehicle of disorder rather than order.

We are therefore deeply concerned about state efforts to mandate that Congress call a convention that would reopen the Constitution and possibly jeopardize its provisions.

I. Background

Unknown to most citizens of the United States, state legislatures have petitioned Congress for a constitutional convention. Only seven more are needed to make up the three fourths required by the Constitution. This would be the first constitutional convention since 1787, which was called to amend the Articles of Confederation. There are two forces behind the movement. One desires to add an amendment declaring a fetus a human person at the moment of conception, thus prohibiting abortions for any reason. Another force seeks an amendment to require a balanced federal budget.

The Constitution provides two methods for proposing amendments. One is the familiar route used to adopt all of the twenty-six present amendments. Five others were approved by Congress but not ratified by the states. Two are still pending. Both methods are described in Article V of the Constitution:

The Congress, whenever two thirds of both Houses shall deem it necessary, shall propose Amendments to this Constitution, or, on the Application of the Legislatures of two thirds

561

of the several States, shall call a Convention for proposing Amendments, which, in either Case, shall be valid to all Intents and Purposes, as Part of this Constitution, when ratified by the Legislatures of three fourths of the several States, or by Conventions in three fourths thereof, as the one or the other Mode of Ratification may be proposed by the Congress. . . .

Since 1787, there have been over 300 applications for a constitutional convention, but no single proposal has ever been endorsed by two thirds of the states at the same time. The closest approach occurred in the mid-1960s, when thirty-three state legislatures petitioned Congress to call a convention to overrule the "one person, one vote" decision of the Supreme Court dealing with equitable apportionment of state legislatures.

II. Reasons for Opposition to a Constitutional Convention

We state the following concerns as our reasons for opposing a constitutional convention:

1. There are virtually no guidelines regarding the specific rules for calling a convention and, if it were called, for determining how it would be run.

Since the language of the Constitution is vague, serious questions have been raised that constitutional scholars and jurists are unable to answer. What constitutes a valid application to Congress by a state legislature for an amending convention? Do all state petitions have to have the same wording, the same provisions, and the same subject matter? If two thirds of the legislatures do adopt a resolution, is Congress obliged to call a convention? Must all applications for a convention on a given issue be submitted to the same Congress, or is an application adopted in 1975, for example, still valid? If an amending convention were called, could it be limited to a single issue, or might it open the entire Constitution for change? How would delegates be selected, and how would votes in the convention be allocated? What would Congress's role be in this amending method? Would disputes over calling a convention and over its procedures be reviewable by the courts?

The complexity of the questions, and the fact that "experts" have no answers, illustrates the seriousness of attempting an uncharted route for changing the most fundamental document of our government.

2. This constitutional convention process of amendment has been a less democratic procedure than the traditional means of amendment.

The fact that in almost 200 years there have been only twenty-six amendments to the Constitution attests to the fact that the traditional amendment route is constructed to ensure wide national debate on each amendment and careful consideration by a three-fourths majority of the legislatures.

The process of calling for a constitutional convention has not been marked by careful consideration and democratic procedures. Of the twenty-seven states that have adopted the resolution, only six legislatures held hearings where the public was able to testify on the implications of the convention. In most instances, there has been only cursory debate before adopting the resolution. In two states, no committees considered the petitions before they were passed by the two bodies of the legislature. Committee reports were issued in only six states, explaining the proposed action. In one state, the senate committee discussed the petition for thirty minutes; the house committee discussed it six minutes.

Further, the people of the United States would have no direct vote on the results of the convention. State constitutional conventions, which are quite common, submit the proposed state constitutional changes to the voters. This has prevented the passage of changes pushed by small pressure groups, frequently over highly emotional issues. But the voters would have no ability to vote on a national constitutional revision, a matter affecting their most precious liberties.

3. Forces behind the call for a constitutional convention are dealing with highly emotional and highly complex issues that should be dealt with in the established manner for amending the Constitution.

Right-to-life advocates, frustrated by their inability to succeed in their goals of eliminating all abortions through the normal legislative process, are now trying the constitutional convention route. Yet such an amendment, declaring the fetus a person from the moment of conception, would be, in effect, to write one theological position into the Constitution. Various faith groups, including The United Methodist Church, do not share that theology. Such a position would be tantamount to declaring an abortion for any reason a murder. It would also inhibit the use of contraceptives such as the intrauterine device (IUD). This would be contrary to the doctrine of separation of church and state embodied in the Constitution and would impinge on freedom of religion, guaranteed in the First Amendment.

While the idea of a balanced federal budget has wide popular support, economists are highly uncertain of its effect on the economy. Many believe that it would not cut spending, as the public believes, but instead might require higher taxes and higher revenues. Both Republican and Democratic leaders oppose such an amendment because of its inflexibility. The budget and the economy are closely interrelated. When unemployment goes up only one percentage point, the deficit swells by some $20 billion due to lost tax revenues and increased social welfare costs such as unemployment compensation. A constitutional amendment would make it impossible to deal with such situations. Congressional leadership also points to the fact that the federal budget could be balanced fairly easily—by eliminating the current $82 billion in aid to state and local governments. But the same states calling for an amendment do not want the budget balanced at the cost of lost revenue to their states.

In summary, the present move toward a constitutional convention is ill-conceived and is being promoted by persons looking for easy solutions to complex problems. The Constitution should not have to suffer at the expense of frustrations that should be dealt with in the normal procedural manner that has served us well for two centuries.

Therefore, be it resolved, that the General Conference:

1. Oppose efforts of state legislatures to petition Congress to call a constitutional convention;

2. Inform local congregations regarding the factors involved in proposing a constitutional convention; and

3. Urge United Methodists to communicate their opposition to such a convention to their state legislatures and, in states that have adopted such a resolution, to urge its withdrawal.

ADOPTED 1980

See Social Principles, ¶ 68B; "The United Methodist Church and Church-Government Relations."

The U.S. Campaign for a Peace Tax Fund

We have long supported those persons who cannot in conscience pay taxes in support of war. We believe they should be granted the same legal recognition as that granted to conscientious objectors to military service. Toward that end, we recognize the work of the National Campaign for a Peace Tax Fund (NCPTF). The NCPTF advocates for legislation by the United States Congress to establish a Peace Tax Fund.

The purpose of Peace Tax Fund legislation is to:

- provide each individual the right not to be coerced into any form of participation in killing other human beings—whether that participation is physical or financial;
- offer conscientious objectors the right to pay their full tax obligation without violating deeply held religious or ethical beliefs; and
- give those who are conscientiously opposed to war because of religious or ethical beliefs the right not to have legal penalties imposed because of those beliefs.

We believe all persons have these rights based in the freedom to exercise their beliefs according to the dictates of conscience. To that end, we support the National Campaign for a Peace Tax Fund and affirm the work it does on behalf of those who conscientiously object to payment of taxes for war.

ADOPTED 1996

See Social Principles, ¶¶ 68G, 69; "The United Methodist Church and Peace"; "Justice, Peace, and the Integrity of Creation."

Penal Reform

Our Lord began his ministry by declaring "release to the captives" (Luke 4:18), and he distinguished those who would receive a blessing at the Last Judgment by saying, "I was in prison and you visited me" (Matthew 25:36). The Christian, therefore, naturally has concern for those who are captive, for those who are imprisoned, and for the human conditions under which persons are incarcerated.

The Social Principles of The United Methodist Church assert the need for "new systems for . . . rehabilitation that will restore, preserve, and nurture the humanity of the imprisoned" (¶ 68F).

There is not one, but many correctional systems in the United States that bear the responsibility for the confinement or supervision of persons convicted of crimes. For the most part, the systems are capable of neither rehabilitating criminals nor protecting society. They are, in fact, institutions where persons are further conditioned to criminal conduct and where advanced skills in crime are taught. More often than not, correctional institutions have created crime rather than deterred criminals. They represent an indescribable failure and have been subjected to a gross neglect by the rest of society.

The Church has participated in the neglect of the correctional system by being blind to the inhumanities that the system perpetuates and being silent about the social ills that it intensifies. The Church has challenged neither society nor itself to accept responsibility for making those critically needed changes in the penal system that would permit it to motivate improvement and offer hope to those detained within it.

Major changes are needed in the nation's correctional systems in order for them to become positive factors in the restoration of persons and the stabilization of society. Support needs to be given to alternatives to incarceration to reduce mounting costs, by using additional rehabilitative resources.

The United Methodist Church calls upon its members to express a practical faith in redemptive love through the supporting of:

1. The greater use of alternatives to pretrial detention for persons accused of crimes, such as: (a) release on recognizance; (b) the setting of reasonable and equitable bail; and (c) the payment of a modest percentage in cash of the designated bail;

2. The use of alternatives to prosecution, such as dispute settlement services and conflict resolution programs, and the diverting of persons formally subject to criminal prosecution for drunkenness, vagrancy, and "juvenile status" offenses into those organized programs which furnish noncriminal justice services; and

3. The use of alternatives to incarceration for those convicted of crimes, such as: fines, payments of restitution to victims of offenders' crimes, social service sentences, and probation.

The United Methodist Church further urges its congregations and members to support those penal policies which:

1. Promote social rehabilitation of convicted persons in preference to punitive confinement;

2. Develop and support a range of community-based alternatives to institutional incarceration, such as work-release programs;

3. Establish and maintain prisons and jails that have healthful and humane surroundings and a climate conducive to human growth and development;

4. Guarantee and maintain the rights of offenders to legal and medical services; guarantee the freedom of expression, association, and religion; protect the lives and persons of offenders from abuse from staff and other inmates; and furnish effective procedures for the redress of grievances;

5. Establish uniform disciplinary procedures within correctional institutions;

6. Provide cooperation with community agencies; and

7. Allow an optimal maintenance of relationships with the outside world, especially to preserve wholesome marriage and family ties; arrange for conjugal visits of husbands and wives following medical examinations and interviews for the purpose of ensuring that mutual desire exists; arrange visits of families with as much privacy as security will permit; and encourage friends and friendly counselors to make visits as well.

ADOPTED 1980

See Social Principles, ¶ 68F; "Criminal Justice"; "Equal Justice"; "The Local Church and the Local Jail."

Police Firearms Policies

We deplore the killing and injuring of police officers by citizens and the unnecessary and unwarranted killing of persons by police. We therefore not only call for the tightening of legal control over citizens' ownership of firearms or of guns, but we also call for the formulation of more clearly defined written firearms policies by every agency of law enforcement in the country.

ADOPTED 1976

See Social Principles, ¶ 68F; "Gun Violence in the U.S."; "Criminal Justice."

Prevention and Reduction of Juvenile Delinquency

WHEREAS, the abhorrent ills of our society (child abuse and neglect, teenage pregnancy, suicide, venereal diseases, drug and alcohol abuse) that relentlessly assail children have a profound effect on the quality of their lives and, without proper intervention, are often manifested in destructive behavior within the school setting; and

WHEREAS, these debilitating effects often become cyclical, appearing in generation after generation, and result in the loss to society of fully functioning and competent adults; and

WHEREAS, our school systems emphasize remediation at the secondary level to prevent delinquency;

Therefore, be it resolved, that all United Methodists work through the appropriate structures and channels to provide guidance counseling at the elementary level of all schools in prevention of delinquency.

Be it further resolved, that all United Methodists work through the appropriate structures and channels to provide guidance counseling at the elementary level of all schools in prevention of delinquency.

Be it further resolved, that United Methodist pastors are encouraged to develop cooperative relationships with persons doing such counseling.

ADOPTED 1984

See Social Principles, ¶ 68F; "Criminal Justice."

Proposition 187 of California

WHEREAS, Proposition 187 of California, approved by the electorate of this state in November 1994, is an attempt against the most elemental Christian moral and human principles that govern our life as a people, requiring even that schools and hospitals become branches of the Immigration and Naturalization Service, as they would be required under this proposition to report children and adults who are not legal citizens; and

WHEREAS, as Christians longing for a heavenly homeland, we are strangers in a foreign land but at the same time present in a world that demands God's will and justice; and

WHEREAS, our Holy Scripture calls us time and time again to the defense of the marginalized of our society—in particular, the poor, the orphans, the widows, and the strangers among us; and

WHEREAS, Proposition 187 of California represents a backward step in our development as a nation seeking interracial harmony; and

WHEREAS, the spirit and intent of Proposition 187 goes against the Social Principles of our United Methodist Church, specifically ¶ 66A, which states: "We recognize racism as sin and affirm the ultimate and temporal worth of all persons. . . . We assert the obligation of society and groups within the society to implement compensatory programs that redress long-standing, systemic social deprivation of racial and ethnic people. . . . to equal opportunities . . . to education and training of the highest quality; to nondiscrimination in . . . access to public accommodations. . . ."; and

WHEREAS, Proposition 187 is being challenged in the courts, and it has been found out of compliance with our constitutional rights;

Therefore, be it resolved, that the General Conference categorically, unequivocally, and totally repudiate Proposition 187 of California and the abusive and alienating spirit that it fosters and represents against Hispanic and other ethnic groups; and

Be it further resolved, that the General Conference make a call to all churches to be witnesses against this and other forms of alienation.

ADOPTED 1996

See Social Principles, ¶¶ 68A, 69A; "Immigrants and Refugees: To Love the Sojourner"; "Immigrants in the United States: Ministries of Hospitality, Advocacy, and Justice"; "Opposition to the Deportation of Salvadoran Refugees from the United States."

Ratification for District of Columbia Representation

The Scriptures tell us clearly that "God shows no partiality" (Acts 10:34). The Social Principles of The United Methodist Church cite "the full and willing participation of its citizens" as a key factor in the strength of our political system.

In keeping with the idea of impartiality and the call for citizen participation, we are concerned about the lagging issue of ratification of the constitutional amendment providing for full representation of the District of Columbia in the Congress. We are well aware that the population of the District of Columbia is powerless with respect to our national legislative body.

In October of 1971, a statement of the Board of Christian Social Concerns of The United Methodist Church asked the United States Congress to "provide the District of Columbia with two voting U.S. Senators plus the number of voting U.S. Representatives it would be entitled to if it were a State." This position was reaffirmed by the Board of Church and Society in October of 1978.

In 1978, the U.S. Congress passed a constitutional amendment providing for full voting representation of the District of Columbia in both the House and the Senate.

This amendment is now before the various state legislatures and, to become law, must be ratified by thirty-eight states by 1985. A number of states have already ratified the amendment.

The District of Columbia contains about 750,000 residents. This represents a population equal to or greater than seven states—each of which has full voting representation in the Congress. Each year, District residents pay more than $1 billion into the federal treasury, yet they are not permitted to have voting representation in the Congress. Such a practice appears to violate our American heritage of "no taxation without representation."

In terms of simple justice, we believe it is appropriate that District of Columbia citizens should have the right to elect national legislators who make the laws under which they too must live. Therefore, we urge all uncommitted state legislatures to ratify the constitutional amendment providing the District of Columbia with full voting representation in the Congress. We further encourage all United Methodists to support their state legislators in this endeavor.

ADOPTED 1980

See Social Principles, ¶ 68B.

Religious Liberty

The United Methodist Church, as a worldwide denomination, declares religious liberty, the freedom of belief, to be a basic human right that has its roots in the Bible. Paul admonished Christians with these words: "Who are you to pass judgment on servants of another?" (Romans 14:4). This understanding is fundamental to our religious heritage, which requires that we honor God, not by placing our demands on all persons, but by making true account of our own selves.

The preamble to the Universal Declaration of Human Rights states that "the advent of a world in which human beings shall enjoy freedom of speech and belief . . . has been proclaimed as the highest aspiration of the common people."

Minimal standards of the right of belief are amplified by the international community in the Declaration on the Elimination of All Forms of Intolerance and of Discrimination Based on Religion or Belief, adopted by the General Assembly of the United Nations on November 25, 1981. It declares that the right to freedom of thought, conscience, religion, or belief is basic to the following freedoms:

1. To assemble and to worship;

2. To establish and maintain places for those purposes;

3. To establish and maintain charitable, humanitarian, and social outreach institutions;

4. To produce and possess articles necessary to the rites and customs of a religion or belief;

5. To write, to issue, and to disseminate relevant publications;

6. To teach religious beliefs;

7. To solicit and receive voluntary financial and other contributions from individuals and institutions;

8. To train, to appoint, to elect, or to designate by succession necessary leaders;

9. To observe days of rest and to celebrate holidays and ceremonies in accordance with the precepts of one's religion or belief;

10. To establish and maintain communications with individuals and religious communities in matters of religion and belief at the national and international levels.

The declaration further establishes the rights of parents to provide religious training for their children.

Our test of religious liberty is not limited by these standards. We also believe that religious liberty includes the freedom to doubt or to deny the existence of God, and to refrain from observing religious practices. Further, we believe that persons of faith have the right to propagate their faith through evangelistic outreach. Persons must be allowed to live within the constraints and the demands of their convictions. We believe it is the right of a person to be allowed to follow the call of conscience when it becomes impossible to live by both the dictates of the state and the decisions of faith.

Threats to Religious Liberty

Religious liberty involves much more than the right to worship within the walls of a house of worship. Religious individuals, institutions, and their members have the right—indeed, the obligation—to be engaged in faith-based witness on issues of state and society. Broad latitude must be allowed in defining this religious function.

Theocracies or other governments and societies that give special privileges to adherents of one religion or ideology have a particular responsibility to ensure and guarantee not only the religious rights, but also the political, economic, social, and cultural rights of those who are not members of the favored group.

A grave threat to religious liberty exists in nation states where all forms of voluntary association—even for purposes of private religious worship—are limited or prohibited. In such situations, special accommodation that uses the United Nations Declaration as a minimum standard must be made for the observance of religious functions.

Religious liberty is menaced in other ways. Governments or political movements have used religious institutions or organizations for their own purposes by compromising their personnel through offering power, or by manipulation, infiltration, or control. Governments also subvert religious organizations by means of surveillance of their legitimate activities through use of informers, covert searches of religious property, and politically motivated threats to the safety of religious leaders or the financial operation of religious institutions. We pledge our continual efforts to protect against these activities.

We recognize that situations exist where religious observances seem to threaten the health or safety of a society. However, the importance of religious liberty dictates that restrictions of religious observances that are alleged to be contrary to government policy on the presumption that health or safety is threatened must be carefully examined. They must only be imposed in the midst of clear and serious danger to society beyond that of the observant adult.

Denominational Action to Expand Religious Liberty

The United Methodist Church places a high priority on the struggle to maintain freedom of religious belief and practice in the world. Religiously observant persons in some societies are denied the rights on which there have been international agreements. Our members have an obligation to speak out on behalf of those for whom such freedoms are abridged.

In carrying out their responsibilities, United Methodists, United Methodist agencies and institutions, shall:

1. Affirm and support these concerns for religious liberty in the ecumenical groups in which we participate;

2. Pursue application of these minimal standards of the human rights of religious liberty in all societies and work toward conditions where governmental units neither inhibit nor encourage religion;

3. Advocate, through education and political action, to gain religious liberty in all places where it is lacking;

4. Extend the compassionate ministry of the Church to persons who suffer because either religious or governmental authorities seek to deny these rights to them, assuming a special responsibility to work on behalf of "unregistered," in addition to governmentally sanctioned, religious institutions;

5. Educate ourselves so that we will be able to identify and respond to violations of religious liberty both in our own and in other societies; and

6. Offer support to the Office of the United Nations Special Rapporteur on Religious Intolerance.

ADOPTED 1988

See Social Principles, ¶¶ 68B, 69A; "The United Methodist Church and Church-Government Relations."

Repression and the Right to Privacy

The Social Principles of The United Methodist Church affirm that "illegal and unconscionable activities directed against persons or groups by their own governments must not be justified or kept secret, even under the guise of national security" (¶ 68C). "We also strongly reject domestic surveillance and intimidation of political opponents by governments in power and all other misuses of elective or appointive offices" (¶ 68A).

The prophets of Israel denounced the repression of the poor, widows, orphans, and others of their society, and our Lord's ministry began with the announced purpose to set at liberty the poor and disadvantaged. In our biblical tradition, we raise the following issues:

Repression

We have lived in a time when the accumulated hopes of racial and cultural minorities, combined with a growing dissent in the United States, were met by mounting fears and rising anxieties of the dominant group within the population. Seized with apprehension, many became obsessed with establishing a climate of security—even by the sacrificing of creating and maintaining justice and protecting the rights and liberties of individuals.

The institutions of this society began to reflect the fears of the majority of the population and established policies and procedures that, in the short range, provided expedient control. These policies, however, were seen as repressive measures by those who sought legitimate rights and new opportunities.

In the immediate past, we sounded a call to concern because we recognized that society can become repressive in nature with hardly a trace of consciousness by the mass of the people, particularly if that people is feverishly fearful and has developed the readiness to accept any measure that seems to offer a new form of protection.

It is deplorable that in a society that is democratic in theory and structure there are signs of increasing repression: dragnet arrests; police and the intelligence community's harassment of minority leaders; charges of conspiracy; summary acquittals of police accused of brutality; the rising militance of rank-and-file police; support for the use of preventive detention; the utilization of wiretaps; censorship of journalism in educational institutions; heavy punitive action against dissidents; the confinement of those who protested within the military forces; the use of police to control dissent within the churches; utilizing grand juries for the purpose of harassment rather than indictment; and the use of church members, clergy, and missionaries for secret intelligence purposes by local police departments, the Federal Bureau of Investigation, and the Central Intelligence Agency.

We affirm the many civil, school, and church authorities who are working toward the elimination of these abuses through their work and example; and we note that many of the most flagrant of these acts of repression no longer occur. Congress, the press, and the American people have begun watching agency activities more closely and with a greater demand for public accountability.

This vigilance must not be relaxed, for if it is, there may be renewed acts of repression and fresh attempts to curtail the rights of citizens whenever redress is sought for economic and social grievances.

Therefore, we urge that all Church members and leaders continue to be sensitive to this situation in their local community and in the nation by:

1. Seeking to understand and undergird responsible institutions and agencies of the community and being supportive of measurements that will improve them and upgrade their personnel; and

2. Establishing programs in the community sponsored by local churches to: (a) educate church members and their wider community about the potential for repression in the institutions of society; (b) study and affirm the biblical and constitutional basis for justice under law; (c) work in state and federal legislatures to bring about just and responsible criminal code revisions that do not reinforce repressive elements in our nation's life; oppose forms of legislation that would legalize repression; support legislation that would prohibit intelligence agencies from conducting surveillance or disruption of lawful political activities or otherwise violating constitutional rights; (d) develop an awareness of the rights and protection citizens should expect; and (e) work for institu-

tional change in situations where rights are not respected and protection is not furnished.

The Right to Privacy

The Christian faith stresses the dignity of and respect for human personality. Invasion of the privacy of an ordinary citizen of society negates this dignity and respect. Further, the Christian faith is supportive of a society that elicits hope and trust, not a society that foments fear and threatens with oppression.

The revelation that intelligence agencies, local police, and the United States Army have, over a number of years, developed a domestic espionage apparatus involving the gathering of information about the lawful political activities of millions of citizens is a cause for concern.

The Constitutional Rights Subcommittee and the Privacy Commission Report provided substantial information that demonstrated that privacy lies in jeopardy as a result of the use of long, personal government questionnaires. Much government data is collected under the threat of jail or fine. As useful as such information may be to the government and to private agencies, the misuse of data banks is an imminent and serious threat to constitutional liberties.

We are concerned about the increased amount of government wiretapping and electronic surveillance that has taken place in recent years.

Although it is now illegal for any governmental unit to engage in any kind of wiretapping without a warrant of a court, we urge restraint in the use of wiretapping and electronic surveillance, for its prevalence creates an air of suspicion throughout the whole society and contributes to the insecurity of law-abiding American citizens.

Therefore, we respectfully request the Congress of the United States to:

1. Enact comprehensive charter legislation for all of the intelligence agencies that would prohibit them from engaging in surveillance or disruption of lawful political activity. We oppose any charter provision that permits intelligence agencies to recruit and use as agents clergy or missionaries;

2. Place statutory limitations upon the demand by governmental bureaus and agencies for personal information about any citizen or family for statistical purposes. When such requests by agencies are for information not required by law, the respondent should be informed that compliance is voluntary. Restrictions should be placed by law on

private agencies in gathering, storing, and disseminating personal information; and

3. Retain the Freedom of Information Act as it is, in support of the right of all citizens to know the actions of their government.

ADOPTED 1980

See Social Principles, ¶¶ 68*A*, 69*A;* "Human Rights"; "Domestic Surveillance."

Separation of Church and State

WHEREAS, The United Methodist Church has historically supported the separation of church and state, including the free exercise of religion; and

WHEREAS, The United Methodist Church has understood this to mean that government must be neutral in matters of religion and may not show preference of one religion over others, for religion in general, or for religion over nonreligion; and

WHEREAS, The United Methodist Church has continued to affirm the position that government may not engage in, sponsor, supervise, aid, or lend its authority to religious expression or religious observance;

Therefore, be it resolved, that the 1996 General Conference, meeting in Denver, Colorado, reaffirm its historic position and oppose any government legislation or constitutional amendment that would change our existing First Amendment rights in regard to the use of public funds to support nonpublic elementary and secondary schools where religion is taught, or in regard to religious observances in public schools.

ADOPTED 1996

See Social Principles, ¶ 68; "Church-Government Relations"; "The United Methodist Church and Church-Government Relations."

Support of Conscientious Objectors to Registration

The United Methodist Church supports all persons who make decisions of conscience in regard to military service. The ministry of the Church is not limited to those who conscientiously serve in the armed forces of their nation. It is also extended to those who, as a matter of conscience, refuse to serve in the armed forces, to cooperate with systems of military conscription, or to accept alternate service (*see* Social Principles, ¶ 68*G;* "The United Methodist Church and Peace," Roman numeral V, section 2).

In order to demonstrate this ministry, institutions of higher education affiliated with the various entities of The United Methodist Church are expected to affirm that participation in systems of military conscription, including draft registration, will not be considered a prerequisite to eligibility either for enrollment or for institutionally controlled student aid funds.

Therefore, be it resolved, that the General Conference of The United Methodist Church encourage all United Methodist institutions of higher education to respect those students who conscientiously refuse to cooperate with the draft registration and provide them equal access to institutional financial aid resources to which they may be entitled.

ADOPTED 1988

See Social Principles, ¶ 68G; "Certification of Conscientious Objectors"; "The United Methodist Church and Peace."

Support Legislation Prohibiting Malicious Harassments

The United Methodist Church encourages and supports the introduction, passage, and funding of legislation that prohibits malicious and intimidating actions that are reasonably related to, associated with, or directed toward a person's race, color, religion, ancestry, national origin, sexual orientation, age, gender, or disability.

ADOPTED 1992

See Social Principles, ¶¶ 66 and 68; "Racial Harassment"; "Sexual Harassment and The United Methodist Church"; "Sexual Harassment in Church and Society in the U.S.A."; "The Church and People with Mental, Physical, and/or Psychological Disabilities."

A Call for Truth, Fairness, and Accuracy

Our Christian heritage includes hearty critique of religious institutions, led by Old Testament prophets, Jesus of Nazareth, Martin Luther, John Wesley, Sojourner Truth, Evangeline Booth, Martin Luther King Jr., and others. Their words and actions were necessary to call the people of God to goals of righteousness, justice, and mercy. Their motives were to reform and heal, to bring purity through the refiner's fire.

The United Methodist Church endorses an open, uninhibited flow of information regarding its policies and actions. The Church's health depends on an informed membership and the opportunity for that membership to participate in a nonthreatening, responsible dialogue with Church agencies and leaders.

Given its firm commitment to fair, accurate, and truthful communication, the Church today is deeply concerned about the miscommunication of information emanating from groups both within and outside the Church. Criticism that is more political than spiritual, more dedicated to tearing down than building up, is divisive and fracturing, rather than reconciling and healing.

Recent attacks on this denomination overlook or downplay the ways God is working through communities of faith. There is a growing spirituality in The United Methodist Church as evidenced by the tremendous success of the DISCIPLE Bible study program, in which many thousands have participated. The Walk to Emmaus, a Christian renewal effort, is experiencing steady growth around the world.

Today's United Methodist Church is doing substantial good around the world. We are in the Midwest, years after devastating floods, helping people recover. We are in South Florida easing the pain of Hurricane Andrew victims. The Church is in Bosnia and Africa. In Oklahoma City, the First United Methodist Church received $100,000 from the United Methodist Committee on Relief (UMCOR) to help recover from the federal building bombing.

The United Methodist Church rests on a strong foundation of seeking to address society's ills. Ours is a communion that provides for diversity, guards the ability of pastors to preach the gospel, and affirms the priesthood of all believers. Our connectional strengths are needed by a world clearly experiencing isolation, alienation, and loneliness. Members deserve to rejoice in what their Church is doing.

We encourage our critics to engage in a dialogue to make our Church stronger. Recognizing the value of true theological diversity, The United Methodist Church calls for a discussion of Church issues, using the honorable principles of truth, fairness, and accuracy in reporting the words and actions of Church people and agencies.

The United Methodist Church recognizes the right of any group to inform those who have common interests. It honors the idea of free speech in an open forum, and it encourages the healthy discussion of diverse viewpoints so long as it is conducted with dignity and respect.

To all who truly love the Church and pray for its future, we say, "Come, let us together listen to the Spirit of God, calling us to New Creation, where none are intimidated and all are valued for their gifts, passion, and viewpoints. Let us share our pain and our dreams, that Christ's new church may be born through the travail."

ADOPTED 1996

See Social Principles, ¶ 68A, C; "Free Flow of Information Among All Peoples of the Earth."

Victims of Crime

Jesus answered the question of "Who is my neighbor" by telling the parable of the Good Samaritan (Luke 10:25-37). The priest and the Levite failed to respond. The Samaritan did respond, and we are to do likewise. The neighbor was the victim of crime—he had fallen among robbers, who not only stole his money but also stripped him, beat him, and left him half dead. The Samaritan had compassion; he stopped, bandaged the man's wounds, cared for him, took him to an inn, and took responsibility for the cost of his stay.

Many people are victims or relatives of victims of crime. They suffer shock and a sense of helplessness. In addition to financial loss, there is a spiritual and emotional trauma and often a lack of support and direction. There is no doubt that many feel frustrated because often there seems to be no provision for them to be heard, or their injuries redressed, and they are not notified of the court procedures.

This is an area where the Church has an opportunity to minister.

Therefore, we call upon the members of The United Methodist Church to minister to the victims of crime and to be advocates for them, and we call upon the General Conference:

1. To direct the General Board of Church and Society to work for the recognition of the needs of victims of crimes and survivors to certain rights;

2. To support laws at both the federal and state levels with respect of compensation of victims of crime and to work for the adoption of such laws in those jurisdictions where there are now no such provisions;

3. To recognize that the constitutional rights of the accused must be provided. Victims of crime or their lawful representative, including the next of kin of homicide victims, are entitled to be kept informed during criminal proceedings, to be present at the trial, and to be heard at the sentencing hearing as well as an impact statement of the time of the parole consideration;

4. To encourage seminaries to develop continuing-education programs on this subject;

5. To direct the General Board of Discipleship to develop guidelines, programs, and study materials for pastors and others in providing spiritual support and understanding for victims and families; and

6. To urge all members of The United Methodist Church to initiate presence, prayers, and support for victims and survivors as well as

strategies to bring about necessary changes in the criminal justice system.

ADOPTED 1988

See Social Principles, ¶ 68F; "Criminal Justice"; "Equal Justice."

Violence in Electronic Media and Film

The Social Principles of The United Methodist Church, in the section on "Media Violence and Christian Values" (¶ 66P), point to "the unprecedented impact the media (principally television and movies) are having on Christian and human values within our society." The paragraph specifically notes the media's depiction of "acts of graphic violence."

In November 1993, the General Board of the National Council of the Churches of Christ in the U.S.A. adopted a policy statement (by a vote of 145-0-0) on "Violence in Electronic Media and Films." As a member of the National Council of Churches (NCC), The United Methodist Church affirms that policy statement. While the bulk of the content in this United Methodist resolution comes from the NCC statement, it was substantially revised at points to reflect the purpose and intent of The United Methodist Church.

Foreword

We live in a climate of violence. Violence is everywhere: in city and suburb, in mean streets and quiet lanes, in private conversations and public media. Our society knows violence through abuse and rape, rising crime rates and diminished trust. We acknowledge that the climate of the psychological violence of words, as well as physical violence, breeds fear and rapidly escalating concerns for personal security. This in turn leads to more violence and contributes to societies' tightening cycle of violence.

Violence is simple and brutal, but its roots are complex. We know it to be bred in families where children and spouses are abused and maltreated, where problems are met with force or threat of force. People who are in submissive positions to authority, actual or perceived, are particularly vulnerable to violence. We know that violence may be related to learning disabilities and chemical dependency. And we know that violence is exacerbated in communities and families living in poverty, and by the prominence given to it in films, television, and other media.

Women often are portrayed in the media as being subjected to sexual violation and violence. These sexual situations would appear to create no harmful effects for women, when in fact the context of the encounter is a power or authority relationship. The electronic media and film often reinforce this authority/victim relationship, depicting it as harmless or neutral.

Violence cannot be reduced to one cause. It is clear, however, that films and television play a role not only in reflecting but also in contributing to a violent and mean world.

Films and Television

Films and television
- *give the only information many of us receive about some aspects of life.* Frequently, there are no other comparable sources of information available on human relationships or complex social issues;
- *model and prompt emotional responses to the realities of individual and social life.* Entertainment that provides a vicarious experience of violence also models a response, often one of anger and retribution;
- *over-represent violence, with television sometimes showing as many as thirty violent acts per hour as preferred solutions to disagreements.* This increases viewer concern for self-protection and a fear of going out alone. In addition, it enhances the acceptance of using violence as a solution to problems;
- *increase an appetite and tolerance for entertainment with a violent content, since the more violence an audience sees, the more violence it will want.* This appetite for violence entails an increased callousness to people who may be hurting or in need;
- *sexualize violence by rendering it pleasurable and/or by depicting an erotic payoff for the protagonists who initiate the sexual violence.*

While films and television are certainly not the only cause of a climate of violence, they bear a considerable share of the responsibility; thus the need for this policy statement.

Our Faith Perspective

According to our biblical faith, every person whom we encounter is precious as one created in the image of God and one for whom Christ died (Romans 5:8-10). Every human group—all races, women and men, gay and straight, just and unjust—accordingly share in this dignity.

The body is essential to the person and is created and redeemed by God (Romans 8:23). Violence against the body, mind, or spirit is an assault against human dignity. The taking of life violates God's image (Genesis 9:6), and cruelty defies the Creator's intentions (Job 31:13-15). Even a slap against a cheek calls forth a moral response (Matthew 5:39).

Human beings, in their separation from God, are prone to violence. The Scriptures provide abundant examples. One person or group continually has an advantage over another, and the human gift of freedom provides the temptation to exercise power against others. When violence is the recourse, the innocent often are hurt. In contrast to the impression often given by the media, deeds have consequences. Violence leads to violence in a climate of revenge, but vengeance belongs to God (Romans 12:19). God's people are called to forgiveness (Matthew 6:12).

Our response to others is one of caring for them as we care for ourselves (Matthew 7:12). Problems are not solved through a self-protective consciousness, but through trust in God (Matthew 5:39-42). They are solved in a context of community, respect, and hearing of one another, and, where necessary, through the provisions of the broader community (Matthew 18:15-20). Any force needed to protect human life must be the minimum required and carried out in this context.

We are to be people of peace (Matthew 5:9). We are people of the story and realize the powerful impact of images. We are about what is true and honorable and just and pure (Philippians 4:8). We are accountable for our words as well as our deeds (Matthew 12:36).

We therefore deplore the competing stories of violence from the media that continue to shape our society. Even in doing so, however, we know that sin still infects and affects us all. Too often we ignore our personal and corporate complicity in violence, blaming others. Too often we are weak and uncertain about our part of the solution.

After all, we Christians

• *support the media industries as consumers, thereby helping to form their financial backbone.* We are part of the audience that media violence attracts;

• *permit and sometimes encourage our children's exposure to media with violent content.* When a child is baptized or dedicated, a congregation promises to nurture and care for the child and to bring the child into faith. We certainly must be concerned about the impact that media have on a child;

• *participate in the media industries through our investments and through our vocations as producers and writers.* We do not always use our power to work for better programming; and

• *shirk our duty as citizens to be vigilant in the pursuit of a common good.*

An Issue of Urgency

Media violence has not abated. Movie rentals and cable television have made explicit violence more available; CD-ROM technology promises to make violence interactive. Network television, over the years, has supplied a steady diet of violence; 70 percent of primetime programs use violence, with an average of sixteen violent acts (including two murders) in each evening's primetime programming.

We affirm our adherence to the principles of an open forum of ideas and the guarantees of the First Amendment to free speech, press, and religion. As objectionable as we find media violence, we do not believe government censorship is a viable or appropriate solution.

We strongly object, however, to what we see as the misuse of the First Amendment, by commercial interests, as a cover for a quest for profit. Free speech and a free press have their places within a context of social responsibility and a concern for the common good. We hold media industries accountable for what they produce and distribute, and we challenge them to act as good citizens in society.

We commit ourselves to working through government and with industry to find ways to respect free expression while abhorring and selectively limiting media violence, the moral equivalent of a harmful substance. We commit ourselves also to support families and churches in their aspirations and strategies for more appropriate media choices.

A Call to Action

In order to be supportive of churches and families and in our dealings with government and industry, we call for media that clearly:

1. Create community and value and develop cultures;

2. Help to remove people and society from the cycle of violence that we understand to have been broken definitively by the cross of Christ; and

3. Respect human dignity and seek to involve people in participatory communication processes that enhance human dignity.

We call for a nationwide approach to media literacy, involving four interrelated components:

1. *Critical viewing*—learning to discern the meanings of media messages;

2. *Critical analysis*—determining the cultural, social, political, and economic influences on a media message;

3. *Creative production skills*—producing films and programs that create community, value cultures, and respect human dignity; and

4. Preparation for *citizenship in a media culture*—understanding how the media work in society; taking personal and public action to challenge government and industry.

Our Challenge to Churches

Our requests of churches are made in light of their role in resisting hate and witnessing to the Prince of Peace. *We call upon churches to:*

1. Provide leadership through congregations, as centers of media literacy;

2. Promote specific electronic media and film programs for pastors and people who teach moral and ethical values that enhance life;

3. Provide assistance to parents of children and youth concerning how families may use television more creatively;

4. Prepare leadership, through media literacy programs in seminaries and universities, and through other means; and to develop and promote media literacy resources;

5. Urge the integration of media awareness and literacy programs as critical components of peace, justice, and advocacy agendas; and

6. Organize their efforts for continuity and wider impact, working ecumenically wherever possible.

Our Challenge to Families

As the primary social unit of our culture, *we ask families to:*

1. Monitor family viewing habits of television, film, and video games;

2. Discuss programs, films, and media experience in relationship to their faith;

3. Participate directly in the media world through conversations with the church, government, and media industries. It helps to let these groups know what is valued and what needs to be changed among the media options; and

4. Protect children from seeing films expressly intended for adults.

Our Challenge to Government

As citizens, we are responsible for our governments. Historically, federal and local governments help maintain order and community standards, including personal safety. However, our requests for government leadership do not diminish our commitment to the First Amendment. Keeping this balance in mind, *we call upon our federal government to:*

1. Lead in the development of media standards through an open, representative, and accessible process;

2. Develop not only regulations but also incentives for producers in order to encourage media choices that build community and enhance human dignity; and

3. Review its mandated task of regulating airwaves that we hold in common. Vigilant supervision, through the Federal Communications Commission, the Federal Trade Commission, and other means, would entail a closer scrutiny of media violence than has been the case.

We call upon our municipal governments to review and discuss media violence, especially when making contracts with the cable television industry.

Our Challenge to the Media Industries

Our requests of media industries are that they reexamine their roles as "corporate citizens." Our expectations are that they will act in a more socially responsible manner. This corporate citizenship has global dimensions because of the extensive products our media export to the rest of the world.

We strongly urge the media industries to contribute to the development of media standards by which we all can live. This includes the film, television, cable television, and video-games industries. *We will support these industries in such efforts through:*

1. Ongoing dialogue with media management and professional media practitioners;

2. Bringing together those who manage the media and the consumers who receive their products;

3. Reinforcing a voluntary approach for protecting children from adult material through the film industry rating board for the Motion Picture Association of America (MPAA). We urge the members of the MPAA to reverse the trend toward the increasingly violent images that now appear in films rated suitable for children. We call upon the

National Association of Theater Owners (NATO) to enforce more diligently the ratings system at the box office to prevent children from exposure to R-rated films intended strictly for adults. We also call for similar standards from the industry producing videotapes;

4. Publicizing advertisers of specific programs that depict significant values of the religious community; and

5. Encouraging investors, media management, and practicing media professionals to acknowledge their responsibility for ameliorating the climate of violence and for developing alternatives to gratuitous violence.

Specifically, we urge that churches holding shares in corporations with media assets ask those corporations to:

1. Adopt public and verifiable community-interest standards;

2. Participate in open discussions on the development of and use of media technology and their implications for our common interests;

3. Provide programming that promotes peaceful alternative resolutions of conflict; and

4. Provide increased programming from international sources to enhance our understanding of our neighbors in the global community.

ADOPTED 1996

See Social Principles, ¶ 66P; "The Church in a Mass Media Culture"; "Sexual Violence and Pornography."

THE WORLD COMMUNITY

Africa Reconstruction and Development

We applaud international efforts to develop a more just international economic order in which the limited resources of the earth will be used to the maximum benefit of all nations and peoples. We urge Christians in every society to encourage the governments under which they live and the economic entities within their societies to aid and work for the development of more just economic orders.

(Social Principles, ¶ 69B)

The continent of Africa is in crisis. The international community singled out Africa as the area of greatest human suffering at the United Nations World Summit for Social Development held in Copenhagen, Denmark, in March 1995. And more recently, the UN System-wide Special Initiative on Africa, jointly launched by the UN and the World Bank on March 15, 1996, has committed up to $25 billion over ten years to respond to Africa's developmental needs in a coordinated way in the following sectors: basic education, basic health, governance, food security, water and sanitation, peace-building, and informatics.

A century of colonial rule, preceded by two centuries of a vicious slave trade and followed by a generation of neo-colonialism, has left much of Africa's social, political, and economic life in a shambles. The decade of the eighties was disastrous. Real wages for Africa's workers fell by 30 percent in a decade, and unemployment quadrupled. Infant mortality rates, a powerful index of human well-being, are now more than three times the rate for Southeast Asia and more than double the rate for Latin America and the Caribbean. A destructive combination of military dictatorship, *apartheid*, economic collapse, social unrest, civil war, and natural disasters created 7 million refugees, 50 million disabled persons, and 35 million displaced people. Armaments that poured into Africa during and following the Cold War are now used by some governments to oppress their own people, by armed bands who enrich themselves at the point of a gun, and in interethnic conflicts.

Archbishop Desmond Tutu, president of the All Africa Conference of Churches, observes with alarm that: The magnitude of the economic crisis is manifest by the rising cost of living; adverse commodity prices; a ruthless free market; the unfair and heavy debt burden; the falling prices of raw materials; the over-burdening of social services; rising unemployment, especially among women and young men; unacceptably high mortality and morbidity rates among children and women; and noticeable increases in general abuse and violence.

Yet the continent is a place of hope and promise. Peace has been achieved in a number of nations that were wracked by civil war for years. Democratic reforms are being demanded by the people of those countries still suffering under military dictatorship and government corruption. Democracy is struggling into life in more than a dozen nations. The whole world is rejoicing at the miracle of liberation in South Africa, as the old wineskins of *apartheid* have been broken. New models of sustainable and equitable development are being created by the people of the continent, as they see the destructiveness of inappropriate Western and neo-colonial models. The continent is rich in natural resources needed by the entire world. Africa is blessed with people of remarkable energy, spirit, and ingenuity. The United Methodist Church, continuing to grow rapidly, is a transforming presence in many countries, influential beyond its numbers, engaging in a holistic Wesleyan ministry of outreach, evangelism, and humanitarian service.

The Copenhagen Commitment

In response to the crisis and mindful of the new possibilities emerging in Africa, governments and nongovernmental organizations meeting at the United Nations World Summit for Social Development made a solemn pledge:

We commit ourselves to accelerating the economic, social and human resource development of Africa and the least developed countries.

To this end, we will:

(a) Implement, at the national level, structural adjustment policies, which should include social development goals, as well as effective development strategies that establish a more favorable climate for trade and investment, give priority to human resource development and further promote the development of democratic institutions;

(b) Support the domestic efforts of Africa and the least developed countries to implement economic reforms, programmes to increase food security, and commodity diversification efforts through international cooperation, including South-South cooperation and technical and financial assistance, as well as trade and partnership;

(c) Find effective, development-oriented and durable solutions to external debt problems, through the immediate implementation of the terms of debt forgiveness agreed upon in the Paris Club in December 1994, which encompass debt reduction, including cancellation or other debt-relief measures; invite the international financial institutions to examine innovative approaches to assist low-income countries with a high proportion of multilateral debt, with a view to alleviating their debt burdens; and develop techniques of debt conversion applied to social development programmes and projects in conformity with Summit priorities. These actions should take into account the mid-term review of the United Nations New Agenda for the Development of Africa in the 1990s[1] and the Programme of Action for the Least Developed Countries for the 1990s,[2] and should be implemented as soon as possible;

(d) Ensure the implementation of the strategies and measures for the development of Africa decided by the international community, and support the reform efforts, development strategies and programmes decided by the African countries and the least developed countries;

(e) Increase official development assistance, both overall and for social programmes, and improve its impact, consistent with countries' economic circumstances and capacities to assist, and consistent with commitments in international agreements;

(f) Consider ratifying the United Nations Convention to Combat Desertification in Those Countries Experiencing Serious Drought and/or Desertification, particularly in Africa,[3] and support African countries in the implementation of urgent action to combat desertification and mitigate the effects of drought;

(g) Take all necessary measures to ensure that communicable diseases, particularly HIV/AIDS, malaria and tuberculosis, do not restrict or reverse the progress made in economic and social development.

---

[1] General Assembly resolution 46/151, annex, sect. II.
[2] Report of the Second UN Conference on the Least Developed Countries, Paris, 3–14 September, 1990 (A/CONF: 147/18), part one.
[3] Ibid.: A/49/84/Add2, annex, appendix II.

United Methodist Response

As Christians, our faith is in the God of Jesus Christ, who stands with the most vulnerable and oppressed people in our societies. Their well-being must serve as a guidepost for justice. God, sovereign over all nations, had made of one blood all the peoples of the earth. United Methodists, therefore, remain ever-vigilant, listening more attentively than ever to churches and movements around the world, as they struggle for social, political, economic, and spiritual development. Therefore, we call upon the United Methodist people, local churches, and agencies to:

1. Participate fully in the Campaign for Africa of the Council of Bishops and the General Board of Global Ministries and urge the continuation of the campaign; and to urge the General Board of Church and Society to advocate for policies that address the economic crises, peacemaking, and human-rights concerns in Africa;

2. Encourage United Methodist churches to increase their participation in programs of emergency relief, aid to refugees, reconstruction, and development through the appropriate units of the General Board of Global Ministries, regional councils of churches, and the World Council of Churches;

3. Encourage United Methodists to participate in Volunteers in Mission programs and educate themselves (through orientation, cultural sensitivity, and contingency planning) for working alongside and empowering African brothers and sisters and their institutions in, for example, reconstructing schools, clinics, and churches. There is also a need to emphasize the importance of preparation for the cross-cultural experience and mutuality of learning for both the volunteer in mission and the receiving partner;

4. Be faithful witnesses to government leaders in every country to the need for concerted national and international efforts toward sustainable, equitable development and reconstruction on the continent of Africa, guided by the Copenhagen Commitment and other bilateral and multilateral initiatives—including the Special Program of Assistance to Africa (SPA) and the new UN System-wide Initiative on Africa;

5. Urge United Methodists to persuade their governments to ratify the United Nations Convention to Combat Desertification in Those Countries Experiencing Serious Drought and/or Desertification;

6. Press the World Bank and International Monetary Fund to reform their structural adjustment programs, which have contributed to debts,

declining economic and health systems, and deteriorating education and infrastructure in African nations;

7. Urge an embargo on present and future arms sales to Africa, and urge measures to rid Africa of the weapons that were poured into the continent, including the land mines that kill innocent people, predominantly women and children;

8. Continue and further develop the General Board of Global Ministries' commitment to comprehensive, community-based primary health care, recognizing the role that poverty, poor sanitation, and polluted water play in the spread of communicable diseases across the continent; the collapse of the health-care systems in many countries; and the ineffectiveness of Western medical models; and

9. Monitor all programs of relief and development, with special attention to these criteria:

(a) give priority to women and children, who suffer the most during times of social unrest and war;

(b) involve full participation of African United Methodists in setting priorities and in designing, managing, and coordinating projects, relying upon their experience, wisdom, and resourcefulness;

(c) design programs to alleviate the root causes of poverty, oppression, and social unrest; and

(d) program for sustainability, both in terms of ecological integrity and the avoidance of dependency by utilizing appropriate technologies that do not require continuing input of resources from other countries.

ADOPTED 1996

See Social Principles, ¶ 69; "The United Methodist Church and Peace"; "Liberia."

The Black Hills Alliance

The Black Hills, historically the sacred, ancestral lands of the Lakota people, is designated a "national sacrifice area" in a federal plan known as Project Independence. Large-scale plans are underway for the mining of uranium, coal, and taconite iron deposits, using open pits, strip mines, and solution mines. It is estimated that within thirty-five years, the water tables will be exhausted. Radioactive byproducts will pollute the air. Unrestricted strip-mining will devastate the land.

We therefore affirm: (1) the right of native people to keep sacred their ancestral burial grounds and their right to determine the responsible use of natural resources; (2) the necessity to consider the long-range consequences of depleting the water supply, as opposed to the short-range benefits of obtaining additional coal and other mineral resources; and (3) the position of the Black Hills Alliance, an organization of persons who live in the Black Hills region who are dedicated to a safe and healthy future for their children, and who maintain research, education, and action projects in support of their cause.

ADOPTED 1980

See Social Principles, ¶¶ 66A and 69A; "American Indian Religious Freedom Act"; "The Fort Laramie Treaty"; "Toward a New Beginning Beyond 1992."

The Building of Settlements in the Occupied Territories

WHEREAS, the continuing efforts by the State of Israel to build settlements in the occupied territories violates both international law and the spirit of the Declaration of Principles, that such efforts are based upon a vision of superiority of Jewish claims to land over the long-standing and recognized claims to the land by indigenous Palestinian people, and that such efforts have a devastating effect on Palestinian communities; and

WHEREAS, the continuing confiscation of private land for the construction of settlements stands as an impediment to peace because it violates both international law and the Declaration of Principles; it destroys the capacity of people in Palestinian communities to work and earn a livelihood; it, along with the restrictions on building placed on the Palestinian communities, forces the emigration of Palestinian people from the occupied territories; and it demoralizes the indigenous Palestinian population; and

WHEREAS, the prophet Isaiah cautioned against coveting the lands and homes of one's neighbors: "Ah, you who join house to house,/who add field to field,/until there is room for no one but you,/and you are left to live alone/in the midst of the land!" (Isaiah 5:8); and

WHEREAS, the continuing confiscation of privately held land for construction of settlements violates basic understanding of human rights, perverts the peace process, destroys the hope of people who are working for and longing for peace, both Israelis and Palestinians, and fosters a sense of desperation that can only lead to further violence; and

WHEREAS, we in the United States are providing financial assistance to the State of Israel that allows for the building of these settlements;

Therefore, be it resolved, that The United Methodist Church opposes continuing confiscation of Palestinian land, the continued building of

Jewish settlements, and any vision of a greater Israel that includes the occupied territories and/or the whole of Jerusalem and its surroundings.

ADOPTED 1996

See Social Principles, ¶ 69; "The Middle East and North Africa"; "Jerusalem"; "Economic Support for Palestinians."

Chungshindae/"Comfort Women"/Sex Slaves Drafted by Japan During World War II

WHEREAS, in Scripture we are exhorted to bring lasting justice to all and to establish justice on the earth and are warned against healing the wound of the people lightly, delivering false peace (Isaiah 42:1-7; Jeremiah 6:14); and

WHEREAS, our Social Principles state, "The Church must regard nations as accountable for unjust treatment of their citizens and others living within their borders. While recognizing valid differences in culture and political philosophy, we stand for justice and peace in every nation" (¶ 69A); and

WHEREAS, The United Methodist Church, taking note of the successful contributions made by the World Council of Churches in supporting the "comfort women" survivors at the United Nations human rights bodies; and also taking note of the recommendations to Japan on the "comfort women" issue made by the United Nations Sub-Commission on Prevention of Discrimination and Protection of Minorities in August 1995, as well as paragraph 147(f)[1] of the Platform for Action adopted by the Beijing United Nations Fourth Conference on Women in September 1995, endorses "the United Nations and its related bodies" and urges the United Nations to "take a more aggressive role in the development of international arbitration of disputes and actual conflicts" (¶ 69D);

Therefore, be it resolved, that the General Conference—its membership, churches, and ministries—become informed on the history of military "comfort women" in Korea and other Asian and Pacific countries and on the plight of the survivors and families of "comfort women";

---

[1] Paragraph 147(f) of the Platform for Action: "Uphold and reinforce standards set out in international humanitarian law and international human rights instruments to prevent all acts of violence against women in situations of armed and other acts of conflict; undertake a full investigation of all acts of violence against women committed during war, including rape, in particular systematic rape, forced prostitution and other forms of indecent assault and sexual slavery; prosecute all criminals responsible for war crimes against women; and provide full redress to women victims.

educate local congregations on Chungshindae/"comfort women"/sex slaves; and hold survivors and their families in prayer;

Be it further resolved, that the General Conference communicate to the United Nations human rights bodies its concern over the inclusion of Japan as a permanent member of the United Nations Security Council until Japan recognizes the act of sexual slavery as a crime against humanity and as a war crime under international humanitarian laws; that the General Conference communicate its support of the Korean Council for the Women Drafted for Military Sexual Slavery by Japan (Korean Council) as it demands that Japan take responsibility for its crimes by immediately passing a bill in the Japanese Diet to apologize and pay redress directly to the individual "comfort women" survivors as the most urgent state responsibility of Japan;

Be it further resolved, that the General Conference support and communicate with Radhidka Coomaraswamy of Sri Lanka, the Special Rapporteur on Violence Against Women (appointed by the UN Commission on Prevention of Discrimination and Protection of Minorities in 1994), and publicize and disseminate her reports to educate members of The United Methodist Church on district, annual conference, jurisdictional, and general board levels as a special study project;

Be it further resolved, that the General Conference communicate with the World/Regional/National bodies of Methodist churches and the Christian Council of Asia, and so forth, and ask them to support the Korean Council's political ideology and activities if they agree with the ideology and activities of the Korean Council.

ADOPTED 1996

See Social Principles, ¶ 69; "The United Methodist Church and Peace."

The Church and the Global HIV-AIDS Epidemic

The United Methodist Church will work cooperatively with colleague churches in every region in response to the global HIV-AIDS epidemic, which is affecting the health and well-being of individuals and communities worldwide. The Old Testament is replete with calls to the nations and religious leaders to address the needs of the people who are in distress, who are suffering and ill. The New Testament presents a Jesus who reached out and healed those who came to him, including those who were despised and rejected because of their illnesses and afflictions. Jesus' identification with those who suffer was made clear in his admonition to his disciples that "just as you do to the least of these, you do also to me" (Matthew 25:40, paraphrased). His Great Commission to his followers to go and do as he has done is a mandate to the church for full involvement and compassionate response.

The Geneva-based World Health Organization estimates that by the year 2000, the number of people infected with the Human Immunodeficiency Virus (HIV)—which causes HIV-related illnesses, including AIDS (Acquired Immune Deficiency Syndrome)—will reach forty million. The suffering being borne by individuals, families, and entire communities, and the strain being placed on health facilities and national economies, call for intensified cooperative efforts by every sector of society to slow and prevent the spread of infection; to provide appropriate care for those already infected and ill; to speed the development of effective, affordable treatment and vaccines to be available in all countries; and to provide support to care providers, communities, health-care workers, health facilities, and programs. The presence of HIV infection has been found in all five geographical regions, and HIV illnesses have been reported to the World Health Organization by nearly 200 countries.

Worldwide, HIV infection has been transmitted primarily through heterosexual intercourse with infected persons, as well as in some regions through homosexual/bisexual sexual contact with infected persons; through blood-to-blood contact, including the transfusion of infected blood and blood products; through infected transplanted organs and donated semen; through the use of infected instruments as well as skin-piercing objects associated with ceremonial or traditional healing practices; through the sharing of infected needles and equipment by injection drug users; from an infected woman to her fetus/infant before or during childbirth, and in some instances, after delivery through infected breast milk.

The impact of HIV infection and related illnesses on economic, social, demographic, political, and health systems is being felt in innumerable ways. Worldwide, women and children increasingly are being affected by the spread of HIV infection. As larger numbers of women of childbearing age are infected and give birth, larger numbers of infants are born with HIV infection. As larger numbers of parents are infected and die, larger numbers of children are orphaned, and extended families are called upon to provide care for greater numbers of family members.

Population growth rates, age structures, labor supply, and agricultural productivity will suffer negative effects as younger-age-group members and women are infected and become ill. The ramification of HIV infection and illness will be particularly grave for families and societies where the extended family is the main or only system of social security and care for family members who are aged or ill and for the nurture of orphaned children.

Gross national products may decrease in areas with high rates of HIV infection, morbidity, and mortality. Crimes of hate and instances of neglect and rejection may increase against gay and bisexual men, injection drug users, prostitutes, and others who are assumed to be carriers of HIV. Available health dollars and resources will be affected in the process of caring for larger numbers of persons with HIV illnesses, owning to the costs of securing, distributing, administering, and monitoring the effects of new treatments and drug therapies as they become more readily available. The advances of the "Child Survival Revolution" may be offset as the health of greater numbers of children are affected. It is not known how health systems in any region will be able to manage the additional caseloads in a world in which as many as forty million people may be infected with HIV by the year 2000. The potential to reject and refuse care to persons with HIV is likely to increase until such time as low-cost, effective vaccines and therapeutic agents are produced and readily available to all.

In its 1988 Resolution "AIDS and the Healing Ministry of the Church," the General Conference affirmed that "the global AIDS pandemic provides a nearly unparalleled opportunity for witness to the gospel and service to human need among persons." Across the world, United Methodist-related public-health specialists, health workers, social workers, teachers, missionaries, clergy, and laity are living and working in cities, towns, and villages where HIV infection and illness are endemic. In all regions, churches; congregations; health facilities; schools; and men's, women's, and youth groups exist that can provide support, nurture, and education in the midst of the HIV epidemic.

The United Methodist Church urges

A. Local congregations worldwide to:

1. Be places of openness where persons whose lives have been touched by HIV infection and illness can name their pain and reach out for compassion, understanding, and acceptance in the presence of persons who bear Christ's name;

2. Provide care and support to individuals and families whose lives have been touched by HIV infection and illness; and

3. Be centers of education, and provide group support and encouragement to help men, women, and youth refrain from activities and behaviors associated with transmission of HIV infection.

B. General program agencies to:

1. Assist related health institutions to obtain supplies and equipment to screen donated blood and provide voluntary HIV testing;

2. Support efforts by projects and mission personnel within regions to promote disease prevention and to respond to the needs of family care providers and extended families;

3. Facilitate partnership relationships between institutions and personnel from region to region, as appropriate, to share models and effective approaches regarding prevention, education, care, and support for individuals and families with HIV infection and illness;

4. Assist health workers to obtain regional specific, timely updates on the diagnosis, treatment, and prevention of HIV infection and illness;

5. Facilitate the sharing of pastoral-care resources and materials dedicated to the care of persons and families whose lives have been touched by HIV;

6. Respond to requests from the regions to develop training seminars and workshops for church-related personnel in cooperation with ecumenical efforts, private voluntary organizations, and programs already existing in the regions; and

7. Advocate national, regional, and international cooperation in the development, availability, and transport of appropriate/relevant equipment and supplies for infection control, disease prevention, and treatment.

C. Annual conferences to:

1. Explore HIV prevention and care needs within their areas and to develop conference-wide plans for appropriate, effective responses;

2. Promote pastoral responses to persons with HIV infection and related illnesses that affirm the presence of God's love, grace, and healing mercies; and

3. Encourage every local church to reach out through proclamation and education to help prevent the spread of HIV infection and to utilize and strengthen the efforts and leadership potential of men's, women's, and youth groups.

D. Episcopal leadership in every region to:

1. Issue pastoral letters to the churches, calling for compassionate ministries and the development of educational programs that recognize the HIV-AIDS epidemic as a public health threat of major global and regional significance; and

2. Provide a level of leadership equal to the suffering and desperation being experienced by individuals, families, and the communities in which they live.

The unconditional love of God, witnessed to and manifested through Christ's healing ministry, provides an ever-present sign and call to the Church and all persons of faith to be involved in efforts to prevent the spread of HIV infection, to provide care and treatment to those who are already infected and ill, to uphold the preciousness of God's creation through proclamation and affirmation, and to be a harbinger of hope, mercy, goodness, forgiveness, and reconciliation within the world.

The United Methodist Church unequivocally condemns the rejection and neglect of persons with HIV infection and illness and all crimes of hate aimed at persons with HIV infection or who are presumed to be carriers of the virus. The United Methodist Church advocates the full involvement of the Church at all levels to be in ministry with and to respond fully to the needs of persons, families, and communities whose lives have been affected by HIV infection and illness. In keeping with our faith in the risen Christ, we confess our belief that God has received those who have died, that the wounds of living loved ones will be healed, and that Christ, through the Holy Spirit, is present among us as we strive to exemplify what it means to be bearers of Christ's name in the midst of the global HIV-AIDS epidemic.

ADOPTED 1992

See Social Principles, ¶ 66Q; "AIDS and the Healing Ministry of the Church"; "Resources for AIDS Education"; "Recognizing and Responding to the Many Faces of HIV/AIDS in the U.S.A."

Consequences of Conflict

WHEREAS, contemporary warfare frequently involves a level of conflict short of formal and massive force engagement of two or more armies; and

WHEREAS, such lower-intensity forms of conflict are frequently undeclared or even covert, and often take the form of tragic civil war in which outside parties may or may not participate; and

WHEREAS, such types of conflict are less amenable to international rules of warfare, particularly regarding the status of noncombatants and prisoners of war;

Therefore, be it resolved:

1. That The United Methodist Church calls upon all who choose to take up arms or who order others to do so to evaluate their actions in accordance with historic church teaching limiting resort to war, including questions of proportionality, legal authority, discrimination between combatants and noncombatants, just cause, and probability of success;

2. That The United Methodist Church urges the governments of the nations in which the Church exists to support negotiations for peace and support the United Nations and other multinational regional peacekeeping forces; and

3. That the General Conference instruct its secretary to send a letter containing the admonition and support outlined above to the chief executive of the above nations and to the Secretary General of the United Nations.

ADOPTED 1992

See Social Principles, ¶¶ 68G, 69C; "The United Methodist Church and Peace"; "Justice, Peace, and the Integrity of Creation."

East Timor

East Timor is part of an island on the far eastern end of the Indonesian archipelago, only 300 miles from Darwin, Australia. It had been under Portuguese control for some three centuries, unlike the other islands of present-day Indonesia, which were all Dutch colonies. During 1974–1975, following a coup and change of government in Portugal, East Timor was in the process of decolonization. There was a brief civil war between the newly formed political parties, which was subsequently won by Fretilin, the party favoring independence. But hardly had Fretilin declared independence for East Timor when, on December 7, 1975, Indonesia launched a massive invasion and annexed the half island. (Ninety percent of the weapons used by Indonesian armed forces were US-made weapons.) Twenty years later, Indonesia continues to occupy East Timor in spite of repeated United Nations resolutions deploring the invasion, affirming the right of the East Timorese to self-determination, and calling on the Indonesian government to withdraw its troops.

The events in East Timor went unnoticed and unreported in the outside world because it was closed off to foreign presence until 1989. However, during the invasion and subsequent occupation, over one third of the population died from killing, starvation, or disease. Timorese culture was suppressed, local languages were discouraged, and the majority of population living in the mountains and forests was forced to come out and resettle in planned villages built by the Indonesian army.

World attention was finally brought to the plight of East Timor when, on November 12, 1991, Indonesian troops massacred between 50 and 250 peaceful demonstrators at the Santa Cruz cemetery in Dili, East Timor. The number of dead has never been determined, because many people who disappeared on that day have not been found. This tragedy was witnessed by Western journalists whose reports, especially videotape taken by British journalist Max Stahl, helped to stimulate international efforts to bring about a just resolution to the problem of East Timor. In 1992, in protest of the massacre, the United States Congress eventually cut off military training (since reinstated by the Clinton administration, in 1994) and instituted a ban on small arms sales to Indonesia.

In January 1995, a delegation from the National Council of the Churches of Christ in the U.S.A. and a representative of the Canadian Council of Churches visited East Timor to express solidarity with the churches and people of East Timor. The region is 90 percent Christian, predominantly Catholic, with a small Protestant minority. The population has come to identify being Catholic with being patriotic and supporting the East Timorese cause. The Roman Catholic Bishop Carlos Ximenes Belo is recognized and respected as the leader and spokesperson of the East Timorese people. It has been said that relations between Catholics and Protestants have not been good. The National Council of the Churches of Christ/Church World Service and Witness (CWS&W) delegation found this to be exaggerated, however, and witnessed many examples of Catholic-Protestant cooperation. The main Protestant church, the Christian Church of East Timor, has begun to find its voice and recently received membership in the World Council of Churches. Previously, it had been represented in religious fora only through the Indonesia Communion of Churches, which always spoke on its behalf.

Human rights groups such as Amnesty International, as well as individual observers, have reported continued serious human-rights abuses against the East Timorese, including beatings, abductions, torture, rape, extrajudicial killing, and imprisonment for any acts of political expression. In addition, the Indonesian government has encouraged thousands of Indonesians from more crowded islands to migrate to East Timor. These transmigrations have displaced many East Timorese from their traditional homes and land, taken over much of the trade, and filled many of the civil service jobs. This has exacerbated the unemployment problem, particularly among the youth, and created social tension that has provided the military with justification for further repression.

Following its visit to East Timor, the NCCC/CWS&W delegation recommended an advocacy effort that calls for the demilitarization of East Timor and supports a process that would lead to the determination of the political status of East Timor, with the full participation of the East Timorese people.

Therefore, be it resolved, that The United Methodist Church, its members, local churches, annual conferences, central conferences, and agencies:

1. *Deplore* the continuing occupation of East Timor and the resultant abuse of human rights and climate of oppression;

2. *Support* the witness of the Christian Church of East Timor and the Roman Catholic Church, and other groups, in their commitment to human rights, peace, and restoration of the East Timorese national identity;

3. *Support* the rights of the East Timorese to self-determination and call for the full participation of the East Timorese people in just resolution of the political status of East Timor;

4. *Urge* the United Nations to intensify efforts to resolve the political status of East Timor;

5. *Support* the East Timorese people and the East Timorese churches who struggle for justice, dignity, freedom from fear, and the preservation of their ethnic and cultural identity;

6. *Celebrate* the membership of the Christian Church of East Timor in the World Council of Churches and its participation in ecumenical bodies in order that this East Timorese church may have an independent voice;

7. *Encourage,* in the spirit of partnership, the Indonesian churches and the Communion of Churches in Indonesia to stand in solidarity with those who are oppressed in East Timor;

8. *Call* on the United States government to cease military aid, including military training, and the sale of arms to Indonesia as long as it continues its de facto military occupation of East Timor; and

9. *Call* on the United Methodists to make efforts in mission, education, witness, and advocacy to alleviate the plight of the East Timorese by:

(a) making available through general boards and agencies resources regarding East Timor to assist United Methodist congregations in initiating programs in education, mission, witness, and advocacy;

(b) working to increase awareness of the ongoing crisis in East Timor among U.S. policymakers, the general public, and United Methodist congregations through general boards and agencies and ecumenical bodies; and

(c) supporting the East Timorese, both within East Timor and in exile, who are struggling to end the Indonesian occupation and attempting to achieve self-determination in their land.

Be it further resolved, that we urge the United States government and other governments to:

1. Take legislative and administrative action to pressure Indonesia to comply with the United Nations resolutions on East Timor, to withdraw its military occupation forces from East Timor, and to cooperate with the United Nations in a process bringing about self-determination for East Timor; and

2. Send copies of this resolution to the Secretary General of the United Nations, the President of the UN General Assembly, the President of the United States, all U.S. Senators and Representatives, and all appropriate ecumenical colleagues.

ADOPTED 1996

See Social Principles, ¶ 69.

Economic Development of Puerto Rico

WHEREAS, Section 936 of the Internal Revenue Code of the United States allows that corporations be established in Puerto Rico with tax exempt benefits to provide employment and economic development through the Caribbean Basin Initiative; and

WHEREAS, these corporations generate approximately 300,000 direct and indirect jobs, which constitute a vital part of the economy of Puerto Rico; and

WHEREAS, the earnings generated by the employees of these companies generate financial benefits for Puerto Rico; and

WHEREAS, the new Republican Congress, with the support of the Commissioner Resident of Puerto Rico, Hon. Carlos Romero Barceló; and the Governor of Puerto Rico, Hon. Pedro Rosselló González, have proposed the elimination of this Section 936 so as to balance the national budget in seven years; and

WHEREAS, the elimination of Section 936 will cause great harm to the economy of Puerto Rico; and

WHEREAS, The United Methodist Church fosters and promotes a society where it is more dignified to work for a living than to depend on others for subsistence;

Therefore, be it resolved, that the funds being deposited in Puerto Rico be kept there so that low-interest loans be available in Puerto Rico for the use of Puerto Ricans; and

Be it further resolved, that the General Conference of The United Methodist Church support the maintaining of Section 936 of the Internal Revenue Code and that this support be communicated to President William Jefferson Clinton and members of the U.S. Congress.

ADOPTED 1996

See Social Principles, ¶ 69; "Puerto Rico and Vieques"; "In Opposition to Building a Radar in the Lajas Valley and the Town of Vieques, Puerto Rico."

Economic Support for Palestinians

WHEREAS, the signing of the Oslo Accord by the PLO and Israel in September 1993 stipulated financial aid for a necessary and rapid improvement in the economy of the occupied territories; and

WHEREAS, external parties, including the United States, at the World Bank Conference in October 1993 pledged 2.4 billion dollars to help revive the failing economy of the West Bank and the Gaza Strip and to provide for immediate and basic needs such as nutrition, housing, health care, sanitation, education, and jobs; and

WHEREAS, delivery of aid has kept pace neither with the promises nor the needs, causing further deterioration of the living standards of the Palestinians, contributing to the unrest and cycle of violence that is making it difficult for the Palestinian National Authority to establish educational systems and other social programs and to implement economic development; and

WHEREAS, continued and, in many cases, intensified closures, confiscation of Palestinian land by the government of Israel, and the importing of foreign workers into Israel to replace Palestinian labor, coupled with economic policies of the Israeli government that hamper economic development in the West Bank and Gaza, have caused a further deterioration of the living standards of Palestinians, an increasing distrust of the peace process and its leaders, and an increasing sense of hopelessness and frustration; and

WHEREAS, we deplore the violence directed toward Israelis and the violence directed toward Palestinians and believe that, even as we hold the perpetrators responsible and accountable, we must address the root causes;

Therefore, be it resolved, that The United Methodist Church insist that the U.S. government release the remaining portion of its aid immediately and encourage other nations to do the same; and

Be it further resolved, that we request that the U.S. government reevaluate the entire structure of aid to the Middle East, one goal being to redistribute the huge amount now given to Israel and Egypt, and a second goal being to consider economic support for the efforts of nongovernmental organizations, including religious institutions, human rights groups, labor unions, and professional groups.

ADOPTED 1996

See Social Principles, ¶ 69; "The Middle East and North Africa"; "The United Methodist Church and Peace."

Encounter with Christ in Latin America and the Caribbean

WHEREAS, colleague churches of Methodist heritage in Latin America and the Caribbean now have extraordinary new opportunities for mission and ministry, with many experiencing marked numerical growth and renewed vitality in witnessing to God's redemptive work through Jesus Christ, our Lord; and

WHEREAS, many of these same churches are struggling with severe financial problems rooted in the massive poverty that besets the majority of peoples in this region of the world; and

WHEREAS, Methodist churches of the Caribbean and Latin America have made costly decisions in their history for self-determination, seeking to incarnate more faithfully within the diversity of nations within this region; and

WHEREAS, the churches represented by the Council of Evangelical Methodist Churches in Latin America and the Caribbean (CIEMAL) and the Methodist Church of the Caribbean and the Americas (MCCA) urgently need sisters and brothers who will share with them in supporting new church development, evangelistic initiatives, and programs that nurture justice ministries and respect for all persons; and

WHEREAS, many of these colleague churches are being led to make costly new commitments in order to strengthen their solidarity and faithful ministry with children, women, and youth;

Therefore, be it resolved, that we will encourage and invite support for the General Board of Global Ministries Permanent Fund called Encounter with Christ in Latin America and the Caribbean (No. 025100), a designated giving channel that provides a special means for current and deferred giving in order to strengthen our shared ministries with the Methodist churches of Latin America and the Caribbean.

ADOPTED 1996

See Social Principles, ¶ 69.

End U.S. Military Presence in Bolivia

Since 1986, the United States has stationed military advisers in Bolivia, originally to fight communist subversion, and currently to fight a "war on drugs."

Because the production of coca is part of the history, culture, and religion of the Bolivian people; and

Because we believe that the war on drugs should be waged in the United States, where money now spent on military efforts in Latin America could better be used for education, drug prevention, and rehabilitation; and

Because efforts in Bolivia could be better used in confronting the corruption caused by the narco-traffickers, the growing consumption of cocaine (1.5 percent of the population is currently affected), and the negative economic impact on the international community; and

Because we believe that the continuing buildup of U.S. military presence in Bolivia is part of a wider strategy of military/political control over governments, popular organizations, and resources, which violates the people's right to self-determination, perpetuates dependence, destroys the social fabric, and becomes an obstacle to a free and independent foreign policy; and

Because the people of Bolivia, who only recently have freed themselves of the power of military dictatorships, strongly object to the presence of U.S. military in their country;

Therefore, we, as concerned members of The United Methodist Church, join with our brothers and sisters in Bolivia in calling for an end to the U.S. military presence in Bolivia that could lead to further militarization of the country and the continent.

ADOPTED 1992

See Social Principles, ¶ 69; "The United Methodist Church and Peace"; "In Support of Self-Determination and Nonintervention."

The Fort Laramie Treaty

WHEREAS, the 1868 Fort Laramie Treaty was entered into by the United States of America, the Lakota Nation, and other Indian nations and was ratified by the Senate of the United States and proclaimed by its president in 1869;

WHEREAS, this treaty affirms the sovereignty of the people of all the nations involved;

WHEREAS, treaties entered into by the United States government are considered to be the supreme law of the land, equal to its Constitution;

WHEREAS, treaties cannot be unilaterally abrogated, according to international law;

WHEREAS, the 1868 Fort Laramie Treaty has never been legally abrogated;

WHEREAS, the 1868 Fort Laramie Treaty has been repeatedly violated and ignored by the United States government;

WHEREAS, these treaty violations have undermined both the moral integrity of the United States government and the respect for its laws by U.S. citizens;

WHEREAS, these treaty violations have resulted in the loss of land and loss of self-government, which have contributed to poverty, ill health, unresponsive educational institutions, loss of self-determination, and loss of life for the Lakota people;

Therefore, be it resolved, that we, the members of The United Methodist Church, recognize and reaffirm the sovereignty and independence of the Lakota people.

Be it further resolved, that we, the members of the General Conference of The United Methodist Church, call on our United States government to recognize the sovereignty and independence of the Lakota Nation through the 1868 Fort Laramie Treaty. We call upon the President of the United States to form a Presidential Treaty Commission to meet with representatives selected by the Lakota people to redress the grievances caused by the U.S. violations of the 1868 Fort Laramie Treaty to the mutual satisfaction of both nations, and to devise and implement specific steps to bring the United States into compliance with its treaty obligations with the Lakota Nation.

ADOPTED 1980

See Social Principles, ¶¶ 66A, 69A; "Rights of Native People of the Americas."

Free Flow of Information Among All Peoples of the Earth

In the international arena there is widespread discussion of what is known as the "new world information and communication order." The discussion involves the worldwide flow of information in the light of such factors as governmental restraints, multinational commercial communication enterprises, and the modern technology of communication. The Church has a witness to bear upon these issues.

I. The Scriptural Base

Scripture is replete with demands for freedom, truth, justice, and fair treatment of others.

The Old Testament records how, in the early history of the Hebrew people, God's law demanded truth, honesty, and equity. In the great nineteenth chapter of Leviticus, God calls for equal treatment of the powerless (verse 15), for love and fair dealing toward the sojourner or stranger (verses 33-34), and for truth and honesty in all dealing (verses 35-36). The Ten Commandments forbid false witness (Deuteronomy 5:20).

The prophets called for justice and righteousness. Amos gave God's Word: "Let justice roll down like waters" (5:24); Micah declared that the Lord required of humans "to do justly, and to love mercy" (6:8, KJV).

In the New Testament, Jesus both demands and promises truth and freedom. In John's Gospel he says, "If you continue in my word, you are truly my disciples; and you will know the truth, and the truth will make you free" (8:31-32). In the Synoptic Gospels, he commands respect for others, especially those who are weak. Each person's responsibility toward the "little ones" (Matthew 18:5-6; Mark 9:42; Luke 17:2) may be seen also as a responsibility toward the powerless. By example, Jesus was an advocate for persons on the margins of society.

Paul, as he wrote the Galatians about freedom in Christ, called his readers to enjoy and use their freedom, but to use it as an opportunity to serve others (Galatians 5:13-15).

As Christians of today, we seek to apply these biblical concepts to the opportunities and problems of the modern media.

II. Our Historic Witness

The United Methodist Church and its predecessor denominations have a long history of defending freedom of religion, freedom of expression, and the rights of persons who are powerless because of political or economic conditions. This concern found expression in the original (1908) Social Creed and successor documents down to the present Social Principles, including today a specific call for freedom of information and protection of the people's right to access to the communication media (¶ 68A). The concern is raised in actions of the 1980 General Conference as recorded in the 1980 *Book of Resolutions*. The resolution on "Church-Government Relations" urges Christians to participate meaningfully in public affairs. The resolution on "The Church in a Mass Media Culture" declares that channels of communication "must operate in open, humanizing ways." In the resolution on Open Meetings, the Church demands of itself the high standard of openness that it commends to others. The 1996 *Book of Discipline* instructs one of the Church agencies to "work toward promotion and protection of the historic freedoms of religion and the press" (¶ 1806.5).

III. Problems in the Flow of Information

Nowhere in the world do people have full and free access to information about people and events elsewhere. Even in the United States, with a tradition of press freedom and constitutional guarantees, our view of the world is circumscribed by what is selected for us by newspaper and newsmagazine editors and by radio/television news producers. A study of datelines in newspaper stories quickly reveals that most of the news pertains to our own country or to Europe, and that news from countries elsewhere is likely to be filtered through Western conduits.

Persons in many countries, especially in developing nations, feel that they seldom have the opportunity to express themselves, or even describe themselves, in their own words and on their own terms. They feel that they are seen mainly through the eyes of foreigners—usually reporters for the commercial news services of Europe and North America.

Many persons live in countries where newspapers and broadcast news are controlled by governments. In many countries, there is outright censorship. Some governments use the mass media for political purposes.

Modern technology, especially computer-based communications and transmission by satellite, makes global communications possible on a scale and with an immediacy never before possible. But the cost is beyond the reach of all but the most affluent countries or corporations. Those who control communication technology have the power to determine what is known about others. The same technology makes it possible to treat information as a commodity to be bought and sold, to be shared or withheld for payment or consideration.

In the United States, the broadcast and print media increasingly have turned viewers and readers into a product to be delivered to the sponsors. As a result, the media's goal becomes to reach and hold the largest possible audience, regardless of other journalistic objectives.

These and other related concerns demand serious thought in all countries, especially those countries that have the power to create and control the media of communication. The light of the Christian gospel must be applied to these questions.

IV. Statement of Principles

In view of inequities in the flow of information among the peoples of the world, and in the light of our own understanding of the gospel, we state these principles:

• All peoples of earth have a right to free flow of information.

• Peoples have a right to originate information and to make statements about themselves in terms of their own culture and self-view.

• Journalists must be given access to information within their own countries and across international frontiers.

• Journalists have a responsibility for accuracy and fairness in all that they write, photograph, edit, publish, or broadcast. Part of this responsibility includes cross-cultural sensitivity and awareness, as well as freedom from language bias.

• The licensing of publications or of journalists violates freedom.

• Information is a human right, and not just a commodity to be bought and sold. (However, those who gather, edit, and transmit information are entitled to fair rewards for their efforts.)

• Every citizen has a right to be informed in order to participate in politics intelligently.

• Censorship by governments or by those who control news media is abhorrent and should not be permitted; neither should there be legal restrictions to the free flow of information. The withholding of information for security reasons must be limited by publicly-stated guidelines.

• Readers and viewers in every land have a right to a broad view of the world, drawing upon multiple sources of information.

• The churches should be primary advocates for a free flow of information and diversity of sources. The churches should oppose the practice of those persons and systems that use media for purposes of human exploitation, political control, or excessive private profit.

V. Recommended Actions

This resolution is commended to the churches and to individual United Methodists for study and action, such as monitoring local and national media and legislation and instituting appropriate follow-up. Dialogue with journalists, publishers, and broadcasters is recommended.

The United Methodist Church must ensure that in its own communications, persons of other countries and cultures speak for themselves.

Individuals, local churches, and local church groups are urged to join with other Christians in their communities in study and action on the issues and principles stated in this resolution.

The results of local study may indicate suggestions to local media. Recommendations may be made to representatives in local, state, or national government. Viewpoints may be registered also with governmental agencies, such as the Federal Communications Commission, and with intergovernmental or international agencies.

General agencies of the Church, particularly United Methodist Communications, the General Board of Church and Society, and the General Board of Global Ministries, are directed to provide coordinated resources and guides for study and action.

ADOPTED 1984

See Social Principles, ¶¶ 68C, 69; "Justice, Peace, and the Integrity of Creation"; The United Methodist Church and Peace."

Global Economy and the Environment

The United Methodist Church has been rightly concerned about the environment and its sustainability, given the rapid depletion of natural resources and the contamination of the air, water, and land. However, we have been slow to recognize the impact of the emerging global economy and its impact upon the environment.

When the economic institutions were contained within the boundaries of countries, governments had the power to regulate. Particularly, in the area of the environment, communities could exercise control so that pollution and waste could be regulated and conservation encouraged. Of course, this adds costs to doing business. However, if everyone is under the same constraints, no one is at a disadvantage.

As countries rush to open up markets in the name of free trade, it is obvious that those countries that have strict environmental regulations are going to be at a competitive disadvantage in attracting and keeping business. Business will seek countries in which to operate that have lower environmental standards and, therefore, lower operating costs. Pressures will increase on countries with higher standards to lower them, and developing countries will be hesitant to enact environmental legislation.

The United Methodist Church therefore recommends:

1. That every country, including the United States, require that there be roughly equivalent environmental standards between itself and any other country with which it enters into a free-trade agreement, so that there is not a competitive disadvantage for the country with the stricter standards. Mechanisms should also be included in the agreement that will allow for further new standards of environmental regulations in the future;

2. That the General Board of Church and Society develop a statement outlining the relationship of the world economy to the environment and communicate this to appropriate governmental agencies and the Church;

3. That the General Board of Church and Society develop study materials for local congregations; and

4. That local congregations study the implications of the global economy on the environment. Study materials might include: *For the Common Good: Redirecting the Economy Toward Community, the Environment, and a Sustainable Future,* by Herman E. Daly and John B. Cobb; *Sustaining the Common Good, A Christian Perspective on the Global Economy;* or materials to be developed by the General Board of Church and Society.

ADOPTED 1996

See Social Principles, ¶¶ 64, 69; "Environmental Justice for a Sustainable Future"; "Economic Justice"; "The United Methodist Church and Peace."

God's Shalom for the People of Central America

The prophet Isaiah spoke of the people rejoicing, building houses, planting the fields, and enjoying the fruit of their labor in peace (Isaiah 65:19-25). It is easy for the people in Central America to identify themselves with the vision of Isaiah. The images of the reign of God depicted by Isaiah point toward the dignified life all human beings have the God-given right to enjoy.

Many expectations of peace arose during the past decade. These expectations were created by peace agreements like Esquipulas, the peaceful transition of political power in Nicaragua, the end of the war in El Salvador, and the peace negotiations in Guatemala. Nevertheless, the reality for most people in Central America is that peace, justice, and the dignified life depicted by Isaiah have become a fleeting hope. There are many reasons for this hope to be ephemeral. Some of the reasons are the unfulfilled promises of judicial reform and land redistribution, and the economic policies that continue to favor the wealthy.

Most of the people of Central America live in situations that cry out for justice. In Nicaragua, El Salvador, and Guatemala, people have endured the loss of family members and the destruction of their environment throughout decades of war. The people of Central America have suffered with the intervention of foreign governments whose surrogate armies kidnapped their children, burned their food supplies, killed countless innocent people, and threatened church members who have dedicated themselves to living out the gospel.

In the aftermath of war, the daily lives of most Central Americans entail facing survival in fractured economic systems with very high unemployment, ingrained structural injustices, suffering drought and illness from the pollution or destruction of their environment, and coping with disabled family members and psychological traumas in systems without health care. The ingrained structural injustices keep the socioeconomic situation in status quo. Massive debts acquired during wartime must be paid off to the World Bank, and loans received from the International Monetary Fund take first priority. Loans from the International Monetary Fund and other international lending institutions increase debt without alleviating human suffering to any reasonable degree or changing significantly the socioeconomic prospects of the poor.

There is no adequate financial support left in the national treasuries to meet economic and social needs of the people due to the austerity measures imposed by the international lending institutions, the payment of past debt, and the lack of priority given to the elimination of dehumanizing conditions.

Multinational *maquiladoras* (assembly plants) take advantage of the meager financial situation in many Central American countries. The *maquiladoras* engage in economic exploitation and deny human and labor rights with impunity because governments permit it and people have no alternatives for income.

God's *shalom* is also denied by the several human rights violations and the rampant violence reported by different religious and human-rights organizations. Military and paramilitary groups in different countries, such as Guatemala and El Salvador, have conducted arbitrary arrests, torture, and extrajudicial executions. Sadly, the United States government, through its Central Intelligence Agency (CIA), has been linked with these groups and individuals that violate human rights. Actions of the CIA and the Guatemalan military have caused unjustifiable loss of life and profound grief for families.

The Church in the Face of Suffering

The Latin American church has borne the cost of discipleship and continues to insist on God's *shalom*. The church in Central America is divided on issues of social, economic, and political justice. Nevertheless, prophetic voices continue to cry out for social and economic justice, adequate health care, and protection of the environment.

God's intention for humanity is expressed in the Old Testament with the all-inclusive word *shalom*, which means wholeness, health, and harmony with God and nature, with oneself, and with others. *Shalom* symbolizes justice and the presence of God. (*Shalom* was Jesus' greeting: "Peace be unto you." "Go in peace." The apostles began their New Testament letters to the churches by saying, "Grace and peace to you from God. . . .") *Shalom* does not exist when there is injustice. Biblical prophets exhorted those in authority to admit their sins and offer restitution to the poor people. Amos declared, "Hear this, you who trample the needy and do away with the poor of the land. . . ." (Amos 8:4-6, New International Version). Micah warned the leaders: "Listen, . . . Should you not know justice, you who hate good and love evil" (Micah 3:1, 2*a*). Isaiah told the leaders of his day: "When you spread out your hands in prayer,/I will hide my eyes from you;/even if you offer many prayers,/I will not listen./Your hands are full of blood; . . ./learn to do right! Seek justice,/encourage the oppressed. Defend the cause of the fatherless,/plead the case of the widow" (Isaiah 1:15,17); and "'It is you who have ruined my vineyard;/the plunder from the poor is in your houses./What do you mean by crushing my people/and grinding the faces of the poor?' declares the Lord, the LORD Almighty"(Isaiah 3:14-15).

Shalom requires respect for the sanctity of life. There will be no *shalom* until the basic human needs of bread, shelter, work, safety and freedom are guaranteed to everyone. The possibility of authentic peace is undermined by the frequent cases of persons living under the threat of death, or being "disappeared," or forced to migrate or live in conditions of miserable poverty. It has been reported that members of the Guatemalan police have threatened citizens, including children, with death if they have witnessed human rights violations perpetrated by the police, frightening them to silence. Another serious threat against *shalom* is the lack of fulfillment of the peace accords. In El Salvador, refugees and ex-combatants have not received land that rightfully belongs to them under the United Nations Land Transfer Program. Many families who seek legal redress have been threatened or ignored.

It is essential to the Central American Peace Process that international financial and political commitments to reconciliation and development continue. The Central American nations remain very fragile. United States aid levels have dropped drastically. To cut funding even more would put the peace processes in jeopardy. Impoverished citizens of the Central American nations would be left without sufficient agrarian, environmental and other developmental funds, thus weakening the peace process as it is starting. There is no government, lawful or unlawful, that can build peace on hunger or the denial of the most basic human rights from its citizens who are in need.

WHEREAS, religious leaders, labor union leaders, peasants, students, merchants, women's associations, etc., in Central America continue to call for a concerted effort to change the course of the political and economic processes toward an alternative that may lead to lasting peace with justice in the region; and

WHEREAS, it is our conviction that injustice, war, and economic and political oppression do not lead to peace; and

WHEREAS, the government of the United States has actively supported war and participated in low-intensity conflict, which includes clandestine and covert operations, support for counter insurgency and counterrevolutionary campaigns, terrorist strikes and other low-level missions, and sparing use of United States soldiers; continues to economically support military forces; and maintains several military bases across the region, particularly in Honduras and Panama;

Therefore, The United Methodist Church calls upon the government of the United States to:

1. Fulfill its obligations to support reconstruction and development for Central American countries to promote healing by all means possible, including a strong United States program in the region;

2. Actively support accords made by the Central American nations in search for peacemaking alternatives other than military;

3. Withdraw all United States military presence in Panama and honor the Torrijos-Carter treaty agreements; and fulfill its responsibilities for damages to human life, property, housing, and the economic system caused by the 1989 invasion;

4. Recognize and respect each nation's sovereignty and rights to self-determination, and refrain from any activity—military, economic or of any other nature, covert or overt—directed against any sovereign state in Central America;

5. Apply human rights certification based upon U.S. law (Section 502b of the Foreign Assistance Act of 1960 as amended) and data from Amnesty International and the United Nations Human Rights Commission as criteria for economic assistance to governments in the region;

6. Protect persons fleeing repression or war in Central America;

7. Encourage multilateral institutions to approve debt reduction for all countries which are impoverished and debt-ridden;

8. Replace the Structural Adjustment Programs, which exacerbate the conditions of poor people, with humane policies that address the social and economic needs of the majority of the people in Latin American nations; and

9. Support United Nations peace talks on Guatemala, and seek the truth about persecution and deaths in Guatemala, including those in which the CIA may have been involved.

We call upon the United Nations to:

1. Continue active support in finding political and financial solutions that ensure the participation of all segments of the population and benefit all;

2. Continue to oversee and report any violations of human rights according to its Human Rights Declaration;

3. Support governmental, nongovernmental and civic organizations of the region in their efforts to work toward a unified solution so that peace and justice may prevail in the region;

4. Work in support of efforts to demilitarize the region and support alternatives for ecologically sound and sustainable economic development; and

5. Support the efforts of organizations in their work to alleviate the plight of Central American refugees.

We call upon The United Methodist Church, working together with the Council of Evangelical Methodist Churches of Latin America and the Caribbean(CIEMAL) and the churches it represents, the Latin American Council of Churches (CLAI), the Caribbean Conference of Churches (CCC), and other ecumenical partners in the region to:

1. Learn about and better understand the hopes and aspirations of the people of Central America;

2. Strengthen our ties of solidarity with the people of Central America by deepening our understanding of the history and cultures of the region;

3. Encourage the use of ecumenical curriculum materials, study guides, and other resources prepared by the general boards and agencies;

4. Encourage annual conferences and Central American churches to continue to support each other through prayer, exchange, dialogue of persons, and the physical accompaniment of persons where appropriate;

5. Increase efforts to assist and participate in the reconstruction of the war-torn nations through sharing of resources;

6. Advocate and support policies and programs by The United Methodist Church directed to the rehabilitation of youth and young adults; victims of war; protection, defense, and promotion of the indigenous communities; and the promotion and support of health and other programs for children and women;

7. Pray that peace, justice, and political solutions leading to development for life prevail in Central America;

8. Support sustainable economic development projects, encouraging the conservation of forests, air, water and agricultural projects;

9. Resource church leadership in environmental resources and ecological programs;

10. Help communities to affirm life and strengthen their hope by supporting production and credit programs of the poor which create jobs, such as micro-enterprises, cooperative and worker ownerships;

11. Nurture self-esteem among street children and youth; and

12. Facilitate projects for marginalized groups to address discrimination and injustice.

ADOPTED 1996

See Social Principles, ¶ 69; "Assistance and Sanctuary for Central American Refugees"; "Immigrants and Refugees: To Love the Sojourner."

Holy Land Tours

Concern has been raised across the Church about special opportunities that are often being missed by United Methodists traveling to Israel/Palestine, often called the Holy Land. Christians indigenous to the area have also sharpened the question by wondering why they are so often ignored by Christian pilgrims to the region. Why, they ask, do travelers tend to honor the inanimate stones that testify to Jesus' life and ministry while ignoring the "living stone," the indigenous Christians who represent an unbroken line of discipleship to Jesus in the land that he called home?

Travelers to this land have the opportunity to be ambassadors of unity and concern to the churches and Christians in a troubled land. They also have an opportunity to learn from the spiritual traditions of the churches indigenous to the Middle East. Further, they have a special opportunity to discover firsthand the realities of a region of deep meaning and vital importance to Christians, as well as to Jews and Muslims.

Therefore, The United Methodist Church:

1. Strongly affirms the resolution of the 1984 General Conference, offering "ecouragement of all leaders of and participants in 'Holy Land tours' to contact indigenous Christian leaders in the Middle East, and to hear the concerns of both the Israelis and Palestinians who live there, as well as visit the biblical and historical sites" ("The Arab-Israeli Conflict," *The Book of Resolutions, 1984;* page 280);

2. Asks the bishops, clergy, members, agencies, and congregations of The United Methodist Church, as they plan visits to the Holy Land, to devote at least 20 percent of the program time to contact with indigenous Christian leaders and to hearing the concerns of Palestinians and Israelis on the current crisis of Palestinian self-determination;

3. Recommends that United Methodists planning individual or group tours to Israel/Palestine consult with the United Methodist liaison in Jerusalem and the Middle East Council of Churches Ecumenical Travel Office to seek opportunities to worship with indigenous

Christian congregations and to visit United Methodist-supported mission sites;

4. Asks the General Board of Global Ministries and the General Board of Church and Society to prepare specific recommendations for United Methodists traveling in the Middle East and other sensitive regions of the world;

5. Recommends that United Methodist-sponsored tours use the denomination's joint seminar program in pre-departure seminars for the travelers; and

6. Urges that travelers use, as advance study materials, positions adopted by General Conference and by general Church agencies relating to the Middle East;

7. Extends sincere appreciation to those United Methodists who have facilitated the implementation of the above recommendations in tours they have sponsored or participated in during the first quadrennium following adoption of this resolution;

8. Expresses deep concern that many tours sponsored or arranged by United Methodist bishops, pastors, and laity do not schedule opportunity for all participants to enter into partnership with the indigenous Christians for the recommended program time and, therefore, fail to "Walk With the Living Stones" in their strides toward Palestinian self-determination, their rich spiritual heritage, and their faithful contemporary witness;

9. Expresses deep concern that evidence continues to accumulate that Christianity is dying in the land of Jesus through economic, social, and political pressures, which have greatly diminished the numbers and percentage of Christians in the Holy Land. United Methodist bishops and other organizers of Holy Land tours have a special responsibility to adhere to these recommendations to strengthen the witness of the remaining Palestinian disciples of the Living Lord;

10. Affirms the presence of The United Methodist Church in Jerusalem through our liaison office;

11. Encourages tour leaders to consult with the United Methodist liaison office in Jerusalem in order to facilitate adherence to these recommendations;

12. Instructs the Joint Panel on International Affairs of our general agencies to monitor and report to the General Conference regarding the implementation of this resolution;

13. Underscores the significance of Bethlehem 2000, which celebrates two millennia of Christianity in the land of Jesus; and

14. Urges close cooperation with the Middle East Council of Churches and other indigenous Christian groups to facilitate informed, alternative travel opportunities to the region.

ADOPTED 1992
AMENDED & READOPTED 1996

See Social Principles, ¶ 69; "The Middle East and North Africa"; "Jerusalem."

In Opposition to Building a Radar in the Lajas Valley and the Town of Vieques, Puerto Rico

WHEREAS, the United States Marines have decided to use 70 percent of the fertile Valley of Lajas to build a radar station, which would nullify use of the land for agricultural purposes; and

WHEREAS, the use of this radar station is not clear at the present time, the information being that it will be used to detect planes coming from South America with drug cargo; and

WHEREAS, this radar station will not only take the Valley of Lajas but will be, in part, located in the island town of Vieques, where the operation of such equipment would generate radiation in such a way that the land, air, and maritime life on this island will be in danger of becoming extinct; and

WHEREAS, all the diverse political, social, and religious communities of Puerto Rico have spoken against the establishment of such a radar station in Puerto Rico; and

WHEREAS, studies made in the United States have proven the ineffectuality of this kind of installation for the purpose designated; and

WHEREAS, the problem of drug addiction and drug trafficking are by nature moral and social problems needing that kind of approach for a solution instead of a technological one; and

WHEREAS, the bishop of the Affiliated Autonomous Methodist Church of Puerto Rico, pastors, and lay leaders of the Church are actively participating, from their faith perspective, in this effort to oppose the building of this radar station;

Therefore, be it resolved, that the General Conference support MARCHA (Methodists Associated Representing the Cause of Hispanic Americans) and those sectors of the Puerto Rican society that oppose the building of the aforementioned radar station, and that copies of this resolution be sent to the President of the United States of America, the governor of Puerto Rico, the media, and the Methodist Church in Puerto Rico.

ADOPTED 1996

See Social Principles, ¶ 69; "Puerto Rico and Vieques."

In Support of Self-Determination and Nonintervention

Interventions of nations into the affairs of other nations, frustrating justice and self-determination, are a reality of our time. The United Methodist Church stands unequivocally against such interventions.

The Hebrew prophets call us to a world in which all peoples are secure in their own land and on their own mountains. God breaks the bars of the yoke of oppression and feeds the people in justice (Ezekiel 34). Our Savior, Jesus Christ, calls us to be peacemakers, to live in justice and in peace with one another (Matthew 5).

The Social Principles of our Church offer guidance:

• "The first moral duty of all nations is to resolve by peaceful means every dispute that arises between or among them. . . ." (¶ 69C)

• "We affirm the right and duty of people of all nations to determine their own destiny. . . ." (¶ 69B)

• "Upon the powerful [nations] rests responsibility to exercise their wealth and influence with restraint. . . ." (¶ 69B)

The United Nations Charter provides mandates. All member states shall:

• settle international disputes by peaceful means;

• respect the principle of equal rights and self-determination of peoples;

• refrain from the threat or use of force against the territorial integrity or political independence of any other state; and

• undertake to comply with the decision of the International Court of Justice in any case to which it is a party.

The Charter of the Organization of American States offers an additional directive:

• No state or group of states has the right to intervene in any way, directly or indirectly, for any reason whatever, in the internal or external affairs of any other state.

In spite of the mandates of international law and the cries of the people for a world of peace with justice, we are faced with continuing interventions of all kinds. These actions undermine international law, breed injustice, frustrate the self-determination of peoples, and are responsible for untold human suffering.

Intervention, as used in this resolution, is defined as the knowing and willful intrusion by one nation into the affairs of another country with the purpose of changing its policies or its culture. It includes any activity—military, economic, political, social, cultural, covert or overt—designed to stabilize or destabilize an existing government.

We are guided in our activities for self-determination and nonintervention by our biblical faith, the Social Principles, and the principles of international law. Specifically, we adopt the following guidelines:

1. The United Methodist Church categorically opposes interventions by more powerful nations against weaker ones. Such actions violate our Social Principles and are contrary to the United Nations Charter and international law and treaties.

2. We oppose clandestine operations, such as political assassinations; political and military coups; sabotage; guerrilla activities; atrocities, particularly those directed at children; paramilitary efforts; military training; weapons support and supply; mining of navigable waters; economic pressures; political or economic blackmail; and propaganda aimed at destabilizing other governments. We oppose activities where national or international intelligence agencies engage in political or military operations beyond the gathering of information.

3. We support multilateral diplomatic efforts—for example, the Contadora peace process and the Afrias Initiative (Esquipulas II), which have been used in Central America as a means of settling disputes among nations. We support regional and international negotiations arranged in cooperation with the United Nations and held without resort to political rhetoric and public posturing.

4. To deepen understanding among nations and to affirm the diversities among peoples, their politics and culture, we support increased contacts between peoples—between East and West, North and South, between the peoples of the Soviet Union and the United States, between the peoples of Nicaragua and the United States, and between the peoples of Afghanistan and the Soviet Union. These contacts could include cultural exchanges, tourism, educational and scientific seminars, and church visitations. We applaud and encourage the development of covenant relationships between United Methodist congregations in countries with differing social or economic systems.

5. We support affirmative United Nations policies and actions to assist peoples of the world, particularly of developing nations, in achieving self-determination. We support the development and implementation of United Nations sanctions against those nations that intervene unilaterally in the affairs of other nations in violation of international law.

6. We support United Nations and regional policies and actions designed to isolate and quarantine any nation that consistently denies fundamental human rights, as enumerated in the Universal Declaration of Human Rights, to any segment of its people. Through collective action, wars fought to achieve justice might be averted or diminished. Such measures include: "complete or partial interruption of economic relations and of rail, sea, air, postal, telegraphic, radio, and other means of communication, and the severance of diplomatic relations" (Article 41, United Nations Charter).

Therefore, we call upon all United Methodists, United Methodist Agencies and institutions, to:

1. Study the issue of intervention and to hold their own governments accountable to the United Nations Charter and other international laws and treaties;

2. Deliver this resolution to their government leaders and to discuss its contents with them, urging its support and implementation; and

3. Monitor their own governments and to support appropriate actions to hold their governments accountable to the United Nations Charter and international laws and treaties.

ADOPTED 1988

See Social Principles, ¶ 69B, D; "End U.S. Military Presence in Bolivia"; "Oppose Food and Medicine Blockades or Embargoes"; "The United Methodist Church and Peace."

Infant Formula Abuse

Breastfeeding is the healthiest, most nutritious method of feeding newborn infants and is virtually universally recommended as the preferential means of feeding infants. Conversely, the misuse of infant formula and bottle-feeding causes health problems, illness, and even death for hundreds of thousands of babies each year. We support full compliance with the WHO/UNICEF Code of Marketing of Breast Milk Substitutes as one vital means of promoting breastfeeding and protecting the health and lives of millions of infants.

During the past decade and a half, The United Methodist Church has developed considerable knowledge in this arena and has worked as an active global advocate for maternal and infant nutrition. In pursuing our goal of proper nutrition for infants, we have supported the elements of the International Code of Marketing of Breast Milk Substitutes, supported UNICEF and their Baby Friendly Hospital Initiative, and challenged infant formula companies to comply with the code and end all practices, in the U.S. and around the world, that undermine breast-feeding. At times our voice has been heard in tones of quiet persuasion in meeting rooms, while at other times it has been a forceful public challenge in arenas such as company stockholder meetings. The Infant Formula Task Force of The United Methodist Church has also engaged in comprehensive monitoring in third world countries of government and corporate adherence to the code.

"Then he took a little child and put it among them; and taking it in his arms, he said to them, 'Whoever welcomes one such child in my name welcomes me, and whoever welcomes me welcomes not me but the one who sent me' " (based on Mark 9:36-37).

Jesus, in these words, confirmed what the Scriptures taught from ancient days, that how one treats the weakest and most helpless—the widow, the orphan, the alien, the child—was an expression of one's respect for God. God through Christ comes to us in the inversion of our images of power and omnipotence, in the persona of one in need of care. Those who cheat, steal, or profit from the weak and helpless are urged to change and, if they remain impervious to correction, are driven out of the community of faithful.

In the present world of impersonal technology and high-pressure global sales strategies, those who deprive the children of their rightful heritage of health may never see the faces of those who suffer by their corporate decisions. But we are called, nevertheless, to hold up before them the children whose lives are stunted by their policies, and to hold them accountable for the wasted lives, the stolen promises, the unnecessary premature deaths. God sets every child in our midst, reminding us that we are accountable to the Most Holy One for how our actions affect the weakest and most helpless of our brothers and sisters.

On the other hand, we are called to love those who cannot take care of themselves, such as infants, for they are powerless, vulnerable, have no claims on us, and cannot reward or repay us.

Children are a gift of God, a precious resource and our planet's future. Every year, hundreds of thousands of newborn infants suffer needless sickness and even death when breastfeeding is not chosen and infant formula is misused. At the United Nations World Summit for Children in 1989, nations agreed to the "empowerment of all women to breastfeed their children exclusively for four to six months and to continue breastfeeding until complimentary food well into the second year." Breastfeeding passes on essential immunities to the infant from the first day of life, reducing infectious diseases and mortality; it also builds a special bond between mother and child.

In a 1991 communication to all heads of state in the world, UNICEF Executive Director James Grant and WHO Director-General Dr. Hiroshi Nakajima stated: "More than a million children would not have died last year if all mothers had been able to effectively breast-feed." Breast-feeding also significantly reduces the prospect of breast cancer.

Conversely, the misuse of infant formula feeding by the use of contaminated water or overdilution of the formula results in the very sickness and death that the WHO/UNICEF letter refers to. Health authorities, supported by our denomination, have vigorously opposed any actions, whether by a government or infant formula company, that discourage breastfeeding or inadequately warn mothers and fathers about the dangers of bottle-feeding.

To express their deep conviction on this issue, the nations of the world voted in 1981 for the Code of Marketing of Breast Milk Substitutes. The code expressly opposes policies such as public advertising, lack of warnings on labels, sample packs to mothers leaving the hospital, promotion of bottle-feeding over breastfeeding in literature, and free supplies of infant formula to hospitals. This code provides a basis of understanding for government health professionals and industry alike.

Recently, WHO and UNICEF launched a Baby Friendly Hospital Initiative to encourage successful breastfeeding.

While infant formula companies have made many changes over the last decade, such as revising labels, ending sample packs to mothers, and public advertising in developing countries, they stubbornly refuse to affirm the universal nature of the code or to put its provisions fully into effect. For example, infant formula companies still provide free supplies of infant formula to hospitals, a vitally important marketing strategy since families usually continue to use the formula they start with in the hospital. WHO and UNICEF both believe these free supplies act to discourage breastfeeding and have recently set the end of 1992 as a deadline for ending free supplies. Industry has pledged its support for this deadline but refuses to end such supplies voluntarily, instead waiting for government agencies to legislate their end. We believe this code violation should be ended speedily; further, we urge companies to unilaterally end free supplies as well as supporting government action to do so.

In addition, there have been new public advertising and marketing campaigns in the United States that violate the code and discourage breastfeeding. Nestle/Carnation, Bristol-Myers Squibb, and Gerber have all begun mass-media advertising of new infant formula products. Claiming their formula is a "complete food," or that "if it isn't from you, shouldn't it be from Gerber?" tens of millions of advertising dollars have been spent to attract consumers to these new formula products. Such campaigns undermine breastfeeding in the pursuit of profit. These deceptive campaigns are vigorously opposed by health professionals, including the American Academy of Pediatrics.

The Church is called to give leadership on this vital issue. After fifteen years of involvement, our expertise and effective public leadership is acknowledged as a vital moral voice. James Grant of UNICEF has commended the religious community's "moral imperative" on infant formula and urged us to continue this urgent work.

Many companies turn to the churches as a moral compass and public litmus test on this issue.

The United Methodist Church affirms the needs for urgent action to support breastfeeding on a global basis and to end policies or practices by governments, corporations, or health authorities that promote bottle-feeding over breastfeeding. While we believe women and families should have information allowing a choice in how they feed their babies, information campaigns and education programs should support the primacy of breastfeeding.

In particular:

1. We recommend the continuation of an Infant Formula Monitoring and Action Committee with representation from a variety of United Methodist agencies to give leadership to the Church in this new quadrennium. The committee is to be convened by the General Board of Church and Society (GBCS) and shall include one person from the 1985–88 Infant Formula Task Force, one person from the 1988–92 Infant Formula Task Force, two persons chosen at large for their expertise on Infant Formula issues, and two members of GBCS.

2. We recommend that The United Methodist Church support WHO and UNICEF in their active initiatives for comprehensive global implementation of the code and the Baby Friendly Hospital Initiative.

3. We recommend that The United Methodist Church urge infant formula companies to implement fully and universally all provisions of the code and in particular cooperate with the WHO and UNICEF goal of ending free supplies of infant formula to hospitals by the end of 1992. These supplies can be ended using a variety of approaches, including government action and unilateral corporate withdrawal of free supplies, to ensure the end of the code abuse. We believe the 1992 deadline should not be negotiable.

4. We urge Nestle/Carnation, Bristol-Myers Squibb, and Gerber to end all public advertising of infant formula in the United States. This advertising violates the code and the stated position of the American Academy of Pediatrics and numerous national health organizations opposing such widespread media advertising, and it promotes new brands of infant formula, undercutting breastfeeding.

5. We urge all United Methodist institutional and individual stockholders in infant formula companies to use their shareholder leverage to encourage code compliance by these corporations, including dialogue and shareholder resolutions with selected companies. Further, we urge our partner churches around the world to raise these concerns with infant formula companies in their nations.

6. We urge all United Methodist-related hospitals to embrace the UNICEF Baby Friendly Initiative, a multipronged program for infant health and breastfeeding.

7. We urge United Methodist agencies to work ecumenically through the Interfaith Center on Corporate Responsibility and in partnership with leadership groups such as UNICEF, WHO, and the American Academy of Pediatrics in support of these goals.

8. We support a campaign of education and advocacy for breastfeeding to help create a culture in the workplace, the church, the hospital, and the home supportive of breastfeeding, and we commend to the churches the work of World Alliance for Breastfeeding Action (WABA), Penang, Malaysia, in this regard.

9. We urge individual United Methodists and appropriate agencies of the Church to voice strong concern to the United States government about the pricing policies of the $2 billion federally-funded WIC program (for women, infants, and children) in light of a 1991 study that revealed a sharp decline in breastfeeding among WIC recipients.

10. We acknowledge the effectiveness of boycott action as a last resort to press corporations to act responsibly and request the General Board of Church and Society to initiate a study to see if the new massive advertising campaigns in the U.S. media warrant such boycott actions.

11. We urge governments and health authorities to take concrete steps to support breastfeeding and to end marketing and promotion tactics leading to bottle-feeding abuses.

ADOPTED 1992

See Social Principles, ¶ 69; "The United Methodist Church and Peace."

Jerusalem

Jerusalem is sacred to all the children of Abraham: Jews, Muslims, and Christians. We have a vision of Jerusalem as a city of peace and reconciliation, where indigenous Palestinians and Israelis can live as neighbors and, along with visitors and tourists, have access to holy sites and exercise freedom of religious expression. The peaceful resolution of the Jerusalem issue is crucial to the success of the whole process of making peace between Palestinians and Israelis.

International consensus and law, in accordance with United Nations Resolution 242, support the view that the Jerusalem issue is unresolved and that East Jerusalem is occupied territory. However, the prospects for a just resolution in accordance with Resolution 242 are being seriously compromised by policies of the Israeli government. These include the confiscation of increasing amounts of Palestinian land, expansion of the borders of Jerusalem to include more and more Palestinian villages and lands (thus forming what is now known as "Greater Jerusalem"), the building of settlements for Jewish families on those lands, closures that prevent Palestinians from traveling to or through Jerusalem, the withholding of basic services from tax-paying Palestinian neighborhoods, the denial of Jerusalem identity cards to Palestinian citizens, and the denial of building permits for Palestinians (causing an increased number of homeless persons and the departure of Palestinian residents from Jerusalem).

Therefore, The United Methodist Church requests that the government of the United States, and other nations as well, urge the state of Israel to:

1. Cease the confiscation of Palestinian lands;

2. Cease the building of new, or expansion of existing, settlements in the occupied territory and Gaza;

3. Lift the closure of Jerusalem to Palestinians;

4. Issue Jerusalem building permits to Palestinians so that they can build and maintain their buildings;

5. Halt the practice of denying Jerusalem identity cards to Palestinian citizens; and

6. Address the problem of homelessness, severe overcrowding, and substandard housing among the Palestinian residents of Jerusalem.

Governments, by their silence and through financial assistance, contribute to the creation of these "facts on the ground," which impede peace and may preclude any hope of Jerusalem's ever becoming the City of Peace and Reconciliation for which we pray. *Therefore,* we urge our governments to:

1. Reject efforts to move embassies from Tel Aviv to Jerusalem;

2. Deduct annually from any Israeli loan guarantees an amount equal to all Israeli settlement spending in that year, including spending for settlements in and around Jerusalem; and

3. Affirm that the status of Jerusalem is unresolved and that East Jerusalem is, indeed, occupied territory.

ADOPTED 1996

See Social Principles, ¶ 69; "The Middle East and North Africa."

Justice for the Reverend Alex Awad

The Reverend Alex Awad is a Palestinian American who was commissioned a missionary in 1989 by the United Methodist General Board of Global Ministries to serve as pastor of the East Jerusalem Baptist Church. Since that time, however, the Israeli government has repeatedly refused to grant him a visa for entry into Jerusalem.

Although the reason given for the refusal relates to visa problems with the Reverend Awad some years past, it is more likely that he is being prevented from pastoring this church because he is the brother of Mubarak Awad, founder of the Palestinian Center for the Study of Nonviolence, who was deported by the Israeli government in 1988. The Reverend Awad has no history of political activity and wishes to assume his role as pastor of the East Jerusalem Baptist Church for religious, and not political, reasons. He and his wife, Brenda, have also been asked to teach at the Bethlehem Bible College.

The Reverend Awad has been formally issued a call by the East Jerusalem Baptist Church to serve as its pastor. His congregation has suffered patiently without a pastor throughout these years as he has petitioned the Israeli government for a visa.

Support for indigenous Christian congregations is especially important during this time of great stress, which has led to increased Christian emigration from East Jerusalem, the West Bank, and Gaza in response to the sufferings of Palestinians under Israeli occupation.

The Social Principles clearly state the moral obligation for all governments to provide freedom of religion: "We hold governments responsible for the protection of the rights of the people to free and fair elections and to the freedoms of speech, religion, assembly, [and] communications media" (¶ 68A). The resolution on "Religious Liberty," in the *Book of Resolutions*, restates and expands the Church's commitment to religious freedom.

Despite numerous pleas from United Methodist Church officials (including a November 1991 meeting of bishops and top mission staff with Israeli embassy officials), U.S. congresspersons, concerned citizens, peace and rabbinical organizations in Israel, and church officials from other denominations in Europe and the United States, the government of Israel has persisted in denial of a visa to the Reverend Awad and his family.

Israel's refusal to grant a visa to the Reverend Awad represents:

1. A denial of the freedom of religion that Israel espouses for Jerusalem;

2. An affront to The United Methodist Church, whose mission board has found him suitable in every way to serve under its auspices and has formally commissioned him and his family to serve in Jerusalem;

3. A spiritual burden upon the congregation in Jerusalem, which has been without a pastor this long period;

4. A source of grave concern as to whether this is part of a policy to intimidate and reduce the Palestinian population of Jerusalem; and

5. A travail for the Awad family and their young children, who have been forced to move at least yearly throughout this time of waiting.

Therefore, The United Methodist Church:

1. Expresses its gratitude for all of those religious groups, government officials, concerned individuals, and organizations who have joined with United Methodist members and officials in calling for an end to this denial of religious freedom and for the granting of a visa to the Reverend Alex Awad and his family;

2. Extends our Church's continuing prayerful concern and support for the Reverend Awad and his family during this difficult time and expresses our deep appreciation for his ongoing ministry of mission interpretation within our Church during this interim period;

3. Protests, in the strongest terms, the refusal of the Israeli government to grant a visa to the Reverend Awad, a commissioned missionary and a United States citizen;

4. Requests that Church agencies, annual conferences, and congregations monitor the case of the Reverend Awad and voice their concern about religious freedom to the Israeli Embassy;

5. Requests that the General Board of Global Ministries, the General Board of Church and Society, and the Council of Bishops intensify their advocacy for the free practice of religion in Jerusalem, the rights of the Palestinian people, and the granting of a visa to the Reverend Awad;

6. Urges all United Methodists who travel to Israel/Palestine to:

(a) share with Israeli authorities their deep concern about this denial of religious freedom; and

(b) use the special opportunity afforded by their travel to learn about and share with the Palestinian Christian community; and

7. Encourages United Methodist congregations to learn about the life and challenges facing Palestinian Christians and other Christians in the Middle East.

ADOPTED 1992

See Social Principles, ¶ 69; "The Middle East and North Africa"; "Economic Support for Palestinians."

Justice, Peace, and the Integrity of Creation

"Justice, Peace, and the Integrity of Creation" was the theme of a process initiated by the World Council of Churches, Sixth Assembly, in Vancouver, Canada, in 1983. In Canberra, Australia, in 1991, the World Council of Churches adopted this emphasis as a priority area for the council's programs. To join the issues of peace, justice, and the well-being of creation is to create a common understanding of this interconnectedness.

A World Convocation was held in Seoul, Republic of Korea, in March 1990 "to engage member churches in a conciliar process of mutual commitment to justice, peace and the integrity of creation." A set of ten affirmations was approved by the convocation for a process of covenanting:

1. We affirm that all forms of human power and authority are subject to God and accountable to people. This means the right of people to full participation. In Christ, God decisively revealed the meaning of power as compassionate love that prevails over the forces of death.

2. We affirm God's preferential option for the poor and state that as Christians our duty is to embrace God's action in the struggles of the poor in the liberation of us all.

3. We affirm that people of every race, caste, and ethnic group are of equal value. In the very diversity of their cultures and traditions, they reflect the rich plurality of God's creation.

4. We affirm the creative power given to women to stand for life whenever there is death. In Jesus' community women find acceptance and dignity, and with them he shared the imperative to carry the good news.

5. We affirm that access to truth and education, information, and means of communication are basic human rights. All people have the right to be educated, to tell their own stories, to speak their own convictions and beliefs, to be heard by others, and to have the power to distinguish truth from falsehood.

6. We affirm the full meaning of God's peace. We are called to seek every possible means of establishing justice, achieving peace, and solving conflicts by active nonviolence.

7. We affirm that the world, as God's handiwork, has its own inherent integrity; that land, waters, air, forests, mountains, and all creatures, including humanity, are "good" in God's sight. The integrity of creation has a social aspect, which we recognize as peace with justice, and an ecological aspect, which we recognize in the self-renewing, sustainable character of natural ecosystems.

8. We affirm that the land belongs to God. Human use of land and waters should release the earth to replenish regularly its life-giving power, protecting its integrity and providing spaces for its creatures.

9. We affirm the dignity of children that derives from their particular vulnerability and need for nurturing love; the creative and sacrificial role that the young people are playing in building a new society, recognizing their right to have a prophetic voice in the structures that affect their life and their community; the rights and needs of the younger generation as basic for establishing educational and developmental priorities.

10. We affirm that human rights are God-given and that their promotion and protection are essential for freedom, justice, and peace. To protect and defend human rights, an independent judicial system is necessary.

The Social Principles of The United Methodist Church clearly reflect our commitment to justice, peace, and the integrity of creation. In addition, The United Methodist Church has demonstrated its support for justice, peace, and the integrity of creation through its complementary Peace with Justice Program.

In affirming its participation in the justice, peace, and the integrity of creation process of the World Council of Churches, The United Methodist Church specifically pledges to:

1. Encourage local churches and individuals to study the documents of "Justice, Peace, and the Integrity of Creation" in order to develop greater understanding and support for those movements of people who struggle for human dignity, liberation, and for just and participatory forms of government and economic structures;

2. Join the worldwide ecumenical movement to articulate its vision for all people living on earth and caring for creation;

3. Urge the General Board of Global Ministries and the General Board of Church and Society to give priority to integrated programs supportive of the four covenants affirmed by the convocation in Seoul, Korea, which advocate:

- a just economic order and liberation from the bondage of foreign debt;
- true security of all nations and people;
- the building of a culture that can live in harmony with creation's integrity; and
- the eradication of racism and discrimination on national and international levels for all people;

4. Urge all United Methodists to implement the Social Principles and General Conference resolutions that address these issues, especially "Economic Justice," "The United Methodist Church and Peace," "Environmental Stewardship," "Global Racism," and "Ecumenical Decade: Churches in Solidarity with Women"; and

5. Urge all United Methodists to join in covenant with Christians around the world to work to fulfill the goals of justice, peace, and the integrity of creation.

ADOPTED 1992

See Social Principles, ¶¶ 64, 67, and 69; "The United Methodist Church and Peace"; "Peace with Justice as a Special Program"; "Environmental Justice for a Sustainable Future."

Liberia

The West African nation of Liberia has been experiencing a brutal civil war since 1989. As a result, there have been hundreds of thousands of casualties, in which 1 in 17 Liberians lost their lives. Over 150,000 people have been displaced within the country, and more than 160,000 people are forced to live as refugees in neighboring African countries.

The economic and social infrastructure is virtually destroyed, including the pertinent services of hospitals and schools. People have been dying on a daily basis from diseases and malnutrition. And with renewed fighting in Monrovia, the capital, cholera is claiming the lives of residents. The closure of industries and business has led to high unemployment and, consequently, a lack of resources for families to buy food and maintain basic life support.

The lives of Liberia's children have been disrupted. Often they were kidnapped and coerced into becoming soldiers. Children participate in and view the grisly murders of relatives and friends. As the war continues, the bombing and destruction of school buildings prevents students from continuing their education.

Worship attendance in the Liberia Annual Conference has gradually declined, because members are fearful to travel distances from their homes to attend services. Church leaders and members have been displaced or have become refugees. Many church leaders remain in Liberia and are ministering to the people during this turbulent period. We commend Liberian Bishop Arthur Kulah, resident bishop of the Liberia Annual Conference, and other church leaders for remaining in the country during the times of heightened civil war and commend their civil-war active participation in the process of peace and national reconciliation.

With the signing of the August 1995 peace accord in Abuja, Nigeria, there was great anticipation among Liberians toward reconstructing their broken nation, improving their standard of living, and maintaining lasting peace. Unfortunately, the civil war resumed in March 1996, threatening the peace accord.

The Social Principles of The United Methodist Church (¶ 69) state that the Church must commit itself "to the achievement of a world community that is a fellowship of persons who honestly love one another. We pledge ourselves to seek the meaning of the gospel in all issues that divide people and threaten the growth of world community."

Such conditions call upon The United Methodist Church to pray, sympathize, and stand in solidarity with over 70,000 Liberian United Methodists and the Liberian nation as a whole. We commit ourselves to:

1. Urge our governments to continue all humanitarian assistance, including medical services, food, and water to the suffering population;

2. Urge the Organization of African Unity and the United Nations to facilitate an immediate disarmament of the warring factions as called for in the Abuja peace accord;

3. Provide financial assistance to pastors and their families;

4. Rebuild churches, parsonages, and church-related institutions;

5. Repatriate, resettle, and provide shelter for refugees, displaced persons, and war victims;

6. Rebuild homes through efforts by Volunteers in Mission and Habitat for Humanity;

7. Assist the transition of soldiers into the civilian sector through counseling, vocational and general education;

8. Engage in reconciliation and healing at a grassroots level between and among various ethnic groups;

9. Train pastors to be agents of reconciliation, peace, and healing;

10. Set up counseling and educational programs to help children, women, and others traumatized by war;

11. Stabilize the country's economic structure by:

(a) calling on the governments and international lending agencies to provide development grants, loans, and to forgive debts;

(b) encouraging private investment in the country;

(c) encouraging United Nations agencies such as the World Health Organization, the United Nations Children's Fund and the United Nations Development Program to generate programs in Liberia; and

(d) helping Liberians establish and maintain their own businesses.

The Liberia Annual Conference was founded by the Reverend Milville B. Cox in 1833. Liberia has maintained close historical ties to the United States and became the first independent republic in 1847.

The Liberia Annual Conference remains committed to finding peace and reconciliation in Liberia. We will advocate public policy, diplomatic relations, economic support, and a negotiated settlement of the Liberian civil war.

ADOPTED 1996

See Social Principles, ¶ 69; "Africa Reconstruction and Development."

The Middle East and North Africa

Introduction

The Middle East and North Africa, the region of the world stretching from Mauritania on the west to Iran on the east and from Turkey on the north to Somalia on the south, holds a special place in the hearts and minds of United Methodists. The Methodist presence in the region dates back to 1887, when the Methodist Church in France answered a request for an organized Protestant church to be engaged in mission in North Africa. The Methodist Church responded by establishing a mission station in the mountains of Kabylia in North Algeria. The mission station provided evangelistic, medical, educational, and technical programs for the whole population. Methodist mission work later spread to other parts of Algeria and Tunisia.

The United Methodist connection to the region dates back to 1924, when United Methodists joined other Protestants in forming the International Missionary Council in North Africa. The Methodist Church in North Africa was also a founding member of the Near East Christian Council (NECC) in 1956. The United Methodist Church maintained its membership in the NECC when it became the Middle East Council of Churches in 1974. Following the 1948 war and the establishment of the state of Israel, The United Methodist Church began responding to the critical needs of hundreds of thousands of Palestinian refugees as well as the other human needs in the region caused by wars, invasions, liberation struggles, natural disasters, and devastating economic and social conditions.

United Methodist engagement in mission in the Middle East and North Africa has challenged our understanding of the theological foundations for our presence there. As we deepened our relationship with the Christians of the region, we gained an appreciation for the life and witness of the indigenous Christian churches there. This broadened our understanding of mission, enabling The United Methodist Church to develop partnerships based on respect and mutuality rather than parochial concerns. For several quadrennia, the General Conference of The United Methodist Church has encouraged United Methodist members, local churches, and agencies to pray for peace and become actively involved in justice and peacemaking efforts in the Middle East. The United Methodist Church has given special attention to the Arab-Israeli conflict and the homelessness of the Palestinian people, with the hope that the resolution of these long-standing conflicts would create the conditions for resolving other crises in the region.

Throughout our history of involvement in the Middle East and North Africa, we have gained a deeper understanding of the region in its full human and spiritual context. We join our Jewish and Muslim brothers and sisters in feeling a deep sense of rootedness to the land where our three religious traditions were born. We also celebrate the diversity of religious customs and traditions in the Middle East and North Africa that provide United Methodists with the opportunity to strengthen our understanding of and commitment to interfaith encounters and explorations. This challenge includes not only Islam and Judaism, but the variety of Christian traditions indigenous to the region as well. Our United Methodist presence is primarily through our relationship with the Middle East Council of Churches (MECC). The MECC is an inclusive fellowship of churches from four Christian families: the Eastern Orthodox, the Oriental Orthodox, the Catholic, and the Protestant.

Over the past four years, the Middle East and North Africa has experienced dramatic and profound political, civil, social, economic, and religious developments. The strategic location of the region, its natural resources, ethnic richness, and religious passions attract a variety of powerful influences and interests from around the world. The result has too often brought exploitation, violence, and death to the peoples there. As we reflect upon these developments in light of our Christian vocation, we are challenged to reexamine and reaffirm our United Methodist commitment to service and witness there.

Sustainable Development

The Middle East and North Africa is diverse in its topography, climate, and physical and social environments, and covers an area approximately equal in size to the United States. The area is defined by a variety of independent states with diverse political systems, ethnic groups, languages, customs, and traditions. These definitions join factors such as rapid population growth; increasing urbanization; scarcity of land, water, and other economic resources; and limits on women's social and economic autonomy in playing a critical role in questions of sustainable development there.

Since the Gulf War of 1990, the social, economic, and political situation has deteriorated drastically. Many countries are facing a major economic crisis that is rapidly getting worse. The struggles of people throughout the region are similar: an extremely high unemployment rate, especially among the young population; falling per capita consumption; shortages of basic food commodities; no access to basic social services; high levels of illiteracy; an absence of accountable government; and governmental corruption.

Against this backdrop of deteriorating social, economic, and political conditions, the region suffers from environmental degradation. Concentrations of air pollutants such as sulfur dioxide and lead are well above levels considered safe. The quality and productivity of agricultural land is threatened by salination. This limits the amount of land available for cultivation, which is already threatened by dwindling sources of fresh water. The water needs of giant and overcrowded cities compete with agricultural methods demanding large amounts of water, resulting in a water shortage of major proportions. Much of the water that is available is highly contaminated from industrial wastes, agricultural pesticides, and other chemicals. While water shortage is a global problem, the political implications are most vulnerable in the Middle East and North Africa where a number of conflicts between states are rooted in disagreements over gaining unrestricted access to sources of water. The results of this environmental crisis are poor health, inferior housing, and poor sanitation for both rural and urban populations, especially those who are marginalized.

As people begin to demand more equitable access to jobs, schooling, housing, and health care, it becomes clear that questions of population and development must be framed within a context of equity. Governments will continue to be unsuccessful in their efforts to slow rates of population growth until policies designed to protect the lifestyles of wealthy elites while ignoring the basic needs of the majority population undergo drastic changes. Family-planning strategies must become more holistic to include factors that influence women's reproductive choices, such as women's other health needs, their education, job opportunities and overall status, and the role that men play in reproductive behavior.

Human Rights Concerns

Over the past decade, the human rights movement in the Middle East and North Africa has expanded rapidly. We applaud the commitment and determination of thousands of individuals and groups dedicated to documenting and publishing information about human rights abuses in their countries. These efforts have enabled people in the West to gain a better understanding of human rights violations. Their work has also helped to challenge stereotypes about Middle Eastern and North African societies.

Perhaps the most destructive of these stereotypes is the notion that political absolutism is generic to the region. There is a pervasive sense that the problem in the region is an absence of civil society— networks of nongovernmental institutions and civic culture to which the state is accountable. However, in fact there are vibrant and diverse communities and nongovernment organizations knowledgeable about and critical of structures of power in and among their own societies.

The commitment to reforming the political and economic problems of the region has been threatening to authoritarian governments bent on maintaining power in the Middle East and North Africa. Many states throughout the region have implemented restrictions on basic civil and political participation, including freedom of expression, freedom of peaceful assembly, and freedom of association. Corrupt justice systems allow politically motivated killings, arbitrary arrest, torture, and denial of fair public trials. The rights of minorities, such as the freedom of religious and ethnic groups to express their culture, practice their religion, and even use their own language, are restricted and denied in many states. Fundamentalist religious groups, intolerant of those who disagree with their vision of society, have used violence to challenge and destabilize existing political orders. The struggle for women's rights has also been long and hard in the region. Women in many countries suffer from restrictions on their movements, activities, and personal freedoms from both the state and religious fundamentalist groups. Immigrant women working in the Middle East are especially vulnerable to human rights violations with little if any access to redress their oppression.

Peace and Justice Concerns

In recent years, The United Methodist Church has become more active in justice and peacemaking efforts in the Middle East and North Africa. The Church has worked with ecumenical and interfaith bodies advocating self-determination for Palestinians, affirming Israel's right to exist within secure borders, calling for region-wide disarmament, and urging the United States government to initiate a U.S. embargo on arms to the entire region.

United Methodists are committed to the objective of a comprehensive Arab-Israeli peace agreement that would bring recognition and security to Israel and national and human rights to the Palestinians. We commend those who have actively worked to end the Israeli occupation of the West Bank, Gaza, Southern Lebanon, and the Golan Heights, while seeking the revocation of those articles in the PLO covenant that call for the destruction of Israel. We commend those who worked faithfully to uphold human dignity and resist dehumanization and demonization. We are hopeful that the signing of the Israel-Palestinian Authority Interim Agreement will begin the long-awaited withdrawal of Israeli forces from the West Bank in partial compliance with United Nations Security Council Resolution 242, the release of Palestinian political prisoners, and the initiation of democratic political rights for Palestinians. The most important issues have not been resolved: Israel's claim to exclusive sovereignty over all of Jerusalem, the presence of existing Israeli settlements and the construction of new ones, the future of the Palestinian refugees in the *diaspora,* and Palestinian national rights. Israelis and Palestinians, the peoples of the three Abrahamic religions, should shape the future status of Jerusalem.

In the aftermath of the Gulf War, we deeply grieve for the Iraqi people. Massive declines in levels of education, health, water purification, and sanitation have hit women, children, and the elderly particularly hard. The imposition of economic sanction on Iraq following the devastating war, compounded by the Iraqi government's abusive and divisive social and political policies, has resulted in massive cases of malnutrition, illness, and death.

We uplift those groups and individuals who have worked tirelessly to bring human dignity, reconciliation, justice, and peace to the region. We are especially mindful of those committed to resolving the conflicts and injustices suffered by people in Algeria, Cyprus, Egypt, Iraq, Kurdistan, Lebanon, Somalia, Sudan, and the Western Sahara. We know that the interest of our governments, including the massive exportation of military weapons and technical assistance to the region, plays a critical role in these conflicts. As citizens, our responsibility is to stand with those laboring to redress all injustices in the Middle East and North Africa.

Call to Action

We call upon United Methodists individually, in their local churches, and through their boards and agencies to take the following actions:

1. Pray for all people in the regions;

2. Continue United Methodist support, through the General Board of Church and Society and the General Board of Global Ministries, working with the people of the region to address their needs;

3. Strengthen our relationship with the Middle East Council of Churches and other indigenous partners in the region;

4. Seek a deeper understanding of the region and its peoples. We ask that leaders of Holy Land pilgrimages and volunteer-in-mission visits contact United Methodist missionaries, representative(s) of the Middle East Council of Churches, and other partner organizations in the region in planning their itineraries;

5. Urge governments to stop military assistance and arms exports to the region, and to support sustainable development initiatives;

6. Urge the United States government to lead the United Nations Security Council in calling for a relaxation of UN economic sanctions against Iraq in order to end the cruel and devastating effect they are having on the Iraqi people, especially on the elderly, women, and children;

7. Urge the Iraqi government to cease its abusive and divisive social and political policies, and to encourage it to bring human dignity and justice to its people;

8. Provide a forum in United Methodist churches for voices of women, especially from Algeria, Egypt, Palestine, Tunisia, and the Western Sahara;

9. Support nongovernmental organizations dedicated to working for peace and justice, reconciliation, and human dignity in the Middle East and North Africa;

10. Urge the United States and other governments to support the internationalization of Jerusalem;

11. Urge the United States and other governments to encourage strongly the state of Israel to cease the confiscation of Palestinian lands; to cease the building of new, or the development of existing, settlements in Gaza and the West Bank, including East Jerusalem; to lift all closures of Jerusalem to Palestinians; to cease the construction of bypass roads connecting Israeli settlements that isolate Palestinian towns and villages; to cease the sealing and demolition of Palestinian homes; to cease administrative detention of men, women, and minors without the right

to a fair trial; to cease the torture of Palestinian prisoners, deportations, and other human rights violations, and to release Palestinian political prisoners;

12. Urge the United States and other governments to encourage strongly the Palestinian National Authority to cease human rights violations, including extrajudicial punishment, abduction, and torture, and call upon the Palestine National Authority to establish a civil and independent judiciary in the West Bank and Gaza; and

13. Organize educational events and community prayers for peace in the Middle East in order to bring together in each community Jews, Muslims, and Christians.

ADOPTED 1996

See Social Principles, ¶ 69; "Jerusalem"; "Economic Support for Palestinians"; "Holy Land Tours."

Mission and Aging of Global Population

The Church is being asked to respond to a rapidly expanding number of older persons throughout the world, many of whom live in precarious circumstances in societies hard-pressed to find the economic resources to cope with them. However, the situation holds possibilities for an invigorated ministry by, for, and with these older persons, and the challenge is to change some of our perceptions of older persons and their abilities as well as our complacence about so-called advanced societies.

A primary reason for the Church to be concerned about the aging of the global population is rooted in the Bible. The creation stories in Genesis were not merely about youth and middle age; they also dealt with the promise of a blessed future. These promises took on more material form in the patriarchal stories where individuals lived hundreds of years—an expression of the belief that life itself was good and therefore extended life was very good. The birth of children to Sarah and other women of advanced age fulfilled God's intent that older persons were of worth all their years. The ninetieth psalm's "threescore and ten,/or even by reason of strength fourscore" (verse 10, Revised Standard Version) was expressed in the context of transient life, but at the same time, life lived confidently in God's care. When Jesus spoke of the commandments, he included honor for father and mother (Mark 10:19, with parallels in Matthew and Luke), and it can be assumed that when Paul spoke of giving "honor to whom honor is due" (Romans

13:7), he meant to include respect for older persons. The term *elder* used in the New Testament gravitated to a title for certain roles in the church, but it could only have been used in a community in which "older" called for honor and reverence.

Through the centuries, the church has held varying attitudes toward older persons, but the strongest traditions were those that accorded dignity to persons in old age. These traditions contributed to our United Methodist Social Principles statement on rights of the aging, in which social policies and programs are called for "that ensure to the aging the respect and dignity that is their right as senior members of the human community."

The facts are clear: Demographic data reveal that every month the world population of older persons, age fifty-five and over, increases by more than one million persons. Eight percent of the increase occurs in so-called developing countries. Today, these countries contain about 370 million older persons, but projections are that by the year 2020 they will contain more than one billion. The rate of growth of older persons is faster in these countries than in others.

Advances in public health and education, as well as control of infectious diseases, have contributed to these changes. Nevertheless, the biblical hope for a blessed old age never becomes reality for many older persons because of extreme conditions of poverty, war, and hunger. Eldercide is becoming more frequent. Social security coverage applies only to a small minority of citizens in some countries.

Many of these older persons live in situations that make them very vulnerable. They live in rural areas, working the land; are predominantly female; and are illiterate. Rural areas have much older populations, since younger people tend to migrate to cities. Older persons are heavily concentrated in agriculture, with manufacturing jobs ranking a distant second. Women outlive men in virtually all countries. Most women past age sixty-five are widows, a trend that is likely to continue. Less than 10 percent of older women in many poor societies are literate. Older persons belong to families, but traditional social support based on family structures is eroding, leaving many in isolation and without persons to care for them in their last years.

Many of these poor societies are more advanced than our own in one respect, however: Older persons are held in love and respect precisely because of their experience and their symbolic place as the wise leaders and survivors of families and communities. Contrast this love and respect with some of the attitudes in the United States and other

Western countries, where old age is depreciated because it is less "productive," and because physical energy and young ideals of style and beauty are held to be more valuable than spiritual energy and the beauty of the inner soul. For this reason, the United States and other societies are "developing" and can learn much from other societies.

Those in the United States can celebrate the improved health and social security provided to older persons in recent decades, as well as the important role that very large nonprofit associations of older persons play in policy development and legislation. Those in The United Methodist Church also celebrate the inclusion of older persons in structures throughout the Church and the increasing quality of care provided for these persons in retirement and older-adult facilities. Gratitude for these advances does not, however, blind us to efforts to depict older persons as benefiting from the plight of the very young, to the low quality of care in many nursing homes, and to outright abuses in families, institutions, and organizations that employ older persons.

The United Methodist Church calls upon

A. Local churches to:

1. Involve older adults intergenerationally and in ways that empower and encourage them to be resources for skills, knowledge, experience, and spiritual insight; and

2. Use resources from general agencies of The United Methodist Church that suggest actions and models for learning from other cultures and countries in their understanding and appreciation of older persons.

B. Annual conferences to:

1. Involve older adults in the full range of programs of the conference, including volunteer-in-mission (VIM) projects; health ministries in which able older adults care for the frail elderly; and use of resources and action suggestions from the Advisory/Coordinating Committee of Older Adult Ministries and its successor in The United Methodist Church; and

2. Ask itinerating missionaries to speak to constructive ways churches in the United States can: (a) learn from the customs, values, and practices of churches in other countries and cultures; and (b) support older persons in these other countries and cultures through Advance Specials, VIM projects, and mission support.

C. All general program agencies of The United Methodist Church to:

1. Identify specific actions in their ongoing programs and ministries by which families on a global basis can be assisted in caring for their frail elderly; and

2. Include older persons in training for care giving in relation to mission and ministry globally.

D. The General Board of Church and Society and the General Board of Global Ministries to:

1. Advocate support for older persons in governmental and nongovernmental organizations, including the United Nations, the U.S. government, and ecumenical and other nongovernmental, international organizations; and

2. Study and share with the whole Church pertinent issues related to the well-being of older persons, such as allocation of governmental resources for support and care, end-of-life issues, and avoidance of ageism in employment and community life.

E. The General Board of Global Ministries to include in mission education:

1. Positive images of older persons in all countries and cultures, along with images realistically depicting the difficulties many of these persons have under conditions of poverty and isolation;

2. Information about the "double bind" in which many poor societies find themselves by virtue of the demands of a growing young population and the demands of a growing older population; and

3. Resources for annual conferences and local churches that provide models for appropriate mission and ministry on the local level, and specific action and program suggestions.

F. All general agencies and all episcopal leadership to:

1. Include older persons as full participants in programs and ministries from planning through decision-making and evaluation;

2. Seek opportunities by which The United Methodist Church can affirm its aging membership, while finding ways by which this membership can collaborate with younger persons in evangelism and renewal of the whole Church, to the end that persons of all ages are called to the discipleship of Jesus Christ; and

3. Lift the prophetic voice of Christian faith in a critique of the limits and values of self-help efforts, such as asking older persons to take responsibility for their own health and well-being, and to proclaim a vision of human community in which older persons are accorded respect and dignity as those made in the image of God and part of the human family.

ADOPTED 1992

See Social Principles, ¶¶ 66E, 69; "Aging in the United States of America"; "The United Methodist Church and Peace."

"New House" of Europe

United Methodism in a New Europe

The United Methodist Church recognizes, with deep gratitude, the positive developments that have taken place in Europe. President Gorbachev accelerated the process toward change with new policies of openness (*glasnost*) and reconstruction (*perestroika*). This process has provided room for development of the liberation movements that have been growing in Eastern Europe. The fall of the Berlin wall was a symbol of a new order. From these changes, a "New House" of Europe is emerging that is reshaping the political, social, and economic fabric of the continent.

We affirm that many people, among them numerous Christians including United Methodists, stood and suffered against oppressing political powers that used coercion to extinguish any spark of opposition.

At the same time, the violence that too often accompanies change causes us grief. There is civil war going on in many parts of Europe. We encourage development and application of peaceful means while change continues in these regions. We point to the liberation movements in central Europe as models for change.

We commend the reconciliation that occurred among the western European nations during the last four decades. However, some countries still struggle for identity and recognition, e.g., the Republic of Macedonia. We are concerned, therefore, that a special effort should be made by governments so that consensus and harmony can now be extended to the whole of Europe. The United Methodist Church needs to raise its members' awareness of the issues, thus involving them in the efforts to build a "new house" in which all people will feel at home. Consensus and harmony can now be extended to the whole of Europe.

The process for change has been strengthened by confidence-building measures promoted within the Helsinki process (the Conference on Security and Cooperation in Europe, or CSCE). Churches in Europe and North America have participated together in that process through The Churches' Human Rights Program on the Helsinki Final Act, a joint program of the Conference of European Churches, the National Council of the Churches of Christ in the U.S.A., and the Canadian Council of Churches.

We are aware of the dangers that continue to threaten the process toward a new Europe: self-serving nationalism, serious economic problems, and social upheaval. The necessary transformation that nations make into market economics will not provide easy answers to their circumstances. We encourage all the peoples in the "New House" of Europe to show concern and support for their neighbors in the struggle for economic, social, and political equality. The current priorities of the Church's human rights program are:

- protection of refugees, migrants, asylum seekers, and displaced people;
- development of the common rule of law in a manner that favors people's well-being;
- religious freedom;
- social policy questions such as capital punishment, conscientious objection, and social rights for all, including justice for women and children; and
- environmental and energy policies for a sustainable way of life.

A strong and united Europe can offer positive support to the developing nations elsewhere in the world. On the other hand, many developing nations see a strong Europe as a potential threat to their interests. We urge the European nations to refrain from economic and other practices that work against the peoples of developing countries.

As United Methodists, we support efforts for the creation of a new world of interdependent regional communities of nations, especially CSCE. This new set of conditions also demands new thinking and behavior on our part, including the acceptance of our responsibilities as The United Methodist Church.

We live in a time in which there is a great need for the gospel of reconciliation, a time when we can share the joys and sorrows of Christians living in faith together, yet having been physically separated for so many years. Now it is possible to recount to each other our past failures and successes as we attempted to be faithful servants of Christ in a divided world.

In the old Europe, there were Christians, both East and West, who were faithful witnesses to the good news of Jesus Christ. Those from the East must be encouraged to maintain that faithfulness and not become beggars dependent upon the largesse of the West. Those from the West must be encouraged to maintain their faithfulness and allow and encourage the independent witness of those in the East.

Contacts between Christians and between churches that were developed at a time of closed political borders are still important. Contacts were established in order to strengthen relationships across those borders. Christians must not now assume that open borders and new political structures have eliminated the need for the continuation of these contacts. Such relationships can also be of exceptional value between churches in Europe and throughout the world.

New relationships among churches must be carefully prepared and implemented through a process of mutual discovery and sharing. They must be based upon the connectional nature of The United Methodist Church.

Valuable and limited church resources (e.g., money, time, travel costs, food) are best used in local ministries rather than in demonstrations of hospitality for visitors.

Relationships often result in partnerships—a mutual sharing between specific congregations. These partnerships must minimize the formation of privileged and nonprivileged churches. Such arrangements are not only unfair but are destructive of the Christian family. Partnerships must not exist solely on the basis of money. Personal contact, exchange of information, and correspondence are as important as material support.

The most important relationship to be developed is the essential understanding that we are all one in Christ. This basic premise of the gospel must be kept without violation. Oneness in Christ is equality.

Ministry in community is the purpose of the Church. Therefore, in all cases the following principles are recommended:

• The offices of the bishops involved, and the appropriate general agencies working together, will arrange and coordinate all partnerships and will provide information on special projects and answers to questions. This procedure will prevent inappropriate concentration of attention on one congregation or pastor.

• All financial contributions will be made through authorized denominational channels.

• Visits between Christians are still needed. However, bishops should be informed of denominational visits.

Enormous challenges lie ahead for European peoples before the goal of a "New House" of Europe is reached, a Europe at peace and with justice. The United Methodist Church is called upon to advance that goal.

ADOPTED 1992

See Social Principles, ¶ 69; "Understanding The United Methodist Church as a Global Church."

Nuclear-Free Pacific

The United Methodist Church affirms its commitment to a nuclear-free Pacific. As Christian people committed to stewardship, justice, and peacemaking, we oppose and condemn the use of the Pacific for tests, storage, and transportation of nuclear weapons and weapons-delivery systems and the disposal of radioactive wastes. We further affirm the right of all indigenous people to control their health and well-being.

ADOPTED 1984

See Social Principles, ¶¶ 64A, 69C; "Nuclear Abolition: Saying No to Nuclear Deterrence"; "The United Methodist Church and Peace."

Oppose Food and Medicine Blockades or Embargoes

WHEREAS, as Christians we have a moral obligation to support life and stand against any force or action that causes suffering and death; and

WHEREAS, some governments and/or groups of nations and/or factions within a country have stopped the flow and free marketing of food and medicines, seeking political gains; and

WHEREAS, such practices cause pain and suffering, malnutrition, or starvation with all its detrimental consequences to the innocent civilian population, especially the children; and

WHEREAS, the blockade of food and medicines is used many times to force riots in the general population, putting them in greater danger; and

WHEREAS, the media have brought to us the terrible images of children and women suffering, sick, and starving due to the blockade of food and medicines in recent conflicts;

Therefore, be it resolved, that as United Methodists, we request the United Nations to declare the practice of impeding the flow or free commerce of food and medicines to be a crime against humanity; and, as such, not to be permitted in or by the Security Council; and

Be it further resolved, that as United Methodists, we request the President of the United States and the United States Congress to abstain from using embargoes or blockades of food and medicines, with no exceptions, as an instrument of foreign policy;

And we, as Christians, call upon world leaders to affirm life, to affirm and guarantee the right of all human beings to have access to food and adequate health care, regardless of their political or ideological views.

ADOPTED 1992

See Social Principles, ¶ 69; "Recognition of Cuba"; "The United Methodist Church and Peace."

Our Muslim Neighbors

Christians are called to initiate and promote better relationships between Christians and Muslims on the basis of informed understanding, critical appreciation, and balanced perspective of one another's basic beliefs.

The Historical Context

United Methodists, seeking to be faithful neighbors and witnesses to other members of the human family, recognize with respect peoples of the religion of Islam, who number about one fifth of the human race.

Christians and Muslims acknowledge common roots, along with Jews, in the faith of Abraham, Sarah, and Hagar. As members of one of the monotheistic world religions, Muslims worship and serve the one God with disciplined devotion. Both Christians and Muslims believe that God is ever-inclined toward humankind in justice and mercy. The two faiths sometimes understand differently the particular ways in which God deals with human beings, but they agree that the proper human response to the Almighty is a life of humble obedience, including repentance, faith, and good works. Muslims believe that in their Scripture, the Qur'an, they find set forth for believers the principles for righteous conduct and a harmonious life in society. The following verses from the Qur'an show that these principles are similar to the ones found in the Christian Scriptures:

O believers, be steadfast witnesses for God with justice. Do not let the hatred of a people make you act unjustly. Be just, for justice is next to piety. (5:8)

Worship only God; be good to parents and kindred, to orphans and the poor; speak kindly to others. (92:83)

Do not mix truth with falsehood, nor knowingly conceal the truth. (2:42)

O believers, fulfill your obligations. (5:1)

Hold to forgiveness and enjoin good; turn aside from the foolish. (7:199)

It may be that God will bring about friendship between you and those whom you hold to be your enemies. (60:7)

The Need for Understanding

United Methodists live together with Muslims in many countries of the world and in a variety of social environments. Indeed, in the United States of America, Muslims comprise one of the most rapidly growing religious communities. In places around the world, Muslims may constitute the majority of the population, and in other places, Christians may be the majority. As believers of the two religions build their lives in the same general area, they are often affected by patterns of religious antagonism inherited from the past history of disputes and misunderstanding between the two.

Also, Muslims and Christians experience varying degrees of political and social discrimination, depending on the particular circumstances of each country. In certain areas of tension—for example, Indonesia, Malaysia, Palestine, Sudan, West Africa, the Philippines, Europe, and the United States of America—believers in the two faiths are caught up in struggles for economic, political, and human rights.

We believe that sustained and ever-renewed initiatives of open discussion and sharing of concerns in interfaith settings contribute to the achievement of social justice.

By this statement, we express solidarity with those of either religion who suffer oppression or discrimination.

By this statement, we make a step toward more hospitable and cooperative relationships and encourage dialogical relations.

Basic United Methodist Documents

A. Called to Be Neighbors

A clear biblical basis for discussion in interfaith settings is set forth in *Guidelines for Interreligious Relationships*:

In conversation with a lawyer (Luke 10:25), Jesus reminded him that his neighbor, the one to whom he should show love and compassion, included a stranger, a Samaritan. Today, Christ's call to neighborliness (Luke 10:27) includes the "stranger" of other faiths. It is not just that historical events have forced us together. The Christian faith itself impels us to love our neighbors of other faiths and to seek to live in contact and mutually beneficial relationship, in community with them.

B. The Social Community

In our United Methodist Social Principles, we affirm all persons as equally valuable in the sight of God and determine to work toward societies in which each person's value is recognized, maintained, and strengthened.

Religious persecution has been common in the history of civilization. We urge policies and practices that ensure the right of every religious group to exercise its faith free from legal, political, or economic restrictions. In particular, we condemn anti-Semite, anti-Muslim, and anti-Christian attitudes and practices in both their overt and covert forms, being especially sensitive to their expression in media stereotyping.

C. Our Theological Task

In our United Methodist Doctrinal Standards, our relationship with adherents of other living faiths of the world is set in the context of our ecumenical commitment. We are encouraged to enter into serious interfaith encounters and explorations between Christians and adherents of other living faiths of the world. Scripture calls us to be both neighbors and witnesses to all people. Such encounters require us to reflect anew on our faith and to seek guidance for our witness among neighbors of other faiths.

When Christians enter into such dialogue, they come to it consciously as they seek to live as one people, under the living God who is the Creator of all humankind, the One "who is above all and through all and in all" (Ephesians 4:6).

This theological understanding compels us to a particular kind of dialogue, one in which we reflect critically upon our Christian tradition, gain accurate appreciation of the traditions of others, and engage with love and generosity of spirit as we seek "to raise all such relationships to the highest possible level of human fellowship and understanding."

Christian-Muslim Discussions

The long-standing commitment of The United Methodist Church to social justice, to theological inquiry, and to just and open relationships places a particular responsibility on its members to develop discussions between Christians and Muslims.

Although the movement is still small, there is increasing evidence that groups of Christians and Muslims are coming together to witness to their faith and acknowledge the power of God in their lives, to identify problems that challenge all on the deepest theological and moral level, and to try to understand better the complex factors that determine the crucial decisions being made by governments around the world.

Through such interactions, Christians and Muslims are finding that working for better exchange of information and for ways to cooperate in solving mutual problems and concerns often leads to discovery and growth, adding to the depth and understanding of each tradition.

If we observe the unfolding of events in today's world and assess Islamic movement as only reactionary and threatening, we will hinder the advancement of justice and peace and neither gain from nor contribute to mutual understanding.

If we develop friendships with Muslims as members of the human community from whom and with whom we have much to learn, we will increase our respect for Islam as a way of life that calls its millions of followers to the highest moral ideals and satisfies their deepest spiritual aspirations.

Action Statement

Local congregations and United Methodist agencies at all levels are encouraged to develop ongoing relationships with Muslims and their respective organizations. They are urged to initiate conversations, programs, and dialogues leading to the understanding of both Islam and Christianity, appreciation of their particular gifts, and discovering of commonalities and differences; and to seek areas of mutual cooperation. They are also urged to exchange information and discuss ways to cooperate when they deal with common problems and concerns.

Recommendations

We request the Council of Bishops to support, participate in, and assist United Methodists in implementing this resolution.

We call upon the General Board of Global Ministries, and particularly its Women's Division, to promote a program of ongoing relationships with Muslim women, seeking areas of mutual concern about how to live ethically, morally, and responsibly in today's world and to join in common struggles for peace and justice.

We urge the General Board of Church and Society to work with Muslims in activities designed to achieve common political, social, economic, and ecological goals.

We urge that the General Board of Global Ministries and the General Board of Church and Society develop advocacy programs on behalf of religious freedom and minority rights, particularly regarding nations that are experiencing crisis in Christian-Muslim conflict in which religious minorities are harassed or persecuted. These advocacy programs should be directed toward, among others, the U.S. Department of State and the United Nations Human Rights Commission.

We recommend that the General Commission on Christian Unity and Interreligious Concerns, as it initiates and engages in dialogue with representatives of Islam, remain mindful of the evangelism imperatives of the gospel and the gospel mandate to seek justice for those who are oppressed.

We recommend that United Methodist Communications, through its Division of Public Media and News Service, monitor and call attention to discrimination against Muslims in both the religious and secular media.

We urge United Methodist members, local churches, and agencies to take the following specific actions:

1. Study Islam, using resources such as: *Guidelines on Dialogue with People of Living Faiths and Ideologies,* World Council of Churches (Geneva: 1990); *God Is One: The Way of Islam,* by R. Marston Speight (New York: Friendship Press, 1989); resources available from the Office of Christian-Muslim Concerns, The National Council of the Churches of Christ in the U.S.A., 77 Sherman Street, Hartford, CT 06105; *Striving Together: A Way Forward in Christian-Muslim Relations,* by Charles Kimball (New York: Orbis Books, 1991); *The Holy Qur'an,* New Revised Edition, trans. 'Abdullah Yusuf ' Alli (Brentwood, MD: Amana Corp., 1989); periodicals such as *The Muslim World Islamic Studies.*

2. Initiate dialogue with Muslims, utilizing as our guide the resolution of the 1980 General Conference entitled "Called to Be Neighbors and Witnesses, Guidelines for Interreligious Relationships," and models of dialogue developed by the General Commission on Christian Unity and Interreligious Concerns.

3. Develop awareness of the concerns of particular Muslim populations through implementation of other applicable General Conference Resolutions in the 1992 *Book of Resolutions,* such as "The Arab-Israeli Conflict"; "The Current Arab-Israeli Crisis"; and "Prejudice Against Muslims and Arabs in the U.S.A."

4. Promote understanding between Christians and Muslims in local communities through:

- arranging visits to local mosques;
- developing and participating in cultural exchanges with Muslims;
- inviting Muslims to social occasions;
- seeking Muslim participation in local interfaith councils and interfaith worship;
- sending messages of greeting and good will to Muslims upon the occasion of their religious festivals;
- encouraging authorities of schools, hospitals, prisons, factories, and places of business and government to respect particular features of Muslim life;
- upholding the dignity of individuals, families, and communities; and
- seeking to remedy situations in which Muslims encounter misunderstanding, prejudice, stereotyping, or even hostility from the neighborhood or population when they desire to express their faith in everyday life.

ADOPTED 1992

See Social Principles, ¶ 66B; "Prejudice Against Muslims and Arabs in the U.S.A."; "The Middle East and North Africa"; "Guidelines for Interreligious Relationships: 'Called to Be Neighbors and Witnesses.' "

Peace, Justice, and the Reunification of Korea

Christians in Korea, rooted in a biblical passion for justice, have spoken prophetically and at great risk about the urgency of the reunification of their nation. Celebrating one hundred years of Korean Methodism in 1985, the Korean Methodist Church, in its Centennial Statement, said:

"Faced as we are with the forty years' tragic division of the Korean peninsula, we express our longing for unification of the nation in any form possible through peaceful means in the earliest possible time. This must be done through establishing a democratic political structure based upon freedom and human rights, and must be fulfilled by working toward the establishment of a just society built for the sake of the people. Therefore, we reject any form whatever of dictatorship. Deploring the long history of our nation in which the reality has been the sacrifice of our country's political life, and now with a definite sense of national self-determination which rejects any domination by the superpowers, we disavow any form of war or the taking of life, and commit the whole strength of the Korean Methodist Church to the peaceful reunification of our country."

Now is a time for repentance, a time for reconciliation, a time for justice, a time for peace. For the nation of Korea, divided for more than forty years, justice, peace and reconciliation are tragically overdue. In 1945 just before the end of World War II, the United States proposed and the Soviet Union agreed to the division of Korea. The division was to have been temporary to facilitate the surrender of Japanese troops in Korea. More than four decades later the country is still divided into the Republic of Korea (ROK) and the Democratic Peoples Republic of Korea (DPRK). The enmity between the superpowers has been played out in the Korean tragedy of war and death, dictatorship and militarization, separation of one people into two hostile camps and divided families with no contact at all. All members of the body of Christ, but especially Christians in the United States, have a special responsibility to support the Korean people in their attempts to build democracy, reduce tension, create trust on the Korean peninsula, heal the divisions and reunite their country. God's reconciling activity in Jesus Christ calls us as Christians to the ministry of reconciliation.

Now is the time of urgency. The hunger for democracy and respect for human rights grows strong and promises political change. In the Democratic People's Republic of Korea, people's struggle for human rights and political freedom is completely repressed, and there is no sign of improvement at this time. In the Republic of Korea, the political situation has been much improved with the constitutional change and the direct presidential election. However, there still exist elements of political repression. The threat to peace remains critical with the world's fifth and sixth largest armies facing each other across the Demilitarized Zone. Nuclear weapons back up 40,000 U.S. troops in the south, and the U.S.S.R. and the U.S. have nuclear weapons in the region targeted on Korea. The 1953 Armistice has not yet led to a peace separation in the body of Christ, so that Korean Christians, who once worshiped and served our Lord together, now live in isolation from one another. Ten million Korean people separated from their families, divided since the 1950s with no contact, are growing older and dying. The divisions deepened with distorted rhetoric.

In many ways, the Korean people, north and south, have expressed their strong desire for reunification. Since 1984, there have been official contacts and conversations on economic and humanitarian issues between ROK and DPRK. Emergency assistance, following devastating floods in the south, was offered by the DPRK and accepted by the ROK. The first government-sponsored exchange of visits between divided family members occurred in 1985. Christians from north and south met in 1986 in Glion, Switzerland, as part of an ecumenical process on peace and the reunification of Korea led by the World Council of Churches. In 1987, both sides offered proposals to lower military tensions on the peninsula.

In 1986, as a result of consultations in Korea, north and south, with Christians and government representatives, the National Council of the Churches of Christ in the U.S.A. (NCCCUSA) adopted an important policy statement on "Peace and the Reunification of Korea." United Methodist representatives participated fully in the development of this statement, in consultations on peace and reunification, and in an official ecumenical delegation to North and South Korea in the summer of 1987.

In support of the Korean people and in cooperation with partner Christian groups, it is recommended that The United Methodist Church, its members, local churches, annual conferences, and agencies undertake the following actions through intercession, education, public advocacy, and support of programs furthering justice, peace, and reconciliation:

1. Engage in prayer of penitence and petition with the Korean people and with Christians in the north and south, scarred and pained by the division of their nation and yearning for reunion, and support the efforts of the Korean Methodist Church and the National Council of Churches of Korea to seek peace and reconciliation;

2. Commend the policy statement on "Peace and the Reunification of Korea" of the National Council of the Churches of Christ in the U.S.A. (NCCCUSA), November 1986, to annual conferences and local churches for study and action. The policy statement affirms the desire of the Korean people for restoration of national unity and reunion of separate families, traces the history of division and hopeful steps toward change, and outlines Recommendations for Advocacy and Action in the areas of "Healing and Reconciliation," "Peace With Justice," and "New Directions for U.S. Policy." Recommendations 3, 4, and 5, which follow, are in line with the policy statement;

3. Participate in the ecumenical effort of the World Council of Churches (WCC) and NCCCUSA to facilitate the reunion of separated

Korean families, including Korean residents in the U.S. and their family members in the DPRK;

4. Urge all governments that have relations with the ROK or the DPRK, or both, to exercise their influence to further mediation, interchange, peace, and reunification;

5. Urge all governments involved to forthright commitment to the following policy directions in support of Korean efforts for peace and reunification:

(a) The peaceful reunification of Korea should be a formal U.S. policy goal;

(b) A Peace Treaty should be signed among the nations involved to eliminate the threat of war, establish an enduring peace, and minimize tension in the Korean peninsula. The Peace Treaty, replacing the existing Armistice Treaty, should be based on the conditions of a Non-aggression Pact between the Republic of Korea and the Democratic People's Republic of Korea, with the full participation of the United States and the People's Republic of China, as well as other related countries;

(c) ROK and DPRK contacts should be encouraged;

(d) Bilateral diplomatic and human contacts between the Republic of Korea and the People's Republic of China and between the Republic of Korea and the U.S.S.R. and bilaterally between the United States and the DPRK should be enhanced;

(e) Upon the ratification of a peace settlement in the Korean peninsula based on the spirit of the Peace Treaty and the Non-aggression Pact, and the restoration of mutual trust between the Republic of Korea and the Democratic People's Republic of Korea, U.S. troops in Korea should be withdrawn, and, accordingly, the U.N. command should be dissolved. At the same time, all nuclear weapons in Korea and all U.S. and U.S.S.R. nuclear weapons targeted on Korea that threaten the survival of the Korean people and those of the world should be removed. Any type of military exercises in Korea that affect the peace of the Korean peninsula should be mutually suspended; and

(f) The U.S. should negotiate to end the war and to seek a comprehensive peace settlement in Korea;

6. Call on governments, churches, and other groups to support the struggle of the people of Korea for human rights and democracy by:

(a) Making efforts to lessen the international climate of polarization, hostility, and fear of war that leads to political repression, imprisonment, torture, the militarization of society, and international acts of political violence in air, sea, and land;

(b) Encouraging dialogue and reconciliation among parties, regions, and classes to resolve long-held grievances and prejudices for the sake of a just, inclusive society;

(c) Emphasizing the importance of open social institutions, including freedom for press, political, academic, religious, and cultural activities, in order to build a strong, unified Korea; and

(d) Supporting international economic relations with Korea that enhance economic justice for workers, farmers, and small businesses and that protect the environment; and

7. Encourage United Methodists to use the occasion of the 1988 Olympics and other opportunities for visitation and interchange to come to a deeper understanding of the Korean situation, the witness of the Church, and the achievements, aspirations, and contributions of Korean people in Korea and in various parts of the world, including the United States.

ADOPTED 1988

See Social Principles, ¶ 69.

The United Methodist Church and Peace

"Peace is not simply the absence of war, a nuclear stalemate or combination of uneasy cease-fires. It is that emerging dynamic reality envisioned by prophets where spears and swords give way to implements of peace (Isaiah 2:1-4); where historic antagonists dwell together in trust (Isaiah 11:4-11); and where righteousness and justice prevail. There will be no peace with justice until unselfish and informed life is structured into political processes and international arrangements" (Bishops' Call for Peace and the Self-Development of Peoples).

The mission of Jesus Christ and his church is to serve all peoples regardless of their government, ideology, place of residence, or status. Surely the welfare of humanity is more important in God's sight than the power or even the continued existence of any state. Therefore, the Church is called to look beyond human boundaries of nation, race, class, sex, political ideology, or economic theory and to proclaim the demands of social righteousness essential to peace.

The following are interrelated areas that must be dealt with concurrently in a quest for lasting peace in a world community.

I. Disarmament

The arms race goes on. However, the danger of a holocaust remains as long as nations maintain nuclear weapons. Meanwhile, millions starve, and development stagnates. Again and again, regional tensions grow, conflicts erupt, and outside forces intervene to advance or protect their interests without regard to international law or human rights.

True priorities in national budgeting are distorted by present expenditures on weapons. Because of fear of unemployment, desire for profits, and contributions to the national balance of payments, the arms industry engenders great political power. Arms-producing nations seek to create markets, then vie with one another to become champion among the arms merchants of the world. Food, health, social services, jobs, and education are vital to the welfare of nations. Yet their availability is constantly threatened by the overriding priority given by governments to what is called "defense."

We support disarmament initiatives that go beyond compliance with international treaties. In particular, we ask that the nuclear powers dismantle nuclear stockpiles to show good faith to the non-nuclear participants of the extended Non-Proliferation Treaty. We have rejected possession of nuclear weapons as a permanent basis for securing and maintaining peace. Possession can no longer be tolerated, even as a temporary expedient. We affirm the prophetic position of our bishops, who said in their statement *In Defense of Creation*: "We say a clear and unconditional NO to nuclear war and to any use of nuclear weapons. We conclude that nuclear deterrence is a position that cannot receive the church's blessing."

The time to test nuclear weapons is past. The Comprehensive Test Ban Treaty must include a prohibition on all tests that release radiation. We condemn those nations that continue to conduct such tests. Their actions show they are not responsible members of the world community. We ask that measures such as embargoes, boycotts, or other peaceful pressures be universally applied against nations that continue to test.

At the same time, nations must provide for more secure control of weapons-grade nuclear materials. It is clear deterrence comes from international controls on materials from which bombs are made.

We support the concept of nuclear-free zones where governments or peoples in a specific region band together to bar nuclear weapons from the area either by treaty or declaration.

World public opinion justly condemns the use of chemical or biological weapons. Governments must renounce the use of these particularly inhumane weapons as part of their national policy.

We support treaty efforts to ban the development, trade, and use of weapons that are inhumane, are excessively injurious, and have indiscriminate effects. Such weapons include land mines, booby traps, weapons with nondetectable fragments, incendiary weapons, and blinding laser weapons.

We are also concerned about the use of inhumane weapons by civilian or military police. Hollow-point ("dumdum") or other bullets designed to maim are not acceptable weapons for use by civilian or military forces. We support measures that outlaw use of such weapons at all levels.

We affirm peoples' movements directed to abolition of the tools of war. Governments must not impede public debate on this issue of universal concern.

The goal of world disarmament demands a radical reordering of priorities coupled with an effective system of international peacemaking, peacekeeping, and peace building. The church must constantly keep that goal before peoples and governments.

II. Democracy and Freedom

Millions of people still live under oppressive rule and various forms of exploitation. Millions more live under deplorable conditions of racial, sexual, and class discrimination. In many countries, many persons, including Christians, are suffering repression, imprisonment, and torture as a result of their efforts to speak truth to those in power.

Action by governments to encourage liberation and economic justice is essential but must be supported by parallel action on the part of private citizens and institutions, including the churches, if peaceful measures are to succeed. Unless oppression and denial of basic human rights are ended, violence on an increasing scale will continue to erupt in many nations and may spread throughout the world. The human toll in such conflicts is enormous, for they result in new oppression and further dehumanization.

We are concerned for areas where oppression and discrimination take place. We, as United Methodist Christians, must build the conditions for peace through development of confidence and trust between peoples and governments. We are unalterably opposed to those who instill hate in one group for another. Governments or political factions must not use religious, class, racial, or other differences as the means to achieve heinous political purposes.

This concern extends to all situations where external commercial, industrial, and military interests are related to national oligarchies that resist justice and liberation for the masses of people. It is essential that governments which support or condone these activities alter their policies to permit and enable people to achieve genuine self-determination.

III. The United Nations

International justice requires the participation and determination of all peoples. We are called to look beyond the "limited and competing boundaries of nation-states to the larger and more inclusive community of humanity" (Bishops' Call for Peace and the Self-Development of Peoples).

There has been unprecedented international cooperation through the United Nations and its specialized agencies as they have worked to solve international problems of health, education, and the welfare of people. The United Nations Children's Fund (UNICEF) is one of the agencies that has been successful in this area.

These achievements are to be commended. However, in other areas, political considerations have diminished the support needed for the United Nations to achieve its goals. Many nations, including the most powerful, participate in some programs only when such action does not interfere with their national advantage.

We believe the United Nations and its agencies must be supported, strengthened, and improved. We recommend that Christians work for the following actions in their respective nations:

• The Universal Declaration of Human Rights is a standard of achievement for all peoples and nations. International covenants and conventions that seek to implement the Declaration must be universally ratified.

• Peace and world order require the development of an effective and enforceable framework of international law that provides protection for human rights and guarantees of justice for all people.

• Greater use should be made of the International Court of Justice. Nations should remove any restrictions they have adopted that impair the court's effective functioning.

• The industrialized world must not dominate development agencies. We support efforts to make controlling bodies of such agencies more representative.

• We support the development and strengthening of international agencies designed to help nations or peoples escape from domination by other nations or transnational enterprises.

• Economic and political considerations greatly affect issues of food, energy, raw materials, and other commodities. We support efforts in the United Nations to achieve new levels of justice in the world economic order.

• We support the concept of collective action against threats to peace. Wars fought in the search for justice might well be averted or diminished if the nations of the world would work vigorously and in concert to seek changes in oppressive political and economic systems.

IV. World Trade and Economic Development

The gap between rich and poor countries continues to widen. Human rights are denied when the surpluses of some arise in part as a result of continued deprivation of others. This growing inequity exists in our own communities and in all our nations. Our past efforts to alleviate these conditions have failed. Too often these efforts have been limited by our own unwillingness to act or have been frustrated by private interests and governments striving to protect the wealthy and the powerful.

In order to eliminate inequities in the control and distribution of the common goods of humanity, we are called to join the search for more just and equitable international economic structures and relationships. We seek a society that will assure all persons and nations the opportunity to achieve their maximum potential.

In working toward that purpose, we believe these steps are needed:

• Economic systems structured to cope with the needs of the world's peoples must be conceived and developed.

• Measures that will free peoples and nations from reliance on financial arrangements that place them in economic bondage must be implemented.

• Policies and practices for the exchange of commodities and raw materials that establish just prices and avoid damaging fluctuations in price must be developed.

• Control of international monetary facilities must be more equitably shared by all the nations, including the needy and less powerful.

• Agreements that affirm the common heritage principle (that resources of the seabed, subsoil, outer space, and those outside national jurisdiction are the heritage of humanity) should be accepted by all nations.

• Multilateral, rather than bilateral, assistance programs should be encouraged for secular as well as religious bodies. They must be designed to respond to the growing desire of the "developing world" to become self-reliant.

• Nations that possess less military and economic power than others must be protected, through international agreements, from loss of control of their own resources and means of production to either transnational enterprises or other governments.

These international policies will not narrow the rich-poor gap within nations unless the powerless poor are enabled to take control of their own political and economic destinies. We support people's organizations designed to enable the discovery of local areas of exploitation and development of methods to alleviate these problems.

Economic and political turmoil within many developing nations has been promoted and used by other powers as an excuse to intervene through subversive activities or military force in furtherance of their own national interests. We condemn this version of imperialism that often parades as international responsibility.

We support the United Nations' efforts to develop international law to govern the sea and to ensure that the world's common resources will be used cooperatively and equitably for the welfare of humankind.

We urge the appropriate boards and agencies of The United Methodist Church to continue and expand efforts to bring about justice in cooperative action between peoples of all countries.

V. Military Conscription, Training, and Service

1. *Conscription.* We affirm our historic opposition to compulsory military training and service. We urge that military conscription laws be repealed; we also warn that elements of compulsion in any national service program will jeopardize seriously the service motive and introduce new forms of coercion into national life. We advocate and will continue to work for the inclusion of the abolition of military conscription in disarmament agreements.

2. *Conscientious objection.* Each person must face conscientiously the dilemmas of conscription, military training, and service and decide his or her own responsible course of action. We affirm the historic statement: "What the Christian citizen may not do is to obey persons rather than God, or overlook the degree of compromise in even our best acts, or gloss over the sinfulness of war. The church must hold within its fellowship persons who sincerely differ at this point of critical decision, call all to repentance, mediate to all God's mercy, minister to all in Christ's name" ("The United Methodist Church and Peace," 1968 General Conference).

Christian teaching supports conscientious objection to all war as an ethically valid position. It also asserts that ethical decisions on political matters must be made in the context of the competing claims of biblical revelation, church doctrine, civil law, and one's own understanding of what God calls him or her to do.

We therefore support all those who conscientiously object to preparation for or participation in any specific war or all wars, to cooperation with military conscription, or to the payment of taxes for military purposes, and we ask that they be granted legal recognition.

3. *Amnesty and reconciliation.* We urge understanding of and full amnesty or pardon for persons in all countries whose refusal to participate in war has placed them in legal jeopardy.

VI. Peace Research, Education, and Action

The 1960 General Conference established the landmark study "The Christian Faith and War in the Nuclear Age." That study said, "The Christian Church and the individual must accept responsibility for the creation of a climate of opinion in which creative changes can occur." It called work for these creative alternatives "our mission field as we live as disciples of the Prince of Peace." In order to create such a climate of conciliation and compromise, we call upon The United Methodist Church, including its agencies and institutions of higher education, in the light of its historical teachings and its commitment to peace and self-development of peoples, to:

1. Seek the establishment of educational institutions devoted to the study of peace;

2. Develop alternatives to vocations that work against peace, and support individuals in their quest;

3. Explore and apply ways of resolving domestic and international differences that affirm human fulfillment rather than exploitation and violence;

4. Affirm and employ methods that build confidence and trust between peoples and countries, including training in multicultural understanding and appreciation of differences, rejecting all promotion of hatred and mistrust;

5. Continue to develop and implement the search for peace through educational experiences, including church school classes, schools of Christian mission, and other settings throughout the Church; and

6. Encourage local churches and members to take actions that make for peace and to act in concert with other peoples and groups of good will toward the achievement of a peaceful world.

ADOPTED 1984
AMENDED & READOPTED 1996

See Social Principles, ¶ 69; "Peace with Justice as a Special Program"; "Justice, Peace, and the Integrity of Creation."

Peace with Justice as a Special Program

Background: From Despair to Hope

Since 1980, we have seen a worsening of living conditions for poor people in the United States and elsewhere in the world. Affordable housing for persons of modest income is becoming scarce. Homelessness is increasing. Unemployment rates for minority youth and persons lacking skills are astonishingly high. Hard-working industrial workers are losing their jobs as a result of global economic change. Hard-working farmers are being displaced from productive land. Family stability is threatened by economic insecurity. The number of single-parent households is on the rise. Immigrants who have come to the United States to escape persecution and to seek economic opportunity face obstacles in law and community acceptance. Many Native Americans, Blacks, Hispanics, and Asians still suffer from discrimination and other manifestations of inequality. So do women. Many millions of persons, particularly elderly persons and low-income women and children, receive inadequate or no health care. Persons have been discharged from mental hospitals with little or no provision of the community-based services they need. Victims of the spreading AIDS epidemic confront prejudice and insufficient care facilities.

Historically, and presently, issues of injustice are disproportionately experienced by racial and ethnic people. A disproportionate number of racial and ethnic persons are victimized by poverty, poor or no health care, violence, limited educational opportunities, and higher frequencies of environmental pollution. Racial and ethnic persons are most severely affected by the militarization of our economy.

Daily we experience the disintegration of creation. We consume the earth's resources without regard to the processes of regeneration of the earth. Regional environmental issues—water scarcity, loss of precious topsoil, pollution of natural resources, the over-harvesting of timber, the encroachment of development in wildlife habitats, and the use of arable land to grow cities and parking lots rather than farms—plague our nation. In other sectors of our world, we see the processes of desertification, acid rain, and loss of tropical rain forest destroying our natural world. The implications and far-reaching effects of global warming put our whole world at risk.

Many of the economic problems and the decline in community services can be traced to the militarization of the U.S. and world economies. The United States has gorged itself with military expenditure but refused to pay the full bill through taxes. As a result, the federal deficit has almost tripled, thus mortgaging the future for coming generations. Similar distortion occurred in the Soviet Union, contributing to its dissolution. It has also happened in a number of third world countries, which can ill afford such waste. For part of the third world, the situation is made worse by civil and regional wars, low-intensity conflicts, and military intervention by the United States and other nations.

While these harmful trends have been occurring, many people in the United States and elsewhere have raised their voices in protest. They have urged an end to nuclear madness, to undue reliance on military force as the primary instrument of foreign policy, to neglect of urgent human needs. The 1984 General Conference of The United Methodist Church spoke out on a number of these issues of peace and justice. The United Methodist Council of Bishops offered a prophetic vision in the pastoral letter and foundation document *In Defense of Creation*. Roman Catholic bishops in the United States have spoken eloquently on the need for a reversal of U.S. nuclear policy and for introduction of greater justice into the U.S. economy. Other religious denominations have added their voices. An increasing number of political leaders are insisting that there must be better ways of conducting the world's business.

Changes taking place in our global community give us hope for potential future reductions in military expenditures. This will free up resources of money and talent to be used for meeting urgent social needs.

This is happening at the same time that an increasing number of persons and institutions are expressing a strong determination and commitment to address the social and economic crisis that confronts the poor, those displaced by economic change, and those who never achieved full equality of opportunity. This, then, has set the stage for a social transformation, for the quest to open the doors of opportunity for all, to distribute resources more equitably, to provide better care for persons in need.

Biblical Basis for Response

The United Methodist Church, with its historic commitment to peace and justice, can and should provide leadership to this social transformation. This heritage is expressed in the Social Principles and the Social Creed. It gained eloquent articulation by the United Methodist Council of Bishops in the foundation document *In Defense of Creation: The Nuclear Crisis and a Just Peace*, which offers a well-grounded biblical analysis for peace with justice. The bishops wrote:

At the heart of the Old Testament is the testimony to *shalom*, that marvelous Hebrew word that means peace. But the peace that is *shalom* is not negative or one-dimensional. It is much more than the absence of war. *Shalom* is positive peace: harmony, wholeness, health, and well-being in all human relationships. It is the natural state of humanity as birthed by God. It is harmony between humanity and all of God's good creation. All of creation is interrelated. Every creature, every element, every force of nature participates in the whole of creation. If any person is denied *shalom*, all are thereby diminished. . . .

The Old Testament speaks of God's sovereignty in terms of *covenant*, more particularly the "covenant of peace" with Israel, which binds that people to God's *shalom* (Isaiah 54:10; Ezekiel 37:26). In the covenant of *shalom*, there is no contradiction between justice and peace or between peace and security or between love and justice (Jeremiah 29:7). In Isaiah's prophecy, when "the Spirit is poured upon us from on high," we will know that these laws of God are one and indivisible:

> Then justice will dwell in the wilderness,
>   and righteousness abide in the fruitful field.
> And the effect of righteousness will be peace,
>   and the result of righteousness, quietness and trust forever.
> My people will abide in a peaceful habitation,
>   in secure dwellings, and in quiet resting places. (Isaiah 32:16-18)

Shalom, then, is the sum total of moral and spiritual qualities in a community whose life is in harmony with God's good creation. . . . (pp. 24, 25–26)

In their analysis, the United Methodist bishops pointed out that when the elders of Israel forsook their moral covenant for warrior-kings, the nation descended into generations of exploitation, repression, and aggression—then into chaos, captivity, and exile in Babylon. Yet we must look to the great prophets of that bitter period of Exile for the renewed vision of *shalom*. If Exodus is liberation, Exile is renewal. Ezekiel and Isaiah (40–66) reaffirm God's creation and redemption as universal in scope. Narrow nationalism is repudiated. Servanthood is exalted as the hopeful path to *shalom* (page 27).

> And the prophets' images—swords into plowshares, peaceable kingdoms, new covenants written on the heart—"forecast the coming of One who will be the Prince of Peace."
>
> And so he comes. He comes heralded by angels who sing: "Glory to God in the highest, and on earth peace!" He invokes the most special blessings upon peacemakers. He exalts the humanity of aliens. He commands us to love our enemies; for he knows, even if we do not, that if we hate our enemies, we blind and destroy ourselves. *Shalom*, after all, is the heart of God and the law of creation. It cannot be broken with impunity. . . .
>
> New Testament faith presupposes a radical break between the follies, or much so-called conventional wisdom about power and security, on the one hand, the transcendent wisdom of *shalom*, on the other. Ultimately, New Testament faith is a message of hope about God's plan and purpose for human destiny. It is a redemptive vision that refuses to wallow in doom. . . .
>
> Paul's letters announce that Jesus Christ is "our peace." It is Christ who has "broken down the dividing wall of hostility," creating one humanity, overcoming enmity, so making peace (Ephesians 2:14-19). It is Christ who ordains a ministry of reconciliation. Repentance prepares us for reconciliation. Then we shall open ourselves to the transforming power of God's grace in Christ. Then we shall know what it means to be "in Christ." Then we are to become ambassadors of a new creation, a new Kingdom, a new order of love and justice (2 Corinthians 5:17-20). . . .
>
> The promise of peace envisioned by Israel's prophets of the Exile at the climax of the Old Testament is celebrated once more at the climax of the New Testament. The Revelation of John, in the darkest night of despair, sings of a new earth, radiant with infinite love and compassion, in which all nations and peoples come together peaceably before the Lord God and in which hunger and hurt and sorrow are no more (Revelation 7). (pp. 27–30)

This is the foundation of faith that enables us in The United Methodist Church to offer hope to those who despair and to bring forth joy to replace sadness. As Saint Francis of Assisi prayed to act in the spirit of Christ, so we too can sow love where there is hatred; where injury, pardon; where darkness, light. As instruments of peace and justice, we can seek to replace discord with harmony and to repair the brokenness that shatters the wholeness of *shalom*.

Program Activities

The General Board of Church and Society will carry out the following "Peace with Justice" activities:

1. Implement "Policies for a Just Peace" as specified in the Council of Bishops' Foundation Document;

2. Implement the process of "Justice, Peace, and the Integrity of Creation" as adopted by the 1990 World Convocation for Justice, Peace, and the Integrity of Creation in Seoul, Republic of Korea;

3. Work for social-justice policies and programs that seek the wholeness of *shalom*, including provision of greater economic opportunity; affordable housing, adequate food; and proper health care for poor people, displaced industrial workers, displaced farmers, and other persons faced with economic insecurity;

4. Work to eradicate attitudinal and systemic behavior patterns that perpetuate the sin of racism as it is lived out in the areas of peace, justice, and the integrity of creation.

To achieve these objectives, the General Board of Church and Society may:

(a) Assist annual conferences, districts, and local churches to organize and carry out peace with justice activities, and to promote the Peace with Justice Special Sunday Offering;

(b) Provide a regular flow of information on public issues to local churches, districts, and annual conferences;

(c) Strengthen its staff capability to act as a public-policy advocate or measures that improve U.S. global relations and move toward nuclear disarmament and measures that provide jobs, housing, food, health care, and income support for lower-income families and individuals; and

(d) Assist annual conferences and/or local churches to assess and respond to the disproportionate effect of injustices on racial and ethnic persons.

For the purpose of financing activities (a) to achieve the "Policies for a Just Peace" contained in the Council of Bishops' Foundation Document *In Defense of Creation*, and (b) to pursue other justice and peace objectives contained within the vision of *shalom* in this same document, revenue shall come from the Peace with Justice offering and other possible sources in accordance with ¶ 267.5 and World Service Special gifts.

Assignment

The Peace with Justice Special Program shall be assigned to the General Board of Church and Society.

ADOPTED 1992

See Social Principles, ¶ 69; "Justice, Peace, and the Integrity of Creation"; "The United Methodist Church and Peace."

Puerto Rico and Vieques

The theme of human liberation is found again and again in the Bible, from Moses' leadership of the Hebrew people out of Egypt to Jesus in the synagogue proclaiming the acceptable year of the Lord.

The United Methodist Church has long stood for an end to colonialism and for the self-determination of all peoples. At the same time, the people of Puerto Rico have lived under the sovereignty of the United States in what can be described as a form of colonialism. Though plebiscites have been held and a degree of local autonomy granted, all of the island's political parties in recent years have expressed their dissatisfaction with Puerto Rico's political status. The situation has been aggravated by the U.S. Navy's bombing practice and related activities on and around two offshore islands, first at Culebra, and now Vieques.

The General Conference of The United Methodist Church:

1. Asks that the people of Puerto Rico be accorded full opportunity for self-determination of their future political status under conditions that assure a genuinely free choice with generous provisions for adjustment to any new status chosen; and

2. Expresses its solidarity with the people of Vieques in their most ardent desire that the United States Navy cease its military activity that adversely affects the citizens of Vieques, and that the United States Navy repair whatever damages it has caused to the people of Vieques.

To these ends, the General Conference directs the attention of United Methodists and the general agencies of the denomination to the need for information and action.

ADOPTED 1980

See Social Principles, ¶ 69; "Economic Development of Puerto Rico"; "In Opposition to Building a Radar in the Lajas Valley and the Town of Vieques, Puerto Rico."

Rape in Times of Conflict and War

Their infants will be dashed to pieces
before their eyes;
their houses will be plundered,
and their wives ravished. (Isaiah 13:16)

Women are raped in Zion,
virgins in the towns of Judah. (Lamentations 5:11)

For I will gather all the nations against Jerusalem to battle, and the city shall be taken and the houses looted and the women raped; half the city shall go into exile, but the rest of the people shall not be cut off from the city. (Zechariah 14:2)

"We believe war is incompatible with the teachings and example of Christ. We therefore reject war as an instrument of national foreign policy and insist that the first moral duty of all nations is to resolve by peaceful means every dispute that rises between or among them; that human values must outweigh military claims as governments determine their priorities; that the militarization of society must be challenged and stopped; that the manufacture, sale, and deployment of armaments must be reduced and controlled; and that the production, possession, or use of nuclear weapons be condemned" (Social Principles, ¶ 69C).

For centuries, women have been raped as an act of violence and a demonstration of power—most especially in times of conflict and wars. Rape has been and is sanctioned by military organizations for the gratification of soldiers as was seen in several Asian countries during World War II. The Comfort Women of Korea are a most blatant example of this practice. Rape during wartime constitutes many individual and group acts of violence perpetrated by soldiers against girls and women of enemy countries or opposing sides, often under orders. Thus rape, in effect, is used as an extension of warfare. But rape is rarely mentioned in resolutions and statements on war and peace. And the conquest of women as spoils of war continues to be tolerated in times of conflict.

Mass rape is an increasingly sophisticated weapon of war, as it is being used in the Bosnia-Herzegovina conflict and in other conflicts—such as Haiti, Georgia (CIS), and Rwanda—in the world today.

Survivors of conflicts speak of rape on the frontline and third-party rape; these rapes are carried out publicly by soldiers to demoralize family members and opposition forces compelled to witness them.

Many stories refer to village communities being rounded up in camps—perhaps a school or community center—where a space is cleared in the middle. It is in this space that public raping takes place. It is reported as repeated and violent and procedural. It is claimed that many of the victims and witnesses know the rapists.

Destruction and violation of women is one way of attacking male opponents who regard the women as their property—and whose male identity is therefore bound to protection of their property.

671

The current tribunals against war crimes undertaken in Rwanda and Bosnia have acknowledged rape as a form of torture, since it is not specifically mentioned in existing international laws.

The United Methodist Church affirms the sacredness of all persons and their right to safety, nurture, and care. And, together with the international community, it is challenged to respond to the rape of women in military conflicts. The extent and frequency of the violation of women in war must not be allowed to deaden sensitivity to this as gross injustice. There must be greater understanding of the use of rape in this manner (as a weapon of warfare). Documentation and analysis of such planned violation of human rights and its root causes must be developed. Strategizing to confront systems that give rise to it and the needs of those who are its victims must be undertaken.

International instruments such as Geneva Conventions must be strengthened to ensure condemnation of rape as a war crime with appropriate enforcement and monitoring.

At local and regional levels, churches and concerned groups must pressure for legal and political decisions to protect victims of rape. It is not sufficient to articulate condemnations of crime; practical actions to effect change must follow.

As part of the overall humanitarian responses to physical and emotional needs, it is a matter of urgency that adequate and appropriate attention be given to the psychological needs of women raped in war.

The task of supporting these survivors—as well as their children, families, and communities—requires massive commitment, resources, and expertise.

We call on The United Methodist Church:

1. To condemn all forms of rape as incompatible with the Church's understanding of the sacredness of life; and to affirm the right of all persons to safety, nurture, and care;

2. To urge the United Methodist Office for the UN to work toward including the condemnation of rape as a war crime in international instruments such as the Geneva Conventions;

3. To urge the General Board of Global Ministries to develop an anthology of theological and biblical perspectives of rape in times of war, written by survivors and other women who have observed and reflected on this grave concern;

4. To urge both the General Board of Global Ministries and the General Board of Church and Society to act as resources for churches who wish to pressure for legal and political decisions to protect victims of rape in times of war; and

5. To urge UMCOR to continue developing assistance and support for women victims of war and their families, to meet their physical and emotional needs. This may mean supporting, as wartime refugees, women who cannot return to their homes because of fear of rape, violence, and condemnation.

ADOPTED 1996

See Social Principles, ¶ 69; "The United Methodist Church and Peace."

Ratification of United Nations Covenants and Conventions by the United States

The United Methodist Church commends the Senate of the United States for actions that completed ratification of the following human rights instruments and allowed its government to deposit instruments of ratification with the Secretary General of the United Nations, who received them on the following dates:

• the International Convention on the Prevention and Punishment of Genocide on November 25, 1988;

• the International Covenant on Civil and Political Rights on June 8, 1992;

• the Convention Against Torture and Other Cruel, Inhuman, or Degrading Treatment or Punishment; and

• the International Convention on the Elimination of All Forms of Racial Discrimination on October 21, 1994.

The Senate has not pursued those steps which will complete ratification of three remaining human rights instruments that have been signed by the President:

• The International Covenant on Economic, Social, and Cultural Rights was signed by President Jimmy Carter on October 5, 1977, and transmitted to the United States Senate;

• The Convention on the Elimination of all Forms of Discrimination Against Women was signed on behalf of President Carter in Copenhagen on July 17, 1980, and transmitted to the United States Senate; and

• The Convention on the Rights of the Child was signed on behalf of President Clinton in New York on February 16, 1995, and transmitted to the United States Senate.

The Senate also has not acted upon the following conventions:

• The Convention on Biodiversity was signed on June 4, 1993, on behalf of President Clinton and transmitted to the United States Senate; and

• The Treaty on the Law of the Sea was signed on behalf of President Clinton on July 29, 1994, and transmitted to the United States Senate.

It is imperative that the United States Senate act promptly to give its "advice and consent" to the ratification of these instruments.

ADOPTED 1996

See Social Principles, ¶ 69D; "The United Methodist Church and Peace"; "In Support of the United Nations"; "Human Rights."

Recognition of Cuba

The United Methodist Church is linked in Christ with The Methodist Church of Cuba. We share a common heritage and mission. We are mutually responsible for the proclamation of God's love and the nurturing of neighbor love.

The Social Principles require us to make the community of God a reality as we "pledge ourselves to seek the meaning of the gospel in all issues that divide people and threaten the growth of world community" (¶ 69). We believe that "God's world is one world" (¶ 69). However, such a world cannot exist if fragmented against the will of God when nations refuse to solve their differences in respectful dialogue and give diplomatic recognition to one another.

For over thirty-five years, the government of the United States has not maintained diplomatic relations with the government of Cuba and has, instead, pursued an economic embargo prohibiting all kinds of trade with Cuba. The Democracy Act of 1992 (22 U.S.C. 6001) has tightened the embargo restrictions by penalizing other countries if their ships stop in Cuba. This policy is heightening tensions in the Caribbean; it also creates tensions between the United States and the many nations that trade or want to trade with Cuba. The objectives sought by the proponents of this policy in the Cold War era were to force a change in Cuban foreign policy and to halt the growth and development of Soviet influence in that country.

WHEREAS, the Cold War is over and there is no Soviet Union exercising any influence on Cuba's foreign policy or posing any threat to the United States; and

WHEREAS, the Cuban government has made significant changes in its foreign and economic policies; and

WHEREAS, The Methodist Church in 1964 made a historical statement entitled the "Re-examination of Policy Toward Mainline China, Cuba, and Other Countries," which said: "The Christian gospel involves reconciliation by encounter and by communication regardless of political considerations. Therefore, we cannot accept the expression of hostility by any country, its policies, or its ideologies as excuses for the failure of Christians to press persistently, realistically, and creatively toward a growing understanding among the peoples of all countries"; and

WHEREAS, the government of the United States is the only major Western country pursuing a policy of nonrelations with Cuba, while Canada, France, Great Britain, Germany, Japan, Mexico, Argentina, Bolivia, and almost all other countries of the Western alliance maintain normal diplomatic and/or economic relations with Cuba; and

WHEREAS, the General Assembly of the United Nations voted successively in 1993 and 1994 for a resolution called "Necessity of Ending the Economic, Commercial, and Financial Embargo Imposed by the United States of America Against Cuba"; in the 1993 resolution, the General Assembly is "reaffirming, among other principles, the sovereign equality of States, nonintervention, and noninterference in their internal affairs and freedom of trade and international navigation" and calling "all States to refrain from promulgating and applying laws and measures" aimed at "the economic, commercial, and financial embargo against Cuba"; and

WHEREAS, the government of the United States has in recent years strengthened its commercial and diplomatic relations with other Communist countries such as China and Vietnam and has also increased contacts and negotiations with North Korea, independently of their foreign policy, which differs and often collides with that of the United States; and

WHEREAS, the Reagan administration declared that the United States will not use food as a foreign policy instrument when it lifted the grain embargo imposed against the Soviet Union by the Carter Administration in order to protest the Soviet intervention in the conflict in Afghanistan; and

WHEREAS, the lifting of the economic embargo against Cuba, a member of the Caribbean Common Market (CARICOM), would help relieve tensions in the Caribbean; and

WHEREAS, the Council of Churches of Cuba, of which the Methodist Church of Cuba is a member, the Cuban Conference of Roman Catholic Bishops, and several other international religious groups and leaders such as CIEMAL, the Caribbean Conference of Churches, and Pope John Paul II, as well as U.S. religious bodies such as the United Church of Christ, the Presbyterian Church (USA), and the American Baptist Churches have stated or passed resolutions in favor of lifting the embargo; and

WHEREAS, the Cuban Democracy Act of 1992 and the 1994 additional measures to tighten the embargo curtail religious freedom by making very difficult the relationship between churches in the United States and churches in Cuba; and

WHEREAS, an abandonment of these hostile measures would facilitate improvements in democratic reforms and human rights in Cuba; and

WHEREAS, the Bible teachings give us the mandate to "love one another, because love is from God" (1 John 4:7), and to practice mercy as the good Samaritan did (Luke 10:25-37);

Therefore, be it resolved, that The United Methodist Church, from its Christian and humanitarian perspective, inspired by the love of God and the historic Methodist commitment to peace and social justice, and in light of historic changes with the end of the Cold War, hereby petitions the President and Congress of the United States to lift its economic embargo against Cuba by repealing the Cuban Democracy Act of 1992 (22 U.S.C. 6001, et seq.) as well as the 1994 additional restrictions and any other laws or measures related to the embargo against Cuba and to seek negotiations with the Cuban government for the purpose of resuming normal diplomatic relations.

Note: The United States broke diplomatic relations with Cuba on January 3, 1961. A partial trade embargo against Cuba by the U.S. government was declared on October 19, 1960. On July 8, 1963, "the Treasury Department, using its authority under the Trading with the Enemy Act of 1917, issues more restrictive Cuba Assets Control Regulations."

(*Cuban Foreign Relations, A Chronology, 1959–1982*)

ADOPTED 1996

See Social Principles, ¶ 69; "Oppose Food and Medicine Blockades or Embargoes."

Removal or Reduction of U.S. Military Bases in Okinawa

Be it resolved, that the 1996 General Conference support the present government of Okinawa and the vast majority of the Okinawan people in their strong, unceasing efforts to achieve the complete removal or substantial reduction of U.S. military bases and U.S. military personnel on the island of Okinawa and other islands in Okinawa Prefecture of Japan, and the return of those lands for peaceful, constructive purposes; and that a copy of this petition be sent to the President of the United States, the U.S. secretary of state, and the U.S. secretary of defense for consideration and action, and that a copy be sent to the Governor of Okinawa and the Prime Minister of Japan for their information.

ADOPTED 1996

See Social Principles, ¶ 69; "The Search for Peace and Justice in Okinawa."

The Search for Peace and Justice in Okinawa

In recognition of the great investment that The United Methodist Church has made in the mission of the Church in Okinawa (Japan) since the turn of the century, with the arrival of the first Methodist missionary, this resolution is presented to request the support of United Methodist congregations for one of the urgent issues in mission of the Okinawa District of The United Methodist Church in Japan, the Christian body with which The United Methodist Church has a cooperative mission relationship.

With 1995 commemorating the fiftieth year since the end of the Battle of Okinawa, the long-term oppressive presence of U.S. military bases in Okinawa has become a critical issue for the entire Okinawan society. In accordance with the Japan-America Security Treaty, which grants the U.S. use of facilities and areas in Japan, the United States military forces occupy a substantial amount of the land area of Okinawa Island, in addition to having exclusive use of designated air and sea space for military training. This vast military presence greatly hinders the development of Okinawa and threatens the livelihood of Okinawan citizens.

Even after Allied occupation ended on the Japanese mainland in 1952, Okinawa remained under complete U.S. military administration for twenty years, until 1972, when the islands reverted to Japanese jurisdiction.

Private property requisitioned by the U.S. military to construct the vast military bases after the war is still held today, denying some 30,000 families the right to live on and utilize their own land. Military aircraft produce ear-splitting noise on a daily basis. Military drills endanger the lives of citizens and destroy the natural environment.

Since 1972, the date of Okinawa's reversion to Japan, U.S. military personnel have committed 4,716 crimes. These crimes, which include robbery, murder, and rape, imperil the fundamental human rights of the Okinawan people.

The September 4, 1995, rape of an elementary school girl by three American military personnel is not an extraordinary case. Such structural violence is inherent in the enforced presence of the U.S. military in Okinawa. The residents of Okinawa living around the bases become the primary targets of this violence, with women and children being especially vulnerable.

This latest rape is only the spark igniting the Okinawans anger over this and past crimes perpetuated upon them by the U.S. military. Okinawan citizens are demanding the reduction of U.S. military bases in Okinawa and also a reappraisal of the Status of Forces Agreement, the document that governs the presence of U.S. military personnel in Japan.

The Okinawa District of the United Church of Christ in Japan considers the militarization of Okinawa to be an issue that the church is called on to address in its mission of peacemaking. Following the resolution acted on by the Okinawa District Executive Committee of the United Church of Christ in Japan, a letter was sent to partner church members in North America, including The United Methodist Church, in the name of the moderator of the United Church of Christ in Japan. This letter appealed for support of Okinawan Christians, who feel that it is no longer possible to coexist with military bases and personnel.

In light of the above, this resolution requests the General Conference of The United Methodist Church to join with Okinawan Christians in urging the following four appeals to the governments of the United States and Japan:

1. A thorough investigation of all crimes and acts of violence committed by U.S. military personnel stationed on U.S. military bases in Okinawa, and an apology and compensation to the victims of the crimes;

2. An immediate cessation of all military exercises that destroy the environment and threaten the daily life of Okinawan citizens;

3. An immediate review of the Japan-America Security Treaty (AMPO) and the Status of Forces Agreement (SOFA), which completely

ignores the laws of Japan, imposing great hardship on the people of Okinawa; and

4. Establishment of a peace not based on military power, and the removal of all U.S. military bases from Okinawa.

ADOPTED 1996

See Social Principles, ¶ 69; "Removal or Reduction of U.S. Military Bases in Okinawa."

Support Amnesty International

WHEREAS, Amnesty International has documented and verified political imprisonments, tortures, and killings over the last few years involving government-linked forces by governments of widely differing ideologies in more than twenty countries on four continents; and

WHEREAS, Amnesty International has mounted a campaign to publicize such crimes against humanity that involve thousands of victims, and in this way to bring pressure upon the governments involved;

Therefore, be it resolved, that The United Methodist Church adds its endorsement and support to Amnesty International, along with that already given by the Central Committee of the World Council of Churches, the National Council of the Churches of Christ in the U.S.A., and the American Baptist Churches, U.S.A.

Be it further resolved, that notice of this support be sent to Amnesty International, U.S.A.; to the Secretary General of the United Nations; and to the media.

ADOPTED 1984

See Social Principles, ¶ 69; "Human Rights"; "In Support of Self-Determination and Nonintervention."

Terrorism

The increase in terrorism from the 1970s through the present has caused fear and desperation among people everywhere, which creates a sense of hopelessness and instability and reveals the weakness in the present world system of international peace and security at home.

The image of God and the sacrifice of Christ bestow a worth and dignity that cannot be rightfully ignored or violated by any human institution or social movement. For this reason, we condemn all acts of terrorism, with no exception for the target or the source.

There is no significant difference between "state terrorism," as the "overkill" response of a state, and group terrorism, whether in the international arena or on the home front.

With these truths in mind, it is important that we, as United Methodist Christians:

1. Examine critically the causes of terrorism, including national and international involvement;

2. Firmly support the United Nations as an agency for conflict resolution and as a viable alternative to resorting to war and/or terrorism;

3. Stand against terrorist acts in the forms of retaliation or capital punishment;

4. Urge the President of the United States to repudiate violence and the killing and victimizing of innocent people;

5. Oppose the use of indiscriminate military force to combat terrorism, especially where the use of such force results in casualties among noncombatant citizens who are not themselves perpetrators of terrorist acts, and urge support of United Nations' Resolution 40-61, which addresses international cooperation regarding terrorist acts;

6. Condemn the use of extremist tactics that resort to violence within our own domestic society as an expression of ideological differences, racism, and anti-Semitism;

7. Direct the General Board of Church and Society to formulate a study to show how to deal with acts of terrorism that we face as a society and give direction as to how the Church and annual conferences' leaders and members can and should respond; and

8. Continue to support the U.S. ban on assault rifles, as they are the weapons of choice by individuals and organizations implementing terrorist activities both at home and abroad.

ADOPTED 1992
AMENDED & READOPTED 1996

See Social Principles, ¶ 69.

Understanding The United Methodist Church as a Global Church

WHEREAS, modern developments in transportation, communications, and technology have brought peoples and nations closer together; and

WHEREAS, globality tends to be understood in The United Methodist Church basically in terms of the United Methodist presence beyond the boundaries of the United States and almost exclusively in relation to those sections of the Church that are structurally within it; and

WHEREAS, there are a number of churches in the Methodist family that out of a sense of calling by the Holy Spirit, a desire to affirm their own identity, and their need for self-determination have elected to become autonomous;

Therefore, be it resolved, that The United Methodist Church:

1. Celebrate the God-given diversity of race, culture, and people at every level of Church life in our worship and other activities;

2. Celebrate the global dimension brought to The United Methodist Church by sisters and brothers from all over the globe and the Native American nations, who are a part of U.S. society and The United Methodist Church;

3. Celebrate the autonomous affiliated Methodist churches and the Central Conference of The United Methodist Church as important expressions of the diversity of cultures and peoples called by God to be the church universal;

4. Work for a future where The United Methodist Church and the autonomous Methodist churches throughout the world, expressing their faith through their unique, God-given culture, will share resources, personnel, and perspectives as equals in their common task of evangelizing all the world;

5. Continue and strengthen its ecumenical commitment; and

6. Embody this vision as possible in all United Methodist programs.

ADOPTED 1992

See Social Principles, ¶ 69; " 'New House' of Europe."

In Support of the United Nations

The United Methodist Church affirms its historic support for the United Nations. We rejoice that since 1945, the United Nations has been a functioning organization working for international peace and justice. In that time, it has

• provided mechanisms for the peaceful settlement of disputes; established peacekeeping forces in troubled areas;

• developed principles of peace-building;

• provided assistance through United Nations Educational, Scientific, and Cultural Organization (UNESCO), United Nations Development Program (UNDP), United Nations Children's Fund (UNICEF), World Health Organization (WHO), and its other agencies to persons who are usually neglected;

• provided a forum for discussion of difficult issues, such as racism, population, and decolonization;

• promoted just and equitable world social and economic systems;

• established internationally accepted standards of human rights for all persons, including women and children;

• forged international treaties on Ozone, Climate Change, Bio-diversity, and The Law of the Sea, and sponsored summits of heads of state and government on issues of children, environment, and social development;

• brought nations together to coordinate the battles against smallpox, polio, childhood mortality, inadequate nutrition, and HIV/AIDS; and

• provided a means of coordination and communication for world Non-Governmental Organizations (NGOs).

International relations are entering a new era. Governments turn to the United Nations as they recognize that they must address problems multilaterally through the use of consultation and compromise. Nations acting together can, for the first time in history, enforce observance of international law. We are encouraged that nations show a new willingness to work together for peace.

We are not convinced that the move toward cooperation among governments is inevitable. Nations still return to unilateral acts of violence. Conflicts persist. The arms buildup has decreased, but it has not ceased. Regional civil and ethnic wars continue to break out. The Security Council does not have the mechanism to implement fully the intent of the charter for collective action. Those aspects of the charter must be implemented which will protect the organization from undue reliance on the military of one or a few powerful states.

The pursuit of peace is thwarted when media-promoted falsehoods about the purpose and possibilities of the United Nations are widely disseminated and believed.

We encourage the governments of the world to say no to nationalistic self-will, to say yes to the ideals and visions of the Charter of the United Nations, and to let it serve as their guide to a new spirit of international cooperation.

To that end:

1. We commend to the churches a wider study of the United Nations in order that Christians might be enabled to work in unity for peace and justice in the world;

2. We reaffirm decisions of the General Conference beginning in 1994 to establish "an international office of education and publicity for peace." Supported by those decisions, the Church established the Methodist Office for the United Nations and, in 1963, constructed the Church Center for the United Nations;

3. We particularly commend the program United Methodist Seminars on National and International Affairs to local church, district, and annual conference groups as a way to experience firsthand the work of the United Nations as it strives for peace;

4. We affirm and support the United Methodist Office for the United Nations as a facilitator and participant in the NGO network;

5. We also reaffirm the importance of celebrating the entry into force of the Charter of the United Nations on October 24, 1945, with an emphasis in local churches on United Nations Sunday, observed on that date or the Sunday preceding it; and

6. We call upon United Methodists to encourage their governments to strengthen the UN by fulfilling all treaty and financial obligations, so that it may more effectively relieve the suffering of millions through better health, protect our planet's environment, promote human rights, and bring about genuine and lasting peace in the world.

ADOPTED 1992
AMENDED & READOPTED 1996

See Social Principles, ¶ 69D; "The United Methodist Church and Peace."

United States-China Political Relations

Our Political Understandings

In late 1978, the governments of the United States and the People's Republic of China (PRC) reached agreement establishing full diplomatic relations. The United States ended official relations—diplomatic and military—with the authorities on Taiwan. (In March 1979, the U.S. Congress passed the Taiwan Relations Act, putting U.S. relations with Taiwan on an unofficial basis.) The United States recognized the People's Republic of China as the "sole legal government of China" but reserved the right, over PRC objections, to sell "defensive" weapons to Taiwan. At the time of normalization, the PRC refused to rule out the possibility of reunifying with the island of Taiwan by force but offered to allow Taiwan to maintain the political, economic, and military status quo if Taiwan were to recognize PRC sovereignty.

This normalization agreement ended a thirty-year period in which formal American commitments to the authorities on Taiwan blocked closer relations with the People's Republic of China. It laid the foundations for a framework of cooperation and exchanges that continues to develop. Highlights include:

• government-to-government agreements covering consular relations and embassies, civil aviation, scientific and technical cooperation, educational exchange, trade and credit, fisheries, and a wide range of other fields;

• substantial expansion of tourism and specialized visits;

• educational programs facilitating nearly 10,500 scholars and teachers (10,000 Chinese, 500 Americans) to be resident in the other country;

• numerous governmental and private institutional exchange agreements in education, the fine and performing arts, cinema, publishing, and so forth; and

• sister state-province and city-to-city agreements calling for various kinds of cooperation.

The rapid growth and elaboration of these bilateral relations has been unusual and, to many, unexpected. While the direction is generally positive and the initial results heartening, the relationship is still in its early stages. Because the PRC and U.S. systems are so different, translating worthwhile goals into concrete practice has often been difficult.

Fundamentally, the two countries have yet to determine what kind of long-term relationship they want. Misperceptions and misunderstandings are all too common on both sides, even on basic principles.

As a case in point, the two sides had sharp disagreements during 1981 and 1982 over the issue of continuing U.S. arms sales to Taiwan. By August 1982, Washington and Beijing had clarified their understanding on this question: The PRC stated that its "fundamental policy" was to "strive for peaceful reunification" with Taiwan. In that context, the U.S. government pledged not to increase and in fact to reduce its sale of arms to Taiwan. But this agreement only holds in abeyance a resolution of the Taiwan issue.

Recommendations on U.S.-China Political Relations

The United Methodist Church:

1. Affirms the establishment of full diplomatic relations between the United States and the People's Republic of China as an important step

toward mutual cooperation and understanding and toward world peace;

2. Advocates that the U.S. government, in accordance with the Joint Communique of December 1978, should continue to deal with the people of Taiwan on an unofficial basis;

3. Recognizes the necessity for China to continue its economic and social development and urges U.S. cooperation to that end within the context of Chinese independence and selfhood;

4. Feels the long-term basis of U.S.-China relations should emphasize people-to-people, educational, social, and economic short-term or expedient military or strategic interests; expresses deep concern about the anti-Soviet rationale used to explain U.S.-PRC relations; opposes the sale of U.S. military equipment to the PRC;

5. Endorses a peaceful approach to ending the long-standing conflict between the governments in the People's Republic of China and in Taiwan while recognizing that the resolution of the status of Taiwan is a matter for the Chinese people themselves, and in that context supports the continued reduction and early cessation of U.S. arms sales in Taiwan;

6. Declares our continuing concern regarding the human rights of all people on both sides of the Taiwan Straits; and

7. Recognizes that U.S.-PRC relations have an important influence on the peace and stability of the Asian region, particularly in Southeast Asia; and urges both the United States and the People's Republic of China to seek peaceful means to contribute to the peace and stability of the region.

ADOPTED 1984

See Social Principles, ¶ 69B; "United States Church-China Church Relations."

United States Church-China Church Relations

Our faith affirmations and historical understandings of a relationship with the church in the People's Republic of China. Throughout the history of the Christian church, changes in the social, political, economic, and cultural environment have elicited new, different, sometimes creative, sometimes destructive responses in the ministry and witness of the church.

The church that re-emerged in the People's Republic of China (PRC) in 1979, having been officially closed during the Cultural Revolution in

1966–1976, is striving to shape a new church, a new ministry, a new witness in China. A fundamental task for United Methodists is to develop the perceptiveness and spiritual depth that will enable us to enter into new relationships with the PRC and with this new church. Entering this new relationship requires an honest examination of past patterns of work and relationships; a rethinking of our understanding of the task of the Church; and an openness to new ways of being, relating, and doing under the guidance of the Holy Spirit.

God's church is called to mission. Individually and together, both the church in the People's Republic of China and the church in the United States are called to find their place in God's mission. This understanding, which forms the basic approach of the United Methodist China Program, is founded on certain affirmations drawn from biblical faith and shaped by our contemporary social and historical context.

I. Our faith is in God, who is One, the only transcending reality, who is Creator of heaven and earth, who has made humankind one, and who continues to work in human history. God's love is expressed in great cosmic and human events; it is also very personal and individual. Created by God, each individual is loved of God, made for God, and drawn to God.

Faith in God as Creator affirms a common humanity with the Chinese people, a recognition that God relates to and has always been at work in Chinese history and culture and in individual persons. Persons in other cultures have much to learn from the Chinese people and from their experiences. Western values and assumptions cannot be projected as universal for all peoples.

II. God has called into being, through Jesus Christ, a particular people, the church, and has made them one and has sent them into the world in mission and service to all humankind. Christians are linked to Christians in every nation and place through Jesus Christ. Living their daily lives in separate nations and cultures, Christians seek relationships that draw them into fuller expressions of unity while allowing for diversity and independence.

Churches within each nation have a primary link with one another and are the body of Christ, the church in that place. They are also linked with churches, the church, in every other nation, and together are the one body of Christ in the world. Their unity is a sign to the world of God's intention to reconcile and unite humankind. As God continues working in human history, creating, judging, reconciling, and redeeming, so the church, and the churches, are called to share in this mission to the world.

Fundamental to the mission are acts of thanksgiving:

We give thanks for all those persons, both indigenous and expatriate, through whose lives and ministries the church has come into being throughout the world.

We rejoice that God stands with all people, especially the poor and the oppressed of the earth.

Christians give thanks wherever the poor of the earth are receiving new life, and affirm this as part of God's work.

Also fundamental to mission are acts of repentance. We are aware of historic links between the missionary movement and Western influence. Christianity must not be used as a tool of Western penetration. While all are sinners and offered God's grace and forgiveness, the church is called to stand especially with those who are "sinned against." As the church renews its covenant of witness, ministry, and mission, it does so with deep repentance and humility, accepting God's forgiveness and seeking the forgiveness of those it has wronged. Trusting God's grace and guidance, the church moves forward with courage to seek new relationships in mission and service.

III. Through the Holy Spirit, the Christian community—within and outside the People's Republic of China—is being challenged to respond in new ways to a new China. Together, the Chinese government and people have brought about many improvements in basic physical needs. The attitudes of the people are also changing. Liberation from foreign domination has brought a renewed sense of pride and dignity in being Chinese. Growing self-reliance in overcoming seemingly insurmountable problems has underscored this feeling of self-respect and self-esteem.

In 1949, many Chinese viewed the church in China as a foreign institution, largely supported by foreign funds and personnel, and closely allied with those who opposed the revolution. While the Chinese Communist Party and the Chinese church differ on their views of religious belief, the Constitution now provides for both the policy and practice of religious freedom.

Chinese Christians now reaffirm their responsibility to bear witness to the gospel in the People's Republic of China through Christian communities that are self-governing, self-supporting, and self-propagating. Responsibility for Christian mission in the People's Republic of China is with the Christians in the PRC. Their leaders want no assistance from outside organizations or individuals without mutual consultation and decision. The Chinese Protestant Three-Self Patriotic Movement and the China Christian Council are institutional expressions of these affirmations.

The life of the church in China, as in other countries, is a precious gift offering a powerful witness to the world. Part of the task of the churches outside China is to receive that witness and to allow time and space for it to grow.

In its centuries-old struggle for survival, China is an inspiration and a challenge to United Methodists. Where is God in the struggle and pathos of the Chinese people? How does the church of Jesus Christ share in this history? Our historical involvement as United Methodists with the people of China offers a rare opportunity for us to look at the ambiguous relationships between the Chinese people and ourselves. It forces us toward a new understanding of faith in the gospel that seeks to unite all things in Jesus Christ. A new understanding is primary in all that we do in cooperation with the people of China and the church in China. Christians in China have requested our new understanding and underlined this need by asking us to pray for them and for ourselves.

Recommendations on U.S. Church-China Church Relations:

1. That The United Methodist Church provide information, guidance, and encouragement to help its constituency understand the struggles of the people of China, and pray fervently with informed sensitivity for the people and the church in China.

The church in the People's Republic of China has declared itself to be self-governing, self-supporting, and self-propagating. The primary responsibility for Christian mission in the People's Republic of China belongs to the church there. We must not act as if the church in the People's Republic of China does not exist, or as if only we are called in mission. We thank God that the church lives in China, and that it is a Chinese church;

2. That The United Methodist Church affirm the selfhood of, respect the autonomy of, and reaffirm our readiness to hear and interact with the church in the People's Republic of China as together we shape future relationships based on mutuality.

Christians in the People's Republic of China have declared themselves to be in a "post-denominational era." There are now no denominations in the People's Republic of China. There is no Chinese body of Christian believers having an agreed-upon polity, creed, rites, and so forth. What future form of organization, doctrine, and/or ritual the church will take has yet to be determined. Chinese Christians are now concerned that they be allowed to determine these issues within their understanding of the Holy Spirit's leading and without foreign interference. The de-emphasis on denominations in the church in the People's Republic of China is a reminder to United Methodists that the whole church of Jesus Christ must manifest unity as a sign and sacrament of the unity of humankind;

3. That The United Methodist Church reaffirm its continuing commitment to work ecumenically with other Christian bodies in relating to the church in the People's Republic of China and with the Chinese people.

Christians in the People's Republic of China have made us sensitively aware of the imbalances of relationships between China and ourselves. They have also pointed out the growing disparities between the rich and the poor nations. They have challenged us to examine our involvement with the poor and oppressed in our own society;

4. That The United Methodist Church recommit itself (a) to a sustained program for awareness of the disparities between the rich and the poor, and (b) to work with faithfulness and integrity to create new attitudes and institutional structures that more perfectly manifest the gospel of Christ that all humankind be united. Such efforts include:

• being sensitive to areas of our national life that exploit peoples of other societies as well as our own;

• standing with the poor and the oppressed in the United States as well as in other countries;

• examining and learning from the accomplishments and the mistakes in past and present missionary efforts in China and other parts of the world; and

• being available for mutual ministry with Christians in China, in the United States, and in other countries; and

5. That The United Methodist Church also commit itself to a strengthened program of communication and dialogue within The United Methodist Church about the People's Republic of China and the church there.

ADOPTED 1984

See Social Principles, ¶ 69B; "United States-China Political Relations."

United States-Mexico Border

The United States-Mexico border is a 2,000-mile-long area where the socio/economic dynamics of two interacting cultures have a negative impact on the quality of life of adjoining populations. This adverse situation has been exacerbated by domestic and international policies espoused by the U.S. and Mexican governments.

The border region is characterized by:
- political domination by a minority of rich and powerful families;
- drastic economic disparity between segments of the population;
- constant deterioration of the health conditions, particularly those affecting the poor;
- high incidence of crime and drug trafficking; and
- high rates of unemployment and underemployment, and (in the United States) the lowest per-capita income.

These detrimental conditions also affect the constant influx of thousands of refugees and undocumented persons coming to the United States seeking safe haven or better economic conditions. This situation of pain and suffering affects millions of women, children, and men residing on both sides of the border. The impact of these dynamics reaches well into the interiors of both countries.

Confronted by this human suffering along the United States-Mexico border region, we recognize that the vision of the "new heaven and new earth" (Revelation 21) will be only an illusion as long as "one of the least" (Matthew 25) continues to suffer.

As Christians and United Methodists, we express our sorrow and indignation and accept the responsibility to use our resources toward the elimination of the root causes creating this tragic human problem. We are particularly concerned about the following conditions:

1. Environmental:

(a) the constant indiscriminate use of pesticides in the growing and harvesting of agricultural products, a problem on both sides of the border; pesticides harmed or restricted in one nation are being exported for use in the other;

(b) the water contamination caused by corporations dumping industrial toxic waste and the flushing of poisonous compounds into the Rio Grande, the Colorado, and other rivers; and

(c) air pollution, a growing problem on both sides of the border.

2. Health:

(a) the use of toxic materials in production without informing workers of their hazards or providing education or proper equipment, leading to a high incidence of birth defects and other health problems;

(b) the high incidence of dysentery, tuberculosis, and hepatitis caused by lack of adequate water-waste facilities, lack of healthy drinking water, hunger, and malnutrition, particularly among the *Colonias*—rural unincorporated areas—and, more specifically, as they affect children;

(c) the lack of minimum adequate and affordable housing for workers in the Maquiladoras, leading to informal shanty towns without sanitation or other social facilities, and the use of unsafe and crowded barracks for workers; and

(d) the strained and inaccessible public services, such as health, education, and welfare, that seem to perpetuate the cycle of poverty and dehumanization.

3. Economic:

(a) wages kept low by repression of workers' bargaining rights, keeping the border region below the average of Mexican industrial wage levels, despite the fact that the Maquiladoras are the second largest producers of export income for the country (after oil), and the largest source of income for the Mexican border region;

(b) the lack of long-range economic and industrial development strategies, making the economies of both sides of the border more dependent on "quick economic fixes" such as "maquiladoras," "quick cash crops," tourism, and services that can help temporarily and superficially, but ignoring the economic needs of most of the present and future generations;

(c) the trade agreements (such as the proposed North American Free Trade Agreement), which may worsen the existing economic dependencies and foster the exploitation of human and natural resources; and

(d) the low educational attainment level, high incidence of illiteracy, the high dropout rate, and the ready availability and constant influx of drugs, which heighten the vulnerability of the low-income population along the border.

4. Political:

the prevalent existence of political styles that benefit only those who want to perpetuate models of feudalistic governments that leave control in the hands of the powerful few, a situation creating the political climate that disempowers the poor.

5. *Civil and Human Rights:*

(a) the constant influx of people from south of the borders, heightening the anxieties of those who perceive immigrants as unwelcomed foreigners who pose a threat to the U.S. social, political, and economic security;

(b) strategies devised by governmental agencies and groups to harass, intimidate, and repress legal and illegal foreign entrants into the U.S. territory; and

(c) the poor administration of justice; the cultural insensitivity of Border Patrol agents; the high incidence of illegal use of force; and the constant violation of the civil and human rights of those detained or deported, creating an atmosphere of tension and distrust that exacerbates the social dynamics, contributing to the polarization between white and nonwhite residents and transients.

As people of faith, we are urged by God through Christ to love our neighbor and to do what we must to bring healing in the midst of pain, and to restore to wholeness those whose lives are shattered by injustice and oppression. "I have come in order that you might have life—life in all its fullness" (John 10:10, Today's English Version).

Therefore, we recommend and urge the Mexican and U.S. governments to:

• develop national and international policies that bring more economic parity between the two countries, as the integral part of any trade agreement;

• appropriate sufficient resources to develop new industrial and economic development programs that are long-range, mutually beneficial, and more sensitive to the well-being of all women, children, and men of that area;

• develop binational and multilateral agreements that improve the quality of life; safeguard the water rights; and prevent the contamination of air, water, and land of the area;

• develop binding and enforceable mechanisms with respect to labor and human rights; agriculture, including farm workers; environmental standards; and health and safety standards for both nations and in any agreements to which they are a party;

• develop national and international policies that facilitate the migration and immigration of peoples across the border without the violation of their rights and aspirations; and

• find alternative and creative ways to reduce the foreign debt of Mexico.

Furthermore, we urge The United Methodist Church to continue its support of the U.S.-Mexico Border Bilateral Advisory Committee within the General Board of Global Ministries to provide coordination and facilitate a holistic approach to addressing the structural causes of the problems in this region.

We further recommend that the General Board of Church and Society, with churches in Mexico, the United States, and Canada, seek ways to network on fair trade, labor and human rights, agricultural, and environmental concerns.

ADOPTED 1992

See Social Principles, ¶ 69; "Immigrants and Refugees: To Love the Sojourner"; "Immigrants in the United States: Ministries of Hospitality, Advocacy, and Justice."

OTHER RESOLUTIONS

Biblical Language

The United Methodist Church affirms the right and custom of the use of biblical language and images in all its forms in worship and in our common life together. Phrases such as "Lord" and "King" and "Father" are an integral part of the rich heritage of the faith. A truly inclusive church will not restrict its people as to what is appropriate and what is inappropriate language and imagery about God. We therefore affirm the use of biblical language and images in all its forms as appropriate for use in hymns, liturgy, teaching, and in all areas of our common life together.

ADOPTED 1988

A Call to Reaffirm the Centrality of Christ

We invite all members of The United Methodist Church to participate in study and reflection on "Our Theological Task" as found in ¶ 63 of the 1996 *Book of Discipline.*

We recognize both the Church's need for theological and doctrinal reinvigoration and the need for a wide range of ongoing theological exploration.

In issuing this invitation, we affirm our baptismal covenant to confess faith in and obedience to Jesus Christ. "A convincing witness to our Lord and Savior Jesus Christ can contribute to the renewal of our faith, bring persons to that faith, and strengthen the Church as an agent of healing and reconciliation. This witness, however, cannot fully describe or encompass the mystery of God" ("Conclusion," ¶ 63).

Our invitation comes because "theology is our effort to reflect upon God's gracious action in our lives" (first sentence, ¶ 63). In response to the love of Christ and in continued faithfulness to Wesleyan tradition, we "seek to give expression to the mysterious reality of God's presence, peace, and power in the world," and to resist evil, injustice, and oppression in whatever forms they present themselves.

We affirm all those who would explore new ways of preaching Jesus Christ, which sets people free from all forms of evil and equips them for a life of holiness.

We join all who profess the apostolic faith, while recognizing that no final definition can be given to the apostolic faith, other than it confesses Jesus Christ. As the center of our faith and obedience, Jesus Christ cannot be replaced by creed, tradition, or even Scripture. From the beginning, Christian faith has been expressed in many diverse forms. Indeed, the earliest Christians were led by the Spirit to the necessity of four equal but different Gospels. Likewise, expressions of faith in our day do not need to be uniform. The test is whether they preach Jesus Christ, and none other.

"We are confident in the ultimate unfolding of God's justice and mercy" ("Conclusion," ¶ 63). In this spirit, we encourage all United Methodists to take up our theological task.

ADOPTED 1996

Make Evangelism the Number One Priority
for the Next Quadrennium

Evangelism shall become the number one priority of The United Methodist Church for the next quadrennium. Evangelism shall also become the number one priority of all our mission work around the world—and of all our commissions, boards, and agencies at all levels—for the purpose of persuading men, women, and children to come to Jesus Christ and so be reconciled to God. It is imperative for us to fulfill the Great Commission, left us by Jesus Christ, God's Son, to go into all the world in the power of the Holy Spirit, to influence the unsaved persons of our world to receive Jesus Christ as Savior and Lord.

ADOPTED 1992

Guidelines: The United Methodist Church and the Charismatic Movement

Introductory Statement

Since its beginning in the early 1960's, the ecumenical charismatic renewal has exerted a continuing influence upon mainline Christian bodies, both Protestant and Roman Catholic. Recent studies by George Gallup indicate approximately 18 percent of United Methodists identify with the movement.

At the 1972 session of the General Conference of The United Methodist church, the Western Pennsylvania Annual Conference brought a petition asking that a position statement be prepared on the posture of The United Methodist Church toward the charismatic movement.

A General Board of Discipleship task force consisting of Don Cottrill, director of services, Youth Ministry Coordinators; T. Poe Williams, assistant general secretary, Local Church Education Training Enterprises; Maxie Dunnam, editor, *The Upper Room*; Horace Weaver, executive editor, Adult Publications; and Ross E. Whetstone, assistant general secretary for Evangelism, admitted the "Guidelines" for consideration by the Board of Discipleship and the General Conference. The task force felt that this position statement should be couched in the context of the theological pluralism which characterizes The United Methodist Church; the current culturally conditioned demands for experiential Christianity, insofar as we respond to them with integrity; and the doctrinal statements, the General Rules and Doctrinal Guidelines as set forth in Paras. 68–70 of the 1972 *Discipline*.

The "Guidelines" portion of this paper, was approved by action of the 1976 General Conference. The paper, "The Charismatic Movement: Its Historical Base and Wesleyan Framework," derived by the Executive Committee of the Division of Evangelism, Worship, and Stewardship and the editors from a paper by Dr. Robert G. Tuttle, is a separate piece not considered to be official in nature but commended to the church for study as background to the "Guidelines."

Glossary

Terminology associated with the charismatic movement is confusing because of varying usage.

Pentecostal refers to the movement which began late in the nineteenth century, resulting in the formation of a number of Pentecostal denominations in the early years of the twentieth century. Classic Pentecostalism affirms what is sometimes spoken of as initial evidence, which includes the concept of a requisite "baptism in the Holy Spirit" that may be expressed by glossolalia or speaking in tongues. The inference that one who does not speak in tongues is guilty of withholding a full surrender of self to the will and purpose of God can be divisive among United Methodists.

Charismatic. While in popular usage the term *charismatic* is often closely associated with *glossolalia,* or speaking in tongues, most persons within the charismatic movement recognize the importance of all the "gifts of the Spirit," affirming that "to each is given the manifestation of the Spirit of the common good" (1 Cor. 12:7). Many elevate the gifts of prophecy, healing, tongues, and interpretation of tongues because of a conviction that these gifts have been neglected by the church and should be reaffirmed.

Charismatic Movement. Throughout this report the term *charismatic movement* is used to identify the movement which began about 1960 in mainline Christian bodies, both Protestant and Roman Catholic, reemphasizing the importance of the gifts of the Spirit in the life of the church.

In a biblical sense there is no such person as a "noncharismatic Christian," since the term *charismata* refers to the gracious gifts of God bestowed upon all Christians to equip them for ministry. The terminology above is used throughout this paper as a concession to popular usage.

Guidelines

We believe the church needs to pray for a sensitivity to be aware of and respond to manifestations of the Holy Spirit in our world today. We are unmindful that the problems of discrimination between the true and fraudulent are considerable, but we must not allow the problems to paralyze our awareness of the Spirit's presence; nor should we permit our fear of the unknown and the unfamiliar to close our minds against being surprised by grace. We know the misuse of mystical experience is an ever-present possibility, but that is no reason to preclude authentic and appropriate relationships with the Spirit.

In facing the issues raised by charismatic experiences, we plead for a spirit of openness and love. We commend to the attention of the church the affirmations of First Corinthians 13, as well as the 1972 *Discipline of The United Methodist Church*, Para. 70: "United Methodists can heartily endorse the classical ecumenical watchword: 'In essentials, unity; in non-essentials, liberty; and, in all things, charity' (love that cares and understands)." Without an active, calm, objective, and loving understanding of the religious experience of others, however different from one's own, reconciliation is impossible.

The criteria by which we judge the validity of another's religious experience must include its compatibility with the mind and the spirit of our Lord Jesus Christ, as revealed in the New Testament. If the consequence and quality of a reported encounter with the Holy Spirit be manifestly conducive to division, self-righteousness, hostility, and exaggerated claims of knowledge and power, then the experience is subject to serious question. However, when the experience clearly results in new dimensions of faith, joy, and blessings to others, we must conclude that this is "what the Lord hath done" and offer him our praise.

Guidelines for All

I. Be open and accepting of those whose Christian experiences differ from your own.

II. Continually undergird and envelop all discussions, conferences, meetings, and persons in prayer.

III. Be open to new ways in which God by his Spirit may be speaking to the church.

IV. Seek the gifts of the Spirit which enrich your life and you for ministry.

V. Recognize that, even though spiritual gifts may be abused, this does not mean that they should be prohibited.

VI. Remember that, like other new movements in church history, the charismatic renewal has a valid contribution to make to the ecumenical church.

For Pastors Who Have Had Charismatic Experiences

VII. Combine with your charismatic experience a thorough knowledge of, and adherence to, United Methodist polity and tradition. Remember your influence will, in large part, be earned by your loving and disciplined use of the gifts, by your conduct as a pastor of *all* your congregation, as well as by your participation as a responsible pastor.

VIII. Seek a deepening and continued friendship with your clergy colleagues within and without the charismatic experience.

IX. Remember your ordination vows, particularly the vow to "maintain and set forward, as much as lieth in you, quietness, peace, and love among all Christian people, and especially among those that shall be committed to your charge." Also, to "reverently heed them to whom the charge over you is committed, following with a glad mind and will their godly admonitions."

X. Avoid the temptation to force your personal views and experiences on others. Seek to understand those whose spiritual experiences differ from your own.

XI. Seek to grow in your skills as a biblical exegete, a systematic theologian, and a preacher in all the fullness of the gospel (Para. 304, *The Book of Discipline*, 1972).

XII. Pray for the gifts of the Spirit essential for your ministry; continually examine your life for the fruits of the Spirit.

XIII. Find significant expressions of your personal experience through ministries of social witness.

For Pastors Who Have Not Had Charismatic Experiences

XIV. Continually examine your understanding of the doctrine and experience of the Holy Spirit so you can communicate this with clarity.

XV. Remember the lessons of church history when God's people rediscover old truths; that the process is often disquieting, that is usually upheaval, change, and a degree of suffering and misunderstanding.

XVI. Seek firsthand knowledge of what the charismatic renewal means to those who have experienced it. Keep your judgments open until this firsthand knowledge is obtained (i.e., by attending and understanding their prayer meetings, etc.). Then observe and respond as a Christian, a United Methodist minister, and as a sympathetic, conscientious pastor. Keep an openness to scriptural teaching regarding the charismatic gifts.

XVII. When speaking in tongues occurs, seek to know what it means to the speaker in his or her private devotional life and what it means when used for intercessory prayer, especially in group worship. We should be aware that speaking in tongues is considered a minor "gift of the Spirit" by many who have charismatic experiences.

XVIII. Seek to know the meaning of the other "gifts of the Spirit" in the charismatic experience, such as the utterance of wisdom, knowledge, the gift of faith, healing, miracles, or prophesying.

XIX. United Methodist pastors should be intentional about the benefits to be derived by a mutual sharing of a variety of experiences which have biblical support. Accordingly, the pastor should seek to keep all meetings called for prayer and fellowship open to all interested members of the congregation.

For Laity Who Have Had Charismatic Experiences

XX. Remember to combine with your enthusiasm a thorough knowledge of an adherence to the United Methodist form of church government. The charismatic movement is closely related to the holiness movement, which is a part of our tradition. Consult with your pastor (or pastors) and if he or she has not also had your experience, help him or her to understand what it means to you. Invite your pastor to attend your group meetings.

XXI. Pray that the Spirit will help you understand, and that he may help you to maintain empathy with your colleagues and all your fellow United Methodists.

XXII. Strive for a scholarly knowledge of scriptural content in combination with your spiritual experiences. "Seek to unite knowledge and vital piety" (Wesley). Strive to integrate your experiences with the theological traditions of our church.

XXIII. Avoid undisciplined undiplomatic enthusiasm in your eagerness to share your experiences with others. Resist the temptation to pose as an authority on spiritual experiences. Failure in this area often causes your fellow United Methodists to accuse you of spiritual pride.

XXIV. Keep your prayer meetings and other gatherings open to all members of your congregation. When noncharismatics do attend, discuss with them the purpose of the meeting with an interpretation of the significance of the content.

XXV. Remember that there are many types of Christian experiences which lead to spiritual growth; charismatic experience is one of these.

XXVI. Accept opportunities to become personally involved in the work and mission of your own congregation. Let the results of your charismatic experience be seen in the outstanding quality of your church membership. Be an obvious enthusiastic supporter of your congregation, its pastor and lay leadership; of your district, your Annual Conference, the General Conference, and mission of each. This may well be the most effective witness you can offer to the validity and vitality of your charismatic experience. Strive to integrate your experience with the theological traditions of our church.

XXVII. It is not necessary to embrace all the usual physical and verbal expressions of Pentecostalism. These singular expressions may at times be a barrier to your witness.

XXVIII. Keep your charismatic experience in perspective. No doubt it has caused you to feel that you are a better Christian. Remember that this does not mean you are better than other Christians, but that you are, perhaps, a better Christian than you were before.

For Laity Who Have Not Had Charismatic Experiences

XXIX. In our Western tradition, we believe God is constantly seeking to renew his church, including The United Methodist Church. Pray that God may make known to your own place in the process of renewal. The advent of the charismatic movement into our denomination is only one aspect of renewal.

XXX. Should some fellow members of your congregation have charismatic experiences, accept them as Christians. Should it edify, thank God.

XXXI. Be aware of the tendency to separate ourselves from those who have experiences which differ from our own. Observe personally the charismatics in their prayer meetings, in your congregation, and in the mission of your church. Examine scriptural teaching about this. Pray about it. Discuss your concern with your pastor. The United Methodist Church is theologically pluralistic.

XXXII. Do not be disturbed if your experience is different from others. This does not mean that you are an inferior Christian. Your function in the work and mission of your congregation calls for many gifts (1 Cor. 12-14). Each Christian is a unique member of the body of Christ.

XXXIII. Should your pastor be a charismatic, help her or him to be mindful of the spiritual needs of all the congregation, to be a pastor and teacher to all, and encourage her or him in preaching to present the wholeness of all aspects of the gospel.

For Connectional Administration

XXXIV. Refer prayerfully and thoughtfully to the other sections of these Guidelines.

XXXV. Remember your pastoral responsibilities toward ordained persons and congregations within the connection, particularly toward those whose spiritual experience may involve charismatic gifts.

XXXVI. Each administrator should consider whether any teaching or practice regarding the charismatic movement involving an ordained minister of a congregation is for the edification of the church.

XXXVII. If there is divisiveness involved in a particular situation, make as careful an evaluation as possible, remembering that there are other kinds of issues which may divide our fellowship. Sometimes tensions and conflicts may result in the edification and greater purity of the church and need, therefore, to be handled wisely and prayerfully by all concerned.

XXXVIII. Administrators and connectional bodies will be required to deal with expressions of the charismatic movement. We urge all involved to seek firsthand evidence about the movement, its meaning for those involved in it, and its value of the particular congregation.

XXXIX. Where an ordained person seems to overemphasize some charismatic doctrines/practices, she or he should be counseled to preach the wholeness of the gospel, to minister to the needs of all the congregation, and as a pastor to grow in understanding of our polity in the mission of the particular Annual Conference.

XL. Annual Conferences may also be faced with a situation where there is a charismatic group within a congregation whose pastor, or whose lay leadership, or both, may be hostile to or ignorant of the charismatic movement. The Annual Conference Board of the Ministry, the bishop, and the district superintendent have a pastoral responsibility to mediate and to guide in reconciliation.

XLI. Pray continuously for sensitivity to the will of, and the leading of, the Holy Spirit.

The Charismatic Movement, its Historical Base, and Wesleyan Framework

Within the last quarter of the twentieth century we have witnessed a unitarian emphasis on the fatherhood of God, a radical evangelical faith in the person of Jesus Christ, and the charismatic expression of the Holy Spirit. Charismatic gifts and experiences, however, are not new to the church. History has revealed certain manifestations of the gifts and experiences of the Spirit, in every century since Pentecost.

In our own time, the work of the Holy Spirit is apparent. Increasingly, United Methodists are holding healing services, participating in prayer and praise groups, and attending Holy Spirit conferences across the country. Interest is high, with testimonies coming from bishops, lay persons, district superintendents, seminary professors, and local pastors. Yet many United Methodist charismatics feel isolated and misunderstood; many noncharismatics feel threatened and/or alienated and hostile. If we can gain perspective from our Wesleyan heritage—significant contribution to the charismatic movement—reconciliation can take place.

Azusa Street, where American Pentecostalism was launched, is to this movement what Aldersgate is to Methodism. The Pentecostal doctrine of subsequence was derived from Wesley's teachings concerning the second blessing, or entire sanctification.

The Historical Base

Methodism provides a highly important tradition for the student of charismatic origins. Wesley's theology of grace is in fact a theology of the Holy Spirit. The terms *grace* and *Holy Spirit* are associated in all of Wesley's writings. Although Frederick Dale Bruner exaggerated a bit to insist that the Pentecostal/charismatic movements are "primitive Methodism's extended incarnation," the fact remains that eighteenth century Methodism gave rise to the nineteenth century American holiness movement, which gave rise to the twentieth century Pentecostal/charismatic phenomena. It was the eighteenth century Methodist quest for an instantaneous experience of sanctification, or second work of grace (rightly or wrongly interpreted), that inspired the nineteenth century American holiness movement. Revivalists like Charles Finney (born in 1792, the year after Wesley's death) used Wesley's theological writings as grist for a holiness emphasis designed to "revive" religion in America. Although Finney's methodology was more significant than his theology upon the Pentecostal/charismatic movement, his popularization of the phrase "baptism of the Holy Ghost" had a close parallel to the Pentecostal emphasis arising out of Azusa Street.

There is some question whether Pentecostalism per se would have occurred had the holiness tradition retained its influence within the local church. By the turn of the twentieth century, however, the decline of Wesley's emphasis on perfection among Methodists, the development of theological views in response to changing cultural conditions, and the apparent wealth and worldliness of the church created considerable spiritual insecurity.

It was also a period of tremendous social change. The American scene was shifting rapidly from an agrarian to an industrial society. The move was from a rural to an urban-centered population, from a relatively homogeneous to a polygenetic people. Anticolonialism was giving way to imperialism, and the laissez-faire policy to the first stages of governmental social regulation. Those changes registered shock most severely, accordingly to W. G. McLoughlin, on the "country-bred, evangelically oriented, intellectually unsophisticated and sentimentally insecure individuals who made up the bulk of the nation's churchgoers."

Many, however, sensed the need to individualize and to create an excitement for the Christian faith in a depersonalized civilization. Pentecostalism, viewed by some as closely akin to a Methodist experiential *theology* and a revivalist experiential *methodology*, was to meet that need, at least in part, and to find response in an experience-hungry world.

Pentecostalism might never have severed itself from mainline denominations, and revivalism might have remained within the established churches, had not many Christians overreacted. The social gospel, born out of revivalism, aligned itself with a more liberal tradition which saw the necessity of stamping out anything that was suggestive of the priest and Levite bypassing suffering humanity. The church became polarized in response to the Pentecostal emphasis. The Pentecostal doctrine, which insists on speaking in tongues as initial evidence of baptism in the Holy Spirit, remains divisive to the present time.

Pentecostal beginnings were spontaneous, scattered, and little noticed. As early as 1896 some revivalists reported experiences of glossolalia in North Carolina. It was not until 1900, however, that any significance was attached to this experience. Charles F. Parham, a young Methodist minister frustrated by the sterility of his own ministry in contract with the power of the apostles, started the Bethel Bible College at Topeka, Kansas. Parham and his students quickly identified Wesley's doctrine of subsequent instantaneous sanctification with Finney's "baptism of the Holy Spirit" and concluded that it should be sought with the evidence of tongues. Parham then opened a second school in Houston, Texas. Among those who came seeking the baptism of the Holy Spirit was W. J. Seymour, a black minister from Los Angeles. After several months of study and prayer he returned to Los Angeles where a revival broke out during a mission at a former Methodist chapel at 312 Azusa Street. That revival lasted three years and the American Pentecostal movement was "officially" launched.

About twenty-five years ago pastors and lay persons within mainline denominations began to confess experiencing various gifts of the Spirit more openly. Rather than leaving for Pentecostal congregations, they chose to remain within their established churches. Thus, the charismatic movement began when individuals across denominational lines—Protestant and Roman Catholic—realized that they shared common experiences. While continuing to support their local churches, they began meeting to discuss those experiences openly.

There are several areas where charismatics identify with their Pentecostal cousins—the emphasis on religious experiences beyond conversion with an openness to spiritual gifts, for example. *But there are significant differences as well.* Pentecostals organize their converts into separate churches; charismatics do not. Charismatics encourage their number to remain within their local churches. Pentecostals have a fairly well-defined theological system. They maintain, for instance, that subsequent to justification there is an instantaneous sanctification experience known as the baptism of the Holy Spirit which *must* be confirmed by speaking in tongues. Charismatics do not. Although charismatics are open to all spiritual gifts and experiences subsequent to conversion, they try not to isolate those gifts and experiences as marks of spirituality. They choose, rather, to interpret them in the light of their own traditions. John Wesley writes:

In [Acts IV] we read, that when the Apostles and brethren had been praying, and praising God, "the place was shaken where they were assembled together, and they were all filled with the Holy Ghost." Not that we find any visible appearance here, such as a had been in the former instance: nor are we informed that the *extraordinary gifts* of the Holy Ghost were then given to all or any of them: such as the gifts of "healing, of working" other miracles, of prophecy, of discerning spirits, the speaking with diverse kinds of tongues, and the interpretation of tongues (I Cor. XII, 9, 10).

Whether these gifts of the Holy Ghost were designed to remain in the Church throughout all ages, and whether or not they will be restored at the nearer approach of the "restitution of all things," are questions which it is not needful to decide. But it is needful to observe this, that even in the infancy of the church, God divided them with a sparing hand. Were all even then prophets? Were all workers of miracles? Had all the gifts of healing? Did all speak in tongues? No, in no wise. Perhaps not one in a thousand. Probably none but the teachers in the Church, and only some of them (I Cor. XII, 28-30). It was, therefore, for a more excellent purpose than this, that "they were all filled with the Holy Ghost."

It was, to give them (what none can deny to be essential to all Christians in all ages) the mind which was in Christ, those holy fruits of the Spirit, which whosoever hath not, is one of His; to fill them with "love, joy, peace, long-suffering, gentleness, goodness" (Gal. V.22-24); to endue them with faith (perhaps it might be rendered *fidelity*), with meekness and temperance; to enable them to crucify the flesh, with its affections and lusts, its passions and desires; and in consequence of that inward change, to fulfill all outward righteousness; to "walk as Christ also walked," in "the work of faith, in the patience of hope, the labour of love" (I Thess. I. 3). John Wesley, Sermons: "Scriptural Christianity," Introduction, 2–4 (S, I, 92–94)

It is in a failure to see the importance of this that some charismatics get into trouble. Ideally, Presbyterian charismatics, for example, interpret their gifts and experiences in light of the sovereignty of God, Roman Catholic charismatics in light of their sacramental theology, and United Methodists in light of John Wesley's theology of grace. Problems arise when charismatics, knowingly or unknowingly, attempt to adopt a more classical Pentecostal line in conflict with their own tradition, and division occurs. Equally devastating is the circumstance in which some charismatics adopt no line at all and become floaters vulnerable to exploitation. They substitute experience for doctrine and are no longer rooted in the traditions that could sustain them.

Our task, therefore, is to provide United Methodists with a clear understanding of our heritage—a heritage that will enable them to interpret charismatic gifts and experiences in a way that is healthy and sound.

A Wesleyan Framework

Charismatics interpret their gifts and experiences in light of their own traditions. When this does not occur, division and/or exploitation sets in. When United Methodists charismatics adopt a classical Pentecostal line, they are no longer United Methodists—at least in the Wesleyan sense. John Wesley said:

"The gift of tongues may," you say, "be considered as a proper test or criterion for determining the miraculous pretensions of all Churches. If among their extraordinary gifts they cannot show us this, they have none to show which are genuine."

Now, I really thought it had been otherwise. I thought it had been an adjudged rule in the case, "All these worketh one and the self-same Spirit, dividing to every man, severally as he will"; and as to every man, so to every Church, every collective body of men. But if this be so, then yours is no proper test for determining the pretensions of all Churches;

seeing He who worketh as He will, may with your good leave, give the gift of tongues, where He gives no other; and may see abundant reasons so to do, whether you and I see them or not. For perhaps we have not always known the mind of the Lord; not being of the number of his counselors. On the other hand, he may see good to give many other gifts, where it is not his will to bestow this. Particularly where it would be of no use; as in a Church where all are of one mind, and all speak the same language."

The Works of John Wesley, Vol X, p. 56

Charismatics must be brought *gently* to an awareness of the inherent possibility of division. When United Methodist charismatics have no theological base—a disease common not only among charismatics—they need to know that, properly understood within the context of our own tradition, their charismatic gifts and experiences will be considered as fresh wind in a church that still has more trouble with ice than fire. John Wesley's theory of grace, properly understood, *can* ground charismatic United Methodists in a tradition that can give direction to their enthusiasm. Let us, therefore, reexamine Wesley's theology of grace in light of the charismatic gifts and experiences.

Wesley's theology of grace is in fact a theology of the Holy Spirit. He believed that Reformation theology was built upon the cardinal doctrine of original sin and that it is God's sovereign will to reverse our "sinful, devilish nature" by the work of his Holy Spirit. He called this prevenient, justifying, and sanctifying grace.

Bound by sin and death, one experiences almost from the moment of conception the gentle wooing of the Holy Spirit—*prevenient grace.* This grace "prevents" one from wandering so far from the Way that when a person finally understands what it means to be justified, the Holy Spirit prompts one's freedom to say yes. For Wesley, this yes was a heartfelt faith in the merit of Christ alone for salvation. It allows the Holy Spirit to take the righteousness that was in Christ and attribute or impute it to the believer—*justifying grace.* For Wesley this begins a *lifelong movement* from imputed to imparted righteousness in which the Holy Spirit moves the believer from the righteousness of Christ attributed through faith to the righteousness of Christ realized within the individual—*sanctifying grace.*

Most students of Wesley are keenly aware of the emphasis he placed upon sanctification. It is precisely at this point, however, that we must not make the same mistake by classical Pentecostals, namely that of isolating sanctification as one other experience beyond conversion. Harald Lindstrom writes in *Wesley and Sanctification* that investigation of Wesley's concept of salvation has been concentrated too often on the new birth and complete sanctification (Christian perfection) as "two isolated phenomena unconnected organically with this doctrine of salvation as a whole." Since both of these events in Wesley's thought may be instantaneous, the gradual process of general sanctification is often minimized. Yet Wesley's emphasis upon the gradual process is obvious, for, though "entire sanctification" is a possibility and goal for all believers, by far the greater number of Christian believers will always be involved in the process. Admittedly, Wesley was a bit unguarded at times when referring to sanctification as an instantaneous experience subsequent to justification. If he were writing today, he would probably place even more emphasis on sanctification as a gradual work of grace characterized by many experiences that keep conversion contemporary.

To understand Wesley's experience of "entire sanctification" is to know how far the Pentecostal baptism of the Holy Spirit falls short, if there are not continuing works of grace. Grace is continual, though it may be perceived episodically. In our study of the charismatic movement it is essential that we do not confuse being "filled with the Holy Spirit" with Wesley's mature doctrine of sanctification. The Spirit-filled life is, rather, a sustained line of gifts, experiences, and divine support, beginning with conversion, constantly moving us toward that goal.

Many charismatics have come to believe that being filled with the Holy Spirit is an experience which begins with justification and continues as a lifelong motivating experience for the believer. For the charismatic, Spirit-baptism is not one but many gifts, not two but many experiences, intended to sustain one day after day. The relevance of Wesley's doctrine can be demonstrated by his statement: "The only way to keep Methodists alive is to keep them moving." Wesley took the expression *moi progressus ad infinitum*—my progress is without end— from Francois Fenelon, the seventeenth century theologian and mystic. Thus, United Methodist charismatics, within the context of their own rich tradition, can never interpret gifts and experiences as signs of superior spirituality making them better than others. Rather, the power of God being sustained within them makes them better than they were.

Conclusion

Pentecostals have a predictable interpretation of the Wesleyan revival. Although Pentecostalism has its roots imbedded within that tradition, it has little in common with Wesley's theology. Charismatics, on the other hand, have a point of reference for understanding their gifts and experiences in a way that is both guarded and open.

United Methodist charismatics and noncharismatics alike should be encouraged. There is no need for battle lines to be drawn. Albert Outler has stated that the charismatic movement might be the catalyst for a third great awakening. He concludes: "What if their charismatic renewal should prove more than a passing fad? Would they be our allies or rivals in our commitments to a church catholic, evangelical, and reformed: catholic in its human outreach, evangelical in its spiritual upreach, reformed in its constant openness to change? If nothing comes of all this, put my comments about it down to a softening of the brain. But if something does come of it, don't say you weren't warned!"

There are blind spots in all of us. Charismatics, for example, have a tendency to exalt a personal gospel; noncharismatics need to remember that opposite of *personal* is not *social* but *impersonal*. The social dimension of the gospel does not bypass the personal; it harnesses it and rides it to the stars. It provides an opportunity for witness and service in the world. In fact, the term *noncharismatic* Christian is a misnomer. All Christians have gifts. *Charismatic,* as earlier defined, refers to those who more explicitly acknowledge and emphasize teaching concerning the power of the Holy Spirit at work within them through such gifts. Surely there are lessons to be learned as well as lessons to be taught, sometimes from mistakes and sometimes from successes. In the meantime, God help us all if we do not practice love and openness. After all, that is what the Spirit-filled life is all about.

ADOPTED 1996

Membership of Gideons International

WHEREAS, Gideons International provides an important ministry in the distribution of Scripture; and

WHEREAS, many United Methodist congregations and individuals support Gideons International through memberships and financial donations; and

WHEREAS, the membership of Gideons International is limited to Protestant business and professional men; and

WHEREAS, their membership criteria stand in opposition to the *Discipline* of The United Methodist Church (*see* Social Principles); and

WHEREAS, the Minnesota Annual Conference and the Minnesota Annual Conference Commission on the Status and Role of Women have taken the position of encouraging the Gideons International to reconsider their membership criteria; and

WHEREAS, the membership criteria of Gideons International detract from the strength of their ministry;

Therefore, be it resolved, that the General Conference of The United Methodist Church and its member congregations strongly encourage Gideons International to open their membership to all Christians, regardless of gender, socioeconomic class, or denominational background.

ADOPTED 1996

The Order of Elder

WHEREAS, the 1988 and 1992 General Conferences enacted legislation (¶ 435.3, 1992 *Book of Discipline*) enabling the whole Church to participate in the ordination of elders (to wit, "The bishops shall be assisted by other elders and may include laity designated by the bishop representing the Church community . . . in the laying on of hands"), thus affirming the ministry of all Christians and dignifying the ministry of the laity; and

WHEREAS, said legislation clearly relegates to each presiding bishop sole prerogative to allow or disallow participation by representatives of the Church community in the ordination of elders; and

WHEREAS, only the Judicial Council may declare a paragraph of the *Discipline* null and void; and

WHEREAS, the Council of Bishops has passed a "covenant for action" (reference United Methodist News Service press release dated May 11, 1993), which effectively discourages its members from choosing to include or not to include laity in the laying on of hands during the ordination of elders;

Therefore, be it resolved, that the 1996 General Conference reaffirm the will of its two predecessor General Conferences with respect to ¶ 435.3 in the 1992 *Book of Discipline;* and

Be it further resolved, that the 1996 General Conference direct the Council of Bishops to rescind its May 1993 "consensus," which runs contrary to ¶ 435.3 of the 1992 *Book of Discipline.*

ADOPTED 1996

Prayer in the Local Church

In the Old Testament, the importance of prayer is shown and told many times. In the New Testament, prayer is taught to and commanded of all who believe. The substance of prayer has been given witness by the saints and servants of the church throughout its history. It is through prayer that every Christian today may actively engage the grace and presence of God, experience a perpetual renewal of his or her faith, and maintain the abundant flow of guidance and strength essential to the dynamic integration of his or her beliefs into Christian living.

Corporate prayer also assumes many roles. Preeminent among these is the responsive grace experienced in the bonding of the members into the church body. From this is often gained inner knowledge of belonging and the cherished feelings that go with Christian love. Further, evangelical grace is manifest in prayers for the community and the unchurched.

The substance of the above is self-evident and of common knowledge. Yet it is found that many United Methodist churches do not have areas of focus, ongoing programs, or organized activities that encourage or support prayer.

The needs for prayer are infinite. The ways to prayer in the local church may greatly benefit from the following:

WHEREAS, the sustained focus and emphasis on programs and activities of prayer in the local church significantly increases the interest in prayer and personal Christian growth; and

WHEREAS, the initiation of programs of prayer in a church will in turn activate a pool of dormant prayer talent that blossoms forth with purpose and energy; and

WHEREAS, basic instruction in the nature and methods of prayer helps many individuals who say they do not know how to pray to find new meaning and commitment to prayer and an enriched spiritual life; and

WHEREAS, normal support of prayer activities creates a variety of new opportunities for greater member-involvement in the ministries of the church; and

WHEREAS, the formal recognition of prayer as a dynamic, sustaining force in a church is universally viable and applicable regardless of size.

In the smallest congregations there will be one or more members who will accept the leadership in this Christian ministry. Large churches have the membership and organizational base to sponsor a wide variety of activities. This can include churchwide special event programs emphasizing prayer in the Christian life, the organization of special prayer projects or vigils to meet the particular or urgent needs of the church, sponsoring area Concerts of Prayer, and in-place formation and training of home prayer teams using members who have restricted or limited travel ability. Other possible activities include the conducting of prayer workshops, seminars, and retreats, as well as the operation of dedicated church facilities for use as a prayer ministries center; and

WHEREAS, established prayer programs and formed prayer groups provide a ready resource and certain response for special Calls to Prayer and other ongoing needs of The United Methodist Church; and

WHEREAS, the organization of specialized prayer groups and church prayer chains requires continuing attention to administrative and leadership duties; typically, this includes the supervision of prayer requests, the enlistment of members, continuing appreciation and motivation, personal renewal, and the ongoing definition of the local church's changing prayer needs and objectives; and

WHEREAS, the formal recognition and commitment of The United Methodist Church to continuing programs of prayer in the local church will cause an increased requirement for study materials, as well as a demand for the development and publication of new materials in the form of guidebooks and advance study aids;

Therefore, be it resolved, that the 1996 General Conference affirm its belief in prayer ministries and that this resolution be published in the *Book of Resolutions.*

ADOPTED 1996

Proper Use of Name: The United Methodist Church

WHEREAS, The Methodist Church and The Evangelical United Brethren Church were united under the name The United Methodist Church in the year 1968 and that the uniting name has great historical significance for both bodies;

Therefore, be it resolved, that insofar as possible, all materials used in correspondence, advertisements, and signs of the said churches and other denominational organizations use the complete proper name, "The United Methodist Church," capitalizing the word *The* when referring to the denomination as a whole.

ADOPTED 1980

Realizing Unity Between Lutherans and United Methodists

WHEREAS, Lutheran and Methodist churches alike arose as reform movements within large church bodies; and

WHEREAS, dialogues sponsored by the Lutheran World Federation and the World Methodist Council culminated in 1984 in the common statement "The Church: Community of Grace," which recommended "that our churches take steps to declare and establish full fellowship of Word and Sacrament"; and

WHEREAS, this common statement was accepted by the World Methodist Council at its meeting in Nairobi in 1986; and

WHEREAS, full fellowship of Word and Sacrament has now been established between Lutherans and Methodists in West Germany (1987), East Germany (1990), Austria (1991), and Sweden (1993); and

WHEREAS, a series of dialogues between The United Methodist Church and the member churches of the Lutheran Council in the U.S.A. held between 1977 and 1979 culminated in the common statement "A Lutheran-United Methodist Statement on Baptism"; and

WHEREAS, the Germany United Methodist Central Conference has voted to become a member of the *Leuenberger Konkordie* (1995), which is a fellowship of eighty Lutheran and Reformed judicatories that accept each other's faith and order; and

WHEREAS, The United Methodist Church believes that Christ wills for the church to be visibly one; and

WHEREAS, throughout the church of Jesus Christ significant ecumenical proposals continue to emerge that envision the achievement of visible unity through a series of covenants and concordats that unite our memberships, ministries, observances of the sacraments, and mission, rather than merge our structures; and

WHEREAS, The United Methodist Church preamble to the Constitution recognizes that "the church of Jesus Christ exists in and for the world, and its very dividedness is a hindrance to its mission in that world"; and

WHEREAS, United Methodists have diligently participated in the development of the common statements between Lutherans and Methodists as a way of reducing the dividedness among Christians; and

WHEREAS, the most recent round of formal Lutheran and United Methodist dialogue ended in 1988 in the United States;

Therefore, be it resolved, that the Council of Bishops and the General Commission on Christian Unity and Interreligious Concerns be in conversation with leadership of the Evangelical Lutheran Church in America about further dialogue between the two churches and work seriously toward a continuation of the formal dialogue.

ADOPTED 1996

Regarding the Service of Holy Communion

WHEREAS, it has been our practice for two centuries to use what the ritual printed in our hymnals has referred to as "the pure, unfermented juice of the grape" for Holy Communion; and

WHEREAS, this terminology was inadvertently omitted when the present hymnal was adopted;

Therefore, be it resolved, that the 1996 General Conference restore this phrase to our ritual by ordering that the words "The pure, unfermented juice of the grape shall be used during the service of Holy Communion" be added beneath the headings "A Service of Word and Table I," "A Service of Word and Table II," and "A Service of Word and Table III."

ADOPTED 1996

Spiritual Directors' Program

WHEREAS, the importance of a person of faith listening to, sharing with, and guiding another is clearly told in the Scripture (as examples, Elijah guiding Elisha, the spiritual friendship of Naomi and Ruth, Jesus leading the Samaritan woman to truth, Philip guiding the eunuch, Paul nurturing Timothy); and

WHEREAS, the church through the ages has benefited from the spiritual guidance given by such prayerful persons as Ignatius of Loyola, Teresa of Avila, Thomas Merton, and Douglas Steer; and

WHEREAS, our own history as United Methodists is informed by John Wesley's probing question, "How is it with your soul?"; by the spiritual nurturing he shared with Peter Boehler; and by the spiritual guidance of the class meeting; and

WHEREAS, many in our dizzying culture are seeking to discern the subtle threads and blessings woven by the mysterious movement of the Spirit; and

WHEREAS, the interest in and training of spiritual directors is beginning to occur in many Protestant circles; and

WHEREAS, a great service could be passed on to the Church through encouragement, networking, information-sharing, and training of spiritual guides;

Therefore, be it resolved, that General Conference recommends that *The Upper Room* explore ways of supplying resources to and networking with United Methodists and others involved in and interested in spiritual direction work; and

Be it further resolved, that General Conference further recommends that *The Upper Room,* in consultation with other boards and agencies (such as the Board of Higher Education and Ministry), plan a consultation/workshop in the next quadrennium that would enhance the gifts and skills of spiritual directors and those interested and serve as a way to link with others for support; and

Be it further resolved, that the costs for these actions be assumed within the normal funding of *The Upper Room* and those boards and agencies consulted.

ADOPTED 1992

A Tithing Church

Scripture

WHEREAS, In Numbers and Deuteronomy, Moses stated all the laws of God that God commanded him to pass on to Israel. After describing the three different kinds of tithes God requires of us, Moses said, "The purpose of tithing is to teach us to always put God first in our lives" (Numbers 18:21-24, adapted), so that "Jehovah, our God, will bless us and our work" (Deuteronomy 14:29, The Living Bible, paraphrased); and

WHEREAS, In the Sermon on the Mount, Jesus proclaimed, "You cannot serve two masters: God and money. For you will hate one and love the other, or else the other way around" (Matthew 6:24, TLB); and

Tradition

WHEREAS, Tithing has been the Christian minimum standard of giving for many years; and

Reason

WHEREAS, In the 1987 Journal of Stewardship published by the National Council of Churches, the giving level per number of The United

Methodist Church ranks twenty-eighth out of the thirty United States denominations reporting; and

Experience

WHEREAS, There is always the need to be continually reminded that God is to be first in our lives;

Therefore, be it resolved, that the General Conference of the United Methodist Church determine that we will be a tithing church and that the practice of tithing be lifted up to each congregation from the pulpit and through other channels of communication, and that workshops on the spiritual blessings of tithing will be held in each annual conference a minimum of once a year as a part of Christian stewardship.

ADOPTED 1988

By Water and The Spirit: A United Methodist Understanding of Baptism

A Report of the Baptism Study Committee

Contemporary United Methodism is attempting to recover and revitalize its understanding of baptism. To do this, we must look to our heritage as Methodists and Evangelical United Brethren and, indeed, to the foundations of Christian tradition. Throughout our history, baptism has been viewed in diverse and even contradictory ways. An enriched understanding of baptism, restoring the Wesleyan blend of sacramental and evangelical aspects, will enable United Methodists to participate in the sacrament with renewed appreciation for this gift of God's grace.

Within the Methodist tradition, baptism has long been a subject of much concern, even controversy. John Wesley retained the sacramental theology which he received from his Anglican heritage. He taught that in baptism a child was cleansed of the guilt of original sin, initiated into the covenant with God, admitted into the church, made an heir of the divine kingdom, and spiritually born anew. He said that while baptism was neither essential to nor sufficient for salvation, it was the "ordinary means" that God designated for applying the benefits of the work of Christ in human lives.

On the other hand, although he affirmed the regenerating grace of infant baptism, he also insisted upon the necessity of adult conversion

716

for those who have fallen from grace. A person who matures into moral accountability must respond to God's grace in repentance and faith. Without personal decision and commitment to Christ, the baptismal gift is rendered ineffective.

Baptism for Wesley, therefore, was a part of the lifelong process of salvation. He saw spiritual rebirth as a twofold experience in the normal process of Christian development—to be received through baptism in infancy and through commitment to Christ later in life. Salvation included both God's initiating activity of grace and a willing human response.

In its development in the United States, Methodism was unable to maintain this Wesleyan balance of sacramental and evangelical emphases. Access to the sacraments was limited during the late eighteenth and early nineteenth centuries when the Methodist movement was largely under the leadership of laypersons who were not authorized to administer them. On the American frontier where human ability and action were stressed, the revivalistic call for individual decision-making, though important, was subject to exaggeration. The sacramental teachings of Wesley tended to be ignored. In this setting, while infant baptism continued not only to be practiced, but also to be vigorously defended, its significance became weakened and ambiguous.

Later toward the end of the nineteenth century, the theological views of much of Methodism were influenced by a new set of ideas which had become dominant in American culture. These ideas included optimism about the progressive improvement of humankind and confidence in the social benefits of scientific discovery, technology, and education. Assumptions of original sin gave way before the assertion that human nature was essentially unspoiled. In this intellectual milieu, the old evangelical insistence upon conversion and spiritual rebirth seemed quaint and unnecessary.

Thus the creative Wesleyan synthesis of sacramentalism and evangelicalism was torn asunder and both its elements devalued. As a result, infant baptism was variously interpreted and often reduced to a ceremony of dedication. Adult baptism was sometimes interpreted as a profession of faith and public acknowledgment of God's grace, but was more often viewed simply as an act of joining the church. By the middle of the twentieth century, Methodism in general had ceased to understand baptism as authentically sacramental. Rather than an act of divine grace, it was seen as an expression of human choice.

Baptism was also a subject of concern and controversy in the Evangelical and United Brethren traditions that were brought together in 1946 in The Evangelical United Brethren Church. Their early pietistic revivalism, based upon belief in the availability of divine grace and the freedom of human choice, emphasized bringing people to salvation through Christian experience. In the late nineteenth and early twentieth centuries, both Evangelical and United Brethren theologians stressed the importance of baptism as integral to the proclamation of the gospel, as a rite initiating persons into the covenant community (paralleling circumcision), and as a sign of the new birth, that gracious divine act by which persons are redeemed from sin and reconciled to God. The former Evangelical Church consistently favored the baptism of infants. The United Brethren provided for the baptism of both infants and adults. Following the union of 1946, The Evangelical United Brethren Church adopted a ritual that included services of baptism for infants and adults, and also a newly created service for the dedication of infants that had little precedent in official rituals of either of the former churches.

The 1960–64 revision of *The Methodist Hymnal*, including rituals, gave denominational leaders an opportunity to begin to recover the sacramental nature of baptism in contemporary Methodism. The General Commission on Worship sounded this note quite explicitly in its introduction to the new ritual in 1964:

> In revising the Order for the Administration of Baptism, the Commission on Worship has endeavored to keep in mind that baptism is a sacrament, and to restore it to the Evangelical-Methodist concept set forth in our Articles of Religion.... Due recognition was taken of the critical reexamination of the theology of the Sacrament of Baptism which is currently taking place in ecumenical circles, and of its theological content and implications.

The commission provided a brief historical perspective demonstrating that the understanding of baptism as a sacrament had been weakened, if not discarded altogether, over the years. Many in the Church regarded baptism, both of infants and adults, as a dedication rather than as a sacrament. The commission pointed out that in a dedication we make a gift of a life to God for God to accept, while in a sacrament God offers the gift of God's unfailing grace for us to accept. The 1964 revision of the ritual of the sacrament of baptism began to restore the rite to its original and historic meaning as a sacrament.

In the 1989 *The United Methodist Hymnal*, the Services of the Baptismal Covenant I, II, and IV (taken from the 1984 official ritual of the denomination as printed in *The Book of Services*) continue this effort to reemphasize the historic significance of baptism. These rituals, in accenting the reality of sin and of regeneration, the initiating of divine grace, and the necessity of repentance and faith, are consistent with the Wesleyan combination of sacramentalism and evangelicalism.

United Methodism is not alone in the need to recover the significance of baptism nor in its work to do so. Other Christian communions are also reclaiming the importance of this sacrament for Christian faith and life. To reach the core of the meaning and practice of baptism, all have found themselves led back through the life of the church to the Apostolic Age. An ecumenical convergence has emerged from this effort, as can be seen in the widely acclaimed document *Baptism, Eucharist, and Ministry* (1982).

Established by the General Conference of 1988 and authorized to continue its work by the General Conference of 1992, the Committee to Study Baptism is participating in this process by offering a theological and functional understanding of baptism as embodied in the ritual of The United Methodist Church. In so doing, the broad spectrum of resources of Scripture, Christian tradition, and the Methodist-Evangelical United Brethren experience has been taken into account. The growing ecumenical consensus has assisted us in our thinking.

We Are Saved by God's Grace

The Human Condition. As told in the first chapters of Genesis, in creation God made human beings in the image of God—a relationship of intimacy, dependence, and trust. We are open to the indwelling presence of God and given freedom to work with God to accomplish the divine will and purpose for all of creation and history. To be human as God intended is to have loving fellowship with God and to reflect the divine nature in our lives as fully as possible.

Tragically, as Genesis 3 recounts, we are unfaithful to that relationship. The result is a thorough distortion of the image of God in us and the degrading of the whole of creation. Through prideful overreach or denial of our God-given responsibilities, we exalt our own will, invent our own values, and rebel against God. Our very being is dominated by an inherent inclination toward evil which has traditionally been called original sin. It is a universal human condition and affects all aspects of life. Because of our condition of sin, we are separated from God, alienated from one another, hostile to the natural world, and even at odds with our own best selves. Sin may be expressed as errant priorities, as deliberate wrongdoing, as apathy in the face of need, as cooperation with oppression and injustice. Evil is cosmic as well as personal; it afflicts both individuals and the institutions of our human society. The nature of sin is represented in Baptismal Covenants I, II, and IV in *The United Methodist Hymnal* by the phrases "the spiritual forces of wickedness" and "the evil powers of this world," as well as "your sin." Before God all persons are lost, helpless to save themselves, and in need of divine mercy and forgiveness.

The Divine Initiative of Grace. While we have turned from God, God has not abandoned us. Instead, God graciously and continuously seeks to restore us to that loving relationship for which we were created, to make us into the persons that God would have us be. To this end God acts preveniently, that is, before we are aware of it, reaching out to save humankind. The Old Testament records the story of God's acts in the history of the covenant community of Israel to work out the divine will and purpose. In the New Testament story, we learn that God came into this sinful world in the person of Jesus Christ to reveal all that the human mind can comprehend about who God is and who God would have us be. Through Christ's death and resurrection, the power of sin and death was overcome and we are set free to again be God's own people (1 Peter 2:9). Since God is the only initiator and source of grace, all grace is prevenient in that it precedes and enables any movement that we can make toward God. Grace brings us to an awareness of our sinful predicament and of our inability to save ourselves; grace motivates us to repentance and gives us the capacity to respond to divine love. In the words of the baptismal ritual: "All this is God's gift, offered to us without price" (*The United Methodist Hymnal*, page 33).

The Necessity of Faith for Salvation. Faith is both a gift of God and a human response to God. It is the ability and willingness to say "yes" to the divine offer of salvation. Faith is our awareness of our utter dependence upon God, the surrender of our selfish wills, the trusting reliance upon divine mercy. The candidate for baptism answers "I do" to the question "Do you confess Jesus Christ as your Savior, put your whole trust in his grace, and promise to serve him as your Lord . . .?" (*The United Methodist Hymnal*, page 34). Our personal response of faith requires conversion in which we turn away from sin and turn instead to God. It entails a decision to commit our lives to the Lordship of Christ, an acceptance of the forgiveness of our sins, the death of our old selves, an entering into a new life of the Spirit—being born again (John 3:3-5,

2 Corinthians 5:17). All persons do not experience this spiritual rebirth in the same way. For some, there is a singular, radical moment of conversion. For others, conversion may be experienced as the dawning and growing realization that one has been constantly loved by God and has a personal reliance upon Christ. John Wesley described his own experience by saying, "I felt my heart strangely warmed. I felt I did trust in Christ, Christ alone for salvation; and an assurance was given me that he had taken away my sins, even mine, and saved me from the law of sin and death."

The Means by Which God's Grace Comes to Us

Divine grace is made available and effective in human lives through a variety of means or "channels," as Wesley called them. While God is radically free to work in many ways, the church has been given by God the special responsibility and privilege of being the body of Christ which carries forth God's purpose of redeeming the world. Wesley recognized the church itself as a means of grace—a grace-filled and grace-sharing community of faithful people. United Methodism shares with other Protestant communions the understanding that the proclamation of the Word through preaching, teaching, and the life of the church is a primary means of God's grace. The origin and rapid growth of Methodism as a revival movement occurred largely through the medium of the proclaimed Gospel. John Wesley also emphasized the importance of prayer, fasting, Bible study, and meetings of persons for support and sharing.

Because God has created and is creating all that is, physical objects of creation can become the bearers of divine presence, power, and meaning, and thus become sacramental means of God's grace. Sacraments are effective means of God's presence mediated through the created world. God becoming incarnate in Jesus Christ is the supreme instance of this kind of divine action. Wesley viewed the sacraments as crucial means of grace and affirmed the Anglican teaching that "a sacrament is 'an outward sign of inward grace, and a means whereby we receive the same.'" Combining words, actions, and physical elements, sacraments are sign-acts which both express and convey God's grace and love. Baptism and the Lord's Supper are sacraments that were instituted or commanded by Christ in the Gospels.

United Methodists believe that these sign-acts are special means of grace. The ritual action of a sacrament does not merely point to God's presence in the world, but also participates in it and becomes a vehicle for conveying that reality. God's presence in the sacraments is real, but it must be accepted by human faith if it is to transform human lives. The sacraments do not convey grace either magically or irrevocably, but they are powerful channels through which God has chosen to make grace available to us. Wesley identified baptism as the initiatory sacrament by which we enter into the covenant with God and are admitted as members of Christ's church. He understood the Lord's Supper as nourishing and empowering the lives of Christians and strongly advocated frequent participation in it. The Wesleyan tradition has continued to practice and cherish the various means through which divine grace is made present to us.

Baptism and the Life of Faith

The New Testament records that Jesus was baptized by John (Matthew 3:13-17), and he commanded his disciples to teach and baptize in the name of the Father, Son, and Holy Spirit (Matthew 28:19). Baptism is grounded in the life, death, and resurrection of Jesus Christ; the grace which baptism makes available is that of the atonement of Christ which makes possible our reconciliation with God. Baptism involves dying to sin, newness of life, union with Christ, receiving the Holy Spirit, and incorporation into Christ's church. United Methodists affirm this understanding in their official documents of faith. Article XVII of the Articles of Religion (Methodist) calls baptism "a sign of regeneration or the new birth"; the Confession of Faith (EUB) states that baptism is "a representation of the new birth in Christ Jesus and a mark of Christian discipleship."

The Baptismal Covenant. In both the Old and New Testament, God enters into covenant relationship with God's people. A covenant involves promises and responsibilities of both parties; it is instituted through a special ceremony and expressed by a distinguishing sign. By covenant God constituted a servant community of the people of Israel, promising to be their God and giving them the Law to make clear how they were to live. The circumcision of male infants is the sign of this covenant (Genesis 17:1-14; Exodus 24:1-12). In the death and resurrection of Jesus Christ, God fulfilled the prophecy of a new covenant and called forth the church as a servant community (Jeremiah 31:31-34; 1 Corinthians 11:23-26). The baptism of infants and adults, both male and female, is the sign of this covenant.

Therefore, United Methodists identify our ritual for baptism as "The Services of the Baptismal Covenant" (*The United Methodist Hymnal*, pages 32–54). In baptism the Church declares that it is bound in covenant to God; through baptism new persons are initiated into that covenant. The covenant connects God, the community of faith, and the person being baptized; all three are essential to the fulfillment of the baptismal covenant. The faithful grace of God initiates the covenant relationship and enables the community and the person to respond with faith.

Baptism by Water and the Holy Spirit. Through the work of the Holy Spirit—the continuing presence of Christ on earth—the church is instituted to be the community of the new covenant. Within this community, baptism is by water and the Spirit (John 3:5; Acts 2:38). In God's work of salvation, the mystery of Christ's death and resurrection is inseparably linked with the gift of the Holy Spirit given on the Day of Pentecost (Acts 2). Likewise, participation in Christ's death and resurrection is inseparably linked with receiving the Spirit (Romans 6:1-11; 8:9-14). The Holy Spirit who is the power of creation (Genesis 1:2) is also the giver of new life. Working in the lives of people before, during, and after their baptisms, the Spirit is the effective agent of salvation. God bestows upon baptized persons the presence of the Holy Spirit, marks them with an identifying seal as God's own, and implants in their hearts the first installment of their inheritance as sons and daughters of God (2 Corinthians 1:21-22). It is through the Spirit that the life of faith is nourished until the final deliverance when they will enter into the fullness of salvation (Ephesians 1:13-14).

Since the Apostolic Age, baptism by water and baptism of the Holy Spirit have been connected (Acts 19:17). Christians are baptized with both, sometimes by different sign-actions. Water is administered in the name of the triune God (specified in the ritual as Father, Son, and Holy Spirit) by an authorized person, and the Holy Spirit is invoked with the laying on of hands in the presence of the congregation. Water provides the central symbolism for baptism. The richness of its meaning for the Christian community is suggested in the baptismal liturgy which speaks of the waters of creation and the flood, the liberation of God's people by passage through the sea, the gift of water in the wilderness, and the passage through the Jordan River to the promised land. In baptism we identify ourselves with this people of God and join the community's journey toward God. The use of water in baptism also symbolizes cleansing from sin, death to old life, and rising to begin new life in Christ. In United Methodist tradition, the water of baptism may be administered by sprinkling, pouring, or immersion. However it is administered, water should be utilized with enough generosity to enhance our appreciation of its symbolic meanings.

The baptismal liturgy includes the biblical symbol of the anointing with the Holy Spirit—the laying on of hands with the optional use of oil. This anointing promises to the baptized person the power to live faithfully the kind of life that water baptism signifies. In the early centuries of the church, the laying on of hands usually followed immediately upon administration of the water and completed the ritual of membership. Because the laying on of hands was, in the Western Church, an act to be performed only by a bishop, it was later separated from water baptism and came to be called confirmation (*see* pp. 729–31). In confirmation the Holy Spirit marked the baptized person as God's own and strengthened him or her for discipleship. In the worship life of the early church, the water and the anointing led directly to the celebration of the Lord's Supper as part of the service of initiation, regardless of the age of the baptized. The current rituals of the Baptismal Covenant rejoin these three elements into a unified service. Together these symbols point to, anticipate, and offer participation in the life of the community of faith as it embodies God's presence in the world.

Baptism as Incorporation into the Body of Christ. Christ constitutes the church as his Body by the power of the Holy Spirit (1 Corinthians 12:13, 27). The church draws new persons into itself as it seeks to remain faithful to its commission to proclaim and exemplify the gospel. Baptism is the sacrament of initiation and incorporation into the body of Christ. An infant, child, or adult who is baptized becomes a member of the catholic (universal) church, of the denomination, and of the local congregation (*see* pp. 729–31). Therefore, baptism is a rite of the whole Church, which ordinarily requires the participation of the gathered, worshiping congregation. In a series of promises within the liturgy of baptism, the community affirms its own faith and pledges to act as spiritual mentor and support for the one who is baptized. Baptism is not merely an individualistic, private, or domestic occasion. When unusual but legitimate circumstances prevent a baptism from taking place in the midst of the gathered community during its regular worship, every effort should be made to assemble representatives of the congregation to participate in the celebration. Later, the baptism should be recognized in the public assembly of worship in order that the congregation may make its appropriate affirmations of commitment and responsibility.

Baptism brings us into union with Christ, with each other, and with the church in every time and place. Through this sign and seal of our common discipleship, our equality in Christ is made manifest (Galatians 3:27-28). We affirm that there is one baptism into Christ, celebrated as our basic bond of unity in the many communions that make up the body of Christ (Ephesians 4:4-6). The power of the Spirit in baptism does not depend upon the mode by which water is administered, the age or psychological disposition of the baptized person, or the character of the minister. It is God's grace that makes the sacrament whole. One baptism calls the various churches to overcome their divisions and visibly manifest their unity. Our oneness in Christ calls for mutual recognition of baptism in these communions as a means of expressing the unity that Christ intends (1 Corinthians 12:12-13).

Baptism as Forgiveness of Sin. In baptism God offers and we accept the forgiveness of our sin (Acts 2:38). With the pardoning of sin which has separated us from God, we are justified—freed from the guilt and penalty of sin and restored to right relationship with God. This reconciliation is made possible through the atonement of Christ and made real in our lives by the work of the Holy Spirit. We respond by confessing and repenting of our sin, and affirming our faith that Jesus Christ has accomplished all that is necessary for our salvation. Faith is the necessary condition for justification; in baptism, that faith is professed. God's forgiveness makes possible the renewal of our spiritual lives and our becoming new beings in Christ.

Baptism as New Life. Baptism is the sacramental sign of new life through and in Christ by the power of the Holy Spirit. Variously identified as regeneration, new birth, and being born again, this work of grace makes us into new spiritual creatures (2 Corinthians 5:17). We die to our old nature which was dominated by sin and enter into the very life of Christ who transforms us. Baptism is the means of entry into new life in Christ (John 3:5; Titus 3:5), but new birth may not always coincide with the moment of the administration of water or the laying on of hands. Our awareness and acceptance of our redemption by Christ and new life in him may vary throughout our lives. But, in whatever way the reality of the new birth is experienced, it carries out the promises God made to us in our baptism.

Baptism and Holy Living. New birth into life in Christ, which is signified by baptism, is the beginning of that process of growth in grace and holiness through which God brings us into closer relationship with Jesus Christ, and shapes our lives increasingly into conformity with the divine will. Sanctification is a gift of the gracious presence of the Holy Spirit, a yielding to the Spirit's power, a deepening of our love for God and neighbor. Holiness of heart and life, in the Wesleyan tradition, always involves both personal and social holiness.

Baptism is the doorway to the sanctified life. The sacrament teaches us to live in the expectation of further gifts of God's grace. It initiates us into a community of faith that prays for holiness; it calls us to life lived in faithfulness to God's gift. Baptized believers and the community of faith are obligated to manifest to the world the new redeemed humanity which lives in loving relationship with God and strives to put an end to all human estrangements. There are no conditions of human life (including age or intellectual ability, race or nationality, gender or sexual identity, class or disability) that exclude persons from the sacrament of baptism. We strive for and look forward to the reign of God on earth, of which baptism is a sign. Baptism is fulfilled only when the believer and the church are wholly conformed to the image of Christ.

Baptism as God's Gift to Persons of Any Age. There is one baptism as there is one source of salvation—the gracious love of God. The baptizing of a person, whether as an infant or an adult, is a sign of God's saving grace. That grace—experienced by us as initiating, enabling, and empowering—is the same for all persons. All stand in need of it, and none can be saved without it. The difference between the baptism of adults and that of infants is that the Christian faith is consciously being professed by an adult who is baptized. A baptized infant comes to profess her or his faith later in life, after having been nurtured and taught by parent(s) or other responsible adults and the community of faith. Infant baptism is the prevailing practice in situations where children are born to believing parents and brought up in Christian homes and communities of faith. Adult baptism is the norm when the church is in a missionary situation, reaching out to persons in a culture which is indifferent or hostile to the faith. While the baptism of infants is appropriate for Christian families, the increasingly minority status of the church in contemporary society demands more attention to evangelizing, nurturing, and baptizing adult converts.

Infant baptism has been the historic practice of the overwhelming majority of the church throughout the Christian centuries. While the New Testament contains no explicit mandate, there is ample evidence for the baptism of infants in Scripture (Acts 2:38-41; 16:15, 33) and in early Christian doctrine and practice. Infant baptism rests firmly on the understanding that God prepares the way of faith before we request or even know that we need help (prevenient grace). The sacrament is a powerful expression of the reality that all persons come before God as no more than helpless infants, unable to do anything to save ourselves, dependent upon the grace of our loving God. The faithful covenant community of the church serves as a means of grace for those whose lives are impacted by its ministry. Through the church, God claims infants as well as adults to be participants in the gracious covenant of which baptism is the sign. This understanding of the workings of divine grace also applies to persons who for reasons of disabilities or other limitations are unable to answer for themselves the questions of the baptismal ritual. While we may not be able to comprehend how God works in their lives, our faith teaches us that God's grace is sufficient for their needs and, thus, they are appropriate recipients of baptism.

The church affirms that children being born into the brokenness of the world should receive the cleansing and renewing forgiveness of God no less than adults. The saving grace made available through Christ's atonement is the only hope of salvation for persons of any age. In baptism infants enter into a new life in Christ as children of God and members of the body of Christ. The baptism of an infant incorporates him or her into the community of faith and nurture, including membership in the local church.

The baptism of infants is properly understood and valued if the child is loved and nurtured by the faithful worshiping church and by the child's own family. If a parent or sponsor (godparent) cannot or will not nurture the child in the faith, then baptism is to be postponed until Christian nurture is available. A child who dies without being baptized is received into the love and presence of God because the Spirit has worked in that child to bestow saving grace. If a child has been baptized but her or his family or sponsors do not faithfully nurture the child in the faith, the congregation has a particular responsibility for incorporating the child into its life.

Understanding the practice as an authentic expression of how God works in our lives, The United Methodist Church strongly advocates the baptism of infants within the faith community: "Because the redeeming love of God, revealed in Jesus Christ, extends to all persons and because Jesus explicitly included the children in his kingdom, the pastor of each charge shall earnestly exhort all Christian parents or guardians to present their children to the Lord in Baptism at an early age" (1992 *Book of Discipline*, ¶ 221). We affirm that while thanksgiving to God and dedication of parents to the task of Christian child-raising are aspects of infant baptism, the sacrament is primarily a gift of divine grace. Neither parents nor infants are the chief actors; baptism is an act of God in and through the church.

We respect the sincerity of parents who choose not to have their infants baptized, but we acknowledge that these views do not coincide with the Wesleyan understanding of the nature of the sacrament. The United Methodist Church does not accept either the idea that only believer's baptism is valid or the notion that the baptism of infants magically imparts salvation apart from active personal faith. Pastors are instructed by the *Book of Discipline* to explain our teaching clearly on these matters, so that parent(s) or sponsors might be free of misunderstandings.

The United Methodist Book of Worship contains "An Order of Thanksgiving for the Birth or Adoption of the Child" (pages 585–87), which may be recommended in situations where baptism is inappropriate, but parents wish to take responsibility publicly for the growth of the child in faith. It should be made clear that this rite is in no way equivalent to or a substitute for baptism. Neither is it an act of infant dedication. If the infant has not been baptized, the sacrament should be administered as soon as possible after the Order of Thanksgiving.

God's Faithfulness to the Baptismal Covenant. Since baptism is primarily an act of God in the church, the sacrament is to be received by an individual only once. This position is in accord with the historic teaching of the church universal, originating as early as the second century and having been recently reaffirmed ecumenically in *Baptism, Eucharist, and Ministry.*

The claim that baptism is unrepeatable rests on the steadfast faithfulness of God. God's initiative establishes the covenant of grace into which we are incorporated in baptism. By misusing our God-given freedom, we may live in neglect or defiance of that covenant, but we cannot destroy God's love for us. When we repent and return to God, the covenant does not need to be remade, because God has always remained faithful to it. What is needed is renewal of our commitment and reaffirmation of our side of the covenant.

God's gift of grace in the baptismal covenant does not save us apart from our human response of faith. Baptized persons may have many significant spiritual experiences, which they will desire to celebrate publicly in the worship life of the church. Such experiences may include defining moments of conversion, repentance of sin, gifts of the Spirit, deepening of commitment, changes in Christian vocation, important transitions in the life of discipleship. These occasions call not for repetition of baptism, but for reaffirmations of baptismal vows as a witness to the good news that while we may be unfaithful, God is not. Appropriate services for such events would be "Confirmation or Reaffirmation of Faith" (*see* Baptismal Covenant I in *The United Methodist Hymnal*) or "A Celebration of New Beginnings in Faith" (*The United Methodist Book of Worship*, pages 588–90).

Nurturing Persons in the Life of Faith. If persons are to be enabled to live faithfully the human side of the baptismal covenant, Christian nurture is essential. Christian nurture builds on baptism and is itself a means of grace. For infant baptism, an early step is instruction prior to baptism of parent(s) or sponsors in the gospel message, the meaning of the sacrament, and the responsibilities of a Christian home. The pastor has specific responsibility for this step (the 1992 *Book of Discipline*, ¶ 439.1*b*). Adults who are candidates for baptism need careful preparation for receiving this gift of grace and living out its meaning (the 1992 *Book of Discipline*, ¶ 216.1).

After baptism, the faithful church provides the nurture which makes possible a comprehensive and lifelong process of growing in grace. The content of this nurturing will be appropriate to the stages of life and maturity of faith of individuals. Christian nurture includes both cognitive learning and spiritual formation. A crucial goal is the bringing of persons to recognition of their need for salvation and their acceptance of God's gift in Jesus Christ. Those experiencing conversion and commitment to Christ are to profess their faith in a public ritual. They will need to be guided and supported throughout their lives of discipleship. Through its worship life, its Christian education programs, its spiritual growth emphases, its social action and mission, its examples of Christian discipleship, and its offering of the various means of grace, the church strives to shape persons into the image of Christ. Such nurturing enables Christians to live out the transforming potential of the grace of their baptism.

Profession of Christian Faith and Confirmation. The Christian life is a dynamic process of change and growth, marked at various points by celebrations in rituals of the saving grace of Christ. The Holy Spirit works in the lives of persons prior to their baptism, is at work in their baptism, and continues to work in their lives after their baptism. When

729

persons recognize and accept this activity of the Holy Spirit, they respond with renewed faith and commitment.

In the early church, baptism, the laying on of hands, and eucharist were a unified rite of initiation and new birth for Christians of all ages. During the Middle Ages in Western Europe, confirmation was separated from baptism in both time and theology. A misunderstanding developed of confirmation as completing baptism, with emphasis upon human vows and initiation into church membership. John Wesley did not recommend confirmation to his preachers or to the new Methodist Church in America. Since 1964 in the former Methodist Church, the first public profession of faith for those baptized as infants has been called Confirmation. In the former Evangelical United Brethren Church, there was no such rite until union with The Methodist Church in 1968. With the restoration of confirmation—as the laying on of hands—to the current baptismal ritual, it should be emphasized that confirmation is what the Holy Spirit does. Confirmation is a divine action, the work of the Spirit empowering a person "born through water and the Spirit" to "live as a faithful disciple of Jesus Christ."

An adult or youth preparing for baptism should be carefully instructed in its life-transforming significance and responsibilities. Such a person professes in the sacrament of baptism his or her faith in Jesus Christ and commitment to discipleship, is offered the gift of assurance, and is confirmed by the power of the Holy Spirit (*see* Baptismal Covenant I, sections 4, 11, and 12). No separate ritual of confirmation is needed for the believing person.

An infant who is baptized cannot make a personal profession of faith as a part of the sacrament. Therefore, as the young person is nurtured and matures so as to be able to respond to God's grace, conscious faith and intentional commitment are necessary. Such a person must come to claim the faith of the church proclaimed in baptism as her or his own faith. Deliberate preparation for this event focuses on the young person's self-understanding and appropriation of Christian doctrines, spiritual disciplines, and life of discipleship. It is a special time for experiencing divine grace and for consciously embracing one's Christian vocation as a part of the priesthood of all believers. Youth who were not baptized as infants share in the same period of preparation for profession of Christian faith. For them, it is nurture for baptism, for becoming members of the church, and for confirmation.

When persons who were baptized as infants are ready to profess their Christian faith, they participate in the service which United Methodism

730

now calls Confirmation. This occasion is not an entrance into church membership, for this was accomplished through baptism. It is the first public affirmation of the grace of God in one's baptism and the acknowledgment of one's acceptance of that grace by faith. This moment includes all the elements of conversion—repentance of sin, surrender and death of self, trust in the saving grace of God, new life in Christ, and becoming an instrument of God's purpose in the world. The profession of Christian faith, to be celebrated in the midst of the worshiping congregation, should include the voicing of baptismal vows as a witness to faith and the opportunity to give testimony to personal Christian experience.

Confirmation follows profession of the Christian faith as part of the same service. Confirmation is a dynamic action of the Holy Spirit that can be repeated. In confirmation the outpouring of the Holy Spirit is invoked to provide the one being confirmed with the power to live in the faith that he or she has professed. The basic meaning of confirmation is strengthening and making firm in Christian faith and life. The ritual action in confirmation is the laying on of hands as the sign of God's continuing gift of the grace of Pentecost. Historically, the person being confirmed was also anointed on the forehead with oil in the shape of a cross as a mark of the Spirit's work. The ritual of the baptismal covenant included in The United Methodist Hymnal makes clear that the first and primary confirming act of the Holy Spirit is in connection with and immediately follows baptism.

When a baptized person has professed her or his Christian faith and has been confirmed, that person enters more fully into the responsibilities and privileges of membership in the church. Just as infants are members of their human families, but are unable to participate in all aspects of family life, so baptized infants are members of the church—the family of faith—but are not yet capable of sharing everything involved in membership. For this reason, statistics of church membership are counts of professed/confirmed members rather than of all baptized members.

Reaffirmation of One's Profession of Christian Faith. The life of faith which baptized persons live is like a pilgrimage or journey. On this lifelong journey there are many challenges, changes, and chances. We engage life's experiences on our journey of faith as a part of the redeeming and sanctifying body of Christ. Ongoing Christian nurture teaches, shapes, and strengthens us to live ever more faithfully as we are open to the Spirit's revealing more and more of the way and will of God. As

731

our appreciation of the good news of Jesus Christ deepens and our commitment to Christ's service becomes more profound, we seek occasions to celebrate. Like God's people through the ages, all Christians need to participate in acts of renewal within the covenant community. Such an opportunity is offered in every occasion of baptism when the congregation remembers and affirms the gracious work of God which baptism celebrates. "Baptismal Covenant IV" in *The United Methodist Hymnal* is a powerful ritual of reaffirmation which uses water in ways that remind us of our baptism. The historic "Covenant Renewal Service" and "Love Feast" can also be used for this purpose (*The United Methodist Book of Worship*, pages 288–94 and 581–84). Reaffirmation of faith is a human response to God's grace and therefore may be repeated at many points in our faith journey.

Baptism in Relation to Other Rites of the Church

The grace of God which claims us in our baptism is made available to us in many other ways and, especially, through other rites of the church.

Baptism and the Lord's Supper (Holy Communion or the Eucharist). Through baptism, persons are initiated into the church; by the Lord's Supper, the church is sustained in the life of faith. The Services of the Baptismal Covenant appropriately conclude with Holy Communion, through which the union of the new member with the body of Christ is most fully expressed. Holy Communion is a sacred meal in which the community of faith, in the simple act of eating bread and drinking wine, proclaims and participates in all that God has done, is doing, and will continue to do for us in Christ. In celebrating the Eucharist, we remember the grace given to us in our baptism and partake of the spiritual food necessary for sustaining and fulfilling the promises of salvation. Because the table at which we gather belongs to the Lord, it should be open to all who respond to Christ's love, regardless of age or church membership. The Wesleyan tradition has always recognized that Holy Communion may be an occasion for the reception of converting, justifying, and sanctifying grace. Unbaptized persons who receive communion should be counseled and nurtured toward baptism as soon as possible.

Baptism and Christian Ministry. Through baptism, God calls and commissions persons to the general ministry of all Christian believers (*see* 1992 *Book of Discipline*, ¶¶ 101–07). This ministry, in which we participate both individually and corporately, is the activity of discipleship. It is grounded upon the awareness that we have been called into a new relationship not only with God, but also with the world. The task of Christians is to embody the gospel and the church in the world. We exercise our calling as Christians by prayer, by witnessing to the good news of salvation in Christ, by caring for and serving other people, and by working toward reconciliation, justice, and peace, in the world. This is the universal priesthood of all believers.

From within this general ministry of all believers, God calls and the church authorizes some persons for the task of representative ministry (*see* 1992 *Book of Discipline*, ¶¶ 108–110). The vocation of those in representative ministry includes focusing, modeling, supervising, shepherding, enabling, and empowering the general ministry of the church. Their ordination to Word, Sacrament, and Order or consecration to diaconal ministries of service, justice, and love is grounded in the same baptism that commissions the general priesthood of all believers.

Baptism and Christian Marriage. In the ritual for marriage, the minister addresses the couple: "I ask you now, in the presence of God and these people, to declare your intention to enter into union with one another through the grace of Jesus Christ, who calls you into union with himself as acknowledged in your baptism" (*The United Methodist Hymnal,* page 865). Marriage is to be understood as a covenant of love and commitment with mutual promises and responsibilities. For the church, the marriage covenant is grounded in the covenant between God and God's people into which Christians enter in their baptism. The love and fidelity which are to characterize Christian marriage will be a witness to the gospel, and the couple are to "go to serve God and your neighbor in all that you do."

When ministers officiate at the marriage of a couple who are not both Christians, the ritual needs to be altered to protect the integrity of all involved.

Baptism and Christian Funeral. The Christian gospel is a message of death and resurrection, that of Christ and our own. Baptism signifies our dying and rising with Christ. As death no longer has dominion over Christ, we believe that if we have died with Christ we shall also live with him (Romans 6:8-9). As the liturgy of the "Service of Death and Resurrection" proclaims: "Dying, Christ destroyed our death. Rising, Christ restored our life. Christ will come again in glory. As in baptism *Name* put on Christ, so in Christ may *Name* be clothed with glory" (*The United Methodist Hymnal,* page 870).

If the deceased person was never baptized, the ritual needs to be amended in ways which continue to affirm the truths of the Gospel, but are appropriate to the situation.

Committal of the deceased to God and the body to its final resting place recall the act of baptism and derive Christian meaning from God's baptismal covenant with us. We acknowledge the reality of death and the pain of loss, and we give thanks for the life that was lived and shared with us. We worship in the awareness that our gathering includes the whole communion of saints, visible and invisible, and that in Christ the ties of love unite the living and the dead.

Conclusion

Baptism is a crucial threshold that we cross on our journey in faith. But there are many others, including the final transition from death to life eternal. Through baptism we are incorporated into the ongoing history of Christ's mission, and we are identified and made participants in God's new history in Jesus Christ and the new age that Christ is bringing. We await the final moment of grace, when Christ comes in victory at the end of the age to bring all who are in Christ into the glory of that victory. Baptism has significance in time and gives meaning to the end of time. In it we have a vision of a world recreated and humanity transformed and exalted by God's presence. We are told that in this new heaven and new earth there will be no temple, for even our churches and services of worship will have had their time and ceased to be, in the presence of God, "the first and the last, the beginning and the end" (Revelation 21–22).

Until that day, we are charged by Christ to "go therefore and make disciples of all nations, baptizing them in the name of the Father, the Son, and the Holy Spirit, and teaching them to obey everything that I have commanded you. And remember, I am with you always, to the end of the age" (Matthew 28:19-20).

Baptism is at the heart of the gospel of grace and at the core of the church's mission. When we baptize we say what we understand as Christians about ourselves and our community: that we are loved into being by God, lost because of sin, but redeemed and saved in Jesus Christ to live new lives in anticipation of his coming again in glory. Baptism is an expression of God's love for the world, and the effects of baptism also express God's grace. As baptized people of God, we therefore respond with praise and thanksgiving, praying that God's will be done in our own lives:

> *We your people stand before you,*
> *Water-washed and Spirit-born.*
> *By your grace, our lives we offer.*
> *Re-create us; God, transform!*

—Ruth Duck, "Wash, O God, Our Sons and Daughters,"
(*The United Methodist Hymnal,* 605); Used with permission.

ADOPTED 1996

Enlist and Involve the Youth in the Life of the Church

Introduction

From August 2–4, 1991, a group of some twenty-five persons who had been active in the youth of the Methodist denominations that merged to form The Methodist Church in 1939 met at Baker University, Baldwin City, Kansas. They came together with the cooperation of Archives and History leaders of the Kansas East Annual Conference to observe the fiftieth anniversary of the founding of the Methodist Youth Fellowship.

Nearly all of them had played a leading role as state student representatives or conference youth presidents in the programs of the predecessor denomination, in the deliberations of the Uniting Conference (1939), in the Youth Study Commission created by action of the 1940 General Conference of the new church, in the work of the general boards as full, voting youth members, and/or in the leadership of the National Conference of the Methodist Youth Fellowship, created to coordinate and represent the youth and student leadership of The Methodist Church.

After the presentation of papers reviewing the youth programs of those days, the group heard from two representatives of the current NYMO youth program: Jenny Devoe, a youth leader from Helena, Montana; and Lynn Strother Hinkle of the NYMO staff in Nashville, Tennessee. They spoke of the program and answered questions at length.

The group also had in their hands copies of a letter addressed by Harold W. Ewing, director of youth work in The Methodist Church during the 1950s, to Ezra Jones of the General Board of Discipleship. In his letter, Dr. Ewing wrote, "We are raising teen-agers in a 'pressure cooker' of cultural problems we have created. The direction of the future may depend upon how the church can minister to them as they develop their values, life style and priorities. Such an EMPHASIS (sic) to involve every board, every conference and every local church in a creative program/ministry with the youth of the church and community."

The discussion of this question led the group of former leaders to contrast the substantial staff and funds devoted in the 1940s and 1950s to work with youth and students with the scanty resources now available on both national and annual conference levels. There was unanimity that United Methodism must place a higher priority on such work if its membership decline is to be reversed.

Therefore, be it resolved, that:

1. the General Conference direct the General Council on Ministries, the General Council on Finance and Administration, the General Board of Discipleship, the General Board of Higher Education and Ministry, and other general agencies to allocate sufficient funds and mobilize the necessary staff and resources for a major emphasis on youth and students commensurate with the risks and problems confronting young people in society today;

2. the General Conference urge the annual conferences to increase their efforts and resources in youth and student work;

3. the General Conference urge that at least one half-time staff position be provided within each conference to work in connection with the conference council on youth ministries and that adequate funding be provided within each annual conference budget for youth ministry as outlined in the *Book of Discipline*;

4. the General Conference encourage local churches to enlist and involve youth in the life and work of their congregations; and

5. that youth ministry be a program emphasis for the 1997–2000 quadrennium.

ADOPTED 1992
AMENDED & READOPTED 1996

See Social Principles, ¶ 66.

TOPICS & CATEGORIES

TOPICS & CATEGORIES

Ecumenical/Interfaith/Cooperative Relations

Education

TOPICS & CATEGORIES

INDEX

747

INDEX